Lecture Notes in Computer Science 797
Edited by G. Goos and J. Hartmanis

Wolfgang Gentzsch Uwe Harms (Eds.)

1124

High-Performance Computing and Networking

International Conference and Exhibition
Munich, Germany, April 18-20, 1994
Proceedings
Volume II: Networking and Tools

Springer-Verlag
Berlin Heidelberg New York
London Paris Tokyo
Hong Kong Barcelona
Budapest

Series Editors

Gerhard Goos
Universität Karlsruhe
Postfach 69 80
Vincenz-Priessnitz-Straße 1
D-76131 Karlsruhe, Germany

Juris Hartmanis
Cornell University
Department of Computer Science
4130 Upson Hall
Ithaca, NY 14853, USA

Volume Editors

Wolfgang Gentzsch
FH Regensburg and GENIAS Software GmbH
Erzgebirgstraße 2, D-93073 Neutraubling, Germany

Uwe Harms
Harms Supercomputing Consulting
Bunsenstraße 5, D-81735 München, Germany

CR Subject Classification (1991): C.2-4, D, F.2, G.1, H.2, J.1-2, J.6, K.6

ISBN 3-540-57981-8 Springer-Verlag Berlin Heidelberg New York
ISBN 0-387-57981-8 Springer-Verlag New York Berlin Heidelberg

Printed in Germany

Typesetting: Camera-ready by author
SPIN: 10131015 45/3140-543210 - Printed on acid-free paper

Preface

High-Performance Computing and Networking (HPCN) is driven by several initiatives in Europe, the United States, and Japan. In Europe several groups, the Rubbia Advisory Committee, the European Industry Initiative, the Teraflops Initiative, and others encouraged the Commission of the European Communities (CEC) to start an HPCN programme. They recognized the economic, scientific, and social importance of the HPCN technology for Europe.

Members of these groups started the first HPCN conference last year in Amsterdam. The other player in this field was Supercomputing Europe, an annual exhibition and conference, that was founded by Royal Dutch Fairs in 1989.

Due to the personal engagement of Bob Hertzberger, University Amsterdam, Dorte Olesen, University Copenhagen, Peter Linnenbank, Royal Dutch Fairs, and others, we succeeded in combining important European HPCN activities to organize the HPCN Europe 1994 in Munich.

The HPCN Foundation is responsible for the Conference and the Technology Demonstrators Display. The Exhibition and the Vendors Session is organized by Royal Dutch Fairs. The Organizing Committee's intention is that HPCN Europe becomes a sister of the well-known American supercomputer events.

This new start inspired many HPCN experts in Europe. More than 60 specialists decided to take an active role in the Advisory Board and in the Programme Committee, to look for interesting contributions in this field. They enthusiastically broadened the base for HPCN in Europe.

As a result of this activity, more than 220 contributions from all over the world have been submitted, and the Programme Committee selected 140 papers and 40 posters. Over 20 well-known experts from Europe and the United States have agreed to present an invited lecture, demonstrating the advantages of using high-performance computers in their industrial and research application fields, including the keynote speakers, Horst Forster, CEC, Geoffrey Fox, NPAC, and David Williams, CERN.

Many different application areas, such as engineering, environmental sciences, material sciences, computational chemistry, electrical CAD, high-energy physics, astrophysics, neural networks and parallel databases are covered in the conference. In the context of real applications, subjects like languages, programming environments, algorithms, compilers, data parallel structures, monitoring, debugging, and benchmarking of parallel systems are discussed as well.

This event would not have been possible without the broad and personal support and the invaluable suggestions and contributions of the members of the Programme Committee and the Advisory Board. In addition, we would like to thank the referees in the Programme Committee, who spared no effort in evaluating so many papers, in a very short time over Christmas.

Many thanks to our sponsors, the CEC and the Royal Dutch Fairs, for their financial support of HPCN Europe 1994; without this support it would have been impossible to start such a considerable initiative. Also, we highly appreciate the personal efforts of Monika Grobecker and Anschi Kögler, who managed the conference secretariat and prepared these proceedings, and Hans-Georg Paap, who decoded and uncompressed nearly 100 Mbytes of papers. Finally, we are pleased to thank the staff from Springer-Verlag for publishing these proceedings just in time.

March 1994

On behalf of the Advisory Board
and the Programme Committee
Wolfgang Gentzsch and Uwe Harms

Committees

Organizing Committee

Chairman: Wolfgang Gentzsch	FH Regensburg
Co-Chair: Bob Hertzberger	University Amsterdam
Co-Chair: Dorte Olesen	University Copenhagen
Local Organizer: Uwe Harms	Munich
Demo-Display: Ad Emmen	SARA Amsterdam
Exhibition: Peter Linnenbank	Royal Dutch Fairs Utrecht

Programme Committee

A. Bachem	University of Cologne
T. Bemmerl	RWTH Aachen
A. Bode	Technical University of Munich
H. Burkhart	University of Basel
E. Clementi	University of Strasbourg and CRS4
I. Duff	RAL-CERC Chilton and CERFACS
A. Emmen	SARA, European Watch
W. Gentzsch	FH Regensburg
U. Harms	Supercomputing Consulting Munich
J. Häuser	FH Braunschweig
B. Hertzberger	University of Amsterdam
A. Hey	University of Southampton
G. Hoffmann	ECMWF Reading
F. Hoßfeld	KFA Jülich Research Center
S. Jähnichen	GMD FIRST Berlin
W. Jalby	University of Versailles
E. Krause	RWTH Aachen
C. Lazou	HiPerCom-Consultants London
G. Meurant	CEA Villeneuve-St-Georges
J. Murphy	British Aerospace Bristol
D. Olesen	University of Copenhagen
R. Perrott	University of Belfast
A. Reuter	University of Stuttgart
D. Roose	KU Leuven
U. Trottenberg	GMD St. Augustin
C. Upstill	PAC Southampton
A. van der Steen	ACCU Utrecht
H. van der Vorst	University of Utrecht
J. Volkert	University of Linz
E. Zapata	University of Malaga

Advisory Board

Contents

17. Numerical Algorithms for Engineering

18. Domain Decomposition in Engineering

19. Parallel Programming Environments

20. Load Balancing and Performance Optimization

Contents of Volume I

1. Keynote Talks

2. HPCN and Visualization in Industry

3. Algorithms for Engineering Applications

7. Material Sciences

8. Weather Simulations

9. Environmental Applications and Climate

12. Database Applications

High Performance Computing and Networking for Numerical Weather Prediction

Geerd-R. Hoffmann

European Centre for Medium-Range Weather Forecasts
Shinfield Park
Reading, Berks. RG2 9AX
England
EMAIL: GEERD.HOFFMANN@ECMWF.CO.UK

Abstract

The size of computer acquired for numerical weather prediction is dependant on the intended use of the forecast. For short- and medium-range weather forecasts, the real-time requirements enforce the use of supercomputers, while for seasonal and climate predictions the requirement for reasonable problem solution times leads to the same conclusion.

Having established the requirement for high speed computing, the relationship to networking is considered, taking into account the intended use of the supercomputers and the international cooperation of the meteorological community.

The current situation of European networking will be confronted with the expectations the weather community harbours, and a wish-list for the future development will be derived.

Keywords: supercomputer, networks, numerical weather prediction

1. Introduction

The computer modelling of the earth's atmosphere relies on the solution of large systems of coupled partial differential equations describing the physical laws and their boundary conditions and on the availability of a good representation of the initial state of the atmosphere, i.e. meteorological observations (see Burridge [2]). The amount of computing to carry out a numerical weather prediction depends on the size and spatial resolution of the model grid, the length of the forecast and the complexity of the model itself. For example, a ten day global weather forecast using a uniform horizontal grid of 60 km and 31 vertical levels requires approximately $1.5*10^{13}$ floating point operations (for details see Bengtsson [1]).

2. Numerical weather prediction

The different types of atmospheric prediction can be broadly classified as follows:

- Short-range weather forecast
  For the short range, i.e. up to 3 days ahead, a detailed prediction for a region has to be computed within a few hours after all meteorological observations in the area have been made. Typically, the model is geographically limited and uses a very high spatial resolution, up to around 10 km. Satellite and radar images may be used for "nowcasting".

- Medium-range weather forecast
  Here, the prediction covers the whole globe and extends up to ten days into the future. Today's finest spatial resolution is around 60 km.
- Long-range weather forecast
  To predict statistics of the weather months ahead or for whole seasons requires the simulation of the oceans as well. Initial studies show that some predictive skill may be achieved in some parts of the world. The atmospheric models are similar to those employed for medium-range forecasting.
- Climate prediction
  To predict what the climate would be like, if certain trends continue, for instance CO_2 emissions, requires the combination of atmospheric, ocean and biospheric models including chemical reactions. Again, the atmospheric models used are very similar to those employed for medium-range weather forecasting except that, due to computer performance limitations at present, only very coarse resolutions can be computed, typically with a horizontal grid of 300 to 600 km.

In all cases, the simulation model will generate the values of predictive variables in the selected resolution for the forecast period. These data will then be used to produce the various forecast results, like weather maps, rainfall charts or temperature distributions. The size of the data sets may vary between a few MB (10^6 bytes) for short-range forecasts to some TB (10^{12} bytes) for climate predictions.

3. Computing requirements

For short- and medium-range weather forecasts, the real-time requirements enforce the use of supercomputers, because the forecast must have been completed well in time before the predicted period. For example, at ECMWF there are only four hours available to complete a global 10 days' weather forecast. Therefore, a computer with a sustained performance over four hours in excess of one GFlop/s (10^9 floating point operations per second) is required. For seasonal and climate predictions, the requirement for reasonable problem solution times leads to the same conclusion.

4. Networking requirements

Having thus established the requirement for high speed computing, the relationship to networking is considered, taking into account the intended use of the supercomputers and the international cooperation of the meteorological community. The following distinction can be made:

4.1. Data acquisition and distribution of results

Meteorological observations are carried out all over the world at regular intervals. In addition, meteorological satellites are orbiting the earth and transmit their measurements to a number of groundstations. The total volume of data thus generated amounts to roughly 500 MB per day at present.

The data generated by a single weather forecast may exceed a GB (10^9 bytes), but the data required for a forecaster in a weather service rarely exceeds a few hundred MB.

Therefore, the major characteristics of the networking requirements can be summarized as real-time continuous traffic, limited number of data sources and sinks, and limited bandwidth (≤ 2 Mb/s).

4.2. Access to data for research purposes

As stated above, the data sets generated by the various forecasting activities may reach TB in size. In addition, it is not known in advance which researcher may request the data.

The networking requirements can therefore be summarized as burst traffic, limited number of data sources and large number of data sinks, and bandwidth of up to 34 Mb/s, depending on the size of the data sets.

4.3. Remote use of installed supercomputers

The supercomputers installed mainly for carrying out the forecast tasks outlined above are also used remotely by researchers to share the expensive resources more widely and to foster European cooperation. In general, the remote user would use his workstation to connect to the supercomputer and use its facilities for numerical simulations and graphical presentation of the results. The work would partially be carried out as batch processing, but for debugging and visualisation interactive use is required.

The networking requirements can be summarized as burst traffic, limited number of supercomputer sites and large number of users, and bandwidth between 64 kb/s and 140 Mb/s.

4.4. Distributed supercomputing ("Metacomputer")

As outlined in Hoffmann [4], the computations in climate prediction could benefit from distributed computing across a number of specialised supercomputers. In this area, the requirements are for burst traffic, small number of connections, very low latency (10^{-6} s) and very high bandwidth (Gb/s).

5. Current status of pan-European networking

Since the meteorological and climate community are international by nature, most of the networking requirements have to be met by international connections. However, at present only the requirements expressed in 4.1. can be satisfied, because the bandwidth available for international links seems to be limited to 2 Mb/s by the Public Network Operators (PNO). Even at this modest speed, the costs are very high in Europe compared to the United States of America where similar links cost only a twentieth of the European price.

Taking into account that most of the traffic described above is bursty and does not require a continuous connection, a shared use of some international network would be advantageous. However, at present the pan-European backbone of the national research networks struggles to achieve an aggregate bandwidth of 2 Mb/s between the connected countries. In practice, this means that a single data transfer during day time will get less than 10 kb/s bandwidth allocated. Furthermore, the split in Europe between two competing backbone providers: Dante and Ebone, exacerbates the situation because gateways with limited capacity have to be used if the "wrong" combination of countries is chosen.

In summary, the current situation of international networking in Europe is characterised by inadequate bandwidth and impracticable management. It is at present not possible to meet the requirements of the meteorological and climate community.

6. Outlook

It is hoped that the activities proposed by the European Consultative Forum for Research Networking (ECFRN) in its report (see ECFRN [3]) will finally be implemented and that the European Union in its 4th Framework Programme will provide data networks in Europe which will also meet the requirements for numerical weather prediction. Without this infrastructure, Europe will fall behind other countries in its research, with potentially serious consequences for its future well-being.

References

[1] L. Bengtsson: Computer Requirements for Atmospheric Modelling. In: Multiprocessing in Meteorological Models. G.-R. Hoffmann, D.F. Snelling (eds.). Berlin Heidelberg New York 1988. pp. 108-116.

[2] D.M. Burridge: The Current State of Meteorological Modelling. In: Multiprocessing in Meteorological Models. G.-R. Hoffmann, D.F. Snelling (eds.). Berlin Heidelberg New York 1988. pp. 117-123.

[3] ECFRN: Computer Networking For European Researchers. The Challenges Ahead. CEC DGXIII. 30 March 1992.

[4] G.-R. Hoffmann: Use Of High-Speed Networks in Climate Research. In: Report of the High Performance Computing and Networking Advisory Committee. Volume 2. Commission of the European Communities. October 1992. Report from the Networks Group. Appendix 1.

High Performance Computing and Networking as Base Element of the Environmental Information System UIS of Baden-Württemberg

Fritz Schmidt

IKE, University of Stuttgart,
Department of Knowledge Engineering and Numerics,
Pfaffenwaldring 31, D-70550 Stuttgart, Germany

Abstract. High Performance Computing and Networking have a long tradition in the state of Baden-Württemberg. They are intensively used in research and development but also through industry and state organisations. It was back in 1989 when the former president of Baden-Württemberg Lothar Späth recognized the practical relevance of HPCN for environmental management systems. Due to this a project was started which had the goal to integrate the CRAY-II computer of the University of Stuttgart as a compute server and the BELWÜ network as high speed data link into the environmental information system (UIS) of the state of Baden-Württemberg. This early integration of HPCN techniques into the UIS proved to be a major design decision and has influenced the development of the system considerably.

1 Introduction

The paradigm underlying environmental modelling has changed over the last few years considerably. Instead of trying to isolate specific effects one now understands the environment as a highly dynamic system with complex structures. On the one hand we are able to identify substructures which can be modelled relatively isolated. On the other hand we have learned that we are able to make responsible decisions only if we develop general views which integrate subsystems representing various environmental areas, various interests and various groups of our society. This is represented in both the structure of the environmental administration and the procedures to reach environmental decision finding. Tools like environmental information systems which support such procedures should reflect this general paradigm rather than being contraproductive. High performance computing and networking offers the opportunity to develop environmental information systems which support scientists and decision makers locally in their specific tasks and in addition provide them with distributed compute and data services which require normally highly experienced specialists and expensive equipment. It is one of the characteristic features of the environmental information system (UIS) of Baden-Württemberg that it was tried to follow this new modelling paradigm right from the beginning. After several years of experiences in both developing and using this system it now can be shown what influences HPCN may have on problem solving.

2 The Environmental Information System UIS of Baden-Württemberg

It is essential to understand the basic philosophy behind the UIS if one wants to understand why HPCN is needed in such a system and how the UIS was influenced by ideas resulting from HPCN. First of all the UIS is a concept. Under this concept more than 200 systems will work together. They are classified into three categories:

- basic systems which support various administrative tasks,
- basic components of environmental information systems, which handle specialized tasks in the environmental sector and
- supra-departmental environmental information systems, which collate specialized items of information as required for the purposes of permeation and interlinking.

Naturally a concept like this has to be developed as a distributed system which is based on intensive use of client-server architectures and high speed networking.

Second the UIS is a framework to integrate measured environmental data, methods to analyze them (primarily graphical and statistical methods) and models and knowledge to interpret, to correlate and to condense data with the purpose to derive information for the various environmental tasks and the decision making. Such model based analyses frequently require up-to-the-minute information on the state and the development of the environment. The symbol of the UIS is the pyramid. Pyramids exist for various aspects including methods and data. One example is shown in Fig. 1.

Of course this pyramid symbolizes the concept rather than the realisation. As mentioned before it is our belief that an implementation can only be achieved successfully if it is done on the basis of a distributed service oriented system. Of course object oriented analysis, design and implementation techniques are most promising tools.

3 Test Beds for the Introduction of High Performance Computing and Networking into the UIS

We have several test beds which can be used to study various aspects of the introduction of HPCN into the environmental information system.

3.1 The High Speed Network of the Faculty Energy Techniques

On a local basis we have installed a high speed network at the Faculty of Energy Techniques at the University of Stuttgart. The main components and partners are shown in Fig. 2. This test bed allows

- to distribute applications,
- to investigate parallelisation techniques at various levels,
- to test communication strategies and networking techniques,
- to organise cooperative development of application software.

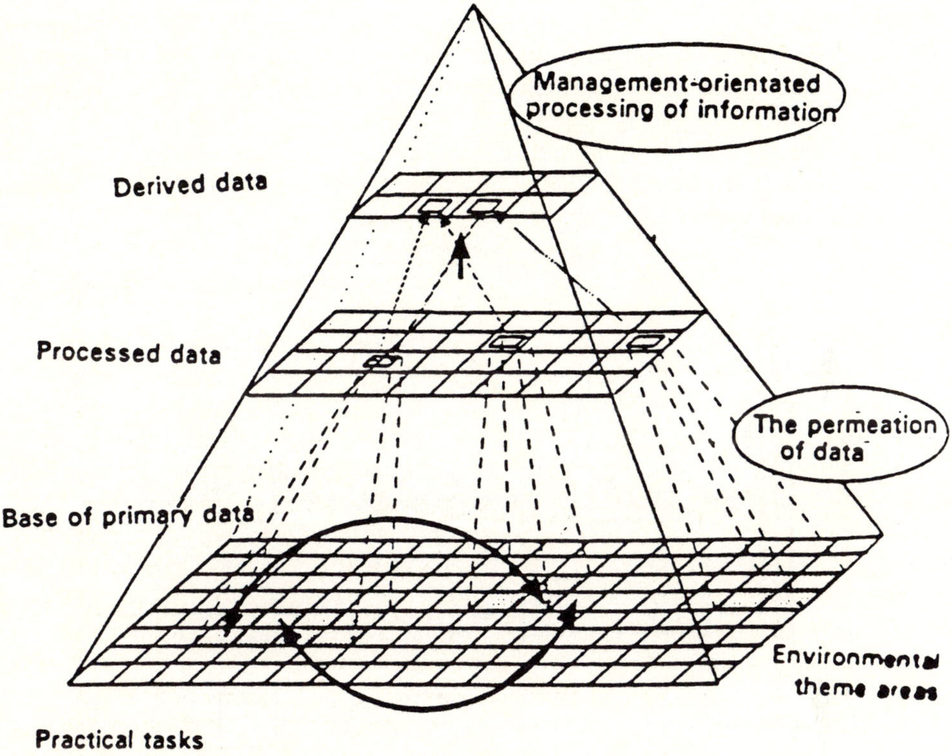

Fig. 1. The Environmental Information System concept requires the management oriented treatment of information and the permeation of the data

3.2 The Nuclear Monitoring System of the State of Baden-Württemberg

One of the basic components of the UIS is the Nuclear Monitoring System of the state of Baden-Württemberg. It is based on approximately 100 measurement stations which surround the nuclear power plants in the state and near its boarders. They produce daily more than 50.000 data which have to be evaluated, condensed, interpreted and stored in data management systems. The measured data include information on emissions, immissions, reactor conditions and meteorological conditions. In addition meteorological data of the German Weather Service (DWD) are provided on a routine basis. All these data are used to monitor the influence of nuclear power

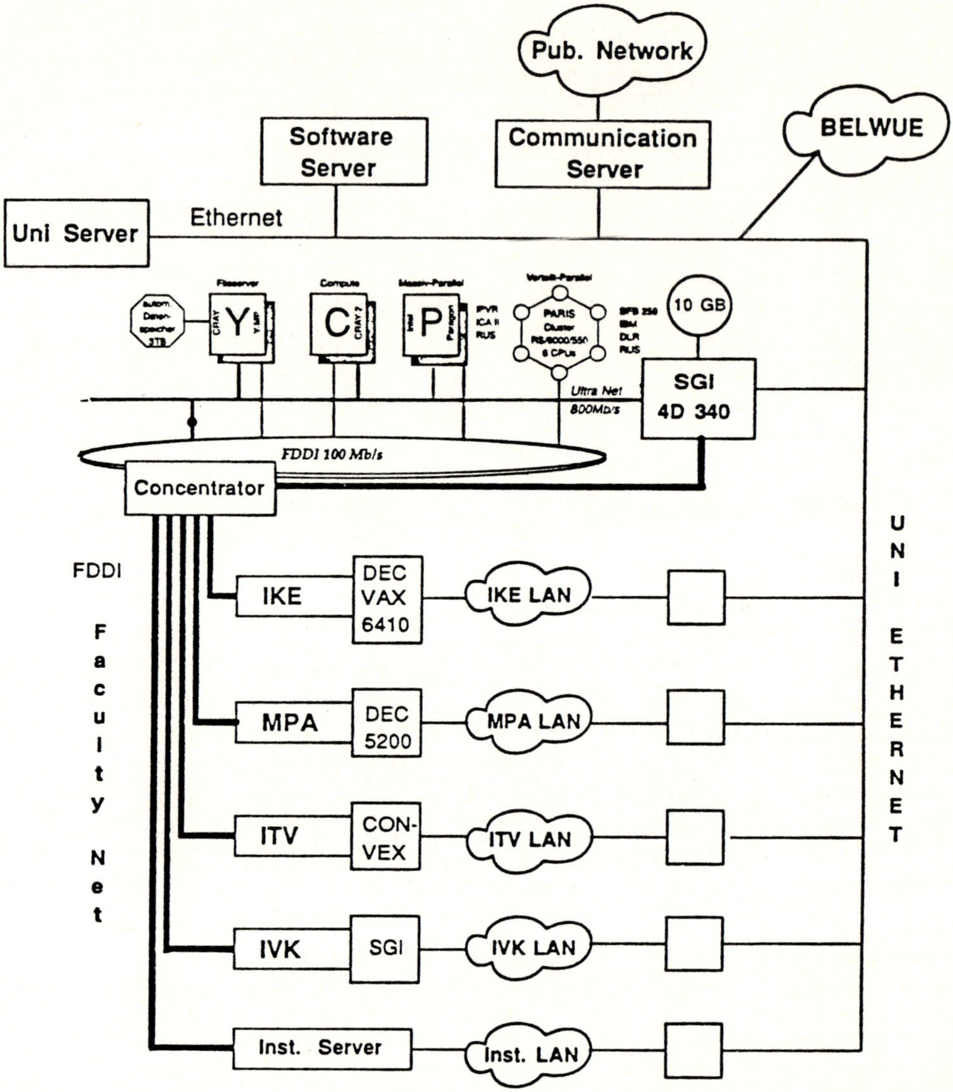

Fig. 2. High Speed Network of Faculty of Energy Techniques

plants on the environment but are available for other purposes too. In the case of an unexpected emission of nuclear material they also can be used to predict the transport of such material and the resulting immissions. From this it is possible to derive counter measures.

Due to the very advanced state of development of this monitoring system it was decided to use this component of the UIS as the application test bed. The special sequence of calculation steps integrated in the test application include

- collection and evaluation of measured emission and immission data,
- collection of local and global meteorological data,
- adaption of local and global meteorological data by meteorological models,
- interpolation of wind fields and transport conditions around an arbitrary location in Baden-Württemberg,
- transport of emittents,
- visualisation and interpretation of intermediate and final results in the context provided by the UIS.

4 Experiences

Both test beds are in operation and continuous improvement since several years. Major results concern:

4.1 General Structure of the UIS

We have proved that the environmental information system of Baden-Württemberg can be realized as a distributed system. The general structure of such a realisation is given in Fig. 3. Major basic systems exist as prototypes already. The backbone net of the system is the "Landesverwaltungsnetz" (LVN) of the state. All major administration units are connected to this. A special shell called TZUI was written to connect UIS components and applications independently from network developments. Two further projects are under way to split UIS applications into services (INSERV) and to integrate UIS applications and other services under one hypertext interface. At present we are experimenting with the World Wide Web system. The realisation of the UIS as a distributed system requires both high speed networks and dedicated compute servers. It allows to integrate all the manpower, knowledge and computer capacity available to solve the tasks of preventive and effective environmental conservation.

4.2 High Speed Networking

Experiments could be performed with the major available network technologies. Of course our results are strongly dependent on the local implementations given in Fig. 2. Typical results are given in Tab. 1.

Tab. 1. Transfer rates between CRAY-2 and SGI 4D-340

Ethernet	540 KB/s
FDDI	2.300 KB/s
ULTRANET	4.600 KB/s

As may be learned from other installations our results indicate that

- ETHERNET can be used most efficiently,
- FDDI is necessary if several users would need the ETHERNET capacity at the same time,
- ULTRANET does not improve data transfer capacities as dramatically as expected.

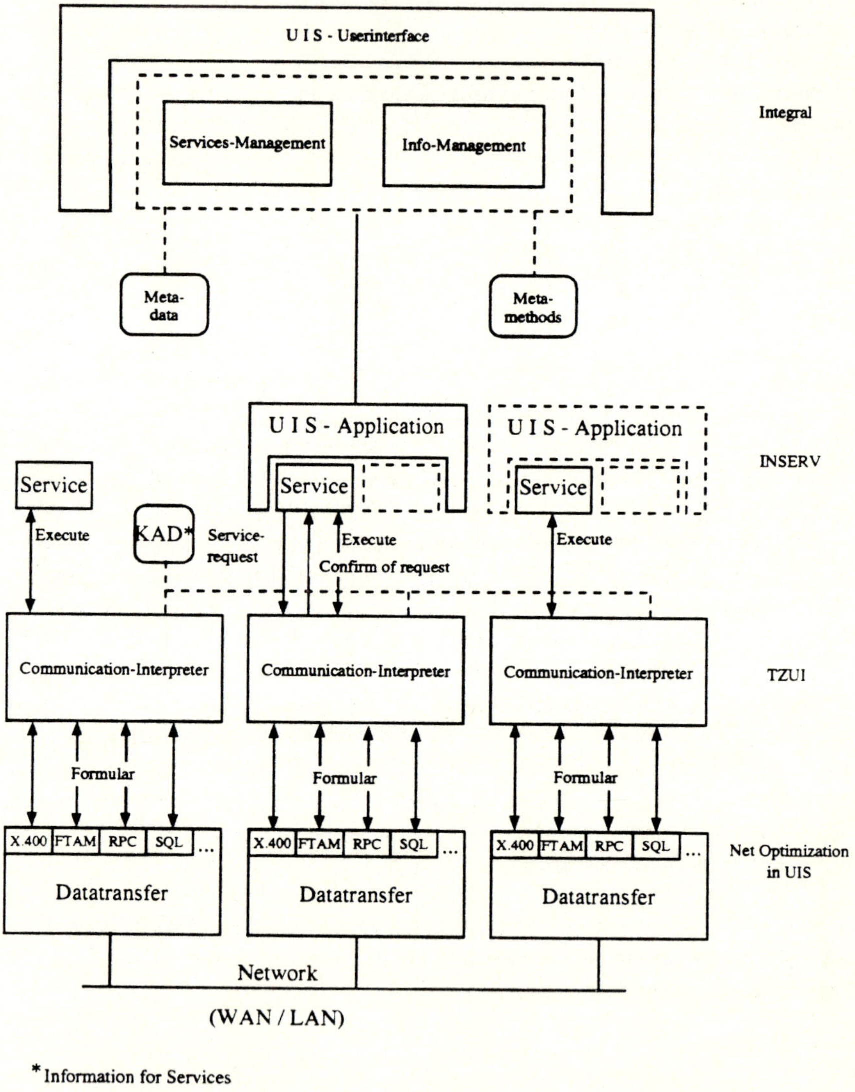

Fig. 3. The UIS Baden-Württemberg as a distributed, service oriented system

4.3 Distributed Computing

The effective solution of complex problems requires vectorisation and parallelisation. It is our basic experience that we should not try to use only one implementation paradigm for systems which are as heterogeneous as environmental systems are. Instead high performance networking will allow us not only to distribute functionalities to several organisations but also to implement such functionalities (or parts of it) on the most suited computers. We have developed a classification scheme which includes parallelisation of instructions (vectorisation), operations (parallelisation) and processes (distribution). From this we can derive the necessity of a heterogeneous computing environment, rules for distributing applications in such an environment and hints how to decide when to parallize, vectorize or to use hardware which is specialized for the solution of a special problem. Also software which supports such a distributed computing is under development and evaluation.

4.4 Towards Tera Computers

During the writing of this paper the state of Baden-Württemberg decided to replace the CRAY-2 computer at the University of Stuttgart by a next generation machine. This new computer will not only allow to start a new area of supercomputing at the university but also give an essential push to the environmental projects of the state. Due to the work described in this paper we are well prepared to integrate the new compute server into the overall UIS strategies, to feed it with data measured in the environment and to make available the new capacities to all those who need it to get more trustworthy solutions of environmental problems. One specific example is given in the following paragraph.

4.5 On-Line Analyses of the Transport of Pollutants

At various occasions we could experiment our ideas under real conditions which included high ranking decision makers and all the time stress which results from unusual events. Due to this experiments it could be proved,

- it is possible to use a distributed computer environment under such conditions;
- the inclusion of HPCN allows to analyze complex situations in time spans which are tolerable for both decision makers and counter measures;
- using HPCN techniques in conjunction with problem dependent visualisation techniques as available in daily used information systems supports the understanding of results from complex simulations and stimulates the decision making process.

5 Acknowledgements

The following people have contributed to this work:

W. Dax, Distributed Computing	(4.3)
O. Kretzschmar, High Speed Networking and Visualisation	(4.2)
W. Scheuermann, High Speed Network of the Faculty Energy Techniques	(3.1)
A. Schuch, General Structure of the UIS and Development of TZUI	(4.1)
S. Schweizer, Validation of Measured and Calculated Data in KFÜ	(3.2 and 4.5)
M. Tischendorf, Development of the UIS and Integration of Services (Projects INSERV and INTEGRAL)	(2 and 4.1)

Their work will be published in a series of doctoral theses to be submitted to the University of Stuttgart in 1994 and 1995.

High Speed Networking for the Research Community in Europe

- A Summary of Existing Approaches and Future Plans -

Klaus Ullmann, DFN-Verein Berlin
January 1994

Abstract. There is a growing gap in transmission capacity between production networks for the research community in Europe and the US. With the exception of the SuperJANET program there is no equivalent to the NSFNET program in Europe. Fortunately an increasing number of countries have identified the need for such an infrastructural tool and a European program has been launched to complement national activities on a European scale. First results should be visible in 1994.

1. Introduction

Within a few years high speed data communication services will play an important role as infrastructural tools for the research community; this role can be compared with the usage of electronic mail services today. The term "High Speed" will be used for communication systems with an access rate far beyond 2Mbps; i.e. it will deal with communication systems with 34Mbps and 140Mbps access rate. Furthermore it will concentrate on production systems and will not describe or assess the huge number of very successful pilot projects in Europe. It is therefore the purpose of this paper to describe the European component of a high speed production communication system for research, addressing both academic and industrial research.

The paper will start with a description of user demands (chapter 2) and will then deal with technical requirements (chapter 3). Chapter 4 will address the situation in the US, chapter 5 will describe the situation in Europe, covering some of the existing high speed activities and plans for new activities. Chapter 6 will summarize the main findings.

2. User Demands

Today the working environment of end users in several disciplines especially those in natural and engineering sciences is ideally suited for high speed communication. The computational tool of an engineer or a scientist is a work station (investment about 10-15KECU) with input/output devices for voice and video.

In the open-domain such an end user will find a tremendous number of high-quality software, which enables him/her to run desktop video conferences, to use multi-media electronic mail, to access multi-media server and to use a growing number of external resources which are inherently based on a multi-media mix of data, voice/music and video information.

Furthermore a number of traditional software packages especially in the engineering disciplines are already taylored to new interfaces, which are closer to human capabilities than those which produce nothing else than huge sets of numbers: Interactive visualisation tools should serve just as one example - these tools normally represent numerical results in coloured pictures or even movies rather than in numbers and matrices.

The end user will find these tools for moderate investments in a modern computing environment, which is defined by a set of specialized servers including compute server, the end user´s workstation and all this networked with an access rate to the local network of 10Mbps to 100Mbps. It is obvious that the parameter "access rate" will be improved within the next years from 100Mbps to 1Gbps.

For an end user there is no technical reason why this environment should not be extended to the wide area, i.e. to the national or even to the international environment, where he/she is anyhow in contact with colleagues. This natural extension of a local environment is the basic source of most wide-area high speed activities worldwide.

3. Technical Requirements

The implementation of 34Mbps networks requires a basic high speed infrastructure frequently addressed as fibre optic infrastructure. In most (not in all) industrialized countries huge projects for the implementation of such infrastructure are under way or close to be finalized.

From a user's point of view the network must react in a controlled way when he sends or receives data to/from the network. Data of the applications described above can be described by its peak load characteristic, i.e. for a few seconds the demand for bandwidth is (very) high, afterwards for a long period low and then suddenly high again. This characteristic can be derived from video applications as well as from visualisation applications or others.

For voice transfer another parameter is important in order to guarantee a certain level of quality of service: Packetized voice has to reach the receiver in sequence without big gaps in delivery, technically addressed as jitter.

For traditional 64Kbps or 2Mbps networks a methodology for modelling such a technical system is well understood - this is not the case for high speed networks with the characteristics described above. In traditional networks both user population and the number of transfer channels can be described with (statistical) big numbers, which results in a specific methodology for the engineering of such systems. As the number of users of 34Mbps technology is small compared to the number of users using traditional communication it is not possible to directly apply existing engineering methodology to the development and management of 34Mbps (and 140Mbps) networks.

4. The Situation in the US

Since three years one of the national networks for the research community, the NSFNET, offers access rates of 45Mbps (i.e.T3) to its users. It is obvious that in such an environment a tremendous number of new applications has grown over the last years. The range of these innovative applications covers spectacular applications like life-transmissions of conferences over NSFNET to really useful tools for multimedia electronic mail, to applications of information interfaces to Gopher or WWW servers. All these applications have in common that they basically require high bandwidth in order to be useful. NSFNET is implementing a 140Mbps production service in 1994 - the public procurement procedure has been started already in 1993.

Two features have to be recognized for an evaluation of US specifics in this field:

a) Compared with Europe the regulatory situation is very much advanced, which is reflected by a competitional situation amongst several providers and hence in significantly lower prices for bandwidth.

b) There has always been substantial central government support during the last 15-20 years for networking - the Clinton/Gore administration´s plans for a National Information Infrastructure are just a (logical) successor of earlier US government programs.

5. The Situation in Europe

5.1 National Plans and their Implementation

An increasing number of countries in Europe have their plans to establish 34Mbps production networks on a national scale. Some of them will be described as examples.

The most advanced system is without any doubt SuperJANET in the UK. At the end of 1993 a 34Mbps production system with access of roughly 70 sites to the 34Mbps service has started its work. Technically this system is based on networked routers (IP, CLNP over SMDS). The next step is the establishment of a 34Mbps ATM network (roll-out of ATM equipment under way) which can be easily extended to 140Mbps. The fibre infrastructure necessary for this step is layed into the ground and a national 140Mbps network for the UK is not far away.

In Norway a couple of research sites covering big parts of the country have been networked with 34Mbps in 1992/1993 sucessfully. The technical characteristic on the actual service level is comparable to that of the SuperJANET.

Holland and France have plans to implement 34Mbps into their national networks very soon. In both countries there are already 34Mbps Metropolitan Area Networks (MANs). The same approach is taken in Germany where regional 34Mbps networks will be established in the context of the national network DFN in 1994. Due to extreme prices for 34Mbps bandwidth in Germany funding for a 34Mbps national network could not be organized so far.

Generally the situation in most European countries is far behind the US. Except for the UK most countries have in common that the regulatory situation is roughly ten years behind the US and as a result of this prices for bandwidth are relatively high.

5.2 Plans for the European Network

There is a common view in Europe that a European overlay structure should combine and interconnect national networks to a common European resource. A couple of reasons favour such a solution, amongst them funding, regulatory and organisational issues.

This approach has been taken in the earlier days of European networking with EARN and has recently materialized again in the EuropaNET, a 2Mbps network operated by PTT Telecom (NL) and managed by DANTE, a group located in the UK but working for a couple of national networks in order to solve their international network problems.

DANTE has recently received the task to perform a study phase for a European 34Mbps network. This network should combine and interconnect national networks starting with those which have established or are soon going to establish national 34Mbps services. Difficulties within this study phase are as follows:

- A couple of PTOs have so far not published tariffs for 34Mbps international lines. They claim that there is no market for 34Mbps lines, a statement which is obviously not true looking at the growing US market.

- A couple of countries do actually not have the technical infrastructure to offer 34Mbps nationally. This is a fact in most central and eastern European countries but true as well for some western European countries.

Norway and the CEC have taken initiative to establish a Eureka project in order to organize funding, most of the European countries have joined this initiative, which has so far been able to materialize the study phase mentioned above. The study phase should be finalized in summer 1994 and there are plans to immediately start the implementation phase. An optimistic assessment says that the first trans European 34Mbps service will be available in 1994 already.

In order to be successful to reduce the gap between Europe and the US it is essential, that

a) the networking community (i.e. the experts) concentrate on technical problems

and

b) that enough funding is available to realize the technical system. First evaluations have shown that an amount of 40-50MECU is necessary to implement a 34Mbps network for Europe.

The National Information Infrastructure Testbed (NIIT)

Mike McKeown

Network Systems Corporation
Kings Ride Court
Ascot
Berkshire
SL5 7JR
UK

Abstract. It has long been accepted that a national transportation infrastructure, including road, rail and air, is vital for any strong industrial economy. However, today's major economic powers, including the USA and EC are becoming increasingly reliant on high technology as a major source of economic wealth. Therefore the provision of a *national information infrastructure* will be as vital to the long term economic growth, as the transportation infrastructure was vital to the original industrial economy.

1 Introduction

On September 15 1993, a number of companies including Network Systems, AT&T, Hewlett-Packard, Digital Equipment Corporation, Sprint and SynOptics, together with several universities, and government labs announced the formation of a consortium called National Information Infrastructure Testbed, or NIIT.

This industry-led group is building a national testbed for the integration of advanced computing and communications technologies, including ATM, Frame Relay and Distributed Computing Environment (DCE), in a nation-wide network that will allow users do real-time collaborative problem-solving.

2 First NIIT Applications

The first NIIT application, Earth Data System, uses both ATM and Frame Relay. It was demonstrated in both Portland and Washington. D.C. in November.

The first application to be put on the testbed is called Earth Data System. This environmental application allows researchers at Oregon State, the University of New Hampshire, Sandia National Laboratories, and elsewhere to combine information on tropical deforestation and ocean pollution. Users can access, view, manipulate, and analyse twenty years' worth of environmental data stored in different locations and in different data bases. This initial application involves nine sites connected by an ATM DS3 network provided by Sprint and a Frame Relay DS1 network provided by

AT&T. Network Systems is providing the backbone routers for the ATM network; these routers will also be the connection points between the two networks. Earth Data System was also demonstrated at the Supercomputing '93 Conference in Portland, Oregon, and in Washington, D.C.

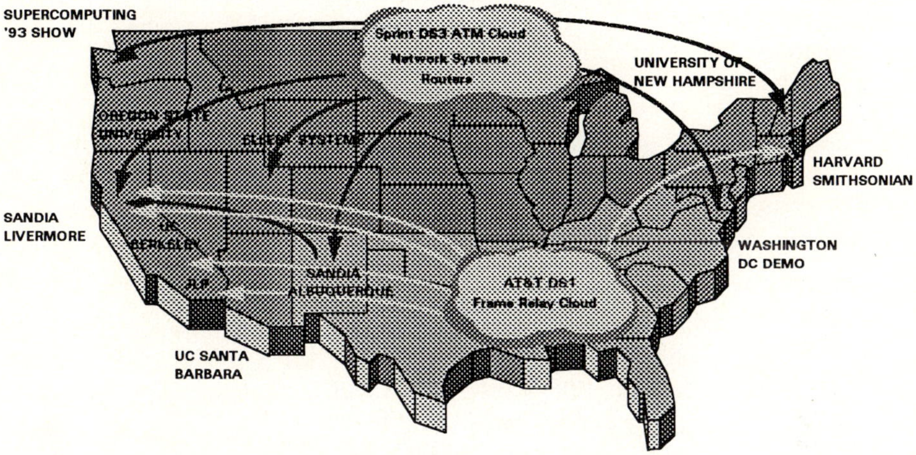

The next application planned for the testbed involves patient records for health care. Other applications will concern education, manufacturing, finance and entertainment.

3 NIIT Objectives

Besides the knowledge gained by the users of the various applications, the group has a number of objectives. First, it will be a real world, practical test of how various computing and communications technologies can be combined over wide areas using a broad range of hardware and software. Second, the companies participating in the testbed can take advantage of what they learn in offering commercial solutions to customers. Third, because of its practical experience, NIIT will be a valuable source of advice to government agencies and advisory commissions on questions of public policy and regulation. Finally, the collective learning gained from the NIIT will have far-reaching economic benefits.

As Lewis Platt, CEO of Hewlett-Packard, said at the announcement, "The existence of such an infrastructure will foster the creation of a wide variety of new information-based jobs and services".

4 How NIIT Came About

NIIT is taking advanced technologies out of the research lab into the main-stream business world. It came about because a small, dedicated group of people with a vision of what was possible got together to build temporary testbed networks known as SCinet at the Supercomputing '91 trade show in Albuquerque and the Supercomputing '92 show in Minneapolis. They built mixed-media, high performance, long distance, heterogeneous networking.

For example, SCinet '92 included the world's longest gigabit-speed LAN, a HIPPI-based network stretching some 43 kilometres. A HIPPI backbone was tied to FDDI rings, Ethernets, cross-country T3 and SMDS connections, and the Internet. The portion of the network on the show floor had over 100 gigabits of available bandwidth.

Besides HIPPI switches, Network Systems provided high-performance routers; SynOptics furnished hubs and concentrators; U S West, AT & T and MCI provided high-speed WAN connections. Ellery Systems, a small software company, provided DCE-based middleware that enabled researchers to access Hubble Space Telescope images and other data from data bases residing in different locations on widely different systems around the country. Another small company, Essential Communications, provided network management equipment. The Smithsonian Astrophysical Observatory, Sandia National Laboratories, and other research facilities provided data, people, and computational power.

In fact, SCinet '92, which ran flawlessly, was even used for Heterogeneous Computing Challenge, a contest among research organisations to see who could make the best use of the network, based on creativity, speed, connectivity, and a real-world applications. The contest was won by the Army High Performance Computing Research Centre and the Minnesota Supercomputer Centre. Overall, SCinet '92 demonstrated that collaborative work could be conducted on such heterogeneous networks using current technology.

But these successes were not widely disseminated, and the network had to be dismantled after a few days. The people who had worked on SCinet got together afterwards and said, "Why not build a more permanent network that could continue to be a testbed?" Such a testbed would accelerate the integration of critical computing and communications technologies and their commercial use. From their discussions in late 1992 and early 1993, NIIT was born.

Today, the NIIT Steering Committee includes a dozen leading companies, and the number of universities and other organisations joining as members at large keeps growing. Aided by the Clinton-Gore administration's interest in developing a National Information Infrastructure, NIIT is in an excellent position for continued growth in size and importance.

5 Why a *National Information Infrastructure*?

The concept of a *National Information Infrastructure* has received backing from the Clinton-Gore administration at the highest level. The vision behind this is two fold; first it is seen as vital for the long term competitiveness of the US economy in the world's high technology market, and second it is an enabler for the constitutional concept that all citizens are equal and should receive equal opportunities. A National Information Infrastructure would allow any citizen access to the best of the US' education and medical systems, irrespective of their geographical location.

5.1 Remote Learning

The US is a geographically large country with Universities spread throughout its boarders. Many of these Universities are recognised as the world's leaders in their fields. Unfortunately students may not be able to attend the best University for their chosen subject, for a number of reasons, which may include; high regional living costs, family ties to their home area and lack of places on the course. This means not all students receive equal opportunities.

With a National Information Infrastructure it will be possible for students to attend one University but still attend courses at other Universities, by use of interactive video systems and electronic / multi-media "books". The Universities themselves will also have easy access to academics who are recognised experts in their field. Currently this is restricted to infrequent and expensive visits on lecture tours. Overall a National Information Infrastructure will increase the standard of education available in the US, which is of course vital to long term economic growth.

5.2 Medical Applications

Similar to the education system, medical experts in particular fields are spread through the US. How much more efficient it would be if many doctors were to specialise in certain areas, but their expertise was available to any hospital within a matter of minutes or even seconds. With huge progress in medical technology it is now possible to transmit high quality image, X-ray and scan images in real time, while the latest computer controlled operating equipment, especially those based on laser technology hold the potential for remote control.

Take the example of an emergency brain operation. A National Information Infrastructure would allow the local surgeon to be guided by one of the country's top brain surgeons, no matter where in the country that surgeon was based. High resolution images would be available in real time to the expert and they would even be able to perform delicate surgical procedures by remotely driving the operating equipment. This could not only directly make the difference between life and death for many patents, but encourage greater specialisation by doctors, thus improving the overall capabilities of the medical community.

5.3 Business Infrastructure

Many of the US' most successful high-tech companies were start-ups only a few years ago. This entrepreneurial sprit is the life blood of the US economy. However it is becoming increasingly expensive to start-up a new company, particularly as it may be expensive to obtain the right staff. The employee situation in particular is a chicken and egg situation - the greatest availability of experienced high-tech employees is typically concentrated in certain areas, such as Silicon Valley and New England. However this concentration has lead to high local costs. Therefore it is very expensive for a new company to start in one of the high-tech areas, but unless they do, it will be much harder to find suitably qualified employees.

However with a National Information Infrastructure it becomes possible for the company to be much more distributed. So while the company may be based in a low cost area, it can draw its top people for all around the country. Everybody then works together in the "virtual office" built on top of the information highway. This can be particularly valuable at the formation of the business, where it is possible to have easy access to contract staff such as consultants for a company "quick start".

5.4 Scientific Research

The scientific community has long been a "global community", with co-operative research being undertaken throughout the country and indeed the world. Many scientific problems, ranging from physics and cosmology to medical research can be solved far faster with a large co-operative team of scientists. Obviously these scientists need to be experts in their field and typically they will be spread throughout many universities, research institutions and commercial companies.

Traditionally forming such large teams of scientists has been a problem, since communication is limited to telephone and email with occasional face-to-face meetings. Today scientific research has many high technology tools at its disposal. This includes graphical simulation tools, often using super-computers, real time data feeds, such as satellite data, while new tools are starting to be used such as video conferencing and electronic "white boards". All these applications require large amounts of network bandwidth through the scientific community and are therefore an excellent application of a National Information Infrastructure. Indeed the Earth Data System described earlier in the paper provides a good example.

6. Conclusion

The National Information Infrastructure Testbed marks the beginning of an exciting new era of data communications, where high technology computer network applications are recognised as vital to the US' long term economic growth and competitiveness. This obviously has implications for other high technology economies, such as the EC. With the US investing in a National Information Infrastructure, the EC will need to match such developments if it is remain competitive in the long term. While currently there are no European initiatives on the scale of NIIT, there are important regional developments, such as the

SuperJANET academic network in the UK, and the Eurescom ATM project being undertaken by all the major PTT's in Europe. Finally new technologies such as SMDS are being rapidly implemented by many PTT's throughout Europe.

Parallel Knowledge Processing in Open Networks

P. M. Borst[1], H.-T. Götz[1], P. S. Sapaty[2], and W. Zorn[1]

[1] Department of Informatics, University of Karlsruhe, 76128 Karlsruhe, Germany, <borst@ira.uka.de>, <goetz@ira.uka.de>, <zorn@ira.uka.de>
[2] Department of Electronic and Electrical Engineering, University of Surrey, Guildford, Surrey, GU2 5XH, England, <p.sapaty@ee.surrey.ac.uk>

Abstract. The objective of this paper is the description of WAVE model and language for highly parallel processing in open computer networks, as well as an efficient distributed implementation of the language. The WAVE language interpreter may be a basic building block for parallel knowledge processing systems working without any centralised resources in an integral logic & data flow mode. Application of the model for intelligent management of distributed computer networks, based on integration of the WAVE interpreters with traditional network management tools, is discussed.

1 WAVE Model and Language for Distributed Processing

Efficient organisation of distributed systems [5] is of growing interest in many scientific disciplines, especially those dealing with local and wide area computer networks. The WAVE paradigm [8-10] is aimed at creation of a universal computational model for parallel supervision of large open systems supported by computer networks. It describes knowledge processing as parallel and recursive navigation of the network topology, in an asynchronous pattern-matching mode, without any centralised supervision, with the WAVE language and intermediate results self-spreading as waves of messages throughout the distributed knowledge and environment. Using this paradigm it is possible to create and process an arbitrary distributed knowledge network (KN) with any local information at nodes and arcs, activate it as a system of communicating processes, and supervise its behaviour on a higher level. It is also possible to dynamically change the network topology, subsequently inject new wave algorithms, integrating within the same program a variety of such layers of creation, processing, modification, inference and supervision. The whole system evolves without any centralised control and covers large territories, its scope and interconnections between parts may not be known in advance and may be dynamically inferred during this navigation process.

WAVE language describes rather *propagation* (parallel and asynchronous) through the distributed network-structured data continuum than the traditional *data processing*. It has a concise syntax and rich navigational semantics and is oriented on direct (especially) hardware interpretation in computer networks.

Main WAVE language features can be described as follows (where braces represent repetitions with a corresponding delimiter, square brackets show an optional construct, and the vertical bar separates alternatives).

```
wave    ->    { {move , } . }
move    ->    unit  act  unit   | [ rule ] ( wave )
```

A WAVE program (*wave*) is a combination of a sequential and parallel (or unordered) composition of space-time actions over a knowledge network called *moves*, with the period and comma used as corresponding delimiters (or operators). Moves are either elementary actions over two local information *units* separated by an *act* symbol, or again (parenthesised) waves. The latter may be prefixed by a *rule* construct establishing proper constraints on the moving language strings, such as splitting them into branches and coordinating their co-operative (parallel or sequential) development in KN, or enabling the string to create or modify the very KN. The rules and their language abbreviations are: SeQuence (SQ), Or Sequential (OS), Or Parallel (OP), And Sequential (AS), And Parallel (AP), RePetition (RP), WaiTing (WT), InDivisible (ID), and CReate (CR).

Acts are selective or broadcasting *hops* in KN (for which the units keep information about the links and nodes to be passed, including different sorts of local and global broadcasting), condition checking *filters* (halting if false), *assignments* (with the result recorded on the first unit), explicit *halts* with a repertoire of echoing termination conditions, or an *external call* permitting to access and exchange information with any other systems and models distributed in networks. There is also a (potentially recursive) mechanism of *injections* of new strings into a moving wave as procedures (as contents of variables) which can be transported with language strings or picked up in nodes of KN during navigation of the latter.

The basic information unit of the language is a *vector* – a dynamic sequence of arbitrary-length values generally defined as strings, concrete interpretation of which depends on the operations involved. This simple data structure with special operations on it, together with the recursive syntax and semantics of the language, is completely sufficient for representing arbitrary network creation and processing algorithms in a distributed environment. A unit can be also expressed by variables being of the three types: *nodal* – dynamically attached to KN nodes and shared by different moving waves, *frontal* – moving with the language strings, and *environmental* (including user terminals) – accessing currently passed resources relating to KN nodes and links.

A wave, starting in one or a number of nodes (from the same or different users) of KN, *self-propagates* throughout the KN accessing only local resources in nodes. Frontal variables accompany the wave and implement local information exchanges between different active nodes of KN. This (generally recursive) navigation process is asynchronously spawning in KN and independently terminating in nodes at which the wave tail becomes empty or a halt has been reached, with the worked parts (heads) of the string excluded from the further propagation.

A variety of programs on complex network topologies have been written in WAVE showing high density of the code (highly parallel and distributed solutions are usually 1-2 orders of magnitude shorter than the corresponding sequential programs in conventional languages).

As an example of a simple WAVE code consider the following program:

```
WT(CR(@#5.F=A.r#2.,(r#3.,r#F))).OS((F=C.#.F<C),T=C)
```

It first creates a triangle network with nodes `5`, `2`, and `3` connected by `r`-type links, starting from scratch (`@`) with `5` and hopping (by `#`) as `5-2-3-5` with using the moving `F`-variable for carrying the address (accessed by `A`-variable) of `5` to provide a loop to the already created node. It then activates all the created nodes in parallel supplying them with the same function which first tests if their neighbours (broadcasting to them by `#` without operands and carrying its own value in the `F` variable) do not have contents bigger than theirs (accessed by `C` variable). If the test is successful, the node outputs its content (`C`), as a unique maximum, to a terminal `T`. So `5` being the issued result. This program may work without any central control and if applied in any point in a computer network will wire the triangle on three computers, the letter finding the maximum value in parallel which will be output by only one of them.

2 Architecture of the WAVE Interpreter

The WAVE model may work in arbitrary computer network topologies where each computer keeps the same copy of the language interpreter as well as part of the knowledge network. The interpreters are operating on the network hosts as daemon processes having access to the network, and to the resources of the local host through the Unix operating system. Wave programs are injected from the hosts by a user interface to the interpreter which also collects the returned results. With a unique colouring of wave strings, many programs may operate in parallel on the network.

The interpreter consists of the six modules (see Fig. 1): Wave Analyser (WA), Network Processor (NP), Data Processor (DP), Track Processor (TP), Storage Manager (SM), and Communication Processor (CP).

Wave Analyser performs syntactical analysis of wave strings, submitting resultant tokens to TP.

Network Processor keeps the logical partition of the data network, executes move operations, and manages colours of propagating wave strings which are dynamically attached to the nodes. Goal addresses are returned to TP, which controls the further propagation.

Data Processor executes assignment and filter operations with automatic type conversions on the operands. Results are stored in variables or returned as logical values to TP, which continues or aborts the processing of the wave string.

Track Processor manages the track forest for distributed control, creating tracks in nodes when executing move operations and splitting into branches. TP controls the propagation on branches by optionally assigned control functions,

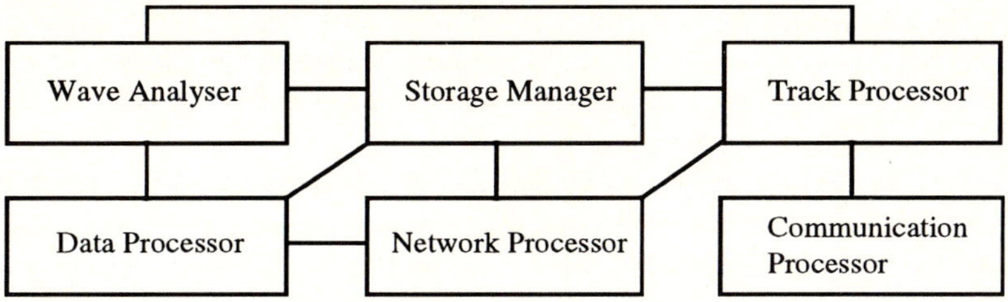

Fig. 1. General structure of the WAVE interpreter

passes suspended wave strings through the track forest to fringe nodes, and merges echoes in tracks with activating garbage deletion.

Storage Manager manages the dynamic memory for all other modules, with mapping the memory addresses to a network-wide unique addressing scheme.

Communication Processor implements the protocols for message exchange with the other interpreters on the network, buffering incoming and outgoing messages and converting wave strings and data between internal and the KN representation.

The WAVE interpreter is currently implemented in C under Unix [3]. Communication is based on the TCP/IP protocol and allows asynchronous message exchange with multiple destinations in both local and wide area networks. An efficient hardware implementation of the WAVE interpreter is currenly being analysed and modelled.

3 Network Management in WAVE

The communicating WAVE interpreters, distributed throughout a computer network and driven by the moving wave strings, may be efficiently used for advanced network management applications [12]. This interpretation network may communicate in multiple points with traditional network management tools like TRANSVIEW [11], extracting higher-order knowledge from the raw data received from the network elements. This knowledge may be subsequently processed on a semantic level with parallel classification and inference mechanisms expressed in the WAVE language.

TRANSVIEW is a commercial network management product based on SNMP (Simple Network Management Protocol) for monitoring and managing network components like bridges, routers, gateways, and Unix systems. The information about the components is stored in a local MIB (Management Information Base) and can be accessed and updated by the SNMP operations GET, GET_NEXT, SET and TRAP, the latter being sent by the components to the management station in case of failure conditions. The system is designed as an open platform and is extendable by the Application Programming Interface providing also an access to the SNMP protocol stack.

The WAVE interpreter has been integrated with the TRANSVIEW system by establishing two channels through Unix for transferring activation code and data between the systems in both directions. The TRANSVIEW manager is accessed by a Unix command, which submits an operation with parameters to TRANSVIEW (e. g. to access data from a network device through the SNMP protocol) and collects the results with returning them to the caller. The Unix command is activated from wave programs by an external call operation which suspends during execution and continues processing with the data received. For the other direction, the TRANSVIEW manager may inject wave strings and data through the interpreter's user interface (say, if some failure conditions on the network occur) and receive the results back for further processing or display. There is no distinguished relationship of client and server, both systems can activate the other ones dynamically, with changing their roles accordingly.

For example, an access of the interface table of a router may be expressed as

```
F=snmp_get;<router name>;<MIB entries>.F?tvex
```

whereby **tvex** is the name of the TRANSVIEW command line interface, **?** is the external call operation of WAVE language, and **F** is a variable to which the result will be assigned after termination of the SNMP GET operation.

While TRANSVIEW accesses local elements of networks collecting large amounts of raw data, the WAVE system generalises this data within a distributed semantic network representation offering top level topology analysis, classification and parallel inference techniques, as well as gobal coordination and recovery functions. Different possible distributed network management architectures resulting from such integration of the network access system and distributed knowledge processing engine are being investigated comprising the following main distributed subsystems: *Knowledge Base System*, *Topology Analysis System*, *Classification & Inference System* using distributed pattern-matching [2] on semantic networks, *Network Modelling System*, and *Recovery System*.

In Fig. 2 a possible communication between distributed WAVE (W) and TRANSVIEW (TW) systems is exhibited. The W-network integrates different domains controlled by the local TW-systems into an overall distributed semantic model coordinated and processed in parallel by the moving WAVE language strings. This model provides a distributed view of the supervised world and may be used, for example, in global traffic simulation and reaction on multiple network failures.

4 Conclusions

The WAVE language and system are currently used for solving a variety of other distributed knowledge processing, inference, reliability, modelling and control problems in distributed computer networks [4]. Parallel and distributed solutions for the main theoretical network analysis problems like those described in [1,7] have been proposed and written in WAVE with possible applications in open and distributed systems.

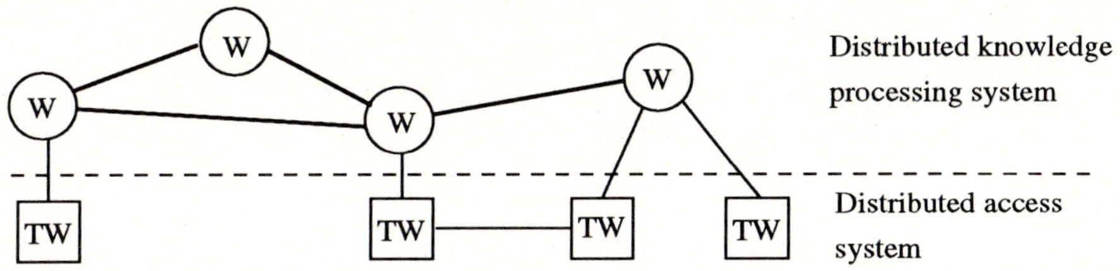

Fig. 2. Possible distributed integration of WAVE and TRANSVIEW systems

The WAVE model, expressing parallel and distributed processing as recursive creation, navigation and pattern-matching of abstract network topologies, hides the traditional process structuring and message passing layers (the latter typical, say, in actors [6]) within the communicating WAVE language interpreters. This provides high efficiency and density of a program code in a variety of applications ranging from modelling and numeric computations on networks to intelligent control, management, and inference in advanced knowledge based systems.

References

1. D. Bertsekas, and R. Gallager, "Data networks", Prentice-Hall, 1992.
2. L. Bic and C. Lee "A data-driven model for a subset of logic programming", ACM Transactions on Programming Languages and Systems, Vol. 9, no. 4, October 1987.
3. P. M. Borst, "The first implementation of the WAVE system for Unix and TCP/IP computer networks", Report 18/92, University of Karlsruhe, Dec. 1992.
4. M. Corbin and P. S. Sapaty, "Using the WAVE paradigm for parallel simulation in distributed systems", Int. Conf. ParCo93, Grenoble, France, Sept. 7-10, 1993.
5. M. S. Fox, "An organisational view of distributed systems", IEEE Trans. Syst., Man, Cybern., Vol. SMC-11, No. 1, Jan. 1981.
6. C. Hewitt, "Viewing control structures as patterns of passing messages", Artificial Intelligence 8 (1977).
7. A. Kershenbaum, "Telecommunications network design algorithms", McGraw-Hill, 1993.
8. P. S. Sapaty, "The WAVE model for advanced knowledge processing", in CAD Accelerators (Ambler, Agrawal & Moore, eds.), Elsevier Science Publ. B.V., 1990.
9. P. S. Sapaty, "A distributed processing system", European Patent No. 0389655, Publ. 10.11.93, European Patent Office.
10. P. S. Sapaty, "The WAVE paradigm", Proc. JICSLP'92 Post-Conference Joint Workshop on Distributed and Parallel Implementations of Logic Programming Systems, Washington, D.C., Nov. 13-14, 1992.
11. "TRANSVIEW-SNMP V1.0A. Programming interface", Publ. by Siemens Nixdorf Infomationssysteme AG, Dec. 1991.
12. W. Zorn, P. S. Sapaty, P. Borst, T. Henrich , "Project DAIMON: Global management in open computer networks", Techn. Report SNI/EK 821 9680/20, University of Karlsruhe, 1991.

Distributed File Caching in Parallel Architectures Utilizing High Speed Networks

Artur Klauser* and Reinhard Posch

Institut für Angewandte Informationsverarbeitung und Kommunikationstechnologie
Technische Universität Graz
Klosterwiesgasse 32/I
8010 Graz, Austria

email: [aklauser,rposch]@iaik.tu-graz.ac.at

Abstract. To obtain well scalable services in distributed and parallel systems, critical parts of these services must be distributed to avoid bottlenecks, thus reducing server processing load and consumed network bandwidth. This work investigates the distribution of the file service by distributed block-level file caches, also called client caches. Fixed-size client caches with various cache coherency schemes are compared with a server cache and a variable-size client cache model, in order to reveal useful caching distribution concepts.

1 Introduction

Parallel architectures and workstation clusters show a number of similarities which make it feasible to investigate both the same way. On the hardware side both consist of a collection of independent compute nodes, interconnected by a high speed network. On the software side there are communication libraries available, like PVM [2], P4, Parmacs, Linda, and soon MPI [7], that provide equal functionality for both types of systems.

To be unrestricted by computers and networks currently in use, this study is based on a simulation approach. The advantages of using a simulator instead of real hardware are obvious. Among these, easy configurability and exact repeatability play an important role.

The simulations are based on a client-server computing model [4]. Our special interest is the file service where block-level caching approaches are investigated. By comparing server caching with a number of client caching models we try to gain insight into distributed caching approaches.

In Sec. 2 the computing model and network structure are presented. Section 3 gives an overview of the implemented caching policies that are compared to each other. The simulator and the file system trace data are introduced in Sec. 4. Section 5 contains results of the simulations and the work is concluded in Sec. 6.

* Partially supported by Computing and Information Services Center, Graz University of Technology.

2 The Computing Model

A general MIMD type architecture with distributed memory, and a point-to-point interconnection network is the basis of this study. Each processing node (PN) consists of a processing unit, local memory, and interfaces to other PNs. Some PNs are also equipped with a disk interface and a physical disk device to form the basis for the block-level file server storage. The only means of inter-node communication is by message passing.

In our concrete case the interconnection network of the Intel Paragon supercomputer has been modeled. It is a direct network with 2D-mesh topology and e-cube wormhole routing supported by dedicated hardware. The simulation model comprises of a 4×4 mesh with 16 PNs.

An important point of the presented network structure is its ability to perform multiple network operations concurrently. Distinct pairs of PNs can communicate at the same time by means of different channels. We assume point-to-point networks to be more appropriate for parallel and distributed systems, as they are more scalable than multidrop networks. The major advantage of multidrop media is their ability to perform 1-to-n communication operations in $\mathcal{O}(1)$ time. Although point-to-point networks limit latency to $\mathcal{O}(\log n)$ time to complete a 1-to-n communication, such operations, however, can be pipelined, yielding the same throughput as multidrop networks.

3 Caching Policies

The following reference models are used in the evaluation process. A more detailed description of the models can be found in [6].

SCO (server cache only): no client caching; no inconsistencies can appear

LOD (local disk): each client has local disk; no coherency traffic modeled; no centralized server; completely distributed file system

NOC (no coherency): client and server caches; no coherency traffic modeled

WTA (write through all): server is always in consistent state; clients write-through shared and private files

WSS (write share sequential): clients write-through shared files only; server is consistent

WSC (write share concurrent): clients do not cache shared files; clients and server are consistent

4 Simulation

The public domain parallel architecture simulator Proteus [3] has been used to evaluate the presented caching policies. Proteus is an execution driven simulator that interleaves the execution of the application with the simulation of the underlying PN hardware and communication subsystem.

The simulated models are fed with the Sprite File System trace data [1] from the University of California at Berkeley. Read and write trace events are fed into the simulator as fast as the simulated caching model is able to handle them. There are two restrictions that bound the event flow into the simulator; on one hand sequential file operations are serialized in the simulator, on the other hand a static limit of maximal 8 outstanding requests from any client is enforced. This limit simulates the maximum number of processes on a client that will perform I/O requests to the server concurrently. This, however, does not restrict the number of processes that run on any node, but is a way to control the mean I/O activity of a client.

5 Results and Discussion

This section compares the hit rates acquired for different caching models throughout the network at the same boundary conditions such as size of the caches, network throughput and latency, disk throughput and seek time.

5.1 Disk Access Traffic

The five client cache models LOD, NOC, WTA, WSS, WSC are simulated with cache sizes ranging from 16 to 8192 blocks per client. The hit rate behavior of all five models, though, shows only a difference of some percent from each other, especially as caches get large enough to hold a relevant part of the clients' working sets. Using a server cache as an additional level of caching reduces these differences still further. This result gives confidence that neither very sophisticated nor very simple coherency schemes do change much in the access traffic to the server disk. The dominant parameter for this traffic is the size of the caches and not the coherency protocol used. Simple coherency protocols can eventually compensate for disadvantages due to inefficient traffic characteristics, by using less space for the implementation and their cache state data, thus leaving more space to allocate to actual cache data buffers.

5.2 Network Load

Comparing the traffic on the network shows a completely different situation. Here we see more sophisticated schemes substantially reducing the traffic on the network. However, it highly depends on type, topology, and speed of the network if these effects are of any severity in the perspective of the whole system. Especially on the simulated network model, the long term utilization of the communication channels is very low, although the request bursts usually found in file access traffic can load the network substantially for short periods of time. With fast networks, e.g. ATM or FDDI, the importance of this factor will shrink even further. The limiting factor in our simulation was more or less the I/O performance of the disk, which was assumed to be several times slower than the network performance.

5.3 Server Cache vs. Fixed-Size Client Caches

Server caching on its own is a very simple means to approach the situation. However, it was found that it is by far better than any of the client caching schemes under consideration, even when using the most optimistic assumptions about additional coherency traffic (LOD). This effect even grows drastically with increasing cache sizes in the system. Large client caches, as used sometimes now and certainly used more often in the years to come, perform more than 3 times worse than server caches with the same total number of cache blocks. This behavior is depicted in Fig. 1.

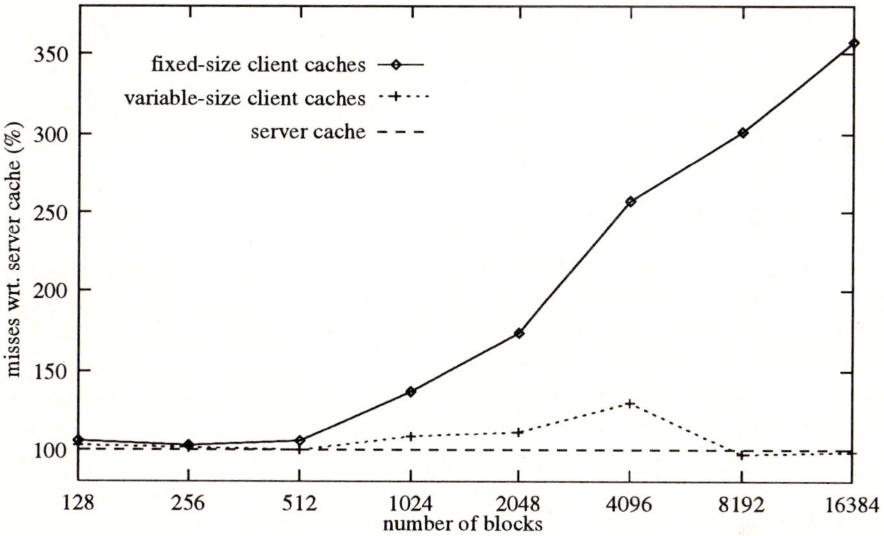

Fig. 1. Fixed and variable-size client cache behavior with respect to server cache.

The reason for this unpredicted behavior is based on the access patterns of the trace data. The traces hold requests coming from a large number of different workstations arriving at the server. Although the number of different sources has been reduced in the simulation to map the traces to a more homogeneous architecture, it still shows an unbalanced static and even more unbalanced dynamic usage pattern. This leads to the effect that some of the clients are in a fairly good usage of their caches, while others completely underutilize their caches, and still others are far from optimal in their cache hit rates because they have to handle much larger working sets. Figure 2 shows the great variety of client cache behaviors with varying cache size. Adding more memory to all client caches only shows significant effects on overutilized caches, while underutilized ones can not make effective use of it. Thus, from a certain point on, adding more memory only is of marginal benefit for the performance of the whole system.

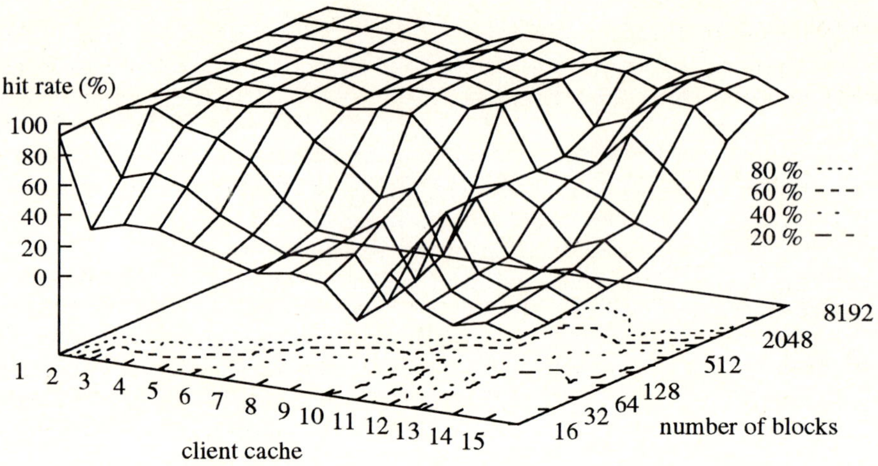

Fig. 2. Influence of the cache size on the hit rates of client caches.

5.4 Variable-Size Client Caches

The previous observations lead to the insight that fixed-size caches are not an especially good idea for efficient client caching schemes. Hence, cache memory has to be balanced between the clients. The optimum, i.e. the minimum total number of misses in the whole system, is reached when the derivatives of the clients' miss functions with respect to the cache size are all equal. The approach taken has similarities to cache partitioning schemes for centralized systems as reported by Stone et al. [8, 9] and Ghanem [5]

Simulation studies with varying cache sizes show that a variable-size client cache scheme exhibits almost the same miss rate as a single big server cache.This is also shown in Fig. 1. Due to the increased reference locality, variable-size client caches even perform better than a server cache for some cache sizes and input data sets.

Although this scheme reintroduces network traffic due to the nonlocal use of memory, it still produces less network traffic than a pure centralized server cache approach, frees the server from the burden of processing every single request in the whole system, and shows much better hit rates than any of the fixed-size client caching approaches discussed before. Moreover, the additional traffic is distributed throughout the whole system and does not introduce new hot spot communication bottlenecks.

5.5 Network and I/O Speed

To be more confident about the simulated computer model some sets of simulations also have been repeated with varying network and I/O bandwidth figures. Variations of the network bandwidth were about three orders of magnitude and variations of the disk throughput were about one order of magnitude. All these simulations show that the miss rates reported in the system are fairly independent of these parameters, with variations being in the range of the accuracy of the simulation, which is predicted as $\pm$ 0.5 % by statistical considerations.

6 Conclusions

A number of fixed-size client caching schemes for parallel architectures or workstation clusters utilizing high speed point-to-point networks with different approaches for the cache coherency problem were compared to a simple centralized server caching scheme and to a variable-size client cache scheme. The variations in miss rate for the different coherency schemes used by fixed-size client caches have been found to be neglectable to the difference between the fixed-size schemes and the centralized server cache. To achieve miss rates in the range of the server cache it is very important to let the clients adjust their cache sizes among each other, such that the total number of misses reaches a minimum. This can be achieved by allowing clients with overutilized caches to use part of the cache memory of clients with underutilized caches. Although this scheme adds additional network traffic, it is shown that it still has advantages over both, centralized server caches and fixed-size client caches.

References

1. Mary G. Baker, John H. Hartman, Michael D. Kupfer, Ken W. Shirriff, and John K. Ousterhout. Measurements of a Distributed File System. Technical report, University of California at Berkeley, Computer Science Division, July 1991. Also appeared in Proceedings of the 13th Symposium on Operating Systems Principles, Oct. 1991.
2. A. Beguelin, J. Dongarra, G. Geist, W. Jiang, R. Manchek, K. Moore, and V. Sunderam. The PVM Project, 1993. Oak Ridge National Laboratory, Oak Ridge, Tennessee.
3. Eric A. Brewer, Chrysanthos N. Dellarocas, Adrian Colbrool, and William E. Weihl. PROTEUS: A High-Performance Parallel-Architecture Simulator. Technical Report MIT/LCS/TR-516, Massachusetts Institute of Technology, Laboratory for Computer Science, September 1991.
4. George F. Coulouris and Jean Dollimore. *Distributed Systems: Concepts and Design*. Addison-Wessley, 1988. ISBN 0-201-18059-6.
5. M. Z. Ghanem. Dynamic Partitioning of the Main Memory Using the Working Set Concept. *IBM Journal of Research and Dev.*, 19(9):445–450, September 1975.
6. Artur Klauser. A Simulation Study for Distributed File Caching in High-Performance Parallel Architectures. Master's thesis, Graz University of Technology, Austria, Department of Applied Information Processing, January 1994.
7. Message Passing Interface Forum. Draft Document for a Standard Message-Passing Interface. Technical report, Univ. of Tennessee, Knoxville, Tennessee, Nov. 1993.
8. Harold S. Stone, John Turek, and Joel L. Wolf. Optimal Partitioning of Cache Memory. *IEEE Transactions on Computers*, 41(9):1054–1068, September 1992.
9. Dominique Thiebaut, Harold S. Stone, and Joel L. Wolf. Improving Disk Cache Hit-Ratios Through Cache Partitioning. *IEEE Transactions on Computers*, 41(6):665–676, June 1992.

Application Fundamentals of Distributed, High-Performance Computing and Networking Systems

H. Westphal and D. Popović

University of Bremen, FB1/NW1, Institute of Automation Technology (IAT), 28359 Bremen, FRG, Tel.: FRG 421/218-3344, FAX: -3601, email: westphal@theo.physik.uni-bremen.de

Abstract. For the application of high-performance, distributed computing systems in solving complex computational problems with high real-time demands and in order to meet the real-time requirements on the underlying communication system the paper deals with application fundamentals of distributed, high-performance computing and networking systems. Evaluation of hard-bounded, worst-case, real-time computing and networking performances and latency and bandwidth evaluation of distributed, high-performance systems shows that such systems have forced us to deal with the propagation delay within the system due to the finite speed of light. The user must pay attention to his file sizes and how latency will affect his applications. At the application level, it is important to use parallelism.

1 Introduction

Engineering, scientific and commercial tasks basically require parallel processing, because sequential processing is not able to meet the real–time requirements in modern application fields like plant automation [4], intelligent systems [7] etc..

Section 2 shows a typical distributed, high-performance computing system. The Fiber Distributed Data Interface (FDDI) real-time traffic requirement evaluation (section 3.1) and the latency/bandwidth evaluation (section 3.2) gives basic system parameters. The quantity of parallel processes, that can be implemented using the T9000 and the FDDI, and a Computing Process Response Time (T_{CPRT}) evaluation is given in section 3.3. A critical Bandwidth (C_{crit}) defines the boundary of a latency-, or bandwidth-limited distributed high-performance computing and networking system (section 3.4).

2 System Elements

Using FDDI [1] ($100 MBaud$) as the networking technology for a distributed, high-performance computing system, serial links of T9000's [3] (80 $MBaud$) are interconnected to serial links of remote T9000's. Fig. 1 shows high-performance computing system C_1 and the remote system C_2 exchanging data by means of Transputer Link Interface TLI_1, a Fiber Optic Link FOL and TLI_2. Processes can intercommunicate via the T9000 *'virtual channels'* and ay number of processes can communicate with any number of transputers.

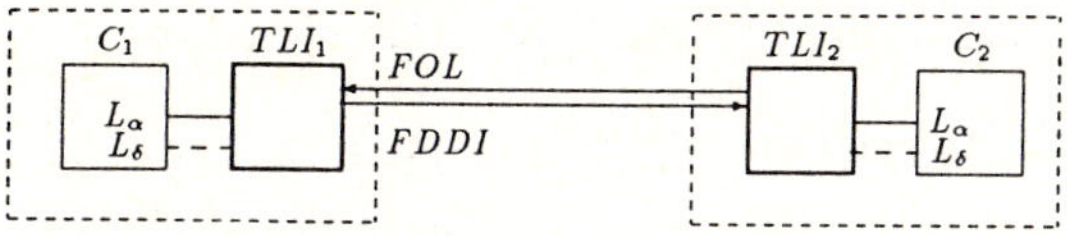

FOL : Fiber Optic Link
C : High-Performance Computing System
TLI : Transputer Link Interface
FDDI : Fiber Distributed Data Interface

Fig. 1. A typical distributed, high-performance computing system

3 Systems Parameter Evaluation

3.1 Real–Time Traffic Requirements of FDDI

The bandwidth available for synchronous traffic is calculated from the current value of the operative token rotation time, *T_Opr* [1] :

$$\mathrm{T_{Opr}} = \sum_{i=1}^{2} \mathrm{s_i} + \mathrm{t_{ov}} \tag{1}$$

N is the number of stations, s_i is the time for which station i can transmit synchronous traffic on each token rotation, t_{ov} consists of the propagation delay, approximately $5,085\mu s/km$, the latency through each station, approximately $0,6\mu s$, and the time required to transmit the token, $0,88\mu s$ [1], for S_{max} we get (s. Figure 2):

$$\mathrm{S_{max}} = \frac{\mathrm{T_{Opr}} - \mathrm{t_{ov}}}{\mathrm{T_{Opr}}} * 100\mathrm{MBaud} \tag{2}$$

The *real–time performance evaluation* is based on estimation of the time delay of the system and on the throughput analysis for transmitting of transputer packets over the FDDI. The delay (from the time a packet from a message of a process is generated at one transputer, until it reaches the remote transputer process, and until the acknowledge of this packet reaches the origin process) is the sum of individual time–delays encountered at each transmission step, we call it the Computing Process Response Time (T_{CPRT}).

Summaring the results, the real–time performance of the system will depend on parameters, specific for the timed token passing protocol (network n) of the Fiber Optic Link (FOL), and the acknowledgement protocol of the transputer (network n). To general performance (p) evaluation the minimum Computing Process Response Time (T_{CPRT}) is given by an one–packet–message process encapsulated in the FDDI protocol, (s. Figure 3). We assume a stable operation state in which each TLI subsequently receives a token, transmitts a frame, and a token. A one–packet–message, composed of a transputer data and Ack packet (312 *bit incl.* 0 – 32 *data bytes*) as INFO in the FDDI frame (224*bit* without INFO), gives a FDDI frame length of 536*bit*, i.e., $5,36\mu s$ transmission time, a ten packet message of $33,44\mu s$ and, a hundred-packet message of $314,24\mu s$ [5].

3.2 Latency and Bandwidth evaluation due to the speed of light

Remote transputer link parameters [2, 5, 6, 7, 4] C (Capacity of the network in Mb/s), b (Number of bits in a data packet), and L (Length of the network in km) give a single critical system parameter a, which is defined as:

$$\mathrm{a} = \frac{5\mathrm{LC}}{\mathrm{b}}. \tag{3}$$

The factor 5 appearing in the equation is simply the propagation delay ($5,085\mu s$ $/km$). This parameter is the ratio of the latency of the link to the time it takes to pump one packet into the link. For the one, ten and hundred packet transputer message (computing message) encapsulated in the FDDI protocol the calculation of the ratio a is shown in table 1. Using the one packet message and a distance of 1000 m the ratio a is approximately 1 (s. table 1). Table 2 shows the ratio $1/a$ (and its diagram) that gives the "FDDI length" of the transputer message (computing message) to the length of the link.

Note that in our one packet computing message one, in our ten packet computing message ten, and in our hundred packet computing message hundred logically parallel transputer processes are encapsulated in the FDDI protocol.

propagation delay / packet Tx time			
C ($Mbit/s$)	b (bit)	t (μs)	a
100	536	5.000	$9.33 * 10^{-1}$
		50.000	$9.33 * 10^{0}$
		200.000	$37.31 * 10^{0}$
	3344	5.000	$1.50 * 10^{-1}$
		50.000	$1.50 * 10^{0}$
		200.000	$5.98 * 10^{0}$
	31314	200.000	$6.36 * 10^{-1}$

capacity (C) (Mb/s)
packet length (b) bits
propagation delay (t) microsec.
ratio (a)

Table 1. a

link buffering / TLI buffer			
bl (m)	m	$1/a$	TLI_1 m TLI_2
2	1000	$1.07 * 10^{0}$	
	10000	$1.07 * 10^{-1}$	
	40000	$2.68 * 10^{-2}$	
	1000	$6.7 * 10^{0}$	
	10000	$6.7 * 10^{-1}$	
	40000	$1.7 * 10^{-1}$	
	40000	$1.57 * 10^{0}$	

FDDI bit length (bl)
link distance (m) meter
ratio ($1/a$)
transputer link interface (TLI)

Table 2. link buffering/TLI buffer

3.3 Response time and bandwidth evaluation versus load

Let us now consider the Computing Process Response Time T_{CPRT} for transputer one,- ten,- and hundred packet messages encapsulated in the FDDI frame. If, as usual, we let ρ denote the system utilization factor, then

$$\rho = \lambda \frac{b}{C}, \tag{4}$$

where λ is the arrival rate (messages per microsecond), and b the number of bits in a packet, and C the channel capacity (Mb/s). Because of the realtime ability of the remote transputer link we assume the boundary condition $0 \leq \rho < 1$.

Table 3 shows for this assumption ($\rho < 1$) the maximum arrival rate λ_{max_m} of messages and λ_{max_p} of packets, encapsulated in the FDDI frame and the approximate maximum number of Virtual Parallel Computing Messages ($VPCM_{max}$) and Virtual Parallel Computing Packets ($VPCP_{max}$) that can be implemented using the T9000.

The computing process response time T_{CPRT} (microseconds) of the remote transputer link, is given by

$$T_{CPRT} = \frac{b}{C(1-\rho)} + \tau, \tag{5}$$

where τ is the propagation delay (i.e. the channel latency) in microseconds. Table 4 shows the T_{CPRT} (in microseconds) for different computing station distances

(d, in km) and for the one,- ten,- and hundred packet transputer message encapsulated in the FDDI ($100Mb/s$) protocol. For a one packet FDDI transputer message ($536bit$, s. Table 4) and a transputer system distance of $1km$ (i.e. a FOL distance of $2km$, $10\mu s$ propagation delay) the T_{CPRT} is $15.36\mu s$. Fig. 3 shows the T_{CPRT} for the one,- ten,- and hundred packet computing message versus the system load ρ for the FDDI remote transputer link and a transputer system distance $1km$. For the T_{CPRT} initial value of $1km$ ($5km$) ($10km$) computer system distance and the one,- (536 bit) ten,- (3344 bit) and hundred (31712 bit) packet computing message refer to Table 4 with the distance (d) of $1km$ ($5km$) ($10km$). The extremely high-load situation is to be avoided for realtime ability.

λ_{max_m}, λ_{max_p}, $VPCM_{max}$ and $VPCP_{max}$						
	C	b	λ_{max_m}	λ_{max_p}	$VPCM_{max}$	$VPCP_{max}$
FDDI	100	536	$1.86 * 10^{-1}$	$1.86 * 10^{-1}$	186567	186567
		3344	$2.99 * 10^{-2}$	$2.99 * 10^{-1}$	29904	299040
		31424	$3.18 * 10^{-3}$	$3.18 * 10^{-1}$	3182	318200

capacity (C) (Mb/s)
arrival rate λ_{max_m} (messages per microsecond)
arrival rate λ_{max_p} (processes per microsecond)
$VPCM_{max}$ (messages per second)
$VPCP_{max}$ (packets per second)

Table 3. λ_{max_m}, λ_{max_p}, $VPTM_{max}$ and $VPTP_{max}$

T_{CPRT}						
d	T_{CPRT}	d	T_{CPRT}	d	T_{CPRT}	b ($FDDI$)
1	15.36	5	55.36	10	105.36	536
	43.44		83.44		133.44	3344
	324.24		364.24		414.24	31424

distance d (km)
T_{CPRT} (microseconds)
packet length (b) bits

Table 4. T_{CPRT}

C_{crit}						
d	C_{crit}	d	C_{crit}	d	C_{crit}	b($FDDI$)
1	54	5	11	10	5	536
	334		67		33	3344
	3140		630		314	31424

distance d (km)
C_{crit} $Mbit/s$
packet length (b) bits

Table 5. C_{crit}

3.4 Critical bandwidth C_{crit}, a boundary for a latency or bandwidth limited link

There are two components, as can be seen from (eq. 5), making up the response time, namely, the queuing-plus-transmission time delay ($\frac{b}{C(1-\rho)}$) and the propagation delay (τ). In accordance with the boundary condition $0 \leq \rho < 1$ we do not have to discuss the queuing delay. We discuss the relative size of each of these and we reffer to regions of bandwidth-limited and latency-limited links (s. Table 2). We define a sharp boundary between these two regions to be a place where the two terms in our equation are exactly equal. From eq. 5 we see that this occurs when the bandwidth of the link takes on the following critical value,

$$\mathrm{C_{crit}} = \frac{\mathrm{b}}{(1-\rho)\tau}. \tag{6}$$

Fig. 4 shows this critical value of bandwidth C_{crit} – for a computing system distance of $1km$, $\tau = 10\mu s$ and the maximum length (b) of the one,- (536 bit) ten,- (3344 bit) and hundred (31712 bit) packet computing message – versus the system load ρ. Above this boundary, the system is latency limited which means that more bandwidth will have negligible effect in reducing the response time, T_{CPRT}. Below this boundary, the system is bandwidth limited which means that it can take of advantage of more bandwith to reduce T_{CPRT}. For the C_{crit} initial value of $1km$, $5km$, and $10km$ computer system distance and the one,- ten,- and hundred packet computing message refer to Table 5.

4 Conclusion

We examined real-time application fundamentals of distributed, high-performance computing and networking systems. The performance evaluation experiment has been carried out with maximum deterministic load using one, ten, or hundred packet processes. The delay between token arrivals will vary according to the load of the network, thus the maximum deterministic load illustrates the worst case, real-time computing process response time of that processes (Fig. 3, Tab. 4). Further we have dealt with the latency and bandwidth in distributed real-time computing (Fig. 4, Tab. 5). One conclusion of this paper is to recognize that the system elements of the remote computing system have forced us to deal with the propagation delay due to the finite speed of light. We must rethink a number of issues. For example, the user must pay attention to his file sizes and how latency will affect his applications and at the application level, it is important to use parallelism (Tab. 3).

References

1. ISO 9314-2. *Information processing systems - Fibre Distributed Data Interface (FDDI) - Part 2: Token Ring Media Access Control (MAC)*, 1989.
2. Leonard Kleinrock. The Latency/Bandwidth Tradeoff in Gigabit Networks. *IEEE Communications Magazine*, April 1992.
3. SGS-THOMSON. *IMS T9000 Transputer*, 1992.
4. H. Westphal. Interfacing Parallel Computers to Fiber-Optic Communication Links for Plant Automation. In *Conference on Control Applications (CCA '94)*, Glasgow, UK, Aug. 24 - 26 1994. Accepted REGULAR paper.
5. H. Westphal and D. Popović. Latency and Bandwidth Evaluation of Distributed Transputer Networks based on FDDI and HIPPI T9000 Links. In R. Grebe, J. Hektor, Susan C. Hilton, Mike R. Jane, and Peter H. Welch, editors, *Transputer Applications and Systems '93, Vol.1*, Transputer and OCCAM engineering series, pages 52–61. IOS Press, Amsterdam Oxford Washington Tokyo, Sept. 1993. Proceedings of the 1993 World Transputer Congress.
6. H. Westphal and D. Popović. Performance evaluation of distributed transputer networks using high performance communication links. In C.A. Brebbia and H. Power, editors, *Applications of Supercomputers in Engineering III (ASE '93)*, pages 425–437. Computational Mechanics Publications, Southampton Boston; Elsevier Applied Science, London New York, Sept. 1993. Third international conference on ASE.
7. H. Westphal and D. Popović. Performance Evaluation of Distributed, Intelligent Real-Time Control Systems. In *American Control Conference (ACC '94)*, Baltimore, Maryland, June 29 – July 1 1994. Accepted REGULAR paper: session FA11, Control of Distributed Parameter Systems.

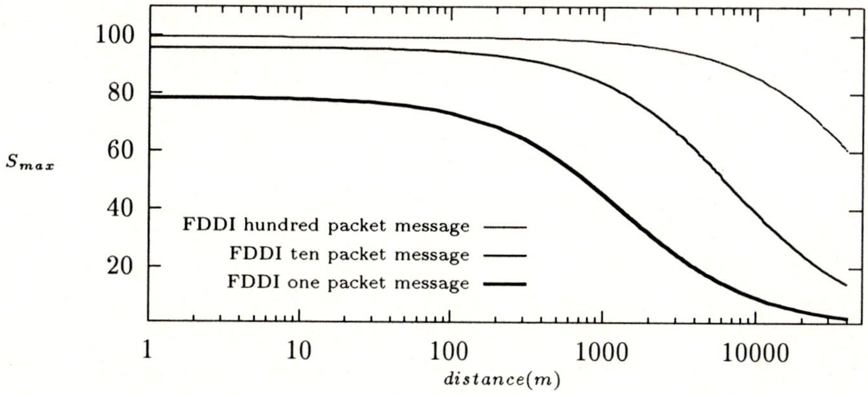

Fig. 2. S_{max} $(Mbit/s)$ versus computing system distance (d), $p = f(r, d, b, n)$

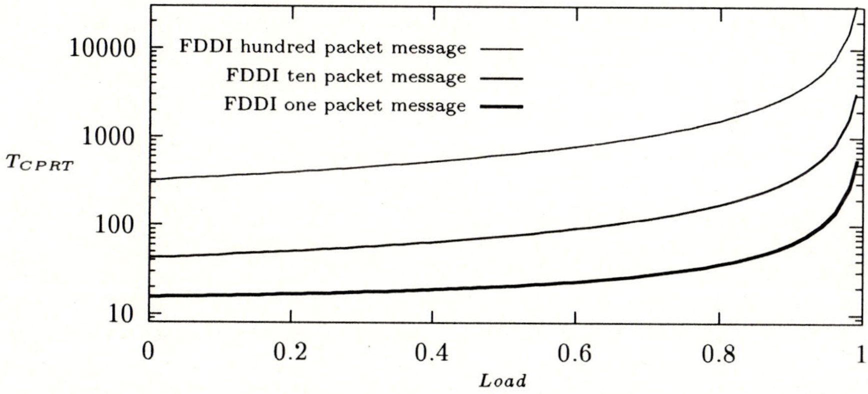

Fig. 3. T_{CPRT} (μs) versus load for a computing system distance (d) of $1km$

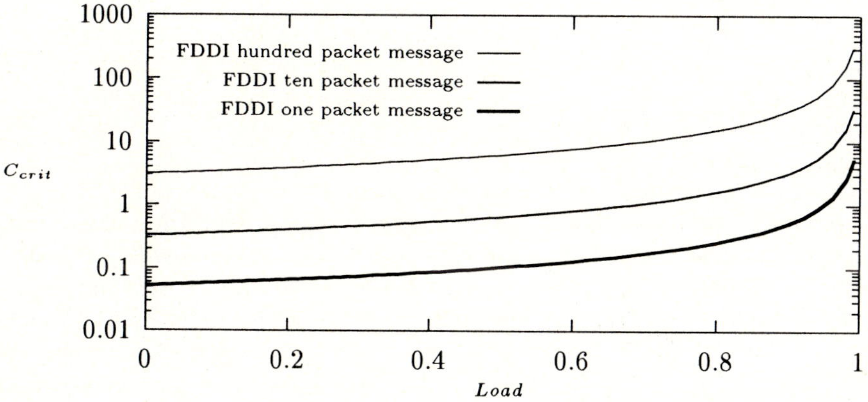

Fig. 4. C_{crit} (Gb/s) versus load for a computing system distance (d) of $1km$

Massive Parallelism with Workstation Clusters – Challenge or Nonsense?

CLEMENS H. CAP*
Department of Computer Science, University of Zurich
Winterthurerstrasse 190, CH–8057 Zurich, Switzerland
e-mail: cap@ifi.unizh.ch, Tel. +41–1–257 43 26

Abstract. Workstation cluster computing recently has become an important and successful technique. The communication bottleneck limits this approach to small and medium sized configurations of up to 30 workstations for most applications. This paper demonstrates that for certain algorithms massively parallel cluster computing using thousands of workstations in the Internet is feasible. It describes structures for the coordination of a large number of geographically dispersed processes. The paper introduces LOLA, a library supporting massively parallel computing in wide area networks, and provides an application example.

1 Introduction

Recent research activities have shown, that workstation cluster computing or *hypercomputing* provides a fair amount of computing power at a reasonable price. [9] reports a performance of more than 1 Gflops in a cluster of 110 workstations and [14] demonstrates, that for certain applications cluster solutions provide a price performance ratio which is two orders of magnitude better than for classical supercomputers. [19] estimates that 90% of Lawrence Livermore National Laboratory's workload can be solved with workstation clusters. On the other hand, [5] shows, that communication represents a severe bottleneck. Since a larger number of processors leads to increased communication, we may expect a limit on the number of workstations.

At first sight massive parallelism with workstations connected by local and wide area networks makes no sense, especially if we use the term massive parallelism for configurations of 500 and more processors. This paper will demonstrate in Section 2 that for special applications massively parallel cluster computation in a WAN indeed is an option and a challenge, whereas for a general approach it makes no sense. Section 3 describes techniques for the development of massively parallel applications in WANs, Section 4 describes concrete library routines and Section 5 discusses practical experiences. The paper closes with an overview of similar research activities and future work.

* Research partially supported by Firma Siemens AG München and Schweizer Bundesamt für Konjunktur und Wirtschaftsförderung, grant numbers 2255.1 and 2554.1.

2 Massive Parallelism in WANs

Computations of two-dimensional heat conduction on a cluster of 40 Sparc workstations produced an average communication bandwidth of 5.288 MBit/sec or 52.88 % of the physical bandwidth of the Ethernet, assuming that communication takes place during the entire run [6], [5]. The peak communication load therefore was still higher. An Ethernet utilization of more than 20 % already is considered a high load. These experiments and analytic performance models indicate, that the communication bandwidth limits the scalability of this approach, since the communication load is proportional to the number of processors. Furthermore the high number of collisions in a heavily loaded Ethernet has an adverse effect on speedup. Similar observations can be made for many applications due to their small grain size and locality [1], [4].

There can be at most 255 workstations in a LAN, and on the average there are about 20 machines in a LAN. Therefore massive parallelism with workstations must use several LANs connected by metropolitan and wide area technology. The following sustained bandwidths were observed in the Internet [12]:

Switzerland	100 kBytes/sec	Transatlantic	$\leq$ 30 kBytes/sec
Europe	1 – 50 kBytes/sec	Transpacific	$\leq$ 3 kBytes/sec

Only special applications with *low communication* demands are reasonable for massively parallel clusters. Depending whether the communication of two processes takes place within a LAN or crosses its borders, differences in the bandwidth of two orders of magnitude may be observed. There are several applications, where the *dominating operations* are comparisons, jumps and integer operations. Their programs are much better adapted to the architecture of RISC workstations with their relatively fast scalar integer units than to the traditional supercomputer: For example the BLASTPM code from molecular biology required 1820 sec. computing time on a Sun 4 workstation and 1522 sec. on a CRAY Y-MP [10]. Similar experiences are reported by [14]. Many problems from *mathematical physics* are concerned with local physical laws and differential equations. The dominating operations are floating point operations and the locality of the physical law is reflected in the algorithm by a high demand for communication. However, a large class of problems from optimization and simulation, from information retrieval, from VLSI layout to the analysis of homology in genetic sequences require only a very small amount of communication and allow a large degree of parallelism.

Consequence: Massive parallelism with workstations in a wide area network is possible, but only for special applications and algorithms.

Presently there are many software packages, assisting the programmer in developing parallel programs for LAN clusters [4], [19]. In principle these systems could also control WAN systems. For practical purposes *wide area communica-*

tion is different from the local area situation for many reasons: The bandwidth in a WAN is one to two orders of magnitude lower and latency is higher by one order of magnitude. In a WAN there can be additional traffic from connected LANs, so there is a higher variation in latency and available bandwidth. Commands which start and terminate processes on remote machines can be delayed for several seconds, and time out mechanisms have delays of up to several minutes.

Although *location transparency* of processes in a cluster is desirable from a software engineering point of view, in wide area massively parallel systems the programmer should know, whether two processes reside in the same LAN or not. Communication and synchronization of processes is much more difficult if it must be achieved across the borders of a LAN and therefore should be adapted to the topology-in-the-large of the WAN.

Small clusters of 5 to 20 machines often belong to one department and may be used in dedicated mode for experimentation. With several hundred workstations there will always be some activity by other users who are likely to revoke the permission for using their machine, if disturbed in their own work. Therefore we must take special care not to produce too much load when the local user needs his workstation. Furthermore problems like looping programs, filling the file system with core dumps, consuming all slots of the process table, using up temporary storage space, flooding networks or extensive swapping lead to more trouble on thousand machines in a WAN than on ten machines in your own LAN. Due to the distributed ownership of a WAN cluster we have less *influence on the configuration* of the machines. In general, superuser capabilities for installing programs or reconfiguring systems are available only for our own workstations. Therefore we must cope with heterogeneous configurations, which cannot be flexibly adapted to our needs. For example, temporary storage space could be found in different parts of the directory structure, network services like name servers could be configured differently or are even disabled.

Due to the large number of different hardware architectures and operating system releases, a *highly portable* programming style is necessary. The *installation* of our software cannot be made by hand on several hundred machines and portable shell scripts must be used to automate this task. In a wide area environment we have less control on remote equipment and a much higher possibility of workstation or network *failure*. Especially, a workstation can be turned off unexpectedly by its user.

Consequence: There is a unique challenge for controlling communication and process activities in a wide area domain which necessitate distinguishing an *inter-LAN* and an *intra-LAN* layer.

3 Managing Massive Parallelism in a WAN

We use three types of processes for controlling the activities of our cluster: *Worker* processes perform the computational work of the application; all the other processes are responsible for the coordination of activities. A single *master* process takes care of all top level system activities, provides a user interface and starts slave and worker processes. The *slaves* coordinate larger configurations, since several hundred workers managed by a single master would produce a bottleneck. Therefore the master starts slaves, preferably a small number in every LAN, and the slaves administrate several dozens of worker processes. Since a master may start workers and slaves and since slaves may start other slaves, the construction of arbitrary tree-structured control hierarchies is possible.

The *communication topology* on the inter-LAN layer is a tree with the master process as root, the workers as leafs and the slaves in between. Workers within a LAN may use their own means of communication to exchange data among them. Since there are several LAN cluster systems like Parform [5], PVM [8], P4 [2] and others [4] we will not further elaborate upon this. Communication on the inter-LAN layer can go *upstream* (up the tree towards the root) or *downstream* (down the tree towards the leafs) and is under the control of the wide area cluster software. Workers controlled by different slaves cannot communicate directly with each other but route their information upstream using the lowest common ancestor in the tree. At first sight this may seem a drawback. However, in practice the structure of the tree will be adapted to the physical layout of the WAN and a direct, point-to-point connection between two workers from different LANs requires the assistance of routing software. In our solution this only becomes more explicit. Furthermore for performance and security reasons many networks are configured so that only servers have direct access to the outer world. In such a situation a direct network connection cannot be established and additional routing processes must be developed. This problem is circumvented by placing the slaves on machines with direct network access. Then data between workers on different LANs automatically are routed by the slaves. The processes are identified by a *hierarchical name space* which provides routing information in the tree.

Before an application can be run, all processes must be *started*. When the master is running, it consults its host file to find out which processes it must start and where. Once a slave is started on a remote machine, this procedure is repeated and after a while the entire tree of master, slaves and workers is operative.

It is imperative to prevent disturbances of other users. Therefore we provide an elaborate *shutdown mechanism* which is triggered on a number of occasions. First, every operating system call requires full error handling. Conditions like "file system full" or "process table full" and signals like "segmentation fault" are observed and caught. All available error information is sent upstream and presented to the user on the machine of the master process. Next, a cleanup procedure is called for deleting temporary files and for killing all other processes running under the same user id. At last the process itself exits. If this shutdown mechanism is triggered in a slave, then the communication connection to its children is lost. When these child processes try to communicate with this slave, they receive an error condition and trigger the shutdown themselves. It is therefore guaranteed, that the shutdown of a non-leaf process eventually leads to a cleanup and shutdown of all processes. A periodic heartbeat enquiry ensures that this mechanism is not delayed arbitrarily. Furthermore, all processes implement a watchdog mechanism. If the watchdog reset has not been called for a certain time the shutdown procedure is triggered.

After startup a process receives information, where and how to establish communication with its parent, starts its own child processes and waits for status information from them. Children that did not provide status information during some period are considered in error. The slave sends a summary of this status information upstream to its own parent and waits for application commands from upstream. It exits, unless a command is received in due time.

This mechanism produces a downstream *wave front* from the root of the tree to its leafs: The master starts slaves, they again start slaves and workers and so on until all processes are running. Then the worker processes start a benchmark to determine the performance with which they might contribute. This information forms an upstream wave front from the leafs to the root. At all branches of the tree a summary of the information received from downstream is composed and sent upstream. Error information is passed upstream for display to the user. Having received the summary information the master broadcasts the application data downstream. When these data finally reach the leafs, the workers start the calculation. When they are finished, the result is sent upstream. The slaves apply an application dependent function to the data they receive from their children and pass the result further upstream. The final result is output by the master process.

In a larger configuration we cannot predict, which workstations will be turned off. Therefore the application algorithm must deal with a *varying number of workers* and cope with the *loss of a worker* process during the calculation. This can be done with a *workpool*: A slave keeps track of some parts of the work. It hands out work to all available workers and receives intermediate results of the computation. It periodically checks, whether there are new workstations, which can be used for the computation, and it keeps track, whether for work handed out eventually a result is returned. If a worker crashes, the slave distributes the respective part of the work to another worker. When a worker crashes all its state is lost. Therefore the slave-worker cooperation must be stateless: The worker must send all information for continuing the calculation back to the salve. An efficient form of this workpool is highly application dependent and is implemented by the application programmer. At the inter-LAN layer no fault tolerance mechanism is used. The slave processes are running on servers or gateways with a connection to the WAN, they generally are more stable than the individual workstations and will not be turned off unexpectedly. The slaves usually produce only negligible computational load and so there is no danger of overloading a server.

The *inter-LAN programming layer* is based on waves which traverse the tree. It provides tree structured communication at low bandwidth and high latency time. Communication between arbitrary processes is difficult to establish for processes in different LANs. The *intra-LAN programming layer* uses the workpool mechanism and can handle every communication topology. It provides a significantly higher bandwidth and smaller latency time. Application algorithms must be adapted to exploit these structures.

We should not *disturb the local user* of a workstation by a compute intensive job. In the host file we can specify the scheduler priority (niceness) for our processes. A sufficiently low priority guarantees, that our process gets a time slice only, when no other process is runnable. This technique works only, when our process consumes just a small percentage of the workstation's RAM; otherwise each time the process must relinquish the CPU to another process, some time must be spent for swapping and paging. A user working with an interactive program is likely to be annoyed by that delay. We can program the workpool, that a machine only gets a piece of work, if it has been idle for at least ten minutes. If the user returns, the workstation signals that it is no longer available and will not finish the assigned task. The workpool will then dispatch this piece of work to a different computer.

4 Library Routines

As *programming language interface* we provide a small set of library routines, which are used to compose master, slave and worker processes. Master and slaves are small programs which can be derived by adapting a template to the specific application, the workers contain the main application code.

Processes on remote workstations can be started using several techniques. The parent process can contact the Internet-demon `inetd`, issue the remote shell command `rsh`, or it can contact the remote shell server `rshd` or the remote execution server `rexecd` directly. Since several sites disabled some of these services such a large choice of methods was necessary. We even worked with a site which had all services disabled, which could remotely start processes. In this situation a user owned and modified Internet-demon of restricted functionality was used instead of the root owned `inetd`. This demon had to be started manually if necessary, or on a regular basis using `at` or `cron` commands. The remotely started processes must establish a communication link with their parent process. Several employed startup techniques, like the `inetd` furnish such a connection, for others, like the `rsh` technique they must be established separately. For every machine the startup and reconnect technique is specified in the host file.

For a remote machine it may take up to one minute until a time out is generated by the local operating system. Therefore we must parallelize the process startup; ten workstations which are switched off could otherwise increase total startup time to more than ten minutes. While we are waiting for an answer from one workstation we can already initiate the startup sequence on other machines. In case of client-server oriented techniques nonblocking socket connection attempts were used. The `rsh` technique may be parallelized running shells in the background. Here care must be taken to disconnect standard input, output and error files from the remote shells to allow an exit of the remote shell before the exit of the issued remote command. Otherwise every remotely started process wastes one slot in the process table of the slave. The routines `startup_kids()` and `reconnect()` are responsible for the described mechanisms.

`receive_upstream (buffer, bufflen)` receives a message from the parent process, `receive_downstream (child_id, buffer, bufflen)` receives a message from a child, `send_upstream (buffer, bufflen)` sends a message to the parent process and `send_downstream (child_id, buffer, bufflen)` sends a message to a child. `flood_downstream (buffer, bufflen)` broadcasts a message to all children. All receive functions are implemented as blocking and all communication functions perform full error handling. They trigger the shutdown mechanism whenever this is appropriate.

`pass_info (app_dep, a, b)` provides the main synchronization function for the wave mechanism and waits for messages from all children of the process in which it is called. As soon as a message arrives it is read and its type and source is decoded from the header. "Pass-through" messages are forwarded upstream to the parent, a technique mainly used for error messages which the processes traditionally would write to standard error. "Status" messages update a table reflecting the state of the immediate children. "Finished" messages trigger the release of the synchronization mechanism and are described below. "Application" messages call an application dependent function for further processing. This function is specified by the pointer `app_dep` and is passed the contents of the message for further processing. The thread of control finally returns to `pass_info`. Control is released from `pass_info` after a timeout, specified by parameters a and `b`, or after every fully operative child process has sent a "finished" message. This mechanism allows to leave `pass_info` earlier than the specified time out and as soon as the children signaled, that they have sent all necessary information. In case an insufficient number of "finished" messages is received, this indicates a problem with one of the children; if appropriate, the shutdown mechanism is triggered. `send_finished()` sends a "finished" message upstream and `send_state_upstream()` sends state information on the process (for workers) or statistical summaries (for slaves) upstream. Both messages are automatically dealt with in `pass_info`.

The master and all slaves collect *state information* on their child processes. They record the number of operative and erroneous processes, the performance of the workstations, the percentage of this performance, that could be contributed to the parallel run and information about the presence and activities of other processes and interactive users. Every process composes a concise statistical summary, which is sent to the parent.

5 Implementation and Practical Experiences

To test our approach, above routines were *implemented* in C for 23 different workstation/operating system combinations and installed on over 800 workstations in 31 LANs of the Internet, situated on all five continents [7], [3]. The system is nicknamed LOLA, which is an abbreviation for loosely coupled large area and was used to develop a prototype for the comparison of genetic and protein sequences.

Portability was astonishingly easy to achieve by a few preprocessor directives. The problems encountered were associated with different paths for include and header files and with system calls like `getrusage`, which only are available on Berkeley-type UNIX implementations. On System 5 and Solaris 2 environments compatibility libraries had to be linked. In general portability was no big issue despite our heavy use of low level network interface routines.

For the *installation* accounts were set up on the remote machines and a master site was entered into the `.rhosts` file. A set of shell scripts was developed for automating the installation: At first various scripts were transferred to the remote hosts via `rcp`. The copied scripts then configured, compiled and installed the software on the target. In order to deal with various different configurations encountered during the installation, we developed a parameter file whose entries allowed a detailed control of installation options. In *heterogeneous* networks we had to ensure, that every machine executes the correct binary. This was especially difficult, when only one machine was connected to the WAN and further copying was necessary to provide workstations of a different architecture with their sources. In networks with *homogeneous* hardware we encountered incompatible versions of runtime systems and shared libraries, which led to error conditions. This was solved with static linking during compilation. Due to the size and heterogeneity of the configuration manual installation via `ftp` or `telnet` or WAN-wide network file systems was no option. However, the necessity of the shell scripts and their functionality became obvious only during our experimentation and so many installations initially were done manually.

The *incoherent configuration* we found in a number of networks was disturbing, but fortunately many departments gave us a helping hand when problems occurred and assisted during the installation wherever they could. We found an alarming number of well known *security holes*, which gives an alarming picture of the state of some academic workstation environments.

We tested our system with an *application from molecular biology*. Given a new gene sequence (in form of a text string) the task is to determine all those genes of a database which are most similar to the given one. This application is very important in modern biotechnology and its background is described further in [11]. The employed algorithm uses dynamic programming techniques and is further explained in [16] and [20]. For parallelization we partitioned the database consisting of 106.684 genes into subsets which were distributed to the individual LANs. The new, given gene was entered at the master and broadcast to the slaves and workers. The slaves told the workers to calculate similarity scores between certain parts of the database and the given gene. This handing out of work was implemented by a workpool mechanism. Finally, the obtained similarity scores were communicated upstream. Every slave determined the best matching genes, so that finally a small set of best fitting genes was output at the master process. The database of a total size of over 100 MBytes was predistributed to the LANs based on a priori performance estimations. Within a single LAN the slaves and the workpool mechanism provided for load balancing between the worker processes. Only the new, given gene and the obtained scores and gene identifiers had to be communicated, so there was no communication bottleneck. The table below shows the speedup obtained in different experiments [7], [3].

Number of Workstations	Parallel Runtime	Runtime on one Sparc 1	Runtime on one Sparc 2	Speedup vs. Sparc 1	Speedup vs. Sparc 2
642	3.2 min	16.4 hours	—	311	—
803	5.0 min	21.5 hours	10.4 hours	258	125
803	18.4 min	6.6 days	3.2 days	515	250

Since this experiment was conducted as *feasibility study*, no effort was made to tune the configuration for high performance. Although in some instances the first LANs were idling already after a fifth of the total execution time, no further load balancing between the LANs was made, and precautions were taken, not to overload the machines and communication links. From this point of view the obtained results are promising. The stability observed throughout the experiments also was astonishingly high.

There are three areas, where the *application* of WAN massively parallel systems is of interest. First, applications which allow a very large degree of parallelism and are well adapted to workstation architectures, similar to our molecular biology example. Second, systems which are WAN based by their infrastructure and data distribution. Examples are name services or wide area library catalogues. Here the emphasis is placed on the distributed aspect rather than on speedup. A third application is parallelism on the supercomputer level. Here the main problem is an imbalanced computation to communication ratio.

It should be possible to setup a WAN massively parallel production system for closed user groups, for example biologists, even across the borders of continents. Small adaptions of network configurations are necessary, in order to obtain higher efficiency. For example, a sufficient number of machines where the slaves will run should have network connection, and at least one disc partition should be mounted by all machines of a LAN for storing shared and temporary data. An acceptable usage policy must be developed for the workstation owners. For example, parallel runs should be restricted to certain times of the day (or rather, of the night or of the weekend) and scheduled to machines, whose performance is not required locally.

6 Similar Work and Further Research

WAN parallelism was studied in [15], [12], [17]. In these experiments a smaller number of *supercomputers* was coupled for determining the structure of large molecules with a modified Hartree–Fock method [12]. Massively parallel approaches were studied with *110 workstations* at the Technical University of Munich [9]. The employed algorithm was optimized to reduce the necessary communication and a special Ethernet topology for the LAN was used. The 1992 winners of the *Gordon Bell prize* [14] made experiments with up to 192 workstations using PVM. In 1993 the first prize of the *Mannheim SuParCup* was awarded to the author of this paper and his collaborator Volker Strumpen for the genetic application described above, using a preliminary version of LOLA.

Encouraged by these scientific activities and awards we want to set up stable test environments to demonstrate that wide area massive parallelism works for *production purposes*. Furthermore we will investigate other kinds of *applications*. However, one must always keep in mind, that at the present, and most likely also the next generation of WAN technology, there is a distinct bottleneck: WAN parallelism is only possible for a small albeit important class of applications. We must live with the realities of installed technology rather than utilize the most advanced techniques which are available. The ever shrinking budgets, however, are likely to promote cluster technologies.

Acknowledgements
I want to thank professors Lutz Richter and Kurt Bauknecht for an environment which is fun to work in and for their interest in my research. The financial support of Firma Siemens AG, München and Schweizer Bundesamt für Konjunktur und Wirtschaftsförderung made this work possible. Volker Strumpen helped with the implementation and installation of the molecular biology example and with measurements. Edgar Lederer provided numerous suggestions. The Suparcup organized by professors Werner Meuer and Wolfgang Gentzsch gave an important stimulus for parts of this work. The measurements could be made when many friends provided us with accounts on their workstations. All their help was and is of high value for our work.

References

1. R. D. Bjornson, Linda on Distributed Memory Multiprocessors. PhD Thesis and technical report YALEU/DCS/RR-931, University of Yale, november 1992.
2. R. Butler, E. Lusk, User's Guide to the p4 Parallel Programming System. Technical report, Argonne National Laboratory, august 1992.
3. C. H. Cap, Massively Parallel Computing in Wide Area Networks. Technical report, department of computer science, University of Zurich, 1993.
4. C. H. Cap, Architekturelle Entscheidungen zur Unterstützung parallelen Rechnens in Workstation Clustern und deren Realisierung in existenten Produkten. Proceedings 2. ITG/GI Workshop Workstations, Hagen 1993, VDE Verlag.
5. C. H. Cap and V. Strumpen, Efficient Parallel Computing in Distributed Workstation Environments. *Parallel Computing*, **19**(11), 1993.
6. C. H. Cap and V. Strumpen, The Parform – A High Performance Parallel Platform for Efficient Computation in a Distributed Workstation Environment. Technical report IFI-TR 92.07 Technical report, department of computer science, University of Zurich, 1992.
7. C. H. Cap and V. Strumpen, Massively Parallel Computing in the Internet – Entry to the SuParCup'93. Department of computer science, University of Zurich, 1993. This entry won the first prize of the SuParCup93.
8. G. Geist and V. Sunderam. The PVM system: Supercomputer Level Concurrent Computation on a Heterogeneous Network of Workstations. *Proceedings of the Sixth Distributed Memory Computing Conference*, IEEE Press, 1991,258–261.
9. M. Griebel, W. Huber, T. Störtkuhl and C. Zenger, On the Parallel Solution of 3D PDEs on a Network of Workstations and on Vector Computers.
10. HPCwire, Comparing the Efficiency of molecular biology sequence-analysis computations. Electronic Newsletter HPCwire, topic 815, March 1, 1993. Further source: SDSC's Computational Science Advances.
11. R. J. Lipton, T. G. Marr and J. D. Welsh, Computational Approaches to Discovering Semantics in Molecular Biology. *Proc. IEEE* **77**(7) 1989, pp. 1056–1060.
12. H. P. Lüthi, J. Almlöf, Network Supercomputing: A distributed-concurrent direct SCF scheme. *Theoretica Chimica Acta* **84**, 1993, pp. 443–455.
13. C. D. Marsan, NSF pursues computing without walls. *Federal Computer Week* **6**(35), 53, november 30, 1992.
14. H. Nakanishi, V. Rego and V. Sunderam, Superconcurrent Simulation of Polymer Chains on Heterogeneous Networks. *Proceedings Supercomputer 92, Minneapolis*, IEEE Press, 1992, 561-569.
15. W. Scott, P. Arbenz, S. Vogel and H. P. Lüthi, Network Supercomputing. *EPFL Supercomputing Review*, november 1991.
16. T. F. Smith, M. S. Waterman, Identification of Common Molecular Subsequences. *Journal of Molecular Biology* **147**, 1981, pp. 195–197
17. C. Sprenger, Netzwerk-Computing. Diploma thesis, Institut für wissenschaftliches Rechnen, ETH Zurich, march 1992.
18. V. Strumpen, Parallel Molecular Sequence Analysis on Workstations in the Internet. Technical report, department of computer science, University of Zurich, 1993.
19. L. H. Turcotte, A Survey of Software Environments for Exploiting Networked Computing Resources. Technical report of the engineering research center for computational field simulation, june 1993.
20. R. A. Wagner and M. J. Fischer, The String to String Correction Problem. *JACM* **21**(2) 1974, pp. 168–173.

Networking Perspectives for Collaborative Supercomputing in European Aerospace Research and Industry

J.P. Peltier[1] Paul Christ[2]

[1] ONERA Office Nationald'Etudes et de Recherches Aerospatiales, France
[2] RUS Rechenzentrum Universität Stuttgart, Germany

Abstract. For some years European aerospace industry and research pursue the idea of an 'EASNet' – an European Aeronautical Supercomputing Network. Within this context, the project RACE 2031 PAGEIN 'Pilot Applications in a Gigabit European Integrated Network' collects a major part of European aerospace research, some manufacturers and two universities. PAGEIN's application environment comprises elements such as supercomputers of different architectures, simulations in computational fluid dynamics (CFD), scientific visualization and cooperative working scenarios including voice and video – to be demonstrated in a high–speed network environment. Using it as a paradigm, the presentation is going to position networking aspects of PAGEIN with respect to history and present state of efforts both within the European aerospace industrial research and CEC level programs towards high–speed network mediated international collaboration.

1 Cooperation in European Aerospace Industry

Aeronautical and space industry is, with nuclear industry, the one relying with the greatest emphasis upon highly sophisticated and integrated simulation tools and has therefore reached maturity in its usage for conception and definition of products.
On the other hand aeronautical industry pioneered in the domain of cooperation, on an European and worldwide scale as exemplified by the Airbus.
But, state of the art in cooperation does not imply technology sharing. And as a matter of fact, it appears that each one of the different European partners has developed, is developing and will still develop specific strong simulation tools. In most cases tools just could not be transferred: Hardware dependant when optimized, often using specific interfaces with local data structures, these very specialized simulation tools could not, at any rate, survive away from their designer's team. The market is not broad enough to justify commercial versions. Moreover they often represent not–for–sale strategic assets.
Given this situation, a major key towards technology sharing is to organize a controlled remote access, open to authorized cooperating teams. Thus, at each step in the definition of a new aeronautical system the conception team will be able to input with its current local data some apprropriate, remote, leading edge simulation tool of a partner.

Hence development of new, leading edge applications of peak expensive supercomputers will be possible on a shared cost basis. Furthermore will be gained, through optimization at all levels, the fraction of performance which in the air–transport business makes the difference: concepts such a hierarchical subcontracting or cooperation without technology – sharing although minimizing information fluxes between European partners, induce a limitation on global system optimization. Intimate 'peer level' cooperation will break this limitation.
This requires the progress one can foresee in the area of broadband computer communication becomes reality in a coordinated manner.
It should be noted that in the past no CEC program yet has adequately addressed wide area communication as such, although RACE, ESPRIT, COST programs had some relevance and some of their successor activities within the context of the evolving 4th Framework Program do explicitely target a European backbone network for research.
But first of all, aeronautical and space industries had to be convinced that, in spite of difficulties, true broadband networking is possible and can be routinely available in Europe – before budgeting any action.
As a result of a CEC initiative to define steps towards cooperative research in order to foster European aerospace competitivity in 1988 a consortium of industries and research institutes has expressed a strong interest for the creation of an 'European Aeronautical Supercomputing Network' – an 'EASNet'.

The presentation will describe the requirements for such a supercomputing network as determined in the EASNet environment and indicate how such a concept stands in European context[3].
Using it as a paradigm the paper will then outline certain aspects of an 'EASNet' covered by the project RACE 2031 PAGEIN so far, its past actions and future plans with respect to the evolving European network scene.

2 Computer Power and Network Bandwidth

2.1 The CFD case

Figure 2 elaborates on Peterson's (NASA Ames) projection on Computational Fluid Dynamics applications for aircraft external flow simulations: such simulations have severely to increase their ability to account for viscosity so as to reach sufficiently accurate drag prediction, as drag commands fuel consumption. Current errors on numerically predicted drag of an aircraft is over ten times the difference in drag over which constructors fight. On the other hand, half of the performance improvement expected in the coming decade for commercial aircraft deals with the aerodynamics; see Fig. 1. The upper curve of Fig. 2 represents the 'proof of principle' performance. Typically a proof of principles demands about

[3] Europe – U.S. competition would deserve a section of its own.

200 CPU hours of a supercomputer, sliced in a number of short runs of typically 3 wall clock hours program execution.
Peterson's projection, based on 1988 algorithms, calls for a 10^{12} improvement in computation efficiency. Such improvement could be obtained combining improvements in algorithms and hardware. Roughly, extrapolating past experience one would expect a balanced hardware/software improvement, eg. 10^6 overall increase in hardware power, 10^6 increase in algorithmic efficiency. Algorithms have already shown significant improvements, and the 10^3 for algorithms with respect to 1988 can be anticipated. Hardware is also expected to exhibit a further 10^3 improvement before the end of decade, most probably by usage of moderately parallel computer in the 100 to 1000 processor range.
Overall improvement of $N = 10^{12}$ would enable to process models be increased by 10^9 in size, but there are doubts that a constant improvement of todays numerical schemes can breaktrough up to 10^6 ratio, while difficulties can also be expected in the efficient interconnection of a million MIMD processors, beyond TeraFlops computers. So, extrapolating far beyond year 2000 is not quite obvious, and direct simulation of Navier Stokes is not for tomorrow. However, rather straight forward is the upcoming overall improvement of $N = 10^6$ which would cope with $10^{4.5}$ in model size, matching the expected 10^3 hardware improvement.

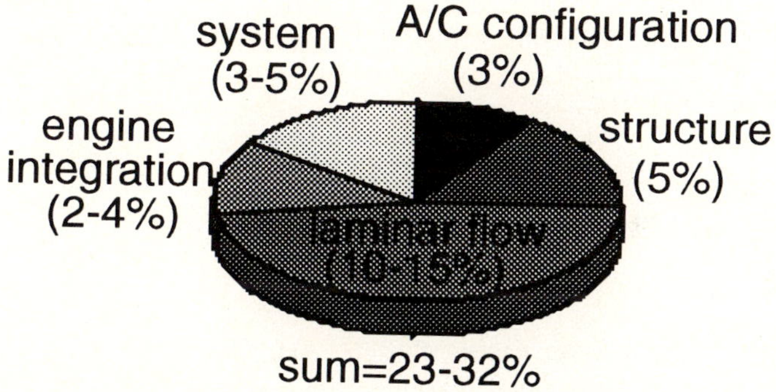

Fig. 1. Expected cost/fuel savings in the 2000's according to Aerospatiale – BAe – Deutsche Airbus

2.2 Going Operational

Peterson's 'diagram can not only be applied to estimate computing requirements for 'proof of principles' cases – which are in limited number on a given supercomputer – but also to estimate computing requirement for industrial usage. Ideally, to be routinely run by industry a simulation which was developed on a 200 CPU hours basis should provide its result within a few tens of minutes; cf. DESIGN curve of Fig. 2. Moreover, to be operated in an automatic design

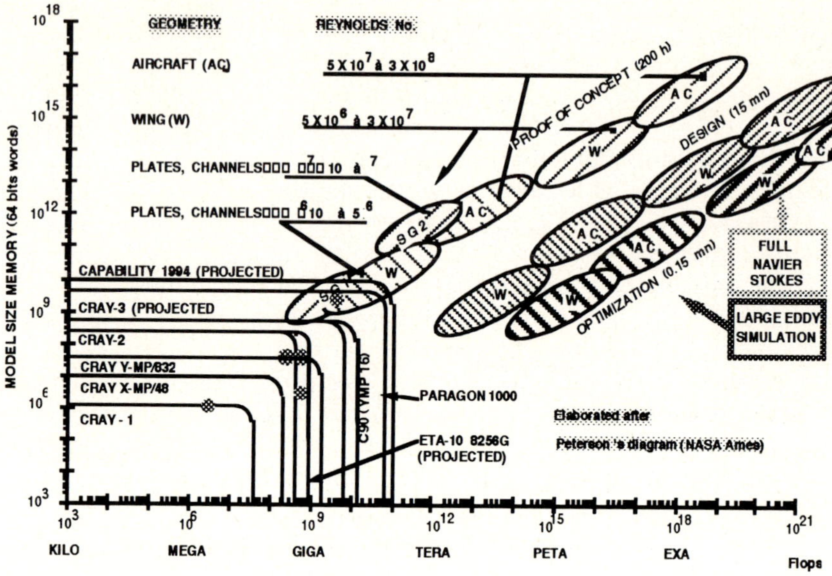

Fig. 2. Increase in computing power required for CFD

process, where performance optimization is sought through iterative execution of simulation cases, an additional minimum improvement of 10 is necessary; cf. OPTIMAZATION curve of Fig. 2.

2.3 Derived Bandwidth

Using the above characteristic cases of high performance computing applications, and assuming a hardware/software evolution in the future compliant with TeraFlops systems available during the second half of the 90's, requirements on bandwidth have been derived as shown in the following table.

Date	Increase Factor N	$N^{3/4}$	Reference Bandwidth	Degraded Bandwidth
1992	1	1	20 Mbit/s	10 Mbit/s
	10	5.6	100 Mbit/s	30 Mbit/s
	10^2	30	300 Mbit/s	100 Mbit/s
	10^3	180	3.500 Mbit/s	300 Mbit/s
1997	10^4	1000	20.000 Mbit/s	1000 Mbit/s
2002	10^5	5600	100.000 Mbit/s	3000 Mbit/s

3 Simulation versus Real Facts

As, in aerospace business, simulation aims at representing reality, simulation tools have to be checked against reality. Actually, validation of large simulation codes represents by itself a stiff challenge. Codes are checked against other pre–validated simultion results or theoretical results whenever possible. In this area, any improvement of validation methods represents a competitive advantage in the end. This is why efficient high peformance computing environment should enable handling of experimental data, including video and sound data.
Such requirements imply appropriate storage and access of experimental data. Once the simulation tool is operational, it can be used in the control loop of a live experiment itself, on a remote basis ideally. This perspective clearly calls for multimedia integrated processes.
Distribution of very large experimental data sets call for broadband networking – but with specific requirements. Large experimental facilities such as wind tunnels in aeronautics or spacelabs in space sciences provide such volumes of data that the best place for storage and post process of data are on the sites where the experiments have been conceived and can best be interpreted. Such distribution of data results in rather steady flow over hours or days, if not month for space measurements, the origin being constant (experimental site or ground station for satellites) destination varying over successive experiments. Such characteristics call for circuit switching rather than for packet switching.
However, if experimenters want real time driving of the experiment, then specifications are quite different: interactive usage, small grain exchanges, latency constraint communication, video access become relevant.

4 Bandwidth alone is not sufficient

Banwidth is a prerequisite, but short of being self–sufficient. To be fully accepted by industry, networks have to be reliable, controllable, cost–efficient, easy to use, secure – and – LAN–WAN–consistent. The latter can be described as coherency of important LAN and WAN attributes as seen by the user.

5 Further Progress – where to go

5.1 Requirements as a Dynamic Process

The frequently asked question 'what are your networking requirements' fails to understand the nature of the problem: the 'final' objective being so distant from current state it is inevitable that any steady and reasonably rapid evolution towards such target will face permanently trade–offs within user's desires/possibilities and recurrent readjustment of target specification on the other. Consequently – 'requirements' have to be evolved as a dynamic process, in a permanent dialog between conceptors, operators and users.

5.2 To Network or not to Network

The dramatic change of working modes in the Aerospace sector potentially caused by the introduction of broadband computer network could be approached by the following steps:

1. Conceive a pre–operational demonstrator
2. Demonstrate with real users – trans–European and with PNO–partnership
3. Build a business plan over the next 10 years
   - Evaluate gains
   - Evaluate cost of change of industry work practices
   - Evaluate return on investment
4. Convince decision makers in industry and government for heavy investment
5. Architecture context–relevant key–products
6. Develop, integrate, test (years!)
7. Introduce tool on pilot aerospace program

6 The PAGEIN Project

Within the context constructed so far and aiming at step 1, 2 and partly 4 of the foregoing list the project RACE 2031 PAGEIN – 'Pilot Applications in a Gigabit European Integrated Network' – was set up by a major consortium from aerospace industry and reserach, two universities and a PNO [4]; see also [1] – [3] of these proceedings. PAGEIN, started in 1992, is a 3 year, 90 men x year project. The initial supercomputer configuration of PAGEIN is shown below in Fig. 3.
The aim of PAGEIN to be a demonstrator of features specific to distributed HPC over broadband networks as needed for aeronautical and space applications has already successfully achieved in national and international demonstrations including CeBIT '93, Interop '93, Paris, and in national testbeds. Networking techniques applied in PAGEIN include wide–area 140 Mbit/s PDH links and 100/140 Mbit/s ATM – both adapted to local Gigabit networks.
At present the PAGEIN consortium is working towards the use of the evolving national and international ATM infrastructures.

7 Summary and Outlook

Problems and potential gains of progressing from present cooperation style in European aerospace industry towards technology sharing by access to advanced simulation, visualization and multimedia facilities via broadband networks have been discussed.

[4] ONERA(F), NLR(NL), CIRA(I), Aerospatiale(F), EANS(F), FCR(F), SLX(F), Stuttgart University(D), Vrije Universiteit Brussel(B), DLR(D), DRA(UK), BA(UK),DA(D), FTE(F)

RACE 2031 project PAGEIN, introduced as a demonstrator of features specific to distributed HPC over broadband networks, will help to focus and keep alive activities of the aerospace sector necessary to profit from the just beginning 'European Network Revolution' as indicated by efforts such as the forthcoming international ATM–field trial and the evolution of the 4th Framework Program of the European Union.

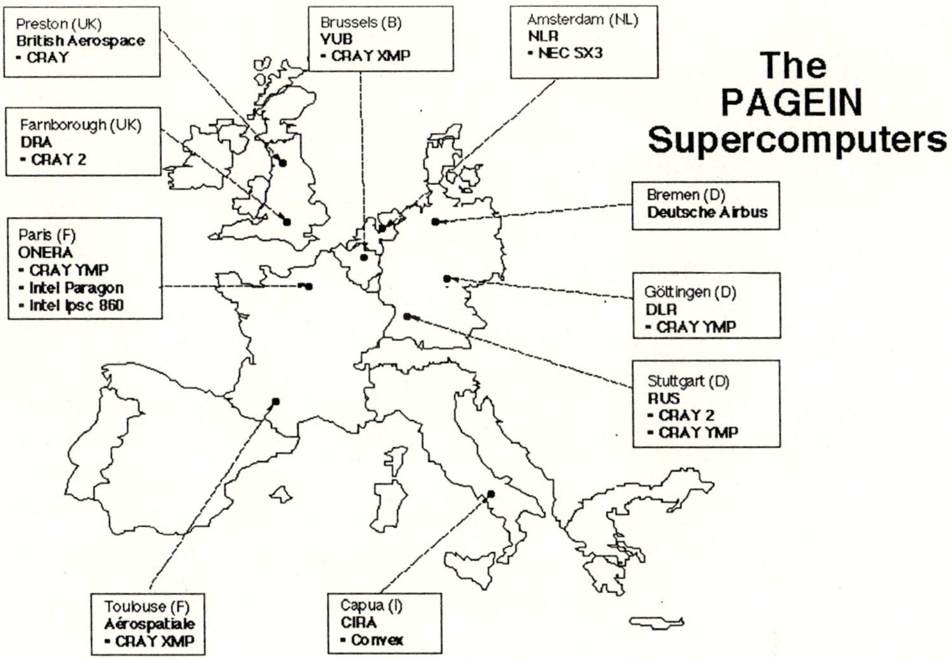

Fig. 3. The PAGEIN initial supercomputer configuration

References

1. Lang, U.: A software environment for cooperative simulation and visualization in the aerospace field. (within these HPCN '94 proceedings)
2. Rill S., Grosso R.: Future aerospace working scenarios using high–speed networks and supercomputers applied to flow simulation for complete aircrafts. (within these HPCN '94 proceedings)
3. Haas P.W., Christ P.: Networking issues in PAGEIN: The 'N' of HPCN. (within these HPCN '94 proceedings)

Future Aerospace Working Scenarios Using High Speed Networks and Supercomputers Applied to Flow Simulation for Complete Aircraft

Stefan Rill, EF 10, Deutsche Aerospace Airbus (DA), Bremen
and
Roberto Grosso, Rechenzentrum der Universität Stuttgart (RUS)

1 Abstract

Aeronautical industry depends on heavy numerical simulation for performance optimization of aircraft beeing designed. In Europe, aircraft conception more and more depends upon effective cooperation between a number of industry and research partners. An effective way to enhance global competitivity is to enable activation of the best simulation tools existing across the community, for definition of a given product. In the scope of this paper we describe the impact that numerical flow simulation already has on the design process of civil transports at DA. It will be demonstrated that, in order to fully exploit the potential of the simulation methods, the interconnection of various design teams with each other and remote supercomputers via a broadband network is a prerequisit. The PAGEIN soft- and hardware environment, that allows international cooperative working in the field of CFD based on international networking, will be presented [1]. It has been developed during the last two years in a European RACE project and is now ready for first industrial pilot applications with the MELINA flow solver of DA.

2 Introduction

Brussels aimes at an interconnection of the European knowledge resources, to preclude isolated national product oriented research. European international cooperation, successfully demonstrated by Airbus Industry since two decades, is now supported by the European Union (EU) with the concentration and interconnection of technological know-how.

Due to ecological and economical considerations, it is of essential importance to reduce the fuel consumption of the new generation of transport aircraft well below todays level. This can only be achieved by applying state-of-the-art technology in the new aircraft. To develop this technology in an economical way requires European international cooperation among the aircraft manufacturers and research institutions. Especially in the aeronautical industries the cost of the pre-design phase is such that it requires international cooperation already in this phase.

The formidable task of reducing aircraft fuel burn below todays level can only be tackled by an interdisciplinary effort because of the strong dependencies between disciplines of aircraft design; like aeroelasticity, structural design and aerodynamics. The biggest contribution is expected to be achieved by applying advanced aerodynamic concepts to the design of new airplanes. Investigations of the improvement potential promise an overall reduction of 20 to 30 percent in lift to drag ratio at a cruise Mach number of M=0.8. Fig. 1 shows the aerodynamic technologies which are relevant for a new generation civil transport.

Improving on most of the shown items means dealing with 3D flow problems with complex flow physics involved that can only be solved by combining advanced technologies like experiments in high quality aerodynamic test facilities and numerical flow simulation by computational fluid dynamics (CFD) applications based on an international cooperation.

In such a perspective, closer and closer ties between pre-design teams will enable the partners to elaborate more and more globally optimal aerodynamic designs, with opposition to suboptimal results after an a priori division and distribution of subsystem definitions over partners. But this close cooperation requires an improved communication infrastructure between the partners.

Within the context of the aforementioned European initiative, multiple European partners have applied at RACE, a European sponsoring agency, for a high speed network application project. Project leader of this PAGEIN project is the french research institution ONERA in Paris and major partners are from the European aerospace industry as well as the "Rechenzentrum der Universität Stuttgart" (RUS). The project aimes to characterize the impact of key features of high performance computing on IBC (Integrated Broadband Communications) usage for aerospace manufacturing.

In the first two years of the project the required soft- and hardware environment has been developed and tested on a research basis. The task of the industry partners was to set up the specifications for such an environment and to consult the research institutions with respect to "real world" applications. In the current, second phase of the project, this technology will directy be applied at DA. The purpose of this paper is to describe todays and future working scenarios as the PAGEIN environment becomes fully operational at Deutsche Aerospace Airbus.

3 Computational Fluid Dynamics in Aerodynamic Analysis and Design

Every other CFD paper starts with the introductory statement that we have observed a tremendous improvement in the efficiency of CFD algorithms as well as in computer hardware in the last two decades. This reveals a trend that certainly has a major effect on the impact of numerical flow simulation on aerodynamic analysis and design of aircraft.

In Fig. 2 the historical development of methods for numerical flow simulation, as they are applied in aerospace industry, is depicted. We distinguish between the capabilty of the methods to treat increasing geometrical complexities of transport aircraft configurations and the power to capture complex flow physics. As expected, we observe a distinct trend towards viscous, compressible flow simulation for complete aircraft configurations. The price we have to pay by increasing geometrical complexity and generality of the physical model, is indicated in terms of the unknown variables in the resulting linear and nonlinear systems of equations.

The treatment of problems like numerical flow simulation for a complete aircraft was made possible by the enormous improvement in soft- and hardware, Fig. 3. Whereas the left side of the chart shows the improvement of algorithms in terms of the efficiency for the solution of large systems of equations as they occur in CFD, the right part shows the speedup of the hardware over the last two decades. After combining both developments, we obtain an overall efficiency improvement of $5*10^6$ over the last two decades. In the CFD community and the computer companies the expectation prevails that this trend will continue into the future, may be even with a faster rate if we think of parallel and massively parallel machines. This will pose tremendous loads on future networks.

Before modern CFD methods where applicable to industrial problems, the aerodynamic design of the aircraft fuselage and wing, as well as the engine integration, where loosly coupled and only after performing expensive and timeconsuming wind tunnel experiments, the aerodynamic design-engineer was able to evaluate the individual components with their mutual interaction.

For the complex problems that the aerodynamicists face today, this approach is no longer feasible. As an example we might mention the large interaction of modern high bypass ratio engines with the flow field around the wing that requires an integrated design of the engine installation and the wing. With the capabilities of modern CFD methods at hand, the aerodynamic design-engineer today has the option to investigate the 3D flow field around the complete aircraft configuration before any wind tunnel experiment. This leads to a *nested iterative design loop* that allows for a preoptimization of the design, completely based on theoretical and numerical tools, before the first expensive and timeconsuming wind tunnel experiment is performed.

An other important aspect in computational aerodynamics is the scientific visualization. Scientists are using numerical simulation facilities to perform their experiments. Especially in the case of CFD codes like MELINA, a 3D simulation can generate many Gigabytes of data which have to be prepared for visualization.

In general the required high-end graphics workstations are connected to a supercomputer with a high-speed channel. The flow simulation is executed on the supercomputer and then the results are processed for viewing. In contrast to that, the future scenario which is under development in the PAGEIN project, is a completely integrated and interactive software environment, where simulation and visualization are different tasks of the same problem to be tackled simultaneously and synchronized by different hardware parts. In this way it is possible to track and steer the application during run time.

4 MELINA - Numerical flow simulation at DA

At DA the Multi-block Euler and Navier-Stokes integration algorithm MELINA, [2] together with the Interactive grid generation system INGRID [3] form the tool package for 3D inviscid and viscous compressible flow analysis.

Viscous and inviscid flow can be modelled by the continuum mechanic's conservation equations for mass, momentum and energy, i.e. the Euler- and Navier-Stokes equations, respectively. In 3D these are five scalar integral equations which are augmented by the thermic and caloric gas equations for ideal gas as material laws to form a closed system.

The MELINA algorithm has been developed at DA based on work at DLR Braunschweig. In order to discretize the physical space, a body fitted finite volume mesh is used. In MELINA the governing equations are discretized with central differences and in order to damp out high frequency oszillations we use a Jameson-typ blended artificial dissipation model. MELINA supports arbitrary multi-block meshes. The convergence in time to a steady state, is accelerated via a multi-grid technique.

The investigation of new aerodynamic design features using 3D computational fluid dynamics applications in the aerodynamic design cycle is already well established at DA. Extensive validation experiments of MELINA, where experimental wind tunnel results were compared to the corresponding simulation data, led to 'faith' in the results by the design engineers.

In Fig. 4 some representativ results of a validation effort for a numerical flow simulation based on the Navier-Stokes equations on a transport aircraft wing-body configuration are depicted. Fig. 4 shows the amount of insight in the flow physics that can be obtained from numerical flow simulations if an appropriate postprocessing is applied. In this particular case we see the skin-friction distribution and the surface pressure distribution on the upper wing side as skin-friction lines and as shaded coloured surfaces, respectively.

5 Future Working Scenarios

As we have seen from the historical retrospective, we have come a long way to reach the capabiltity for viscous, transonic flow simulation around aircraft. But we have not yet reached our final goals. Further developments should aim in two different directions:

1. Increasing the speed of numerical simulations: An impression of the aeronautical engineers targets can be drawn from Fig. 5 where the required computer speed for interdisciplinary unsteady problems like aeroelasticity is shown. In the same picture relief is indicated by the advent of massively parallel computers.

2. Improving on the integration of interactive CFD-simulations and 3D-visualization into the product design process: This includes userfriendlyness of the simulation program and especially the grid generation, which is one

of todays major bottlenecks in CFD application. Although we find *concurrent engineering* in every modern management treatise, numerical flow simulation still is not enough integrated into the interdisciplinary engineering process of transport aircraft. This is especially due to the fact that there is no complete geometry definition of the aircraft available in the early conception phase.

Especially the second item stresses the demand for a physical interconnection of the various disciplines of aircraft design and manufacturing within the individual company and with participating partners in the "outside world" via broadband networks. Fig. 6 shows how networking will enable concurrent engineering in aircraft design.

At this point we should pause and concentrate again on the question of cooperative working as developed in the PAGEIN project. What do we expect ? How will it look like ? One imagines the following scenario: scientists and engineers sitting in front of multimedia workstations are using numerical simulation tools to perform experiments in computational aerodynamics involving large amounts of data. The results are viewed and animated using high-performance graphics workstations, which are connected to supercomputers via high speed networks. Tracking and steering are fundamental requirements for this scenario. Tracking allows the scientist to visually follow his or her flow simulation so it can be stopped and restarted, in case that undesirable results are obtained. Steering goes one step further and allows the scientist to change parameters of the flow solver as it executes. An example of this might be increasing the angle of attack of an aerodynamic body. The scenario applies at European scale. Different research and design groups distributed all around Europe are working on the same problem interactively *as if they are in the same room.* For communication purposes a video conferencing functionality has to be part of the software system.

6 The PAGEIN environment

From the considerations above, it is clear that different aspects of the same problem have to be solved by different specialized hardware, such as vector and parallel supercomputers as number crunchers and high-end graphics workstations for the visualization tasks. On the other hand cooperation means geographically distributed parties taking part on the same application. In order to integrate all these aspects, a software environment is under continuous development within the PAGEIN project. During the design and implementation phase an object-oriented paradigm was adopted. Many different modules constitute the fundament of the system architecture. Data transport between processes in the simulation and visualization pipeline is achieved by introducing the concept of a data space. For synchronization and coordination of the computing processes the message passing mechanism is used.

The main part of the system is a control process called controller, which is in charge of all the administrative tasks, such as starting a process etc. Direct connections exist between the controller and all other modules. Through these links each module is provided with the necessary information to carry out its activities. The control process is in charge of synchronization and timing of the system.

The concept of a distributed data space is realized according to an object oriented database approach. The whole management of the data objects of the application that have to be transferred between modules, is done by a process called data manager. For this purpose, the data manager is connected directly to each module running on the same machine and to data managers on remote machines taking part in the application.

The computing tasks are performed by the application modules. One of these modules is the simulation code MELINA of DA running on a supercomputer. There is no direct communication between the application modules. The application modules communicate with the controller via message passing. In order to access data objects in the data space they have to negotiate with the data manager.

Usually, only one user interacts with an application, thus only one user interface is needed. In a cooperative working environment, it has to be considered that several users interact with the application simultaneously. In this case the system has several user interfaces which have to be coordinated. All the user interfaces, as many as parties in the application, are synchronized by the controller for input and output of information.

One of the many different applications carried out in the frame of the PAGEIN project showed at the CeBit'93 fair in Hannover the benefits that scientific and industrial research can take from supercomputer simulation and visualization on a distributed environment with CSCW (Computer Supported Colaborative Work) facilities. The experiment carried out was a CFD simulation at the supercomputer center of the University of Stuttgart and the visualization as well as the colaborative work at the Hannover fair between two parties. In Fig. 7 one can see the hardware configuration taking part in the application for performing an experiment in computational aerodynamics. The computer power needed for that experiment was two vector machines, a Cray-2 as number cruncher and the Cray-YMP as fileserver, and a massive parallel computer, the Paragon of Intel, at Stuttgart and two high-end graphics workstations at the fair. The network configuration between Stuttgart and Hannover included FDDI, ATM and VBN technologies, see Fig. 7.

7 Conclusions

The purpose of the paper was to sketch future working scenarios with respect to numerical flow simulation of complete aircraft. We have shown that CFD has reached a mature level of sophistication to allow for viscous flow simulation about complete aircraft. In order to fully exploit the potential of CFD and in order to concentrate European know-how in this field, we have also seen that it is of essential importance to interconnect various national and international design teams via broadband networks like in the PAGEIN project.

The authors think that the pilot application of MELINA in the PAGEIN environment is only the tip of an iceberg. The exploitation of the interconnection of remote teams and disciplines via networks might be the key to concurrent engineering. It is easy to think for example of an online monitoring of wind tunnel experiments with the option of interactive control of the experiment. Another application that goes far beyond the described pilot application is to integrate much of the work that has to be done in the various aircraft design disciplines in one *software-based general development platform.* The contributions of different departments might then be modules that could be "plugged" to the platform to perform the desired task. With this strategy, that relies on the kind of environment developed in PAGEIN, true interdisciplinary engineering could become reality.

References

[1] Grosso, R., Lang, U., Ryan, J. "CFD Experiment in a Distributed Simulation and Visualization System", *Proc. European Simulation Symposium ESS'93*, Delft, Holland, Oct. 1993.

[2] Rill, S., Becker, K., "MELINA A Multi-block, Multi-grid 3D Euler Code with Sub Block Technique for Local Mesh Refinement", ICAS Paper 92-4.3.R,*ICAS92*, Beijing, 1992.

[3] Becker. K., "Interactive Algebraic Mesh Generation for Twin Jet Transport Aircraft", *Proc. 3rd Int. Conf. Num. Grid Generation*, Barcelona, June 1991.

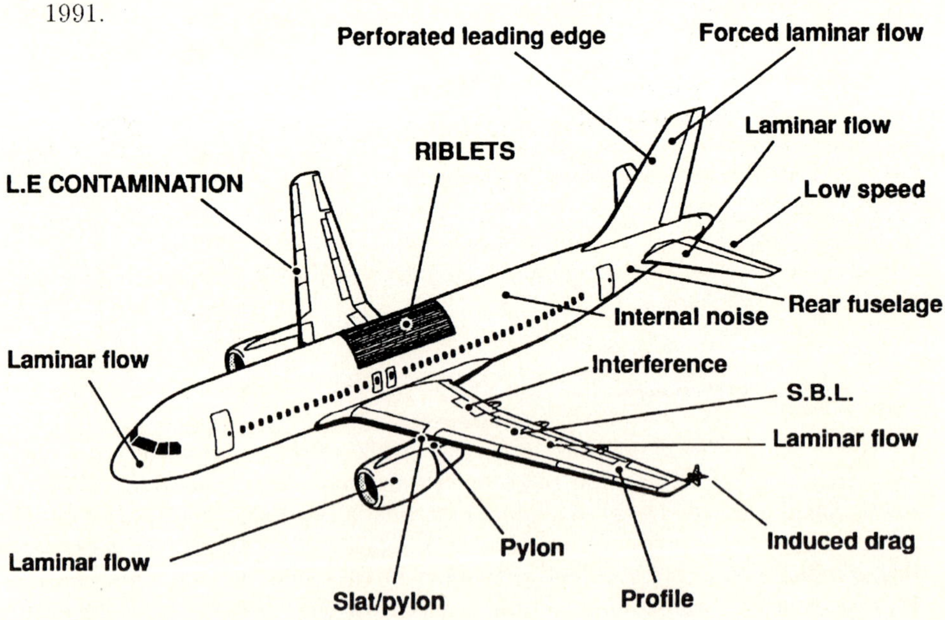

Figure 1: Options for aerodynamic improvement of civil transports.

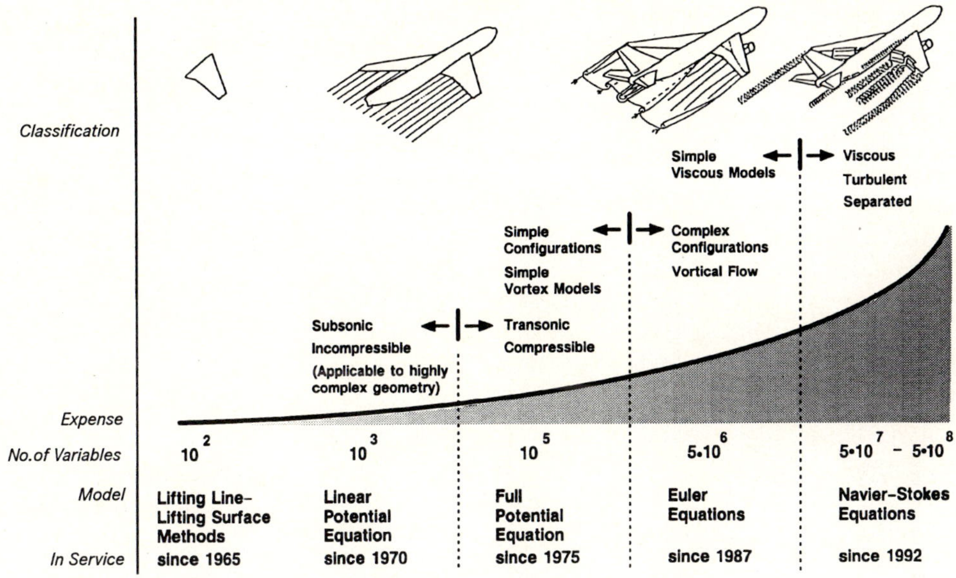

Figure 2: History of numerical flow simulation methods.

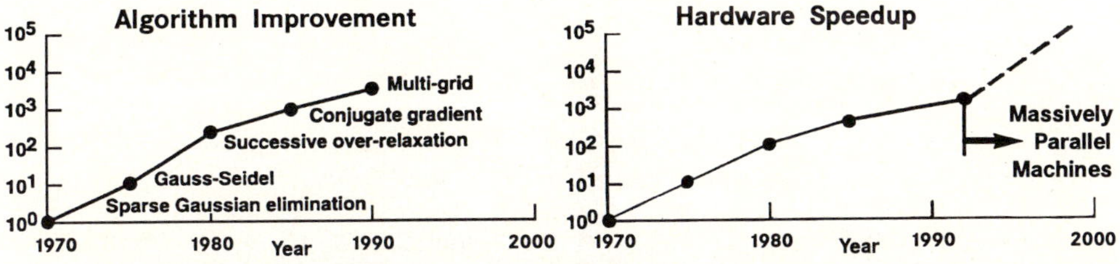

Figure 3: Hardware and algorithm efficiency.

Figure 4: Skin-friction distribution over upper wing side, $M_\infty = 0.75, Re = 3 * 10^6$.

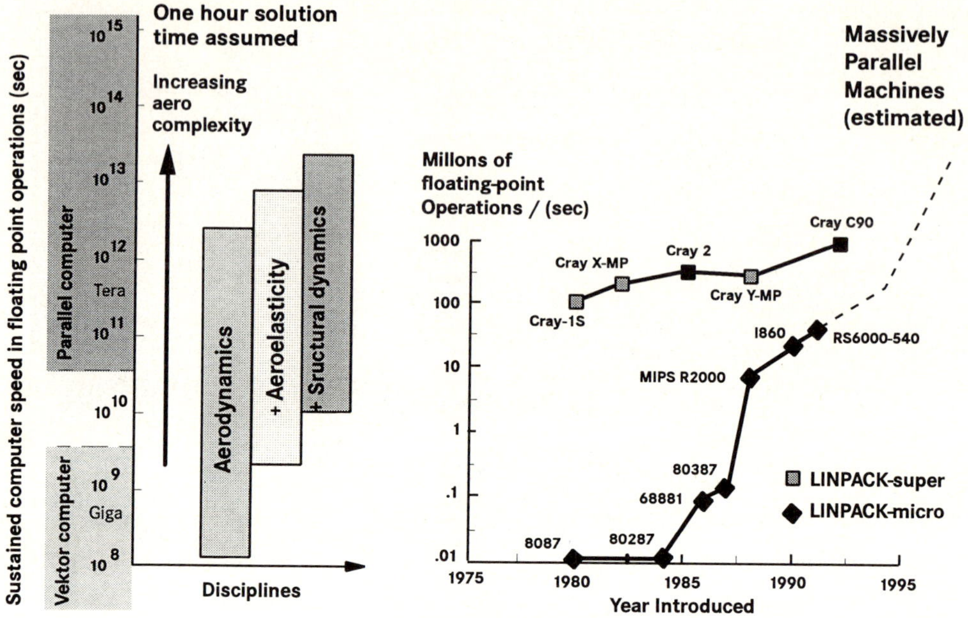

Figure 5: Required computer speed for interdisplinary problems.

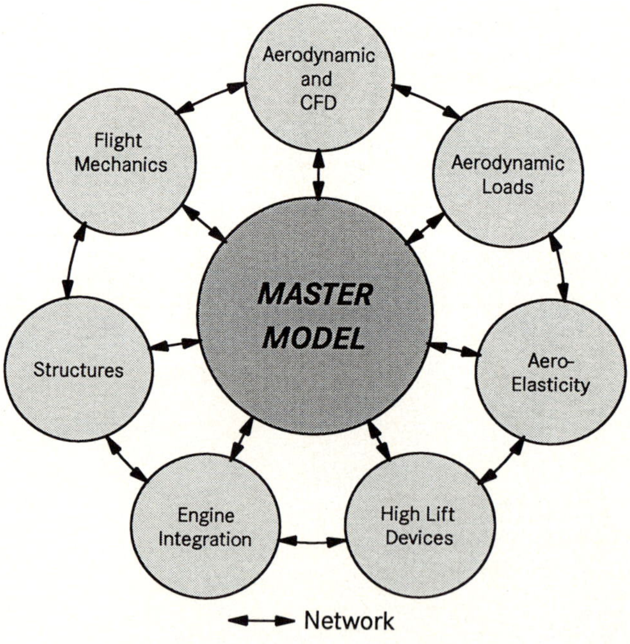

Figure 6: Networking between disciplines - a prerequisit for concurrent engineering.

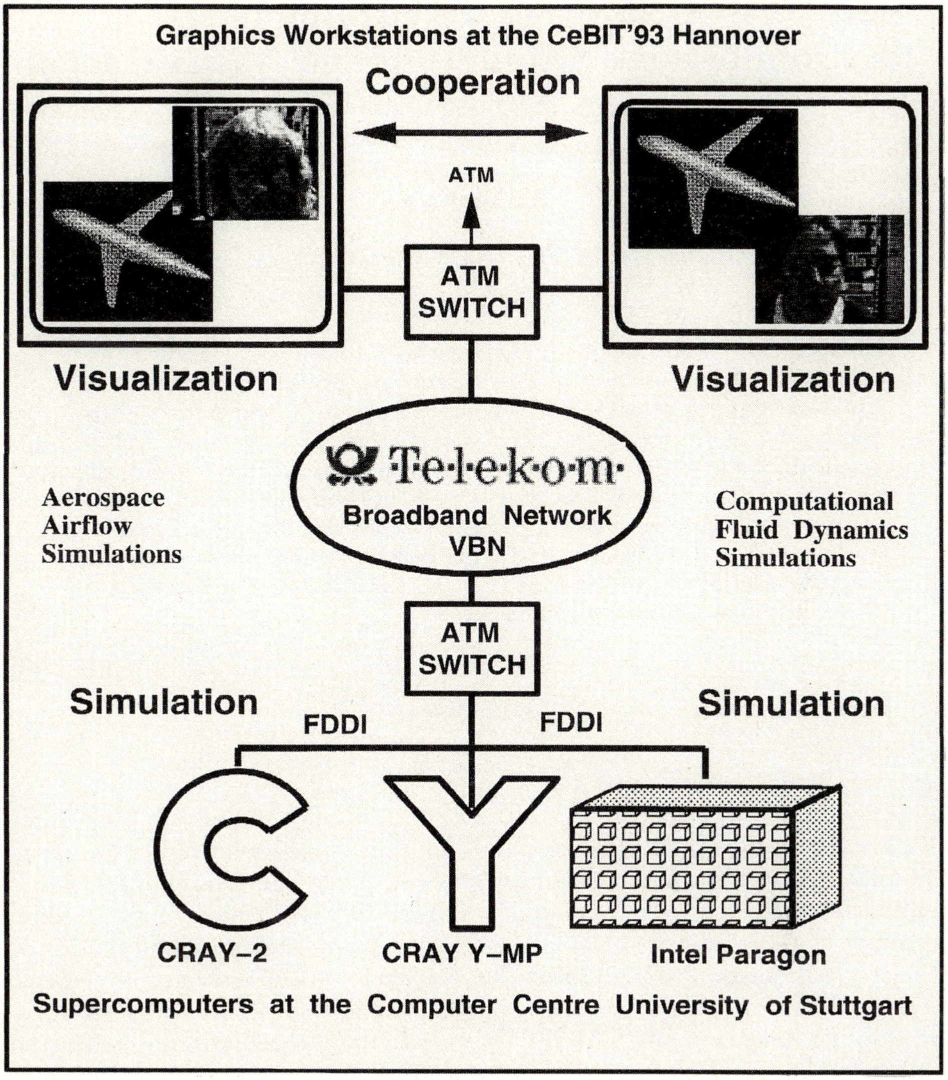

Figure 7: Trans-European cooperative working in aerospace industry.

A Software Environment for Cooperative Simulation and Visualization in the Aerospace Field

Ulrich Lang

Rechenzentrum Universität Stuttgart, Germany

Abstract. Within the PAGEIN project a software environment is developped, that allows to integrate supercomputer simulations and their analysis using different visualization methods in a cooperative working mode. To discuss ongoing simulation and visualization audio-/videoconferencing is closely integrated. The architecture of the software environment is described. Special emphasis has been put on the optimal usage of different network technologies, supercomputer capabilities as well as high end workstations with multimedia support. Some measurement results are presented based on the distribution of processes in a heterogeneous hardware environment.

1 Introduction

1.1 Project Aims

The PAGEIN project (R2031) is sponsored by the Commission of the European Communities within the RACE programme (Research and Development in Advanced Communications Technologies in Europe). PAGEIN aims to characterize the impact of key features of high-performance computing on IBC (Integrated Broadband Communications) usage for aerospace manufacturing. The major sectors for user oriented experiments include remote supercomputing, heterogeneous cooperative computing and group work in applied research and industrial predesign. The applications include visualization of large data sets to illustrate fluid flow and flight dynamics.

The project follows a user oriented, rapid prototyping, testbed approach. Originally it was intended to have a high speed interconnection between ONERA (France) and RUS (Germany) as a testbed. Due to costs this was not possible up to now.

Project leader is ONERA[1], with RUS[2] being the second biggest partner. The other partners are from the European aerospace research centers, European aerospace industry and European telecommunication companies. The project is structured into application and network oriented workpackages.

[1] Office National d'Etudes et de Recherches Aerospatiales

[2] Rechenzentrum Universität Stuttgart

PAGEIN intends to demonstrate effective use of a high-speed broadband trans-european interconnection, to utilize the resources of interconnected cooperating supercomputers, and to experiment with sofisticated use of remote supercomputers including groupware multimedia scenarios (packetized voice and video within the end systems). This collaborative European R&D work paves the way for high power workstation and ATM communications by the mid nineties. Future IBC projects can continue this work by integrating such key features in comprehensive industrialized applications, and contribute to standardization activities.

1.2 Application Scenario

Aerospace industry relies heavily on cooperation. This implies a sharing of know-how and resources among partners during a limited duration of time. The controlled access to technologies such as simulation codes without passing it on to partners is required. Also the colocation of engineering groups from one partner to another should be kept at a minimum.

A working environment should be established, which fulfils the needs of the following scenario.

International scientific research and development projects with multiple partners are conducted in close cooperation. The projects are based on supercomputer simulations. Large amounts of data from simulations and experiments have to be managed and analysed using distributed hardware and software environments. A group of scientists or engineers is sitting in front of multiple multimedia workstations located at different points in Europe. The workstations are connected to a European high speed network. Cooperatively simulations are executed and the results are analysed. The engineers should have the same impression as working together in the same room in front of the same workstation, talking with each other and seeing each other. In addition the multimedia support will allow to integrate video recordings of past happenings like control experiments for the computer simulations. Thus the comparison of video datastreams and visual representations of simulations should be possible. Sources of the different media datastreams are also distributed across the network.

1.3 Project Structuring

To handle the different aspects of the scenario appropriately the project is structured into multiple workpackages with close relationship between each other. Within the application oriented workpackages multiple experiments are defined. These workpackages are:

- the Scientific Visualization Workpackage,
- the Multimedia Workpackage and
- the Supercomputer Workpackage.

In this paper we will concentrate on the activites in the visualization and multimedia workpackages.

2 Architectural Model

Scientific visualization should not be handled separately, but should be closely integrated into the overall process of scientific problem handling (see [1] and [2]). An architectural model of the software environment to perform the overall work is defined. It is designed to integrate all processing steps from simulation via post-processing to visualization. It is based on a heterogeneous networked hardware environment of parallel and vectorizing computers, fileservers and workstations. The environment should allow to compare performance numbers and costs for different distributions of processing steps accross the available resources. Thus experience is gained to better judge the future possibilities. An envisaged software environment should allow to perform all the necessary measurements.

Figure 1 depicts the architecture. The drawing contains three workstations with users participating in a cooperative working session. The session is managed by one centralized controller. For every cooperating partner a separate user interface process (UI) produces the same visual representation. To allow a flexible distribution of processing steps on different machines, modules are implemented as separate processes (shown as boxes A – E). Scientific data is stored as objects in shared data space, which is logically spread across all participating machines. Data Manager (DM) processes are responsible for the consistency of the data space.

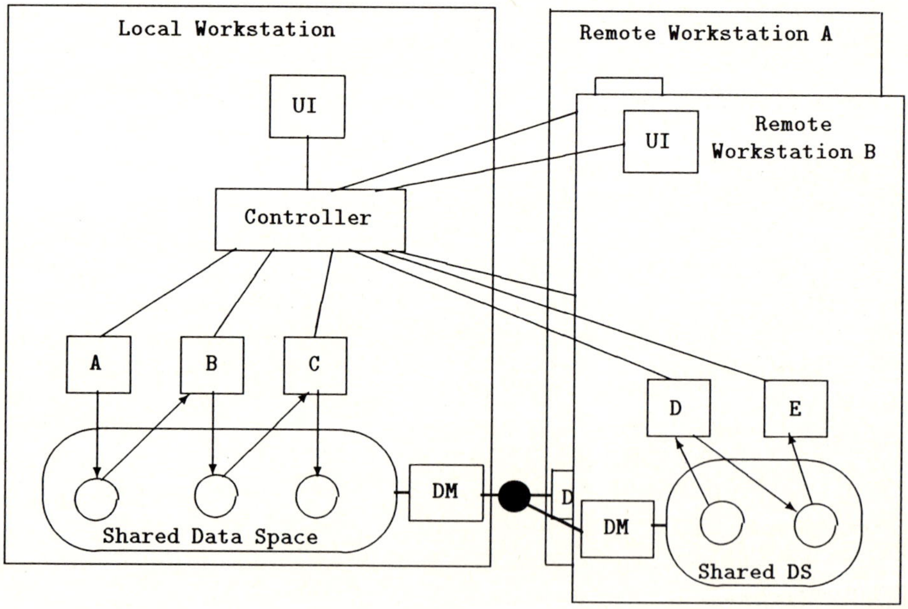

Fig. 1. Architecture of the cooperative simulation and visualization environment

3 Technical Approach

Functionalities and structure of available software packages have been compared with this architectural model (see [3]). None of the packages contained a distributed working mode together with cooperative working, conferencing functionalities and multimedia capabilities. As source code is typically not available for commercial packages, it was not possible within the project to extend such packages to conform to the PAGEIN architectural model. Instead it was decided to split the work in the visualization workpackage in parallel activities. Some partners extend their already available single computer based visualization packages in comparison with the architectural model, while another group implemented the architectural model in a sequence of rapid prototyping steps with increasing functionality. The implementation of the data management, controller and user interface is located at RUS, the application modules are contributed by the other partners from the aerospace research centres. The series of implementations can be characterized by an increasing number of functionalities from the following list:

- Arbitrary distribution of asynchronous processes across machines
- Distributed data management
- Optimal usage of different network types
- Separate communication channels for data and control flow
- Cooperative working capabilities
- Handling of time dependent data
- Partitioned data objects for parallel and overlapped processing
- Integration of conferencing functionality

4 Implemented Software Environment

4.1 User Interface

A user interface process allows a user to model his task by combining iconic representations of the modules in a visual programming environment. By visualy connecting the process icons the topology of the overall processing is defined. The workstation screen snapshot in Fig. 2 contains among others the user interface window with connected process icons. All user interactions are handled localy, thus reducing the network trafic. For cooperative multiuser sessions information is passed on to the controller, which informs the other UIs to synchronize their windows. A master/slave relationship is implemented as cooperation policy, allowing only one partner to control the environment, while the others are informed about the current state by seeing the same screen representations. The master part can be passed to other partners.

4.2 Controller

The controller represents the central part of the system. It has the knowledge about the topology of the processes to be executed. It establishes the distributed processsing environment, starts all processes, connects all data managers and informs all the other processes about their tasks when appropriate. Thus the other processes can have a rather limited knowledge about the overall environment, which keeps their implementation simple. The controller tells each module when to perform their task, which data objects to operate on and which to produce. At the end of a cooperative working session, the controller finishes all processes and saves required states for later restarts. All user input is passed via the controller, which spreads it to the other user interface processes. In addition the input is interpreted and results in actions within the environment.

4.3 Data Manager

The data manager is responsible for the access and storage of data objects from modules. In addition data managers copy data objects between machines, if the requested data object is currently on another machine. Type conversion is done transparently making optimal usage of available machine capabilities (e.g. vectorized conversion of Cray floating point fields). A consistency managment of data objects takes care of multiple instances of an object on different machines.

4.4 Conferencing Support and Multimedia Functionalities

To enable cooperative working within the environment, audio communication is a minimal requirement. The addition of video conferencing allows a behaviour more closely resembling the cooperation of partners within one room. The audio-/video-conferencing functionalities are based on the integration of the INRIA Videoconferencing System IVS into the software environment. The exchange of multimedia datastreams is initiated by the controller and performed by the data managers.

Digitized video recordings of real live experiments such as in wind tunnels or water channels will be stored as data objects in the software environment. This will allow to compare the experiment with the visualization of a computer simulation. The synchronization of both views is an important issue here.

5 Performed Measurements

Up to now distributed processing experiments in a heterogeneous hardware environment have been performed. The measurments clearly show the benefit of using high speed networks, such as Ultranet for large datasets. For a certain test case size the simulation code PEGASE is 52 times faster on a Cray YMP then on a single Mips R4000 processor. Compared to Ethernet FDDI usage improved the transfer performance by a factor of 2 - 3, Ultranet by a factor of 5 - 6. Compared to the workstation performance for the simulation all other times could be ignored. While for non optimal distribution of processing steps the usage of faster networks gives a bigger performance improvement, an optimal distribution reduces the effect of faster network to a certain degree.

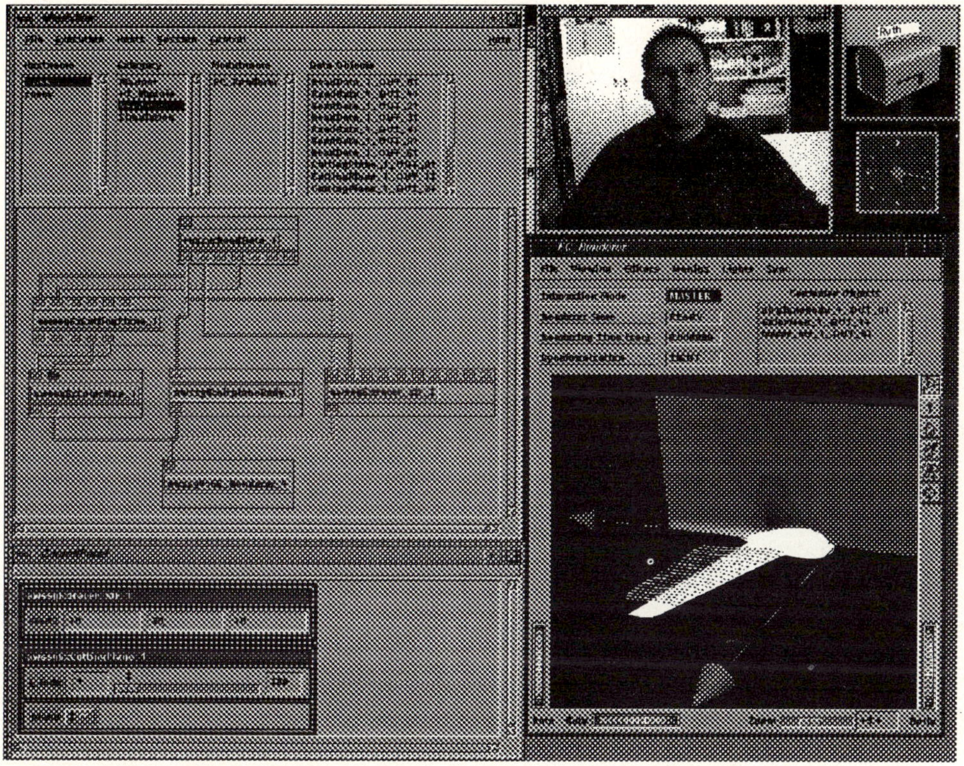

Fig. 2. Screen snapshot of working session using the software environment

The next experiments to be performed this year will extend to joint viewing and cooperative working modes. Additional users will influence the behaviour of the software environment and the measurements to be performed.

6 Conclusions and Aknowledgements

The designed software environment represents an implementation of different concepts, that evolved from previous projects of the involved partners. It allows to do perform measurements and basic research in areas where we recognized that much more experience had to be aquired for future developments. These developments will now be based on a firm platform. Industrial partners have gained enough confidence to use the platform for the integration of their working codes with the intention to gain experience in their dayly work.

The PAGEIN project represents a common effort of many partners, which had an important part in the definition of realistic future working scenarios. Many partners are additionaly involved in designing and performing experiments. Sample data sets and modules have been contributed for the experiments to establish an environment with a realistic background. I would especially like to thank the members of the RUS visualization department Roberto Grosso, Ruth Lang, Harald Nebel, Dirk Rantzau, Lei Wang and Andreas Wierse for their major role in the design and implementation of the software environment.

References

[1] Lang, U., Lang, R., Rühle, R.: Scientific Visualization in a Supercomputer Network at RUS. Computer & Graphics Special Issue on Supercomputer and Graphics, Volume 17, Number 1, 1993, Pergamon Press

[2] Lang, U., Lang R., Rühle R.: Integration of Visualization and Scientific Calculation in a Software System. in "Visualization '91" Conference Proceedings, IEEE Computer Society Press, San Diego, Oct. 1991

[3] Wierse, A., Lang U., Rühle R.: Architectures of Distributed Visualisation Systems and their Enhancements, 4th Eurographics Workshop on Visualisation in Scientific Computing, Abingdon, UK, April 1993

Mechanisms. Before gaining access to shared objects, a module has to enter a SDS, referenced by a name. When it no longer needs to access objects, it leaves the space. For that purpose, a module uses requests of the following type (C++ alike syntax has been used in the examples of this paragraph):

```
SharedDataSpace SDS1(data-space-name);
SDS1.EnterSpace();
-- reference objects belonging to SDS1 --
SDS1.LeaveSpace();
```

In order to access an object, a module has to open it first, possibly creating it, in which case a structure has to be specified, in terms of pieces (number, sizes, basic types). Once processing an object is completed a close operation has to be issued. The corresponding requests are the following:

```
Object SHOB1(SDS1, object-name [,pieces-structure]);
SHOB1.OpenObject();
-- access pieces of SHOB1 --
SHOB1.CloseObject(destruction);
```

Between OpenObject and CloseObject calls, the module can access pieces of the object. Pieces are accessed by only one module at a time (mutual exclusion of modules). The system takes care of the validity of this assess. Therefore, a module first requests access to the piece, and finally sends another request once it has completed the operations it had to perform on it, so that other modules can access the piece again. When a piece has been acquired, the data it holds are available to the module by the use of a mere pointer. Therefore, it can perform any action on it, except re-sizing the area or moving the pointer. The following requests are used:

```
Piece PIEC1(SHOB1,piece-number);
BasicType *data = PIEC1.GetPiece(mode [,testflag][,tag-range]);
-- work on the data: data[xx] = yy; --
PIEC1.ReleasePiece(destruction [, newflag][, newtag]);
```

The system provides the user with multiple ways of selecting a piece from an object. First of all, it is possible to specify a mode of access, as blocking or non-blocking. This means that if the piece of the specified number is not immediately available (because it is held by another module or it does not satisfy the criteria described below), a call to GetPiece with a blocking mode will wait for the piece to become available, whereas a non-blocking mode will cause an unsuccessful return. Besides, two values are attached to a piece: a flag (group of bits) and a tag (numerical value). The piece will be made available to the module on a Get-Piece call only if its tag is in the tag-range and its flag verifies the formula

```
(testflag && flag)== TRUE
```

Note that the use of testflag and tag-range is optional.

Two types of flags are defined: free flags, whose meaning is chosen by the user, and special flags, describing the status of a piece on a system point of view (for e.g. created).

The piece selection mechanism has been defined so that it allows the handling of time-dependent objects, for which tags can be used as computational time-step information. Besides, it is also possible to realize non-deterministic access to pieces, by iterative non blocking requests until finding a piece that meets a condition (flag). By this means, automatic load balancing is achieved: complex requests can be expressed using this mechanism, like for example: I (module) want to access any piece of object O that is available for processing. Finally, the implementation of application synchronization (triggering of modules) can be done without any external mechanism, by the use of special flags and blocking facilities.

2.3 Implementation

A first implementation is currently undertaken by the Visualization Group of ONERA, aiming at validating the mechanisms described, so that maximal performance is not a crucial condition for the prototype.

Mutual exclusion for pieces access and coherence: This is achieved by the principle of no data replication. The contents of a piece can only be found in one place. If needed, it migrates from a local data space to another when access requests occur.

Communication: In our first implementation, when data communication is needed, shared memory is used if possible (processes running on the same machine), and PVM 3 otherwise. In order to overcome PVM overhead, more basic communication primitives should be used instead in the future.

3 Implementation of Distributed Operators

We introduce now an example of application of visualization running currently at ONERA under the DS2 system. Focusing especially on consumer-producer aspects of the processing remains our primary aim all along this discussion.
The purpose of the selected algorithm is: to compute isovalues associated with a mesh topology first, then to display the resulting isosurface. To each vertice of the given mesh is attributed a scalar value depending on vertice coordinates and possibly many more parameters. Then an algorithm is used which takes the latter vertices, scalars and a thresold value as input and eventually produces triangles as output from which an isosurface may be displayed.
With traditionnal sequential programming one would probably gather mesh, isovalue and display processing into a unique package. However we can clearly state

from the many stages of processing within our application that a somewhat more appealing solution, at least, is available. Assuming that each stage of processing may lead to an independent application module we view now our visualization problem as a dataflow problem.
However, instead of pipelining processes we simply spawn them, entering or leaving a shared data space when necessary; each process relates to appropriate objects, opening and closing them where needed all along the stages of processing. Then pieces are accessed through *get* and *release* requests, thus hiding communication concerns. Data hold within pieces are used in between get and release requests.
A reader process gets mesh topology information from a file. Then it slices the mesh into smaller parts which are stored each into a piece of a Mesh object (flag set to *created*). An isosurface process gets all the *created* pieces of the Mesh object on which it is allowed to work. Then from data stored into the Mesh piece an isosurface algorithm is used which produces triangles. Each packet of triangles is stored into the first available (flag set to *empty*) piece of a Triangle Object (flag is then set to *done*). The display process gets all the *done* pieces of a triangle object according to ranking order. Each piece is released with flag state set to *empty*.
This processing can be iterated over with time steps values as shown below throuh excerpts of pseudo-code. It should be noticed that as many isosurface-computing processes as the number of pieces into the Mesh object are possibly running.

```
note: default system value for tag and flag for each piece is assumed
      to be 0 when creating objects.

 process READER:
   Object& meshObject(
     dataSpace, "Mesh", CREATE_OBJECT | DESTROY_OBJECT, descriptor
    );
   ...
   for each piece of object meshObject{
     Piece& slice = meshObject.GetPiece(
       piece-number, non-blocking-request, no-test
      );
     ...
     meshObject.ReleasePiece(
       slice, conservative-release, set flag to CREATED
      );
    }

 process ISO:
   Object& meshObject(dataSpace, "Mesh");
   ...
```

```
    for each piece of object meshObject I have to work with{
     Piece& slice = meshObject.GetPiece(
       piece-number, blocking-request,
       test for a flag value of CREATED
      );
     ...
     meshObject.ReleasePiece(slice, destructive-release);
    }
  Object& trianglesObject(dataSpace, "Triangles");
  ...
  for each time step{
    for each piece of object meshObject I have to work with{
      boolean exit;
      do{
        int status;
        Piece& pieceTriangles = trianglesObject.GetPiece(
          piece-number, non-blocking-request,
          test if tag value is current time step
           and test if flag value is EMPTY,
          status
         );
        if (status){ ...;  exit=true; }
        trianglesObject.ReleasePiece(
          slice, conservative release, set flag to DONE
         );
      } while not exit;
    }
  }

process DISPLAY:
  Object& trianglesObject(
    dataSpace, "Triangles", CREATE_OBJECT | DESTROY_OBJECT, descriptor
   );
  ...
  for each time step{
    for each piece of object meshObject I have to work with{
      Piece& pieceTriangles = trianglesObject.GetPiece(
        piece-number, blocking request,
        test if tag value is current time step and flag is DONE
       );
      ...
      trianglesObject.ReleasePiece(
        slice, destructive release,
        set flag to EMPTY and set tag to current time step+1
       );
    }
  }
```

4 Conclusions and Further Developments

In a close future, a second implementation should allow other types of requests, like non-exclusive concurrent access for modules who don't modify data (read-only) in order to improve performance, reducing bottlenecks. In that case, several copies of the contents of a piece can be found in the modules' address-space at a give time, but only one of them will be valid over time: all the others will be discarded when read to maintain the consistency.

However, the first tests we did based on DS2 proved to be promising, compared to the goals we had. They were especially efficient in terms of automatic distribution of pieces between processes. Currently, a more detailed analysis of the behaviour of DS2 concerning load-balancing is performed.

After DS2 is stabilized, we plan to build a layer on top of it, allowing to handle higher-level objects, like grids or images, making use of the decomposition facilities offered by DS2. This would make modules implementation easier, and would lead to a real reusability of code.

This work has been made possible through funding by EEC Race 2031 Project, and we would like to thank Sylvain Gaultier and Marcel Hollard from ONERA Visualization Group for their help in the development of respectively the portable graphics library we used, and the DPVS system.

References

1. Beguelin, A., Dongarra, J., Geist, G.A., Manchek, R., Sunderam, V.S.: A User's Guide to PVM Parallel Virtual Machine. Oak Ridge National Laboratory Internal Report. June 1992.
2. Butler, D.M., Pendley M.H.: The Visualization Management System Approach to Visualization in Scientific Computing. Computers in Physics. pp40-44. Sept/Oct 1989.
3. Causse, S., Hollard, M., Grave, M.: Experimenting Distributed Visualization with a PVM Based System. ONERA Internal Report. December 1992.
4. Causse, S., Juaneda, F., Grave M.: Partitioned Objects Sharing for Visualization in Distributed Environments. in Frontiers in Data Visualization : Rosenblum and al. Eds. Academic Press. 1994.
5. Duclos, A.M., Grave M.: Reference Models and Formal Specification for Scientific Visualization. in Scientific Visualization: Advanced Software Techniques: P. Palamidese Ed. Hellis Horwood.
6. Haber, R.B., McNabb, D.A.: Visualization Idioms: A Conceptual Model for Scientific Visualization Systems. in Visualization in Scientific Computing: Nielson and al. Eds. IEEE Computer Society Press. 1990.
7. Schroeder, W.J., Lorensen, W.E., Montanaro, G.D., Volpe, C.R.: VISAGE: An Object-Oriented Scientific Visualization System. Proceedings IEEE Visualization'92 Conference. Boston, Ma. 1992
8. Upson, C., Faulbaher, T., Kamins, D, Laidlaw D., Schlegel, D., Vroom, J., Gurwitz, R., van Dam, A.: The Application Visualization System: A Computational Environment fo Scientific Visualization. IEEE Computer Graphics & Applications. Vol 9(4). July 1989.
9. The Khoros Group: Khoros Manual. Department of Electrical and Computer Engineering, University of New Mexico, Albuquerque. March 1992.

Networking Issues in PAGEIN: The "N" of "HPCN"

Peter Haas and Paul Christ[1]

Rechenzentrum Universität Stuttgart, Allmandring 30,
D-70550 Stuttgart, Germany

Abstract. European projects such as RACE 2031 PAGEIN - multimedia supported collaborative supercomputing, simulation and visualization in aerospace research and industry are essentially dependent on networking facilities – locally, nationally and internationally. The paper is going to present measurements carried out in the context of PAGEIN with respect to a variety of performance parameters such as throughput or latency. Results both from local "Gigabit networks" and wide area high-speed networks will be presented.

1 Introduction

The aerospace research oriented RACE 2031 project PAGEIN - Pilot Applications in a Gigabit European Integrated Network – comprises elements such as supercomputers of different architectures, simulation in computational fluid dynamics, scientific visualization, multimedia databases and co-operative working scenarios including voice and video. In a series of networking oriented workpackages PAGEIN is going to set up, demonstrate and make available to interested parties a – preferably – international testbed.

Within this context local networks at HIPPI performance level and PNO-provided WAN-infrastructures such as PDH transmission systems, Metropolitan Area Networks, evolving national and international ATM-field trials are of permanent and actual interest to PAGEIN as potential constituents of the "N" of the HPCN paradigm.

Accordingly, first the G=Gigabit/s components of the PAGEIN testbed are analyzed, namely the HIPPI channel and the UltraNet, the first commercially available Gbit/s network. In a second part the MAN is dealt with. The third part overviews the local ATM network recently installed at the University of Stuttgart and its inclusion in a joint demonstration with RACE 2060 CIO at the CeBIT '93 fair.

2 HIPPI Standards Overview

The High Performance Parallel Interface (HIPPI), American National Standards Institute (ANSI) draft standard X3T9.3, will likely become the standard communication channel for high-speed computer systems. The HIPPI is an open standard defining the physical and logical link layers of a 100-Mbyte/s network using multiple twisted-pair copper cabling at distances up to 25 m [1]. A fiber optic HIPPI specification is also under development, which will extend the HIPPI channel to distances up to 10 km [2].

The HIPPI physical layer is characterized by a 32-bit dual-simplex point-to-point interface, clocked at a rate of 25 MHz. Dedicated hardware signals facilitate connection setup and release, as well as data flow control; connection setup time is typically less than 500 ns. Therefore, crossbar switches are the most common interconnection mechanism used with HIPPI [3].

The HIPPI Framing Protocol provides a connectionless data service and best-effort delivery of data [4]. An eight-byte frame header identifies the upper layer protocol to which a protocol data unit (PDU) belongs. The HIPPI Link Encapsulation defines the the format and interface for transporting IEEE 802.2 logical link control (LLC) PDUs over HIPPI [5]. Eight forwarding classes are used to distinguish, e.g. among ordinary data PDUs, inter-hub control PDUs, and PDUs for services that require bandwidth guarantees such as speech or packet video. Consequently, network-layer information, such as an entire IP datagram, is itself encapsulated into LLC PDUs. Work is going on within the Internet Engineering Task Force on an Internet Draft, describing the host interface to switched networks, based on the HIPPI-SC and HIPPI-LE draft standards [6].

Point-to-point throughput of up to 655 Mbit/s can be shown with maximum-sized TCP/IP packets between Cray supercomputers. High-performance workstations, like the IBM RS/6000 Model 590, have achieved memory throughputs of 220 Mbit/s. Since each packet is nearly as big as the entire window in a standard TCP connection, these speeds are only possible if a TCP window scale factor is used, RFC 1323 [7].

2.1 UltraNet

HIPPI is a data channel, not a network medium. However, it has important networking roles to play. It is one of several available interfaces to the proprietary UltraNet of Computer Network Technology. UltraNet is best described as a hub-based network. A hub contains an arbitrated, parallel bus system that incorporates several types of adapters. Link adapters provide a maximum of 16 serial links and are used for hub interconnection. Up to four serial links can be combined (striped) to provide a 1-Gbit/s data rate. Workstations with an internal link interface are also connected by link adapters. Channel oriented computers connect to the hub-based bus via high-speed parallel channels like HIPPI or the IBM Block Multiplexing Channel (BMC). The Graphics Display Device contains a frame buffer that supports 24 bits of color and a resolution of 1280 x 1024 pixels. It operates up to 125 Mbyte/s, or about 24 frames/s.

All types of adapters are equipped with a protocol processor that implements the ISO TP4 and the Internet TCP transport protocol in firmware. The transport implementation allows to use most of the capacity of the Ultra data link or the host channel, whichever is less. The user transport interface on UNIX systems is a modified BSD socket library.

The protocol processor in the link adapters does not have any transport level responsibility and therefore is used for packet switching on the Ultra MAC-layer (bridging function). The bridging function is self-configuring and can support up to 100.000 packets/s. Network loops are not allowed, but redundant links may be kept in standby mode. A basic description of the UltraNet architecture can be found in [8].

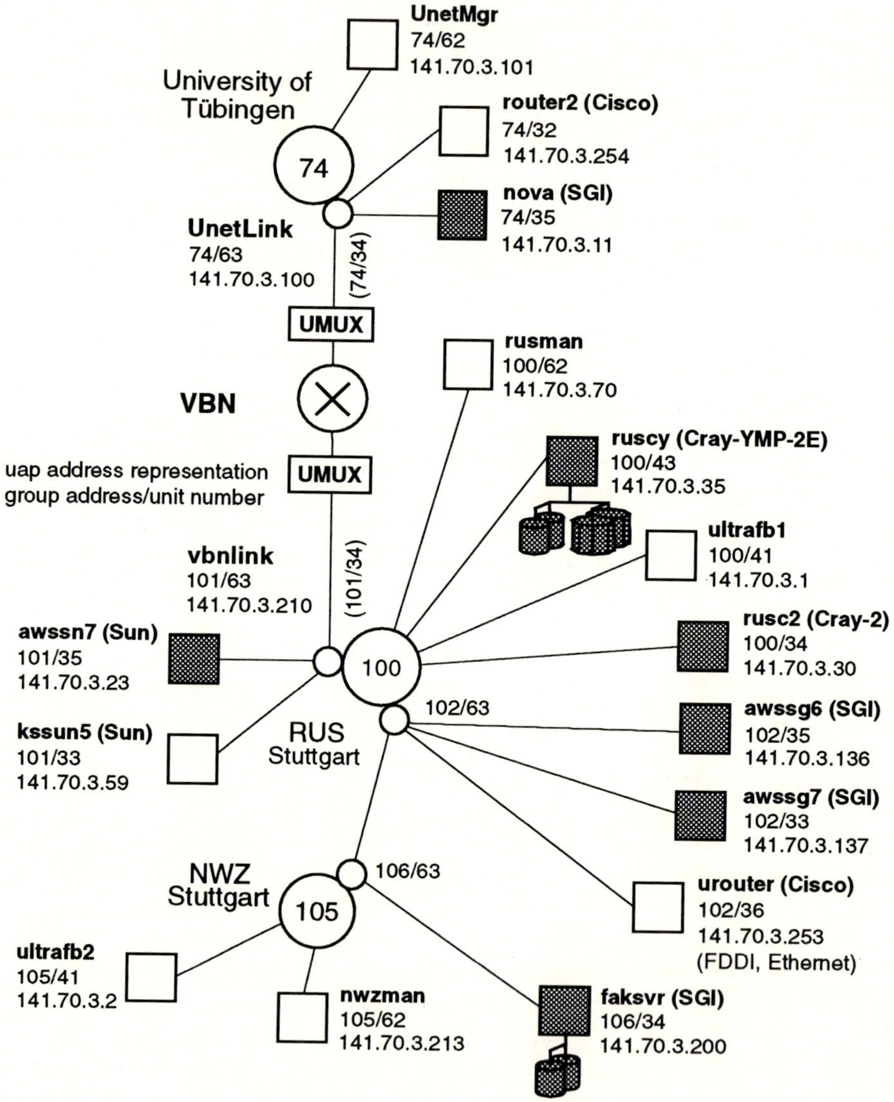

Fig. 1. UltraNet configuration at the University of Stuttgart computer center

In Fig. 1 we show the current UltraNet configuration at the University of Stuttgart computer center (RUS). The UltraNet provides the highest level of network interconnection between a Cray-2 and a Cray-YMP file server and also attaches to a number of Silicon Graphics and Sun Microsystems workstations. The next lower network levels in speed are indicated by the FDDI ring and Ethernet that can be accessed by means of a Cisco router. Of course, the two Cray supercomputers are equipped with network interfaces of their own going directly to FDDI, Hyperchannel and Ethernet (not shown). With the help of multiplexors developed in the framework of PAGEIN [9], a remote UltraNet, using the switched broadband network (VBN) of the Deutsche Bundespost Telekom, was set up between Stuttgart and Tübingen. This non-trivial configuration could serve as a regional PAGEIN testbed – in case of lack of an international one.

In Fig. 2 we provide a generic view of memory-to-memory performance between Cray supercomputers and SGI workstations, respectively. Please note, that memory-to-memory transfers between SGI workstations across the 50-km VBN will achieve more than 80 percent of the physical link speed of 100 Mbit/s. We have added the Cray memory performance over the local UltraBus and also the local FDDI ring to underscore the performance of the VBN link.

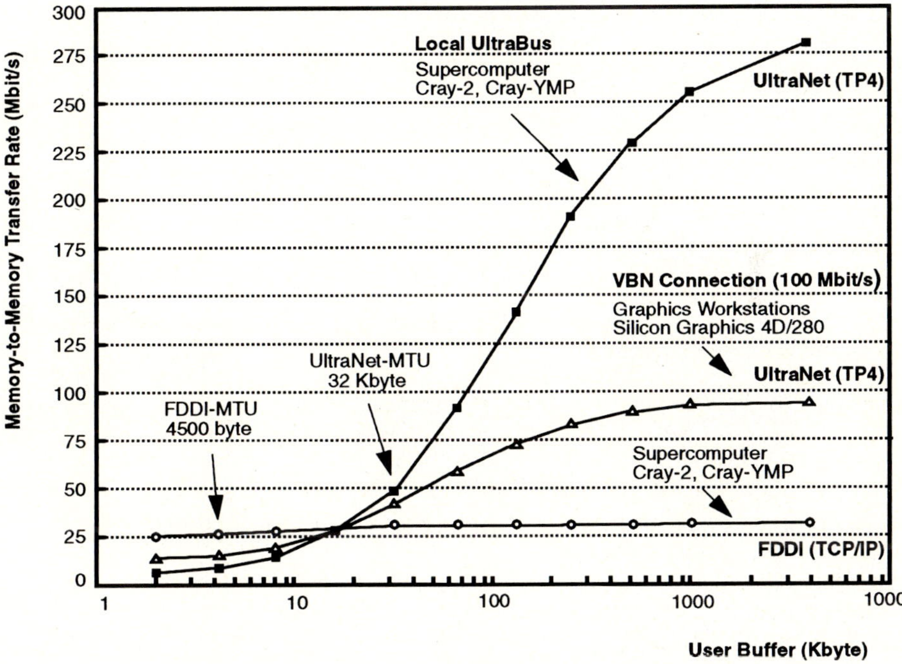

Fig. 2. Performance of remote UltraNet connection via VBN

3 The Stuttgart Metropolitan Area Network

As mentioned above, one of the proposed alternatives for a PAGEIN testbed, initially to include the University of Stuttgart computer center (RUS) and ONERA, was the extension of the Stuttgart Metropolitan Area Network (MAN) field trial. In the following, we therefore derive the performance limits of IP-based user traffic across the MAN. Such measures are felt of being especially interesting in the present context because they do represent the first numbers for "cell-based", i.e. ATM-like switching equipment. Throughout the text ALCATEL/SEL terminology is used [10].

Concerning the round-trip delay and throughput measures, consider Fig. 3 showing a test environment that has been set up in the Stuttgart MAN. The core part of the MAN is made up of two Edge Gateways (EGWs) that are connected by a folded 34-Mbit/s Distributed Queue Dual Bus (DQDB) network. Both customer sites, the debis computer center, Untertürkheim, and RUS, access the MAN by means of bridged Ethernets connected to the local Customer Gateways (CGWs). Protocol processors (PPAUs) are responsible for segmentation and reassembly of user datagrams. Two IBM RS/6000 workstations, located at RUS, are used as traffic generators. About 50 km apart, a Cray-YMP supercomputer in the debis company responds to this traffic. A total of four IP routers are in the network path in addition to the MAN's two CGWs and two EGWs.

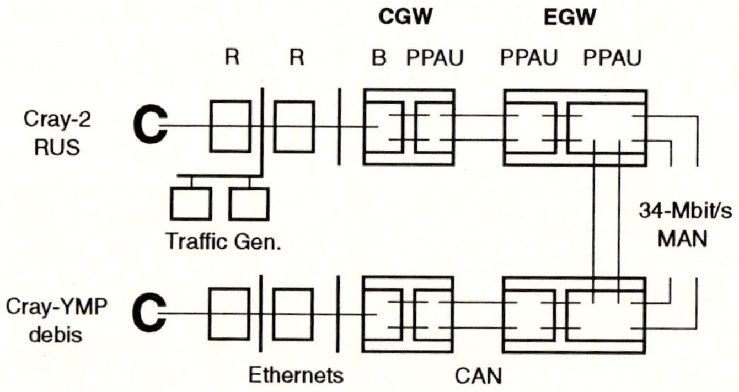

Fig. 3. Supercomputer test configuration in the Stuttgart MAN

As can be seen from Fig. 4, the IP maximum throughput shows a severe limitation for small packets (CGW's bridge). IP throughput is acceptable for maximum-sized packets, however, the round-trip time on Ethernet may reach 50 ms under load conditions. Therefore, user applications, like FTP, will have to support TCP windows in excess of 64 Kbyte.

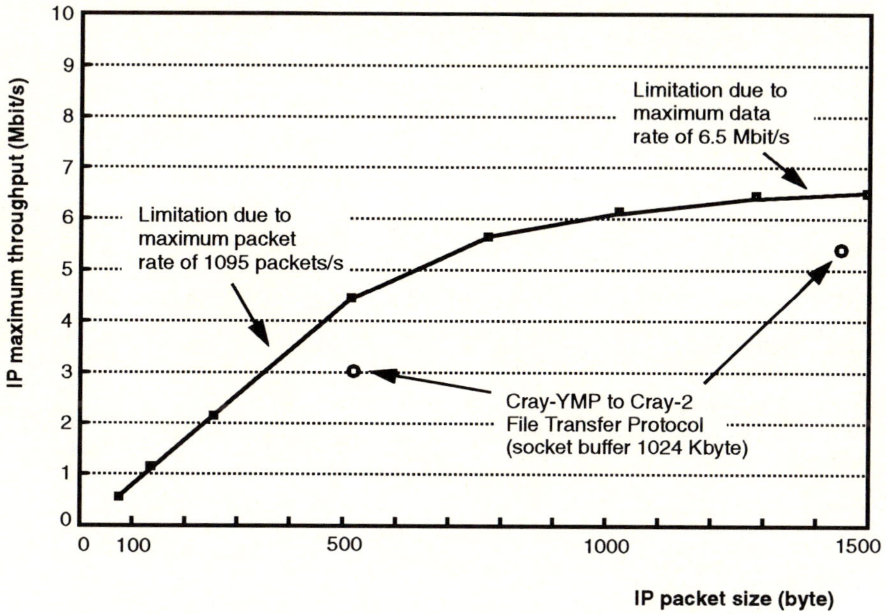

Fig. 4. MAN maximum IP throughput and file transfer performance

4 The PAGEIN CeBIT '93 - a Remote Local ATM-trial

After the announcement of an international ATM field trial of five European telecoms in autumn 1992, finishing its specification phase as early as summer 1993, and the installation of the first international ATM-oriented demonstration projects based on 34-Mbit/s PDH transmission infrastructures by the end of 1993 [11], international ATM networks are of growing interest to PAGEIN.

As a first step towards this goal, in cooperation with RACE 2060 Coordination, Implementation and Operation (CIO) a local ATM testbed has been set up at RUS. Together with CIO, this testbed has been demonstrated at the CeBIT '93 fair according to the following Fig. 5.

The ATM-testbed so far is a homogeneous one comprising switches and interfaces for SUN and SGI workstations from Fore Systems [12], [13], [14], [15].

According to the ATM UNI specification [16], Fore Systems is using the TAXI chip set from Advanced Micro Devices for physical framing. The bits are transferred over the FDDI physical interface using 4B/5B NRZI coding. Currently, connections with 100 Mbit/s and 140 Mbit/s are supported. It is therefore, that a variant of the multiplexor used for UltraNet remote connections [9], is capable of acting as a mapper for the German switched broadband network, VBN, or naked 140-Mbit/s PDH infrastrucures. Second generation ATM host interfaces, like Fore Systems SBA-200 [17], are expected to deliver about 50 Mbit/s data throughput on the application level.

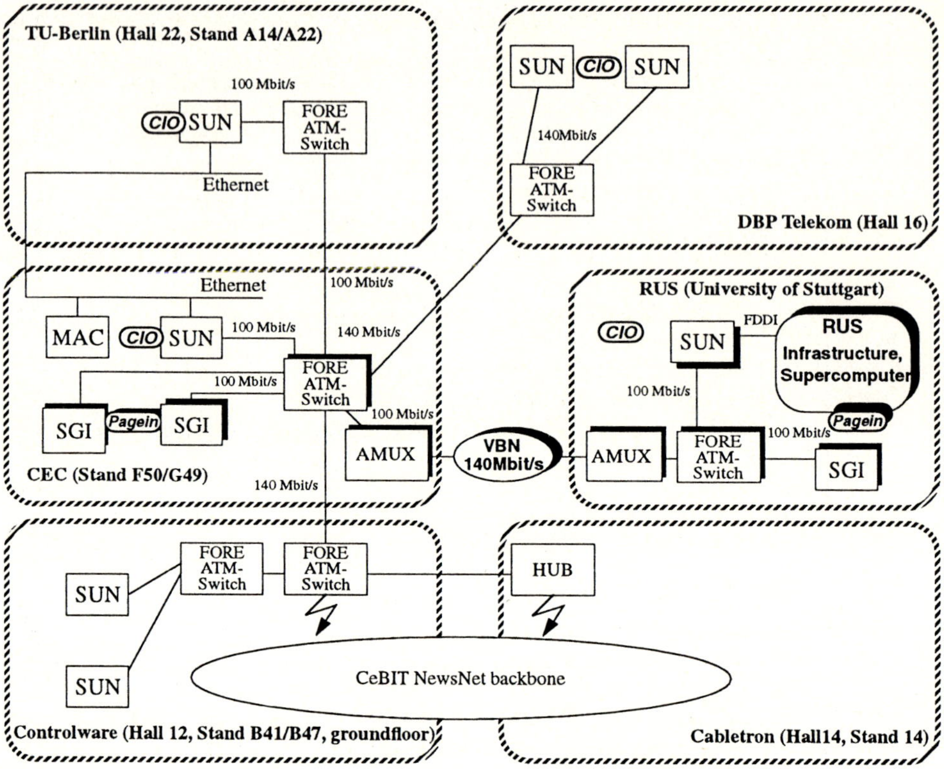

Fig. 5. PAGEIN ATM demonstration at CeBIT '93 together with RACE 2060 CIO

References

1. ANSI X3.183-1991: HIPPI-PH: Mechanical, Electrical, and Signalling Protocol Specification. Working Draft Proposal, June 1991
2. ANSI XT9.3: Serial-HIPPI: Serial HIPPI Implementors Group. Revision 1.0, May 1991.
3. ANSI X3.222-199x: HIPPI-SC: Physical Switch Control. Working Draft Proposal, December 1991

4. ANSI X3.210-199x: HIPPI-FP: Framing Protocol. Working Draft Proposal, February 1992
5. ANSI X3.218-199x: HIPPI-LE: 802.2 Link Encapsulation. Working Draft Proposal, July 1991
6. Renwick, J., Nicholson, A.: IP and ARP on HIPPI. Network Working Group. Internet Draft, Revision 2.0, June 1992
7. Jacobson, V.: TCP Extension for High Performance. RFC 1323
8. Beach, B.: ULTRANET: An Architecture for Gigabit Networking. Proceedings of the Fifteenth Conference on Local Computer Networks, Minneapolis, September 1991
9. Christ, P. et al.: Broadband Interworking Interface Prototype. RACE Document R2031/RUS/DS/L/004/b1, July 1992
10. SEL/ALACTEL: ALCATEL Metropolitan Area Network. Technical Report, SEL Department VS/PM, Version 1.1, April 1991
11. RACE 33rd RCM: ISABEL, BETEL, TIRONET, HP-Vision Project presentation. Project Line 8 presentations. Brussels January 26–27, 1993
12. Fore Systems, Inc.: ASX ATM Switch Architecture Manual. Release: 2.0. Pittsburgh 1992
13. Fore Systems, Inc.: DEVICES AND NETWORK INTERFACES. FSI Release 2.0. Last change: April 10, 1992
14. Fore Systems, Inc.: SBA-100 SBus ATM Computer Interface. User's Manual. Version: 1.0. Pittsburgh 1992
15. Fore Systems, Inc.: SPANS: Simple Protocol for ATM Network Signalling. Version: 2.1. Pittsburgh 1992
16. ATM Forum: ATM User-Network Interface Specification. Version 2.0. June 1, 1992
17. Bonaventure, O.: Performance Measurements of AAL4 and AAL5 on Fore SBA-200. RACE Document R2060/ULg/CIO/IN/R/0010, February 1994

Wavelet interactive in-line analysis with Pégase

F.X. Roux, J. Ryan, B. Troff, T.H. Lê, K. Dang-Tran

ONERA, 29 Av. de la Division Leclerc
BP 722 - 92322 Chatillon Cedex, France

Abstract. The present development partly achieved within the framework of the european RACE/PAGEIN project, is aimed at demonstrating the feasibility of Direct Numerical Simulation techniques for future industrial developments, when combined with modern supercomputer technology and High Performance Computing Networking, enabling massive data transfers between vector and/or parallel supercomputers.
The fast Navier-Stokes solver *PEGASE*, developed at ONERA and running on a Cray computer, has been parallelized to run on MIMD computers in a distributed environment including a Wavelet Analysis Module linked in-line with high performance graphics workstations. As the simulation develops in time, wavelet analysis is concurrently performed, flowfield structures may be interactively visualized without interrupting the numerical simulation.
The experiments conducted here on a local aera basis may be considered as a prerequisite to future communication between remote computing sites via very high speed networks.

1 Introduction

The application of supercomputer technology to aerodynamic design has created the field of computational fluid dynamics. Practitionners of the science simulate flows of fluid by solving the basic equations of fluid motion.

Within the last few years, Direct Numerical Simulation of turbulent flows achieved by solving the unsteady three-dimensional Navier-Stokes equations has proven to be a feasible tool for fundamental research and a potential tool of strong industrial interest. In fact, it appears as a key technology for future industrial developments, which combined with efficient visualization tools will have a definite impact on industrial productivity.

At present, it is clearly recognized that it cannot be used cost-effectivily without a High Performance Computing Networking (HPCN), enabling massive data transfers between vector and/or parallel supercomputers.

The present development is aimed at demonstrating the feasibility of this concept. It has been partly achieved within the framework of the european RACE/PAGEIN project (Pilot application on a Gigabit European Integrated Network) [1] [2]. This part of the project is specifically devoted to the implementation of a simulation code and of an analyzing code on a MIMD iPSC860 or PARAGON supercomputer for communication and visualization tests on a local aera basis. It may be considered as a prerequisite to future communications between remote computing sites via very high speed networks.

The Aerodynamics Department of ONERA has developed the PEGASE code, a fast Navier-Stokes solver for DNS and Large Eddy Simulation (LES) of turbulent flows implemented on a Cray computer. A sophisticated analyzing tool for the structure analysis of spatially highly intermittent turbulent flow fields has been also developed, based on the Wavelet Transform. This tool may also be used for a more compact representation of data with a minimal loss of information if data compression and transmission are of interest.

In collaboration with the Computer Science Department, these two main modules have been implemented on an iPSC860 and a PARAGON computer (the first module uses most of the processors in message passing mode for communication and the second one is implemented on a single processor) and linked in-line with a visualization module issued from the PAGEIN environment [2] [9].

Section 2 outlines the basic numerical method and details the parallel features of the implemented version 1.1 of the PEGASE code and its application to the three-dimensional simulation of a temporal mixing layer. Section 3 outlines the wavelet analysis tool and its application to the mixing layer vorticity field. Section 4 demonstrates the feasibility of the distributed environment including the in-line wavelet analysis with high performance graphics workstations.

2 Flow Code Pégase

2.1 Basic Numerical Method

The PEGASE 1.1 Navier-Stokes solver for direct numerical simulation of incompressible flows [7] was used to perform computations on the 3-D mixing layer configuration. The basic form of the code solves the Navier-Stokes equations, in conservative form, on an uniform non-staggered grid with a finite-difference method. All the spatial derivatives are approximated by centered second-order accurate operators. First derivatives are discretized with a strongly coupled 26-point stencil scheme. The use of such a scheme permits to obtain oscillation-free results. Time cycles are carried out with a first order forward Euler scheme. Incompressibility is enforced by employing a first-order time accurate projection method. The pressure is calculated from the Pressure Poisson Equation by a Bi-CGSTAB solver [9]. Details of the method and validation benchmarks are available in [7].

Periodic boundary conditions are prescribed in streamwise and spanwise directions and non-reflecting condition is used on top and bottom boundaries.

The initial condition is a tanh velocity field with a superimposed 3-D perturbation.

2.2 Pegase on a MIMD Machine

The strategy chosen for parallelization for three-dimensional calculations is that of non-overlapping pencils over a two-dimensional array of processors. This configuration seemed the most efficient for the implementation of the iterative method used to compute pressure. Though this technique implies more modifications of the original CRAY code than the choice of overlapping pencils, it allows a greater number of points in the physical domain and less computations for the same amount of communications.

Computation of spatial derivatives (a second order finite differences 26 point scheme) has been rewritten:

- contributions of border points (between subdomains) to computations of derivatives of points situated in other processors are first computed, and asynchronously sent. Derivatives at inner points are then computed then border points derivatives are computed, the necessary contributions having also been read asynchronously. (By asynchronous, one means that the send and receive calls return immediately, allowing the program to do further work while the message is processed.)

For center border points, see figure 1, (at a point represented by a black square), derivatives are computed in the following way. (Points in the second direction of space which is left uncut are not shown).

- Contribution c2 is sent to domain A. Computations involving points in domain B are made.
- Contribution c1 is then received and added.

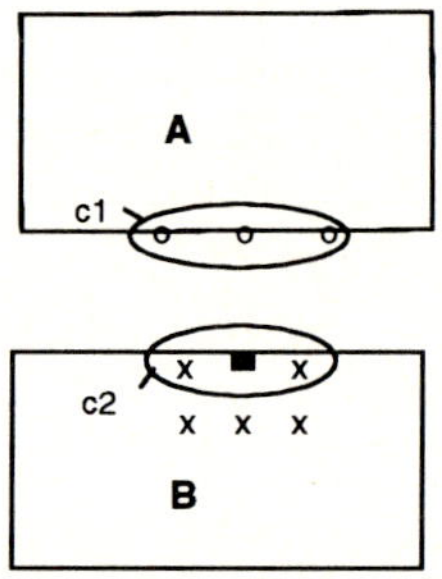

Fig. 1. Computation of derivatives at center border point

For corner points, see figure 2, involving three different domains, computation is done in several steps.

- At first , contribution c2 is sent to domain A while contribution c5 to deritatives of points in domain D is sent. In c5 is included contribution c3.
- In domain D contribution c5 is received and added to contribution c4 which is then sent to domain B.
- In domain B, contributions from domain A are received and added to computations involving points in the domain.
- Contribution c22 is sent to domain D, and contribution c4 is read and added.

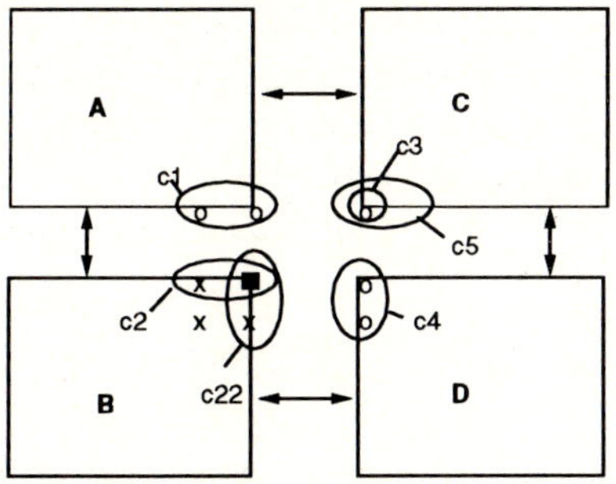

Fig. 2. Computation of derivatives at corner points

3 Wavelet Analysis Tool

In opposition to the classical Fourier transform used for the scale analysis and the computation of Eulerian statistics of homogeneous fields, the wavelet transform presents itself as an attractive and more and more popular tool for analyzing inhomogeneous fields, simultaneously in space and scale.

The present application uses cost-efficient orthonormal wavelet decomposition and recomposition algorithms detailed in [3], based on the theory of multiresolution analysis in [4] and [5]. This theory enables to decompose any (real square integrable) function $f \in L^2(R)$ as:

$$f(x) = \sum_j \sum_s d_{j,s} \psi_{j,s}(x)$$

where $\psi_{j,s}$ (with j, s integers), obtained by dyadic dilations and integer translations of a basic 'wavelet function' ψ :

$$\psi_{j,s} = 2^{j/2} \psi \left(\frac{x - s2^{-j}}{2^{-j}} \right)$$

is an orthonormal basis of $L^2(R)$. Currently used Wavelets ψ are generally oscillating and rapidly decaying functions localized both in physical space (at some location x_ψ) and in Fourier space (at some location k_ψ) so that $\psi_{j,s}$ is localized at $x_{j,s} = (x_\psi + s)2^{-j}$ in physical space and behave in spectral space as a band-pass filter centered at wave-number $k_j = k_\psi / 2^{-j}$. Thus wavelet coefficients $d_{j,s}$ capture information in the viscinity of point $x_{j,s}$ and wave-number k_j corresponding to scale 2^{-j}.

Moreover, orthogonality implies conservation of energy and recomposition of the original function from wavelet coefficients without loss of information, or recomposition of a filtered function corresponding to one chosen scale or a range of scales of interest (a propriety which will be used in the present application).

The wavelet decomposition-recomposition algorithm due to Mallat [2] relies on the fact that f may be also decomposed as:

$$f(x) = \sum_{J} c_{J,s}\phi_{J,s}(x) + \sum_{j>J}\sum_{s} d_{j,s}\psi_{j,s}(x)$$

In a manner similar to $\psi_{j,s}$, $\phi_{J,s}$ (for any interger value of J), obtained by dyadic dilations and integer translations of a basic 'scale function' ϕ :

$$\phi_{J,s} = 2^{J/2}\phi\left(\frac{x - s2^{-J}}{2^{-J}}\right)$$

is an orthonormal basis of a subspace V_J where the functions are known up to details at scale 2^{-J}. This function behave in spectral space as a low-pass filter up to a wavenumber $k'_J = 2^{-J}k_\phi$,($k_\phi \sim k_\psi$).

Consequently, at any level J a function belonging to V_J and containing details up to scale 2^{-J} may be decomposed into the sum of a function belonging to V_{J-1} containing details up to scale $2^{-(J-1)}$ and a function containing extra details at scale $2^{-(J-1)}$ belonging to a subspace W_{J-1}. V_{J-1} and W_{J-1} being orthogonal, V_J may be written as their direct sum:

$$V_J = V_{J-1} \oplus W_{J-1}$$

¿From the $N = 2^p$ values of a function given on a regular grid and belonging to a subspace V_p of $L^2(R)$, the Mallat decomposition algorithm [2] used in the present application defines a succession of embedded subspaces $\{\cdots V_{J-2} \subset V_{J-1} \subset V_J \cdots\}$. At each J level coefficients $d_{J-1,s}$ and $c_{J-1,s}$ are computed in a recursive way from known values of coefficients c_J via two discrete convolutions using two discrete filters depending on the particular (ϕ, ψ) chosen pair. Conversely, coefficients $c_{J,s}$ are computed from known values of $d_{J-1,s}$ and $c_{J-1,s}$ in the case of a recomposition.

In practice and following [6] periodized spline wavelets are used. Convolutions with periodized discrete filters are then computed in spectral space by Fast Fourier Transforms and multidimensional analyses are performed on the basis of tensor-products of the one-dimensional analysis (see [3] for more details). These choices result in efficient fast two-dimensional or three-dimensional algorithms for wavelet analysis of periodical functions.

Many fundamental quantities relevant to the dynamics of turbulent flows may be computed from the wavelet coefficients (such as local enstrophy or energy spectra, local Reynolds numbers...). In the present application, the analysis tool is restricted to the detection and visualization of flow structures at different scales in a three-dimensional mixing layer flow evolving in time as described in §5.

4 In-line Integration

The simulation code is integrated in a distributed environment including an in-line wavelet analysis with high performance graphics workstations. This is based on the message passing mechanism (PVM). For more details on the distributive environnement, see [9].

As the simulation develops in time regularly sending velocity or pressure fields, a scale wavelet analysis is concurrently performed. For example, PEGASE runs on $N-1$ processors on the iPSC860 while the wavelet code runs simultaneously on the Nth processor (or on Cray or an Silicon Graphics workstation). The local fields computed by PEGASE are interpolated on the wavelet grid and sent to the last processor where there are assembled and analyzed (during this stage PEGASE continues its advance in time). Results of this analysis are then sent to a visualization module.

Interactivity guided by continuous visualization is created with the possibility of changing the analyzed variable or the wavelet analysis scales without interrupting the numerical simulation. All the numerical fields are stored periodically so that when the flow develops in complexity, it is possible to go back in time to do a finer analysis of the on-going phenomena.

5 Results

5.1 Direct simulation experiments and visualizations

A direct simulation of a 3-D mixing layer evolving in time has been carried out on a $71 \times 43 \times 85$ grid. A planar mixing layer with a "tanh" mean velocity is perturbed with a strongly 3-D perturbation. As the flow evolves in time, non-linear interactions of these perturbations lead to a complex, fully 3-D flow field with coherent structures at different scales which are analyzed by the wavelet tool.

Figure 3. displays the isovalue 3. of the enstrophy field (square of the vorticity distribution). At time t=12 a main spanwise vortex (y-direction) has formed. The 3-D character of the flow is evidenced by the appearence of secondary streamwise vortices (x-direction). This field has been decomposed by the wavelet transform on a $(64)^3$ grid and recomposed after filtering scales larger than scale 2^{-5}.

Figure 4 displays the iso value 4.10^{-2} of the small structures detected by the wavelet transform. These small structures are absent from the core of the main vortex but are localized partly in the secondary vortices and mainly in the complex reconnection region with the main vortex.

5.2 Cost of Pégase

- On Cray YMP, with one processor, PEGASE runs at approximatively 190 Mflops, and costs 2.10^{-6}s per point and per time step (for an average of 10 iterations when solving the pressure).

- On iPSC860, for a 64 bit accuracy (similar to that of the Cray), the modified code is four times less expensive when using the 128 processors, thus a performance of 760 Mflops is reached. Cost does not increase much with the number of processors as communications are mostly local.
- On Paragon, performances are improved over the iPSC860 by a ratio of 25% as message passing are optimized and processors are more powerful.

5.3 Cost of the Wavelet Analysis Tool

- On Cray YMP, with one processor, and using the Fast Fourier Transform the cost of a Wavelet Analysis is 8s .
- On a Silicon Graphics workstation the cost is about 50 times the cost on Cray YMP
- On ipSC860, using one processor, the cost is weakly less than the cost on the workstation.

In view of the costs mentionned above, in-line analysis of the flow computed on iPSC860 may be performed approximatively every 500 time steps.

6 Conclusion

The PAGEIN prototype is of great interest for massive data generating and analyzing codes. The possibility of interactive visualization and computation allows better control of the process. But safegards such as on-line time dependent measure of error [10] should be devised so that the beauty of the visualizations does not affect accuracy of the results.

Acknowledgment

The authors thank M. Do-khac and C. Basdevant who provided the wavelet analysis code for the present application.

References

1. Cosnuau A. , D'Anfray Ph., Berrino U. , Causse S. , Goirand A. , Grave M. , Hollard M. , Lang U. , Ryan J. , Troff B. , Tromeur-Dervout D. , Wierse A. : Networked Supercomputing Report., December 92. European contract, project number R2031.
2. Spaa J., Westenberg G., Grosso R., Keymeulen D., Lang U., Pottiez M., Seitz B., Vucinic D., Wierse A., Cosnuau A. : Heterogeneous Visualization Specifications, December 92. European contract, project number R2031.
3. Do-Khac M. , Basdevant C. , Perrier V. , Dang-Tran K. : Wavelet analysis of 2D turbulent fields. To appear in PhysicaD, 'Chaotic Advection, Tracer Dynamics and Turbulent dispersion'. Ed. A. Provenzale, A. Vulpiani, A. Babiano.
4. Mallat S. , IEEE Transactions on Pattern Anal. Machine Intell. 11-7 (1989)1

5. Meyer Y. : Ondelettes et opérateurs. Hermann (1990).
6. Perrier V., Basdevant C.: La décomposition en ondelettes périodiques, un outil pour l'analyse de champs inhomogènes. Théorie et algorithmes. Aerospatial Research 3 (1989) 53
7. Lê, T.H., Troff, B., Sagaut, P., Dang-Tran K., Ta Phuoc Loc :PEGASE; a Navier-Stokes solver for direct numerical simulation of incompressible flows, submitted to Int. J . Numer. Methods Fluids
8. Van der Vorst, H., Bi-CGSTAB: a fast and smoothly converging variant of Bi-CG for the solution of nonsymetric linear systems, SIAM J. Sci. Statist. Comput., 13 (1992), 631 -644
9. Causse S., Juaneda F., Grave M. : Implementation of visualization tools in a distributed environment. To be published in the HPCN Europe '94 proceedings.
10. Zienkiewicz O. C. and Zhu J. Z. : The Three R's of Engeneering Analysis and Error Estimation and Adaptavity, Computer Methods in Applied Mechanics and Engeneering 82 (1990) 95-113, North-Holland

Fig. 3. Enstrophy field (iso value 3.)

Fig. 4. Enstrophy field recomposed with smallest scales (iso value 4.10^{-2})

European HPC Competitiveness Centres for Industry

Alfred Scheidegger
Swiss Scientific Computing Center, CSCS

Industry is facing several challenges in their strive for competitiveness. Ever faster technology leaps are building barriers in the effort to realise technology strategies. New, innovative products are not only requiring a faster *time-to-market* but also costeffective production. Innovative products are characterised more and more by their interdisciplinary technology. Often, technological hurdles are bypassed by adjusting the desired product to the available in-house technology.

Table 1: Developments in the field of technology

- Accelerated technological change
- Reduced life cycle of products
- Faster dissemination of Intellectual Property
- Increased financial resources
- Raised risk in R & D
- Global Market
- Augmented number of interdisciplinary products/technology

Improving the efficiency of the R&D process is presently a major issue for industrial corporations. Furthermore, a number of leading service and financial institutions are presently transforming their organisations in function of the introduction of scientific methodologies and are putting similar demands for productivity on research. There are serious questions as to the efficiency of R&D and, above all, on the path from research to development. In Europe in particular, there is growing dissatisfaction for the ability to turn the EC research investment into marketable products. Many leading companies have started a process of analysing their research effort in order to improve its productivity.

Computational science plays a central and growing role in the R&D process. Its importance is twofold. First, it greatly enhances the rate and the quality of scientific discoveries, producing knowledge that would otherwise be very difficult or even impossible to acquire. At the same time, it institutionalises the process of research. Second, computational science greatly expedites the process of turning the results of research into products as it generates a type of knowledge of immediate use in product design and manufacturing. The design and manufacturing processes are shortened and quality is improved.

Table 2: Aspects of computational science in industry

- Specific problem solving
- Saving of time
- Cost factor
- Quality
- Innovation
- New decision process
- Environmental aspects

As statistics show, the ratio between the available super computer power, as measured in Gigaflops, and the nation's GNP is higher in Japan than in the USA and Europe. Japanese industries use more super computer power than their American or European competitors of comparable size. The heavier use of super computing in Japan is correlated to its higher spending in R&D as a percentage of GNP with respect to Europe and the USA.

The structure of R&D

Product development is generally done using established and validated design methodologies while industrial research sets out to solve well defined problems for which there is no known solution. In the present R&D scenario, applied research is problem-driven and is generally related to specific industrial endeavours. Computational science-based R&D can be segmented in the following basic areas:

- the development of general purpose computational methods;
- the development of applications and computational methods to solve specific problems;
- the solution of specific problems using established methods;
- the definition of new design methodologies and applications;
- full-fledged product development.

A vast amount of industrial research is still done using simulation to find facts, while most creative work is executed off-line. It is, however, fundamental to realise that there is the possibility of a major shift in the research paradigm that will bring most of the R&D process on-line. Implementing this change is a major effort in terms of methods, but also in terms of organisation. It would be beneficial if the research community could get in tune with industry and would start scientific endeavours having in mind their industrial use from the beginning.

Industry and public research

Computational science has created enormous expectations that seem not to be matched by actual results. How can the visionary Grand Challenges be reconciled with industrial reality? In many cases, the cost of developing the basic know-how of a new technology like computational science is simply to high for most companies. Industry can reap the best fruits of simulation only through a difficult process of integration that will require a substantial maturity of technologies.

Most applications of present industrial interest were originally developed in government laboratories and research institutes. This trend is likely to continue. Large labs and super computer research centres must fill the role of visionary innovators. In this endeavour, research must come closer to industry in the development of methods which facilitate industrial exploitation. Examples of such research are in the fields of environmental problems, design of drugs and materials, and the improvement of making use of energy.

Presently, most investments go to applied research of industrial interest executed, however, with academic methods. Through computational science, science has reached the stage where technology adopts methods that are very close to theoretical first principles and whose application requires a sophisticated mathematics. The ability to couple a goal-oriented industrial mentality with rigorous theoretical thinking has become fundamental.

Efficient technology transfer by co-operation of industry with public organisations

A competitive co-oporation has to transfer technology quickly and efficiently. Technology transfer does not only work through joint ventures or merger and acquisition. Public organisations can also be a partner. Opportunities for an industry-academy co-operation do exist and can have tremendous advantages, but also pitfalls. Co-operations allow to follow more closely the company's strategic orientation, and generate knowledge and technology.

Table 3: Advantages of industry-academy co-operation in computational science

Strategic	- Enhancement of competitiveness
	- Mastering of technology leaps
	- Realisation of technology strategy
	- Environment for new ideas
	- Knowledge/technology transfer
	- Critical mass
	- Risk reduction
	- Saving of time
	- Problem solving parallel, not serial
Problem-solving	- Cost reduction for investment/project

Co-operation between industry and public research is not new and has been practised since long, however, the success rate is modest. Where are the reasons? Academic institutions are still labelled with scientific freedom, which all to often is misunderstood as a freedom without responsibility towards economy and welfare. As a consequence, only a very limited understanding of industrial problems and applications could so far be built up. A professional attitude towards project management is rarely formed and the ethics of confidentiality is still unpopular in the academic environment.

Table 4: Critical factors of industry-academy co-operation in computational science

Industry	- Bad past experience
	- Mouse-ownership syndrome
	- Flexibility
	- Trust in and interest of partners
	- Competence of partners
	- Win-win situation
	- Institutionalised technology transfer
	- Ivory tower syndrome
	- Security/confidentiality
	- Project management
Academy	- Understanding of industrial applications

On the other hand does industry still hesitate to give away really important problems for solving under a collaborative program. Trust has to be built up - an undertaking, which asks for a strong technology marketing by the academic institution. Often can also a strong internal resistance, the *mouse-ownership-syndrome,* be found in corporations which inhibits the development of a collaborative spirit. Many HPC centres are hardware-based, related to an university, and its staff tied into academic projects. Under these circumstances, the necessary industrial spirit can hardly gain a foothold. Cost-effectiveness and a spirit for deadlines are rarely understood principles.

A centre needs excellent staff, an understanding of industrial applications, and research efforts that are in line with the demanded application areas. Expertise in certain application domains is a key issue to provide industry with the necessary problem-solving capacity. It further needs a well established technology marketing structure and the courage, to expose to the free market and the rules of economy. Quality is evaluated differently by industry and academy. To attract customers, efforts to build a platform of trust is necessary, often with preceding trial periods. The willingness to undergo such procedures, while governmental funding is still flowing excessively is neither common nor easy.

Despite all these difficulties, successful co-operations are possible, and are practised primarily in the US. The research centres Cornell Theory Centre (CTC), Lawrence Livermore National Laboratory (LLNL), and the Beckman Institute at Caltech are representing three different models of co-operation between public research and industry. CTC offers mainly the know-how of the prestigious Cornell University, the Beckman Institute performs applied research in advanced fields with the specific objective of taking it to market, and LLNL is a huge research centre with enormous resources developed for military use that the Government wants to turn into civilian use. All of them can show success stories of collaboration with industry. Other centres that merit to be mentioned are the National Centre for Supercomputing Applications at the University of Illinois at Urbana-Champaign, which is the most successful at marketing joint research with industry, and the San Diego Supercomputer Centre, where the major motivation for using the Centre's resources is apparently cost cutting.

European HPC Competitiveness Centres for Industry

Computational science is a relatively new technology and its broad implementation in industry has started only recently. Until computational science is not well developed with respect to the number of applications as well as to user-friendly user-interfaces, companies do well to turn with their needs to HPC centres. With a highly skilled scientific staff and a state-of-the-art hardware and software environment, the centres can, in a collaborative effort, be capable to solve industry's problems.

Not only scientific and engineering problems can be solved by a well managed co-operation, but computational science can be introduced into all kinds of industrial processes ranging from R&D, innovation management, to decision-making in finance and corporate processes. The definition and implementation of information technology structures and methodologies have to be adapted by industries. Co-operations serve as a bridge between research in computational science methodology and industrial applications. By collaborating with industry, the HPC centres become of central importance in the efforts of the European industry for competitiveness. Industry desperately needs such HPC Centres. Together with industry, these centres will become Competitiveness Centres, and numerous such centres are ideally forming a network covering Europe. The centres should maintain a number of industrial partnerships. The promotion of a new breed of computational scientists that accepts the challenges of industrial applications will be central for success.

If Europe's industry shall be competitive, the intense employment of computational science is a must. The HPC Competitiveness Centres for Industry can build the bridge from research to industry application in order to solve industry's problems and help industry to introduce computational science on a broad basis into all kinds of processes. The spirit for solidarity and the understanding and mastering of management issues finally decides on the success.

An Open High-Performance Computing Infrastructure in Industry

R. Iffert

debis Systemhaus CCS GmbH, RRZ München, P.O. Box 500640, 80976 München

U. Harms

Supercomputing-Consulting, Bunsenstr. 5, 81735 München

Abstract: debis Systemhaus CCS is supplying centralized computing power to the different branches of the Daimler-Benz Holding throughout Germany. In the Munich area these services are delivered to the aircraft and aerospace industry (DASA). A Cray C 90 is operated in Stuttgart. After installing a Cray Y-MP2E as the successor of the Siemens-Nixdorf VP 200 (Fujitsu), that had been in operation since 1985, the infrastructure was changed drastically. The UNIX workstations in the research departments of the customers and the IBM MVS systems in the central computer center had to be connected with the new supercomputer. The design and realization considerations concerning the supercomputer, workstation-clusters, mainframes and high-speed networking in industrial services will be presented and discussed in this paper. Further enhancements in the infrastructure e.g. massively parallel processing systems are now possible without major difficulties.

1. Introduction

In the past, scientific computing was offered on MVS, VMS and initial UNIX platforms. For this purpose, several different network architectures had to be maintained; a big SNA network, a DEC network and finally a small, but fast growing

TCP/IP network. The goal was to integrate, via supercomputing, all of these networks and operating environments.

In the time period from 1985 to 1992 the computer world had changed dramatically with the increase in computing power and memory size with workstations. The research departments in industry installed their own workstations to develop programs, solve smaller problems directly and perform pre- and post-processing. These systems used the operating system UNIX and could not then easily be connected to the MVS-based supercomputer. Moreover, new structures in the computer field as client-server-technology, file serving and high-speed networking had proved to be very useful.

2. Considerations for an open infrastructure

All these facts had to be considered, to achieve a user-oriented supercomputing that connects the old MVS-systems and the UNIX-workstations. The whole environment had to be expandable and open to new computer architectures, systems and operating systems. Two alternatives had been discussed, to install a vector supercomputer or to offer workstation-clusters. The solution: integration of both systems in the central computer center.

The central computer center has a lot of advantages:
- data security
- controlled access to the computer center
- controlled access to the computers
- regular and controlled archiving and backup of files
- migration aids
- advisory services
- education and documentation
- development of user interfaces

Providing these services through the supercomputer center allows the users engineers, mathematicians and physicians, to concentrate on their aerodynamic or engineering problems and not to operate high-speed workstations.
In the first stage the Cray is connected to a MVS host by a direct channel (4.5 MB/sec) connection. This preserves the old (VP 200) environment. The user at an IBM 3270 terminal can continue his work in the well known environment. Another advantage is found in the archiving and backup of files. This can be done in the normal way by robots, the operators are familiar with these procedures. Furtheron the Cray can be accessed via the Cray MVS-station software and a user interface called FORCOS. The workstations located in the computer center are connected directly to the UNIX supercomputer. This is nothing new and has often been implemented in computer centers.

3. Networking

The new and interesting aspect is to be found in the Low Speed Channel (LSX) that is directed to a Data Exchange Box (DX-box) delivered by Network Systems. This flexible router with a bandwidth of about 100 MB/sec contains a TCP/IP coprocessor. The DX-box allows IBM blockmultiplex, the Serial Optical Channel Converter (SOCC) of IBM, Ethernet, FDDI, Token Ring and serial lines (2 Mbit/sec). This way the local and remote LANs can be connected and the box can serve as the heart of a workstation cluster. The MVS hosts and the systems in Ottobrunn (a distance of about 40 km between Allach and Ottobrunn) are connected directly by TCP/IP. In this way the TCP/IP access to IBM and Cray world was implemented, see figure 1, Scientific Computing Environment, First Step Towards Realization.

In a second stage of our installation more computers can be connected to the DX-box directly. These might be file-servers, single workstations with a local disc, big workstation-clusters, user- or computer center-owned, and finally massively parallel systems, when and if the industrial need is defined.

An alternative is offered by the FDDI ring in the computer center. It can be connected by a router to the users FDDI ring, see figure 2, Scientific Computing Environment. Even smaller departments can integrate their LAN with the high-speed networks at the center. A new service is offered: the users can install their own machines in the center's computer room, see figure 3, Scientific Computing Environment, Coarse Network Backup. There they can participate in all the goodies of the center, for example, security, archiving, uninterruptible power supply. The centralized computer center can offer valuable services even in a downsizing environment.

The user only needs office communications, graphics, text processing and programme development facilities on his desk. The computers, the high-speed networks and special systems are operated by the center that also provides support. These services offer a new opportunity to the computer centers, that are beeing decentralized and downsized by the new trends in the data processing environment.

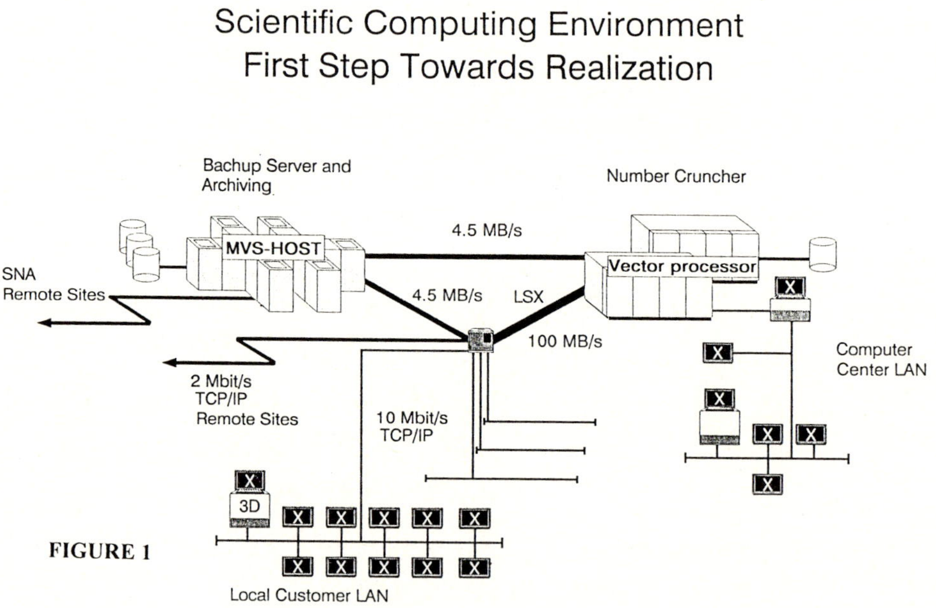

FIGURE 1

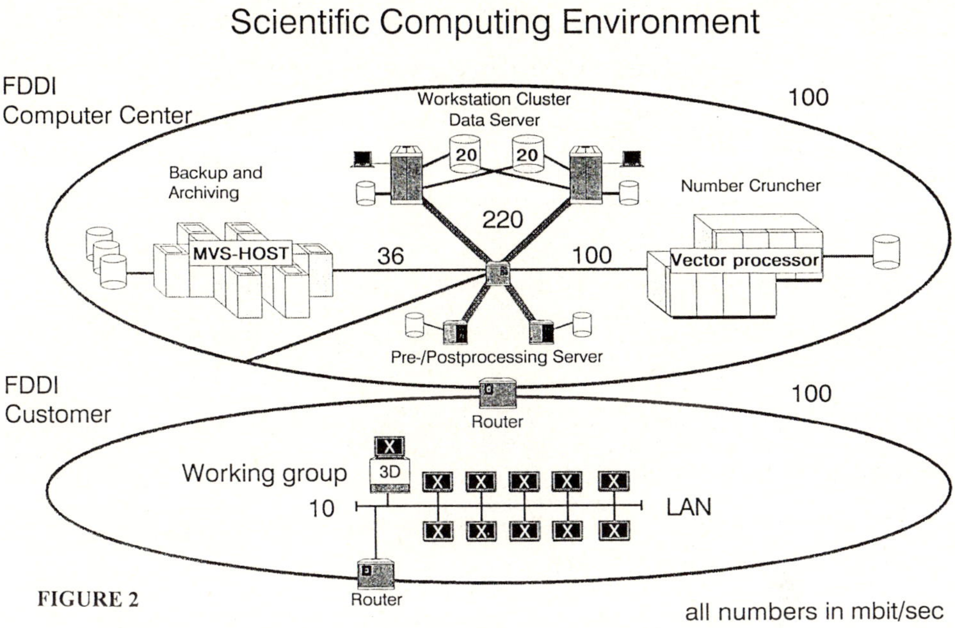

FIGURE 2

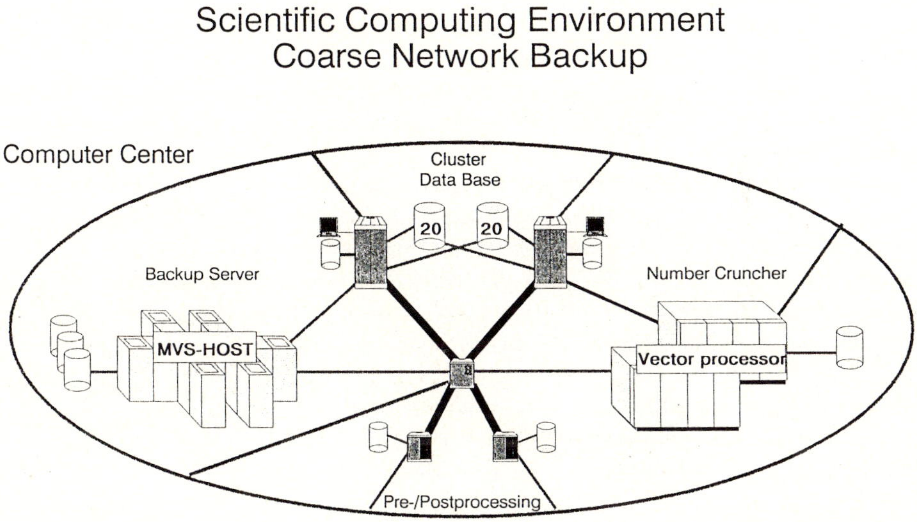

FIGURE 3

A catalog of classifying characteristics for massively parallel computers

Tilmann Bönniger[1], Rüdiger Esser[2], Dietrich Krekel[1]

[1] Regionales Rechenzentrum an der Universität zu Köln, Robert-Koch-Str. 10, D-50931 Köln, E-mail: {Boenniger,Krekel}@rrz.Uni-Koeln.DE
[2] Zentralinstitut für Angewandte Mathematik, Forschungszentrum Jülich GmbH, D-52425 Jülich, E-mail: R.Esser@KFA-Juelich.DE

Abstract. In order to facilitate an application-oriented assessment of high-performance massively parallel computing systems, a catalog of about 350 classifying characteristics concerning the architecture and software environment of such systems has been compiled. The data required for the catalog allow a rather complete and homogeneous description of a massively parallel system to be established. This article contains an overview of the catalog and the hardware model on which it is based.

1 Introduction

Since a new generation of high-performance massively parallel systems (MP systems) has recently become commercially available and claims to be an effective alternative to traditional vector supercomputers, application developers as well as computing centers have to decide whether this new technology can serve their needs. In order to facilitate the assessment of MP systems, we established a catalog of classifying characteristics and prepared a comparative description of some specific MP systems on the basis of the catalog [2], similar to earlier work for vector supercomputers [1]. The data required for the catalog allow a rather complete and homogeneous description of a massively parallel system to be established. In contrast to the data sheets provided by the manufactures, the catalog facilitates the comparison of MP systems even if they have different architectures. What is more, gathering the data required for an MP system makes it possible to understand this system much better. In the process of selecting an MP system, this collection of data complements performance measurements with benchmark programs from the intended application area.

This paper contains an overview of the catalog and of the hardware model forming its basis. In another paper [3], the data required for the catalog have been gathered for three commercially available MP systems: Intel Paragon XP/S, Kendall Square KSR1, and Thinking Machines CM-5. That article also includes textual descriptions of the three MP systems based on the classifying characteristics as well as figures showing their overall architecture, processing nodes, vector units and memory hierarchy.

Table 3: Parallel programming concepts, tools, and libraries

Support for programming models	**Other tools**
SIMD parallel model	**Native communication libraries**
Data parallel model	message passing
MIMD shared memory model	informational routines
Message passing model	global synchronization
Program development tools	global operations
name (type; functionality; runs on)	remote message passing
Debugging tools	**Optimized application libraries**
name (type; functionality; runs on)	node libraries (type; functionality)
Performance analysis tools	parallel libraries (type; functionality)
name (type; functionality; runs on)	**Possible handicaps**
Portability tools	
name (type; functionality; runs on)	

The group *application software* is a difficult topic. One has to be careful with manufacturer lists of available software, sometimes a package is running on a single node only. Parallelized and optimized versions of existing application packages are very scarce, which - from an economic point of view - is quite understandable. And the user base for new massively parallel applications has been small until now. The group *configurations* reveals what the manufacturers offer as minimal, typical and maximal system configuration. Last but not least the group *performance* tries to provide some typical computation and communication performance data derived from available documentation.

References

[1] T. Bönniger, R. Esser, and D. Krekel, CRAY Y-MP, NEC SX-3 und Siemens VP S, Vergleichende Darstellung von Höchstleistungsrechnern, Wirtschaftsinformatik (März 1990) 273-286.

[2] T. Bönniger, R. Esser, and D. Krekel, CM-5, KSR1, and Paragon XP/S: a comparative description of massively parallel computers on the basis of a catalog of classifying characteristics, to appear in Parallel Computing.

[3] T. Bönniger, R. Esser, and D. Krekel, Catalog of classifying characteristics for massively parallel computers: CM-5, KSR1, and Paragon XP/S, Arbeitsbericht RRZK-9302, Regionales Rechenzentrum an der Universität zu Köln, Dezember 1993

[4] A. Choudhary, Parallel I/O Systems, Journal of Parallel and Distributed Computing 17 (1993) 1-3.

[5] A. S. Tanenbaum, Distributed Operating Systems Anno 1992. What Have We Learned So Far? in: Distributed Computing, Practice and Experience, Proceedings of the Autumn 1992 OpenForum Technical Conference, Utrecht, November 23-27, 1992, 1-14.

Building a Parallel Computing Environment from Heterogenous Resources

Kimmo Koski

Center for Scientific Computing (CSC),
P.O.Box 405, Tietotie 6, FIN-02101 Espoo, Finland
e-mail: Kimmo.Koski@csc.fi

1 Introduction

During the recent years parallel processing and lately especially massively parallel processing has been discussed intensively. In certain application areas the need for parallel usage is emerging due to the parallel nature of the problem or high cost of vector supercomputers. However, the massively parallel computer systems have not yet been able to demonstrate mature and adequate computing environment to solve problems from various different application areas. Also it is still unclear to which direction and in which time frame the parallel compiler technology and architechtures are evolving.

Most high-performance computing centers are today running a set of different (mainly UNIX based) resources, like vector supercomputers, massively parallel computers, shared memory multiprocessors and efficient RISC workstations. Their basic problem often is how to run the load in the most suitable computer for this particular problem in order to use the environment as efficiently as possible. This interoperability of different kinds of resources is called Metacomputing.

The optimal usage of parallel processing in a Metacomputing environment raises also several questions. Some of the parallel systems are also used in serial mode so that the task is executed on one node same time than part of the machine executes parallel jobs. In the case of a large set of heterogeneus jobs this brings out the need to consider the throughput capacity obtained from serial usage versus the faster problem solving (but probably more resource consuming) time of parallel usage. One of the key questions is how to balance both the parallel and serial as well also interactive and batch usage optimally across different set of resources.

There are also different approaches to parallel computing. The usage can be moderate using, for example, a small set of processors and shared memory which has already been done for several years. More interesting cases are related to the usage of tens, hundreds or even more processors within the same computer system or possibly across different computer systems. In some cases to build a parallel computing environment has to be realized with quite a moderate budget which makes possibilities to use some of the already existing equipment appealing.

Today the number of different parallel computing and programming tools has grown considerably. Although this kind of tools offer various means to parallelize code and run the jobs in heterogenous platforms, lack of standards still create a somewhat unclear vision about the direction where parallel computing is heading.

2 Motivation of building the environment from heterogeneus resources

Presently the scientific computing environments are often dominated by either large and expensive vector computers, multiprocessor servers or clusters of efficient workstations. Traditional massively parallel computers have not fulfilled their promises to spread quickly around the market, mainly due to their difficult user interfaces and lack of software. In many cases purchased MPP computers are serving as a playground for message passing type programming or very specific applications, and this kind of MPP usage is likely to continue for the next two or three years.

On the other hand it is inevitable that high performance computing is increasingly using more parallelism due to the fact that one processor peak performance is expensive to achieve and processors are also getting near to their practical limits. Also some problems are by their nature suitable for parallel processing. It is necessary for all the high performance computing centers to build an environment for parallel computing due to the inevitable development towards increasingly more massive parallelism.

The state of the massively parallel computing industry is at the moment very unstable. The traditional MPP vendors, such as Intel, Thinking Machines, Meiko, Maspar, Kendall Square Research and some others, are attacked by new products made by vendors previously known for their vector processor supercomputers, like Cray T3D, Convex Exemplar, Fujitsu VPP500 and IBM SP systems among others. The market and especially profits from MPP systems are obviously too small for such a large vendor base. The future will likely reduce the number of the vendors, and I would not be surprised in case the amount of them after two years would be half of today's number.

At the same time as MPP vendors are suffering from hard competition and decreasing profits, some centers are suffering from degreasing investment funds. Thus it is not always possible to purchase a MPP system for dedicated use. This makes it appealing to provide an environment by building it from existing resources by coupling them together or by obtaining such a MPP system which has a high one processor performance so that the system can efficiently take care of serial jobs in addition to parallel tasks. This kind of solution represents also relatively low risk: if the parallel usage does not seem to attract users you can always use the high one processor performance system as a throughput machine for serial load.

The development of different interconnections and switches will make it possible to couple different systems together more tightly than before. In some of the clustered systems the latencies have decreased from hundreds to tens of microseconds getting near to the 'traditional' MPP systems latencies. In a few years timeframe it might not be possible to make very much difference between the systems we today call clusters with high performance interconnection and those which we name massively parallel computers. Thus in the future when the interconnections and communication systems have about similar latencies and capabilities it might also become attractive to couple together processors from different computer systems and use this kind of entity as a parallel computing resource in stead of purchasing a dedicated MPP system.

3 Parallel computing tools

During the last few years there has been many efforts in designing appropriate tools for the parallel computing environment [1]. Several research projects and computing centers have come out with different systems from which the most popular public domain software package is Parallel Virtual Machine (PVM) from the University of Tennessee [2]. In addition to the public domain packages a set of commercial packages have been published such as Express from Applied Parallel Research (GENIAS GmbH in Europe) [3] and PARMACS from Pallas GmbH [4].

These different tools provide a possibility to use several types of computers together and this way to build a parallel computing resource. However, in many cases the parallel usage is limited by the communication latencies between nodes and by the speed of connections. The tools are also often quite difficult to use and require much effort from the end user, their command language is also not consistent with each other. An effort to ease the PVM usage by an interface called EASYPVM has been made at Center for Scientific Computing by Sami Saarinen [5]. A standardisation effort for message passing programming, Message Passing Interface (MPI) [6], has been started, but it will still probably take some time before this standard is generally used.

In addition to the parallel computing tools there is a set of other programming tools which are directed to help the user to write more efficient code, modify old programs or locate the critical parts of the code. The variety of these tools is large and the optimal selection is not obvious. One of the most known is Forge-90, an interactive parallization tool package.

In the future it is probable that parallel computing capabilities and advanced programming features will be included into the compilers. Standard compilers, Fortran-90 and High Performance Fortran (HPF), will probably be used on a variety of different computing resources thus providing the end user a relatively easy to use, standard interface to a parallel computing resource. However, compiler development and standardisation efforts are slow and it will still take some time before compiler technology has reached the sufficent level of effectivity and automatisation.

At the moment it would be useful to be able to predict the future and choose a set of tools that will probably exist in the future in such a way that the work done during the next two years can be profited from with the future systems [7].

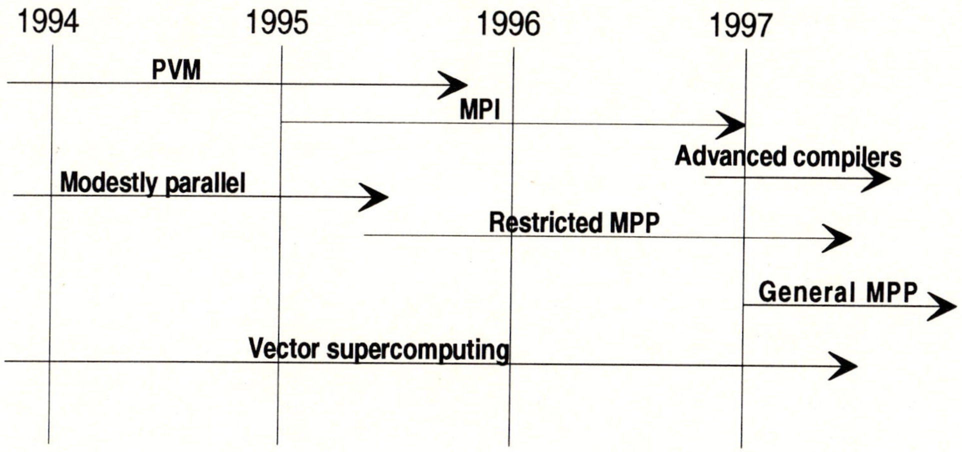

Fig. 2. Assumed timeframes for the development of parallel computing environment. These assumptions are based on various discussions with several people involved with computer industry and research. Estimates for the parallel computing environment have been made also at CSC and the presented timeframes are likely to become more specific and exact with the replacement project of CSC's current supercomputer during 1994.

8 Acknowledgements

I would like to thank especially scientific director Risto Nieminen and application specialist Sami Saarinen from CSC about lots of useful comments and discussions about this subject.

9 References

1. Louis H. Turcotte: A Survey of Software Environments for Exploiting Networked Computing Resources. Engineering Research Center for Computational Field Simulation. June 1993.
2. Al Geist, Adam Beguelin, Jack Dongarra, Weicheng Jiang, Robert Manchek & Vaidy Sunderam: PVM 3 User's Guide and Reference Manual. Oak Ridge National Laboratory, May 1993.
3. Writing Programs for Parallel and Distributed Computing. Course Material. Parasoft Corporation. 1993.
4. Comparison between PVM and PARMACS. Report. Pallas GmbH. 1993.
5. Sami Saarinen: EASYPVM - EnhAnced Subroutine librarY for PVM. Conference presentation at HPCN Europe. April 1994.

6. Jack J. Dongarra et. al. : Message Passing Interface (MPI). Standards draft. 1993.
7. Kimmo Koski, Klaus Lindberg, Sami Saarinen: Effective Use of Supercomputing Resources. CSC Research reports R01/93.
8. Kimmo Koski: Metacomputing Technologies at Center for Scientific Computing in Finland. CSC Research Reports R02/93.

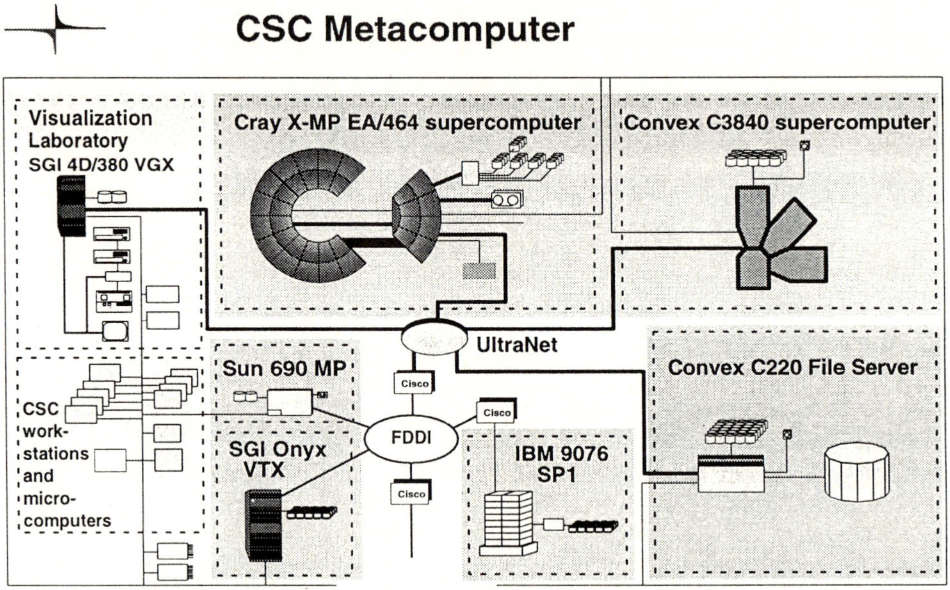

Mohawk Power Corporation), electronic access to image libraries (Kodak), fraud detection in health care payments (Booz, Allen & Hamilton, The Federal Bureau of Investigation), financial modeling in the stock market (NPAC and IBM), electromagnetic simulation (Syracuse Research Corporation), collaborative cardiology and heart surgery (Veterans Administration Hospital, NYNEX), and combining electronic entertainment with education (Abrams Gentile Entertainment and NPAC itself).

Cluster Management Software for Open Object Oriented Systems *

Andrzej Uszok, Andrzej Król, Krzysztof Zieliński

University of Mining & Metallurgy
Institute of Computer Science, Al. Mickiewicza 30
30-059 Kraków, Poland
email: kz@daisy.ics.agh.edu.pl

This paper addresses an issue of a cluster management software which supports parallel jobs processing in an object-oriented environment. A job submitted for computation represents a collection of communicating objects that cooperate with each other to perform a task.

The cluster management software consists of two related parts, i.e. load monitoring (LM) system and object dispatcher, called load balancer (LB). The following assumptions have been taken as a design decisions: the cluster management software has been designed as an object-oriented framework for applying various monitoring strategies and load sharing algorithms; the monitoring functions [1] have been limited only to external activity of computational objects expressed in terms of their resource requirements; user written application software should run without any changes under the proposed management system.

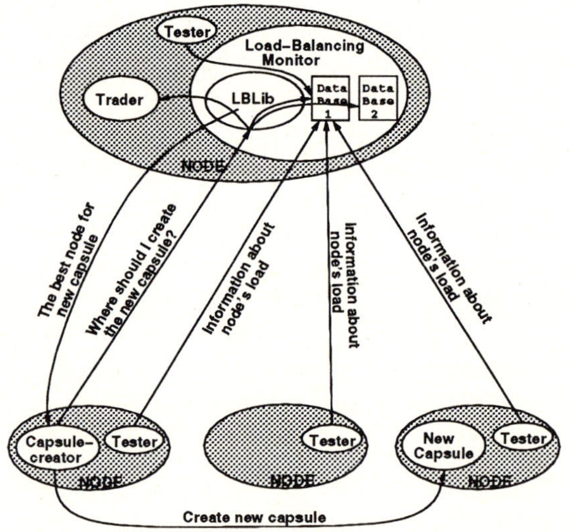

Fig. 1 Overview of Cluster Managment System

An implementation of the system is based on ANSA [2] and represents an extension of the original functionality of the software's version 4.0 with monitoring and LB modules. The described version of the implementation has centralized architecture (Fig. 1). LM system has been written as an ANSA application. Load, treated as a vector of parameters is measured on every computer in the cluster. This is done by special capsules, called *Tester*, which use *rstat* function or read directly from the system's kernel. *Testers* send collected information about system state to a central data base. Another data base contains information about nodes' resources. These data are used for calculation of various metrics of aggregated nodes' load. Various updating strategies of these data

* This work was sponsored by KBN under grant no.: 8 S503 015 06

bases (periodically, on request and event-driven) may be applied during work of this system.

LB module – *LBLib*, using metrics calculated by LM, makes decision about placement of each new object created in the system. When an application sends a request for a new service, the server object may be created on the best node according to the currently active load-sharing strategy.

An extended version of the LB system in which objects can migrate to less loaded nodes during their activity has also been designed and is being implemented.

Two programming styles are provided for the application programmer: transparent and non-transparent usage of management functions. The transparent mode makes it possible for all applications to use provided management functions in implicit form. Hence any existing ANSA programs may use the management software without any changes. For this purpose an application program is processed with the specially designed preprocessor which automatically finds the operations of new objects creation and replaces them with the calls to the management system. In the non-transparent mode an application programmer should explicitly insert calls to the management functions into a program. Available functions are: *BestNode*, *NodesList*, *GoodNodes*, *NewGoodNodes*, *BadNodes* and *StillGoodNodes*. These operations return subset of nodes according to actual arguments and the active load-sharing strategy. Achieved information may be useful in making decision about the creation of new objects in a system.

The implemented management software has been tested for some typical applications for instance processing farm computation. To get more general evaluation of the implemented software and various monitoring and LB strategies applicability, a simulator of cluster load has been also implemented (in ANSA).

The presented idea of management software for a cluster of workstation may be easily implemented in a modern CORBA environment [3]. Most of our current solutions may be applied without any changes. Some extension are also possible because of a distributed nature of the CORBA (Orbix [4] – implementation of CORBA is used), availability of filtering mechanism and Dynamic Invocation Interface. Our current work concentrate on making this management system available not only in ANSA environment but also in other distributed computing system. An effective control of cluster's load will be possible only if all applications running in a network are manageable.

References

1. Masoud Mansouri-Samani, Morris Sloman, Monitoring Distributed Systems, Imperial College Research Report No DOC92/23, April 1993.
2. Application Programmer's Manual – ANSAware 4.0, APM Ltd. Cambridge UK, March 1992.
3. Draft Common Object Request Broker Architecture Revision 1.1, OMG Report 91-12-1, OMG Inc., December 1991.
4. The Orbix Architecture, IONA Technologies Ltd., August 1993.

Transmission rates and performance of a network of computers

K. Boryczko[1], M. Bubak[1], M. Gajęcki[1], J. Kitowski[1,2], J. Mościński[1,2] and M. Pogoda[1]

[1] Instytut Informatyki, AGH, al. Mickiewicza 30, 30-059 Kraków, Poland
[2] A.C.K. CYFRONET, ul. Nawojki 11, 30-950 Kraków, Poland

Abstract. Transmission rates for two communication schemes: ping/pong and ring transfer have been measured on multiprocessors and clusters of workstations. Performance of a network of computers as a tool for numerically intensive computing has been evaluated on the basis of SLALOM and EP–NAS parallel benchmarks.

1 Introduction

Performance of programs running on a network virtual computer often suffers a lot from overhead of communication so it is worth finding out to what limits one can increase number of processing elements and still get more speedup. As factory data are usually too optimistic, we have measured transmission rates for two frequently used communication arrangements: exchange between two processors (nodes) and simultaneous transfer on a ring of processors.

The performance evaluation of parallel machines and networks of computers is a much more complicated task than benchmarking sequential or vector machines [1, 2]. Many benchmarks are known for sequential, vector and multiprocessor architectures. We have adopted two of the well known, classical benchmarks – SLALOM and EP kernel from NAS benchmarks and tried to compare on that base the network of heterogeneous computers with other machines.

2 Specification of communication tests

Two communication scenarios were analysed: simple transfer between two processing nodes in a ping-pong manner (*PP* scheme) and simultaneous transfer on a logical ring of nodes (*RING* scheme).

In the *PP* scheme, message of given length is sent from one node (say A) to another (say B) and then immediately resent back to node A. Wall-clock time of several hundred of such transmissions is measured by node A and average transfer rate is calculated. There are no simultaneous message transfers in this scheme hence results obtained from the *PP* test give only rough estimate of communication system performance.

In the *RING* scheme we have N computing nodes. Each of them, say i–th, (virtually) simultaneously sends a message of equal length to one of its neighbours (say $(i+1) mod N$ - th node) and receives identical message from the other neighbour $((i-1+N)modN)$. In this way simultaneous cyclic shift of distributed data is being performed. Wall-clock time of several hundred such shifts is measured by node 0 and average data transfer rate is calculated.

3 Benchmarking the distributed architecture

3.1 Distributed SLALOM benchmark

SLALOM [3, 4] is a benchmark based on fixed time rather then fixed problem comparison. As originally implemented, SLALOM used a direct solver (by LDL factorization) for solving a set of linear equations. For a problem of size n patches the computational complexity grows as n^3. Application of the iterative conjugate gradient method results in lowering the complexity to $o(n^2)$. For comparison of the methods MFLOPS cannot be compared directly, so the number of pathes should be used.

We adopted the nCUBE version of the algorithm with direct solver by LDL factorization. In the distributed algorithm the plane (x, y) is divided into squares of patches allocated on different computers and communication is organized at domain boundaries. k_x and k_y are numbers of computers in tiles in x and y directions. Numbers of patches in x and y directions are the same, $n_x = n_y$, and number of patches for $k = (k_x, k_y)$ computer in x and y directions are $n_{k_x x}$ and $n_{k_y y}$. For the algorithm without load-balancing (LB) $n_{k_x x} = n_{k_y y}$, so the equal squares of patches are allocated on the computers. The cost of computing on k computer depends on $n_{k_x x} \times n_{k_y y}$; changing $n_{k_x x}$ and $n_{k_y y}$ one can adapt the demand to the current load of the computers. In the proposed algorithm static LB is adopted, i.e. during the first phase of the benchmark a short test of SLALOM is run to define the proper batch for the computers by $n_{k_x x}$ and $n_{k_y y}$ choice.

3.2 Distributed EP kernel

The Embarrassingly Parallel (EP) kernel from the NAS parallel benchmarks [5, 6] generates pairs of Gaussian random deviates and tabulates them in successive square annuli. The original EP kernel has been rewritten from Fortran 77 into C language. On every node the complete program is executed with the original loop 150 distributed between the nodes, see Fig.1 (**NN**$= 2^{m-m_b}$).

Problem size, $n = 2^m$, defines the number of complex pairs of uniform (0,1) random numbers used for generation of Gaussian random deviates and $n_b = 2^{m_b}$ is the size of each batch of uniform random numbers. m_b can be set for convenience on a given system, since it does not affect the results. `lnt` and **`unt`** arise from the LB applied for the network of computers.

Two methods of static LB are applied. In every case the first phase of the run is to obtain the effective speed measure of computers of the network during their normal load. For this purpose a short test is run on the computers just before the basic benchmark to get `lnt` and **`unt`**. In the first method the test is

```
DO 150 K = 1, NN
...................
------------------------------------
for (k = lnt; k < unt; k++)
...................
```

Fig. 1. Distribution of the 150 loop of EP kernel to sequential chunks, with boundaries defined by different `lnt` and `unt` for each computer separately.

based on floating point multiplication, division and logarithm; each operation is invoked 1000 times. The second method of LB is based on EP kernel run for small problem size ($n = 2^{16}$, $m_b = 8$).

4 Results

4.1 Transmission rates

Communication tests were performed on typical multiprocessor machines represented by Intel iPSC/860 and Transtech transputer boards, and on clusters of workstations connected via Ethernet network, represented by Sun SPARCstation IPX and IBM RS/6000. Table 1 presents more detailed specification of hardware and software used.

Computer(name)	Transmission medium speed	Communication tool applied
Intel iPSC/860 (iPSC)	22 Mbit/s	iPSC/2 C
Transtech transputer board (T800)	20 Mbit/s	3L C
SUN SPARCstation IPX (IPX)	10 Mbit/s	pvm 3.1
IBM RS/6000–320 (RS6)	10 Mbit/s	pvm 3.1

Table 1. Specificaton of software and hardware used in communication experiments.

Results of the tests are presented in terms of effective data transfer rate T_r. In the case of the *RING* scheme, T_r concerns the data transfer between neighbouring nodes

Fig. 2 presents T_r dependency on the message length for all hardware platforms and for two schemes (*PP* and 6-element *RING*). In Fig. 3 the results for the workstation clusters are shown again with different scale. All curves in Fig. 2 and Fig. 3 approach some asymptotic values that establish the highest transfer rates obtained on each platform. In the *PP* case for iPSC the highest $T_r > 20 Mbit/s$ for long messages is obtained while transputers turn out to be more effective for shorter messages (below $2KB$). A few times lower transfer rates for clusters of

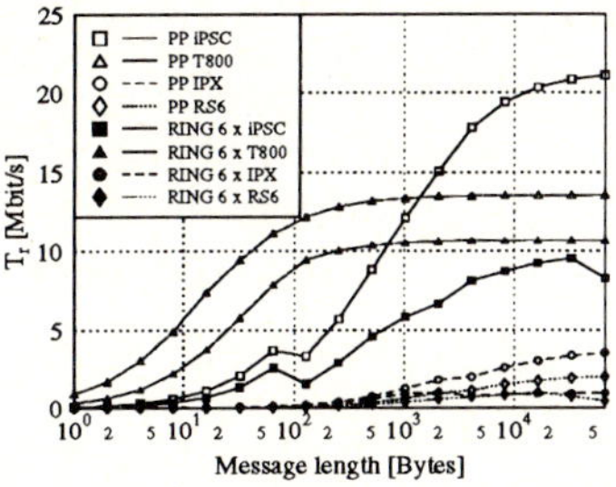

Fig. 2. Comparison of transmission rates for point-to-point and ring communication schemes on parallel computers and networked workstations.

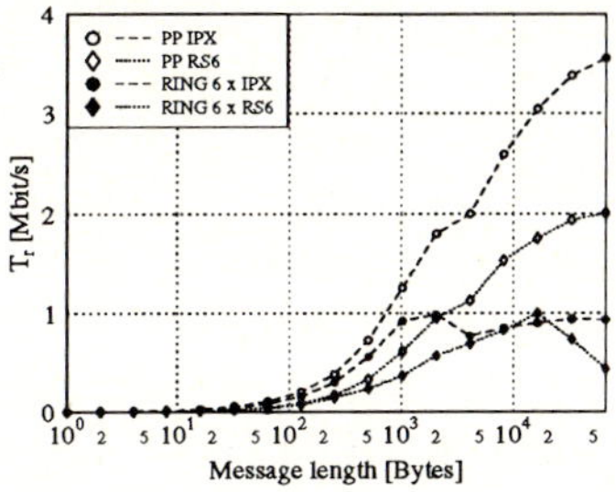

Fig. 3. Comparison of transmission rates for point-to-point and ring communication schemes on networked workstations.

workstations than multiprocessors result from lower bandwidth of interconnecting network and long message startup time. IPX and RS6 differ in transfer rates, though the same type of network was used for interconnection.

Significant T_r drop is observed in *RING* scheme when compared to *PP* on the same platform, and again, transputers outperform iPSC. This effect is due to the transputer ability to transmit and receive data in parallel (which was used in the implementation *RING* test on transputers). In the case of networked workstations, the drop is small for short messages (below $1KB$), where message startup time is dominant, and it becomes very significant for longer messages.

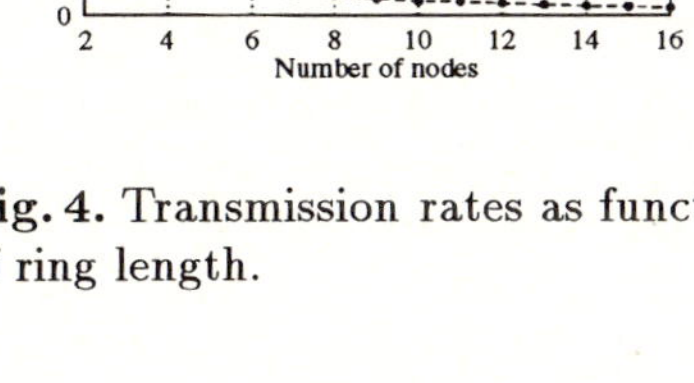

Fig. 4. Transmission rates as functions of ring length.

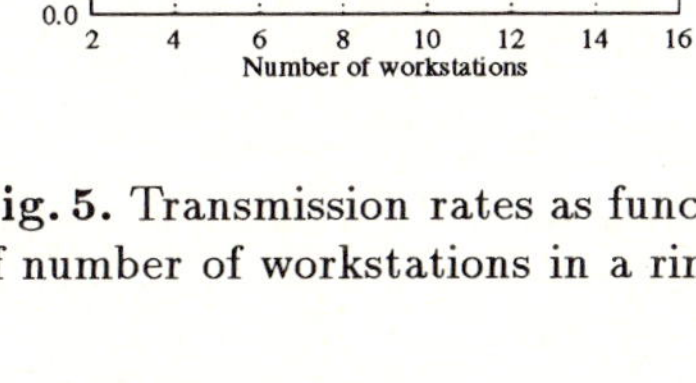

Fig. 5. Transmission rates as functions of number of workstations in a ring.

Figs. 4 and 5 present transmission rates in *RING* scheme as functions of number of nodes for an $8KB$-long message. This kind of study helps to answer the question if data transfer between pairs of nodes goes on in parallel (which should manifest in constant $T_r(N)$). As can be seen in Fig. 4, multiprocessor architectures reveal this desirable behavior and (except for $N = 2$) transputers give a little higher T_r than iPSC. Certain drop of T_r for transputers at $N = 10$ follows from placement of transputers $No.11 \div 16$ on an additional board.

The most important result presented in Fig. 5 was obtained for IPX ring. Transmission rates are constant up to certain number of workstations and then decrease as $1/N$.

4.2 Distributed SLALOM benchmark

The benchmarks have been run on heterogenous network of workstations and Convex C3210 computer (Table 2) under PVM 2.4 programming environment [7].

Computer (name)	Clock, MHz	RAM, MB	OS and opt. level
SUN SPARCstation SLC (SLC)	20	8	SunOS v4.1.1; –O3
SUN SPARCserver 470 (S470)	40	48	SunOS v4.1.1; –O3
SUN SPARCstation 2 (SS2)	40	32	SunOS v4.1.1; –O3
SUN SPARCstation IPX (IPX)	40	48	SunOS v4.1.3; –O3
IBM RS/6000–320 (RS6)	20	16	AIX v3.1; –O
HP Apollo 9000/720 (HP9)	50	16	HP-UX 8.05; –O
CONVEX C3210 (C2)	40 (ns)	128	ConvexOS 10.0; –O2

Table 2. Computers in the network.

Standard C compilers from the Unix operating system were used; the results are averaged over 3-5 trials. For test purposes we also ran the original C language sequential SLALOM code (with conjugate gradient method) on the computers of our network.

Computers	MFLOPS [3, 4]	MFLOPS
HP9	—	4.1
RS6	5.6 (xlf)	3.9
SS2	—	1.4
S470	—	1.4
SLC	—	0.7
SUN 4/370, 25 MHz	1.75 (ucc)	—

Table 3. Performance of sequential SLALOM (conjugate gradient method).

In Table 3 these results are compared with those known from the literature – we believe that the difference in performance arises from the different compilers: `xlf` Fortran 77 compiler for RS6 and `ucc` for SUN 4/370 were used [3, 4].

No.	Computers in the network	without LB Patches	without LB MFLOPS	with LB Patches	with LB MFLOPS
1.	S470, C2, SS2, SLC	42	0.61	—	—
2.	S470, C2, RS6, SLC	42	0.63	151	2.2
3.	S470, C2, RS6, RS6	129	1.72	387	4.1
4.	S470, C2, RS6, HP9	131	1.70	394	4.3
5.	S470, C2, 4*RS6, 2*SS2	107	1.47	475	6.3

Table 4. Performance of distributed SLALOM without and with load-balancing using LDL method. Standard load. PVM v2.4.

Some results of the distributed SLALOM (with LDL method) are presented in Table 4. No optimization of the algorithm for vector processing was performed, only –O2 was applied. MFLOPS are based on the wall-clock time. In the first phase of the runs with the static LB – the test cases of 15 s were performed. We studied the performance of the network of heterogeneous computers starting with configuration with low-end machines and further replace them by the computers with higher performance. For the algorithm without LB the performance is limited by the slower computer in the network. Using the algorithm with LB one gets the significant increase in performance in spite of the standard load of the computers.

For nCUBE 2 with 4 processors (20 MHz, Fortran+coded BLAS) the performance in (Patches / MFLOPS) is 560/3.8 [4]. It is roughly similar to 475/6.3 obtained for 8 networked computers (item 5 in Table 4). For MasPar MP-1 (12.5 MHz, C) with 2048 processors one gets 1055/22 [4], which means that in the reported experiments the tested network is rated higher than 0.45 Patches performance and 0.28 MFLOPS performance of MP-1 with 2048 processors. Due to the standard load of the computers of the network the distributed performance is close to its lower limit.

Parallel efficiency for nCUBE is rather low, especially for Patches measure. For nCUBE with one processor the measure is 354/1.13 [4].

4.3 Distributed EP kernel

Results of the EP kernel runs on the network of computers (with PVM v2.4) are presented in Fig.6, for $n = 2^{24}$, $m_b = 16$ and 64 bit arithmetics. S470, C2, SLC and two RS6 (Table 2). Compilation on C2 was done with –O2 option only, neither modification of the algorithm nor vector directives were applied. Timings are averaged over 3-5 runs in every case.

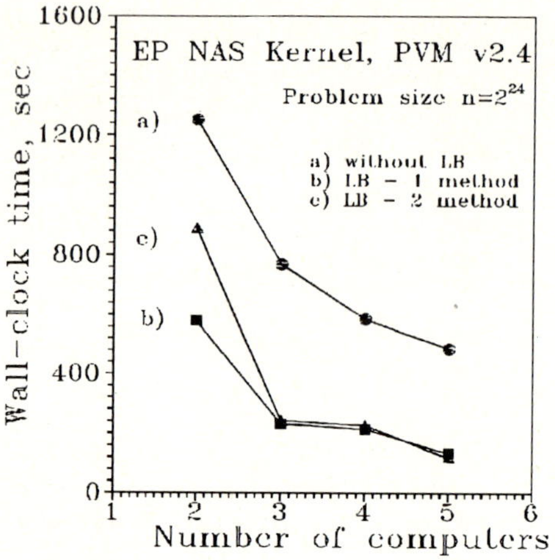

Fig.6.Wall-clock time for EP kernel on network of S470, C2, RS6, SLC, RS6.

	cpu time, s	
	$n = 2^{24}$	$n = 2^{28}$
Computer	$m_b = 16$	$m_b = 19$
RS6	315.4	$\sim$ 5000.
S470	719.1	$\sim$ 14000.
SLC	1319.	—

Table 5.Performance of the sequential EP kernel.

Two methods of static LB are applied. They are compared with results without any LB procedure, in which intervals `unt - lnt` (see Fig.1) are the same for every computer. Both methods of the static LB decrease the wall-clock time in similar way, thus the form of the static load-balancing procedure does not influence much the efficiency of the distributed EP kernel.

Computer	Number of processors	Execution time, s [5] (Fortran 77)	Wall-clock time, s (C language)
BBN TC2000	64	284	—
CM-2	32K	50.9	—
iPSC/860	128	61.3	—
Y-MP	1	150.1	—
Y-MP	8	20.1	—
Computer network	5	—	2960

Table 6.Performance of the parallel EP kernel for $n = 2^{28}$ problem size.

For the problem size $n = 2^{24}$ and $m_b = 16$, the results can be informally compared with those obtained from sequential processing (Table 5) and others presented in [5] for one processor of the Cray Y-MP, for which EP benchmark (in Fortran 77) takes 11.6 s cpu time. Although it is unusual to compare cpu with wall-clock time, we can estimate that 5 networked computers (with the standard load) for which the wall-clock time is equal roughly to 125 s, are rated higher than 2.5 performance of IBM RS/6000-320 and higher than 0.1 performance of the Cray Y-MP.

In Table 6 the wall-clock timing is shown for the problem $n = 2^{28}$ and $m_b = 19$ run on the same network of 5 computers during the standard load. It is compared with the execution time for different multiprocessors [5]. Estimating, the network for this greater problem size is rated higher than 0.05 of Cray Y-MP with one processor. In practice, job turnover time could be similar for CRAY Y-MP and the network of computers.

5 Conclusions

The measured transmission rates as functions of message length and number of nodes on multiprocessors and on homogenous networks of workstations enable choice of communication schemes with the highest possible ratio of computation to communication. The performance measures of distributed computations obtained with SLALOM and EP – NAS benchmarks on the heterogenous network of workstations and Convex C3210 demonstrate its usefulness for numerically intensive computing.

Acknowledgments
The authors gratefully acknowledge Mr. W. Alda and D. Nikołow for the assistance during the computer experiments and the ACK CYFRONET Staff for help in distributed experiments with C3210. This research was partially supported by KBN grants PB 8 S503 0(15, 21, 23) 05.

References

1. Hockney, R.W.: HPC benchmarking performance parameters and results. Talk at *SUP'EUR 93 Conference*, Vienna, September 26-29, 1993
2. Hollingsworth, J.K., Lumpp Jr., J.E., and Miller, B.P.: Performance measurement of parallel programs. in Tvrdik, P. (ed.): ISIPCALA'93 - International Summer Institute on Parallel Computer Architectures, Languages, and Algorithms, *Prague, Czech Republic*, July 5-9, 1993, pp. 239-254
3. Gustafson, J., Rover, D., Elbert, S., and Carter, M.: SLALOM – Surviving Adolescence. Supercomputing Review **Dec. 91** (1991) 54
4. The SLALOM Benchmark Report. unpublished results (1990)
5. Bailey, D.H., et al.: The NAS parallel benchmarks – summary and preliminary results. private information
6. Bailey, D.H., et al.: The NAS parallel benchmarks. Report RNR-91-002 Rev.2 (1991), NASA Ames Research Center, Moffett Field
   NAS parallel benchmark results. Proc. Supercomputing'92 (1992) 386-393
   NAS parallel benchmark results. IEEE Parallel and Distributed Technology, **Feb. 1993** 43-51
7. Sunderam, V.S.: PVM: a framework for parallel distributed computing. Concurrency: Practice and Experience, **2** (1990) 315-339

Measurement of Communication Rates on the Cray T3D Interprocessor Network

Robert W. Numrich[1] and Paul L. Springer[2] and John C. Peterson[2]

[1] Software Division, Cray Research, Inc., Eagan MN, USA
[2] Jet Propulsion Laboratory, California Institute of Technology, Pasadena CA, USA

Abstract. We measure communication rates for the Cray T3D interprocessor network. First we design experiments with no contention on the network to establish the achievable fraction of the peak hardware rate. Then we increase the contention with a sequence of experiments designed to measure the robustness of the network. We analyze the results in terms of the Hockney parameters, r_∞ and $n_{1/2}$.

1 Introduction

The Cray T3D is a massively parallel MIMD computer system with physically distributed but globally addressed memory. It is scalable from 16 to 1024 nodes with two processors per node. Each processor is a 64-bit DEC Alpha microprocessor [11] with a frequency of 150 MHz. The Alpha processor has a direct-mapped data cache organized into 256 lines with 32 bytes per line. Programs can invalidate the local cache as needed to maintain coherence. The Alpha processor manages a virtual address space through an onboard address translation buffer.

Each processor on a node owns a single bank of local DRAM memory external to the Alpha processor. The memory interface between the Alpha processor and local memory is Cray custom circuitry based on the same technology used in Cray's vector-parallel machines. This circuitry extends the local virtual address space to a global address space. It uses five bits of the virtual address to point into a look-up table containing remote processor numbers and codes defining functions to be performed remotely. Each processor can directly read from or write to any other processor's memory. To help manage cache coherency among processors, at the user's discretion, the support circuitry allows remote data entering a processor's local memory to invalidate the corresponding cache line.

The physical nodes are connected through a three dimensional torus. If there are k nodes in each of the three dimensions, such a network is known as a k-ary 3-cube [3]. The network operates independently of the Alpha processors but at the same frequency. The network interface and the network switch, shared by two processors on a node, are Cray custom circuitry.

Data travels from node to node in packets with no processor interrupts along the way nor on arrival at the destination. The packets contain routing information directing them to the correct destination node. They follow a dimension-order routing algorithm, traveling first in the X dimension, then turning the corner to the Y dimension, and finally turning to the Z dimension. The operating system defines routing tables in each node with optimized paths between nodes.

Channels between nodes are two bytes wide operating at 300 MB/s, inbound and outbound in each of six directions. The sustainable rate, determined by the circuit logic in the network interface and the relative size of payload to routing information within each packet, is about 160 MB/s inbound to a node and about 130 MB/s outbound from a node. If both processors on a node are active, the sustainable rate is about 73 MB/s per processor.

We made our measurements on the machine installed at the Jet Propulsion Laboratory, California Institute of Technology. This machine has 128 processors arranged as a double copy of a 4-ary 3-cube: $2 \times (4 \times 4 \times 4)$.

2 Description of Experiments

We describe five experiments, labeled A-E, that measure the performance of the Cray T3D interconnection network. Some of the experiments generate little or no contention among packets on the network. Other experiments generate either moderate or heavy contention.

In experiment A, a single processor on one node writes data to a single processor on the adjacent node, one hop away. All other processors are quiet so there is no contention on the network. Data packets exit the node along one channel and acknowledgement packets return along the other channel.

In experiment B, all processors are active. Each processor picks a partner two nodes away in the X dimension, two away in the Y dimension, and two away in the Z dimension. Two processors share the network interface at each node. If the routing tables are set correctly, contention on the network is negligible.

In experiment C, each processor adds one to its own number and picks that processor as a partner. This kind of communication is common in many programs. Not all partners are one hop away. The partner for an even numbered processor is on the same node so data does not travel outside the node at all. The partner for an odd numbered processor, not at the end of a physical dimension in the torus, is one hop away. The partner for an odd numbered processor, at the end of a physical dimension in the torus, is two and sometimes three hops away. Contention on the network is moderate.

In experiment D, each processor picks a random partner. More than one processor may pick the same random partner so that occasionally several processors line up in front of the same inbound channel. Contention on the network is heavy.

In experiment E, processor zero is quiet while all other processors simultaneously write into its memory. The active processors transmit data at a low rate as they wait in line at the single channel into processor zero's memory. But processor zero sees a packet arriving from somewhere almost all the time so its incoming rate is high.

We use a basic set of communication primitives to move data from local memory on one processor to local memory on another processor. We wrote these primitives in Alpha assembler for speed but we call them from C or Fortran. Using the normal Alpha load and store instructions, they read data from local memory into local registers and write to remote memory; or they read data from remote memory into local registers and write into local memory. By setting a function code in the external circuitry, they process a long transfer by cutting it into cache line pieces and transmitting one cache line per packet onto the network. The entire transfer requires no interrupt to the operating system on either the sending or receiving side. Writing to remote memory is faster than reading from remote memory because the Alpha processor stalls on a local cache miss.

For a fixed transfer length, we measure the average time to write 1000 times to the remote processor. We flush the cache before each transfer to be sure the data travels from memory to memory and not from cache to memory. We do not include the time to flush the cache in the measured time. We subtract the overhead of the timer routine, about 0.5 μs, but do not subtract the overhead of the routine performing the actual data transfer. The measured time includes the time for an acknowledgement to return from the remote processor.

3 Results of the Experiments

From the measured time t and the transfer length n, we compute the transfer rate, $r = n/t$. Figure 1 shows the results for the transfer rates as functions of transfer size. Marked points represent the measured rates and the curves through the points are the result of a linear regression analysis described in the next section.

For experiment A, only processor zero is active and the rate approaches 126 MB/s, a value just below the hardware limit of 130 MB/s. For experiment B, the rate approaches 73 MB/s, the peak sustainable hardware limit with two active processors, implying that the routing tables are set so that there is no contention on the network. For experiment C, the rate approaches 57 MB/s, slightly below experiment B, because some processors go two or three hops rather than just one causing mild contention. For experiment D, the rate approaches 31 MB/s because random traffic causes heavy contention on the network. For experiment E, the rate into processor zero approaches 153 MB/s very close to the peak hardware limit of 160 MB/s. On the other hand, the rate out of the active processors is 127 times smaller than this value.

The measured results fluctuate slightly about their average values. To look at this behavior, we modified experiment A so that processor zero writes to each remote processor in turn. Figure 2 shows the fluctuation of the zero-length latency, defined in the next section, as a function of the location of the remote processor. The latency changes at most by four per cent for any direction in the machine. The erratic, not quite periodic, fluctuations about the average are a reflection of the physical geometry of the 4-ary 3-cube.

We also modified experiment D. For fixed length $n = 1000\ \mathrm{w}_{64}$, we measured times for a large number of transfers. Figure 3 shows the resulting discrete probability density function. The density function is fairly tight around the average $\bar{r} = 35$ MB/s with standard deviation $\sigma = 12$ MB/s. It is nonuniform with many packets hitting a wall of contention as they randomly work their way through the network.

4 Analysis of the Results

The Hockney parameters, r_∞ and $n_{1/2}$, are an excellent pair of parameters for characterizing our results [8]. To obtain these parameters, we perform linear regression on the measured data using the form

$$t = t_0 + n/r_\infty. \tag{1}$$

From the two primary quantities, t_0 the zero-length latency and r_∞ the asymptotic transfer rate, we compute the derived length

$$n_{1/2} = t_0 r_\infty. \tag{2}$$

Table 1 lists the results of the linear regression.

Table 1. Hockney Parameters

Experiment	A	B	C	D	E
r_∞ (MB/s)	126	73	57	31	153
t_0 (μ s)	2.7	2.5	2.3	2.2	0.2
$n_{1/2}$ (w_{64})	43	23	16	9	4

Dividing the transfer length n by the time t of definition (1) and using definition (2) for $n_{1/2}$, we obtain the rate in the form

$$r = r_\infty/(1 + n_{1/2}/n). \tag{3}$$

We might have performed a nonlinear regression using equation (3) to find r_∞ and $n_{1/2}$ as primary quantities. In that case, $t_0 = n_{1/2}/r_\infty$ is a derived quantity. We did not perform the nonlinear regression. We drew the curves in Figure 1 using the function defined by equation (3) with the values of the parameters in Table 1.

Sometimes the use of dimensionless variables reveals similarities among different physical experiments [1]. We have three quantities, r_∞, $n_{1/2}$ and t_0, that characterize our experiments. Only two are independent. Expressed in units such that $r_\infty = n_{1/2} = 1$, so that rates are scaled by $1/r_\infty$ and lengths by $1/n_{1/2}$, all five experiments are described by the same dimensionless function. Following Hockney [5], we define the pipe function

$$\text{pipe(x)} = 1/(1 + 1/\text{x}). \tag{4}$$

Then equation (3) becomes

$$r/r_\infty = \mathrm{pipe}(\mathrm{n}/\mathrm{n}_{1/2}). \tag{5}$$

Figure 4 shows the results of the five experiments in dimensionless form. Our five experiments are scaled variations of the same experiment described by the pipe function.

5 Summary and Conclusions

We have described a sequence of experiments to measure communication rates for the Cray T3D interconnection network. We have demonstrated that a single processor can sustain inbound transfer rates of about 153 MB/s and outbound transfer rates of about 126 MB/s. With all processors active, we have measured sustained rates of 57-73 MB/s depending on the level of contention on the network. With heavy contention, such as that encountered for random traffic, we have measured rates of about 31 MB/s. For comparison, an incomplete list of reports on communication measurements on other machines includes [2, 10, 4, 7, 6].

We have measured zero-length latencies equal to about 2.5 microseconds for memory to memory transfers. The latencies are small because the hardware supports a global address space directly available to user code. Because the startup time is small, the length required to reach half the asymptotic rate is small and the rise to the asymptote is fast. Moving small amounts of data around the machine is efficient.

We have demonstrated that the three dimensional structure of the network results in only small variations in latencies across the machine. The time required to read or write data anywhere in global memory is essentially uniform. Furthermore, the network maintains robust rates even under random traffic with heavy contention on the network. The discrete probability density functions for random traffic have interesting, nonuniform structure similar to results observed in shared memory vector machines [9].

References

1. P. W. Bridgman, *Dimensional Analysis*, Yale University Press, New Haven, 2nd ed., 1931.
2. S. Chittor and R. Enbody, *Performance evaluation of mesh-connected wormhole-routed networks for interprocessor communication in multiprocessors*, Supercomputing '90, (1990), pp. 647–656.
3. W. J. Dally, *Performance analysis of k-ary n-cube interconnection networks*, IEEE Transactions on Computers, 39 (1990), pp. 775–785.
4. R. W. Hockney, *Synchronization and Communication Overheads on the LCAP multiple FPS-164 computer System*, Parallel Computing, 9 (1988/9), pp. 279–290.
5. ——, *Performance Parameters and Benchmarking of Supercomputers*, Parallel Computing, 17 (1991), pp. 1111–1130.

6. ——, *The Communication Challenge for MPP: Intel Paragon and Meiko CS-2*, Parallel Computing, (1994), pp. –. to appear.
7. R. W. Hockney and E. A. Carmona, *Comparison of Communication on the Intel iPSC/860 and Touchstone Delta*, Parallel Computing, 18 (1992), pp. 1067–1072.
8. R. W. Hockney and C. R. Jesshope, *Parallel Computers 2: Architecture, Programming and Algorithms*, Adam Hilger/IOP Publishing, Bristol & Philadelphia, 1988.
9. R. W. Numrich, *Cray-2 memory organization and interprocessor memory contention*, in Linear Algebra, Markov Chains, and Queuing Models, C. Meyer and R. Plemmons, eds., Springer-Verlag, 1992, pp. 267–294.
10. R. Ponnusamy, R. Thakur, A. Choudhary, and G. Fox, *Scheduling regular and irregular communication patterns on the CM-5*, Supercomputing '92, (1992), pp. 394–402.
11. R. L. Sites, *Alpha Architecture Reference Manual*, Digital Press, 1992.

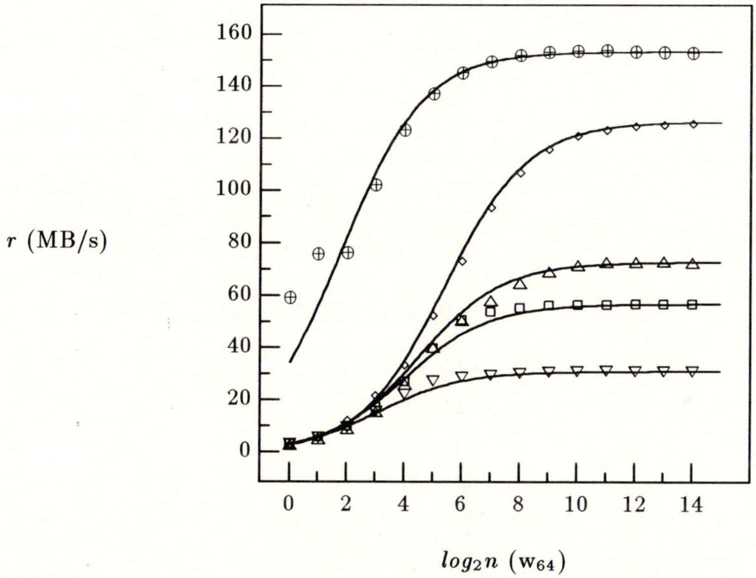

Fig. 1. Transfer rate r as a function of transfer length n for the five experiments described in section 2: (⋄ A), (△ B), (□ C), (▽ D), (⊕ E). The rates are average rates over all active processors except for experiment E. Its rates are the total rates into processor zero from the other 127 active processors.

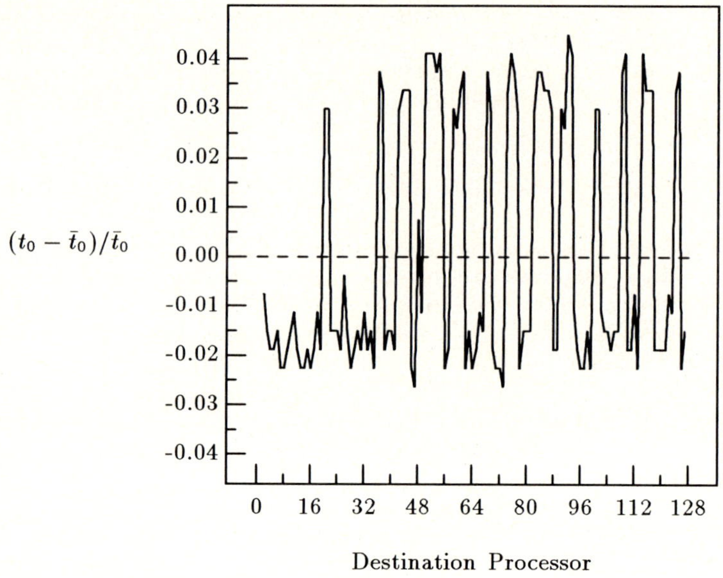

Fig. 2. Fluctuation about the average latency $\bar{t}_0 = 2.7\mu s$ as a function of destination processor as measured by modified experiment A.

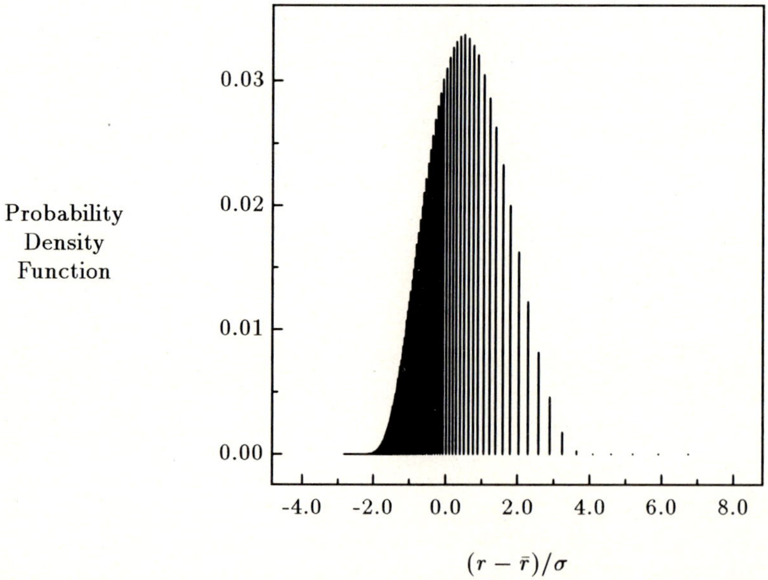

Fig. 3. Discrete probability density function, obtained from modified experiment D, for transfers of length $n = 1000\ w_{64}$ to random processors. The average rate is $\bar{r}$=34.6 MB/s and the standard deviation is σ=11.8 MB/s.

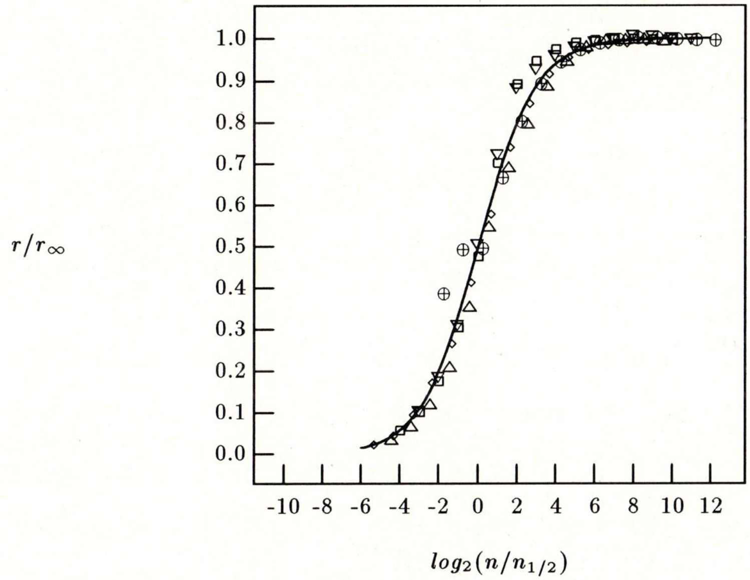

Fig. 4. Scaled transfer rate, r/r_∞, as a function of scaled transfer length, $n/n_{1/2}$ for all five experiments: (◇ A), (△ B), (□ C), (▽ D), (⊕ E). The solid curve is the pipe function defined by equation (4).

An Evaluation of the Meiko CS-2 Using the *GENESIS* Benchmark Suite

Mark Baker & Richard Cloke
High Performance Computing Centre
University of Southampton
Southampton, SO9 5NH, UK

Tel: +44 703 593226
Email: M.A.Baker@soton.ac.uk

Abstract

This paper describes the evaluation of a Meiko CS-2 using the *GENESIS* Benchmark Suite. In the first half of the paper we describe and discuss both the CS-2 and the *GENESIS* Benchmark Suite. In the second half of the paper we report on our benchmarking experiences with the *GENESIS* suite on the CS-2. Finally we draw a number of conclusions about the CS-2.

---

1. An Overview of the Meiko CS-2

1.1 Introduction

The Meiko CS-2 is MPP system which can be categorised as a general purpose distributed memory MIMD supercomputer. The CS-2 is typical of the latest generation of MPP systems in that it maintains a linear scalability of a distributed memory multi-processor as well as having a powerful vector capability. It can also be programmed under a shared memory paradigm.

1.2 CS-2 Structure

The CS-2 has a highly modular structure centred around a basic module which has slots for up to four processing boards. Each board can hold from one to four processing elements (PEs). Each module has its own power supply, cooling system, switch network, I/O and control. A module is capable of using a wide range of standard peripherals, such disks, tapes, CD-ROM and various S-BUS I/O options. The modules are rack mounted in groups of four and can be interconnected to build larger systems. The operating system is based on Solaris 2 from SunSoft.

1.3 Processing Elements

Each processing board consists of one or more RISC CPUs (there is an optional vector processing capability) and a dedicated communications processor, the Elan, to interface to the communications network. Each board also has an interface to a control network and an I/O bus used for Boot ROM and a real-time clock. There are three types of boards:

1.3.1 Vector (VP) - This board consists of a SuperScalar SPARC processor which shares tri-ported memory with two Fujitsu μvector processors. Each VP is independent and operates asynchronously from the SPARC. The VP is used for vectorisable applications.

1.3.2 SPARC with I/O (DINO) - This board consists of a SuperScalar SPARC processor with a number of I/O devices (SCSI, Ethernet & SBUS). This *DINO* is used for I/O intensive scalar applications.

1.3.3 Quad SPARC - This board consists of four SuperScalar SPARCs each with their own memory. These PEs are used for computationally intensive scalar applications.

1.4 The Configuration of the CS-2 at Southampton

The CS-2 at Southampton University was purchased initially as an evaluation platform for two ESPRIT-3 projects based on MPP architectures. Figure 1 shows the configuration of the CS-2 at Southampton in Q2 '94. It should be noted that each Vector PE has it own disk which is used for temporary file and system swap space.

2. An Overview of the *GENESIS* Benchmark Suite

2.1 Introduction

The *GENESIS* Benchmark Suite [1] was assembled to fulfil a need for evaluating the performance of distributed memory MIMD systems on scientific and engineering applications. The suite was initiated under an ESPRIT-2 project (P2702) called *GENESIS*. The codes within the suite were written by a number of project partners including the University of Southampton. There are three types of benchmarks included in the suite:

- Synthetic codes - these are used to measure basic machine parameters.
- Application kernels - these are frequently used algorithms.
- Compact applications - these are full application codes.

In the present release of the *GENESIS* suite two versions of the codes are available: distributed codes written in Fortran 77 with PARMACS 5.1 message passing macros; and, data parallel versions written in High Performance Fortran (HPF). In this paper only the former version will be considered. The suite uses mainly double precision arithmetic, and there are both sequential and distributed versions of each of the codes, where applicable. The fundamental measurement used by all the *GENESIS* benchmarks is the elapsed "wall clock" time to finish. Due to the short nature of this paper a selection of results from the synthetic and kernel codes will be presented.

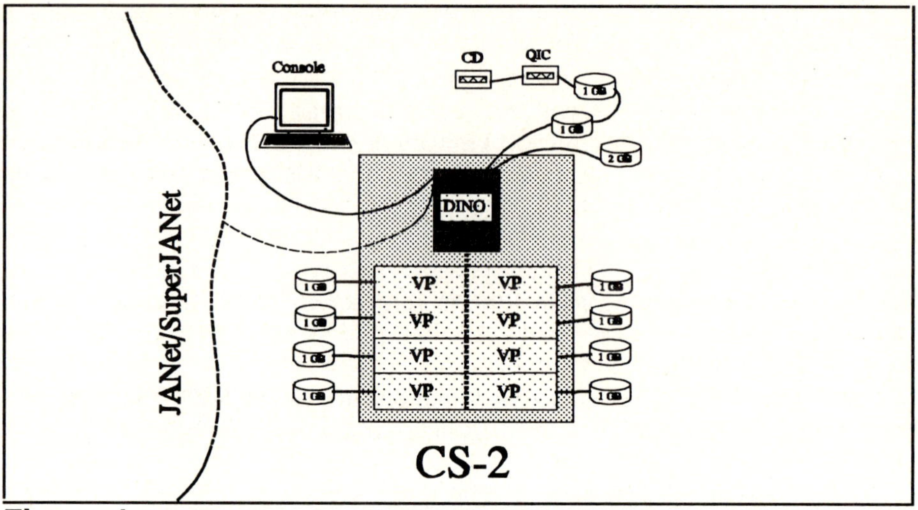

Figure 1 Southampton's CS-2 System Configuration

2.2 Synthetic Codes

2.2.1 Performance Parameters (r_∞ & $n_{1/2}$) - The parameters r_∞ and $n_{1/2}$ are used in both *comms1* and *rinf1* as performance metrics. r_∞ *is* the asymptotic performance rate (in Mflop/s or MBytes/s) which is approached as the vector length, *n*, becomes longer. $n_{1/2}$ (the half performance length) expresses how rapidly, in terms of vector length, the actual performance, *r*, approaches r_∞ [2].

2.2.2 Comms1 - This benchmark measures the basic communication properties of a computer network by performing the 'pingpong' experiment between a neighbouring pair of nodes. A message of varying length is sent to a neighbouring node, and immediately returned after the data has become available to the receiving user program. Half the time for this pingpong exchange is recorded as the time to send a message from one node to a neighbour. This time is fitted by least-squares to the straight line relation (equation (1)):

$$t_n = (n + n_{1/2}) \;/\; r_\infty \qquad (1) \qquad\qquad r = r_\infty / (1 + n_{1/2}/n) \qquad (2)$$

where r_∞ is the asymptotic stream rate (MBytes/s), and $n_{1/2}$ is the message length (Byte) giving half the asymptotic performance. This corresponds to an average performance, *r*, as a function of message length, *n*, For short messages the value of r_∞ may be high but will not be achieved because of the effect of $n_{1/2}$ via equation (2).

2.2.3 Rinfl - The performance of vector operations on a processor can be characterised by the parameters described in section 2.3.1. Here r_∞ is the asymptotic performance (MBytes/s) obtained as the vector length tends to infinity. For finite vector lengths this maximum performance will not be realised due to the start-up time associated with vector operations. The use of vectors whose length is less than $n_{1/2}$ will result in significant loss in performance. The execution time, t, and performance, r, for a vector of length n are given by equations (1) and (2) respectively.

In this benchmark $n_{1/2}$ and r_∞ are derived from a least-squares fit of time against vector length. The value of $n_{1/2}$ will vary with different vector operations. Seventeen different tests are incorporated for different expressions which could potentially be vectorised by a compiler.

2.2.4 Synch1 - This benchmark measures the overhead for global synchronisation by measuring the rate at which the PARMACS `BARRIER` statement can be executed, as a function of the number of processes (nodes) taking part in the global barrier synchronisation. The benchmark repeats a sequence of 10 `BARRIER` statements 1000 times.

2.3 Applications Kernels

2.3.1 Fft1 - This benchmark is based on the classical radix-2 1-dimensional *fft* algorithm by Cooley and Tukey.

2.3.2 Pde2 - This program solves a 2D Poisson equation using a multigrid method and incorporates a mixture of fine and coarse grids to accelerate the solution process.

2.4 GENESIS future development.

The *GENESIS* suite is continuing to evolve, the work is being carried out at Southampton's HPC Centre. Release 2.4, which will include new versions of many of the synthetic codes will be available in April '94. Release 3.0 will be available in June, this version will include PVM versions of all the synthetic and kernel codes. It is anticipated that MPI versions of these codes will be available towards the end of 1994. Further information about the suite and results are stored on the *GENESIS* Benchmark Information Service (GBIS) at Southampton University. GBIS can be accessed via email to *netlib@par.soton.ac.uk* or `xnetlib` pointed at *par.soton.ac.uk*.

3. GENESIS Benchmark Results

3.1 Introduction

In this section a selection of the benchmark results for the CS-2 are presented. Firstly we show the performance of single nodes (both scalar and vector) and then we move on to look at multi-node performance.

3.2 Single Node Performance

3.2.1 Introduction - To benchmark a single node we used the *GENESIS* code *rinf1* and the more widely known *Linpack*d benchmark. The performance figures that are derived reflect the type of processor, its clock speed and the quality of the compiler.

3.2.2 Linpackd - This well-known standard benchmark in which the solution of a (n x n) dense set of linear equations by Gaussian elimination is calculated will be presented at the conference.

3.2.3 Rinfl - The r_∞ figures for the scalar node are fairly consistent across all the operations, with most lying in the range of 7 to 12 Mflop/s. The vector figures are spread across a wider range, with the peak performance equalling 69.8 Mflop/s (double precision). As expected the value of $n_{1/2}$ is much greater for the vector node. The performance figures for the vector node were taken using an early version of the Portland Group automatic vectorising compiler and could be improved markedly with the use of optimised BLAS libraries and compiler directives.

Operation	**r_∞ (Mflop/s)**		**$n_{1/2}$ (Bytes)**	
	VPU	Scalar	VPU	Scalar
Contiguous DYADS	26.27	7.36	294	2
Contiguous TRIADS	38.66	9.22	277	0
TRIADS (stride = 8)	21.03	9.48	153	1
Contiguous 4-OP	50.97	11.55	249	0
Inner Product	69.80	23.86	408	2
1st Order Recurrence	38.42	9.46	267	0
Matrix Mult (mid - product)	33.33	11.53	256	0
Contiguous SAXPY	50.52	10.47	311	1

3.3 Multi-Processor Benchmarks

3.3.1 Comms1 - As it can be seen from the results for the CS-2, a high price is being paid for implementing the PARMACS message passing interface. The *PARMACS* message startup, and thus $n_{1/2}$ is nearly nine times higher than the lower levels communications via the Elan Widget set, although these figures will improve with future implementations of PARMACS. The maximum streamrate, r_∞, is high for both implementations. The CS-2's performance compared to those from other vendors will be presented during the conference.

Vendor	**r_∞ (MBytes/s)**	**$n_{1/2}$(Bytes)**	**Startup(μs)**	**Comments**
CS1	1.24	361	291.0	PARMACS
CS-2	44.31	470	10.6	Elan Widget set
	42.38	3845	90.7	PARMACS

7 Performance Tuning

The code in Figure 1 is a straightforward implementation of the table based approach. However, we were able to further improve its performance by an additional factor of three using a variety of tuning and algorithmic techniques. The optimized inner loop is shown in Figure 2. The code is unrolled so that in one iteration of the loop, four random numbers are generated and two Gaussian pairs are processed. The EP computation is overlapped with the random number generation for the next iteration. In the original code, a pair of random numbers (xj, yj) was considered only if it was inside the unit circle ($t < 1.0$). This conditional execution resulted in a significant delay. The range of t is from 0 to 2 and 78% ($\pi/4$) of the time, t is less than one. If we do the computation for all values, we are doing some additional computation, however, the overall code executes faster. We therefore need to define the function $f(t)$ for $t > 1.0$. Table indices corresponding to $t > 1.0$, were assigned table values of 15.0. This results in calculated bin indices l and $l1$ to be in the range 10 to 15, which is outside the range of interest. Furthermore, for $t > 1.0$, l is always equal to $l1$ and therefore the function $f(t)$ is never explicitly calculated.

A major source of inefficiency in the original code is due to the overheads associated with the conversion from a floating point number to an integer. This conversion is required to get the table index and the bin index. The compiler calls a function routine which takes many cycles. In this conversion, the function routine has to take into account all possibilities including negative integers and overflows. However, in our case, the integers are always small and positive. For a 52-bit positive IEEE floating point number x, $2.0^{52} + x = 2.0^{52} + int(x)$, provided that the arithmetic is done in the chop mode. If this result is stored back into memory, then its low order 32 bits represent the integer part of x, when $x \leq 2^{31} - 1$. These bits are then loaded in a fixed point register. This store/load combination could introduce several cycles of delay and the code must be scheduled to do useful work during this period.

A careful examination of the code will reveal several other tuning techniques which are generally applicable to high performance RISC workstations. This code executes in 68.1 seconds on RS/6000 model 590. This represents a factor of 17.94 performance improvement over the original code. Based on the performance data contained in [5], on this benchmark, RS/6000 model 590 outperforms Cray Y-MP by almost a factor of two.

```
c    ar1 has been equivalenced with ir1 and ar2 with ir2.
c    This has been done to efficiently implement float to
c    integer conversion. The entire program is executed
c    in the "chop" arithmetic mode. The random numbers
c    for the first iteration are generated outside the loop.

      do 4 i = 1, n, 2                   ! Process two pairs in the loop.
         t1 = x1*x1
         t2 = y1*y1
         dc = dcon3 + a * xk             ! dcon3 = 2.**53, a = 5.**13
```

```
      dc3 = dcon3 + a3 * xk          ! a3 = a**3 mod 2.**46
      t1 = t1 + x2*x2
      t2 = t2 + y2*y2
      dc2 = dcon3 + a2 * xk          ! a2 = a**2 mod 2.**46
      dc4 = dcon3 + a4 * xk          ! a4 = a**4 mod 2.**46
      ar1 = t1 + dcon                ! dcon = (2.**52)*(table spacing)
      ar2 = t2 + dcon                ! table spacing = 1/ntab, ntab = 8192
      x3 = max(x1,x2)
      sd = dc - dcon4                ! dcon4 = 2.**53 - 1.
      sd3 = dc3 - dcon4
      sd2 = dc2 - dcon4
      sd4 = dc4 - dcon3
      y3 = max(y1,y2)
      ii1 = ir1(2)                   ! table index = low order bits of ar1
      ar1  = x3*tab(ii1+1) + dcon2
      dd1  = x3*tab(ii1) + dcon2     ! dcon2 = 2.**52
      ii2 = ir2(2)                   ! table index = low order bits of ar2
      ar2  = y3*tab(ii2+1) + dcon2
      dd2  = y3*tab(ii2) + dcon2
      x1 = a * xk - sd               ! x1, x2, y1, and y2 are random
      y1 = a3 * xk - sd3             ! numbers in the range (-1,1).
      x2 = a2 * xk - sd2             ! These are used in the next iteration
      xk = a4 * xk - sd4             ! xk is the next seed in the range (0,1)
      x1 = dabs(x1)
      y1 = dabs(y1)
      x2 = dabs(x2)
      y2 = xk - done
      id1 = ir1(2)                   ! Update statistics assuming that
      id2 = ir2(2)                   ! there is no rare case fix-up.
      q1(id1) = q1(id1) + 1          ! To avoid store/load delay penalty
      q2(id2) = q2(id2) + 1          ! collect statistics in two different
      y2 = dabs(y2)                  ! arrays q1 and q2.

c in the rare case where we are close to a bin boundary
c do full precision calculation and correct the statistics
      if(dd1.ne.ar1) goto 101        ! The bin indices l and l1 are
      if(dd2.eq.ar2) goto 4          ! compared in floating point.
       goto 201                      ! If no rare cases, loop is complete.
101    q1(id1) = q1(id1) - 1         ! undo the statistics
       ar1 = x3*(dsqrt((-2.d0*dlog(t1))/t1))+dcon2
       id1 = ir1(2)                  ! Update the statistics based on
       q1(id1) = q1(id1) + 1         ! full precision calculation.
       if(dd2.eq.ar2) goto 4
201    q2(id2) = q2(id2) - 1
       ar2 = y3*(dsqrt((-2.d0*dlog(t2))/t2))+dcon2
       id2 = ir2(2)
       q2(id2) = q2(id2) + 1
4     continue
```

Figure 2. The final tuned code for the EP Benchmark

8 Performance Comparison on Scalable Parallel Machines

The above code has been implemented on IBM SP1 scalable parallel machines. These machines have RS/6000 model 370 workstations as their compute node. On this benchmark, a single 370 compute node outperforms Cray Y-MP. The following table compares the performance of a 64 node SP1 with other parallel machines. The performance data on other machines is obtained from [5].

Table 1. EP Class A Benchmark Performance on Parallel Machines

System	Nodes	Time in Seconds
IBM SP1	64	1.7
CRAY Y-MP	8	15.9
CRAY C-90	16	2.5
CRAY T3D	128	4.8
Intel Paragon	512	5.2
KSR1	128	18.1
TMC CM-5	512	1.4

References

1. Bailey, D.H., Barszcz, E., Barton, J.T.,Browning, D.S., Carter, R.L., Dagum, L., Fatoohi, R.A., Frederickson, P.O., Lasinski, T.A., Schreiber, R.S.,Simon, H.D., Venkatakrishnan, V., Weeratunga, S.K.: The NAS Parallel Benchmarks. Int. Journal of Supercomputer Applications. (1991) 63-73
2. Bailey, D., Barton, J., Lesinski, T., Simon, H.: The NAS Parallel Benchmarks. NASA Technical Memorandum, 103863, Ames Research Center, Moffet Field, CA 94035-1000 (July 1993)
3. Gustavson, F.G., Shearer, J.B., Zubair, M.: Performance of EP: A NAS Parallel Benchmark on a Cluster of RS/6000. Internal Report, IBM T.J. Watson Research Center, Yorktown Heights, NY 10598 (1992)
4. Agarwal, R.C., Gustavson, F.G., Zubair, M.: Fast Embarrassingly Parallel Pseudo Random Number Generator Using Fused Multiply-Add on RS/6000. manuscript under preparation, IBM T.J. Watson Research Center, Yorktown Heights, NY 10598 (1994)
5. Bailey, D.H., Barszcz, E., Dagum, L., Simon, H.D.: NAS Parallel Benchmark Results 10-93. RNR Technical Report RNR-93-016 (Oct. 1993)
6. Agarwal, R.C., Cooley, J.W., Gustavson, F.G., Shearer, J.B., Slishman, G., Tuckerman, B.: New Scalar and Vector Elementary Functions for the IBM System/370. IBM Journal of Research and Development. (1986) 126-144.

Evaluation of Parallel Operating Systems

C. Lazou[1] and G.R. Nudd[2]

[1] HiPerCom Consultants, 10 Western Rd., London N2 9HX, UK
[2] University of Warwick, Coventry CV4 7AL, UK
Tel: +44 203 523193, Fax: +44 203 525714,
Email: warwick_peps@dcs.warwick.ac.uk

Abstract. This paper is part of a wider report prepared for the ESPRIT III project #6942 (PEPS) by HiPerCom Consultants and the Computer Science Department, University of Warwick. The report identifies and describes the current framework and classifications of Parallel Operating Systems and message passing tools used by Distributed Memory Parallel Processor Systems. It then assesses the impact on efficiency caused by overheads of identified Operating Systems and parallel programming paradigms.

1 Parallel Operating Systems

1.1 General Issues

In High Performance Computing, parallel distributed MIMD systems are on the agenda. New hardware and software systems are being produced opening new vistas and creating market opportunities. Solutions for scientific problems (e.g. Climate), needing Teraflops of numeric calculations are becoming feasible. Object-oriented languages have simplified object representation from the real world and given a fillip to the development of many appliances with visual sensors. Multi-media devices are changing the way information is stored and accessed. Both text and images can be interspersed, accessed and edited on-line at the click of a mouse. The reward for harnessing these developments is market supremacy.

Software costs represent some 80life-cycle. Computer users are foremost interested in cost/performance potential from their computer systems gained in an easy familiar environment. They need to solve their particular problems with as little effort as possible protecting their software investments, and solving their problems quickly, to gain competitive edge. This is why efficient multi-programming Parallel Operating Systems, and parallel developments in languages and databases, have a pivotal role.

Those vendors' whose products are constructed with inherent flexibility, enabling enhancement of customer services with reduced costs are likely to be the winners in these markets.

1.2 Preserving and Exploiting Parallelism

There are four system entities that can be distributed; the processing, the data, the hardware, and the control (e.g. the Operating System and program paradigms for languages). Distributing one of these entities is not sufficient to exploit parallelism and classify the system as distributed. There must be unity in the underlying system mechanism such that it presents a total distributed operating system environment, with minimal system overheads, whether this is used on tightly coupled hardware or as part of a loosely coupled network of hardware. In particular, there must be transparent local and remote resource creation, access, and destruction; and it should be possible to create seamless resource structures which span both hardware and software systems.

1.3 Motivation for Parallel Distributed Computing

There are at least three strong forces driving the evolution of hardware and software for distributed and resource sharing computing:

- 1.3.1 Financial
- 1.3.2 Technology
- 1.3.3 User Requirements

1.4 Summary

In practice, large scale systems, do not operate as stand-alone. They are often part of a heterogeneous resource sharing network environment which is constantly evolving. This network environment is in reality the computing system. Therefore, minimising the costs in time and people necessary to develop, integrate, and maintain this network environment, is an important requirement for assessing whether computing is cost effective. Solving "mission critical" problems, often depending on high performance processing, specialised storage and I/O resources across a network on time, is another.

Both the rate of change and hardware capabilities, provided by the computer industry, are increasing. For these to be useful, integration in the total system environment must be easy and transparent. Procedures to assure high reliability, availability and simplified maintenance are therefore essential. To achieve this, increased modularity and redundancy is necessary.

To meet the user and system requirements articulated above, vendors are providing products offering a Virtual Shared Memory (VSM) model and associated implementation. The user is offered a single logical shared and non-shared memory distributed multiprocessor computer. This logical computer provides network or location transparent resource access, but the implementation mechanisms tend to have associated overheads. For distributed computing to be cost effective efficient distributed operating systems are needed which minimise these overheads. The impact of these overheads on system performance are being studied and assessed.

JNNIE: EVALUATION OF SCALABLE PARALLEL PROCESSING ARCHITECTURES

Steven Hotovy(1) and Thomas Sterling(2)

[1] Cornell Theory Center, National Science Foundation, USA
[2] USRA CESDIS, National Aeronautics and Space Administration, USA

Abstract. The Joint NSF-NASA Initiative in Evaluation is a research program to evaluate the effectiveness of Scalable Parallel Processing systems in performing real-world scientific problems. This paper presents the objectives, methodology, and early results of this important study.

1 JNNIE

Major scientific and engineering applications, at one time beyond the reach of even the fastest supercomputers, are now at the threshold of being realized as peak performance of scalable parallel processing (SPP) architectures surpass peak performance of 100 GigaFLOPS. It is an urgent question as to whether SPP systems will remain difficult-to-program special purpose devices of limited applicability for real-world scientific and engineering work. The United States Federal HPCC program has established a joint initiative between the National Science Foundation (NSF) and the National Aeronautics and Space Administration (NASA) to resolve this question. Drawing on the combined resources, computational testbeds, talents, and applications for the communities the two agencies represent, the Joint NSF-NASA Initiative in Evaluation (JNNIE) is engaged in a one and half year task to develop detailed assessments of the major commercial SPP systems. The critical areas of evaluation are effectiveness of execution, scalability, and ease-of-use. Each agency is providing approximately 10 significant application programs that reflect important computationally demanding problems within their respective communities. This paper presents the objectives, methodology, and early results of the JNNIE study.

2 SPP Architectures

The SPP family of architectures is based on the premise that a new generation of high performance computers can be synthesized from very large arrays of workstation-class processors integrated by high speed interconnect networks. While a limited number of successful application ports have been documented, a number of factors may combine to make this approach generally infeasible. Specifically, the added complexity of managing parallel activities and resources over a space that is physically distributed incurs performance degradation through latency, contention, overhead, and starvation. Together, these influences can inhibit effective computation, limiting performance to unacceptable levels. Compounding these problems is that microprocessor architectures employing cache mechanisms for latency hiding are based on program behavior not necessarily typical of large scientific problems. The assumptions of program temporal and spatial locality from which cache structures were derived appear less than valid for some important scientific problems. But with cache miss penalties approaching 50 cycles for the highest speed microprocessors and latencies far more extreme for distributed memories, poor locality can easily result in sustained performance an order of magnitude below published peak performance.

3 Evaluation

Execution time, the first of the JNNIE focus areas, is characterized as an execution budget; the time division of processor cycles and the way they are used. Scaling is the sensitivity of performance to perturbations in resource and problem size. This leads to an understanding of bounding limits to performance gain. Usability, the second JNNIE focus area, is difficult to quantize but is critical to determining the ultimate success of SPP systems as general high performance computing systems. This paper will present the results of a survey conducted during the Fall of 1993 among computational scientists that provides an important examination of the user community's perceptions of the factors that determine usability of the SPP systems.

The execution budget characterization used by JNNIE is a new hierarchical and recursive delineation of processor cycle usage. The paper presents this methodology in detail with examples. At each level (node of an abstract execution tree) the cycles are demarcated in terms of useful work, overhead work, and idle (or starvation) cycles. One way to consider it is the work that would be performed on a uniprocessor to achieve the same end. Overhead is defined as work that is performed to manage parallelism. It is found that if one looks at the top level, overhead itself can be divided at a more detailed level into these three parts as well. This simple abstraction provides guidance in identifying salient parameters of system operation and defining metrics for experimentation.

4 Conclusions

This joint study involving two major agencies is likely to produce some of the most detailed and complete data in the near future for evaluating scalable parallel processing systems. These results are important to applications programmers, system software designers, computer architects, system vendors, and the the engineering/scientific community at large. This will be the first paper to begin to reveal the results of this important study.

Recent developments in hybrid CG methods

Henk A. Van der Vorst

Utrecht University, Mathematical Institute, Budapestlaan 6, Utrecht, the Netherlands

Abstract. In many relevant large scale computations one has to solve very large linear nonsymmetric systems. Often there is no alternative but to solve these systems by some iterative solution method. In the past few years new methods have emerged that can be seen as combinations of standard Krylov subspace methods, such as Bi-CG and GMRES. One of the first hybrid schemes of this type is CGS, actually the Bi-CG squared method. Other such hybrid schemes include BiCGSTAB (a combination of Bi-CG and GMRES(1)), BiCGSTAB(ℓ) (Bi-CG combined with GMRES(ℓ)), and the nested GMRESR method (GMRES preconditioned by itself or other schemes). These methods have been successful in solving relevant sparse nonsymmetric linear systems.

After a presentation of some recent methods we will discuss briefly implementation issues of the Krylov subspace methods, including possibilities for distributed parallel computation.

1 Introduction

Our attention will be focussed on variants of Bi-Conjugate Gradients (Bi-CG) methods [13, 10] and of Generalized Minimum Residual (GMRES) methods [16]. Bi-CG is attractive because of short recursions, but it does not minimize the residual in a reasonable norm, while GMRES minimizes the residual over the search space, at the cost of long (expensive) recursions. Variants of both methods have been proposed that strive for either to obtain some degree of minimization in Bi-CG-type methods or to shorten the recursions in GMRES. Good examples of a (local) minimization approach with Bi-CG are QMR [11] and the BiCGSTAB method [23]. The latter method can be viewed as a combination of Bi-CG and GMRES(1). An approach to obtain shorter recursions with GMRES is the nested GMRESR method [24], which can be seen as GMRES preconditioned by GMRES again (or by any other method of choice).

Bi–CG has two break–down conditions, one of which can be removed by a look–ahead strategy, the other can be removed by solving the reduced system in a different way, as in QMR [11] or [2]. A weak point in BiCGSTAB is that it introduces one more break–down possibillity on top of these, namely when the GMRES(1) part, or rather GCR(1) part [9], of the algorithm stagnates. This may happen, for instance in advection dominated pde–problems. Gutknecht [12] has suggested to combine Bi–CG with GCR(2): BiCGSTAB2 to overcome this problem. If this idea is implemented in a different manner, a very competitive BiCGSTAB variant is obtained, which is easy to implement. This is a particular class of the broader family BICGSTAB(ℓ) introduced in [17]. In [17] it is shown that it is relatively easy to obtain other obvious variants, like Bi-CG with GCR(4), etc., which may be attractive if one has memory space available.

For GMRESR we will discuss a further improvement obtained by preventing the preconditioning iteration scheme to construct search directions in previously explored subspaces by maintaining orthogonality in the outer iterations as well as in the inner iterations [5].

In our presentations we we do not explicitly consider preconditioning. If a suitable preconditioner is available, then any of our schemes may be applied straight away to the preconditioned system (replace the matrix and the right hand side by the preconditioned ones). To identify and construct suitable preconditioners, specially for parallel applications, may be a very difficult problem. We refer to [7] for some hints for the construction of parallel preconditioners.

2 Bi-CGSTAB2 and variants

The residual $r_k = b - Ax_k$ in the Bi-Conjugate Gradient method, when applied to $Ax = b$ with start x_0, can be written formally as $P_k(A)r_0$, where P_k is a k-degree polynomial. These residuals are constructed with one operation with A and one with A^T per iteration step. It was pointed out in [19] that with about the same amount of computational effort one can construct residuals of the form $\tilde{r}_k = P_k^2(A)r_0$, which is the basis for the CGS method. This can be achieved without any operation with A^T. The idea behind the improved efficiency of CGS is that if $P_k(A)$ is viewed as a reduction operator in Bi-CG, then one may hope that the square of this operator will be a twice as powerful reduction operator. Although this is not always observed in practice, one typically has that CGS converges faster than Bi-CG. This, together with the absence of operations with A^T, explains the success of the CGS method. A drawback of CGS is that its convergence behavior can look quite erratic, that is the norms of the residuals converge quite irregularly, and it may easily happen that $||r_{k+1}||_2$ is much larger than $||r_k||_2$ for certain k (for an explanation of this see [21]).
In [23] it was shown that by a similar approach as for CGS, one can construct methods for which r_k can be interpreted as $r_k = P_k(A)Q_k(A)r_0$, in which P_k is the polynomial associated with Bi-CG and Q_k can be selected free under the condition that $Q_k(0) = 1$. In [23] it was suggested to construct Q_k as the product of k linear factors $1 - \omega_j A$, where ω_j was taken to minimize locally a residual. This approach leads to the BiCGSTAB method. Because of the local minimization, BiCGSTAB displays a much smoother convergence behavior than CGS, and more surprisingly it often also converges (slightly) faster. One weak point in BiCGSTAB is that we get break-down if an ω_j is equal to zero. One may equally expect negative effects when ω_j is small. In fact, BiCGSTAB can be viewed as the combined effect of Bi-CG and GCR(1), or GMRES(1), steps. As soon as the GCR(1) part of the algorithm (nearly) stagnates, then the Bi-CG part in the next iteration step cannot (or only poorly) be constructed.
Another dubious aspect of BiCGSTAB is that the factor Q_k has only real roots by construction. It is well-known that optimal reduction polynomials for matri-

ces with complex eigenvalues may have complex roots as well. If, for instance, the matrix A is real skew-symmetric, then GCR(1) stagnates forever, whereas a method like GCR(2) (or GMRES(2)), in which we minimize over two combined successive search directions, may lead to convergence, and this is mainly due to the fact that then complex eigenvalue components in the error can be effectively reduced.

This point of view was taken in [12] for the construction of the BiCGSTAB2 method. In the odd-numbered iteration steps the Q-polynomial is expanded by a linear factor, as in BiCGSTAB, but in the even-numbered steps this linear factor is discarded, and the Q-polynomial from the previous even-numbered step is expanded by a quadratic $1 - \omega_j^{(1)} A - \omega_j^{(2)} A^2$. For this construction the information from the odd-numbered step is required. It was anticipated that the introduction of quadratic factors in Q might help to improve convergence for systems with complex eigenvalues, and, indeed, some improvement was observed in practical situations (see also [14]).

However, our presentation suggests a possible weakness in the construction of BiCGSTAB2, namely in the odd-numbered steps the same problems may occur as in BiCGSTAB. Since the even-numbered steps rely on the results of the odd-numbered steps, this may equally lead to unnecessary break-downs or poor convergence. In [17] another and even simpler approach was taken to arrive at the desired even-numbered steps, without the necessity of the construction of the intermediate BiCGSTAB-type step in the odd-numbered steps. Hence, in this approach the polynomial Q is constructed straight-away as a product of quadratic factors, without ever constructing a linear factor. As a result the new method BiCGSTAB(2) leads only to significant residuals in the even-numbered steps and the odd-numbered steps do not lead necessarily to useful approximations.

In fact, it is shown in [17] that the polynomial Q can also be constructed as the product of ℓ-degree factors, without the construction of the intermediate lower degree factors. The main idea is that ℓ successive Bi-CG steps are carried out, where for the sake of an A^T-free construction the already available part of Q is expanded by simple powers of A. This means that after the Bi-CG part of the algorithm vectors from the Krylov subspace $s, As, A^2s, ..., A^\ell s$, with $s = P_k(A)Q_{k-\ell}(A)r_0$ are available, and it is then relatively easy to minimize the residual over that particular Krylov subspace. There are variants of this approach in which more stable bases for the Krylov subspaces are generated [18], but for low values of ℓ a standard basis satisfies, together with a minimum norm solution obtained through solving the associated normal equations (which requires the solution of an ℓ by ℓ system). In most cases BiCGSTAB(2) will already give nice results for problems where BiCGSTAB or BiCGSTAB2 may fail. Note, however, that in exact arithmetic, if no break-down situation occurs, BiCGSTAB2 would produce exactly the same results as BiCGSTAB(2) at the even-numbered steps.

BiCGSTAB(2) can be represented by the following algorithm:

x_0 is an initial guess; $r_0 = b - Ax_0$
$\hat{r}_0$ is an arbitrary vector, such that $(r, \hat{r}_0) \neq 0$,
e.g., $\hat{r}_0 = r$
$\rho_0 = 1; u = 0; \alpha = 0; \omega_2 = 1$
for $i = 0, 2, 4, 6, \ldots$
$\rho_0 = -\omega_2 \rho_0$
even Bi-CG step: $\rho_1 = (\hat{r}_0, r_i); \beta = \alpha\rho_1/\rho_0; \rho_0 = \rho_1$
$u = r_i - \beta u$
$v = Au$
$\gamma = (v, \hat{r}_0); \alpha = \rho_0/\gamma$
$r = r_i - \alpha v$
$s = Ar$
$x = x_i + \alpha u$
odd Bi-CG step: $\rho_1 = (\hat{r}_0, s); \beta = \alpha\rho_1/\rho_0; \rho_0 = \rho_1$
$v = s - \beta v$
$w = Av$
$\gamma = (w, \hat{r}_0); \alpha = \rho_0/\gamma$
$u = r - \beta u$
$r = r - \alpha v$
$s = s - \alpha w$
$t = As$
GCR(2)-part: $\omega_1 = (r, s); \mu = (s, s); \nu = (s, t); \tau = (t, t); \omega_2 = (r, t)$
$\tau = \tau - \nu^2/\mu; \omega_2 = (\omega_2 - \nu\omega_1/\mu)/\tau; \omega_1 = (\omega_1 - \nu\omega_2)/\mu$
$x_{i+2} = x + \omega_1 r + \omega_2 s + \alpha u$
$r_{i+2} = r - \omega_1 s - \omega_2 t$
if x_{i+2} accurate enough then quit
$u = u - \omega_1 v - \omega_2 w$
end

For more general BiCGSTAB(ℓ) schemes see [17, 18].
Another advantage of BiCGSTAB(2) over BiCGSTAB2 is in its efficiency. The BiCGSTAB(2) algorithm requires 14 vector updates, 9 innerproducts and 4 matrix vector products per full cycle. This has to be compared with a combined odd-numbered and even-numbered step in BiCGSTAB2, which requires 22 vector updates, 11 innerproducts, and 4 matrix vector products, and with two steps of BiCGSTAB which require 4 matrix vector products, 8 innerproducts and 12 vector updates. The numbers for BiCGSTAB2 are based on an implementation described in [14].
Also with respect to memory requirements, BiCGSTAB(2) takes an intermediate position: it requires 2 n-vectors more than BiCGSTAB and 2 n-vectors less than BiCGSTAB2.

For distributed memory machines the innerproducts may cause communication overhead problems (see, e.g., [4]). We note that the Bi-CG steps are very similar to conjugate gradient iteration steps, so that we may consider all kind of tricks that have been suggested to reduce the number of synchronization points

caused by the 4 innerproducts in the Bi-CG parts. For an overview of these approaches see [3]. If on a specific computer it is possible to overlap communication with computation, then the Bi-CG parts can be rescheduled as to create overlap possibillities:
1. the computation of ρ_1 in the even Bi-CG step may be done just before the update of u at the end of the GCR part.
2. The update of x_{i+2} may be delayed until after the computation of γ in the even Bi-CG step.
3. The computation of ρ_1 for the odd Bi-CG step can be done just before the update for x at the end of the even Bi-CG step.
4. The computation of γ in the odd Bi-CG step has already overlap possibillities with the update for u.
For the GCR(2) part we note that the 5 innerproducts can be taken together, in order to reduce start-up times for their global assembling. This gives one iteration of the BiCGSTAB(2) method a (slight) advantage over two iterations of BiCGSTAB. Furthermore, we note that the updates in the GCR(2) part may lead to more efficient code than for BiCGSTAB.

3 GMRES in combination with BiCGSTAB

In [24] it is shown how the GMRES-method [16] can be combined (or rather preconditioned) with other iterative schemes. The iteration steps of GMRES (or GCR) are called outer iteration steps, while the iteration steps of the preconditioning iterative method are referred to as inner iterations. The combined method is called GMRES$\star$, where $\star$ stands for any given iterative scheme; in the case of GMRES as the inner iteration method, the combined scheme is called GMRESR in [24].
Similar schemes have been proposed recently. In FGMRES [15] the update directions for the approximate solution are preconditioned, whereas in GMRES$\star$ the residuals are preconditioned. The latter approach offers more control over the reduction in the residual, in particular break-down situations can be easily detected and remedied.
In exact arithmetic GMRES$\star$ is very close to the Generalized Conjugate Gradient method suggested in [1]; GMRES$\star$, however, leads to a more efficient computational scheme.

The GMRES$\star$ algorithm can be described by the following computational scheme:

x_0 is an initial guess; $r_0 = b - Ax_0$;
for $i = 0, 1, 2, 3, ...$
    Let $z^{(m)}$ be the approximate solution of $Az = r_i$
    obtained after m steps of an iterative method.
    $c = Az^{(m)}$ (often available from the iterative method)
    for $k = 0, ..., i-1$
        $\alpha = (c_k, c)$

$$c = c - \alpha c_k$$
$$z^{(m)} = z^{(m)} - \alpha u_k$$
$$c_i = c/||c||_2;\ u_i = z^{(m)}/||c||_2$$
$$x_{i+1} = x_i + (c_i, r_i)u_i$$
$$r_{i+1} = r_i - (c_i, r_i)c_i$$

if x_{i+1} is accurate enough then quit

end

There are several approaches to generate efficient code for the orthogonalization step with all its innerproducts (the 'for $k =$' loop). It turns out that this step can be organized so that start-up times for the communication on distributed memory machines can be reduced. For details on this we refer to [6].

A sufficient condition to avoid break-down in this method ($||c||_2 = 0$) is that the norm of the residual at the end of an inner iteration is smaller than the right-hand residual: $||Az^{(m)} - r_i||_2 < ||r_i||_2$. This can easily be controlled during the inner iteration process. If stagnation occurs, i.e. no progress at all is made in the inner iteration, then it is suggested in [24] to do one (or more) steps of the LSQR method, which guarantees a reduction (but this reduction is often only small).

The idea behind this combined iteration scheme is that we explore parts of high-dimensional Krylov subspaces, hopefully localizing the same approximate solution that full GMRES would find over the entire subspace, but now at much lower computational costs. The alternatives for the inner iteration could be either one cycle of GMRES(m), since then we have also locally an optimal method, or some other iteration scheme, like for instance BiCGSTAB. As has been shown in [22] there are a number of different situations where we may expect stagnation or slow convergence for GMRES(m). In such cases it does not seem wise to use this method.

On the other hand it may also seem questionable whether a method like Bi-CGSTAB should lead to success in the inner iteration. This method does not satisfy a useful global minimization property and large part of its effectiveness comes from the underlying Bi-CG algorithm, which is based on bi-orthogonality relations. This means that for each outer iteration the inner iteration process has to build a bi-orthogonality relation again. In [20] it has been shown for the related Conjugate Gradients method that the orthogonality relations are determined largely by the distribution of the weights at the lower end of the spectrum and on the isolated eigenvalues at the upper end of the spectrum. By the nature of these kind of Krylov processes the largest eigenvalues and their corresponding eigenvector components quickly do enter the process after each restart, and hence it may be expected that much of the work is lost in rediscovering the same eigenvector components in the error over and over again, whereas these components may already be so small that further reduction in those directions in the outer iteration is waste of time, since it hardly contributes to a smaller norm of the residual.

This heuristic way of reasoning may explain in part our rather disappointing experiences with BiCGSTAB as the inner iteration process for GMRES$\star$.

In [5] it is proposed to prevent the outer search directions explicitly from being reinvestigated again in the inner process. This is done by keeping the Krylov subspace that is build in the inner iteration orthogonal with respect to the Krylov basis vectors generated in the outer iteration. The procedure works as follows.
In the outer iteration process the vectors $c_0, \ldots, c_{i-1}$ build an orthogonal basis for the Krylov subspace. Let C_i be the n by i matrix with columns $c_0, \ldots, c_{i-1}$. Then the inner iteration process at outer iteration i is carried out with the operator A_i instead of A, and A_i is defined as

$$A_i = (I - C_i C_i^T)A. \tag{1}$$

It is easily verified that $A_i z \perp c_0, \ldots, c_{i-1}$ for all z, so that the inner iteration process takes place in a subspace orthogonal to these vectors. The additional costs, per iteration of the inner iteration process, are i innerproducts and i vector updates. Note that on distributed memory machines these innerproducts can be taken together, so that the start-up times for communication can be minimized. In order to further save on the innerproduct computations, one should realize that it is not necessary to orthogonalize with respect to all previous c-vectors, and that "less effective" directions may be dropped, or combined with others. In [5] suggestions are made for such strategies.
Of course, this orthogonalization approach for the inner iterations should only be considered in cases where we see too little residual reducing effect in the inner iteration process in comparison to the outer iterations of GMRES$\star$.

4 Numerical Examples

4.1 BiCGSTAB variants

In our example we have applied the methods BiCGSTAB, BiCGSTAB2, and BiCGSTAB(2) to the problem ORSREG1 from the Harwell-Boeing Sparse Matrix Collection [8]. The problem has not been preconditioned, and the right-hand side was chosen such that the solution is a vector with all ones. The results are given in FIGURE 1.

4.2 Hybrid GMRES methods

This problem is taken from [23]. The linear system comes from the discretization of

$$-(Au_x)_x - (Au_y)_y + Bu_x = F$$

on the unit square, with $B = 2\exp 2(x^2 + y^2)$. Along the boundaries we have Dirichlet conditions: $u = 1$ for $y = 0, x = 0$ and $x = 1$, and $u = 0$ for $y = 1$. The functions A and F are defined as shown in Fig. 3; $F = 0$ everywhere, except for the small subsquare in the center where $F = 100$. The stepsize in x-direction and in y-direction is $1/81$. Modified Incomplete LU Decomposition was used as the preconditioner.

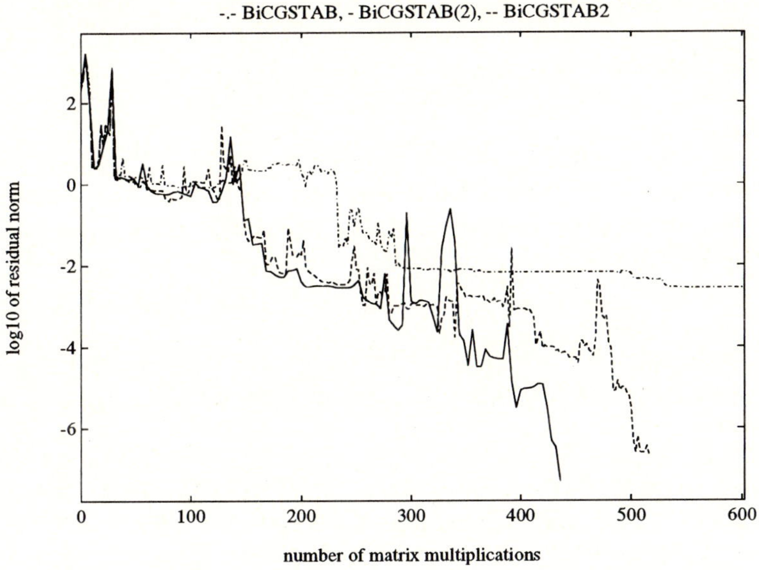

Fig. 1. Convergence plot for example 1.

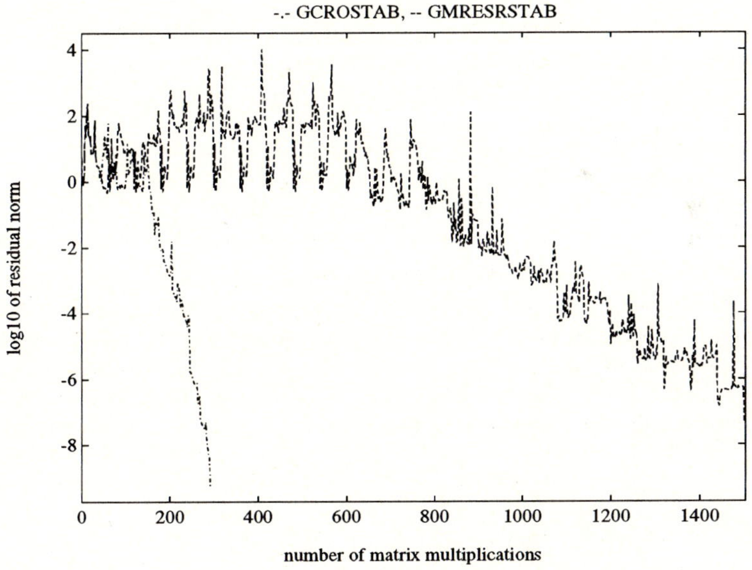

Fig. 2. Convergence history for problem 2

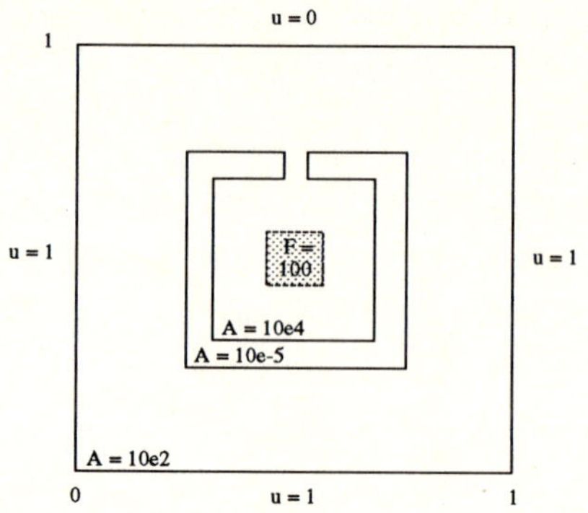

Fig. 3. Coefficients for problem 2

In Fig. 2 a convergence plot is given for the GMRES$\star$ variants: the methods GMRESRSTAB and GCROSTAB. The GMRESRSTAB method is the variant with BiCGSTAB as the inner iteration process. GCROSTAB is a variant of GMRESRSTAB, where the inner iterations are kept orthogonal to the outer iteration process.
In this example the following strategy was taken for the number of iterations in the inner process:

- For GMRESRSTAB we ended an inner iteration after either 30 steps or a relative improvement of the residual of 0.01;
- For GCROSTAB we ended an inner iteration after either after 20 steps or a relative improvement of the residual of 0.01.

For a more elaborate discussion, see [5].

References

1. O. Axelsson and P. S. Vassilevski, *A black box generalized conjugate gradient solver with inner iterations and variable-step preconditioning*, SIAM J. Matrix Anal. Appl., 12(4):625–644, 1991.
2. R. Bank and T. F. Chan, *A composite step Bi-Conjugate Gradient algorithm for nonsymmetric linear systems*, to appear.
3. R. Barrett, M. Berry, T. Chan, J. Demmel, J. Dunato, J. Dongarra, V. Eijkhout, R. Pozo, C. Romine and H. van der Vorst, *Templates for the Solution of Linear Systems: Building Blocks for Iterative Methods*, SIAM, Philadelphia, 1993.
4. G. C. Crone and H. A. van der Vorst, Communication aspects of the Conjugate Gradient method on distributed memory machines, submitted to Supercomputer.
5. E. de Sturler and D. R. Fokkema, *Nested Krylov methods and preserving the orthogonality*, Technical Report Preprint 796, Utrecht University, Utrecht, 1993.
6. E. de Sturler and H. A. van der Vorst, *Reducing the effect of global communication in GMRES(m) and CG on parallel distributed memory computers*, Technical Report Preprint 832, Utrecht University, Utrecht, 1993.

$x_0 = 0;\ r_0 = b; p_{-1} = 0;\ \beta_{-1} = 0;\ \alpha_{-1} = 0;$
Solve s_0 from $Ls_0 = r_0$;
$\rho_0 = (s_0, s_0)$;
Solve w_0 from $L^T w_0 = s_0$;
For $i = 0, 1, 2, \ldots$
    $p_i = w_i + \beta_{i-1} p_{i-1}$;
    $q_i = Ap_i$;
    $\gamma = (p_i, q_i)$;
    $x_i = x_{i-1} + \alpha_{i-1} p_{i-1}$;
    $\alpha_i = \frac{\rho_i}{\gamma}$;
    $r_{i+1} = r_i - \alpha_i q_i$;
    If norm of r_{i+1} small enough then
        $x_{i+1} = x_i + \alpha_i p_i$;
        stop;
    Solve s_{i+1} from $Ls_{i+1} = r_{i+1}$;
    $\rho_{i+1} = (s_{i+1}, s_{i+1})$;
    Solve w_{i+1} from $L^T w_{i+1} = s_{i+1}$;
    $\beta_i = \frac{\rho_{i+1}}{\rho_i}$;
endfor;

Table 2. Parallel implementation of the preconditioned CG algorithm

Results of some numerical experiments

We carried out some experiments on distributed memory systems: a 4 processor (i860) Meiko CS and a 512 processor (T805) Parsytec GCel-3/512. The speedups obtained on the Meiko for the implementation of CG and PCG according to table 2 are shown in table 3. These are speedups obtained from timings of the method until convergence (i.e. $||r|| \leq 10^{-8}$). Since the preconditioning is different on different numbers of processors, the number of iterations of PCG may differ with the number of processors involved.

order of matrix A	CG		PCG	
	2	4	2	4
256	0.29	0.12	0.4	0.24
10000	1.69	1.92	1.45	2.40
90000	1.93	3.23	1.67	3.13

Table 3. Speedup on 2 and 4 processors on the Meiko for CG and PCG

We have also implemented the PCG algorithm on $p \times p$ processor-grids on the Parsytec (see table 4). One processor could not store systems of order larger than 23000. The timings for $N > 23000$ on 1 processor were obtained by extrapolation.

N	1 proc time (in sec.)	16 proc speedup	64 proc speedup	256 proc speedup
1024	3.04146	4.65		
16384	167.488	11.22	25.38	
36864	556.358	12.32	34.05	
102400	2534.25	13.53	43.67	
262144	10297.9	14.37	50.36	138.93
331776	14650.8	14.53	51.50	
692224	43942.9		56.58	
1048576	81807.6			193.89

Table 4. Speedup parallel implementation preconditioned CG on the Parsytec.

As mentioned before the preconditioning matrix is dependent on the number of processors involved. The more processors, the more iterations are required to attain convergence. In table 5 the increase of iterations is shown.

N	1 proc steps	16 proc increase	64 proc increase	256 proc increase
1024	32	60.6		
16384	113	30.1	70.0	
36864	167	24.0	50.9	
102400	274	16.1	32.1	
262144	435	10.6	20.7	44.4
331776	489	9.6	19.0	
692224	703		10.4	
1048576	864			19.8

Table 5. increase of iterations (in %) due to the use of a local preconditioner

The speedups for one iteration are much better. On 16 processors, the speedup per iteration reaches 15.9, on 64 processors 62.4 and on 256 processors 232.3.

Conclusions

From these experiments one may conclude that the geometric parallelization of the PCG algorithm with Block Incomplete Choleski may lead to good speedups. However, the number of iterations needed to reach convergence grows unacceptably when using many processors, especially for small systems. Acceptable speeds on many processors, can only be obtained if one increases the problem size. The better the preconditioning, the lower the number of iterations and thus the better the performance.

A straightforward analysis of the performance on P processors shows that for a constant number of processors best efficiencies are reached when the problem size is as large as possible. However, for every problem with a constant size, there is an optimal number of processors to use.

One way of improving the performance on more processors is to choose a different preconditioning matrix with a similar structure (so that solving the lower triangle systems can still be performed in parallel), and with a better influence on the convergence behaviour. Research in this field is still being conducted.

Acknowledgment

I want to thank prof. Henk A. van der Vorst, who aroused my enthousiasm for large scale computing and assisted my work on CG and preconditioned CG.

References

1. E. F. D'Azevedo and C. H. Romine, *Reducing communication costs in the conjugate gradient algorithm on distributed memory multiprocessors*, Oak Ridge National Laboratory, ORNL/TM-12192, sept. 1992.
2. A. T. Chronopoulos, C. W. Gear, *S-step iterative methods for symmetric linear systems*, Journal of Computational and Applied Mathematics 25 (1989), p. 153-168.
3. J. W. Demmel, M. T. Heath and H. A. van der Vorst, *Parallel numerical linear algebra*, Acta Numerica, Vol. 2, 1993, p. 111-199.
4. J. J. Dongarra, I. S. Duff, D. C. Sorenson and H. A van der Vorst, *Solving linear systems on vector and shared memory computers*, SIAM, Philadelphia, 1991.
5. Y. Saad, *Krylov subspace methods on supercomputers*, SIAM Journal on scientific and statistical computing 10 vol 2 (1989), p. 1200-1232.
6. E. de Sturler, *A parallel restructured version of GMRES(m)*, technical report 91-85, University of Delft, Delft, 1991.

Communication Cost Reduction for Krylov Methods on Parallel Computers

E. de Sturler[1] and H. A. van der Vorst[2]

[1] Swiss Scientific Computing Center CSCS-ETHZ, Via Cantonale, CH-6928 Manno, Switzerland
[2] Mathematical Institute, Utrecht University, Budapestlaan 6, Utrecht, The Netherlands

Abstract. On large distributed memory parallel computers the global communication cost of inner products seriously limits the performance of Krylov subspace methods [3]. We consider improved algorithms to reduce this communication overhead, and we analyze the performance by experiments on a 400-processor parallel computer and with a simple performance model.

1 Introduction

In this paper, we study possibilities to reduce the communication overhead introduced by inner products in Krylov subspace methods and the influence of this reduction on the performance. We use the iterative methods GMRES(m) [7] and CG [6] as representatives for the two different classes of Krylov subspace methods (i.e. with short and with long recurrences).

We will restrict ourselves to problems that have a strong data locality, which is typical for many finite difference and finite element problems. A suitable domain decomposition approach preserves this locality more or less independent of the number of processors, so that the matrix vector product requires communication with only a few nearby processors.

2 Reformulation of Algorithms

We investigate two ways of improvement. The first way is to reschedule the operations such that we can overlap communication with computation. For CG this is done without changing the numerical stability of the method [2]. For GMRES(m) it is achieved by reformulating the modified Gram–Schmidt orthogonalization (MGS) [3, 4], after generating a basis for the Krylov subspace using polynomials for stability. The second way, for GMRES(m), is to assemble the results of the local inner products of a processor in one message and accumulating them collectively.

For GMRES(m), the steps that differ from the standard algorithm are given in Fig. 1. A good strategy for the selection of the parameters d_i (for the polynomials) is discussed in [1]. We can implement the MGS by first orthogonalizing all

{ create polynomial basis: }
$\hat{v}_1 = v_1 = r/\|r\|_2$
for $i = 1, 2, \ldots, m$ do
    $\hat{v}_{i+1} = \hat{v}_i - d_i A \hat{v}_i$
end

{parallel modified Gram-Schmidt: }
for $i = 1, 2, \ldots, m$ do
    split $\hat{v}_{i+1}, \ldots, \hat{v}_{m+1}$ into two blocks
    local inner products (LIPs) block_1

    $\| \left\{ \begin{array}{l} \textit{accumulate LIPs block\_1} \\ \textit{compute LIPs block\_2} \end{array} \right.$

    update $\hat{v}_{i+1}$; LIP for $\|\hat{v}_{i+1}\|_2$;
    place this LIP into block_2

    $\| \left\{ \begin{array}{l} \textit{accumulate LIPs block\_2} \\ \textit{update vectors block\_1} \end{array} \right.$

    update vectors block_2
    normalize $\hat{v}_{i+1}$
end

Fig. 1. The generation of the basis vectors and the implementation of the MGS

parCG:

    Choose $x_{-1} = x_0$;
    $r_0 = b - Ax_0$;
    $p_{-1} = 0; \alpha_{-1} = 0$;
    $s = L^{-1} r_0$;
    $\rho_{-1} = 1$;
    for $i = 0, 1, 2, \ldots$ do
(1) $\rho_i = (s, s)$;
        $w_i = L^{-T} s$;
        $\beta_{i-1} = \rho_i / \rho_{i-1}$;
        $p_i = w_i + \beta_{i-1} p_{i-1}$;
        $q_i = Ap_i$;
(2) $\gamma = (p_i, q_i)$;
        $x_i = x_{i-1} + \alpha_{i-1} p_{i-1}$;
        $\alpha_i = \rho_i / \gamma$;
        $r_{i+1} = r_i - \alpha_i q_i$;
(3)   compute $\|r\|$;
        $s = L^{-1} r_{i+1}$;
        if accurate enough then
            $x_{i+1} = x_i + \alpha_i p_i$
            quit
    end;

Fig. 2. The parCG algorithm

basis vectors on the first vector, then on the second, and so on, because we have all the basis vectors available. This permits the collective accumulation of large groups of inner products instead of the one-by-one accumulation in standard GMRES(m) with MGS. We can improve the MGS even further by splitting the orthogonalizations on one vector in two groups. Then we can overlap the accumulation for one group with the computations for the other group, as is shown in Fig. 1. We refer to this version of GMRES(m) as parGMRES(m).

We follow the approach suggested in [2] to reduce the communication overhead for preconditioned CG. We assume that the preconditioner K can be written as $K = LL^T$. We overlap the communication in the inner products at lines (1), (2) and (3) with the computations in the following line; see Fig. 2. We split the preconditioner to create an overlap for the inner products (1) and (3), and we create extra overlap possibilities by doing the update for x corresponding to the previous iteration step after the inner product (2). We refer to this version of CG as parCG.

3 Performance Model

We will model the performance of one cycle of GMRES(m) and parGMRES(m), and of one iteration of CG and parCG using equations derived from [5]. The purpose of this model is to provide insight in the parallel performance, not to give very accurate predictions. Most notably it ignores the communication in the matrix-vector product. For GMRES(m) this is not important, but for CG this leads to predictions that are too optimistic. The runtime of GMRES(m) is given by

$$T_P = \left(2(m^2+3m)+4n_z(m+1)\right) t_{fl}\frac{N}{P} + \left((m^2+3m)(t_s+3t_w)\right)\sqrt{P}, \tag{1}$$

where N is the total number of unknowns, P is the number of processors, m is the restart parameter, n_z is the average number of non-zeroes per row of the matrix and in the preconditioner (ILU or LL^T), t_{fl} is the (average) time for a double precision floating point operation, and t_s and t_w are the message start-up time and the word transmission time (between neighbouring processors). The factor $\sqrt{P}$ comes from the use of a square processor grid; it is the order of the diameter of the processor grid (graph). The runtime of the parGMRES(m) version is given by

$$\begin{aligned} T_P = {} & (m^2+4m+4n_z(m+1))t_{fl}\frac{N}{P} + \\ & \max\left((m^2+2m)t_{fl}\frac{N}{P} + 16mt_s + (8m^2+40m)t_w\,,\right. \\ & \left.(4mt_s + (2m^2+10m)t_w)\sqrt{P}\right), \end{aligned} \tag{2}$$

where max() depends on whether there is enough local work to overlap all communication. The runtime of CG is given by

$$T_P = (9+4n_z)t_{fl}\frac{N}{P} + 6(t_s+3t_w)\sqrt{P}. \tag{3}$$

The runtime of parCG is given by

$$T_P = (9+2n_z)t_{fl}\frac{N}{P} + \max(2n_z t_{fl}\frac{N}{P} + 24(t_s+3t_w), 6(t_s+3t_w)\sqrt{P}). \tag{4}$$

The speedups curves from the model are given in Figs. 3 and 4. We used the following parameter values (from the experiments), $N = 10000$, $m = 50$ for (par)GMRES(m), $n_z = 5$, $t_{fl} = 3.00\mu s$, $t_s = 5.30\mu s$, and $t_w = 4.80\mu s$.

The speedup of GMRES(m) levels off very quickly due to increasing communication costs. The speedup of parGMRES(m) stays very close to perfect speedup until the number of processors reaches the point where we can no longer overlap all communication (the acute point); this is where the two arguments of the max() in (2) are equal. We see that the speedup of parGMRES(m) then also starts to level off.

For CG and parCG, we see the same effects as for (par)GMRES(m). The number of processors where we can no longer overlap all communication is smaller, because we have less computation to overlap with.

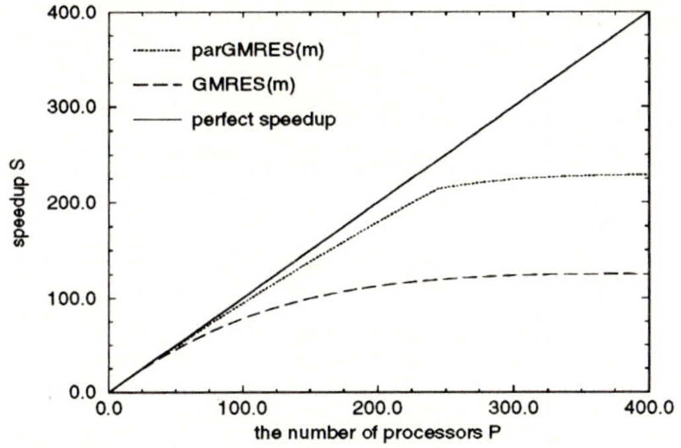

Fig. 3. The modeled performance of GMRES(m) and parGMRES(m)

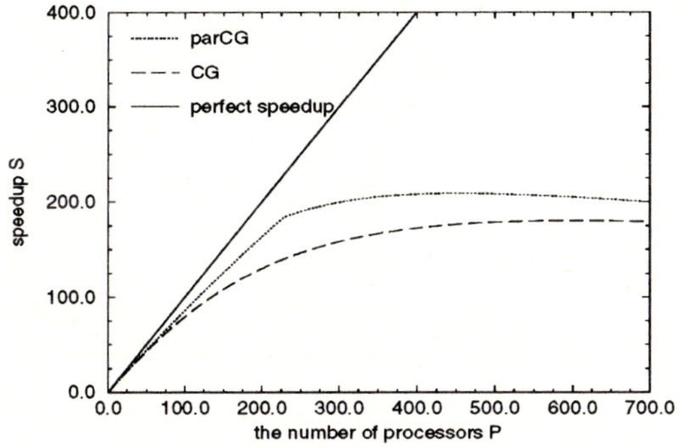

Fig. 4. The modeled performance of CG and parCG

4 Results

Below, we give results on a 400-transputer (T800) Parsytec Supercluster at the Koninklijke/Shell-Laboratorium in Amsterdam. The processors are connected in a fixed 20×20 mesh, of which arbitrary submeshes can be used. We have solved a convection diffusion problem (only diffusion for CG) with 10000 unknowns discretized by finite volumes, resulting in the familiar five-diagonal matrix.

Table 1 gives the measured runtimes for one cycle, the speed-ups, and the efficiencies for GMRES(50) and parGMRES(50). The speed-ups and efficiencies are computed relative to the estimated, sequential runtime of the GMRES(50) cycle, $T_1 = 190.$ s, because the problem did not fit on a single processor. The cost of communication spoils the performance of GMRES(m) completely for large P, as shown in Fig. 3. The performance of parGMRES(m) is much better. The speedups for 100 and 196 processors are almost optimal, because all communication can be overlapped. As predicted by the performance model, we

Table 1. measured runtimes for GMRES(m) and parGMRES(m)

processor grid	GMRES(50)			parGMRES(50)		
	T (s)	E (%)	S	T (s)	E (%)	S
10 × 10	2.47	76.8	76.8	1.93	98.2	98.2
14 × 14	1.90	50.9	99.8	1.05	92.1	181.
17 × 17	1.66	39.5	114.	0.891	73.6	213.
20 × 20	1.75	27.1	108.	0.851	55.7	223.

cannot overlap all communication for 289 processors, and the efficiency starts to decrease; for 400 processors the speedup is not much better. Note that, except for 100 processors, the runtime of GMRES(50) is about twice that of parGMRES(50). The estimated runtimes for GMRES(50) and parGMRES(50) are given in Table 2. A comparison with the measured timings indicates that the model is quite accurate. For 400 processors, neglected costs start playing a role.

Table 3 gives the measured runtimes for one iteration step, the speedups, and the efficiencies for CG and parCG. The speedups and efficiencies are computed relative to the measured, sequential runtime of the CG iteration, which is given by, $T_1 = 0.788$s. We observe that the performance of CG also levels off quickly, even though the number of inner products is small. This is in agreement with the performance model; see also [3]. As indicated in Fig. 4, if we increase P the difference in runtime between CG and parCG increases until we can no longer overlap all communication, then the difference decreases again. In the parCG algorithm, we only try to overlap communication, mainly by overlap with the preconditioner. The preconditioner used is not very expensive,so the potential improvement is relatively small. Note, however, that this improvement comes virtually for free. Moreover, when the computation time for the preconditioner is large or even dominant, the improvement may also be large. For many problems this may be a realistic assumption.

In Table 4 we show estimates for the runtimes of the CG algorithm and the parCG algorithm. Just as for (par)GMRES(m), the estimates for (par)CG are relatively accurate except for the 20 × 20 processor grid. Again, this is probably caused by costs neglected in the model.

Table 2. Estimated runtimes for GMRES(m) and parGMRES(m)

processor grid	GMRES(50) (s)	parGMRES(50) (s)
10 × 10	2.42	2.01
14 × 14	1.70	1.08
17 × 17	1.54	0.853
20 × 20	1.52	0.828

Table 3. Measured runtimes for CG and parCG, speed-up and efficiency compared to the measured, sequential runtime of CG

processor grid	CG T (ms)	CG S	CG E (%)	parCG T (ms)	parCG S	parCG E (%)
10×10	10.7	73.6	73.6	10.2	77.3	77.3
14×14	6.90	114.	58.3	5.84	135.	68.8
17×17	6.09	129.	44.8	5.29	149.	51.5
20×20	5.59	141.	35.2	5.04	156.	39.1

Table 4. Estimated runtimes for CG and parCG

processor grid	CG (ms)	parCG (ms)
10×10	10.7	10.0
14×14	6.66	5.57
17×17	5.71	4.66
20×20	5.00	4.25

5 Conclusions

We have studied the implementation of GMRES(m) and CG for distributed memory parallel computers. These algorithms represent two different classes of Krylov subspace methods, and their parallel properties are quite representative. The experiments show how the global communication in the inner products degrades the performance on large processor grids. This is also indicated by our performance model. We have considered alternative algorithms for GMRES(m) and CG in which the actual cost for global communication is decreased by reducing synchronization and start-up times, and overlapping communication with computation. Our experiments indicate this to be a successful approach.

References

1. Z. Bai, D. Hu, and L. Reichel. A Newton basis GMRES implementation. Technical Report 91-03, University of Kentucky, 1991.
2. J. W. Demmel, M. T. Heath, and H.A. van der Vorst. Parallel numerical linear algebra. *Acta Numerica* Vol 2, Cambridge Press, New York, 1993
3. E. De Sturler. A parallel restructured version of GMRES(m). Technical Report 91-85, Delft University of Technology, Delft, 1991.
4. E. De Sturler. A parallel variant of GMRES(m). In R. Vichnevetsky, J. H. H. Miller, editors, *Proc. of the 13th IMACS World Congress on Computation and Applied Mathematics* , IMACS, Criterion Press Dublin 1991, pp 682–683.
5. E. De Sturler and H. A. Van der Vorst. Reducing the effect of global communication in GMRES(m) and CG on Parallel Distributed Memory Computers. Technical Report 832, Mathematical Institute, University of Utrecht, Utrecht, 1993
6. M. R. Hestenes and E. Stiefel. Methods of conjugate gradients for solving linear systems. *J. Res. Natl. Bur. Stand.*, 49:409–436, 1954.
7. Y. Saad and M. H. Schultz. GMRES: a generalized minimal residual algorithm for solving nonsymmetric linear systems. *SIAM J. Sci. Statist. Comput.*, 7:856–869, 1986.

Parallel Arnoldi Method for the Construction of a Krylov Subspace Basis: an Application in Magnetohydrodynamics

J.G.L. Booten [1], P.M. Meijer [2], H.J.J. te Riele [1] and H.A. van der Vorst [3]

[1] Center for Mathematics and Computer Science,
P.O. Box 94079, 1090 GB Amsterdam, the Netherlands
[2] FOM Institute for Plasmaphysics,
P.O. Box 1207, 3430 BE Nieuwegein, the Netherlands
[3] Mathematical Institute, University of Utrecht,
P.O. Box 80.010, 3508 TA Utrecht, the Netherlands

Abstract. In a recent article [6] a new method was proposed for computing internal eigenvalues of symmetric matrices. In the present paper we extend these ideas to non-hermitian eigenvalue problems and apply them to a practical example from the field of magnetohydrodynamics (MHD). The method is very suitable for an efficient parallel implementation. We give some results for the time-consuming kernels of the underlying orthogonalization process, the Arnoldi method, obtained for an MHD problem on a distributed memory multiprocessor.

1 Introduction

The numerical solution of large-scale eigenvalue problems has many applications in both science and engineering. For a recent overview of some application areas, see [9]. In the field of linear magnetohydrodynamics (MHD), which concerns the study of the interaction of an ionized gas, a so-called plasma, with a magnetic field, the finite element discretization of the partial differential MHD equations gives rise to a generalized non-hermitian eigenvalue problem (see e.g. [1]). Over the last years the demand for solving increasingly larger eigenvalue problems in MHD is growing. Meanwhile considerable progress has been made in the techniques to implement numerical algorithms for large eigenvalue problems on parallel computers. For a recent review in this area, see [2].

The most commonly used algorithms to solve non-hermitian eigenvalue problems are referred to as Arnoldi algorithms. The basic idea is to reduce a general non-hermitian large matrix A to upper Hessenberg form H, after which the eigenvalues are determined for the much smaller projected matrix H. The eigenvalues of this matrix tend to converge to the dominant eigenvalues of the original matrix A. For obvious reasons the method is usually applied in an iterative way. The basis upon which the upper Hessenberg matrix is built is the so-called Krylov subspace basis. The eigenvalues of H are the Ritz values of A with respect to the Krylov subspace. The orthogonal projection method of the original matrix onto the subspace is known as the Arnoldi method. The Arnoldi method is the most time-consuming part in the Arnoldi-based algorithms for solving non-hermitian eigenproblems. It should be noted that the Arnoldi method is also applied as the orthogonalization scheme in the well-known GMRES algorithm [8] for solving general nonsymmetric large linear systems of equations.

In many applications one is not particularly interested in the dominant part of the eigenvalue spectrum, but only in an internal branch. A commonly followed procedure [9] is to shift the original matrix by a value close to the eigenvalues in the interesting part of the spectrum, invert the shifted matrix in order to make the desired eigenspectrum dominant and perform the standard Arnoldi algorithm for the inverted matrix. In MHD the interesting part of the spectrum is the so-called Alfvén branch. In [5] this part of the spectrum was computed applying the implicitly restarted Arnoldi method [10] with a complex shift and invert strategy. The most expensive part in the shift-and-invert Arnoldi method [9] is inverting the shifted matrix: first one has to perform an LU-decomposition of the shifted matrix, followed by solving lower and upper triangular systems of equations. Furthermore, the latter operations make this method unfavourable for an efficient implementation on a distributed memory computer [2].

In a recent paper [6] Paige, Parlett and Van der Vorst demonstrated that the zeros of the iteration polynomial associated with the minimum residual approximation to the solution of a symmetric indefinite system of equations converge slowly, but monotonically to eigenvalues of the coefficient matrix close to the origin. The computation of these eigenvalue approximations, introduced by the authors of [6] as the *harmonic* Ritz values, offers new possibilities for the determination of internal eigenvalues. In the present paper we have investigated whether these ideas could be extended to the non-hermitian case. In the next section we briefly discuss the method and illustrate it with an example from MHD. In the final section we describe the implementation of the time-consuming kernels of the Arnoldi method on a distributed memory machine for the MHD-type matrices. Also timing results are presented.

2 Arnoldi Method for Internal Eigenvalues

If we perform i steps of the standard Arnoldi process [3, 9] with a general $n \times n$ matrix A and a unit two-norm starting vector v_1, we obtain an orthonormal set of basis vectors $v_1, v_2, \ldots, v_i, v_{i+1}$. The first i vectors span the Krylov subspace $K_i(A; v_1)$. Define the $n \times j$ matrix $V_j = [v_1, \ldots, v_j]$. Then from the Arnoldi process the following relation can be derived [9]:

$$AV_i = V_{i+1}\hat{H}_i, \tag{1}$$

with $\hat{H}_i$ an $(i+1) \times i$ upper Hessenberg matrix, whose upper $i \times i$ part we denote as H_i. Using the orthonormality of the basis, we obtain:

$$V_i^H A^H A V_i = \hat{H}_i^H V_{i+1}^H V_{i+1} \hat{H}_i = \hat{H}_i^H \hat{H}_i \equiv M_i^2. \tag{2}$$

From this equation we see that the columns of $AV_i M_i^{-1}$ form an orthonormal basis for $AK_i(A; v_1)$, since we have

$$M_i^{-1} V_i^H A^H A V_i M_i^{-1} = I_i, \tag{3}$$

with I_i the $i \times i$ identity matrix. Using this basis and the relation

$$V_i^H A V_i = V_i^H V_{i+1} \hat{H}_i = H_i \tag{4}$$

it is straightforward to obtain the orthogonal projection of A^{-1} onto $AK_i(A; v_1)$ (see also [6]):

$$M_i^{-1}(AV_i)^H A^{-1} AV_i M_i^{-1} = M_i^{-1} H_i^H M_i^{-1}. \tag{5}$$

Solving the eigenvalue problem for the projected matrix $M_i^{-1}H_i^H M_i^{-1}$, or, which is similar, for the matrix $M_i^{-2}H_i^H$, gives the Ritz values of A^{-1} with respect to $AK_i(A; v_1)$. These Ritz values should be good approximations for the extreme eigenvalues of A^{-1}. Their reciprocals are the harmonic Ritz values and should therefore be good approximations for the eigenvalues of A closest to the origin.

Note that the procedure described above enables us to compute approximations for eigenvalues close to any point in the spectrum of A, simply by performing the method with a shifted matrix $A - \sigma I$. Also note that we avoid explicit inverting of a matrix, which makes the method more appropriate for an efficient parallel implementation than the shift-and-invert method.

We have tested the method for a small problem from MHD (order 416) taken from [5]. We used subspace iteration, restarting at each step with a linear combination of four eigenvectors associated with the four eigenvalues closest to the shift. We were able to reproduce the spectrum obtained in [5]. However, the Krylov dimension had to be set at 125 and convergence turned out to be very slow as displayed in fig. 1. A similar behavior was observed in the symmetric case [6], apart from the fact that the convergence is far from monotonic in the present example.

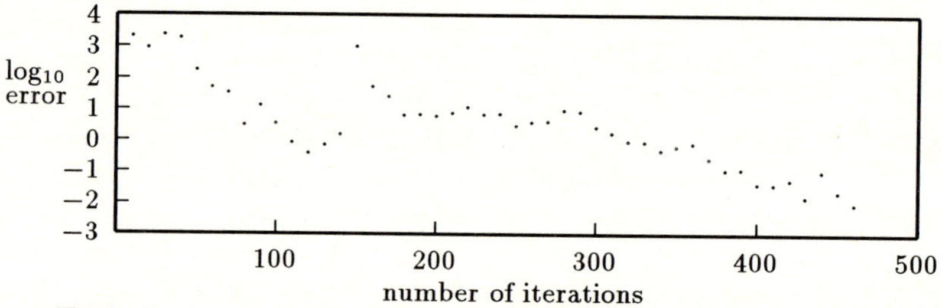

Fig. 1. Typical convergence behavior for a harmonic Ritz value, computed with the present Arnoldi method.

3 Parallel Implementation

We have implemented the basic operations of the Arnoldi method on a parallel distributed memory system. Results are given for the application to the MHD-type matrices, which are of block-tridiagonal shape (with rather dense blocks). The numerical experiments were carried out on a Parsytec GC_{el} (located at SARA, the Academic Computer Center Amsterdam), a distributed memory machine consisting of 512 nodes, each having 4 Mbytes local memory. The processors were configured in a 2d-grid topology.

The blocks in the MHD matrices are of the order $16N_F$, with N_F the number of Fourier modes, see also [7]. Let N_G denote the number of grid points in the finite element discretization of the MHD equations, which is the number of rows

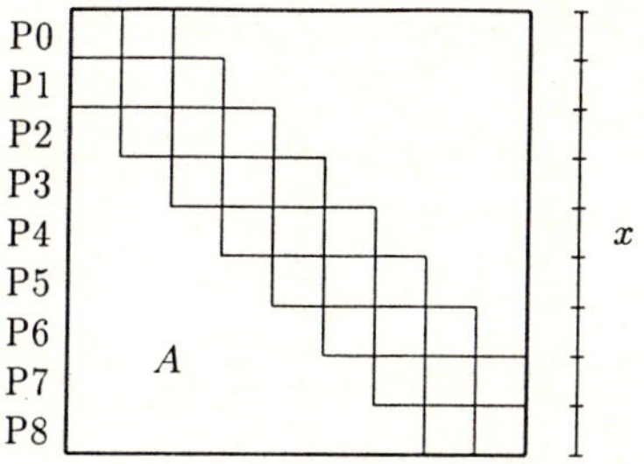

Fig. 2. Data layout on the processors.

of blocks in the matrices. Then the order of the matrices is given by $N = 16 N_F N_G$. We store an equal number of rows of blocks on each processor and for vectors x we assign the corresponding segment to the processors. We choose the problem size such that the number of processors divides N_G exactly. An example of the data layout is given in fig. 2 with $N_G = 9$ and a 3×3 processor grid.

The time-consuming kernels in the Arnoldi method consist of matrix-vector products, inner products and vector updates. The parallel implementation of the matrix-vector products for the MHD-type of matrices does not pose any serious problems, since a strong data locality can be preserved and each processor only has to perform nearest neighbor communication. Therefore, a pipeline has to be embedded in the 2d-grid topology. Only four communication steps have to be performed to evaluate the matrix-vector product, independent of the number of processors.

In the evaluation of the vector updates no communication is involved and thus the implementation of this kernel is optimal.

However, for the inner products the situation is entirely different. Inner products are needed on all processors. Each processor has to evaluate its local part, after which the local inner products have to be accumulated on one processor for instance and the global inner product has to be broadcasted again to all processors. Therefore, when going to larger processor grids, the inner products can be a serious bottleneck and a considerable degradation of the performance of the algorithm can occur, as we shall illustrate below. The accumulation of local inner products on a $p \times p$ grid requires p communication steps when p is even and $p+1$ steps when p is odd. This is shown in fig. 3 for a 5×5 grid. Broadcasting of the global inner product requires the same number of communication steps. This can be illustrated by reversing the direction of the arrows in fig. 3.

In table 1 we present the execution times for the matrix-vector product (MV) and the inner product (IP) obtained for three fairly large MHD problems ($N = 20480$, $N = 40960$ and $N = 81920$) on different processor grids. These problems could not be dealt with on smaller grids than the ones shown, because this would exceed the local processor memory. Also the execution rates (in Mflops) are given. The number of floating point operations for the matrix-vector product equals $4 \times 2 \times (16N_F)^2(3N_G - 2)$ and for the inner product $4 \times 2 \times 16 N_F N_G$. The factor 4 is due to the (double) complex arithmetic, which we use.

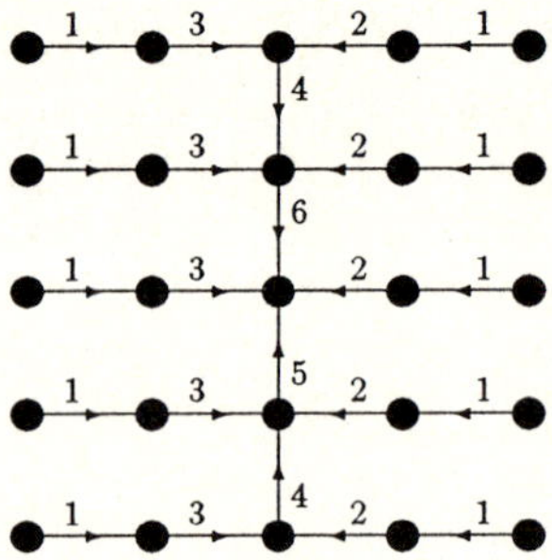

Fig. 3. Accumulation of local inner products on a 2d-grid topology.

Table 1. Timing results for the matrix-vector product (MV) and the inner product (IP) for different MHD problems on a $p_1 \times p_2$ processor grid.

			MV		IP	
N_F	N_G	$p_1 \times p_2$	time[ms]	Mflops	time[ms]	Mflops
5	256	8×4	4111	9.5	7.46	22.0
		8×8	2061	19.0	5.39	30.4
		16×8	1036	37.9	5.42	30.2
		16×16	522	75.1	6.15	26.6
5	512	8×8	4111	19.1	8.16	40.1
		16×8	2061	38.1	6.81	48.1
		16×16	1036	75.8	6.84	47.9
		32×16	519	151.3	9.00	36.4
10	512	16×16	4077	77.1	8.23	79.6
		32×16	2048	153.4	9.69	67.6

From the table we clearly see that the execution time for the MV product scales almost perfectly linear with N_G and N_F^2 if we keep the number of processors fixed. If we compare the performances of the MV product for a fixed problem size ($N_F = 5, N_G = 512$) we observe an almost ideal relative speed-up of 7.92 in going from 64 to 512 processors. For the largest problem size we obtained a maximum performance of 153.4 Mflops for the MV product, which corresponds to 38% of the peak performance of the Parsytec.

For the inner products the performance is much worse as can be seen from the last two columns in the table. If we increase the number of processors for a fixed problem, the execution time decreases initially. However, at a certain stage the communication starts to dominate the computation in the evaluation of the inner product and the execution time increases again. Note that for small processor grids the performance of the IP is better than for the MV product, because only the BLAS level 1 library is available on the Parsytec at the moment.

As we illustrated in section two, the dimension of the Krylov subspace in the Arnoldi algorithm for computing internal eigenvalues has to be rather high. This means that for the construction of the last basis vectors a large number of inner products (and vector updates) have to be evaluated corresponding to only one matrix-vector product. Consider for instance the largest MHD problem in table 1 and the construction of a Krylov subspace basis of the order 100. From the timings of the matrix-vector product and the inner product on the largest processor grid (last row of the table) we observe that the evaluation of the inner products for constructing the last vector of the basis amounts to roughly half the time of the matrix-vector product. This would certainly lead to a serious degradation of the algorithm. A way to get around this difficulty is to create a Krylov subspace basis first and orthogonalize the basis afterwards, see e.g. [2]. A similar procedure has been applied in the s-step Arnoldi algorithm described by Kim and Chronopoulos [4]. The number of global communications due to the inner products is brought down from $O(i^2)$ to $O(i)$, i being the Krylov dimension.

References

1. J. Cullum, W. Kerner, R. Willoughby: A generalized nonsymmetric Lanczos procedure. Computer Physics Communications 53, 19–48 (1989)
2. J.W. Demmel, M.T. Heath, H.A. van der Vorst: Parallel numerical linear algebra. Acta Numerica 2, 111–197 (1993)
3. G.H. Golub, C.F. van Loan: Matrix Computations, 2nd ed. Baltimore: The Johns Hopkins University Press 1989
4. S.K. Kim, A.T. Chronopoulos: An efficient parallel algorithm for extreme eigenvalues of sparse nonsymmetric matrices. The International Journal of Supercomputer Applications 6, 98–111 (1992)
5. M.N. Kooper, H.A. van der Vorst, S. Poedts, J.P. Goedbloed: Application of the implicitly updated Arnoldi method with a complex shift and invert strategy in MHD. FOM Preprint PP 93/061 (1993)
6. C.C. Paige, B.N. Parlett, H.A. van der Vorst: Approximate solutions and eigenvalue bounds from Krylov subspaces. To appear. Linear Algebra and its Applications (1994)
7. S. Poedts, P.M. Meijer, J.P. Goedbloed, H.A. van der Vorst, A. Jacoby: Parallel magnetohydrodynamics on the CM-5. This conference.
8. Y. Saad, M.H. Schultz: GMRES: a generalized minimal residual algorithm for solving nonsymmetric linear systems. SIAM Journal on Scientific and Statistical Computing 7, 856–869 (1986)
9. Y. Saad: Numerical methods for large eigenvalue problems. Manchester: Manchester University Press 1992
10. D.C. Sorensen: Implicit application of polynomial filters in a k-step Arnoldi method. SIAM Journal on Matrix Analysis and Applications 13, 357–385 (1992)

A Scalable Paradigm for Effectively-Dense Matrix Formulated Applications

G. Cheng, G. C. Fox and K. A. Hawick

Northeast Parallel Architectures Center
Syracuse University, 111 College Place,
Syracuse, NY 13244-4100, USA.
Tel. 315-443-3933, Fax. 315-443-3933,
Email: hawick@npac.syr.edu

Abstract. There is a class of problems in computational science and engineering which require formulation in full matrix form and which are generally solved as dense matrices either because they are dense or because the sparsity can not be easily exploited. Problems such as those posed by computational electromagnetics, computational chemistry and some quantum physics applications frequently fall into this class. It is not sufficient just to solve the matrix problem for these applications as other components of the calculation are usually of equal computational load on current computer systems, and these components are consequently of equal importance to the end user of the application. We describe a general method for programming such applications using a combination of distributed computing systems and of more powerful back-end compute resources to schedule the components of such applications. We show how this not only improves computational performance but by making more memory available, allows hitherto impracticably large problems to be run. We illustrate this problem paradigm and our method of solution with problems in electromagnetics, chemistry and physics, and give a detailed performance analysis of a typical electromagnetics application. We discuss a method for scheduling the computational components using the Application Visualisation System (AVS).

1 Introduction

Consider a typical problem in electromagnetics simulation involving the computation of a scattering field pattern from a conducting object. The scatterer could be as simple as an open-ended waveguide or as complex as a full aircraft. The general formulation of such a problem is to find some appropriate discretisation scheme to represent the geometry and to solve the appropriate equations. In this particular case, Maxwell's equations for the electric field must be solved subject to the appropriate boundary conditions [12].

Many application problems can be formulated as matrix equations including many of the field equations and partial differential equations arising in science and engineering. For some of these the problem is most efficiently expressed not as a fully stored matrix but as the field variables themselves. A typical example of this would be a wave equation in an elastic media stored as a displacement field and with a local updating algorithm used on the discretised mesh. The matrix formulation of this problem results in a multiply-banded matrix which would be wasteful of storage.

Some problems are so complicated in terms of the algorithm that they must be formulated as a full matrix which itself may have a sufficiently simple structure that some storage packing can be applied and a sparse matrix solver algorithm applied. Matrices like this often arise in computational fluid dynamics or structural engineering applications where finite elements or volumes are employed. The resulting matrix is by no means trivial but can be factored efficiently by an advanced sparse technique such as the frontal method [7]. In other problems it is not obvious how to exploit the sparsity for an efficient solution, and the matrix must be solved as though it was dense. It is this last case we wish to consider in more detail.

Parallel Solvers

On serial implementations and to a certain extent on traditional vector systems the matrix-solving component often dominates the application's computational complexity to such an extent that it is sufficient to focus all effort on this part of the application alone in terms of efficient coding and algorithms. A great deal of effort has been expended in writing fast efficient matrix factorisation and solver codes and libraries. There has been sufficient awareness of the importance of this problem that factorisation and solver code has been written for many of the parallel and high performance computing systems available today either as a portable library [4] or as proprietary code optimised specifically for one vendor's machine [22, 20]. Vendor-supplied code often has the additional capability to work with matrix sizes larger than the available machine memory. These so called out-of-core solvers typically make use of low level system facilities to be able to move blocks of the matrix between an attached high speed disk and the distributed node memory. Although the communications limitations inevitably degrades performance over an in-core solution, the capability of solving a very large problem size at all can be very valuable.

Generally these packages (for in-core solution) are excellent and can be applied very effectively to solve the matrix which lies at the heart of the application. However, by using such an efficient solver, and by reducing the time taken in the factorising and solving phases of an application, the other parts, which may have been very minor on a serial implementation, now become as significant in terms of compute time on a parallel system.

Computational Phases of an Application

A typical application code might have four identifiable phases: assembling the matrix; factorising the matrix; solving one or more right hand sides (RHS) using the factored matrix; and disassembling the solution into the desired form. If the problem is characterised by the matrix edge size n, which might be the number of elements, patches or nodes depending on the particular problem, then the number of computational operations in each of these will typically be of order n^2 for the assembly, n^3 for the factorisation, n^2 for the RHS solution and of order n or sometimes n^2 for the disassembly of the solution. On a serial implementation the time to completion for each of these phases of the computation is just proportional to the operation count. For a parallel computer system, processors can be added to reduce the effective powers of n in the factorisation and RHS solution phases by one. Our main point in this paper is that the matrix assembly and possibly the disassembly too, must be similarly reduced in completion time or the benefits of using the parallel factorisation and solve will be wasted.

The total time to completion for the application is generally the only matter of interest to the end user, and so it is necessary to consider all phases of the computation. In a particularly complex problem with an irregular mesh for example, the matrix assembly may in fact have the same power of n dependence as the factorisation, but may in fact be weighted by a higher constant if for example some particularly expensive operations such as square roots or trigonometrical functions are involved.

Problem	A	B	C	D
N	126	280	861	1087
A Assembly	4.598	22.711	158.362	2124.677
b Assembly	0.011	0.129	1.545	6.734
Factor	0.129	0.701	12.597	81.544
Solve	0.026	0.190	2.837	14.486
Disassembly	1.603	0.118	1.177	8.293

Table 1. Times (seconds) for components of a CEM Simulation Code

We illustrate this phenomena with some times (table 1) taken from running a method of moments computational electromagnetics code on an Intel iPSC. Our (prototype) parallel implementation uses a COMPLEX version of the ScaLAPACK library codes described in [4], The distribution of compute times for the various algorithmic components shows how the matrix factorisation is still dominated by the time to assemble the matrix at small to medium problem sizes. This is no longer true for very large problems sizes, but the regime of interest to us is close to the cross over point, and it is important to consider parallel implementations of the matrix assembly too.

In addition there are some applications which will require the solution of many medium sized matrices and where the matrix assembly will continue to dominate the completion time for the whole application.

Memory Considerations

A further consideration arises from the storage requirements of our problem. A typical implementation of a matrix factoriser/solver will be able to partition the n^2 storage required to store the matrix itself across the distributed memory of its processors and thus allow a very large matrix to be stored. Some of the effort in achieving this will again be lost however, if the solution and RHS vectors are not also partitioned. Furthermore if the assembly and/or disassembly is not also similarly partitioned, then these phases of the computation must be carried out on a single compute node of the system. This is viable on some hybrid systems where there is a definite "master/slaves" relationship between the compute nodes of the system so that there is one or more nodes with extra memory. This is sometimes the case on systems which employ a so-called "front-end" which can be heavily configured with memory. Nevertheless it is likely that unless the overall machine's memory configuration can be easily changed or tuned for one particular problem, then some benefit of using a distributed memory parallel computer system will be wasted.

For very large systems which must use an out-of-core solver, these arguments are no longer so simple. In such a case the performance degradation due to communications between node memory and even the fastest available concurrent file systems is considerable, This degradation may affect the matrix assembly, factorisation, RHS solution and solution-disassembly in a very machine-dependent manner. This will be determined by the particular memory/disk/caching system and hierarchical structure on a given architecture. Characterising this and designing an optimal portable solution is a very difficult problem at present and we do not consider this further here.

Scheduling Computational Tasks

Our solution to this class of problems is to consider the scheduling of the phases of the computations on a hetero-architecture where distributed workstations for example are used in conjunction with a high performance computer system to overlap as much of the computation as possible and minimise the total time to completion.

It is often possible to partition the problem assembly phase into computationally distinct tasks. An important example concerns the assembly of the RHS vectors in contradistinction to assembly of matrix itself. It may be possible to farm out these tasks to separate compute nodes. This is particularly attractive on a parallel system which allows the compute nodes to act independently as well as in the loosely synchronous fashion necessary for the factorisation and solution phases.

Certain problems may also allow the matrix itself to be decomposed as a sum of sub-matrices, and it is also computationally advantageous to treat these sub-matrix assemblies as separate tasks.

The design goal is generally to achieve the lowest possible time to completion of the *whole* application code. This is generally consistent with making the most efficient use of *all* parts of the hetero-architecture including the concurrent file system if one is available *and* the distributed compute resources (front-end or additional workstations) *as well* as the main back-end compute engine. It is consequently necessary to exploit any task parallelism that presents itself as well as the data parallelism generally employed in the factorisation and RHS solution.

2 Application Visualisation System and Compute Modules

It is not desirable for the end-user of an application code to have to make extensive configurational changes to the code to allow its efficient execution on our proposed heterogeneous system. Indeed it is preferable that this scheduling be done at as high a level as possible within the application code, and be easy for the programmer to tune too.

Our approach involves using the Application Visualisation System (AVS) [1] to control the modular application components. This is discussed below.

3 Industrial Applications Examples

A number of industrial applications that employ dense matrix methods are reviewed in [10]. In this section we illustrate the our paradigm using a specific electromagnetics problem. We also discuss the paradigm's applicability to problems in computational chemistry.

Computational Electromagnetics and Radar Cross-Sections

Electromagnetic scattering (EMS) is a widely encountered problem in electromagnetics [12, 15, 24], with important industrial applications such as microwave equipment, radar, antenna, aviation, and electromagnetic compatibility design.

Consider the following specific electromagnetics problem. Above an infinite conductor plane, there is an incident EM field in free space. Two slots of equal width on the conducting plane are interconnected to a microwave network behind the plane. The microwave network represents the load of waveguides, for example, a microwave receiver. The incident EM field penetrates the two slots which are filled with insulating materials such as air or oil. Connected by the microwave network, the EM fields in the two slots interact with each other, creating two equivalent magnetic current sources in the two slots. A new scattered EM field is then formed above the slots. We simulate this phenomena and calculate the strength of the scattered EM field under various physical circumstances. The presence of the two slots and the microwave load in this application requires simulation models with high resolution and therefore a high performance computing system.

Automatic Differentiation on Distributed Memory MIMD Systems

Luigi De Luca and Piero Fiorino

Department of Electronics, Informatics and Systems
University of Calabria - 87036 Rende (Italy)
E-mail : deluca@deis2.deis.unical.it

Abstract

The main target of this paper is to develop an innovative software for the Automatic Differentiation of separable functions, exploiting the parallel features of a distributed memory parallel system (MIMD architecture).
The developed software, written in Fortran, uses the *Express* tool, thus being easily portable on the several parallel systems supporting *Express*. It consists of a set of subroutines calculating the function, gradient and hessian values; due to its user friendly interface, it is greatly suitable for using inside Fortran iterative algorithms needing these values; it is not necessary any pre-compiling phase.

Introduction

The term Automatic Differentiation outlines a particular algorithm for differential calculus. Through the computation of the derivatives of elementary functions, obtained by the successive decomposition of the original function, it is possible to reconstruct the derivative values in a given point for very complex structured functions as well as for simple functions.
The Automatic Differentiation techniques are a good alternative to the other methods. In fact, these techniques allow computing of the exact derivative values without symbol handling, but through numerical operations only. There are no numerical approximations but those connected to the arithmetic accuracy of the machine. Moreover, the computational effort to evaluate the derivative values could be greatly lower than using finite differences methods.
The specific contexts which can obtain benefits from the use of the Automatic Differentiation are:

- non-linear optimization problems;
  "real-time" problems in which it is necessary to obtain reliable and fast solutions;
- analysis of dynamic system controlled by differential equations, such as applications of the structural analysis and fluid-dynamics.

AutoDif: an Automatic Differentiation Software Tool

There are several papers concerning the automatic differentiation; in particular, many works are related to the automatic differentiation theory. The contribution of this work consists in the development and the implementation of a parallel approach to Automatic Differentiation technique, for the computation of the gradient and the hessian of a function

$$f\colon \mathrm{R}^n \rightarrow \mathrm{R}$$

in a distributed memory multiprocessor system; moreover, the implementation supplies a user friendly interface: in fact, it includes a sort of compiler so that the user only has to write the input function in a file with a shape similar to mathematical formalism; the program reads this function and codifies it to successive automatic differentiation (see fig. 1). Using the software inside iterative algorithms, this phase will be executed only once, before starting iterations.

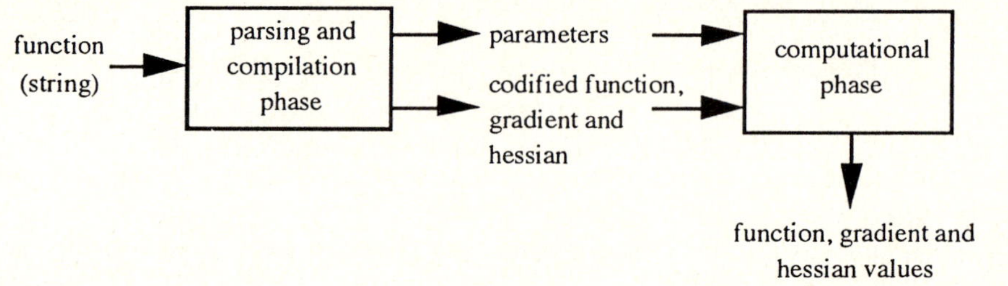

Fig. 1

The automatic differentiation technique being used is the *reverse mode*[6] both for gradient and hessian calculation[2].
The functions considered in this paper belong to the class of the "separable" functions with a sparse-structured hessian, in the form of:

$$f = \sum_{i=1}^{n} f_i$$

where each f_i depends from x_i and a small number of other independent variables; all the f_i have the same structure. For example:

$$f(x) = \sum_{i=2}^{n} x_i (\sin(x_{i+1}) - \cos(x_{i-1}))$$

This kind of functions, massively used in the optimization problems, has a particular structure giving a good exploitation of the parallel machine capabilities.

Computing System and Software

The computational experiments were carried out on a INMOS T800 transputer network clocked at 25 MHz. The software environment used for developing the parallel code is *Express* 3.0 and the *3L fortran compiler* .

Test Problems

Several test problems, with different characteristics, were considered. They are characterised by the possibility of changing the number of variables and represent meaningful tests due to their analytical structure. For all the test functions, the number of variables selected was: 50, 100, 150, 200. The available memory prevented the possibility to increase the number of variables.

Numerical Results

The numerical results are collected with the aim to point out the numerical behaviour of the Automatic Differentiation techniques in a parallel environment, using an increasing number of processors.
In the tables shown below, referred to some of the considered test problems[7], the CPU time and the speed up factor have been reported for different numbers of processors in the transputer network and for different problem sizes.

Brown function

N/proc	1	2	4	8
50	0.146	0.076	0.043	0.028
100	0.296	0.152	0.081	0.049
150	0.445	0.228	0.121	0.070
200	0.594	0.303	0.160	0.092

time table (sec.)

N/proc	1	2	4	8
50	1.00	1.92	3.40	5.21
100	1.00	1.95	3.65	6.04
150	1.00	1.95	3.68	6.36
200	1.00	1.96	3.71	6.46

speed up table

Extended Powell function

N/proc	1	2	4	8
50	0.103	0.053	0.030	0.025
100	0.214	0.115	0.066	0.043
150	0.317	0.167	0.094	0.056
200	0.428	0.220	0.123	0.074

time table (sec.)

N/proc	1	2	4	8
50	1.00	1.94	3.43	4.12
100	1.00	1.86	3.24	4.98
150	1.00	1.90	3.37	5.66
200	1.00	1.95	3.48	5.78

speed up table

Quadratic function

N/proc	1	2	4	8
50	0.033	0.018	0.012	0.012
100	0.065	0.035	0.022	0.018
150	0.098	0.053	0.032	0.023
200	0.130	0.070	0.041	0.030

time table (sec.)

N/proc	1	2	4	8
50	1.00	1.83	2.75	2.75
100	1.00	1.86	2.95	3.61
150	1.00	1.85	3.06	4.26
200	1.00	1.86	3.17	4.33

speed up table

Chained Rosenbrock function

N/proc	1	2	4	8
50	0.123	0.065	0.037	0.025
100	0.249	0.128	0.070	0.043
150	0.375	0.192	0.103	0.062
200	0.500	0.256	0.137	0.080

time table (sec.)

N/proc	1	2	4	8
50	1.00	1.89	3.32	4.92
100	1.00	1.95	3.56	5.79
150	1.00	1.95	3.64	6.05
200	1.00	1.95	3.65	6.25

speed up table

Repeated Rosenbrock function

N/proc	1	2	4	8
50	0.067	0.037	0.022	0.017
100	0.133	0.069	0.040	0.027
150	0.200	0.105	0.058	0.038
200	0.267	0.138	0.076	0.047

time table (sec.)

N/proc	1	2	4	8
50	1.00	1.81	3.05	3.94
100	1.00	1.93	3.33	4.93
150	1.00	1.90	3.45	5.26
200	1.00	1.93	3.51	5.68

speed up table

Extended Wood function

N/proc	1	2	4	8
50	0.838	0.431	0.223	0.121
100	1.729	0.880	0.457	0.249
150	2.620	1.328	0.681	0.364
200	3.511	1.777	0.913	0.482

time table (sec.)

N/proc	1	2	4	8
50	1.00	1.94	3.76	6.93
100	1.00	1.96	3.78	6.94
150	1.00	1.97	3.85	7.20
200	1.00	1.98	3.85	7.28

speed up table

Conclusion

In conclusion, it is worth mentioning some aspects of the present work. The basic result and the original note of this work is the development of a parallel software tool for the numerical evaluation of function, gradient and hessian in a distributed memory parallel computing system. On the bases of the numerical results we can conclude that the parallel implementation turns efficient and reliable. Future works regard: the extension of the Automatic Differentiation to a broad class of functions than the separable one; the interfacing and the experimental use of these techniques within iterative optimization algorithms to have a comparison, in terms of efficiency and convergence to the optimal solution, with other derivative methods such as the finite differences ones.

References

[1] Bartholomew-Biggs, M.C.-Dixon, L.C.W.-Maany, Z.A.-Mohesininia M., Three papers on Automatic Differentiation Presented on the IFAC Symposium on "*Dynamic Modelling and Control of National Economics*", Edinburgh Scotland. Report n. 223, July 1989, Numerical Optimisation Centre, The Hatfield Polytechnic.

[2] Christianson B., *Automatic Hessians by Reverse Accumulation.*, Report n. 228, April 1990, Numerical Optimization Centre, The Hatfield Polytechnic.

[3] Dixon L.C.W., *Automatic Differentiation and Parallel Processing in Optimisation.* Report n.180, April 1987, Numerical Optimisation Centre, The Hatfield Polytechnic.

[4] Fischer H., *Automatic Differentiation: How to Compute the Hessian Matrix.*, Report n. 26, 1987, Technische Universitat Munchen.

[5] Fischer H., *Automatic Differentiation: Parallel Computation of Function, Gradient and Hessian Matrix.*, Parallel Computing 13 (1990), North-Holland.

[6] Griewank A., *On Automatic Differentiation.* Preprint MCS-P10-1088, October 1988, Mathematics and Computer Science Division, Argonne National Laboratory.

[7] Morè, J.J., Garbow, B.S., and Hillstrom, K.E., *Testing Uncostrained Optimization Software*, ACM Transaction on Mathematical Software, Vol. 7, p. 17, 1981.

[8] Rall L.B., *Automatic Differentiation: Techniques and Applications.* Lecture Notes in Computer Science, p. 120, Springer-Verlag, Berlin, 1981.

Optimisations for the Memory Hierarchy of a Singular Value Decomposition Algorithm Implemented on the MIMD Architecture

Adam Czezowski and Peter Strazdins

Department of Computer Science
Australian National University
GPO Box 4, Canberra, ACT, 2601

Abstract. This paper shows several optimisations to the Hestenes parallel algorithm for Singular Value Decomposition (SVD). The central principle in all of the optimisations presented herein is to increase the number of columns being held in each level of the parallel memory hierarchy. The algorithm was implemented on the Fujitsu's AP1000 Array Multiprocessor, but all optimisations described can be easily applied to any MIMD architecture with mesh or hypercube topology, and all but one can be applied to register-cache uniprocessors also.

1 Introduction

The Hestenes SVD algorithm applied to a given $M \times N$ $(M \geq N)$ matrix A is to compute V and to overwrite A with AV, where $A = U\Sigma V^T$, $U^T U = V^T V = I_n$ and the diagonal matrix Σ gives the singular values of A. In the parallel implementation of Hestenes algorithm [1], the columns of A (and V) can be divided into 'blocks' which are distributed two per processor, and these two blocks are then orthogonalised against each other. After exchanging blocks among cells, the orthogonalisation process is repeated until all pairs of columns of A are rotated against each other. The algorithm iterates until the matrix A becomes orthogonal. In [2] we describe in detail implementations used as a starting point to the optimisations presented below.

2 Optimisations for the Memory Hierarchy

In Hestenes algorithm, the number of floating point operations is proportional to ω^2, where ω is the number of columns stored at a particular level of the memory hierarchy. Therefore, we can enhance the performance of the algorithm by increasing ω. Let us introduce a data reuse factor $\mathcal{R}$ as a general measure of algorithm performance at a particular memory hierarchy level. $\mathcal{R}$ is defined as the ratio of the number of floating point operations performed on a set of data, kept in that level of the hierarchy, to the number of 'load' operations required to put (and maintain, in the case of the cache level) the data at that level.

All the techniques presented in this paper are described in detail in [3] and are applied to both the A and V matrices.

By using a $P_x \times P_y$ rectangular processor configuration, where $P_y > 1$, $P_x P_y = P$ and $\omega_{comm} = N/P_x$, instead of a linear configuration of P processors where $\omega_{comm} = N/P$, we increased $\mathcal{R}_{comm}$, and, for the case where both blocks of A fit in cache, $\mathcal{R}_{cache}$ by a factor of P_y and consequently reduced execution time by more than 10% for the optimal aspect ratios of $P_y : P_x = 1 : 2, 1 : 1$. The tradeoff in this technique is the introduction of vertical communication to compute the inner products of columns required for rotation angle calculation.

In the case where both blocks are not small enough to fit into the cache, we must also use partitioning methods [3], i.e. (1) further divide the blocks of the matrix A into sub-blocks that fit within the cache, and (2) reorganise the computation to minimise cache misses. Partitioning improves $\mathcal{R}_{cache}$ by a factor of $\omega/4$ where ω is the number of columns of A that can fit in the cache. This reduced execution time by 25% and raised the cache hit ratio by 3% to 99.2%.

At the register level, two column rotation, which is the basis of Hestenes algorithm, causes poor data reuse and in effect degrades overall algorithm performance. By rotating four columns together simultaneously, data reuse at the register level, $\mathcal{R}_{reg}$, can be improved by a factor of 3, for rotation angle calculation, and by a factor of 2, for actual column rotation. Despite the overhead of 2 additional rotation angle calculations per 4 rotations, four column rotation reduces the execution time by a further 22%.

However, the introduction of 'scaled columns' [2] and four column rotations potentially affects the numerical properties of the algorithm, i.e. possibly introduces round-off errors. In practice, we found that the accuracy was preserved regardless of the method used, the convergence rate was not adversely affected by any optimisation and it even improved in four column rotation method by 10%.

3 Conclusion

The results obtained show that, both in theory and in practice, to increase the number of columns being held in each level of the parallel memory hierarchy leads to better reuse on that level, and hence to better performance of Hestenes SVD algorithm. We expect that similar principles can be used to enhance performance of other linear algebra algorithms implemented on various parallel architectures.

References

1. Brent, R.P., Luk, F.T.: The Solution of Singular-Value and Symmetric Eigenvalue Problems on Multiprocessor Arrays SIAM Journal of Scientific and Statistical Computing **6** (1986) 69–84
2. Czezowski, A., Strazdins, P.: Ways of enhancing performance of a Singular Value Decomposition Algorithm on the AP1000 Array Multiprocessor. Transputer and Occam Engineering Series **31** (1993) 83–88 (ISSN:0925-4986)
3. Czezowski, A., Strazdins, P.: Optimisations for the memory hierarchy of a Singular Value Decomposition Algorithm implemented on the MIMD Architecture. ANU, Department of Computer Science Technical Report **TR-CS-94-03** (1994)

Parallelization and Data Locality of a Multigrid Solver on the KSR1

Ulrich Schwardmann

Gesellschaft für wissenschaftliche Datenverarbeitung Göttingen

The multigrid algorithm is known as a fast method for the solution of differential equations with boundary conditions. For the temporal simulation of physical systems for instance, where an accurate solution is needed for each time step, a fast code, handling big data arrays, is especially necessary. The Poisson equation on a given domain with Dirichlet conditions on the boundary is a famous paradigm of the elliptic boundary value problem. The goal here is the description of the parallelization and optimization process for the multigrid poisson algorithm, as it was published by Stüben and Trottenberg in [2], on a parallel computer with virtual shared memory concept like the KSR1. This summarizes the results of [1].

The first step in our process of parallelization was to use the automatic parallelization facility of the Fortran preprocessor KAP and to run the code parallel on four cells. Because of supposed data dependencies the automatically chosen tiling strategy did not lead to any significant speedup.

After implementing some minor changes on the original code the parallelization of the multigrid method was done by dividing the grids into tiles.

Tiling the data space is possible only, if there are enough columns of the grid to be distributed to the cells. The multigrid cycle has therefore to be performed in a hybride way, with serial code for the coarser grids and parallel code for the finer grids. The parallel relaxation was used here only for grid levels greater or equal to six, the parallel interpolation and restriction between grid levels five and six and higher.

One has to care here for data affinity, a special form of data locality. In order to avoid further and repeated movement of the data, distributed over the cells, which has to be done between each relaxation and interpolation resp. restriction process, an efficient parallelization had to be done coherently for all parts of the cycle.

The tiling was done with slice strategy along the columns of the grid. Only with a large number of tiles (≥ 32) the number of boundary cells in a complete division along columns increases in such a way, that a rectangular division of the grid will become significantly more efficient.

The parallelization of the multigrid solver with slice strategy was then tested on a various number of cells. Remarkeble here is the achieved *superlinear* speedup, which is due to the increased memory bandwidth by the parallel data access (see figure 1).

In order to further increase the performance of the multigrid algorithm we made some experiments in optimizing the most time consuming part of the algorithm, the relaxation. Subpage alignment and manual loopunrolling did not lead to any significant improvement. The change of the data structure of the grid array into a field, efficient for most vector computers, makes the algorithm on the KSR1 even slower for all grid levels.

Therefore the improvement of data locality turned out to be the key to get better performance. For each call the red-black relaxation steps twice with stride two through the whole data area. On finer grids this means, that all data has to be moved twice into the subcache. A better reuse of data in the subcache can be achieved by using a macro pipeline on the columns of the grid, as one can see in figure 2.

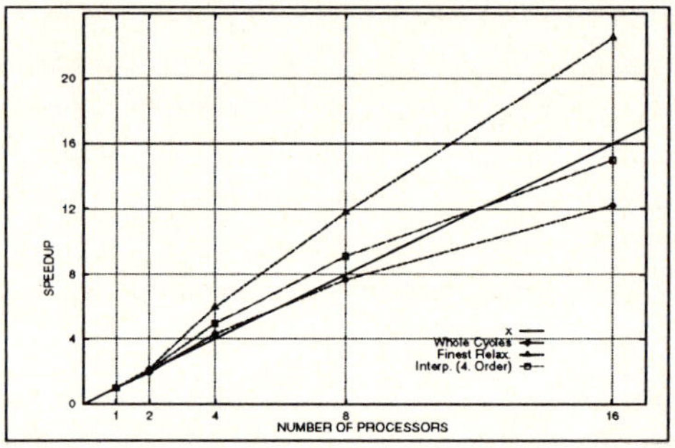

Fig. 1. *Speedup of the parallelization along columns on a various number of processors for all cycles up to level 10, for the 4. order interpolation and the relaxation on level 10.*

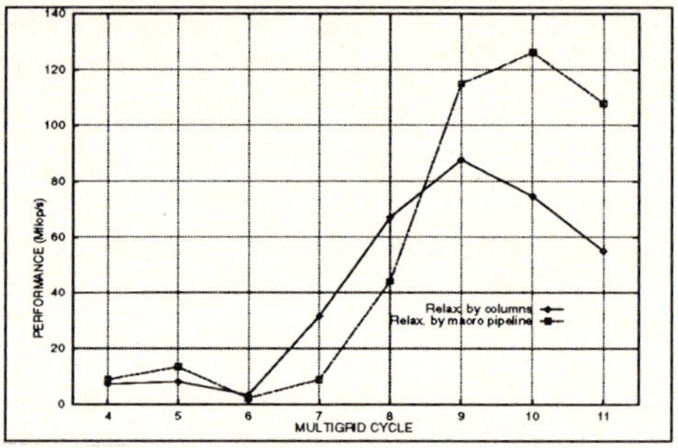

Fig. 2. *Performance on 16 cells of the parallel relaxation on the various grid levels (up to grid level 10), unoptimized version versus optimized version by macro pipelining.*

As a concluding remark one can say, that because of its complex memory hierarchie, the key to achieve high performance on parallel computers like the KSR1 is the optimization of data locality.

Although the relaxation dominates the computing time, optimization of data locality means firstly, that *all* participating subroutines must be included into the parallelization process of the multigrid method, in order to minimize communication costs. Furthermore the grid has to be tiled in such a way, that cache and subcache usage is optimized and the communication cost is minimized. Proceeding like this a speedup of 11.50 for the full multigrid method on 16 cells was produced on the KSR1. By improving data locality inside the relaxation algorithm, a significantly higher speedup of 13.27 for the whole multigrid algorithm could be achieved.

References

1. U. Schwardmann, *Parallelization of a multigrid solver on the KSR1*, Supercomputer 55, X-3, pp. 4-12.
2. K. Stüben and U. Trottenberg, *Multigrid methods: Fundamental algorithms, model problem analysis and applications. In: W. Hackbusch and U. Trottenberg (eds.): Multigrid Methods*, Berlin: Springer (1982) pp. 1-176.

ON THE PARALLEL EVALUATION OF RECURRENCES

Ayşe Kiper
Department of Computer Engineering
Middle East Technical University
06531 Ankara , TURKEY

(email : ayse@vm.cc.metu.edu.tr)

Recurrences constitute an important class of computational problems which arise in a number of numerical analysis problems such as the solution of equations by Gauss elimination, matrix and vector manupulations, iterative methods and the evaluation of polynomials.

The use of new computer systems namely multi processor systems can not be avoided to solve recurrences as in other computational problems. Advances in parallel computing lead the researchers to study and develop parallel algorithms for solving recurrences. In the last decade, a number of articles has been published most of them are being on particular recurrence cases. The aim of preparing this paper is to classify and discuss the existing methods referring to as many papers as possible have appeared in the literature.

A recurrence can be defined as a sequence of evaluations in which the latest term of the sequence depends on one more of the previously computed terms. Formally, the recurrence equations can be defined as the solution of some problems which are expressed as a sequence $x_1, x_2, \ldots, x_n$, $x_i \in R$ where each x_i $(i = 1, 2, \ldots, n)$ may depend on the x_j which $j < 1$.

A general recurrence system R <n, m> of order m with n equations, can be expressed as

$$R\langle n,m\rangle : x_k = H\,[\underset{\sim}{a}_k\,;\, x_{k-1}, x_{k-2}, \ldots, x_{k-m}]\,, \quad (1 \leq k \leq n) \tag{1}$$

with m initial conditions $x_{m+1}, x_{m+2}, \ldots, x_0$. H is called the recurrence function, $\underset{\sim}{a}_k$ is a vector of parameters which are independent of the x_i.

If the recurrence system $R<n,m>$ is linear, then the simple definition

$$R<n,m> : x_k = \begin{cases} 0 & \text{if } \; k \le 0 \\ b_k + \sum\limits_{j=k-m}^{k-1} a_{kj}\, x_j & \text{if } \; 1 \le k \le n \end{cases} \tag{2}$$

can be given with $m \le n - 1$.

If $A = [a_{ik}]$, where $a_{ik} = 0$ and for $i \le k$ or $i - k > m$ and $\underset{\sim}{x} = [x_1, \ldots, x_n]$ and $\underset{\sim}{b} = [b_1, \ldots, b_n]^T$ then (2) can be written as

$$\underset{\sim}{x} = A\,\underset{\sim}{x} + \underset{\sim}{b} \tag{3}$$

When $m = n - 1$, the system is called an "ordinary linear system of recurrence equations" and denoted by $R<n>$.

This work is an overview on the parallel evaluation of recurrence relations. As some problems could originally be formulated by recurrences, some others, although they explicitely (or originally) are not of that type, but can be reduced to recursive forms after series of manupulations. As an example we may mention "The Parallel Solution of Tridiagonal Systems". This process may lead a simpler solution and may allow use of parallel systems.

In literature, recurrences can be regarded as a time consuming class of problems. The advances in the area of "Parallel Computing" have led the researchers to develop parallel algorithms for recurrences. The aim is to reduce the computing time making use of technical properties and facilities of available parallel systems.

In recent years, various papers have been published on the parallel treatment of recurrence relations. All these requires a study and an analysis of these problems under the light of latest developments both in computer architectures and in the design of algorithms.

In this work, a brief presentation and the classification of recurrence relations are given. Some problems, solutions of which can be reduced to recurrences are described and presented with examples. An up to date classification of parallel approaches and of parallel algorithms for recurrence problems of various nature are studied. A discussion and a comparison of parallel methods referring to advantages and disadvantages and the use of new architectures for applications are also included.

Implementation of a Parallel Euler Solver with GRIDS

U. Geuder, M. Härdtner, B.Wörner, R. Zink

Institute of Parallel and Distributed High-Performance Systems
University of Stuttgart, Breitwiesenstraße 20-22, D-70565 Stuttgart
email: grids@hermes.informatik.uni-stuttgart.de

Abstract. We present the basic concepts of the GRIDS parallel programming system and the underlying programming model. A suitable formulation of a finite-volume Euler solver on two-dimensional unstructured grids is developed. The, mostly declarative, representation of the resulting cell-centered scheme with flux splitting and explicit time integration in the GRIDS programming model is described. An efficient parallel execution can be achieved automatically by the system for workstation clusters and parallel supercomputers. Performance results on parallel architectures of both types are shown.

Introduction

In absence of automatically parallelizing general compilers, explicit parallel programming introduces high complexity in programming. Many efforts to overcome these difficulties are ongoing. One approach is to provide specialized programming models with an expressiveness that is adapted to a class of algorithms. Associated programming systems are then enabled to parallelize automatically by exploiting knowledge on the algorithm structure and the problem-inherent parallelism common to all applications of the selected class.

GRIDS is an architecture-independent programming system for iterative computations in technical and scientific applications on unstructured grids. The parallelization strategy in GRIDS is grid partitioning, i.e., the results are independent of the number of processors participating in a computation. For typical programs of the class a good parallel performance is obtained but not necessarily the best achievable [2].

In this paper we describe the formulation of a finite-volume Euler solver on two-dimensional unstructured grids based on work done by Hammond and Barth [4]. We discuss the implementation with the GRIDS programming system and show performance results for different parallel architectures.

1 GRIDS Programming Model

The central concept of the programming model is the integration of neighborhood with respect to the unstructured grid into the programming model. Topological neighborhood defines the possible data access patterns during the execution. It describes implicitly all data dependencies between topological elements that are relevant for the generation of efficient parallel execution schemes.

This concept is strengthened by another important feature of the GRIDS programming model: the separation of the topology description from the formulation of algorithms. Separating the topological and the algorithmic part effectively means separating the handling of parallelism from the sequential algorithms. The topology can be managed by the GRIDS system instead of being coded into the application program. A description of the GRIDS programming model, the complete definition of the accompanying user interface, and an overview of the implementation can be found in [1].

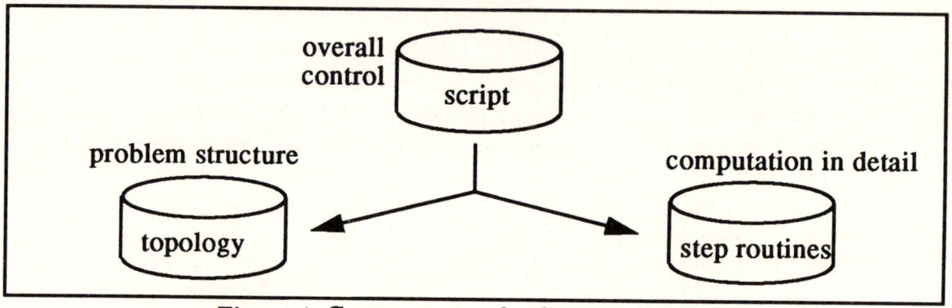

Figure 1 Components of a GRIDS program

Figure 1 shows the main components of a GRIDS program.

- The topology declaration provides information about data dependencies that can be used by the programming system to generate efficient parallel code and schedule it accordingly.
- The algorithms to be executed locally on each topological element are represented by problem-specific iteration procedures. Computations are broken up into steps according to the change of state that must be visible to the neighbors. Different procedures can be invoked as steps in different phases of the overall computation.
- The script contains a set of declarations defining, from a global point of view, which algorithms (step routines) are to be executed on which topological elements. The semantics in the script is a strictly parallel execution of steps.

All parallelization-specific tasks such as data partitioning, processor mapping, load balancing, message passing, and synchronization are implemented in the system. Therefore, they are no longer in the responsibility of the application programmer. Next we describe the development of suitable computing schemes.

2 Finite Volume Euler Solver

For the implementation in the GRIDS system consider the integral form of the Euler equations of gas dynamics in a general region Ω with bounding curve $\partial\Omega$:

$$\frac{d}{dt}\int_{\Omega} \boldsymbol{u}\,da + \int_{\partial\Omega} \boldsymbol{f}(\boldsymbol{u}, \boldsymbol{n})\,dl = 0 \tag{2.1}$$

In this equation, $\boldsymbol{u}$ represents the vector of conserved variables for conservation of mass, momentum, and energy. The flow of mass, momentum and energy through a surface with normal orientation $\boldsymbol{n}$ is represented by the vector function

$f(u, n)$. Equation (2.1) is applied to each control volume c_i of a tessellation of region Ω, yielding (2.2).

$$\frac{d}{dt}\int_{c_i} u\,da + \int_{\partial c_i} f(u, n)\,dl = 0 \tag{2.2}$$

In Godunov's method [3] the conserved variables are averaged in the control volume c_i. Applying equation (2.2) we get an evolution equation for the integral cell averages $\tilde{u}$ (2.3).

$$\frac{d}{dt}(\tilde{u}A)_{c_i} + \int_{\partial c_i} f(u, n)\,dl = 0 \tag{2.3}$$

To proceed in time we must evaluate the flux integral on ∂c_i. The numerical flow normal to the edges of a control volume is calculated by flux splitting and the approximate Riemann solver developed by Roe [7].

The boundary conditions are those described by Jameson et al. [6], Jameson and Baker [5] and are only outlined briefly here. At the inner boundary there is no flux through the wall. However the pressure terms are necessary to calculate the contributions to the momentum equations. At the exterior boundaries extrapolated and fixed Riemann invariants are introduced to reduce the reflection of outgoing disturbances.

This leads to the following overall structure of the algorithm:

1. Flux evaluation on each edge. The boundary ∂c_i of a control volume consists of a collection of edges from the tessellation or its dual.
2. Collection of all flux contributions of the edges and time stepping. To perform this evolution in time one is free to choose the time-stepping scheme e.g. explicit Euler, Runge-Kutta,..

In a finite-volume formulation, given the tessellation of the region, two schemes are used for the definition of the control volumes and the representation of the flow. We will describe the implementation of a cell-centered formulation where the cells of the tessellation are directly used as control volumes and the flow variables are associated to the midpoints of cells. A node-mesh scheme where the control volumes are defined as mesh-cells of the dual of the tessellation and the flow variables are stored at the nodes of the tessellation is as well suited for the GRIDS programming model as the cell-centered scheme described below.

3 Implementation with GRIDS

The steps of an implementation in the GRIDS system are the following: first the structure of the underlying topology is declared; the calculations on grid element types are broken up into steps; the overall structure of the iterations is expressed in the script; calculations within the step routines are implemented, and finally the problem geometry (region) is discretized and the resulting grid described using a GRIDS readable topology definition.

For the implementation of grid-based algorithms, first all necessary types of topological elements have to be determined. Analyzing for elements with semantic differences leads, for the Euler solver, to two types of topological elements and their associated data: node elements with coordinates and cell elements with some geometric data and the conserved variables of the flow. While on the node elements no calculations are performed, on the cell elements the calculation of the flux and time integration is executed.

Next is the analysis of the data access structures. A node element does not access any data, since no operations are performed on its variables, the coordinates. A cell element needs access to data associated to node elements (coordinates) to initialize geometric information like area and edge normals. The data of other cell elements (conserved variables) are accessed to evaluate the flux at the edges. This data access patterns are expressed in the grid declaration by two different types of topological neighborhood relations, one from cell elements to their adjacent node elements and one from cell elements to their neighbor cells.

An analysis of the calculations during the iteration phase reveals that with careful arrangement of the operations only a single step is required, which is executed on the cells. In this step first the fluxes for all edges of the cell are calculated from the data values of neighboring cells at the last iteration. In the second part of this step the evolution in time is performed. The boundary conditions can be handled by evaluating topological information about the neighbors. The calculation of flow is changed accordingly.

Of course, the description of the overall iteration from a global perspective needs only a single phase. The single step routine is executed on all cells. Next, the new values of the conserved variables associated to the cells are made visible to the neighbor cells for the next iteration. The strictly parallel semantics in the script assures that no contention is occurring i.e no access conflicts on the variables emerge.

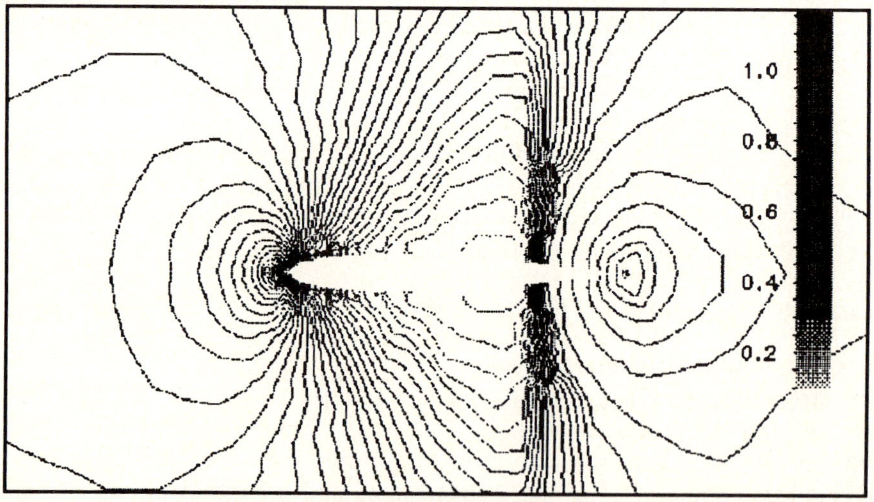

Figure 2 Transonic flow around NACA12 profile $m_\infty = 0.85$; $\alpha = 0^o$

The topology definition is simply a representation of the tessellation in GRIDS format.

Remember, this description of the implementation refers only to the GRIDS programming model. If the algorithm is expressible in this programming model the generation, optimization and efficient parallel execution of the code can be automatically performed by the programming system.

4 Numerical Results and Performance Evaluation

The computed solution for a transonic flow around a NACA12 profile in Figure 2 shows the characteristic mach number distribution for this problem and a good capturing of shocks. The topology consists of 9480 node elements and

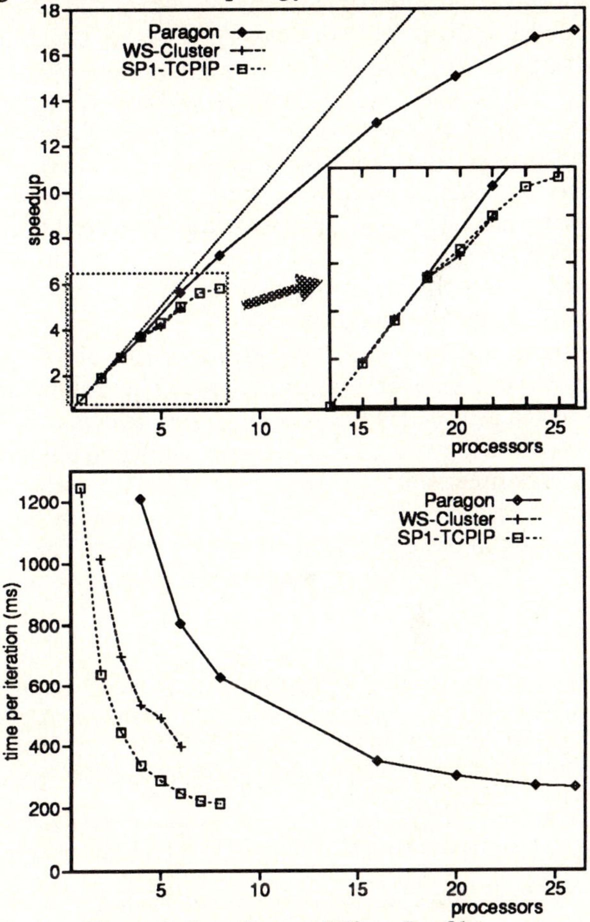

Figure 3 Speedup and Time Profile

18560 triangle elements.

While the structure of the parallel machine is not reflected at the programming model level, in the GRIDS project implementation work has been concentrated on MIMD systems with distributed memory. At the moment, prototype implementations of the GRIDS system exist for TCP/IP, the NX communication library of the Intel Paragon XP/S parallel computer, and PVM.

The (wall-) times were measured on a workstation cluster consisting of 6 IBM RS/6000 Model 570 connected with ethernet, a 8 processor IBM SP-1 using TCP/IP over the high performance switch and on the Intel Paragon with up to 26 processors. The same problem with 1000 iterations was computed; input and output operations were not contained. Of course, the numerical results were the same for all configurations. No parallel architecture with an optimized, native PVM was available, therefore the TCP/IP version of GRIDS was always faster.

The speedup achievable on the workstation cluster and on the SP-1 is comparable. These configurations have powerful processors but TCP/IP introduces a very high latency in the communication. The high bandwidth of the SP-1 did not give any advantage, since message latency is the bottleneck in this case. Of course this will change with the usage of an optimized communication library. The high speedup, with up to 26 processors on this problem, for the paragon is due to the slower processor nodes and a short message latency. Scalable parallel execution control and adaptive optimizations enable the GRIDS system to exploit this automatically.

The importance of optimizations by the system in the case of larger partitions is immediately clear by looking at the absolute computing times. The reduced number of powerful processors that are useful for this problem size can only be caught up by realizing much higher parallelism on the Intel Paragon. With large partitions on fewer processors the system is able to hide, to some extend, the message delay by overlapping communication with computations.

For further enhancements of the numerical efficiency of the used Euler scheme the system will reach similar parallel efficiencies, assuming the algorithms are expressed in the GRIDS programming model. The same holds for the parallel execution of the GRIDS program on other (new) parallel architectures.

5 References

1. U. Geuder, M. Härdtner, B. Wörner, R. Zink, *GRIDS User's Guide*, computer science report 4/1993, department of computer science, University of Stuttgart, Mar. 1993
2. U. Geuder, M. Härdtner, B. Wörner, R. Zink, *The GRIDS Approach to Automatic Parallelization*, Proc. of 4th Workshop on Compilers for Parallel Computers, Delft, Dec. 1993
3. S.K. Godunov, *A Finite Difference Method for the numerical Computation of Discontinous Solutions of the Equations of Fluid Dynamics*, Matematicheskie Sbornik, Vol. 47, 1959
4. S. Hammond, T. Barth, *Efficient Massively Parallel Euler Solver for Two-Dimensional Unstructured Grids*, AIAA Journal Vol. 30, No. 4, April 1992, pp. 947-952
5. A. Jameson, T.J. Baker, *Solution of the Euler Equations for Complex Configurations*, Proceedings of AIAA 6th Computational Fluid Dynamics Conference, AIAA, New York, 1983, pp. 293-302
6. A. Jameson, W. Schmidt, E. Turkel, *Numerical Solution of the Euler Equations by Finite Volume Methods Using Runge-Kutta Time Stepping Methods*, AIAA Paper 81-1259, 1981
7. P. Roe, *Approximate Riemann Solvers, Parameter Vectors and Difference Schemes*, Journal of Computational Physics, 43, pp. 357-372, 1981

Distributed Mapping of SPMD Programs with a Generalized Kernighan-Lin Heuristic *

Johan De Keyser and Dirk Roose

Dept. of Computer Science, K.U.Leuven, Belgium

Abstract. Mapping a parallel algorithm onto a parallel computer is known to be NP-hard. In this paper we propose a parallel mapping technique based on a generalization of the Kernighan-Lin heuristic. The properties of a mapping cost function are thereby exploited.

1 Problem Formulation

The *mapping problem* for parallel programs is defined as : distribute the tasks among the processors for minimal execution time. Partitioning by Recursive Bisection (PRB) and by Pairwise Mincut (PPM) [2] are Kernighan-Lin based heuristics (developed for graph partitioning) which we have adapted to the mapping problem. PPM is discussed here in detail.

The P-processor computer has a topology described by distance function Δ and is characterized by $\tau = t_{comm}/t_{calc}$, the ratio of communication to calculation speed. The algorithm has a *task interaction graph* $(\mathcal{G}, \rightarrow)$ of degree G, with weight matrix Λ; diagonal elements represent computation costs (in units of t_{calc}), while off-diagonals are communication costs (in units of t_{comm}). Mapping then consists of finding a partitioning $\mathcal{S} = \{S_k\}$ which minimizes

$$C^2_{map} = \frac{1}{P}\sum_{k=1}^{P}(\sum_{g_i \in S_k} \Lambda_{ii})^2 + \frac{\tau^2}{P} \sum_{k,l=1;k\neq l}^{P} (\sum_{g_i\in S_k, g_j \in S_l} \Lambda_{ij}\Delta_{kl})^2 .$$

2 Mapping Heuristics Based On Pairwise Mincut

With the auxiliary quantities $L_k = \sum_{g_i \in S_k} \Lambda_{ii}$, $L_{kl} = \sum_{g_i \in S_k, g_j \in S_l} \Lambda_{ij}$, $l_i = \Lambda_{ii}$ and $l_{ik} = \sum_{g_j \in S_k} \Lambda_{ij}$, the cost change resulting from moving graph node g_i from partition or cluster S_0 to S_1 is :

$$\begin{aligned}\Delta C^2_{map} = \tfrac{1}{P}[&2l_i(l_i - L_0 + L_1) + 2\tau^2(l_{i0} - l_{i1})(l_{i0} - l_{i1} + 2L_{01})\Delta^2_{01} \\ &+2\tau^2 \textstyle\sum_{k>1} l_{ik}\left((l_{ik} - 2L_{0k})\Delta^2_{0k} + (l_{ik} + 2L_{1k})\Delta^2_{1k}\right)].\end{aligned} \quad (1)$$

This value depends on all clusters S_k connected to g_i. Similarly, moving g_i affects the evaluation of cost changes in all cluster pairs with such an S_k.

* This work was supported by FKFO grant nr. 9.008.91N (Lotto) and the Belgian incentive programme on Interuniversitary Poles of Attraction (IUAP 17), initiated by the Belgian State – Prime Minister's Service – Science Policy Office. The scientific responsibility is assumed by its authors.

Algorithm 1 Construction of the configuration change sequence

```
procedure mincut_sequence_for_mapping(P,S,(S_0,S_1),Z,T)
  n ← #S_0 + #S_1; m ← min{Z,n}
  /* compute cost quantities */
  unlock all g_i ∈ S_0 ∪ S_1; compute L_k and l_jk, ∀k, ∀g_j ∈ S_0 ∪ S_1
  /* construct the sequence */
  for i = 0,...,m − 1 do
    /* select best configuration change */
    best_gain ← ∞
    for g_j ∈ S_0 ∪ S_1, g_j unlocked do
      compute gain for a transfer of g_j to the other cluster
      if gain < best_gain then best_gain ← gain, j* ← j
    end for
    λ^(i) ← transfer g_j*; μ^(i) ← best_gain; γ^(i) ← dependency_order_of(λ^(i), T)
    /* recompute cost quantities */
    lock g_j*; recompute L_0, L_1, L_01, and L_0k and L_1k ∀k
    recompute l_j0 and l_j1 for g_j ∈ S_0 ∪ S_1, Λ_ji ≠ 0, g_j unlocked
  end for
  return λ,μ,γ
end procedure
```

2.1 Bi-partitioning with the Kernighan-Lin mincut heuristic

Let $P = 2^p$. Consider a set $\mathcal{T} = \{t_k\}$ of $P/2$ disjoint cluster pairs. This set is organized as a binary tree, each leaf node t_k being labeled with b_k, the binary representation of k. The distance function $\hat{\Delta}(t_k, t_l) = \lfloor \log_2(b_k \texttt{ xor } b_l) \rfloor$ represents the height of the smallest subtree containing t_k and t_l.

The Kernighan-Lin procedure [3, 5] constructs a sequence λ of n *configuration changes* $\lambda^{(i)}$ for $t_k = \{S_0, S_1\}$ $(n = \#S_0 + \#S_1)$. The resulting cost change is the *gain* $\mu^{(i)}$. Denoting by $\Gamma^{(i)}$ the set of cluster pairs where cost evaluation is affected by $\lambda^{(i)}$, $\gamma^{(i)} = \max_{t \in \Gamma^{(i)}} \hat{\Delta}(t, t_k)$ is called the *dependency order*. The configuration changes in λ do not necessarily yield cost improvements. We construct a new sequence of $\bar{n}$ *block changes* $\bar{\lambda}^{(j)} = \{\lambda^{(m_j)} \ldots \lambda^{(m_j+n_j-1)}\}$, $m_j = \sum_{i=0}^{j-1} n_i$, with *block gain* $\bar{\mu}^{(j)} = \sum_{i=1}^{n_j} \mu^{(m_j+i-1)} < 0$ and *block dependency order* $\bar{\gamma}^{(j)} = \max_{i=1,\ldots,n_j} \gamma^{(m_j+i-1)}$. We assume that no block change can be further subdivided into smaller profitable subsequences.

We use a mincut variant in which configuration changes are individual graph node transfers (see algorithm 1) [4]. $\lambda^{(i)}$ is selected as the transfer yielding maximum $-\Delta C_{map}$. We construct sequences of limited length $Z \ll n$, which hinders the hill-climbing ability of the algorithm only slightly (most block changes contain only a few transfers [6]). Upon transfer of g_i from S_0 to S_1, the auxiliary quantities are recomputed in $\mathcal{O}(G) + \mathcal{O}(P)$ time [2]. Gain evaluation then is $\mathcal{O}(P)$ (equation (1)). Algorithm 1 is of order $\mathcal{O}(PGn)$ if Z is constant.

Algorithm 2 Non-interfering subsequence selection

```
procedure select_subsequences(λ̄^[k],φ,T)
  for t_k ∈ T do N_0^[k] ← 0
  /* select changes of increasing dependency order */
  s ← 0
  repeat
    /* start new subsequences */
    for t_k ∈ T do
      if N_0^[k] = 0 and φ_s^[k] = 0 and φ_{s+1}^[k] ≠ 0 then N_0^[k] ← 1, l_0^[k] ← s
    /* bottom-up pass */
    for i = 1,...,s do
      for j = 0,...,2^{p-i-1} - 1 do
        eliminate_interfering_changes(j2^i,j2^i,j2^i + 2^{i-1}) (cf. table 1)
    /* check stop condition */
    finished ← ∧_{j=0}^{2^{p-s-1}-1} (N_s^[j2^s] = 0)
    /* top-down pass */
    for i = s,...,1 do
      for j = 0,...,2^{p-i-1} - 1 do
        propagate_selected_changes(j2^i,j2^i,j2^i + 2^{i-1}) (cf. table 2)
  until s = p or finished
  /* determine selected subsequences */
  for t_k ∈ T do
    λ̃^[k] ← if N_0^[k] = 0 then ∅ else first φ_{L_0^[k]+1}^[k] changes from λ̄^[k]
  return λ̃^[k]
end procedure
```

2.2 Interference between simultaneous mincuts

Parallel heuristics require a technique to avoid interference between simultaneous mincuts. The Kernighan-Lin heuristic yields $\bar{\lambda}^{[k]}$, $\bar{\mu}^{[k]}$ and $\bar{\gamma}^{[k]}$ for each cluster pair. We select non-interfering block changes from among these. The $P/2$ selected subsequences $\tilde{\lambda}^{[k]} \subset \bar{\lambda}^{[k]}$ of length $\tilde{n}^{[k]} \leq \bar{n}^{[k]}$. are non-interfering if

$$\forall t_k, t_l \in \mathcal{T} : \forall i \in \{0, \dots, \tilde{n}^{[k]} - 1\} : \hat{\Delta}(t_k, t_l) \leq \bar{\gamma}^{(i)[k]} \Rightarrow \tilde{\lambda}^{[l]} = \emptyset.$$

Dependencies are represented by the *dependency array* ϕ : $\phi_j^{[k]} = \min_{\bar{\gamma}^{(i)[k]} \geq j} i$.

Our selection algorithm is based on the binary tree introduced earlier. For tree node k at level i (from 0 for leaf nodes to $p-1$ for the root), we define $N_i^{[k]}$ to be the number of cluster pairs (leaves of the subtree) for which block changes have been accepted; $sw_i^{[k]}$ indicates whether these pairs are in the left or right subtree, or in both. If $N_i^{[k]} = 1$, we define $l_i^{[k]}$ to be the minimum dependency order of this subsequence. A detailed description is given in algorithm 2).

Table 1. Eliminating interfering marked change sequences of order s

left child	right child	tree node	
$N_L = 0$	$N_R = 0$	$N = 0$	
$N_L = 0$	$N_R = 1\ l_R$	$N = 1$	$l = l_R$ sw =RIGHT
$N_L = 1\ l_L$	$N_R = 0$	$N = 1$	$l = l_L$ sw =LEFT
$N_L = 1\ l_L < s$	$N_R = 1\ l_R < s$	$N = 2$	sw =BOTH
$N_L = 1\ l_L = s$	$N_R = 1\ l_R < s$	$N = 1$	$l = l_R$ sw =RIGHT
$N_L = 1\ l_L < s$	$N_R = 1\ l_R = s$	$N = 1$	$l = l_L$ sw =LEFT
$N_L = 1\ l_L = s$	$N_R = 1\ l_R = s$	$N = 1$	choose LEFT or RIGHT
$N_L > 1$	$N_R = 0$	$N = N_L$	sw =LEFT
$N_L = 0$	$N_R > 1$	$N = N_R$	sw =RIGHT
$N_L > 1$	$N_R = 1\ l_R < s$	$N = N_L + 1$	sw =BOTH
$N_L > 1$	$N_R = 1\ l_R = s$	$N = N_L$	sw =LEFT
$N_L = 1\ l_L < s$	$N_R > 1$	$N = N_R + 1$	sw =BOTH
$N_L = 1\ l_L = s$	$N_R > 1$	$N = N_R$	sw =RIGHT
$N_L > 1$	$N_R > 1$	$N = N_L + N_R$	sw =BOTH

Table 2. Propagating accepted change sequences at level i

tree node	left child	right child
$N = 0$	-	-
$N = 1$ sw =LEFT L	$N_L = 1\ L_L = \max\{i, L\}$	$N_R = 0$
$N = 1$ sw =RIGHT L	$N_L = 0$	$N_R = 1\ L_R = \max\{i, L\}$
$N > 1$ sw =LEFT	-	$N_R = 0$
$N > 1$ sw =RIGHT	$N_L = 0$	-
$N > 1$ sw =BOTH	-	-

2.3 The PPM algorithm

PPM improves a given initial partitioning in a number of passes until no further improvement is achieved. In each pass the mincut procedure is applied to every pair of partitions ($P - 1$ simultaneous mincut steps with $P/2$ mincuts each [5], see algorithm 3). Less iterations are required as a better initial partitioning is available. A parallel implementation is given in [2]. If the number of PPM passes is of order $\mathcal{O}(n^{\kappa_0} G^{\kappa_1} P^{\kappa_2})$, the parallel complexity is $\mathcal{O}(n^{\kappa_0+1} G^{\kappa_1+1} P^{\kappa_2+1})$.

3 Experimental Results

Extensive tests with this mapping technique have been conducted in [2]. Here, we summarize the results for an adaptive grid steady Euler solver. This code starts from a given initial grid, partitioned using inertial recursive bisection. The flow is computed with a 4-stage Runge-Kutta time-integration scheme based on a first-order finite volume discretization with van Leer flux vector splitting. Run-time grid refinement is based on the streamwise entropy gradient. The new grid is partitioned by hierarchical inertial recursive bisection [1] (inertial bisection of the largest parts). The grids have $N = 444, 958, 1867, 4506, 11259, 30207$ cells,

Algorithm 3 A mincut step with $P/2$ simultaneous configuration change sequences

procedure mincutstep(P,$\mathcal{S}$,$\mathcal{T}$,Z)
  $p \leftarrow \log_2 P$
  /* *simultaneous construction of configuration change sequences* */
  for all $i = 0, \ldots, 2^{p-1} - 1$ **in parallel**
    $\lambda^{[i]}, \mu^{[i]}, \gamma^{[i]} \leftarrow$ mincut_sequence($P, \mathcal{S}, t_i, Z, \mathcal{T}$)
    $\bar{\lambda}^{[i]}, \bar{\mu}^{[i]}, \bar{\gamma}^{[i]} \leftarrow$ construct_block_change_sequence($\lambda^{[i]}, \mu^{[i]}, \gamma^{[i]}$)
  end for
  /* *select and perform non-interfering subsequences* */
  $\tilde{\lambda}^{[i]} \leftarrow$select_subsequences($\bar{\lambda}$, $\bar{\gamma}$,$\mathcal{T}$)
  for all $i = 0, \ldots, 2^{p-1} - 1$ **in parallel**
    $gain^{[i]} \leftarrow$ apply_subsequences($\tilde{\lambda}^{[i]}$,$\tilde{\mu}^{[i]}$,$\mathcal{S}$)
  end for
  $gain \leftarrow \sum_i gain^{[i]}$
  return gain
end procedure

partitioned in $n = 2, 4, 8, 23, 57, 144$ parts; the task interaction graphs have $G = 1, 2, 4, 10, 9, 11$ respectively. For supersonic flow through a channel, the fourth grid and its partitioning are shown in Fig. 1.

A 4-stage Runge-Kutta time step requires about 2800 flops per cell; let there be n_{inner} internal cells and n_{bdry} cells along the domain boundary of a partition. Communication of 4 numbers is required in each Runge-Kutta stage; let the interface between parts i and j have n_{ij} edges. The weight matrix has $\Lambda_{ii} = 2800(n_{inner} + n_{bdry})$ and $\Lambda_{ij} = 16n_{ij}$.

Fig. 2 shows the value of C_{map} : mappings are good as long as n/P is large enough (cf. change of slope in Fig. 2); if not, load balance is poor. The mapping time for the largest grid was less than 0.07 % of the problem solution time on a 32-processor iPSC/860. The parallel efficiency $\epsilon_p = \frac{T(N,1)}{P \cdot T(N,P)}$ ($T(N, P)$ is the time to perform a time-integration for a problem of size N on P processors) is shown in Fig. 3, reflecting the bad load balance for small n/P.

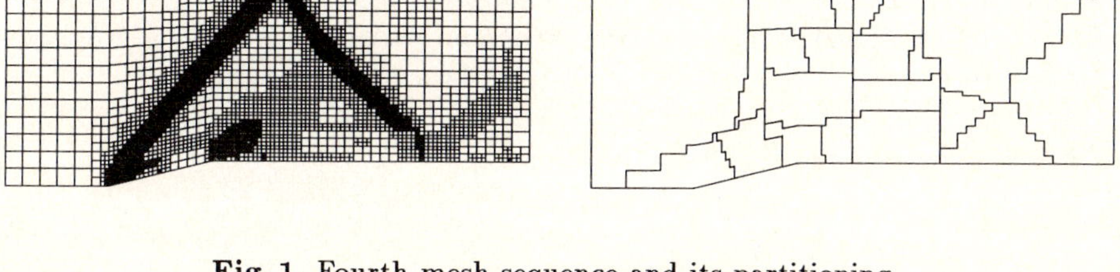

Fig. 1. Fourth mesh sequence and its partitioning

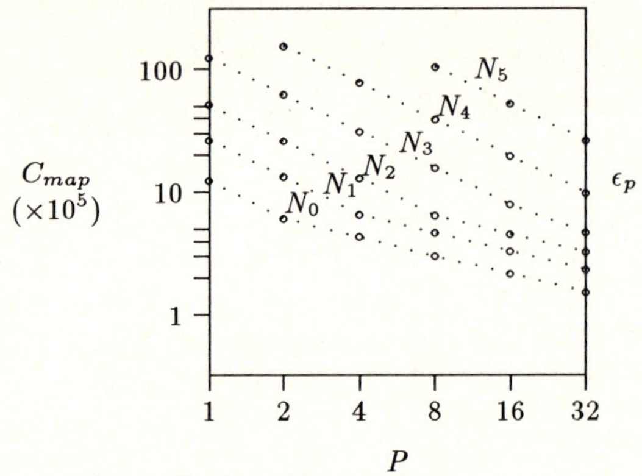

Fig. 2. Single-grid mapping cost

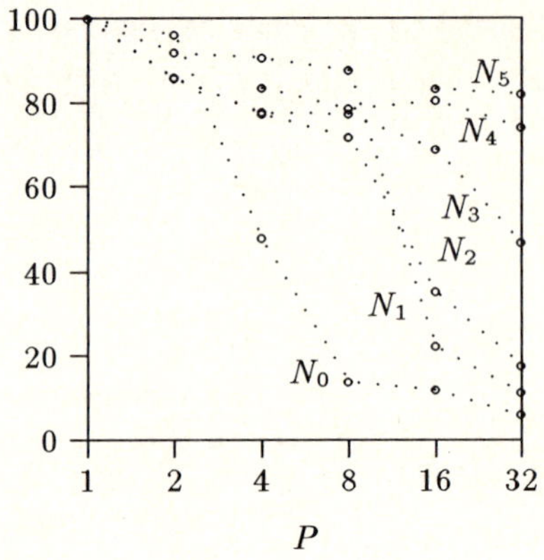

Fig. 3. Single-grid efficiency

4 Conclusion

A Kernighan-Lin mincut variant has been used in conjunction with an algorithm for avoiding interference between simultaneous changes in order to solve the mapping problem. The mappings obtained prove to be of good quality. PPM, PRB and extensions to run-time remapping are discussed extensively in [2].

References

1. J. De Keyser and D. Roose. Incremental mapping for solution-adaptive multigrid hierarchies. In *Proceedings of the Scalable High Performance Computing Conference '92*, pages 401–408. IEEE Computer Society Press, 1992.
2. J. De Keyser and D. Roose. Distributed mapping of SPMD programs with a generalized Kernighan-Lin heuristic. Report TW XYZ, K. U. Leuven, Leuven, Belgium, 1994.
3. B.W. Kernighan and S. Lin. An efficient heuristic procedure for partitioning graphs. *Bell Systems Tech. J.*, 49(2):291–308, 1970.
4. P. Sadayappan, F. Ercal, and J. Ramanujam. Cluster partitioning approaches to mapping parallel programs onto a hypercube. *Parallel Computing*, 13(1):1–16, 1990.
5. P. Sadayappan, F. Ercal, and J. Ramanujam. Parallel graph partitioning on a hypercube. In J. Gustafson, editor, *Proceedings of the 4th Distributed Memory Computing Conference*, pages 67–70. Golden Gate Enterprise, CA, 1990.
6. R. Van Driessche and R. Piessens. Parallel graph partitioning with the Kernighan-Lin heuristic. Report TW 203, K. U. Leuven, Leuven, Belgium, 1994.

Mesh Decomposition and Communication Procedures for Finite Element Applications on the Connection Machine CM-5 System

Zdeněk Johan[1], Kapil K. Mathur[1],
S. Lennart Johnsson[1]* and Thomas J.R. Hughes[2]

[1] Thinking Machines Corporation, 245 First Street, Cambridge, MA 02142, USA
[2] Division of Applied Mechanics, Stanford University, Stanford, CA 94305, USA

Abstract. The objective of this paper is to analyze the impact of data mapping strategies on the performance of finite element applications. First, we describe a parallel mesh decomposition algorithm based on recursive spectral bisection used to partition the mesh into element blocks. A simple heuristic algorithm then renumbers the mesh nodes. Large three-dimensional meshes demonstrate the efficiency of those mapping strategies and assess the performance of a finite element program for fluid dynamics.

1 Introduction

Data distribution is a crucial issue when implementing finite element techniques on distributed-memory parallel computers. Communication between processing nodes can become a bottleneck if the finite element data structures are not carefully mapped to the processing nodes. In order to minimize this bottleneck, we have developed a set of data mapping strategies and implemented them on the Connection Machine CM-5 system. Special library communication routines taking advantage of data locality to reduce data transfer between processing nodes are used to perform the gather and scatter operations found in finite element applications. Decomposition timings for large tetrahedral meshes are presented, as well as the effect of data mapping on the performance of a finite element program for computational fluid dynamics.

2 Data Mapping Strategies

Both elements and nodes of an unstructured mesh are mapped onto the vector units of the CM-5 system. We have designed a two-step procedure which performs these mappings:

1. First, the mesh is decomposed into element blocks made of adjacent elements.

---

* Also affiliated with the Division of Applied Sciences, Harvard University

2. The mesh nodes are then mapped onto the vector units using the mesh partitioning as a criterion for chosing the placement of each node.

The objective of these mappings is to achieve as much locality between the nodes and the elements as possible to minimize data transfer through the CM-5 data network. In order to achieve the best computational load balance possible in the finite element program itself, we constrain the elements and the nodes to be uniformly distributed across the vector units, i.e., all vector units hold the same number of elements (resp. nodes) except for the last one which gets whatever elements (resp. nodes) remain. The implementation of both mapping strategies is done on the CM-5 system itself.

2.1 Mesh Partitioning

The recursive spectral bisection (RSB) algorithm was chosen as the basis of the data mapping strategies described in this paper. The RSB algorithm was proposed by Pothen, Simon and Liou for reordering sparse matrices [1]. Simon then applied it to unstructured mesh partitioning [2]. The RSB algorithm has since found wide acceptance in the scientific community because of the high-quality partitionings it generates.

The RSB algorithm is based on a graph representation of the mesh topology. It is therefore insensitive to regions of highly concentrated elements or to element distorsion. In our implementation, the graph is generated through the *dual mesh connectivity*, which identifies the elements sharing a face with a given element. In this representation, the mesh elements become the graph vertices and the internal faces correspond to the graph edges. The mesh partitioning is performed using an iterative process which decomposes the whole mesh into two partitions, each of which in turn is decomposed into two partitions, and so on. This process ends when there are as many partitions as vector units in the CM-5 configuration considered. Each iteration of the process just described involves several computational steps:

1. Possible disconnections in a partition are identified using a frontal algorithm.
2. The smallest non-zero eigenvalue and its associated eigenvector (also called the *Fiedler vector*) of the Laplacian matrix $\mathbf{L}$, defined as

$$L_{ij} = \begin{cases} -1, & \text{if elements } i \text{ and } j \text{ share a face;} \\ 0, & \text{otherwise.} \end{cases} \tag{1}$$

$$L_{ii} = -\sum_{\substack{j=1 \\ j \neq i}}^{n_{\rm el}} L_{ij} \tag{2}$$

   are computed using the Lanczos algorithm. Each Lanczos step includes three dot-product operations, one matrix-vector product and an eigenanalysis of the tridiagonal matrix generated by the Lanczos process.
3. After convergence of the Lanczos algorithm, the components of the Fiedler vector are ranked, and this ranking is used to reorder the dual mesh connectivity.

4. The graph is then split in two, and this process is repeated on each subgraph.

The RSB algorithm can be computationally intensive since a series of eigenvalue problems have to be solved. In order to keep the partitioning time as small as possible, we have implemented the RSB algorithm on the CM-5 system in a data-parallel fashion. In this implementation, all elements of the mesh are treated in parallel. It implies a two-level parallelization: one level on the partitions generated at a given stage of the decomposition process and the other on the elements in each partition. Most of the resulting code is written in the CM Fortran language [3], except the eigenanalysis of the tridiagonal matrix which is implemented in CDPEAC (a macro-assembler) [4]. Details of the implementation can be found in [5].

2.2 Node Renumbering

Once the elements have been reordered to obtain element blocks, the mesh nodes are renumbered using the following procedure:

1. Each element is assigned the element block number to which it belongs.
2. Each element sends the block number to the nodes it is associated with. Nodes receiving the same block number from their neighboring elements are marked as "interior nodes" and their location code is the block number received. The other nodes are marked as "boundary nodes" and they choose their location code at random from the block numbers they received.
3. Nodes are ranked based on their location code with the constraint of having interior nodes ranked before boundary nodes for the same location code.
4. Nodes are assigned to the vector units based on their location code in the order obtained at Step 3. Since all nodes may not be assigned during this phase because of the load-balance constraint described at the beginning of Section 2, this strategy forces interior nodes to have a greater probability than boundary nodes of being assigned to the same vector unit as the elements they are associated with.
5. Nodes which have not been assigned during Step 4 are distributed among the vector units which still have room left.

This procedure can be easily implemented in a data-parallel fashion, parallelization occuring over the elements for Steps 1 and 2 and over the nodes for Steps 3 through 5.

2.3 Partitioning Example

Both examples presented in this paper have been run in 64-bit arithmetic on a 32-processing node CM-5E system. This system is a prototype used internally at Thinking Machines and has the following hardware characteristics:

1. A processing node running at 39 MHz and composed of a SuperSPARC microprocessor controlling four vector units and 32 Mbytes of memory (which can be upgraded to 128 Mbytes), yielding a peak 64-bit floating-point performance of 156 Mflops/s/pn. Systems shipped to customers will have processing nodes running at 40 MHz.

2. A new network interface chip which can inject larger packets into the data network at a faster rate. The operating system running on the CM-5E at the time we performed the numerical tests (CMOST 7.3 beta 2.9) had the large packet mode disabled.
3. A SPARCstation 2 control processor. Systems shipped to customer sites will have SPARCstation 10 control processors.

The software and hardware restrictions of this CM-5E prototype should have little impact on the performance of the problems presented in this paper.

A tetrahedral mesh of an assembly part composed of 19,793 nodes and 81,649 elements, courtesy of Mark Shephard (Rensselaer Polytechnic Institute), was used as a partitioning illustration (see Fig.1). The graph representation of this mesh has 152,878 edges. The decomposition into 32 subdomains depicted in Fig.2 shows the quality of partitioning. Note that 128 subdomains are actually needed on a 32-node CM-5E, but the resulting picture is too confusing to be shown here. The total cost of partitioning the mesh into 128 subdomains is 24.6 seconds, making the RSB algorithm a competitive strategy for mesh decomposition. At this level of partitioning, there are 10,648 cuts in the graph, which represents 7.0% of the total number of graph edges. Detailed timings based on CM elapsed times (which correspond to the elapsed execution times while the program is not swapped out by the operating system on the processing nodes) are presented in Tables 1 and 2. Figure 3 presents the cost of the RSB algorithm as the bisection procedure progresses. The $O(\log_2(\text{no. of partitions}))$ cost seen in this figure is due to the two-level parallelization of the RSB algorithm. The time spent renumbering the nodes using the algorithm presented in Section 2.2 is 0.2 seconds.

Table 1. Assembly part. CM elapsed times for different parts of the RSB algorithm for a partitioning into 128 subdomains on a 32-node CM-5E system.

	Timings	Percentage
ident. of connected blocks	5.7 s	23.2%
comp. of Fiedler vector	16.8 s	68.3%
data ranking/reordering	1.3 s	5.3%
miscellaneous	0.8 s	3.2%
Total	24.6 s	100.0%

Table 2. Assembly part. Cost analysis for the computation of the Fiedler vector.

	Timings	Percentage
matrix-vector products	8.2 s	48.8%
dot-products	3.7 s	22.0%
eigenanalyses	1.5 s	8.9%
SAXPYs and miscellaneous	3.4 s	20.3%
Total	16.8 s	100.0%

3 Fluid Dynamics Application

We have implemented in CM Fortran a finite element program for solving the compressible Euler and Navier-Stokes equations [6,7]. It is based on the Galerkin/least-squares formulation proposed by Hughes et al. [8] and Johnson et al. [9]. In the case of steady flow computations, an implicit time-marching scheme is used to reach steady-state. A preconditioned matrix-free GMRES algorithm is employed to solve the nonsymmetric systems of equations arising from the finite element discretization. The gather and scatter operations are performed using special communication procedures available from the Connection Machine Scientific Software Library [10].

To illustrate the performance improvements achieved by proper data mappings, we have computed the inviscid flow around a Falcon Jet flying at Mach 0.85 and at an angle of attack of 1 degree on a 32-node CM-5E system. The mesh, courtesy of Dassault Aviation, has 19,417 nodes and 109,914 tetrahedra (see Fig.4 for a view of the surface mesh on the airplane). A one-point integration rule was used on the elements. A freestream uniform flow was chosen as initial condition, and the solver was marched 50 time steps at a CFL number of 10, which was sufficient to reach steady-state. Two computations were performed successively using the following mapping strategies (referred to as Strategy 1 and Strategy 2, respectively):

1. Random mapping of elements and nodes to the processing nodes.
2. Mapping of elements and nodes according to the procedures described in Section 2.

Timings for the data mapping and the finite element solver (which is a series of gather/compute/scatter cycles) are given in Table 3. This example shows that proper mapping can improve overall speed of the program by more than a factor of two, even if the partitioning time is included in the total time. In the case of Strategy 2, the computation part of the solver achieves 39.5 Mflops/s/pn. The gather and scatter operations yield bandwidths of 24.7 Mbytes/s/pn and 20.0 MBytes/s/pn, respectively. The overall performance of the finite element solver is 1.0 Gflops/s, which is 20% of the peak hardware performance. Substantial computational efficiency can therefore be achieved on distributed-memory computers for finite element applications as long as a careful mapping of the data structures is performed.

Table 3. Falcon Jet. CM elapsed times for different parts of the finite element program run on a 32-node CM-5E system.

	Strategy 1	Strategy 2
data mapping	—	35 s
gather operations	202 s	17 s
computations	180 s	177 s
scatter operations	234 s	26 s
Total time	10 min 16 s	4 min 15 s

References

1. Pothen, A., Simon, H.D., and Liou, K.-P.: Partitioning sparse matrices with eigenvectors of graphs. SIAM J. Matrix Anal. Appl. **11** (1990) 430–452
2. Simon, H.D.: Partitioning of unstructured problems for parallel processing. Comput. Systems Engrg. **2** (1991) 135–148
3. CM Fortran Language Reference Manual, Version 2.1 (Thinking Machines Corporation, 1994)
4. VU Programmer's Handbook, CMOST Version 7.2 (Thinking Machines Corporation, 1993)
5. Johan, Z., Mathur, K.K., Johnsson, S.L., and Hughes, T.J.R.: An efficient communication strategy for finite element methods on the Connection Machine CM-5 system. Comput. Methods Appl. Mech. Engrg. (in press)
6. Shakib, F., Hughes, T.J.R., and Johan, Z.: A new finite element formulation for computational fluid dynamics: X. The compressible Euler and Navier-Stokes equations. Comput. Methods Appl. Mech. Engrg. **89** (1991) 141–219
7. Johan, Z., Hughes, T.J.R., Mathur, K.K., and Johnsson, S.L.: A data parallel finite element method for computational fluid dynamics on the Connection Machine system. Comput. Methods Appl. Mech. Engrg. **99** (1992) 113–134
8. Hughes, T.J.R., Franca, L.P., and Hulbert, G.M.: A new finite element formulation for computational fluid dynamics: VIII. The Galerkin/least-squares method for advective-diffusive equations. Comput. Methods Appl. Mech. Engrg. **73** (1989) 173–189
9. Johnson, C., Szepessy, A., and Hansbo, P.: On the convergence of shock-capturing streamline diffusion finite element methods for hyperbolic conservation laws. Math. Comp. **54** (1990) 107–129
10. CMSSL for CM Fortran: CM-5 Edition, Version 3.1 (Thinking Machines Corporation, 1993)

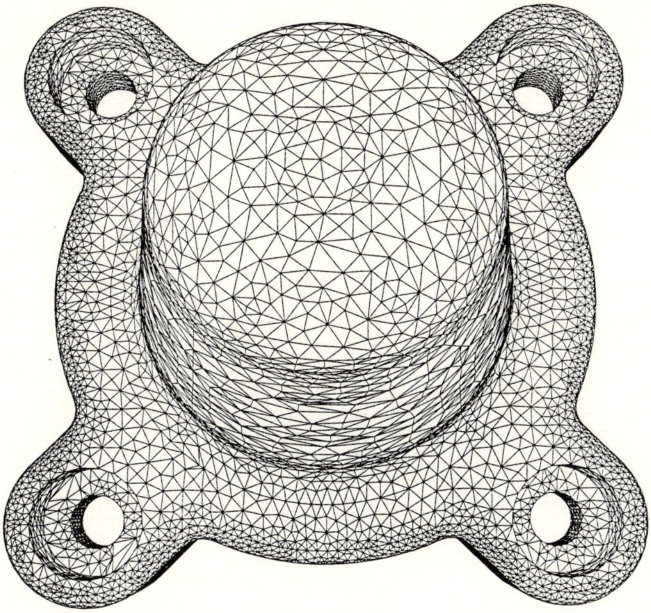

Fig. 1. Assembly part. View of the surface mesh.

Fig. 2. Assembly part. Decomposition into 32 partitions.

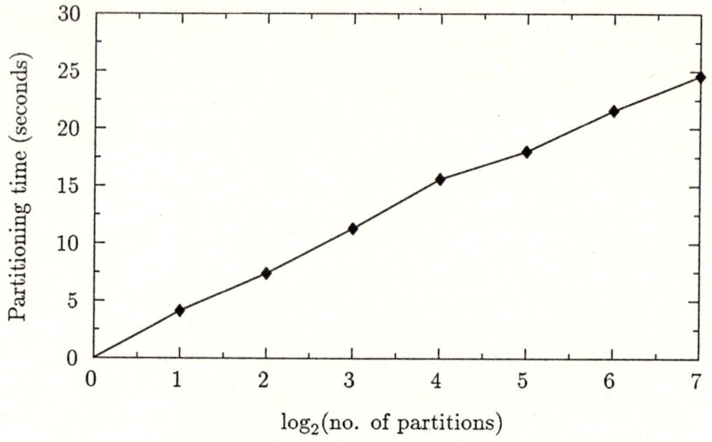

Fig. 3. Assembly part. Partitioning cost as a function of recursive bisection on a 32-node CM-5E.

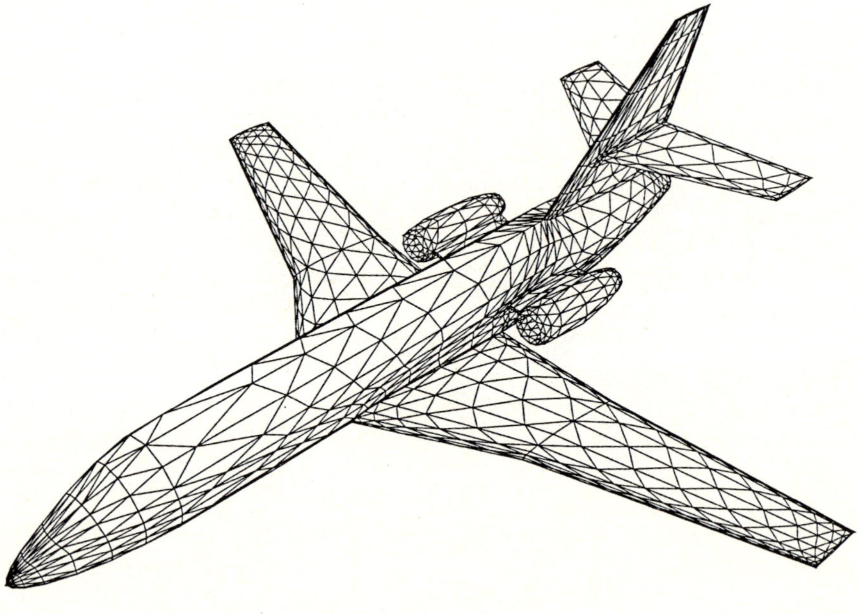

Fig. 4. Falcon Jet. View of surface mesh.

CAPTools - semiautomatic parallelisation of mesh based computational mechanics codes

M.Cross, C.S.Ierotheou, S.P.Johnson and P.F.Leggett

Parallel Processing Research Group, University of Greenwich, London SE18 6PF, UK

Abstract. An overview of a suite of Computer Aided Parallelisation Tools (CAPTools) is presented for the parallelisation of FORTRAN based structured mesh computational mechanics codes. In recognition of the limitations of automatic compilers, CAPTools is a semiautomatic, interactive system which embeds user supplied knowledge into its detailed dependence analysis. Applying the decomposition paradigm, then the addition of masks and communication calls yields generic parallel source code for a DMS.

1 Introduction

Despite the attractive performance measures of distributed memory systems (DMS) they have not had the impact on the HPC community that might have been anticipated. The main reason for the slow take-up of parallel technology has been the difficulty of implementing existing codes on such systems efficiently. This effort has been fraught with difficulty and the task of implementing and testing a parallelisation strategy was a tedious and error prone task.

In an ideal world the implementation of software on a parallel system would require no more effort than is currently required on a conventional scalar system. In the past decade a number of research programmes have pursued the concept of parallelisation compilers; the most notable examples include - Paraphrase, a multi-pass paralleliser developed by Kuck et al [1]; The KAP paralleliser [2] using the theory of dependence analysis and its application to parallel code generation; Parallel Fortran Converter (PFC) developed by Kennedy et al [3] and work on the SUPERB compiler by Zima et al [4].

Parallel compilers based upon the above research are very powerful in some respects and extremely restricted in others. The core of any parallelising compiler is the dependence analysis and many decisions in the analysis involve a knowledge of program variables, about which no information is explicitly available. As such, this results in the conservative assumption of a data dependence which could influence adversely the quality of the consequent parallel version. New parallel languages may smooth the route to parallel software; unfortunately, it does not relieve the programmer from many of the tasks involved in the development and implementation of parallelisation strategies. Moreover, new languages do not help the vast scientific/engineering community with a huge array of existing FORTRAN software.

The alternative to full parallelising compilers or new languages is to use a set of tools to assist and, as far as is practical, to automate the parallelisation process. Recently, the FORGE90 parallelisation analysis system has been launched. The effectiveness of FORGE90 is based on the power of its analysis. Its current version is constrained in a number of ways. For example, its DMS parallelisation is based on localised loops with independent data decompositions, and little communications optimisations. CAPTools (Computer Aided Parallelisation Tools) is also based on the fact that the process of code parallelisation can not, in general, be fully automated [5,6,7,8,9,10]. Information from the programmer is vital during the process of parallelisation and, therefore, a dialogue is an essential component. At the heart of CAPTools is a very sophisticated interprocedural dependence analysis based upon advanced symbolic algebra techniques, combined with a powerful inference engine to elicit and embed user supplied information in the knowledge base. It is the dependence analysis which enables the generation of high quality parallel codes which are almost as efficient as any hand parallelisation.

2 Overview of CAPTools Structure

The main aims of CAPTools are the following:-

- No end-user knowledge of parallel execution.
- Parallelise the **entire** code, not just the solver.
- There should be no loss in efficiency in using CAPTools as opposed to a manual parallelisation.
- There is a need for essential user input to assist in the parallelisation.
- The generated parallel code should be generic and similar to the serial code.

Figure 1 shows an overview of the structure of CAPTools. The main components of the tools comprise:-

- Detailed control and dependence analysis.
- User specification of a parallelisation strategy.
- Automatic insertion of parallel control and dataflow structures.
- Automatic adaption of serial code to produce parallel code.
- Code optimisations e.g. loop splitting, loop interchanging, etc.

Although CAPTools is designed for any application, it is currently used in the field of computational mechanics. The current version uses a mesh decomposition for both structured and unstructured meshes, and the code generated is for a DMS.

2.1 Summary of Dependence Analysis

The dependence analysis can be as basic or as extensive as the paralleliser desires. The options available are:- To perform symbolic variable equality tests; Perform tests to set the exact dependence attribute to dependencies; A full interprocedural analysis to transfer information across routine boundaries; Use of the symbolic inequality disproof algorithm together with knowledge provided from the user, extracted from the control flow and assumed as part of the extended Banerjee test; Use the inference engine to exploit more complex knowledge from the control flow etc; Trace variables through conditional assignments.

The MPI Standard for Message Passing *

Rolf Hempel

GMD (German National Research Centre for Computer Science), Postfach 1316, 53731 Sankt Augustin, Germany

Abstract. The growing number of different message–passing interfaces make it difficult to port an application program from one parallel computer to another. This is a major problem in parallel computing. The open MPI forum has developed a *de facto* message–passing interface standard which was finalized in the first quarter of 1994. All major parallel machine manufacturers were involved in the process, and the first implementations are already available.
This article gives an overview of the MPI initiative. The main aspects of the standard are presented, with emphasis on those features which go beyond current practice.

Introduction

Message passing is the most efficient and most general programming paradigm currently used on parallel machines with distributed memory. In the absence of a message passing standard the broad variety of vendor–specific interfaces inhibits the portability of application programs. As the developers of large software packages cannot afford to write machine dependent code, the missing portability is a major hindrance in the development of parallel computing.

In 1992 the international initiative MPI (Message Passing Interface) was started by the Center for Research in Parallel Computing at Rice University and Oak Ridge National Laboratory [3, 1]. The goal is to define a message passing interface which then will be implemented and supported by all hardware manufacturers. This way a *de facto* standard would be established, and the bureaucratic overhead and the delays associated with an official standardization process could be avoided.

The organization of the MPI process follows closely that of the HPF forum. In particular it is open to everybody, and voting rules are democratic. Most of the discussions go on via email, but the decisions are made at regular meetings, which during 1993 were held every six weeks at Dallas. The result of this first phase of MPI is a preliminary standards document [4] which was presented during the Supercomputing Conference 93 in Portland, Oregon, in November 1993.

In January 1994 the first European MPI meeting was held at INRIA Sophia Antipolis, France. It was combined with a workshop which gave European users

* This work was supported by the Commission of the European Community through Esprit project P6643 (PPPE)

the opportunity to learn about MPI and to give their comments on the current draft standard. The resulting requests for changes were then discussed in the MPI committee. This led to final changes to the draft at a meeting in the USA in February.

This paper presents the basic features of MPI, and discusses how they can be used in application programs.

Overview of MPI

MPI is intended to be the standard message passing interface for high–level applications and parallel libraries. It was not the design goal to support low–level features to be used by parallelizing compilers. The focus of MPI is the point–to–point communication between pairs of processes, and collective communication within process groups. More advanced concepts allow creating those groups, and giving them topological structure.

On the other hand, apart from a basic SPMD process model, no provision is made for dynamic process creation. Other important features like parallel I/O are not yet included in MPI, because the committee felt that those concepts are not mature enough for standardization, or that there was not enough time available during the first MPI phase. It is the intention of the MPI forum to cover those topics in a second phase, MPI–2, which will probably begin in the second half of 1994.

Among the major problems in the MPI process was the growing number of functions in the interface. On one hand, the definitions must be flexible enough to handle efficiently all kinds of applications on very diverse hardware platforms. If, on the other hand, the interface becomes too complicated, users will be deterred from using it. The solution followed by MPI is the organization of the interface functions in two layers. The high–level functions look similar to commonly used message–passing libraries. Thus, a change from such an interface to MPI is expected to be relatively easy. This MPI level is intended for the regular user.

The low–level functions make the whole MPI functionality available to the expert user. Parallel library writers, for example, can optimize the efficiency of their routines using low–level communication functions. In this case the investment of additional programming work can be amortized by freqent reuse of the library.

Groups, Contexts, and Communicators

A group in MPI is an ordered set of processes, each of which is assigned a rank within the group. The initial group contains all processes. Group manipulation functions can be used to dynamically create subgroups, or to build unions of groups.

Communication contexts allow the insulation of the message traffic in different parts of an application. In this way the messages sent within a parallel library routine, for example, cannot be intercepted inadvertently by a receive in the user code.

A communicator is a combination of a process group and a context. It defines the scope of a communication operation. In a point–to–point operation the destination is defined by the communicator together with the rank of the target process within the associated group. In a collective operation all processes of the process group participate in its execution.

Point–to–Point Communication

Sending and receiving a single message between two processes is the basic communication mechanism in MPI. Messages are identified by an integer tag, which may be wildcarded on a receive. Three semantically different send/receive mechanisms are available:

- asynchronous type: MPI_SEND/MPI_RECV. This is the basic pair of communication functions which best reflects current programming practice. The sender process is blocked only until the send buffer can be reused without altering the content of the message. The receiver process is blocked until the message has been completely received. Since the system may copy the outgoing message into system space before delivering it to the receiver, this send/receive pair does not guarantee a synchronization point between the sender and receiver processes.
- synchronous type: MPI_SSEND/MPI_SRECV. No system buffering is necessary in this case. The sender process waits until the receiver issues the corresponding receive. Then the message is transferred without additional copying. It depends on the application whether the obviated memory copy outweighs the time lost by synchronization. This type of communication is what users from the Transputer world are most acquainted with, and, in fact, this feature was brought into the standard by the British MPI participants.
- ready–receive type: This last option can only be used if the sender process knows that the receiver has already posted a matching receive. Therefore, it should be applied with special care. The advantage is that the system can use a simplified communication protocol. The data can be transferred immediately without a preceeding handshake between sender and receiver. This feature has been introduced by Intel for their Touchstone Delta and Paragon computers, and users claim to save up to 20 percent communication time.

Orthogonally to the three options the send/receive can be chosen to be blocking or non–blocking. In the blocking case, the send buffer can be reused immediately after the user process regains control. On the receiver side, the buffer contains the complete message on return from the receive function.

The non–blocking variants only start the send/receive in the background, and the user process continues immediately. At that point it is not safe, however, to reuse the send buffer, because the data may not yet have been copied.

Similarly, the receive buffer may not yet contain the message. The completion of the communication operation can be interrogated or waited for by use of additional functions. The non–blocking functions allow overlapping local computations with communication. This is particularly useful if the hardware contains dedicated communication processors.

A very general construction mechanism allows complicated message structures to be defined to MPI. Thus, in most cases it is not necessary to copy the message contents into contiguous memory before a send.

Collective Communication

All processes in a process group are involved in a collective communication operation. A collective function must be called as if it contained a group synchronization, but this property is not guaranteed. The available functions are summarized in Tab. 1.

Table 1. Summary of the most important MPI collective communication functions

Function	Description
MPI_BARRIER	Synchronization of all processes within a group
MPI_GATHER	Each process sends a message to a "root" process, which stores the messages in rank order
MPI_SCATTER	Inverse operation to MPI_GATHER. The send buffer of the root process contains a message section for each process in the group. Every process receives its section.
MPI_REDUCE	Performs a reduction operation over all group processes. The operation can be selected from a set of predefined arithmetic and logical operators. Alternatively, the user can define their own reduction function (MPI_USER_REDUCE).
MPI_SCAN	Parallel prefix operation. The operation returns in process with rank `i` the reduction of the values in the send buffers of processes with ranks `0` ... `i-1`. The possible operation types are the same as for MPI_REDUCE

Process Topologies

Many numerical applications have a geometrical background. For example, the parallelization of a PDE solver on a three–dimensional grid leads to a corresponding arrangement of the processes. The most natural way of addressing those processes is to specify their coordinates in the grid, as opposed to their linear ranks in the group. Also, a collective shift operation is only meaningful in conjunction with a topological process structure. Similar as in the PARMACS interface [5], MPI supports the setup of general Cartesian process structures, as well as arbitrary process graphs [2].

Process topologies in MPI are assigned to process groups. Process ranks in a group are ordered by topology locations. Topologies are created and deleted at run–time, and a process can be in more than one topology at the same time. Often a group has to be split into subgroups along coordinate lines in a Cartesian topology. An example for using the MPI function MPI_CART_SUB is the creation of row or column subgroups in a two–dimensional process grid. Since group boundaries limit the scope of collective operations, those subgroups can be used to limit operations like broadcast to all processes in the same matrix column.

As an example for the general graph case, the left picture in Fig. 1 shows the geometry of a fluid flow problem around an airfoil. The parallelization is done by domain splitting, each resulting subdomain being assigned to a process. The right picture shows the abstract process structure. Graph edges connect neighboring processes.

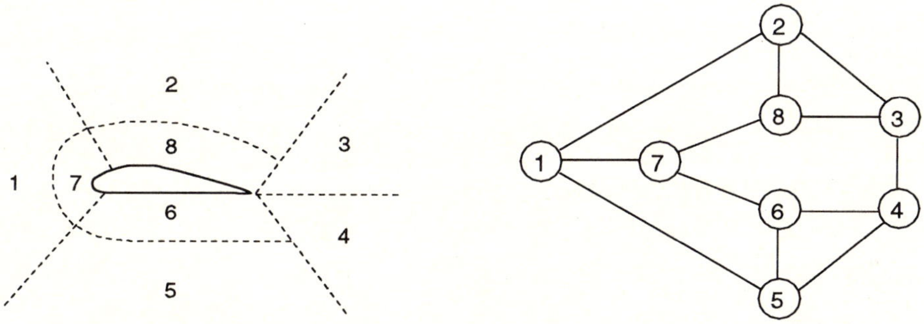

Fig. 1. Block structured domain around an airfoil, and the induced process topology

As a consequence of the locality principle of PDE applications, a process in the graph topology tends to exchange most messages with its direct neighbors. Thus, the topology information can be used by an MPI implementation to minimize the message traffic by placing those processes onto neighboring hardware processors.

References

1. Walker, D.: Standards for Message Passing in a Distributed Memory Environment. Tech. Rep. TM-12147, Oak Ridge National Laboratory, August 1992
2. Hempel, R.: A Proposal for Virtual Topologies in MPI1. Tech. Rep., GMD, November 1992

3. Dongarra, J., Hempel, R., Hey, A., Walker, D.: A Proposal for a User-Level, Message Passing Interface in a Distributed Memory Environment. Tech. Rep. TM-12231, Oak Ridge National Laboratory, February 1993
4. The MPI Forum: MPI: A Standard Message–Passing Interface. Tech. Rep., The University of Tennessee at Knoxville, November 1993
5. Calkin, R., Hempel, R., Hoppe, H.-C., Wypior, P.: Portable Programming with the PARMACS Message–Passing Library. Special Issue on Message–Passing Interfaces, Par. Comp. (1994), to appear

A Comparison of the Iserver-Occam, Parix, Express, and PVM Programming Environments on a Parsytec GCel

P.M.A. Sloot, A.G. Hoekstra, and L.O. Hertzberger

Parallel Scientific Computing & Simulation Group, Department of Computer Systems, Faculty of Mathematics and Computer Science, University of Amsterdam, Kruislaan 403, 1098 SJ Amsterdam, the Netherlands, tel.:3120-5257463, fax.: 3120-5257490, email: peterslo@fwi.uva.nl

Abstract

We compare the Iserver-Occam, Parix, PVM, and Express parallel programming environments on a Parsytec GCel with 512 T805 transputers. The comparison will be made by a detailed analysis of the performance of one particular application. In our approach we start with this application and isolate the basic (environment dependent) building blocks. These basic building blocks, which depend on floating point performance and communication capabilities of the environments, are analysed independently. We have measured point to point communication times, global communication times and floating point performance. All information will be combined into a time complexity analysis, allowing us to compare the environments on all relevant degrees of functionality. Together with demands for portability of the code, and development time (i.e. programmability), an overall judgement of the environments can be made.

1 Introduction

Real success of Massively Parallel Processing critically depends on programmability of the parallel computers and on portability of parallel programs. We are made to believe that "parallel computing has come to age". Although it is safe to say that parallel hardware has reached a convincing stage of maturity, both programmability of the parallel hardware and portability of parallel programs still pose serious problems to developers of parallel applications.

Today, an application programmer is usually faced with a situation as drawn in figure 1. A parallel computing platform supports native environments, which allow very low level programming, or allow a more abstract view of the hardware. Furthermore, generic environments, also available on other platforms, can be used.

These environments can be grouped in order of decreasing hardware visibility and increasing portability. Of course, one expects that the price to be paid for portability is a decrease of control of the hardware and associated degradation of performance.

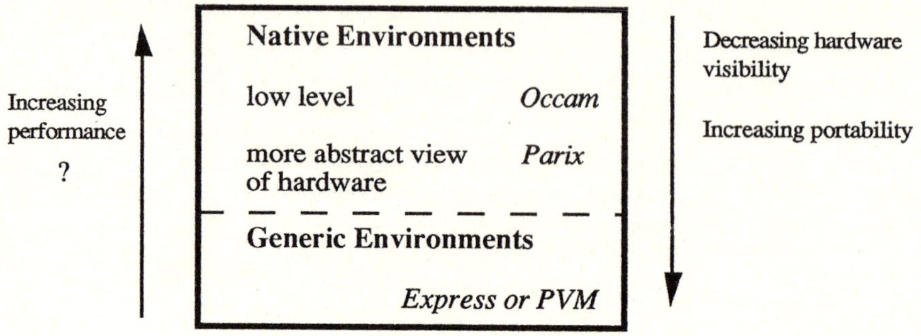

Fig. 1. a typical situation encountered by application programmers of parallel systems.

In this paper we will compare two native environments, Iserver-Occam [1] and Parix [2], with two generic environments, Express [3] and PVM [4]. All experiments are executed on the Parsytec GCel. As part of a contract with Genias, Sloot et al. ported PVM to the GCel [5].

Our experiments allows us to judge the trade-off which clearly exists between native environments, usually offering a better performance at the price of extensive programming effort, and generic environments which allow to develop more portable programs. In this paper we will briefly describe our methodology and summarise the most important results. Reference [6], chapter 6 contains further details.

As a representative case study we have implemented, in the four environments, an application from Physics: Elastic Light Scattering simulations using the Coupled Dipole method [6, 7, 8]. This application is a real application (in the sense that it is used for actual production), the time complexity of the program is predictable, it contains global communication routines, and it does not exhibit (severe) load imbalance.

The run time of the parallel Coupled Dipole implementation is determined by the floating point performance τ_{calc}, i.e. the time to perform a floating point operation, and global communication times (specifically a vector gather operation). In the Iserver-Occam and Parix implementation the global routines are explicitly implemented using (nearest neighbour) point to point communications. In Express and PVM we rely on the available global communication routines. In order to compare the environments we have measured floating point performance, basic communication routines, global communication routines and finally the execution time of the parallel Coupled Dipole method.

6 References

1] Inmos Ltd, *OCCAM® 2 Reference Manual* (Prentice Hall, 1988).

2] Parsytec, "The PARIX programming environment," In *Transputer Systems - ongoing research* (IOS Press, A. Allen Ed., pp. 218-230, Amsterdam, Oxford, Washington, Tokyo, 1992).

3] J. Flower and A. Kolawa, "A packet history of message passing systems," Physics Reports **207**, 291-304 (1991).

4] J. Dongarra, G.A. Geist, R. Manchek, and V.S. Sundaram, "Integrated PVM Framework Supports Heterogeneous Network Computing," Computers in Physics 7, 166-175 (1993).

5] P.M.A. Sloot, for more information, please send email to peterslo@fwi.uva.nl.

6] A.G. Hoekstra, "Computer Simulation of Elastic Light Scattering: Implementation and Applications", Ph.D. thesis, University of Amsterdam, the Netherlands, 1994.

7] A.G. Hoekstra and P.M.A. Sloot, "New Computational Techniques to Simulate Light Scattering from Arbitrary Particles," in *Proceedings of the 3rd International Congress on Optical Particle Sizing '93 - Yokohama*, Ed. M. Maeda, 1993, pp. 167-172.

8] A.G. Hoekstra and P.M.A. Sloot, "Simulating Elastic Light Scattering Using High Performance Computing Techniques," in *European Simulation Symposium 1993*, Ed. A. Verbraeck and E.J.H. Kerckhoffs, Society for Computer Simulation International, 1993, pp. 462-470.

Message-Passing-Systems on Workstation Clusters and Parallel Computers - The Impact of Software- and Network-Architectures on Applications

Michael Resch, Alfred Geiger, Jörg Zikeli

RUS,

Allmandring 30, D-70550 Stuttgart,

e-mail: resch@rus.uni-stuttgart.de, geiger@rus.uni-stuttgart.de, zikeli@rus.uni-stuttgart.de

Abstract. Parallel computer systems have reached a share of interest that is already far beyond the sacred halls of universities and research laboratories. The amount of performance delivered today theoretically allows for the tackling of so called grand challenge problems. But there is still the software-gap that keeps us from fully exploiting the performance of such systems.

Message-passing has become the most popular programming-paradigm to overcome this problem. One hardware-approach that is driving the development of parallel systems and parallel software is clusters of workstations. Being available nearly everywhere, they offer the opportunity to get parallel performance without additional costs.

1 Introduction

One way of closing the software-gap is by completely redesigning the physical and mathematical models and thus completely rewriting the codes. However, there is the large amount of available serial code and the high costs in terms of money and terms of time for a complete redesign. Also there is an inherent contradiction between optimisation for a specific hardware and portability. Due to the short hardware and long software innovation-cycles portability is a very critical issue.

So what is needed to make parallel systems work is a migration path from serial computing to parallel computing on the one hand and some sort of interface that hides the underlying architecture thus allowing a less experienced user still to get some performance out of the machine on the other hand.

The most important programming-models for a migration path as described above today are the Data Parallel model (e.g. HPF), Message-Passing (MP) and the arising Shared Virtual Memory (SVM). All these rely to a certain extent on the exchange of messages - either explicitely by the user or by the system and hidden from the user.

2 Message-Passing-Systems

We concentrate on message-passing as the explicit handling of messages by the user. The reasons for this are portability issues to a very broad range of different hardware-platforms.

SVM and Data-Parallel models are consumer-driven models and therefore have very hard needs concerning the communication-speed and latency. Message-passing however is a producer-driven model and therefore allows it to a skilled user to have an arbitrary amount of overlap between communication and computation. By this, good results can already be achieved on very low-cost hardware like clusters. The paper concentrates on three well-known message-passing interfaces which have a different nature, but are usable on a broad variety of hardware.

- PVM (Parallel Virtual Machine) from ORNL [1] has become a secret standard for message-passing systems. Since it is freely available, it has spread all over the academic community and beyond. PVM has been ported to a big variety of currently available machines ranging from workstations to MPP-systems. The highlight of PVM is its usability in heterogenous environments. However, its functionality is limited.
  Due to its wide spreading, hardware vendors of parallel machines have implemented specially designed versions of PVM intended to better exploit their hardware-architectures.
  PVM/6000 (PVM6K) is a message-passing system specially designed for IBM Power parallel systems and IBM RISC System/6000 clusters [2]. It is able to take full advantage of fast networks for workstation clusters. Furthermore, PVM6K does not use TCP/IP to exchange data like PVM does but, instead, goes directly to the lowest network layers.
  The native message-passing-system of the Cray T3D is from the user's view an extended version of PVM. The implementation however is in no relationship at all with the standard version of PVM. The extensions of Cray-PVM consist of communication-mechanisms which were added to the traditional mailbox model of PVM. Most important are channel-oriented communication (similar to Transputer-based systems) and one-sided puts and gets to and from the memory of other nodes (SM-MP). These features are possible on the T3D because of it's unique hardware synchronisation mechanisms.
- NX from Intel [3] is an example of a formerly native message-passing system specially designed for Intel's massively parallel systems. It offers a broad range of features and makes advantageous use of the hardware it was designed for. Because of its high functionality and maturity it was recently ported to Meiko systems and several workstation platforms [4] thus allowing its use on clusters of workstations too. This enables cheaper development and testing phases.
- MPI (Message-Passing Interface) [5] currently under discussion by the Message-Passing Interface Forum (MPIF) is intended basically to become the standard for message-passing. It is much more flexible than PVM and NX and several vendors are in the process of implementing message-passing tools based on the currently available draft. MPI aims to allow for a unique message-passing interface for the user on all parallel systems. The first implementations of a subset for RS6K are already available [6].

3 Parallel platforms

Message-passing on three parallel hardware architectures was investigated.

- In a joint project of IBM, DLR, RUS and a Special Research Project about "High Temperature Problems of Re-Usable Space Transportation Systems" at the University of Stuttgart, a cluster of 6 IBM RS/6000-550 was installed called PARIS (PArallel RISc). Each of the machines has 128 MB main memory and 1 GB disk space. Only one of the machines allows user login while the others may only be used as additional nodes in a dedicated message-passing environment. All the machines in the cluster are connected via both Ethernet (10 Mb/s) and FDDI (100 Mb/s). Additionally three of them are connected via a special high speed point-to-point interconnect network SOCC (Serial Optical Channel Converter, 225 Mb/s) from IBM.

  A special issue with clusters is, that the interconnection networks are almost standard LANs. The main problem for this approach ist the lack of scalability, the loose coupling of the machines and the lack of software tools. If the message-passing interface sits on top of standard protocols, there is an additional software layer between the application-code and the hardware which leads to longer paths and therefore higher latencies. We present an analysis of latency and bandwidth for the three message-passing systems PVM, NX and MPI. The effects of special protocols are analyzed with the example of PVM/6000.
- The Paragon XP-S we use at Stuttgart consists of 4 service nodes and 72 compute nodes (i860XP) connected via a scalable high-speed network. Each compute node has 32 MB of main memory. The interconnection-network has the form of a 2-D-mesh, the intersection-points of which are formed by mesh-routing-chips with switching times in the range of 10ns. Each router is connected to its four neighbours and one compute-node with a bidirectional link of 200 MByte/s in each direction.
- The Cray-T3D, to which we have external access, has the architecture of a 3-D-torus. The bandwidth of each link in this machine is 300 MByte/s and each node consists of two processing-elements gaining their power from DEC alphas. Global sychronisation mechanisms allow for latencies, which are orders of magnitudes below those of machines without this feature.

4 Latency and Bandwidth

Basic measurements for latency and bandwidth were done for the architectures and message-passing systems described above to give an impression on the performance of message-passing for the user. Testing was done using a standard ping-pong example for varying sizes of messages.

	enc/route	enc/direct	noenc/route	noenc/direct
latency (μsec)	4825	1875	4590	1920
bandwidth (MB/sec)	0.34	0.5	0.5	1.0

For the PARIS-cluster the impact of different communication parameters of PVM was tested. The user may choose whether to encode (enc) or not encode (noenc) data before sending them. One may furthermore decide about the routing of the message. Messages may either be routed via the PVM-demon (route) or may be sent directly from task to task (direct). Results for Ethernet are given in the table above.

For a homogenous hardware environment as treated here data encoding is of no importance. Encoding of data typically takes about 0.5μsec per byte on an RS/6000-550. For detailed information see [7]. To use a direct task-to-task connection instead of making use of the PVM-demon normally doubles the performance of message-passing as can be seen from the table. This is also true for FDDI and SOCC.

Table 2 shows the impact of different networks in the PARIS-cluster. Performance figures are given for different message-passing systems. The comparison shows results for Ethernet, FDDI and SOCC. Values are without data encoding using direct routing.

Network	Ethernet			FDDI		SOCC	
MP-System	PVM	NX	MPI	PVM3	PVM6K	PVM3	PVM6K
latency (μsec)	1920	99000	2500	1850	960	1700	535
bandwidth (MB/sec)	1.0	0.9	0.26	2.6	5.9	2.8	9.3

The specially designed PVM6K is able to exploit the performance of FDDI and SOCC to an acceptable extent. PVM3, NX and the available early implementations of MPI do not take care of the underlying hardware and thus do not yield satisfying results for latency and bandwidth in the benchmark tests. The following figure shows bandwidth for varying message sizes.

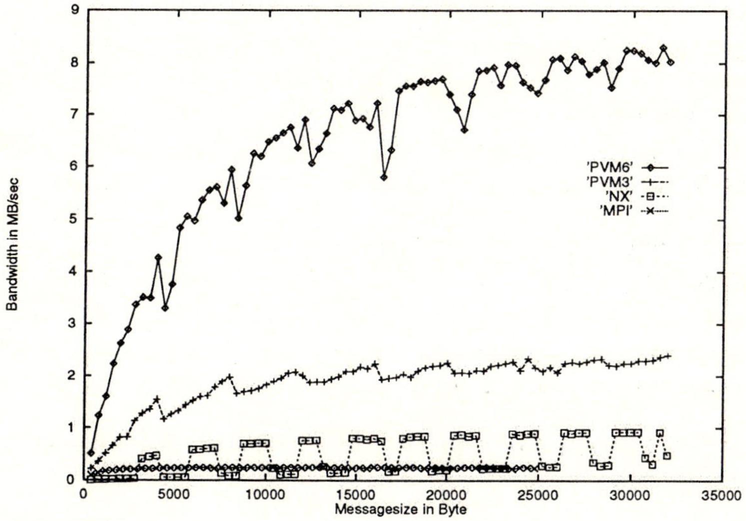

One goal of the study was to compare specially designed software and standard software. The next table summarizes results for different hardware and message-passing systems.

Hardware	RS6K		PARAGON		CRAY T3D	
MP-System	PVM3	PVM6K	PVM3	NX	Cray-PVM	SM-MP
latency (μsec)	1700	535	750	160	84	3
bandwidth (MB/sec)	2.8	9.3	2.4	65	34.8	98.5

A comparison of the best message-passing system for each of the three different parallel hardware architectures is shown in the next figure.

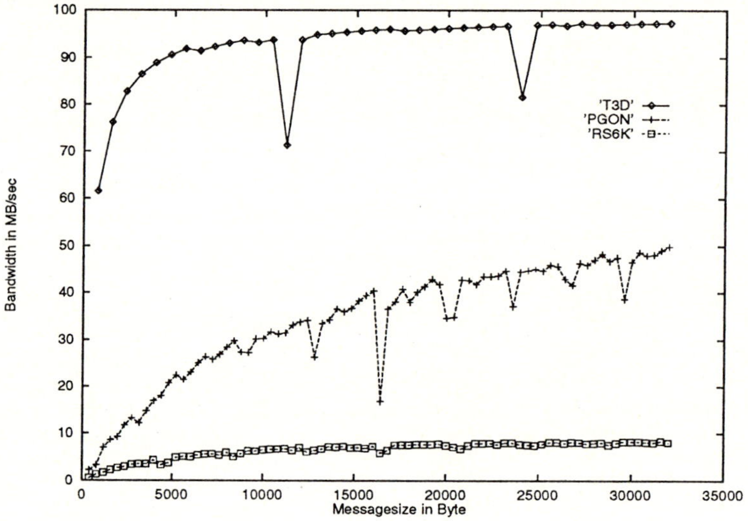

5 Applications

5.1 Multigrid

This example is a model of an application-kernel typical for modern multi-level algorithms: The solution of a 2-D Poisson-equation with a standard multigrid method. It puts extreme stress to parallel systems for the following reasons:

- Only one and also a very simple differential equation leads to a very small amount of work per gridpoint and therefore a very bad communication to computation-ratio in domain-decomposition.
- Most work is done on the coarser grid-levels, decreasing vector lengths on the single PEs and also leading to a higher surface to volume ratio per domain.

The intention of this example is to find out whether workstation-clusters and parallel-systems with low communication-performance are suited to modern algorithms with low numerical complexity.

As multigrid-methods are in the category of latency-bound algorithms, we did as much latency-hiding as was possible in the underlying message-passing-system. With intel's NX-model this was much easier than with PVM because of the possibility of non-blocking receives, which allow it very easily to overlap the communication with the computation on the inner region of each domain.

As long as we are on finer grid-levels this overlapping will be fine, whereas on the coarsest grid-levels all gridpoints will be situated in the domain-boundaries, therefore there is no overlap as there is no more inner region. Anyway all communications can still happen in parallel, if the interconnection-network allows this, so we expect a constant communication-overhead if we have at least three domains.

The following results are scaleup-curves (our goals are large problems) for a distributed-memory parallel-computer (intel Paragon) and a workstation-cluster (IBM RS/6000-550) with three different interconnection-networks. Furthermore for comparison two speedup-curves (which is the appropriate measure for shared-memory-systems) on a Cray-2 are included. As our intention was not to test the scalability of the algorithm itself but to test the scalability of certain parallel architectures for this kind of algorithms we decided to take a fixed number of iterations.

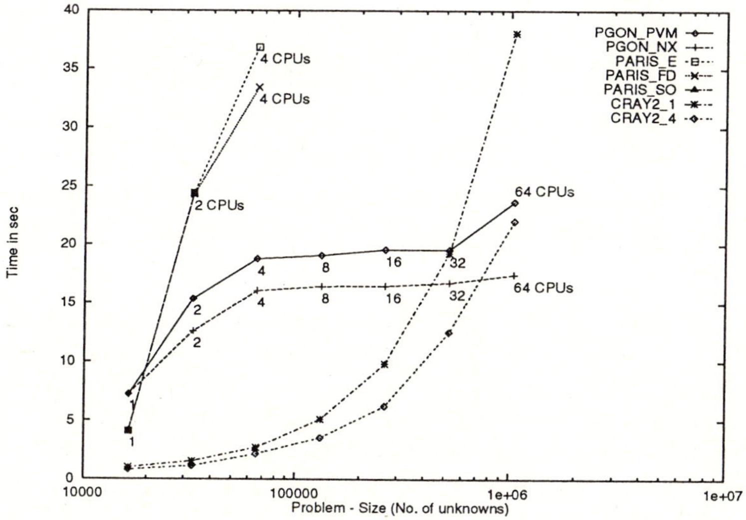

The intel Paragon shows nearly constant times for four domains and beyond for both, NX and PVM as programming-interface. As the lines for PVM and NX don't diverge, latency and not bandwidth is the problem. The reason for this conclusion is, that the work on the coarsest grid-levels is the same for all problem-sizes leading to a constant offset.

Although the IBM POWER-architecture is better suited for red/black-Gauss-Seidel type algorithms as used in the smoother than the more vector-like i860XP, it can easily be seen that this kind of algorithm is beyond the limit of workstation-clusters. This is not only due to the high latencies, but also the non-scalable interconnection-networks which lead to nearly no decrease in slope between two and four nodes.

The Cray-2, as a machine which is two generations old is suffering from short vector-lengths and can no more compete with MPPs, even on such a typical shared-memory-problem.

5.2 NSFLEX

NSFLEX(Navier-Stokes-Solver using characteristic FLux EXtrapolation) is a solver to simulate compressible inviscid and viscous flow [8]. A finite volume code is used together with a multiblock strategy. An implicit solver runs independently on each block thus leading to an explicit behaviour. Update of overlapping boundaries is done after each time step.

# proc	PGON		RS6K	
	PVM3	NX	PVM3	PVM6
1	10082		6632	
4	2670 (3.8)	2437 (4.1)	1612 (4.1)	1588 (4.2)
8	1237 (8.2)	1210 (8.3)		
16	656 (15.4)	595 (16.9)		
32	480 (21)	343 (29.4)		
64	532 (19.0)	303 (33.3)		

The values in the table are CPU-times in seconds. Numbers in brackets give the speedup. For PVM3 on the Paragon the time for spawning the slaves has been included. This is about three seconds per node. Subtracting this "startup" time yields much better speedup results for PVM3.

The code involves only a very low amount of communication and is therefore very tolerant to the interconnection-network behaviour.

References

1. Al Geist et. al., PVM 3 User's Guide and Reference Manual, ORNL/TM-12187, May, 1993.
2. M. Bernaschi, G. Caliari, G. Richelli, PVM/6000 User's Guide and Subroutine Reference, Release 1.0, November 15, 1993.
3. intel Paragon OSF/1, FORTRAN System-Calls Reference Manual.
4. Georg Stellner, Stefan Lamberts and Thomas Ludwig, NXLIB Users' Guide, Inst. für Informatik, Technische Universität München, October, 1993.
5. Message Passing Interface Forum, Document for a Standard Message-Passing Interface, University of Tennessee, Knoxville, Tennessee, November, 1993.
6. William Gropp and Ewing Lusk, A Test Implementation of the MPI Draft Message-Passing Standard, ANL-92/47, December 1992.
7. A. Geiger, M.M. Resch, PARIS: Erfahrungen mit einem parallelen RISC-Cluster an der Universität Stuttgart, Workshop Parallelrechner, Braunschweig, 1993.
8. A.Bode, M.Lenke, T.Michl, S.Wagner, Implicit Euler Solver on Alliant FX/2800 and Intel iPSC/860 Multiprocessors, in E.H.Hirschel, Flow Simulation with High-Performance Computers I, Notes on Numerical Fluid Mechanics, Vol. 38, Vieweg 1993.

EASYPVM
EnhAnced Subroutine LibrarY for PVM

Sami Saarinen

Center for Scientific Computing (CSC),
P.O.Box 405, Tietotie 6, FIN-02101 Espoo, Finland
e-mail: Sami.Saarinen@csc.fi

Abstract. EASYPVM is a message passing library built on top of the Parallel Virtual Machine (PVM) version 3.2. The purpose of EASYPVM is to considerably facilitate the use of PVM-programs by supplying a small set of functions that hide the details of PVM-message passing syntax and process creation. It provides a very coordinated and clear message passing programming approach and eliminates the need of any unnecessary parameters in message passing calls. EASYPVM also introduces some important global commmunication routines and has a very simple interface to PICL/ParaGraph message tracing postprocessor.

1 What is EASYPVM ?

EASYPVM is a message passing library built on top of the Parallel Virtual Machine (PVM) version 3.2. EASYPVM is a simplified message passing interface for those PVM programmers who are aiming to port, test and run MPP-programs on the cluster of workstations, but who are not fully satisfied with the functionality that PVM provides by default.

EASYPVM is in principle available for any platform where PVM is ported. It can be used from C, C++ or Fortran programs. Unlike PVM, EASYPVM-calls are *similar* in any of the aforementioned languages[1]. The performance of EASYPVM is determined by the underlaying PVM-implementation. Also, an EASYPVM-application can still call any of the PVM-routines.

EASYPVM is currently ported for SGI (the development machine), SUN4, IBM RS/6000, Cray, Convex, HP PA-RISC and DEC ALPHA platforms. To obtain a copy of this public domain product, use anonymous ftp (`ftp.funet.fi (128/214.248.6)` under directory `/pub/csc/software/easypvm`. It has been tested with PVM 3.2.6.

2 EASYPVM in more detail

EASYPVM offers the following features that are not available in PVM or would have otherwise required re-inventing the wheel every time a new PVM-program is coded:

[1] Possible name clashes are handled via C-preprocessor.

- A simplified process creation under
  - HOST-NODE programming model
  - NODE-only programming model through generic HOST-program
- Graceful process exits with the careful PVM-daemon shutdowns
- Generic `send()/recv()` -routines that access data in elements rather than bytes
- Global operations including global syncronization, sum, prod, dot product, max/min, concatenation and complete exchange
- `send()/recv()` -operations with 2D-matrix sub-blocks
- Broadcast, Multicast, Store-Forward, SendRecv -functions
- Simple activation of the performance monitoring via PICL/ParaGraph

2.1 Process creation and exit

The underlying logical processor topology in EASYPVM is a 3D-torus found also in the Cray T3D architecture. The so called nearest neighbour -functions and rank indexing of the NODE-processes guarantee flexible access of any NODE-process in a logical *computational cluster.*

EASYPVM is capable for HOST-NODE and NODE-only (SPMD or non-SPMD) approaches. A single HOST can be a user written program or so called **pvmserver**, a generic HOST-program that automatically drives and terminates the NODE-programs. Furthermore, a user written HOST-program can operate simultaneously with several clusters of NODE-programs which need not to be aware of each others.

One weakness in the pure PVM is a process creation. Every time a HOST process creates one or several NODE-processes, nearly all of the following steps must be repeated:

1. Get my PVM task id via `XXXmytid()` -call [2]
2. Get my PVM parent process id from the `XXXparent()` -call
3. Call `XXXspawn(...)` to create the NODE processes
4. Multicast task ids of the NODE processes to every NODE that were just created so that every NODE knows about its siblings

This can be expressed in EASYPVM by a simple subroutine call and providing so called NODE Definition File (`ndffile`) for the HOST process:

```
character*(*) ndffile
CALL createproc(ndffile)
```

Alternatively an SPMD-model can be adopted. In this case the HOST calls `loadproc()` with two parameters: NODE-program executable name and how many copies of the NODE should be initiated.

In the NODE -side the repeated steps are usually:

[2] `XXX` refers to `pvmf` in Fortran or `pvm_` in C/C++ -languages

1. Get my PVM task id via `XXXmytid()` call
2. Get my PVM parent process id from `XXXparent()`
3. Receive task ids of the sibling NODE processes

These can be hidden by the following call:

```
CALL attachproc(me,nproc)
```

This connects the NODE-programs to the PVM-complex and all sibling-related information are made available to them. After the call, the parameters `me` and `nproc` contain the rank of the process (`0..nproc-1`) and how many NODE-processes actually form a computational cluster.

Thus these simple looking function calls hide all the handshaking details from the programmer, who is only responsible for creating the appropriate `ndffile` just before starting his application. An `ndffile` contains typically information about logical 3D-torus dimensions, NODE-executable names and parameter list and on which computers NODEs should be initiated.

For leaving the PVM-complex, EASYPVM offers routine `detachproc()`. This notifies automatically the HOST-process so that the HOST can decrement its counter of the still active NODE-processes. If `detachproc()` was *not* called by the user, then EASYPVM-library takes care of this upon process' exit.

`detachproc()` only leaves the PVM-complex, not exits the process. If program needs to be terminated explicitly, for example, because of some abnormal operation, EASYPVM has another routine available: `killproc(`*procno*`)`. This terminates any process that is a member in a computational cluster; also itself.

Additional features to manage graceful exit and shutdown of any pending PVM-daemons, are implemented via signal handlers in EASYPVM-library and through the system level command `pvmclean`. Both of them guarantee that no processes will remain hanging after abnormal situations. The former one will caught any interrupt signals issued from the keyboard (like `CTRL-C`) or other abnormal situations like segmentation violations. The `pvmclean` does a post-cleaning of any pending processes by killing the PVM-daemons and running down the PVM-complex gracefully.

2.2 Generic message passing calls

With the term *generic message passing* is meant a feature, where a programmer fixes certain data type for subsequent data communication. Data is sent or received using generic `send()` and `recv()` functions and the length of the data arrays is expressed in elements (words) rather than bytes. This offers a nearly trivial port to machines with different word lengths (e.g. Cray vs. other systems) or data representation (e.g. low vs. big-endian).

A typical PVM-application contains several message passing calls that are repeated over and over again, thus making PVM-application hard to read, longsome to code and (thus) errorprone. For example before sending the message, one should do in PVM:

1. initiate a message buffer
2. pack message into that buffer
3. send buffer to a specific destination

This requires (in most cases) three PVM-library calls. In PVM a single message can be formed of different data types. This feature is, however, very seldom used in a real application. For that reason EASYPVM offers a subroutine call `setdatatype()` which fixes the data type for the subsequent message passing operations. A Fortran-code may look like as follows:

```
DOUBLE PRECISION A(N)
... do something with your data A ..
CALL setdatatype(REAL8)      ! Sets data type for subsequent operations
CALL send(dest,100,A,N)      ! Data type is REAL8
... do something else with your data A ..
CALL send(dest,200,A,N)      ! Data type is still REAL8
```

EASYPVM is also capable sending or receiving matrix blocks. Using function calls `send2d()` and `recv2d()` a specific sub-block of a matrix can be accessed. This simplifies programming in many linear algebra applications.

In addition, functions to `broadcast()` or `multicast()` data arrays are available. Also a special function that forwards the just received data buffer before starting to unpack it for itself is available (`storefwd()`). For simple data exchanges function `sendrecv()` can also be used. It simply combines `send()` and `recv()` into one function.

2.3 Global Operations

EASYPVM provides many common global communication routines like global syncronization, summation, product, min-max and concatenate functions. All these functions are also generic, that is, exactly the same function call is suitable for `INTEGER`, `REAL` or `DOUBLE PRECISION` data types, as well as for different `COMPLEX` data types.

If all NODE processes share the same (SPMD-)code, one can syncronize processes in the following manner[3]:

```
CALL gsync()
```

Only after all processes have reached this point in the source code, the NODEs can proceed their execution. This feature is available in a very difficult manner through dynamic process groups in PVM 3.x and was called `barrier()` in older PVM 2.4.x.

Global summation, product, min/max are also available through a single, generic library call (unlike in the Intel's NX-library). It is under user responsibility to assure that the correct data type is in use. A code for `INTEGER` summation may look like as follows:

[3] The routine is exactly the same that is found in Intel's (message passing) NX-library.

```
INTEGER MYVAR, RESULT, mynode
MYVAR = mynode()
CALL setdatatype(INTEGER4)
CALL gsum(MYVAR,1,RESULT)  ! Perform global summation with INTEGERs
```

As result each of the NODE processes have the sum of *local* `MYVAR`'s accumulated in the `RESULT`-variable. It should be noted that the program is essentially the same for the `REAL`-variables, except that function call `setdatatype(INTEGER4)` must be replaced by `setdatatype(REAL4)`.

With the nearest neighbour capability in EASYPVM is meant a set of functions which return the rank index of every nearest neighbour process in a logical 3D-torus. For example, exchanging data with the neighbour processes in left (`west()`) and right (`east()`) sides can be coded as follows:

```
REAL*8 U(0:N+1,0:Mlocal+1)
CALL setdatatype(REAL8)
if (me .lt. nproc-1) then
  CALL send(east(),100,U(1,Mlocal),N)
endif
if (me .gt. 0) then
  CALL recv(west(),100,U(1,0),N)
  CALL send(west(),200,U(1,1),N)
endif
if (me .lt. nproc-1) then
  CALL recv(east(),200,U(1,Mlocal+1),N)
endif
```

2.4 Performance tracing via PICL/ParaGraph

For time being no acceptable way of doing performance tracing is available in PVM. This means difficulties in detection of the communication bottlenecks. Or in tracing which process is sending messages to whom. Or what has been the volume of the communication. EASYPVM removes this hurdle.

By default EASYPVM-library routines are compiled to include performance tracing function calls, that produce PICL[4]-formatted timing records for every communication call issued from a NODE-program. After the run these records are merged and sorted in a timestamp-order for the subsequent post-processing with ParaGraph-tool.

Performance tracing is off by default, but can be activated in a *run-time* by simply defining an environment variable `EASY_PICLTRACE`.

3 Summary and Conclusions

EASYPVM offers a simple way to extend capabilities of the popular PVM. It facilitates testing and porting of the distributed memory programs in a workstation cluster environment written for the "real" MIMD/MPP-systems.

[4] Portable Instrumented Communication Library.

Table 1. A summary of the most important functions in EASYPVM

Function call	Short description
`createproc('ndffile')`	Creates NODE-processes via `ndffile`
`loadproc('a.out',num)`	Starts `num` '`a.out`'-procs
`attachproc(me,nproc)`	NODE becomes a member of a cluster
`mynode()`	Returns rank index of my process
`myhost()`	Returns PVM-task id of my creator
`numnodes()`	Returns number of NODEs in a cluster
`detachproc()`	Leave computational cluster
`killproc(procno)`	Kill specific process in a cluster
`send(dest,msgtag,data,nelems)`	Sends `data` of `nelems` to `dest`
`recv(source,msgtag,data,nelems)`	Receives `data` from `source`
`broadcast(msgtag,data,nelems)`	Broadcast data to sibling NODEs
`setdatatype(type)`	Sets data type for subsequent `send()/recv()`
`getdatatype()`	Gets data type currently active
`setstride(stride)`	Sets stride for subsequent `send()/recv()`
`getstride()`	Gets stride currently active
`probe(source,msgtag)`	Blocking test of received messages
`iprobe(source,msgtag)`	Non-blocking test of received messages
`recvinfo(bufid,source,msgtag,nbytes`	Information about received message
`gsync()`	Global syncronization within a cluster
`gsum(input,nelems,output)`	Global, elementwise sum of input
`gprod(input,nelems,output)`	Global, elementwise product of input
`gmin(input,nelems,output,where)`	Global, elementwise min and its location
`gmax(input,nelems,output,where)`	Global, elementwise max and its location
`gdot(input1,input2,nelems,output)`	Global dot product
`gcol(data,nelems,output,noutput`	Global concatenation of local vectors
`gcolx(data,nlengths,output`	Global concatenation of local vectors (fast version)
`gcxch(data,blksize,datatransp`	Complete exchange ("transpose")
`east(),west(),north(),south(),up(),down()`	Direction functions in a 3D-torus
`getprocdim(nx,ny,nz)`	Size of the logical 3D process torus
`getprocpos(my_x,my_y,my_z)`	My position in a 3D-torus

EASYPVM also removes most the PVM-programming burden, but also creates some new barriers related to mixed data type packing that is already available in PVM. However, the nature of EASYPVM is not to restrict PVM-programming in any way, thus all functions available in PVM, are still fully available for EASYPVM applications.

DynamicPVM

Dynamic Load Balancing on Parallel Systems

Leen Dikken[1], Frank van der Linden[2], Joep Vesseur[2] and Peter Sloot[2*]

[1] Shell Nederland Informatieverwerking
Rijswijk
[2] Parallel Scientific Computing and Simulation Group,
Faculty of Mathematics and Computer Science,
University of Amsterdam
Kruislaan 403, 1098 SJ, Amsterdam

Abstract. This paper describes DynamicPVM, an extension to PVM (Parallel Virtual Machine) [1] . PVM enables users to write parallel applications using message passing primitives and statically places the parallel tasks on a collection of nodes. System schedulers schedule atomic jobs over a predefined number of nodes. DynamicPVM addresses the problem of scheduling parallel tasks over a set of nodes. It therefore has to integrate a process checkpointing, migration and restart restart mechanism with the PVM runtime support system. DynamicPVM facilitates an efficient use of existing computational resources for computational jobs consisting of parallel subtasks. Typical target HPC platforms for DynamicPVM are multi user, multi tasking, loosely coupled processors.

Introduction

The number of workstations in industrial and academical institutions has grown tremendously over the past years. A migration from centralized mainframes to collections of these high-performance workstations connected by LANs is taking place. These new loosely coupled parallel systems require new programming environments that provide the user with the tools to explore the full potential of the distributed resources.

Although these parallel programming systems provide the user with large amounts of processing power, the behaviour of these systems under changes of the environment dramatically influences the usability and efficiency of the system.

Environmental changes (e.g. increase of demand for processing power or a decrease of the number of available processors) impose the necessity to migrate tasks between nodes in order to improve the resource utilization. DynamicPVM aims to add system scheduling mechanisms on top of tasks running in parallel on this new type of parallel system.

* All correspondence with regard to this work can be addressed to this author at peterslo@fwi.uva.nl

Our primary objective is to study models describing systems like DynamicPVM that dynamically adapt to changes in the environment. To validate these models, experiments with actual implementations of such dynamic systems are required. The work described here presents a pilot implementation of DynamicPVM.

The choice for PVM is motivated by the fact that at the time of writing it is in use by more than 10,000 users and thus is considered as the *de facto* standard environment for parallel programming. The process migration primitives used in DynamicPVM are based on the checkpoint-restart mechanisms found in a well established global scheduling system, Condor [2].

In Table 1, several different aspects of load managing for the three systems discussed in this paper are shown.

	Condor	PVM	DynamicPVM
intended usage	longer running background jobs	parallelized distributed application programs	
unit of execution	job	task	
load managing objective	load distribution	load decomposition	both
schedule policy	dynamic load sharing	cyclic allocation	dynamic load balancing
schedule objective	resource utilization	application response time	both
performance objective	efficiency	effectiveness	both

Table 1: Aspects of load managing in Condor, PVM and DynamicPVM.

Parallel Virtual Machine: Runtime Support System for Parallel Programs
PVM offers primitives for remote task creation and inter process communication (IPC) to the user. Both point to point communication and broadcasts are supported. Newly created tasks are assigned to the available nodes using a cyclic assignment policy; PVM does not integrate any load information of the nodes into the assignment policy. Once a job is started, it runs until completion.

PVM as such does not support operations on files but PVM tasks can share files through the Network File System (NFS). Terminal I/O is transparently redirected to the terminal where the job was initiated, the *PVM console*.

At startup time each processor in the PVM pool runs a PVM-daemon representing that node. Requests to create a new PVM task onto a host are sent to the host's daemon which executes the requested binary. The daemon also takes care of IPC generated by or addressed to tasks on the host: tasks direct their communication to their local daemon which takes care of delivery to the daemon of the destination task. The remote daemon delivers the message to the destination task.

PVM uses XDR [4] as eXternal Data Representation, therefore messages can easily be sent between different architectures, thereby facilitating the use of heterogeneous processor pools. Apart from IPC using the PVM daemons, users are also able to initiate their own communication channels (TCP connections) which require no intervention of the PVM daemons.

Condor: Runtime Support for Job Scheduling
Condor stems from the observation that many of the—constantly increasing number of—workstations in academic institutions are lightly loaded on the average. Most workstations are intended for personal usage, which has a typical activity pattern where machines are only used for a small part of the day. As a consequence many cycles are idle or unused during the day. Typical figures of large pools of workstations have a mean idle time of 80% [2].

To address this problem, Condor implements a global scheduling based on dynamic load balancing by job migration. Condor monitors the nodes in its pool keeping track of their load. New jobs are spawned on lightly loaded nodes and tasks from heavy loaded machines can be migrated to lighter loaded ones. When Condor detects interactive usage of a workstation all jobs are evacuated in order to retain the sympathy of the workstation's owner. To implement this job migration Condor creates checkpoints on a regular basis. These checkpoints can be restarted on another machine.

The Condor scheduler consists of both a centralized and a distributed part. Each node in the pool runs a small daemon that gathers statistics about the node and forwards this information to the central scheduler. This information is used optimize the available processing power.

System calls made by a Condor process are redirected to the host that initiated the job. In this way the user is freed from the complications of the checkpointing mechanism since it is completely transparent to the job.

Using Condor, it is not possible to migrate jobs consisting of parallel tasks that cooperate to complete a job since Condor does not provide any IPC primitives and the standard UNIX IPC primitives are host-addressed and therefore not suited for migrating tasks.

Combining PVM with an extended version of Condor's checkpoint-restart facility makes it possible to apply global scheduling to parallel tasks.

DynamicPVM: Runtime Support System for Job Scheduling of Parallel Tasks

In DynamicPVM we add checkpoint-restart primitives to the PVM environment. Most of PVM's features are compatible with the checkpoint-restart mechanism we use, with the exception of the inter process communication. We present a protocol that ensures that no messages get lost whenever a task is migrated. This protocol involves a special role for the PVM-daemon that initiated the computation, the Master-daemon. We also present an extension to the PVM IPC routing mechanism in order to redirect messages to the new host after a task has migrated.

DynamicPVM's task migration facility consists of four principal components:

1. A global scheduler that initiates job migration (not addressed in this paper)

2. Task checkpointing including a method to indicate checkpoint save moments
3. Actual Task migration
4. Task restart and updating of routing tables to indicate the task's new location.

Task Checkpointing
Checkpoints are created using the standard Condor checkpoint code. This code creates a core-dump of the task onto a shared file system (NFS). Condor appends extra information to the core in order to be able to restore the state of the process when it is restarted again.

Checkpointing cooperating tasks introduces new conditions compared with checkpointing stand-alone tasks. Checkpoints should be avoided, e.g., when a task is communicating with another task. To enable DynamicPVM to determine which situations are save to checkpoint, we have introduced the concept of critical sections. When a task is inside such a critical section, any checkpoint request is postponed until the task leaves the critical section. All PVM communication routines are contained in critical sections.

In the absence of a global scheduler, the task itself initiates any possible checkpoint requests by calling a new routine `pvm_move`.

As soon as the task initiates a checkpoint it sends a message to all tasks with which it shares a communication channel. These remote tasks will then close the channel and issue an `accept` call in order to re-establish the connection as soon as the task is restarted.

Task Migration
The main objective of the DynamicPVM task migration protocol is to guarantee migration transparency, i.e. to allow the movement of tasks within the system without affecting the operation of tasks in the system. With respect to a PVM task selected for migration this implicates transparent suspension and resumption of execution. With respect to the total of cooperating PVM tasks in an application communication may be delayed but not fail due to the migration of one of the tasks.

First we create a new task context at the new node by sending a message to the remote PVM daemon. The task's new daemon is now able to receive any packets for the migrated task.

Next, the new routing information is sent to the task's new daemon, the Master PVM daemon and finally updated in the routing tables of the task's old PVM daemon. All messages directed to the migrating task will from now on be send to the new node.

At this point the task is actually checkpointed and written to disk.

Task Restart
As soon as the checkpoint is finished, the task's new daemon is notified. It then restarts the task which restores any saved state information including the re-establishment of any communication channels that were closed at checkpoint

time. The daemon then delivers any messages that arrived during the creation of the task's checkpoint.

Any future messages that are directed to the task's old daemon will fail. Whenever this happens, the sending daemon will contact the Master daemon to obtain the task's new location to which the message will be directed next.

Current Status and Ongoing Research

DynamicPVM is currently implemented on a cluster of IBM RS/6000, AIX32 machines [3]. Due to a conflict between Condor's restart mechanism and PVM's startup code, we are currently not able to checkpoint tasks that perform file-I/O.

Tests performed with the pilot implementation strongly support the usability of our integrated approach. In the very near future we will design additional experiments for quantitative testing of the behaviour of DynamicPVM.

Our final goal is to use probabilistic models of jobs in a dynamic environment and validate them by experiments with an actual implementation. We have added several primitives to PVM that allow us to monitor PVM tasks. Using these primitives we will implement a scheduler based on our models. Simulations using our models will gain us insight in the behaviour of DynamicPVM and will be used to improve the scheduling mechanism. The scheduler is a topic of future research, and it is expected to be dealt with in the coming months.

References

1. V. S. Sunderam. *PVM: A framework for parallel distributed computing*, Concurrency: Practice and Experience, vol. 2(4), pp. 315–339, December 1990.
2. M. J. Litzkow, M. Livny. *Condor — A hunter of idle workstations*, 8th International Conference on Distributed Computing Systems, San Jose, California, June 1988.
3. L. Dikken, *DynamicPVM: Task Migration in PVM*, Technical Report, Shell Research, ICS/155.1, November 1993.
4. Sun Microsystems, *XDR: External Data Representation standard*, Sun Microsystems, Inc., 1987, RFC 1014.

A Large-Scale Metacomputer Approach for Distributed Parallel Computing

Volker Strumpen

Institut für Wissenschaftliches Rechnen,
ETH Zürich, CH-8092 Zürich, Switzerland

Abstract. In this paper, a new architecture for metacomputing is proposed, designed to integrate heterogeneous resources of the Internet. The goals of this metacomputer are the orchestration of very large amounts of workstations and the integration of supercomputers into a pool of resources for distributed parallel computing. Based on a tree shaped logical interconnection topology, the system provides not only a parallel programmer interface but also a simple user interface to administrate large systems.

1 Introduction

One of the most exciting developments in the area of parallel computing is the recent emergence of distributed parallel computing. A particular variant, called *metacomputing* [5], refers primarily to the software layer which provides a transparent environment of various heterogeneous resources, distributed geographically and loosely coupled through networks. The ideal metacomputer is a system that provides not only transparency to users as well as programmers, but also guarantees high performance by means of efficient utilization of the underlying hardware. The system proposed here is based on a tree structured process topology, logically superimposed over the Internet. The user is provided with a view on a tree hierarchy of directories, and the parallel programmer with a tree hierarchy of processes, on top of which arbitrary application topologies can be configured transparently. This ensures a simple user interface, as well as scalability and fault tolerance, which are fundamental properties for a large system consisting of thousands of machines.

To access a large network of machines, control of the resources in a simple and uniform way is essential. Within a LAN, users rely on conveniences like uniform permissions and authentication, or a network file system. Using UNIX remote services `telnet`, `ftp`, `rlogin` or `rsh` across LAN borders, it quickly becomes difficult to cope with various operating system or library versions, file systems, or diverse userids and passwords. Software management tasks such as compiling codes for numerous binary incompatible machines, or version control, are error-prone. Resource management is already important for a limited number of different machines within a LAN, but appears indispensible when coupling a number of LANs with many different machine architectures. Therefore, a an appropriate user interface has to be offered.

means of structuring a large network, for example, by assigning subdirectories to LANs. Second, the virtual file system can be seen as a single directory structure, providing a global directory name space. Each entry is uniquely related to a directory of the underlying local file system.

Changing from one machine to another requires only a change of the current working directory. Executing a command on a remote machine is completely hidden from the user. The communication kernel routes the command to the machine given by the current working host. After command execution, the results are returned and displayed at the root node.

The virtual file system furthermore enables partitioning of the metacomputer for parallel computations. For selective use of machines, the user can deactivate and reactivate subdirectories of the virtual file system. The user chooses a partition of the metacomputer by deactivating all directory entries of machines that shall not be used. A parallel computation running, for example, on THE PARFORM [2] runtime system automatically selects machines from the pool of activated machines in a location transparent way, thereby using a subset of the set of activated machines, which is a subtree of the tree of accessed machines.

4.3 The Command Interpreter

Serving the needs of a very large distributed system, the command interpreter by default submits commands in a non-blocking manner, i.e. the shell at the root node is not blocked until the command terminates. There are two reasons for this design decision. First, parallelism at the command level cannot be exploited using blocking command submission. Second, Internet connections to remote machines may cause inconvenient response times. Non-blocking commands allow for submission of sequential and parallel jobs, and their concurrent execution. Blocking command submission is offered explicitly to ensure command execution in a predefined sequence. The concept of non-blocking and blocking command submission is similar to background and foreground processes in UNIX systems, respectively. However, the default mode of UNIX is foreground processing, in PARC non-blocking command submission.

The command interpreter accepts two different categories of commands, PARC commands and UNIX commands. PARC commands effect the virtual file system. The most fundamental commands, such as `ls`, `cd`, `pwd` or `cp` are currently implemented. They offer a UNIX-like environment with different, yet similar semantics. For example, `ls` lists the host names of the current working directory of the virtual file system. `cd` changes the current working host by changing the current working directory of the virtual file system. `cp` uses UNIX copy within the scope of one network file system, and transfers compressed files across local file system borders by means of TCP streams. Original UNIX commands are executed on the current working host by the local UNIX system. The similarity between PARC and UNIX commands maintains consistency of the user interface, and permits a transparent implementation.

4.4 The Runtime System

PARC is being implemented (1) to learn about effects and limits of very large distributed systems especially with respect to parallel computing, and (2) to ease the implementation and analysis of different runtime systems, such as for parallel databases and parallel programming languages. Several programming paradigms exist that may be suited for metacomputing, among them distributed shared memory or process group oriented programming. However, we do not know yet whether and how a large scale metacomputer can be programmed efficiently in general.

The layered structure of PARC provides access to different interfaces, especially the UNIX system layers, for the sake of efficiency. Currently, THE PARFORM [3] application programmer interface is ported onto PARC. Here, for instance, message passing is directly implemented on top of UNIX system calls, inducing no more overhead than a function call and eventually data marshalling.

Parallel applications are configured on top of the control tree. A subset of activated hosts is chosen for a parallel computation automatically. This ensures transparency, although this principle will be violated to integrate vector computers and parallel architectures. When starting an application, the processes of the control tree `fork` a child process that executes the application process. This mechanism also permits efficient dynamic process creation. The application processes inherit the tree shaped interconnection structure of the control tree. If requested by the application program, additional stream connections are established between them. This can be impossible across LAN borders, if machines are not directly connected to the Internet. In such cases, the underlying control tree routes the corresponding messages. Thereby, arbitrary application process topologies are supported. The separation of application processes and PARC kernel processes guarantees orthogonality with respect to kernel and application process control and communication.

5 Conclusions and Future Work

The PARC metacomputer with its communication kernel, virtual file system, command interpreter and runtime system components has been presented. The user interface with the virtual file system and the command interpreter proved to be a valid technology. The development of efficient runtime systems for parallel programming languages remains a fascinating challenge. An intricate task is the interface definition of the PARC kernel layers, because it depends on the needs of different abstractions and programming models. Ongoing work investigates the integration of supercomputers into the metacomputer. The goal is to provide a uniform interface on top of different machine architectures. Efficiency shall be maintained by utilizing low-level primitives that exploit machine specific hardware mechanisms.

Acknowledgement

Thanks to Peter Arbenz and Walter Gander for providing me with a fantastic working environment, and Tom Casavant for stimulating discussions and proof reading. Parts of this work have been conducted at the Institut für Informatik, University of Zurich, funded by Siemens AG (ZFE), Germany, and the Schweizer Bundesamt für Konjunkturfragen, Grant No. 2254.1. Thanks to Kurt Bauknecht, Clemens Cap, and Lutz Richter for this possibility.

References

1. Bhoedjang R., Rühl T., et al.: Panda: A Portable Platform to Support Parallel Programming Languages. In: Proceedings of the USENIX Symposium on Experience with Distributed and Multiprocessor Systems. San Diego, CA, 1993, pp.213–226
2. Cap C.H., Strumpen V.: Efficient Parallel Computing in Distributed Workstation Environments. Parallel Computing **19**(11) (1993) 1221–1234
3. Feitelson D.G., Rudolph L.: Distributed Hierarchical Control for Parallel Processing. IEEE Computer **23**(5) (1990) 65–77
4. Peterson L., Hutchinson N., et al.: The *x*-kernel: A Platform for Accessing Internet Resources. IEEE Computer **23**(5) (1990) 23–33
5. Smarr L., Catlett C.E.: Metacomputing. Communications of the ACM **35**(6) (1992) 45–52
6. Strumpen V.: Parallel Molecular Sequence Analysis on Workstations in the Internet. Techrep **93.28**, Department of Computer Science, University of Zurich, 1993

Developing Applications for Multicomputer Systems on Workstation Clusters

Georg Stellner, Arndt Bode,
Stefan Lamberts and Thomas Ludwig*

Technische Universität München
Institut für Informatik
Lehrstuhl für Rechnertechnik und Rechnerorganisation
D-80290 München
nxlib@informatik.tu-muenchen.de

Abstract. Much computational power on state-of-the-art multicomputers like the Paragon is wasted with porting applications. Using networks of workstations is an attempt to withdraw this workload from multicomputer systems. Therefore an environment is needed which provides the programming interface of multicomputers on coupled workstations. The paper describes the design and implementation of the NXLib environment which allows to use Ethernet coupled workstations as a development platform for applications targeted for Intel Paragon systems.

1 Motivation

A drawback of multicomputers is that porting existing applications onto those systems often requires enormous efforts. Applications have to be parallelized which leads to frequent test runs during the implementation. Therefore, much workload on multicomputer systems consists of test and debugging runs. To withdraw some of this load, an environment is needed which allows the implementation of applications for multicomputer systems on different hardware platforms.

Today, typical environments in universities and companies consist of several networked workstations. The basic architecture of multicomputer systems and coupled workstations is similar: independent processing elements (nodes or workstations) which are interconnected. In difference to the multicomputers' high performance interconnection network, workstations currently use a slower interconnect. In addition the network has to be shared with other machines and users which are also connected to the network.

State-of-the-art multicomputers like the Paragon offer a proprietary message passing environment. An implementation of that library on coupled workstations would allow for using interconnected workstations as a development platform for applications where the production code should finally run on a multicomputer

* This project was partially funded by a research grant from the Intel Foundation.

system. In addition to that, it is also applicable to use interconnected workstations as additional computational resource. The performance constraints of coupled workstations restricts this to applications with limited demands concerning computational power and a coarse grained or medium grained granularity of parallelism.

In the following we will describe the design and implementation of the Paragon NX communication library for workstation nets. Therefore we first give a short description of the Paragon and its software environment. After that, we introduce the design and implementation of the NXLib package for coupled workstations. Some performance figures of the current NXLib release are provided in chapter 4. Finally, the last chapter summarizes and gives an outlook on future work.

2 The Paragon and its Message Passing Interface

To get a better understanding of NXLib's design and implementation, we first present a short overview on the Paragon and the NX message passing library [1]. The nodes of a Paragon system are interconnected in a two-dimensional mesh topology, which is subdivided into three partitions: the I/O partition, the service partition and the compute partition (see fig. 1). Usually the largest partition in a

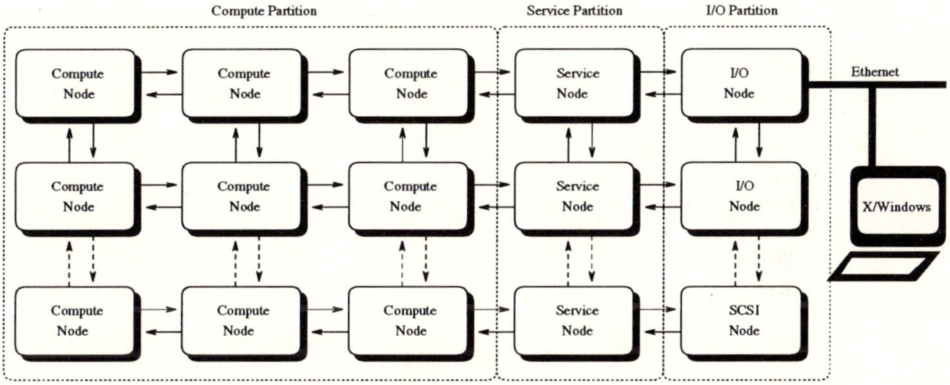

Fig. 1. Different partitions in a Paragon system

configuration is the compute partition. Parallel user applications are executed on the nodes in this partition. In contrast to that, interactive processes are executed on the nodes in the service partition. Finally, the nodes in the I/O partition are used to connect I/O devices.

Parallel user applications on the compute partition make use of Intel's message passing library which is derived form the NX/2 of the iPSC systems [3]. Apart from synchronous, asynchronous and interrupt-driven communication calls, NX provides calls for process management.

3 Design and Implementation of NXLib

In the following sections a short introduction to the design and implementation of NXLib is given. For a more detailed discussion refer to [5].

3.1 The node model

In the following the meaning of some frequently used terms will be explained. A parallel application on a Paragon system consists of two parts. The application processes on the compute partition and the controlling process of the application on one node of the service partition. In the following discussion the term *Paragon node* will be referred to as the collection of a hardware Paragon node, the operating system kernel and a set of application processes running on top of that.

The basic means to model Paragon nodes on coupled workstations is virtualization. Consequently, the term *virtual Paragon node* (VPN) describes a *Paragon node* on a workstation. The hard- and software properties of a *Paragon node* which are not available on a workstation are virtualized in the following way. A natural approach to model them is to introduce a daemon process which virtualizes the node hardware and the operating system. The calls of the application processes to NX communication routines are transformed into requests to the the daemon. In such an implementation every system call would require an

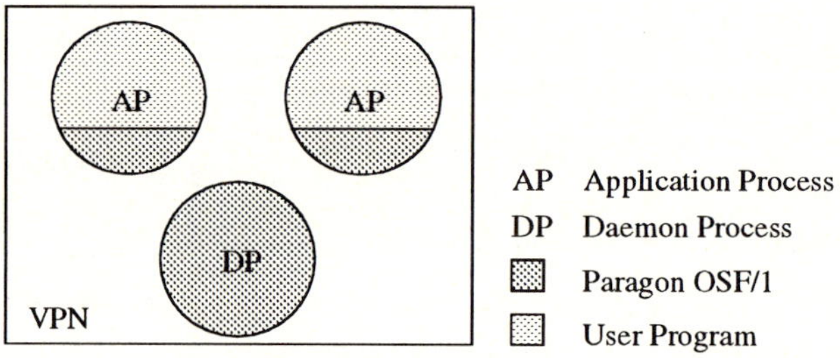

Fig. 2. Processes and the distribution of the operating system on a VPN

interprocess communication. To reduce the amount of interprocess communication parts of the operating system's tasks have been moved into the application processes like illustrated in fig. 2.

3.2 Layers of NXLib

An important issue for a message passing library for coupled workstations is portability and flexibility. A layering of the message passing library has been designed to cover both aspects. Figure 3 shows the layers of the NXLib environment. The basis form the standard UNIX system calls. To achieve a great flexibil-

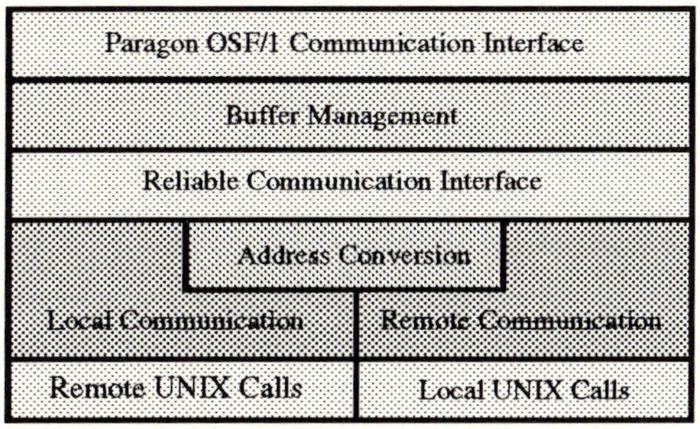

Fig. 3. Layers of the NXLib environment

ity concerning the communication protocol which is used for the implementation NXLib distinguishes between local and remote communication. Within the local and remote communication layer a protocol specific addressing scheme is used. The reliable communication layer provides reliable point-to-point communication calls disregarding the location of the communication partners. The reliable communication interface still uses the Paragon addressing scheme. The address conversion layer has been introduced to map Paragon addresses to corresponding protocol specific addresses. In addition to its address conversion task this layer also distinguishes whether a communication is local or remote. Provided with that information the reliable communication layer can invoke the appropriate local or remote communication calls.

The Paragon OSF/1 communication interface finally provides the user calls which are available on a Paragon system. The calls of the buffer management to insert and delete messages into the message table are used to map messages to corresponding user calls. All user communication calls interface the communication system via the message table.

3.3 Modeling Paragon partitions

In addition to the partitions which were introduced in section 2 it is also possible to define sub-partitions of the compute partition. In a workstation environment mapping files can be used to simulate such partitions. Within that file a mapping of virtual node numbers to workstations is provided. Thus, the mapping table defines a *virtual compute partition*.

A problem occurs for the service partition. It is not part of the Paragon partition management which is available for the user. Consequently a different means has to be provided to establish a *virtual service partition*. This is simply done by defining the machine where the application has been started as the *virtual service partition* of the *virtual Paragon* on the workstations.

3.4 NX message passing calls on workstations

An important issue for message passing libraries is the performance of the communication calls. Both local and remote communication use TCP sockets because this protocol achieves high throughput rates. To reduce the latency it is desirable to use direct paths between communication partners. Every stage in an indirect scheme increases the latency as additional calls have to be performed. On the other hand, on most UNIX systems the number of socket descriptors is limited. A full interconnection of all application processes would therefore drastically reduce the number of processes in an application. Establishing and terminating a communication link between two processes for every communication call is not feasible either as this would introduce much additional effort for every communication.

The basic assumption of our implementation is that typical parallel applications have a regular communication structure in the sense that certain processes regularly communicate with each other. Thus, two processes are either connected and use this communication path frequently during the computation or they do not communicate at all. Consequently, communication paths need only to be created for those processes that wish to communicate. As the communication structure of an application can not be determined at start time, the interconnection of the processes can certainly not be done during the initialization of the application. So the communication paths between processes are set up on demand during run time. Once established a connection between two processes is kept until the application terminates. Building up the connections on demand has the advantage that all interacting processes are fully interconnected. So communication latencies can be kept minimal for established communication links. Finally, as only those processes are interconnected which need to communicate more processes can participate in an application. The only drawback is that the first communication between two processes is more expensive than the following because the connection has to be set up.

4 Applications and Performance

To evaluate the NXLib environment we have used two coarse grain applications which we have running on Paragon systems: NSFLEX [2] and MUMUS [4]. In both cases only minor changes to the makefiles were necessary to compile and link the source code. After the compilation the applications can be started like on a Paragon system by specifying the name of the executable at a shell prompt. To select a virtual partition the same command line switch like on a Paragon can be used. Instead of the partition name the mapping file has to be specified. In a similar way the number of processes which should be created during the start up can be specified with the appropriate Paragon command line switch.

The performance comparison is based on the solution of the same problems on both platforms. To achieve comparable results the problems were solved on a four node Paragon partition and on four Sun Sparc 10. These were the most powerful machines and the maximum number which were at our disposal. Computations on more machines, which included some Sun SLC, made obvious that the performance is driven by the slowest machine in the configuration. On the Paragon its OSF/1 release 1.0.3 was running whereas the Suns executed the SunOS 4.1.1

operating system kernel. With these operating systems a single Paragon node can achieve a floating point performance which is up to three times better than a single Sparc 10. Fig. 4 illustrates the results of the computations.

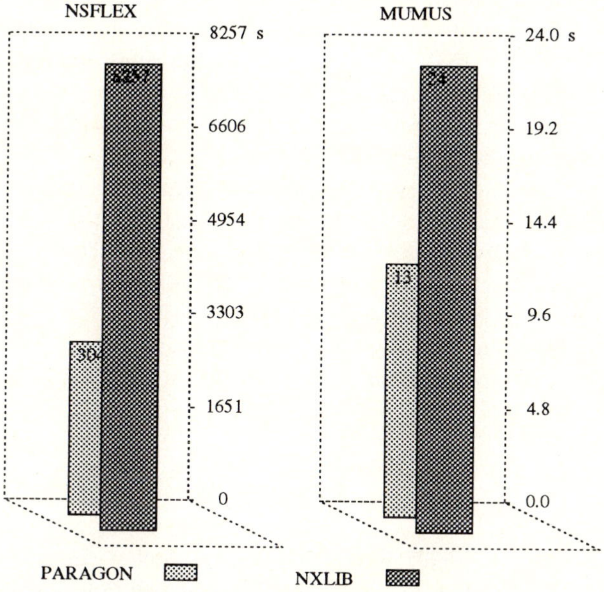

Fig. 4. Comparison of the execution times of MUMUS and NSFLEX on a Paragon and a network of workstations

For NSFLEX the Paragon system is nearly three times as fast as the workstations. For the computation of the given problem with MUMUS the workstations need about twice the time as the Paragon. Taken into consideration the performance of applications on coupled workstations using NXLib seems very promising. These results have to verified on larger clusters and more powerful machines than the Sparc 10.

5 Conclusion and Future Work

The NXLib environment allows for using a network of workstations for mainly two purposes. First, the network of workstations can be used to develop software which should finally run on a Paragon system. Workload can therefore be withdrawn from the multicomputer system. The CPU time which is gained by shifting the development of applications to workstations can be used for production runs of computational intensive problems. Second, instead of using the workstations merely as a development platform they can also be used as a production environment for certain applications. Especially coarse grain applications can achieve good speed-ups on a workstation environment.

Basically NXLib offers the same programming environment as a Paragon system. Virtualization is the basic means to achieve this. Therefore, source code which has been implemented using NXLib can be ported to a Paragon without any changes.

An important issue for scientific and commercial applications is the support of parallel I/O. Due to the restricted network bandwidth of bus coupled workstations it is not feasible to use a single disk as I/O facility. A more interesting approach would be to use the local disks of the workstations and to set up a virtual Paragon file system on these disks. Concepts for disk and file striping in such an environment must be examined therefore.

Up to now there is no support for the programmer during the implementation process of an application. Efficient coding is an important issue for software projects. Thus, the support of a tool environment which assists the programmer during all steps in the software life cycle is very desirable. Tools which can be used to visualize or debug parallel applications require the possibility to gather run-time information. This can either be done on-line with a monitoring system or off-line through trace files. In both cases an instrumentation of NXLib is necessary to produce the data.

References

1. Intel Supercomputer System's Division, 15201 N.W. Greenbrier Parkway, Beaverton, OR 97006. *Paragon OSF/1 C System Calls Reference Manual*, 1 edition, April 1993.
2. T. Michl, S. Maier, S. Wagner, M. Lenke, and A. Bode. Dataparallel Navier-Stokes Solutions on Different Multiprocessors. In ASE'93, editor, *Applications of Supercomputers in Engineering*, September 1993.
3. Paul Pierce. The NX/2 Operating System. In *Proceedings of the 3rd Conference on Hypercube Concurrent Computers and Applications*, pages 384–391. ACM, 1988.
4. M. Schumann, M. Kiehl, and R. Mehlhorn. Performance Evaluation of NXLib Using Parallel Multiple Shooting. [6], pages 58–64.
5. G. Stellner, S. Lamberts, A. Bode, and T. Ludwig. Design and Implementation of NXLib. [6], pages 6–17.
6. G. Stellner, M. Schumann, S. Lamberts, T. Ludwig, A. Bode, M. Kiehl, and R. Mehlhorn. Developing Multicomputer Applications on Networks of Workstations Using NXLib. SFB-Bericht 342/17/93 A, Technische Universität München, 80290 München, December 1993.

System Support for Distributed Computing*

Silvano Maffeis

Department of Computer Science
University of Zurich
Winterthurerstr. 190, CH-8057 Zurich
maffeis@ifi.unizh.ch

Abstract. This paper hints at models and mechanisms which are part of current distributed systems research, and which may be of interest in the area of distributed, parallel computing as well. In this context, an experimental toolkit which allows for object-oriented programming of distributed, failure-resilient applications is presented. The toolkit, called ELECTRA, supports novel features like object-oriented communication, object-groups, and reliable multicast. We will compare the performance of a compute intensive application implemented on ELECTRA, on PVM, on a transputer, and on two different LINDA systems.

1 Introduction

Some authors make a distinction between *distributed systems* (DS), and *parallel distributed systems* (PDS). DS can be defined as general purpose systems, where distributed activities interact with one another to achieve some common goal. PDS can be defined as distributed systems whose main goal is to achieve maximum performance to solve a specific problem.

We feel that a fundamental distinction between DS and PDS is difficult to maintain, since both sorts of systems have many properties in common. For example, PDS benefit from the models and mechanisms which are being developed in the field of DS research. Examples are process groups [3] for achieving failure resilience, and causal communication [12, 22] for guaranteeing a consistent ordering of messages when several senders interact with several receivers in an asynchronous fashion.

In loosely coupled systems, failures should be seen as the normal case and not as an exception. Most of today's programming environments for PDS do not provide appropriate mechanisms for building failure resilient, robust applications. In contrast, during the past years DS research has addressed problems related with failures in loosely coupled, asynchronous systems, both from the theoretical and programmatical point of view. Models like *virtual synchrony* [4] or *pseudo synchrony* [16], and programming systems like CONSUL [16], DELTA-4

* This work is supported by *Siemens AG ZFE, Germany*, by the *Union Bank of Switzerland*, and by the *Eidgenössisches Volkswirtschaftsdepartement, Kommission zur Förderung der wissenschaftlichen Forschung (KWF), Switzerland*, Grants No. 2255.1, 2554.1

[18], Horus [23], Isis [3], and Transis [1] are the result thereof. We feel that these models and systems should as well be considered for the building of robust and efficient PDS. In the remainder of the paper, we will sometimes use the more general term DS to denote PDS as well.

The next section introduces a general purpose, object-oriented programming environment, called the Electra toolkit, which is based on mechanisms like process groups and virtual synchrony. Later we shall demonstrate how a parallel application implemented with this toolkit scales in a loosely coupled system.

2 The Electra Toolkit

Electra is a general-purpose, object-oriented toolkit for distributed systems which is in development at the University of Zurich, Switzerland. This section gives an introduction to the key aspects of Electra. For details refer to [13, 14, 15].

Unlike systems such as Pvm [20] or Linda [7], the Electra toolkit was not designed for parallelizing compute intensive applications on distributed systems only. Electra aims at different kinds of so-called *directly distributed systems* [5], *i.e.*, systems where distributed threads of execution interact directly with one another while continuously respecting constraints on their joint behavior. Parallel distributed applications are hence a good example of directly distributed systems. Electra offers a generic, object-oriented framework with which different kinds of distributed applications can be built.

2.1 Object-Oriented Communication

Electra allows to model a DS as a set of interacting C++ objects. Objects may have an *active* or a *passive* role. Applications can issue operations on remote, active objects. The invocation of an operation on a remote object is carried out using a syntax similar to and in many cases even identical with conventional C++ method invocations, which we call *Remote Method Calling* (RMC) [13]. To communicate with a remote object, the programmer invokes the methods of a local *proxy* object. The proxy presents a logically local access point to a remote object, and it has the same interface as the remote object. RMCs can take as arguments an arbitrary number of C++ base types and passive C++ objects, and may return an arbitrary number of base types and passive objects. RMCs can be carried out in a blocking or in a non-blocking fashion.

2.2 Interface Definition Language

The interface of an active object is declared using Corba-IDL [9]. A Corba-IDL compiler is used to automatically generate the Electra C++ code which is needed to marshal parameters of an RMC, transferring the data over the network, and to unmarshal the parameters at the receiver's site.

Advantages of having an IDL and a stub generator are that the programmer is not forced to write marshaling code, and that typechecking of RMC parameters can be performed at compile-time. Further, it becomes unnecessary to use a self-describing network representation like XDR [8], where each data element is labeled with its type. The stubs at both ends do not require this information since their code was derived from a common interface description. An IDL also allows to use conventional programming languages for implementing the behavior of an object, which was specified with the IDL. In addition, an application can access objects regardless of the programming language the object was implemented with.

2.3 Object-Groups

ELECTRA offers *object-groups* [15] for implementing failure resilient applications and load-sharing. An object-group consists of a set of object-instances which cooperate to achieve some common purpose. Each member of the group may be instantiated on a different host, and group members fail independently from each other. For example, a critical object in a PDS may be replicated and instantiated as an object-group. Applications may access the object as long as at least one member of the group is operational (k-way resilience).

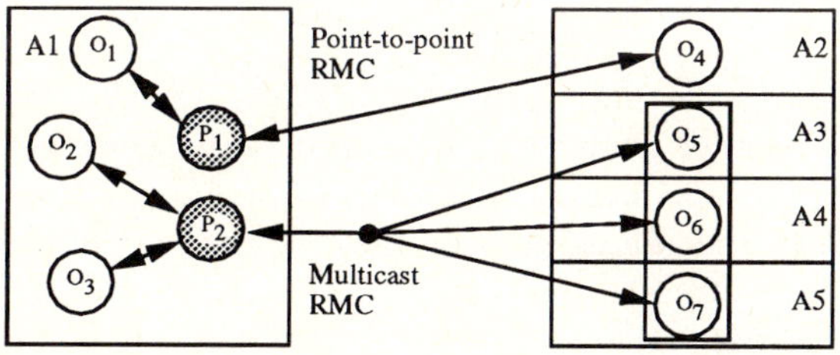

Fig. 1. Remote Method Calling by proxy objects. Proxy P_1 interfaces to a single object whereas P_2 interfaces to an object-group. O_i denotes an ELECTRA object, and A_i an address space.

The proxy objects we mentioned in Sect. 2.1 also hide replication from user programs, which is demonstrated by Fig. 1. This means that an application communicates with an object-group in the same manner it communicates with a singleton object. Operations on object-groups are transparently transmitted to each group member using order-preserving, reliable multicast [10, 12, 22].

Failure tolerance is not the only benefit of object-groups. When an object in a parallel distributed application becomes overloaded, it can be replaced by an object-group which parallelizes the task the overloaded object has. Since ELECTRA proxy objects offer replication transparency, applications which used the replaced object must not be modified to work with the object-group. Thus, parallelism and load sharing can be increased step by step by replacing overloaded singleton objects with object-groups.

2.4 Multi-Threading

Electra objects are multi-threaded, which allows for several methods of an object being active at the same time, and therefore for parallelism inside an object. In Electra, multi-threaded objects come at the price that programmers must explicitly deal with concurrency control. To synchronize activities inside an object, counting semaphores, locks, and event counters are provided.

2.5 Scalable Naming Scheme

Within Electra applications, human readable names are used to identify objects. An object name obeys to the form `<Domain>:<Path>`. For example, the name `"ifi.unizh.ch:/pds/worker81"` refers to the object `"/pds/worker81"` running within the domain `"ifi.unizh.ch"`. Scalability of the naming service is achieved by partitioning the name space into *administrative domains*. Normally, an administrative domain comprises the Electra objects instantiated within a LAN, and Electra applications may thus comprise several LANs. A special Electra object, called the *master trader*, acts as the name server for a specific domain.

2.6 Machine Independence and Portability

Low-level mechanisms for managing threads, process-groups, and for reliable multicast are not part of Electra. An important design goal of Electra is portability to different platforms which offer these low-level mechanisms. Examples of existing platforms which provide most of the low-level primitives needed by Electra are Amoeba [21], Consul [16], Delta-4 [18], Horus [23], Isis [3], Panda [2], and Transis [1].

The Electra toolkit builds upon a *virtual machine layer*, which is implemented in the form of a small set of interacting C++ objects. To port Electra to a specific platform, one needs to implement a specific *adaptor object*, which maps the generic primitives defined by the virtual machine layer onto the real primitives offered by the platform (see Fig. 2).

Electra can also be ported to systems which offer only a small fraction of the needed primitives, for example to Pvm or to the bare Unix[2] IPC mechanisms. In this case, more effort must be invested into the development of a suitable adaptor. For example, an adaptor could be implemented to have Electra applications run on distributed memory multiprocessor systems as well.

2.7 The Horus Toolkit

To implement an Electra adaptor for a platform such as Horus [23] is straightforward. Horus is the redesign of the well-known Isis [3] toolkit, and is in

[2] Unix is a trademark of Unix Systems Laboratories, Inc.

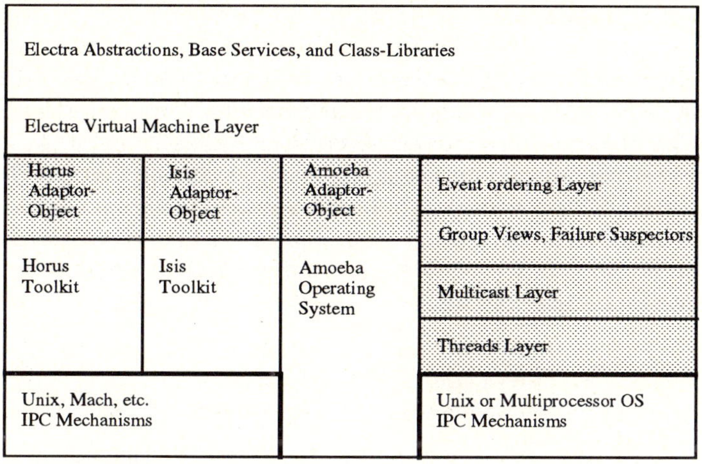

Fig. 2. Architecture of the ELECTRA toolkit. The functionality in the shaded areas is provided by adaptor objects.

development at Cornell University, Ithaca, New York. HORUS consists of several layers, the topmost one allowing for virtual synchronous [4] execution of distributed applications. This is the layer HORUS programmers are usually confronted with. The layers below offer functionality like failure suspectors, consistent group view management, light weight processes (threads), light weight process groups (thread-groups), reliable multicast, and asynchronous message passing.

Furthermore, HORUS supports a variety of UNIX operating systems, like SunOS, HP/UX, AIX, different microkernel operating systems, like MACH, CHORUS and AMOEBA, and communication architectures like the x-kernel [11].

Different communication protocols can dynamically be selected from within HORUS, for example TCP, UDP, Deering-IP, and MACH messages. If multicasting is supported by the underlying communication hard- or software, HORUS makes use of it. If no support is provided, multicasting is transparently simulated using point-to-point messages.

3 Performance Evaluation

To obtain a first impression of the scalability of parallel applications implemented with ELECTRA, a partial differential equation solver (PDES) was implemented in the form of a group of cooperating ELECTRA objects. The PDES was originally implemented on top of PVM, SCA Network LINDA[3] [17], POSYBL-LINDA[4] [19], and on a transputer[5] as part of the research project described in [6]. For our

[3] from Scientific Computing Associates, Inc., New Haven, CT.

[4] from the Department of Computer Science, University of Crete, Greece.

[5] a Parsytec MC-2/32-2 transputer with 32 T-800 processors.

purposes, we simply ported this PDES code to ELECTRA.

The transputer based implementation mainly served as a reference model. All the other experiments were performed on the same workstation network, which consisted of 38 SUN SPARCstation 1 computers interconnected by a 10 mb/sec Ethernet. The experiments were carried out on a dedicated network, which means that users were prevented from using the network during the experiments.

More specific, the considered application is a PDES from the theory of heat conduction. Imagine a rectangular grid with a certain initial temperature distribution on it. Applying the PDES, we computed the heat distribution several times to investigate how the heat on the grid changes over time.

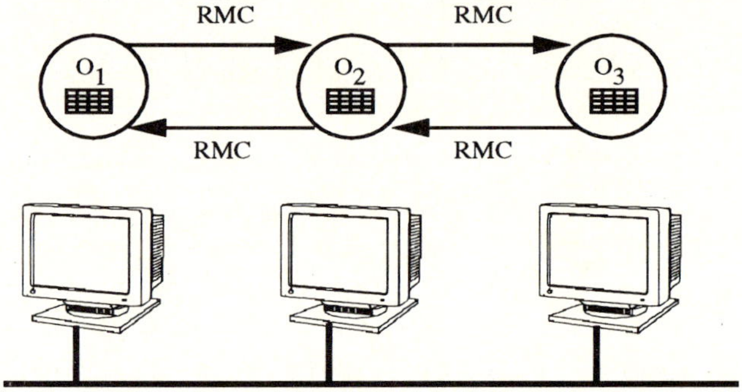

Fig. 3. Interaction patterns between the workstations. O_i denotes a worker-object.

The application is parallelized by partitioning the grid into vertical slices, and by assigning each slice to a worker-object on a different workstation. A worker-object computes the heat situation on its slice, and communicates the left grid-boundary to its left neighbor and the right grid-boundary to its right neighbor (supposing the worker-object is not at an outermost position) using non-blocking communication. Then, the worker-object must block until it receives the left and the right grid-boundary from its left and right neighbor, respectively. After this, the worker-object can compute the next time iteration, and so on. The outermost worker-objects use a constant right or left boundary condition. Figure 3 depicts the described situation. For more details on the computed application refer to [6].

The ELECTRA based implementation of the PDES uses blocking and non-blocking RMC to communicate the grid-boundaries. C++ classes were realized to encapsulate the grid, the grid slices, and the worker-objects. Message passing is used in the PVM based application. Within the LINDA application, the tuple space was used mainly for exchanging the boundaries. Finally, the PDES was implemented on the transputer using the OCCAM communication primitives.

Figure 4 demonstrates the speedup graph for the various implementations of the same PDES. We chose a grid size of 3800 per 100 and computed 500 time iterations. The graphs associated with the transputer, PVM, and with the LINDA implementations are results of the experiments described in [6], which were carried out on the same workstation network as the ELECTRA experiment.

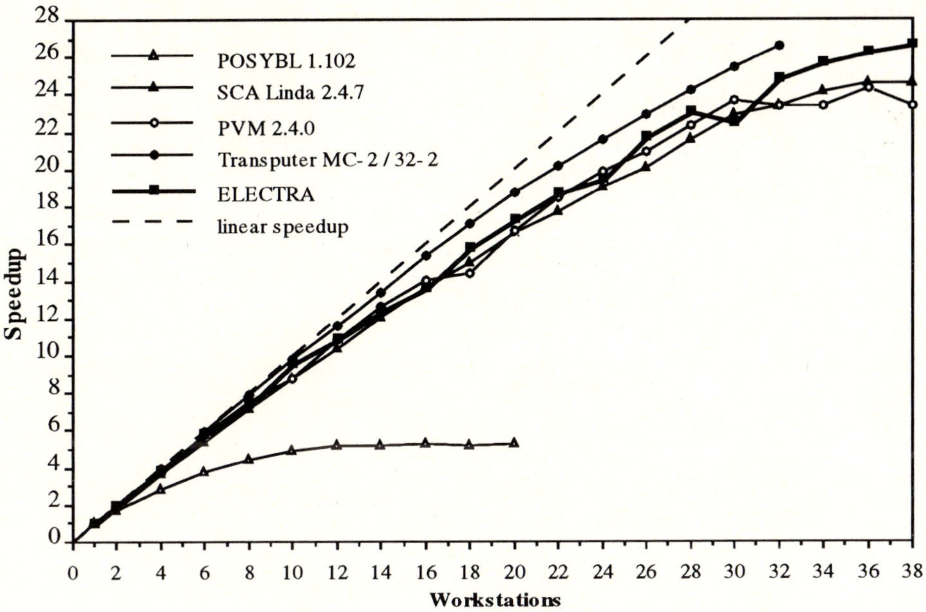

Fig. 4. Speedup of the distributed PDE application.

To obtain a distinct speedup value, the total execution time of the application was measured. This execution time did not include the time to startup worker-objects on the workstations.

4 Conclusions

The speedup curves in Fig. 4 show that for the PDES application implemented on a workstation network, ELECTRA achieved the highest speedup on 32 to 38 nodes[6]. This even though object-oriented communication was practiced and that ELECTRA is conceived for various kinds of directly distributed systems, not only for the ones which aim at achieving high speedups. The ELECTRA system we used is based on the HORUS platform (see Sect. 2.7), which has proven to allow for the implementation of efficient and robust distributed systems in workstation networks.

The public-domain LINDA implementation called POSYBL attained a very low speedup, whereas the same application implemented on the commercial network

[6] The knees in the ELECTRA graph for 24 and 30 workstations are due to a weakness in the HORUS flow control layer. The weakness has been eliminated in a newer version of HORUS, which was not available at the time the measurements were carried out.

LINDA system from SCA [17] scaled remarkably well. POSYBL is a pragmatic and simplistic approach to the implementation of the tuple space abstraction. SCA Network LINDA is a sophisticated implementation of the tuple space abstraction which includes various optimizations to minimize network communication. The speedup of PVM and SCA LINDA differ only slightly, event though LINDA provides a shared tuple space abstraction.

Unfortunately, many programming models and platforms for parallel computing in workstation networks do not provide mechanisms for building robust applications in environments such as large workstation networks, where failures occur frequently. Examples of such mechanisms are object-groups, reliable multicast, and virtual synchrony.

Since ELECTRA is based on platforms like HORUS and ISIS, it provides these mechanisms while offering a high level of abstraction and support in reusing software components. Our experiments demonstrate that a toolkit can provide these mechanisms and still achieve performance comparable to low-level programming systems like PVM, which do not provide important mechanisms like virtual synchrony and group communication.

References

1. AMIR, Y., DOLEV, D., KRAMER, S., AND MALKI, D. Transis: A Communication Sub-System for High Availability. In *22nd International Symposium on Fault-Tolerant Computing* (July 1992), IEEE.
2. BHOEDJANG, R., RUHL, T., HOFMAN, R., LANGENDOEN, K., BAL, H., AND KAASHOEK, F. Panda: A Portable Platform to Support Parallel Programming Languages. In *Symposium on Experiences with Distributed and Multiprocessor Systems IV* (San Diego, CA, Sept. 1993), USENIX.
3. BIRMAN, K. P. The Process Group Approach to Reliable Distributed Computing. *Communications of the ACM 36*, 12 (Dec. 1993).
4. BIRMAN, K. P., AND JOSEPH, T. A. Exploiting Virtual Synchrony in Distributed Systems. *ACM Operating Systems Review 21*, 5 (Nov. 1987).
5. BIRMAN, K. P., AND JOSEPH, T. A. Exploiting Replication in Distributed Systems. In *Distributed Systems*, S. Mullender, Ed. ACM Press, 1989.
6. CAP, C., AND STRUMPEN, V. Efficient Parallel Computing in Distributed Workstation Environments. *Parallel Computing 19*, 11 (Nov. 1993). Springer Verlag.
7. CARRIERO, N., GELERNTER, D., AND AHUIJA, S. Linda and Friends. *IEEE Computer 19*, 8 (Aug. 1986).
8. CORBIN, J., Ed. *The Art of Distributed Programming.* Springer Verlag, 1991. SUN Technical Reference Library.
9. DIGITAL EQUIPMENT CORP., HEWLETT-PACKARD CO., HYPERDESK CORP., NCR CORP., OBJECT DESIGN INC., SUNSOFT INC. *The Common Object Request Broker: Architecture and Specification*, Dec. 1991. Revision 1.1, OMG Document Number 91.12.1.
10. HADZILACOS, V., AND TOUEG, S. Fault-Tolerant Broadcasts and Related Problems. In *Distributed Systems*, S. Mullender, Ed., second ed. Addison Wesley, 1993, ch. 5.
11. HUTCHINSON, N., AND PETERSON, L. Design of the x-kernel. In *Proceedings of SIGCOMM'88* (Stanford, CA, Aug. 1988).

12. LAMPORT, L. Time, Clocks and the Ordering of Events in a Distributed System. *Communications of the ACM 21*, 7 (July 1978).
13. MAFFEIS, S. Electra – Making Distributed Programs Object-Oriented. In *Proceedings of the Symposium on Experiences with Distributed and Multiprocessor Systems IV* (San Diego, CA, 1993), USENIX.
14. MAFFEIS, S. Remote Method Calling and Object Group Communication. ECOOP Workshop on Object-based Distributed Programming, Kaiserslautern, Germany, July 1993.
15. MAFFEIS, S. A Flexible System Design to Support Object-Groups and Object-Oriented Distributed Programming. In *Proceedings of the ECOOP '93 Workshop on Object-Based Distributed Programming* (1994), R. Guerraoui, O. Nierstrasz, and M. Riveill, Eds., Springer-Verlag. To Appear.
16. MISHRA, S., PETERSON, L. L., AND SCHLICHTING, R. D. Consul: A Communication Substrate for Fault-Tolerant Distributed Programs. Tech. rep., Department of Computer Science, The University of Arizona, 1993.
17. PANEPINTO, J. UNIX Linda Enables Parallel Processing. *Digital News & Review*. Digital Equipment Corporation.
18. POWELL, D., ET AL. The Delta-4 Approach to Dependability in Open Distributed Computing Systems. In *Digest of Papers, FTCS-18* (Tokyo, 1988).
19. SCHOINAS, G. Issues on the implementation of POSYBL. Tech. rep., University of Crete, Greece, 1990.
20. SUNDERAM, V. PVM: A Framework for Parallel Distributed Computing. *Concurrency: Practice and Experience 2*, 4 (1990).
21. TANENBAUM, A. S. *Modern Operating Systems*. Prentice-Hall, 1992.
22. VAN RENESSE, R. Causal Controversy at Le Mont St.-Michel. *ACM Operating Systems Review 27*, 2 (Apr. 1993).
23. VAN RENESSE, R., BIRMAN, K. P., COOPER, R., GLADE, B., AND STEPHENSON, P. Reliable Multicast between Microkernels. In *Proceedings of the USENIX Workshop of Micro-Kernels and Other Kernel Architectures* (Seattle, Washington, Apr. 1992).

Assembly Environment for Development of Application Parallel Program

V.E.Malyshkin
Computing Center, Siberian Division
Russian Academy of Sciences
630090, Novosibirsk, Russia
Universiti Sains Malaysia, 11800 Penang, Malaysia
E_mail: malysh@comcen.nsk.su
malysh@cs.usm.my

ABSTRACT

Integrated system (Assembly System) to support technology of application problem parallelization, development (assembly) of parallel programs, turning to available resources of specific multiprocessor system in the course of their execution is presented. Contrary to partitioning assembly approach support synthesis (in a broad sense) of entire problem decision on the basis of elemental ready made fragments. It enable us to use the unified technology for solution of wide range application problem (in seismic data and image processing, nuclear physics, modeling of natural phenomena etc.) in the framework of the same parallel programming system. Our approach is a generalization of our experience in solution of large-size problems.

Keywords: Assembly parallel programming, Parallel computing technologies, Parallel software.

1. Introduction.

Assembly approach to the development of application parallel program is considered. Assembly approach is a generalization of our experience in development of parallel software and solution of big size problem in seismic data and image processing, modeling o natural phenomena (particle-in-cell method), nuclear physics, geophysics, electrophysics, quantum chaos. The main goal of our investigation is a solution of wide range of big size problems in science and applications, using unified technology of problem parallelization and parallel program creation. This approach was realized in the course of development of scalable high performance multiprocessor system (MPS) SIBERIA [1,2] and its parallel software. Above mentioned problems were solved on this MPS.

We proceed from the assumption that we need and we can assemble specific MPS (installation) oriented to a very effective solution of a specific problem from chosen area. We believe that user must use the same facilities to create his program for different architectures. We can't support this approach from a system software now for any architecture but it turns out that it can be supported for wide and important classes of architectures and problems. Another reason to assemble large MPSs also arise if the volume of existing computation must be drastically increased on the basis of hardware and software in current use.

This work was done in the framework of the academic research project Assembly Systems: ASSY which is funded by Russian Academy of Sciences. It was intended for studying assembling phenomena in parallel processing

2. The elements of assembling.

The following constituents of assembling can be listed.

2.1. Separation of fine grain and coarse grain computations. Fine and coarse grain computation must be executed on the different level of hardware and software. Fine grain computation of any problem must be encapsulated inside a module. This module can be realized very effectively on specialized processor element(PE). Parallel program must be assembling out of such ready made modules. The system of modules of a program will define a system of interacting processes (coarse grain computations). It means for realization of specific problem a specific nonhomogeneoue MPS with specialized PE must be assembled. Encapsulation of fine grain computation provide the possibilities to use formal methods of parallel program construction[3].

2.2. Separation of semantics and scheme of computation. Fine grain computation define a semantics (functions) of computations. Therefore on coarse grain level only a scheme (non-interpreted or semi-interpreted) [4] of computations is assembled. It means that methods of automatic synthesis of programs [3] can be used and standard schemes of parallel computations can be accumulated in libraries.

2.3. The regular method of MPS assembling. Diversity of different structures of MPSs and algorithms (structures of data transferring between processor elements and between processes) is too big and their structures do not always match each other. The consequence of unmatched structures of algorithm and MPS is a slump of MPS performance. Thus, restrictions must be imposed on the structure of MPS to fix minimum communications between PEs and to define conceivable extensions of communication lines. Knowledge of MPS structure provide the possibility to create parallel programs tuning on the available resources of MPS in the course of execution. These restrictions can be described as a set of rules for MPS assembling.

2.4. Parallel program assembling out of ready made modules.

Application program must be assembled out of ready made modules as a wall is laid from the bricks. It's known an entire computation can be automatically divided into fragments (partitioning) for very simple regular clases of algorithms usually represented as a systems of recurrent equations with linear dependencies between indexes[5,6]. Assembled computation keeps the "seams" of assembling. They give to compiler the information for automatic dividing entire computation in elementary fragments (as data as program code) which can be executed on separate PEs.

2.5. Mapping assembling. Parallel program must be tunable on the available resources of the specific installation. To provide this property first of all the structure of application algorithm must be restricted in order to be matched to MPS structure. Our experience have shown that such reasonable restrictions can be found and wide class of numerical algorithms can be transformed to satisfy to the restrictions. In this case it will be possible to accumulate a library of standard mappings and assembly of mapping of entire computation out of them.

3.Assembly parallel programming system INIA. Realization of approach.

Assembly approach was applied for the development of MPS SIBERIA [1,2], its parallel software and for solution big size problems .

3.1. Hierarchical MPS assembling. Hierarchical MPS is defined in two steps. At the first step the basic elementary "building blocks" of the system are selected. The first "building block" is the host computer (HC) with the complete set of peripheral devices and well-developed external communications. The second component is represented by PEs. Each PE is high-performance processor with the main memory and control units of its own. PE operation is controlled by HC which initiates PE, transfers programs and data to the PE, synchronizes the computation, at the same time PE as a slave computer may even fail to have its own i/o devices. At the second step the options of connections of "building blocks" are defined. There are two allowed types of connections. Radial connections provide the host-slave interaction between HC and PEs. Similar PEs constitute a subsystem, there can be several subsystems. The other type of connection is interprocessor interface. It provides the high data rate of exchange between the PEs inside the subsystem of similar PE bypassing the HC and providing effective interaction of the lower-level processors.

The above connections present only the general connections between the components of MPS. Their set can be increased. Every PE in its turn can have a complicated structure, in this case there also must be a host and slave processors. Thus the allowed MPS must have a hierarchical structure with connected PE (Fig. 1 and 2).

3.2. Linear Algorithms. The restrictions imposed on the structure of the algorithm - conditions of algorithm linearity - are as follows:

1. All the processes of the algorithm must be linearly ordered.

2. Only linear interactions between processes are allowed, i.e. if the i-th and j-th processes a_i and a_j interact, then $j \leq i+m$, m is a constant of the algorithm. Therefore if algorithm is being mapped in the MPS resources and the processes $a_{i-m},\ldots,a_i,\ldots a_{i+m}$ will are assigned to the processors, then all the interactions of a_i can be performed [Fig.3].

Consider the following example. Let A be a matrix whose elements must be sequentially recalculated (filtration of a kind): A(i,j)Filter(A). This is not a linear algorithm. Algorithm is linearized through encapsulation of fragments of regular computation and their inclusion into a new operation with a greater volume of computations. The matrix A is subdivided into overlapping layers (several adjoining rows or columns) $A_1, A_2, \ldots, A_k$ (Fig. 4). In each layer A_r, r1,2,...,k, all computations inside Ar are performed by the process *ar* , processes *a1* ,*a2* ,...,*ak* are linearly ordered, there are no interactions. If number of applied filters is large the number of columns in the overlapping can be great. To reduce this number the overlapped columns must be recovered by means of exchange between the processes a_{i-1}, a_i, a_{i+1}. In this case linear interactions between processes will arise. Many mass current used practical algorithms can be linearized in such a way. Conditions of algorithm linearity provide effective automatic mapping of computation on available resources of specific MPS installation and assembling of whole mapping.

Mahanti and Daniels [14] introduced some new algorithms for the parallel search on SIMD data-parallel computers. Two main phases can be distinguished during the iterative-deepening parallel search

1. *The search phase:* Where each processors conducts its search.
2. *The load balancing phase:* Whenever one or more processors become idle a load balancing procedure is invoked.

In this paper, we introduce general methods for load balancing data for SIMD data-parallel computers or synchronous distributed multiprocessors.

Notations For the rest of this article, we use the following notations. n is the total number of processors, P_i denotes the processor number i and N is the total load of the system.

2 Global Load Balancing Algorithms

The load balancing phase (the migration phase) is invoked by a triggering mechanism. The load balancing phase sends data from one processor to another one in order to decrease the imbalance of the system. When the data can migrate all over the system, the strategy is called global. In general, the global policies allow a better redistribution of work among the system because there is no idle area which is out of the redistribution zones. We present two global algorithms, the rake algorithm allowing an almost-perfect redistribution of work and the matching algorithm.

2.1 The Rake Algorithm

The aim of this scheme is to redistribute almost-perfectly the work among the processors so that we do not need to load balance too often. At the end of the work redistribution phase the processor load will be close to N/n. For the rake scheme, every processor is involved in the load balancing phase. The algorithm works as follows in a ring, every processor transfers in a torus-way all the data above the average value to their right neighbour. On a grid, the algorithm is realized as 2 applications of this basic algorithm on a ring, one for each dimension of the grid. We show in [5] that for a n processors ring, an perfect load balancing was achieved in fewer than n steps.

2.2 The Matching Algorithm

The Matching works as follows: each time we load balance we try to match overloaded processors with idle ones. Several versions of this algorithm have already been presented [10, 17, 14]. Our implementation differs because only the processors with a weight above the average value of the system will give some data to the idle processors. Furthermore, the Matching algorithm gives a certain amount of holes to idle processors and tokens to overloaded ones and then associates heavily overloaded processors with processors having a great deficit and lightly overloaded processors with lightly underloaded processors in a parallel way to speed up the load balancing phase.

3 Distributed Load Balancing Algorithms

The main disadvantage of the global migration strategy is that the scability is weak [1]. Moreover, in massively parallel architecture a local near-neighbour communication network is sometimes available and is often quicker than the global communication network. For example, 2 communication networks are available on the MasPar data-parallel computer. The X-Net communications which allow each PE to access a PE in one of the 8 directions and the Global Router which allows a global communication between any 2 PEs. As a general rule, the X-Net allows high speed communication and is very efficient for local and uniform communications [7, 18].

With a local migration policy, on the one hand the system is able to react quickly to lightly unbalanced situation but on the other hand a more heavily unbalanced case is overcome with more steps than with a global policy.

3.1 The Local Algorithm

This strategy is a local, distributed, near neighbour approach. We present this scheme for a grid computer (2 dimensions). The grid is divided into small overlapping domains. A domain (an island of redistribution) is a set of processors. The aim of this scheme is to achieve a situation in which the maximum weight difference between processors in the same domain is the smallest possible. In our case, each processor has got 4 neighbours and belongs to 5 overlapping domains. Each domain is centred on an idle processor so that its neighbours will send to it a part of the data they own.

3.2 The X-Local Algorithm

As a matter of fact, we did not have good results with the previous algorithm. We face some problems where there were large areas of idle or very underloaded processors and disjoint large areas of overloaded processors. In that case, the previous scheme behaves very poorly and it takes quite a long time for the system to converge to a steady state. In order to palliate to this problem, we extend the Local algorithm in the following way.

Instead of exchanging the data with its neighbour processors, every processor will be able to send data to to more distant processors. In order to preserve the regularity of the communications, every processor will exchange its data with processors at the same distance. By doing this, we facilitate the transfer of data from overloaded area to underloaded zones. A path is defined to indicate the "lenght" of the transfers and will be updated after each load balancing phase. It is important to note that the scheme efficiency is highly dependant of the path function.

4 Experimental results

We implemented the Mandelbrot set computation on a 1024 processors MasPar MP-1. This is a typical example of no *apriori* knowledge. A good description of the Mandelbrot set implementation can be found in [21, 3]. For each point z in the complex plane, we recursively compute the following operation $z = z^2 + c$ where c is a constant. The computation is stopped for a point as soon as $|z| > 2$ or as soon as the number of iterations needed is over a fixed threeshold.

The MP-1 is a Single-Instruction Multiple-Data stream computer which means all the processors execute the same instruction. The processors are arranged in a two-dimensional torroidal matrix called the PE array. Two communication networks are avalaible, the X-Net network has a built-in direction of communications and is often used for local communications while the Global Router is for general purpose. In general, X-Net communications are faster than Global Router communications.

There are some important criterions to measure the performance of our load balancing schemes: speedup, utilization ...

Speedup The speedup is the ratio of the time taken by the algorithm on one processor divided by the time taken on n processors.

$$S_n = \frac{T_1}{T_n}$$

where T_1 is the time taken by a sequential implementation of the algorithm T_n is the time taken by the parallel algorithm on n processors.

The main part of the algorithm is made of points computation. If t_{calc} is the time taken for a unit of computation, the speedup can be written as:

$$S_n = \frac{N^1_{\text{iter}} \times t_{\text{calc}}}{N^n_{\text{iter}} \times t_{\text{calc}}}$$

where N^1_{iter} is the number of iterations needed to complete the program on one processor, N^n_{iter} is the number of iterations for the parallel program.

However as [14] pointed it out, the speedup does not take care of the load balancing time. So, we introduce the balancing speedup (S'_n) which deals with the time wasted during the load balancing phases.

$$\begin{aligned} S'_n &= \frac{T_1}{T_n+T_{\text{lb}}} \\ &= \frac{T_1}{T_n} \times \frac{1}{1+\frac{T_{\text{lb}}}{T_n}} \\ &= S_n \times \frac{1}{1+\frac{T_{\text{lb}}}{T_n}} \end{aligned}$$

where T_{lb} is the total time spent during the load balancing

Utilization The processor utilization is defined as the average percentage of iterations the processors are busy during the execution of the parallel algorithm.

$$U = \frac{N^1_{\text{iter}} \times 100}{N^n_{\text{iter}} \times n}$$

Computation Time for solving the Mandelbrot Set 256 × 256 from −2.0 − 1.25*i* to 0.5 + 1.25*i*							
Algorithm	pts/PE	MAXITER	N^1_{iter}	N^n_{iter}	S_n	S'_n	% Util.
NONE	64	100	1.9E6	6400	300	300	29.5
NONE	192	100	5.7E6	19200	300	300	29.5
Rake	64	100	1.9E6	2780	690	600	67
Rake	192	100	5.7E6	8080	712	621	69.5
Matching	64	100	1.9E6	2860	670	655	65.5
Matching	192	100	5.7E6	8240	698	677	68
Local	64	100	1.9E6	6400	300	290	29.5
Local	192	100	5.7E6	19200	300	281	29.2
X-Local	64	100	1.9E6	3320	578	551	56
X-Local	192	100	5.7E6	8700	661	612	65

Table 1. Mandelbrot Results

Results

The table 1 shows some of the results we obtained for solving the Mandelbrot sets on the 1k MasPar MP-1 computer. Another point to note is that in order to spend not much time in checking the global convergence of the processors, only every 20 iterations we check the global convergence. Furthermore, the load balacing schemes can be called only every 50 iterations. We use a static triggering mechanism, as soon as 10% of the processors are idle, the load balancing scheme is called.

Table 1 shows that with the "naive" classical parallelization very few processors really do some work. At average more than 2/3 of the processors will be idle waiting for the others to finish their work. With a good load balancing policy, we increase the utilization of the processors up to 70 % (Rake algorithm) and we obtain a high load balancing speedup of 677 wich means an efficency of 0.66, a much better value than the naive parallelization.

5 Conclusion

In this paper, we present several methods for load balancing data in a SIMD computer. There are two types of approach; either global or local. With an easy example, we showed that dynamic load balancing for SIMD data-parallel computers can really improve the performance of the system and is as efficient as in the MIMD case. We plan to work on the constraint load balancing. For example, in image processing, a pixel value is not only dependent of its value but also of its neighbour values. In such cases, a pixel value is neighbour-dependent and must be moved with much care.

References

1. A. Corradi, L. Leonardi, and F. Zambonelli. Load balancing strategies for massively parallel architectures. *Parallel Processing Letters*, 2, 1992.

2. George Cybenko. Dynamic load balancing for distributed memory multiprocessors. *Journal of Parallel and Distributed Computing*, 7, 1989.
3. Alan Dewdney. Computer recreations: A computer microscope zooms in for a look at the most complex object in mathematics. *Scientific American*, page 16, August 1985.
4. Raphael Finkel and Udi Manber. DIB-a distributed implementation of backtracking. *ACM Transactions on Programming Languages and Systems*, 9(2), 1987.
5. Cyril Fonlupt, Philippe Marquet, and Jean-Luc Dekeyser. Dynamic data redistribution on SIMD data-parallel computers. Technical report, Université de Lille I, Lille, France, 1993.
6. M.R. Garey and D.S. Johnson. *Computers and Intractability: A Guide to the theory of NP-Completeness.* Freeman, 1979.
7. Cyril Gavoille. Evaluation of the MasPar performances. Technical report, Ecole Normale Supérieure de Lyon, Lyon, France, February 1992.
8. Dimitris Gerogiannis and Stelios C. Orphanoudakis. Load balancing requirements in parallel implementation of image feature extraction tasks. *IEEE Transactions on Parallel and Distributed Systems*, 4(9):994, September 1993.
9. Wouter Joosen, Stijn Bijnens, and Pierre Verbaeten. A reusable load balancer for parallel search problems. In *Euromicro 93*, Barcelona, September 1993.
10. George Karypis and Vipin Kumar. Unstructured tree search on SIMD parallel computers: A summary of results. In *Supercomputing 92*, 1992.
11. Richard E. Korf. Depth-first iterative-deepening: An optimal admissible tree search. *Artificial Intelligence*, 27:97, 1985.
12. Vipin Kumar and V. Nageshwara Rao. Parallel depth first search. part II. *Int'l Journal of Parallel Programming*, 16(6), 1987.
13. F. Lin and R. Keller. The gradient model load balancing method. *IEEE Transactions on Software Engeneering*, 13(1):32, January 1987.
14. Ambuj Mahanti and Charles J. Daniels. A SIMD approach to parallel heuristic search. *Artificial Intelligence*, 60:243, 1993.
15. Lionel M. Ni, Chong-Wei Xu, and Thomas B. Gendreau. A distributed drafting algorithm for load balancing. *IEEE Transactions on Software Engeneering*, 11(10), October 1985.
16. D. Nicol and J. Saltz. Dynamic remapping of parallel computations with varying resource demands. *IEEE Transactions on Computers*, 37(9):1073, September 1988.
17. Curt Powley, Chris Ferguson, and Richard Korf. Depth-first heuristic search on a SIMD machine. *Artificial Intelligence*, 60, 1993.
18. Lutz Prechelt. Measurements of MasPar MP-1216A communication operations. Technical report, Universität Karlsruhe, 1992.
19. R.McConnell and R.H. Perrott. A hybrid load balancing scheme for distributed memory multiprocessors. Technical report, The Queen's University, Belfast, Northern Ireland, 1993.
20. Eli Shamir and Eli Upfal. A probabilistic approach to the load-sharing problem in distributed systems. *Journal of Parallel and Distributed Computing*, 4, 1987.
21. Sherryl Tomboulian and Matthew Pappas. Indirect addressing and load balancing for faster solution to mandelbrot set on SIMD architectures. In *Frontiers 91*, 1991.
22. Shirley A. William. *Models for Parallel Systems.* Wiley, 1990.

Distributed Scheduling for Multicomputers

Laurent Philippe and Guy-René Perrin

University of Franche-Comté, F-25030 Besançon
e-mail: philippe@comte.univ-fcomte.fr

Abstract. Load sharing or load balancing are generally described as ways to get better execution performances : lots of experimentations have been successfully carried out, usually on networks of workstations. In this article we present new aspects of the load balancing issue when applying it to multicomputers. The main constraints and motivations for a load balancing service on multicomputers are studied. We show that this service could rise to a distributed scheduling service, integrated in the operating system and could avoid the hard process mapping task. A description of a load balancing implementation under Chorus/MiX is given.

Introduction

New architectures - networks of workstations or multiprocessors generate new issues in resources allocation, because of the number and the distribution of the resources. In the case of distributed architectures none of the issues are easy to solve because the system can not access the state of all remote nodes in order to globally manage a resource. Some of these issues have already been described in the literature. For instance, load sharing or load balancing is generally described as a way to get better execution performances or to allocate unused machines. Lots of experimentations have been successfully carried out, usually on networks of workstations, but not followed by a large diffusion due to ownership constraints implied by the workstation concept. Thus, taking benefit of unused machines, without truly balancing the load, is probably enough.

In this article we present new aspects of the load balancing issue when applying it to multicomputers. Using load balancing as a support we show that it could rise to a distributed scheduling service, integrated in the operating system. In the first part, we point out the main requirements when implementing a load balancing service for multicomputers and we present a survey of load balancing solutions, in the light of these requirements. The second part describes our studies on the design of a distributed scheduler for multicomputers.

1 Load balancing on multicomputers

Multicomputers are often dedicated to specialized applications. However, they are more and more based on general purpose microprocessors, so they can be used for general purpose applications (as an execution server in network of workstations for instance). In that case, the operating system must be general purpose oriented and it must provide some support to users. Load balancing is one of the services which will facilitate the multicomputer use.

1.1 Motivations and constraints

Outside of better execution performances, load balancing may be justified, on multicomputers, by a global management of the execution resource. In multicomputers, the nodes are located in the same cabinet. The machine appears to be a unique machine, even if it is composed of several nodes. There is no ownership constraint on multicomputers : the set of processors is shared by the users. So, the load service is in charge of scheduling the allocation of processes to nodes.

To be efficient on multicomputers, load balancing algorithms must provide some basic properties :

Scalability is essential for algorithms implemented on multicomputers. To p-reserve its interest, the algorithm must not be limited to some classes of architectures and must be efficient for small sized networks as well as large sized networks. This mean that the number of nodes involved in an exchange must be independent of the total number of nodes.

Fault-tolerance, as scalability, is essential for algorithms managing multicomputers. In a system composed of several hundreds of nodes, the probability of a node breakdown is higher than on a standard computer. Thus the load balancing service of a node must be able to dynamically be started (or stopped) and participate to the whole load management.

Stability is needed by the limited knowledge of the global load. A stable algorithm will avoid unnecessary process transfer : for instance, transferring processes from site A to site B and from site B to site A in a few time. An unstable algorithm may generate an excess of work by spending more time in load displacement. Unstability is generally carried out by an over-reacting algorithm or by a lack of check before a load transfer.

Scattering is a key to achieve good load balance but it is not or seldom treated in the load balancing literature. Scattering is the ability of the algorithm to scatter the load when a peak appears or to avoid geographic build-ups in load. To achieve an efficient scattering the information exchange must not be limited to the closer nodes but rather involve distant nodes.

1.2 Implications of multicomputers constraints

The global problem of load balancing can be divided in several independent subproblems such as load estimation, displacement policy, etc. In this part we show the implications of multicomputers properties on the issues a load balancing service yields.

Load estimation

The load of a site depends on the amount of used resources :

• the processor load is surely an essential value because we aim at managing the allocation of nodes in term of execution resources,

• the amount of free memory is also a resource use estimator but less significant in case of large memory spaces and MMU,

• the network load may be important for communicating processes but the local load is not ever significant : messages can pass through the node without being intended to it.

In [?], the authors compare different load balancing algorithms. They point out that sample policies, using not much informations, give acceptable results compared with complex algorithms.

Exchange of values

Most of the work done on load balancing was concerned by the exchange of load values. The instant of exchange may be **Periodic**, if the values are exchanged at each period, or **On-demand**, if the load values are exchanged when the node becomes over- or under loaded. The periodic policy may anticipate a load variation by frequently comparing the local and global loads. On the other hand, it reacts more slowly than the on-demand policy to a sudden load imbalance.

The scalabity of the exchange of value depend on the number of nodes implied in an exchange. In **pairing**, load values are exchanged with one site, chosen randomly or by round robin in a set of sites, for instance the neighbors. This policy is scalable - the cost of exchange will not vary with the nodes count - but not efficient. An improvement is proposed by [?] : each site maintains a load table where load values of sites are recorded. The exchange of values may be limited to the **Neighborhood** when the communication network does not provide routing facilities[?]. In case of direct communication between all nodes, this policy is too expensive because it implies several displacements of the same process before achieving a good load distribution. Moreover this policy does not provide a global view of the load. In **Limited Bidding**[?], an overloaded node sends load propositions to a randomly chosen set of nodes. This case is similar to the pairing policy with a better knowledge of the global load because the exchange is done with more than one site. In any case, **Broacast** must be avoided if there is no dedicated hardware.

Displacement policy

Several studies has been done to compare remote execution and process migration [?] and no consensus has been found. Some argue that process migration is too expensive to be used. Otherones show [?] that it is interesting in particular cases. On multicomputers, where instances of the process executable file are not spread on each node (these instances must be loaded from a remote disk in most of the cases), the duration of process migration may be comparable to remote execution : the differences are in freezing the process and in transferring uninitialized data. A load balancing service based on remote execution will provide good stability by limiting load transfers, but process migration will be necessary to achieve a true distributed scheduling : process migration interact with local schedulers to implement a global or distributed scheduling. Using both policies is a good solution : a first load balance is done by remote execution and migration is used just for optimizing the balance.

2 Distributed scheduling implementation

The concepts we developed previously were used as a base for a distributed scheduling implementation. It lies on a simulation and an actal implementation in Chorus/MiX on a iPSC/2.

2.1 Distributed scheduling simulation

In order to better understand the behavior of load balancing algorithms on multicomputers, we have simulated three algorithms, chosen on the criterions developed in ??. The first one is based on random pairing, the second one on limited bidding and the last one on random pairing with load tables exchange. The same simulations have run without load balancing in order to compare the performances improvement.

An exponential law has been used to generate processes and their life time. Processes are executed keeping the time sharing allocation of processors, thus our aim is to truly simulate distributed scheduling. The duration of process migration, remote execution and message exchanges are parameters of the simulation.

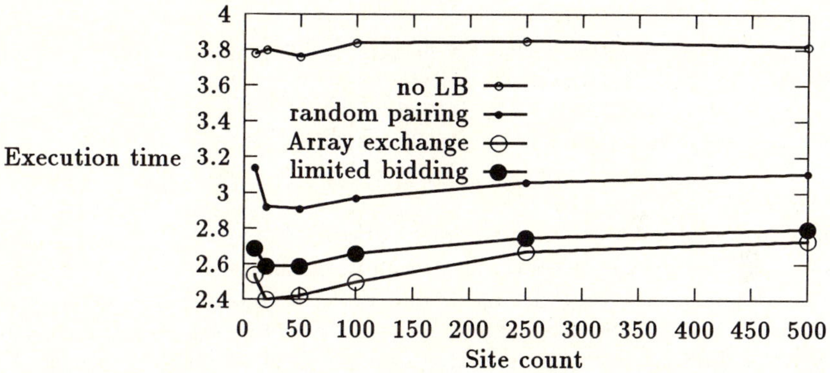

For instance, the preceding curves are obtained with 0.8 % of load. We can state that the behavior and the performances of a load balancing algorithms seem to become stable above 250 sites. If proven this result will be useful to multicomputers with thousands of nodes. Works is on going in this domain.

2.2 Implementation of a load management

According to the previous study on load balancing algorithms, we have developed a process migration facility and a load balancing manager for the Chorus/MiX system on the iPSC/2. These implementations are a first approach to delimit issues encountered when developing a load balancing service.

A. Process migration facility

We have developed a process migration service for Chorus/MiX. The implementation has been done on a iPSC/2.

Transfer algorithm

The transfer algorithm is subject to several constraints :

• the algorithm can not rely on the use of a disk to satisfy several multicomputers configurations, in particular the ones with few disks,

• to satisfy the needs of dynamic reconfiguration the algorithm must tolerate faults. So it can not have residual dependency,

• to optimize the use of the network, the algorithm must limit message exchanges.

Actually several migration algorithms have been described in the literature. Generally, they imply either residual dependencies [?][?] or increase network load [?]. Thus we have implemented the most sample algorithm which consist in sending all the system and memory context of the process to its destination node.

Some performances

Computing the duration of a process migration is not easy because the migration runs on two sites. In the following table, the local execution of a process is compared with the execution of a process which has been migrated there and back to a remote site (no lazy transfer is used). Time is given in milliseconds.

Size of process	time without migration	time with migration	duration of a migration
21 Ko.	15250	15700	225
49 Ko.	15250	16000	375
106 Ko.	16000	17200	600

Thus a migration represent less than 5 percent of a process in a first, unoptimized implementation. We must notice that migration performances are closely tied to communication performances which are 9.6 ms for 4 Ko. In conclusion we can say that the cost of a process migration does not seem to be too expensive. We must also notice that the Chorus/MiX operating system provides a good support, to implement a process migration facility, through an extensive use of transparent communication services.

B. The Load Manager

Global view

The Load Manager (LM) has been developed in the shape of a new server for the Unix sub-system of Chorus. The first implementation uses the algorithm described in [?] : a random pairing with load table exchange to optimize the diffusion of load values. A periodic load exchange is used. In the first implementation, described here, the load balance is done by using remote execution which is a service of the Chorus/MiX system. To ensure fault tolerance properties to load management, none of the message exchanges will block. Thus, if a site is down the LM will just loose its message but not its control.

Analysis

The LM has been implemented on a iPSC/2 under the Chorus/MiX operating system. The tests were done on a sixteen nodes machine but it runs on a height node machine as well. The LM is portable and can be used for other multicomputers. We intend to use it on a machine with height, transputer based, nodes. Functions implemented by the LM are independent, thus they can evolve separately. Changing the load balancing algorithm will then be possible without implying a great effort. The use of the load balancing service on the iPSC/2 has shown that it is a key to achieve distribution transparency on multicomputers.

Conclusion

This paper delimits the needs and motivations for load balancing on multicomputers. The main result is that load balancing is definitely the key to provide a transparent execution of processes on several nodes. Thus, a true distributed scheduling means that the same chance will be given to all the processes : the system will fairly share the execution time.

References

[Barak85] A. Barak and all *A Distributed Load-balancing Policy for a Multicomputer* Software Practice and Experience July 85

[Doug91] F. Douglis and all *Transparent Process Migration: Design Alternatives and the Sprite Implementation* Software Practice and Experience August 91

[Eager86] D. L. Eager and all *Adaptive Load Sharing in Homogeneous Distributed Systems* IEEE transactions on software engineering, May 1986

[Krue88] P. Krueger and all *A Comparison of Preemptive and Non-Preemtive Load Distributing* 8th ICDCS San Jose, CA June 88

[Lela86] W. E. Leland and all *Load-Balancing Heuristics and Process Behavior* ACM SIGMETRICS 1986, Raleigh, NC

[Lin86] C. H. Lin and all *Gradient Model: a Demand-driven Load Balancing Scheme* 6th ICDCS, Cambridge, MA May, 86

[Phil93] Laurent Philippe *Contribution à l'étude et à la réalisation d'un système à image unique pour multicalculateur* Phd Thesis University of Franche-Comté Janurary 93

[Thei85] M. Theimer and all *Preemptive Remote Execution Facilities for the V System* ACM Press: Operating System review December 1985

[Zaya87] E. Zayas *Attacking the Process Migration Bottleneck* 11th ACM SOSP, Austin, Texas November 1987

A Tool for Optimizing Programs on Massively Parallel Computer Architectures

Olav Hansen

Institut für Informatik der Technischen Universität München,
D-80290 München, Germany, Email: hansen@informatik.tu-muenchen.de

Abstract. In this paper a tool is introduced that is capable of measuring and describing program execution on massively parallel computing systems. It allows to focus measurements on relevant points of execution by specifying behavioral attributes. Relevant aspects of the scalable implementation of this tool are described and an example of its application is given.

1 Introduction

Developments in the field of supercomputing during the last couple of years showed that new classes of applications (The Grand Challenges) gain importance that demand for new dimensions in computing power. These demands can only be saturated by applying massive parallelism to the solution of such problems. We consider the use of at least a few hundred processors to be massively parallel. Today several commercially available hardware platforms exist that offer massive parallelism. Although still a lot of improvements on the hardware side are desirable, e.g. lower communication latencies, the main problems have to be solved in developing applications that utilize the theoretical performance capabilities of such systems.

State of the art in parallel programming are programs with explicit synchronization and message passing mechanisms. Code produced by automatic parallelization tools so far does not reach the efficiency of programs parallelized manually. The programming paradigm that is best suited to utilize the performance capabilities of massively parallel systems is the SPMD paradigm [Kar87].

The development of efficient parallel programs has to be supported in all phases of the program design and coding. In this article we focus on tools that support the optimization process of programs that have been coded and are being executed on massively parallel hardware platforms. We especially regard how the optimization of applications that are programmed according to the SPMD paradigm is supported.

First we will give a short survey on existing performance measurement tools. We address the execution analysis methods these tools offer, how these methods fit the needs of the class of applications mentioned above and the implementation problems that come up when dealing with tools for massively parallel systems.

In the next section we will describe the new version of our performance measurement tool PATOP [BHL90] which is available for Parsytec T805 and

PowerPC based parallel computing systems. It allows to focus measurements on points of interest in the system by specifying behavioral attributes rather than location. This makes it scalable to arbitrary system sizes. Behavioral attributes are given as thresholds to the results of other measurements. Thus a direct link between results of different measurements can be made that enables the user to link global system behavior to the execution of individual program parts. We will also show how the distributed measurement evaluation and the on-line mode of operation enable the tool to handle the implementation problems of tools for massively parallel computing platforms.

Finally we will show how the tool can be used to identify performance bottlenecks. We will show this for an implementation of the traveling salesman algorithm that performs well on small numbers of processors and gets severe and unexpected performance problems for bigger numbers of processors.

2 State of the art in performance measurement tools

Tools like Paragraph [HE91] [RAA+93] and the tools belonging to the EXPRESS environment [Par92] support two levels of system representation in detecting and tracking down performance bottlenecks. On the first level profile data for the complete program execution is presented. On this level it is possible to evaluate the system performance and to identify the processor states and nodes that cause performance losses. Paragraph offers a big set of different displays for looking at different aspects of the measured values. On the next level process and processor states and interactions are displayed in detail over a time axis. On this level it is possible to identify the sequence of actions of the program that cause the efficiency losses detected before.

Both tools can handle and display data just for a limited number of nodes, because they are trace based and work with common trace files for all nodes. Another major issue that limits their scalability is the big gap between overview values and detailed values about processor states and interaction. There is no structured way to find the interesting points in space and time, starting from system related overview displays.

The IPS-2 system [MCH+90] supports a stepwise refinement process in detecting and tracking down performance bottlenecks. It is possible to look at data of the complete system, individual nodes, processes and procedures. Profile values can be produced to identify the processor states and nodes that cause performance losses. Values with high resolution in time can be produced to identify the program phases where performance losses occur. Finally with process and procedure related values it is possible to detect the program parts that cause performance losses.

IPS-2 is in principle able to handle any number of nodes. Performance bottlenecks can be tracked down in space and time by stepwise refinement. The implementation is scalable because trace data is stored and processed in a distributed way. The distributed storage of data is possible because IPS-2 is implemented for workstations in a network where every workstation has its local disk space.

IPS-2 still lacks a method to find performance bottlenecks that are not bound to a certain location. Such performance bottlenecks may appear in SPMD style programs when the performance loss is due to the execution of a certain part of the program. In SPMD style programs any part of the program may be executed on any node at some point of time.

The Quartz System [AL90] extends the gprof [GKM82] method to the requirements of parallel systems. It has a very sophisticated calculation scheme for processor utilization that adds idle processor states to the processor utilization of the procedures that cause them. With this it helps a user in optimizing his program by showing him the procedures that are relevant for optimizing, but for calculating its values it requires information about the global state of the system at any point of time. In distributed memory systems this information is not available when recording the data and in order to calculate it after execution, unrealistic amounts of trace data would have to be collected. For this reason Quartz only works on shared memory systems. It is also difficult to find temporary performance bottlenecks that are due to data distributions. Such performance bottlenecks are also very common to SPMD style programs.

3 A scalable tool for optimizing parallel programs

The new version of our performance monitoring tool PATOP supports the search for performance bottlenecks in SPMD style programs in a scalable way. It is scalable in respect to its implementation and in the way it supports a programmer in detecting the performance bottlenecks in his program.

PATOP allows the measurement of CPU utilization, communication delays, external I/O delays, data transfer rates and delays in parts of the program that are defined by user inserted statements. These measurements can be done in relation to the complete program or individual procedures.

As a first analysis step PATOP supports the evaluation of the overall system performance by giving overview information on the overall resource utilization. This information can be displayed with any resolution in respect to time. It is also possible to look at the distribution of the resource utilization in respect to the nodes of the system. The main point of interest is the utilization of computational resources; the utilization of other resources becomes interesting, when searching for the reasons for insufficient utilization of computational resources.

When performance bottlenecks have been discovered, the next step in analysis is to focus measurements on the intervals and nodes where interesting utilization values are measured. This relates interesting utilization values to the results of other measurements and to the program parts that are executed. The focusing is done by specifying behavioral attributes as thresholds to results of a measurement. An example for a measurement that is focused through an behavioral attribute is:

> The average delay of processes in external I/O operations on all nodes that are more than 50% idle.

The behavioral attribute is evaluated for each measurement interval and only those nodes are considered in the measurement, where the condition of the behavioral attribute is fulfilled. It is possible to combine more than one condition to one attribute. The concept of the behavioral attributes makes it possible to focus measurements on points of interest independently from the size of the system. It allows to draw links between global system behavior and the execution of individual program parts in a structured way.

The class of applications massively parallel computing systems are needed for are long running programs that repeat the same execution cycles over and over again. Of interest are only performance bottlenecks that appear regularly or continuously and thus have a noticeable impact on the execution time of the program. This makes it possible to operate PATOP in an on-line mode where at one time only those measurements are performed that are also displayed in the user interface. This technique reduces the amount of measurement data to be handled to a fraction of the data that would have to be recorded to operate PATOP in an off-line mode.

All measurement values are produced in a distributed fashion in cooperation between the node monitors. The monitors can produce global sums, distribution values and attributed average values. For this every node monitor gets a position in a spanning tree; it receives values from its predecessors, reads and evaluates its local values, combines them with the received values and sends them to its successors. No further postprocessing has to be done outside of the node monitors, and still the additional overhead produced by the postprocessing of values is very small.

PATOP is being implemented for the Parsytec GC Power Plus based on PowerPC 601 and 4 INMOS T805 processors. The PowerPC processors do the computation, the inter node communication is done via the links of the T805 processors. A version of PATOP with the functionality described above exists for T805 based Parsytec systems that run under the PARIX parallel operating system. The user interface part of PATOP is based on OSF/Motif and runs on SUN workstations.

4 Example session

The traveling salesman problem deals with the minimization of the overall distance that has to be traveled when visiting a fixed number of cities in an arbitrary order and returning to the starting point. There exists no efficient algorithm to solve this problem. All possible tours have to be calculated in order to find the minimal one. For this reason the time necessary to calculate the solution increases exponentially with the size of the problem.

The given parallel version of the algorithm distributes the solution space among parallel processes over a spanning tree. When one process finds a solution that is shorter than the shortest solution found by any process so far it broadcasts this solution to all other processes. When a process detects that all solutions in his solution space are longer than the shortest one that has been found it gives up on his solution space and asks the successing node in the spanning tree for a part of that one's solution space. This gives the algorithm an integrated dynamic load balancing mechanism that works in a distributed way and it was expected that the algorithm is scalable to big system sizes. The algorithm was implemented in C using the communication primitives of the PARIX operating system.

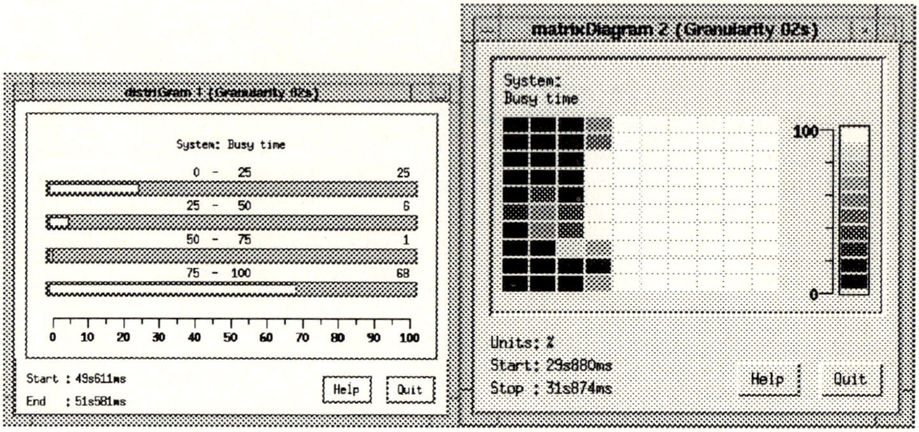

Fig. 1. Matrix and distribution diagrams showing the CPU utilization

The program was executed on 100 nodes of a Parsytec GCel when measuring its performance with PATOP. The utilization of the computing resources of the system showed phases where it was going down 25 percent and then increased again after a while. Looking at the distribution of this utilization it showed that some nodes were almost completely idle during these phases while the rest stayed completely busy (left part of figure 1). Looking at the matrix diagram it turned out that certain regions at the edges of the system were idle during these phases (right part of figure 1). The matrix diagram shows color coded values for the nodes of the system in a 2 dimensional grid. The grid represents the physical interconnection structure of the system. The spanning tree of the traveling salesman algorithm was mapped onto the grid structure of the system in a way that successor and predecessor processes in the tree are mapped onto neighboring nodes in the grid structure. In different phases of the program execution and for different problems other parts of the tree were becoming idle.

The first guess was that the load balancing mechanism was not working for some reason. This assumption could be proved wrong by measuring the message transfer on the idle nodes (selected measurement in figure 2). For this an attributed measurement was used to do the node selection; the condition in the attribute was the busy time being below 60 percent. The measurement showed that the idle nodes were getting the new subdomains of the solution space they requested for. On the other hand, when measuring what program parts the idle nodes were blocked in it showed that they were blocked in a receive call in will be created during program execution. The *Reduction Unit* (described in Sec. 3.3) evaluates the program stored in the Graph, and interacts with the *Thread Pool* (Sec. 3.3) as well as the *Communication Unit* (Sec. 3.4). The Communication Unit is responsible for sending messages to other processors and receiving messages which are temporarily buffered in a *Mailbox* (Sec. 5).

3.2 Parallel Program Structure

In the parallel program, the local component of the data structure (= local data) being transformed is preallocated, and stored in the Graph. The way it is transformed during program execution is described in (Rabhi, Schwarz [1993]).

During a local transformation data, held on other processors, will be needed. These values are provided as *extra parameters* to the transformation function. When the function is executed, these values are unlikely to be already available. This however, does not cause a problem in *lazy* functional languages since values can be represented in unevaluated form. The extra parameters symbolise the communication requirements of the parallel program, and are made explicit in the implementation.

The basic model assumes that a value will be requested when execution cannot continue without it. This means, that the extra parameters contain function calls to a request function which will be executed when referenced. However, the skeleton often provides sufficient information to exactly predict the communication needs, hence values can be sent in advance. In these cases, the extra parameters are represented by *blocked nodes* being automatically overwritten by values received from other processors. The extra parameters are created by the `SIT_skel_fun` function, before the transformation function is executed through `CREATE remote values` (see Fig. 2).

Automatically receiving values implies that there are *threads*[1] for sending values to other processors. In order to achieve this — before the transformation function is executed — so called *update*-threads are created for all distinct values that must be sent to other processors. Each update-thread has two lists (waiting-destinations, *dwait*, and requesting-destinations, *dreq*) attached to it, as well as a function application (*f localData localData'*) that evaluates to the value to be exported. The *dwait* list contains all processors that are known to need the value, and the *dreq* list contains the processors that will request the value if needed. The *dreq* list is necessary, to keep all processors independent of each other, and allowing them to carry out garbage collection based on local information only.

Once activated, an update-thread first evaluates the value to be exported, and then sends it to each processor specified in the *dwait* list, whereby these destinations get deleted from the list. When a request message is received, the sender will be removed from the *dreq* list and inserted into the *dwait* list, so that the requested value can be subsequently sent. An update-thread terminates after the two lists have become empty.

The model described above works fine, if all values to be requested will eventually be requested. However, some values will never be requested because of

[1] Throughout the paper, the term *thread* is used for separate sequential activities within an abstract machine.

```
SIT_skel_fun localData =                        where
  if (NOT finished)                               localData' = transform [r_1 .. r_n] localData
  then                                            s_1 = update (f_1 localData localData' )
    {CREATE remote values [r_1 .. r_n]}                     dwait
    {SPARK update threads [s_1 .. s_n]}                     dreq
    SIT_skel_fun localData'
  else                                            s_2 = ...
    return_and_terminate localData
```

Fig. 2. Parallel program structure

lazy evaluation, or they are shielded by if-statements and will never be required. This would eventually lead to a thread overflow. Therefore, when a processor reaches garbage collection, it sends the identifiers of all values represented by *graph-nodes* containing request calls, and still being referenced, to the processor from where it will request the value. By this method, the receiving processors can find out and delete the destinations from the *dreq* list that are no longer required. The overall structure of the parallel program is shown in Fig. 2.

3.3 Reduction Unit

After the initialisation process which distributes the data elements to the Graph in the abstract machines, and creates a Thread Pool entry for the **SIT_skel_fun** function, control is handed over to the *Reduction Unit*. The Reduction Unit selects the (up to now only) thread and starts executing it. As mentioned in Sec. 3.2, *update*-threads are created for all distinct values to be sent to other processors, before the transformation function will be called.

Evaluation of a thread continues until a value that is referenced is either not yet available (*blocked node*) or has to be requested first. In the latter case, a request message will be sent, and the node will be marked as blocked. In either way, the current thread is suspended, and will only be reawakened after the required value has become available.

This means that a new thread has to be selected from the *Thread Pool*. This will most likely be one of the update-threads that have already been sparked. An update-thread will first evaluate the value to export, which however, does not amount to extra work, as the value is part of the local graph and would have to be evaluated anyway. Only *strict* values are sent to other processors to avoid the problems caused by sending pointers to unevaluated expressions. However, this can lead to problems with recursive data structures to which special attention has to be paid.

An update-thread with an empty *dwait* list changes its status to suspended and gives up the CPU. Update-threads which have evaluated the value to be exported do not have to store their entire thread context when giving up the CPU, as future invocations will not involve any further evaluation but will only send values to other processors.

Threads which are currently suspended, are re-enabled after the corresponding data values or request messages have been received from other processors.

3.4 Communication Unit

The *Communication Unit* — responsible for sending and receiving messages — is activated by the Reduction Unit if the execution of a thread cannot continue, or if an update-thread has to send its evaluated data value to other processors. For every data value to be received, the Communication Unit maintains some information which is created when the *blocked node* for this value has been created, or a request call has been executed. A received data value is then passed to the Reduction Unit, along with the stored information to overwrite the blocked node. In case a request message is received, the address of the sender and the identifier of the value requested will be passed to the Reduction Unit (see Sec. 3.2). Every value has a unique identifier, so that it is known which data value has been received or requested.

The Communication Unit only executes code which never results in blocking. After it has resolved all pending communication events, control is returned to the Reduction Unit which will then select a new thread for execution.

3.5 Program-Mapping onto a Physical Architecture

For the mapping of the problem onto a physical hardware architecture, it is assumed — in the easiest case — that there are as many *physical* processors available as *virtual* processors, and that the communication pattern matches the interconnection network. In case of more *virtual* processors than physical ones, the Graph in the abstract machine must be capable of handling a cluster of local data elements, hence supporting several virtual processors.

4 Advantages of the Method & Related Work

The outlined implementation method exploits all the information given by the behaviour of the SIT skeleton to produce an efficient implementation. The advantages of this approach over standard parallel graph reduction are in particular, all parallelism contained is exploited, all data is as local as possible, less communication overhead as communication calls are made explicit, and garbage collection is simplified, since only strict values are communicated. Also, the problem of array access and (destructive) update in $\mathcal{O}(1)$ does not arise, as the original data structure is broken up into its scalar components that can easily be accessed.

There are a number of projects underway involving skeletons in one or another form. These include, most notably, the work of (Darlington *et al.* [1993], Kelly [1989], and Bratvold [1993]).

5 Project Status

The initial prototype will run on a network of Sun SPARC workstations. The *abstract machine* has been implemented using the C language, where the functional language code is compiled into C using the Glasgow Haskell Compiler (Partain [1992]). The components of the abstract machine are implemented as one UNIX process, and use the recent port of GRIP (Hammond [1993]) to PVM (Beguelin *et al.* [1991]) as a basis.

The prototype will utilise the thread-management code of GRIP for implementing the *Reduction Unit* and the *Thread Pool*. It will also use a subset of the message-passing functions of GRIP which itself makes use of PVM. However, since GRIP only employs *synchronous* communication they have to be modified that *asynchronous* communication — as expected by the implementation method — is possible. The *Mailbox* of the abstract machine uses the buffering mechanism of PVM for incoming messages, and therefore need not to be implemented.

6 Conclusion

A method has been proposed that exploits all the given information and parallelism contained in the skeleton, in order to produce an efficient implementation. The use of skeletons could therefore help to overcome the applicability of functional languages in parallel programming. Furthermore, array access and update in $\mathcal{O}(1)$ comes as a byproduct for free.

Adopting this approach, an implementation should produce better performance results than those of native functional language implementations. It also gives the user a powerful tool to write parallel programs without being concerned about implementation details (deadlocks, synchronisation), and without incurring the typical functional language penalties.

The disadvantage of the method is that it is restricted to a specific skeleton. Other skeletons would have to be considered separately. Future work will include assessing the performance of the prototype on some typical SIT applications.

References

A. Beguelin *et al.*, *A User's Guide to PVM Parallel Virtual Machine*, Oak Ridge National Laboratory, July 1991.

D.I. Bevan *et al.*, Design principles of a distributed memory architecture for parallel graph reduction, *The Computer Journal*, **32**(5), pp. 461-469, 1989.

T.A. Bratvold, A Skeleton Based Parallelising Compiler for ML, In Proc. *5th Int. Workshop on Implementation of Functional Languages*, TR 93-21, University of Nijmegen, pp. 23-33, September 1993.

M. Cole, *Algorithmic skeletons: a structured approach to the management of parallel computation*, Research monographs in Parallel and Distributed Computing, Pitman, London, 1989.

J. Darlington *et al.*, Parallel Programming Using Skeleton Functions, In Proc. *PARLE '93*, Springer Verlag, Munich, June 1993.

K. Hammond, Getting a GRIP (DRAFT), Department of Computer Science, University of Glasgow, 1993.

W.D. Hillis and G.L. Steele Jr., Data Parallel Algorithms, *Communications of the ACM*, **29**(12), pp. 1170-1183, December 1986.

P. Kelly, *Functional Programming for Loosely-coupled Multiprocessors*, Research monographs in Parallel and Distributed Computing, Pitman, London, 1989.

W. Partain, The Glasgow Haskell Compiler, The GRASP project, Department of Computer Science, University of Glasgow, 1992.

F.A. Rabhi, Exploiting parallelism in functional languages: a "paradigm oriented" approach, In Proc. *Abstract Machine Models for Highly Parallel Computers*, T. Lake and P. Dew (Eds), Oxford University Press, 1993.

F.A. Rabhi and J. Schwarz, "Paradigm-Oriented" Design of Parallel Iterative Programs Using Functional Languages, In Proc. *Applications of Supercomputers in Engineering III*, C.A. Brebbia and H. Power (Eds), Computational Mechanics Publications/Elsevier Applied Science, September 1993.

A Dynamic Task Allocation Scheme in Beneš-Type Nonblocking Networks *

Tse-yun Feng ** and Yanggon Kim

The Pennsylvania State University, University Park PA 16802, USA

Abstract. Due to the *uniqueness* of a path between a pair of input/output terminals in cube-type networks, conflicts in the network are the main bottleneck in the performance of a highly-parallel multiprocessor system. In order to provide more flexibilities in realizing conflict-free connection patterns for a permutation, we consider rearrangeable nonblocking networks with $(2\log_2 N - 1)$ stages. Based on an $N \times N$ Beneš network, a new dynamic task allocation scheme is shown to avoid both an intertask conflict and an intratask conflict. In addition, this scheme guarantees the independent partitioning of a MIN for an individual task. Therefore, the hot spot problem of a task caused by nonuniform memory traffic does not affect the other tasks and the effects of switch and/or link faults in the network is confined to a single task.

1 Correlations Between Stages in an $N \times N$ Beneš Network

Let a connection pattern of a 2×2 switching element be denoted as s^{α}_{β} where α and β stand for an input position and an output position in a switching element, respectively. If a path comes in through the upper input position of a switching element, then $\alpha = 0$. Otherwise, $\alpha = 1$. The value of β is assigned in the same way as α and it represents the output position instead of the input position.

Theorem 1. *For a given pair of input/output terminals in an $N \times N$ Beneš network, if $\beta = 0$ ($\beta = 1$) at the ith-stage switching element, then $\alpha = 0$ ($\alpha = 1$) at the $(2\log_2 N - i)^{th}$-stage switching element where $1 \leq i \leq (\log_2 N - 1)$.*

This theorem implies that an $N \times N$ Beneš network can be decomposed into two $N/2 \times N/2$ subnetworks according to the values of β at the 1st stage and the values of α at the $(2\log_2 N - 1)^{th}$ stage. This 2-way decomposition is done recursively. According to a given permutation, the number of possible different connection patterns without conflict is varied. The *degree of flexibility* of a permutation is defined as the number of different connection patterns without conflict for a given permutation.

* This work was partially supported by the National Science Foundation under Grant CDA-9320642.

** Presently at NSF/CISE/CDA, Arlington, VA 22230, on leave from The Pennsylvania State University.

Theorem 2. *In an $N \times N$ Beneš-type network, the maximal degree of flexibility is $2^{(N/2)(\log_2 N-1)}$. And the number of permutations with the maximal degree of flexibility among $N!$ permutations is 2^{N-1}.*

Using the above two theorems, a $(2\log_2 N - 1)$-bit self-routing tag, $T = t_1 t_2 \cdots t_{(2\log_2 N-1)}$, for a given pair of input/output terminals can be generated as follows. The value of t_i, $1 \leq i \leq (\log_2 N - 1)$, is determined by the value of β of a switching element at the ith stage and $t_{(\log_2 N)} t_{(\log_2 N+1)} \cdots t_{(2\log_2 N-1)} = d_1 d_2 \cdots d_{\log_2 N}$ where $D = d_1 d_2 \cdots d_{\log_2 N}$ is the output terminal number.

2 A Dymanic Task Allocation Scheme

Previous research efforts on a task allocation advocate for the cube-type networks[1]–[4]. Assume that in order to run a task of size $K = 2^k$, we select K memory modules(MMs) and K processors(Ps) by an allocation rule where the logical names of the processors are the same as the selected memory modules. For the matching pattern as a logical naming scheme between a MM and its matching P, we use a mapping fuction such that a MM and a P are in the same relative position, i.e., *identity* permutation. Selecting MMs for a task, the allocation strategy is as follows:

1. Let k be the demension of a task size. That is, the task requests 2^k MMs.
2. If there is a set of 2^k MMs avaiable whose binary numbers contain the most significant $(n - k)$ bits in common, allocate it.
3. If not, decompose the request size by the factor of 2 and allocate the corresponding set of MMs to subtasks together.

3 Conclusion

Reducing both the intertask conflict and the intratask conflict in multitasking system improves a whole system utilization and a throughput of a system. A major advantage on using the $N \times N$ Beneš network for the communication is to realize any permutation without conflict. The overhead for setting a conflict-free connection pattern when a permutation changes is minimized by the task scheme proposed.

References

1. Tuomenoksa, D.L.,Siegel, H.J.: Task Scheduling on the PASM Parallel Processing System. IEEE Trans. Software Eng. **11** (1985) 145–157
2. Premkumar, U.V., Browne, J.C.: Resource Allocation in Rectangular SW Banyans. Proc. Int. Symp. on Computer Architecture (1982) 326–333
3. Jeng, M., Siegel, H.J.: A Distributed Management Scheme for Partitionable Parallel Computers. IEEE Trans. Parallel and Distributed System **1** (1990) 120–126
4. Chang, Y., Bhuyan, L.N.: Extending Multistage Interconnection Networks for Multitasking. Proc. Int. Conf. Parallel Processing (1992) 155–158

A METHODOLOGY FOR DIMENSIONING SPMD DISTRIBUTED SYSTEMS APPLIED TO INDUSTRIAL APPLICATIONS

PINTI Antonio & GROSSETIE Jean-Claude

JOINT RESEARCH CENTRE - EURATOM - TP 361
21020 ISPRA (VA.) - ITALY
UNIVERSITE DE HAUTE-ALSACE - FST - TROP
68093 MULHOUSE CEDEX - FRANCE

Abstract : This paper presents a methodology for dimensioning distributed systems applied to industrial applications which can be parallelized in Single Program Multiple Data (SPMD) mode on parallel architecture. This method has been used to dimension a real-time application implemented and working on the European parallel T-node computer.

1 Introduction

The aim of this study is to develop a method to determine the minimum number of processors which are necessary to satisfy the time constraints imposed by an application. For this purpose, a mathematical algorithm based on simplex optimisation technique has been developed [3]. The method described may be used to estimate the computation time of an industrial application parallelized in SPMD mode and simulated on MIMD or SIMD machines communicating in "rendezvous" mode. The architecture of the network of processors may be a pipeline or a tree [2] depending upon the number of communication links used. The distribution of elementary work tasks is proportional with respect to all the network processors [1].

2 Methodology

To use this method, exact knowledge of the different parameters of the computer and sequential algorithm is required, especially the link data flow, the number of links, the computing time of the sequential algorithm, the computing time of an elementary process and the number of data to transmit. This is due to the fact that inter-processor communications in parallel systems consume a considerable time and therefore intrinsically limit the system. This time is defined by the linear function T=ß +Lt {a} with ß the initial delay of the channel, L the length of the message in bytes, and t a constant which is a function of the transfer time of one byte. The minimum calculation time T*cm* is defined as follows:

$$Tcm = \frac{Tseq}{Np} + f(R, L, Te, Tr)$$

$\frac{Tseq}{Np}$ is equal to the optimum calculation time. The time lost in transfer of data and synchronisation between processors is a function of *f* which has the following parameters: **R** the node level, **L** the number of links used per processor, **Te** the time needed to transfer all the input data on a link and **Tr** the time needed to transfer all the results on a link. **Te** and **Tr** are calculated with {a} for a number of data to be transferred. The function cost, *f* is calculated for different cases with R≥ 1:

f(L, R, Te, Tr) = [R + (L-2) n] Te + [S1(L, R) - (L-2) S2(L, n)] Tr

and n an integer given by the following order relations:

- $n = 1$ if $Te < N(L, 2)\,Tr$
- $N(L, n)\,Tr < Te \leq N(L, n+1)\,Tr$ $\quad (n \in [2, ..., R-1])$
- $n = R$ if $N(L, R)\,Tr < Te$

where : $S1(L,R) = \sum_{k=1}^{R} uk$ with $u_0 = 0$ et $uk = (L-1)(u_{k-1} + 1)$

$N(L,v) = \sum_{k=1}^{v} wk$ with $w_1 = 1$ et $w_k = (L-1)\,w_{k-1}$

$S2(L,n) = \sum_{k=2}^{n} N(L,k)$

3 Application and results

This method has been applied in order to design a parallel 3D interpolation algorithm which in turn has been used to study a real-time 3D image synthesis process. The time constraint imposed was to calculate this interpolation in less than 0.5 seconds. Fig. 1 gives the calculation time for the following parameters:

-T*seq*=5 sec.; L=4; Te=64 µs; Tr=16,64 ms

One can see that the calculation time is minimum for 9841 transputers. If one takes into account exclusively the results concerning the total execution time, one can say that in the case studied, the full optimum network is obtained by using 9841 transputers. However, for such a configuration more than 99% of the running time is lost in transfer of data and synchronisation of the transfer procedures. Figure 1 also indicates that 13 transputers are sufficient to satisfy the time constraints imposed by the application.

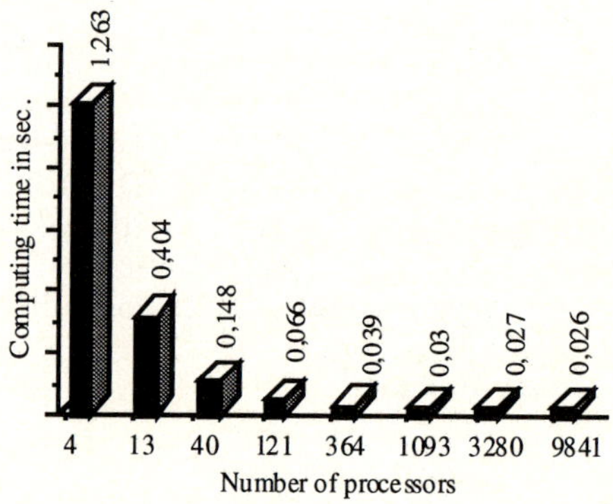

Fig. 1

4 Conclusion and prospects

This methodology can be used in all industrial applications which can be parallelized in the SPMD mode. Moreover, with this approach it is possible to determine the number of processors necessary to satisfy the time constraint. The method can be directly applied to image processing, image synthesis, signal processing, neural networks, and other algorithms where the number of identical operations is significant.

5 References

1. O. KRAMER, H. MUHLENBEIN : Mapping strategies in message-based multiprocessor systems, Parallel Computing 9, 213-225.
2. L. D. WITTIE : Communication structures for large networks of microcomputers, IEEE trans. on comp., vol. C-30, n. 4, 264-273.
3. R. FLETCHER : Practical methods of optimisation - vol. 1 & vol. 2, Ed. John Wiley & Sons.

Do-Loop-Surface: An Abstract Performance Data Visualization

Oscar Naím and A.J.G. Hey

Department of Electronics and Computer Science
Mountbatten Building, Lab. 4037
University of Southampton, Southampton S09 5NH, UK
Email: on92r@ecs.soton.ac.uk

Abstract. Performance is a critical issue in current massively parallel processors. However, to get adequate performance is not an easy task and performance tools are required in order to help the programmer to *understand* the behaviour of a parallel program.

In recent years, a wide variety of tools have been developed for this purpose including tools for monitoring and evaluating performance and visualization tools. However, these tools do not provide an abstract representation of performance. Massively parallel processors could produce a huge amount of performance data and sophisticated methods for representing and displaying this data are required.

The Do-Loop-Surface (DLS) display is an abstract representation of the performance of a particular do-loop in a program and it is implemented using AVS, a Data Visualization Tool. In this paper, this new representation is presented and used in order to improve the performance of a Matrix Multiply parallel algorithm.

1 Introduction

Performance visualization is the use of graphical display techniques for the analysis of performance data in order to improve understanding of complex performance phenomena [15]. Performance visualization systems for parallel programs have been helpful in the past and they are commonly used in order to improve parallel program performance. However, despite of the advances that have been made in visualizing scientific data, techniques for visualizing performance of parallel programs remain *ad hoc* and performance visualization becomes more difficult as the parallel system becomes more complex.

In this paper, the Do-Loop-Surface representation of the performance of a particular do-loop in a program is presented as an alternative to provide an abstract representation of performance (at least of the performance of a particular do-loop or kernel in a program), using an existing Data Visualization Tool for this purpose. The aim of a performance data representation is to *reveal* the meaning of performance data.

2 Do-Loop-Surface

A Do-Loop-Surface (DLS from now on), is an abstract representation of the performance of a particular do-loop in a program. This surface is created by measuring the elapsed time per iteration for every processor and representing this data as a 3D display.

By representing a do-loop using a DLS, the user can view a complete execution of the program in a single picture and looking at this display from the right perspective may uncover unknown bottlenecks. A new and evocative vocabulary that explains the particular features of the display is also incorporated (e.g. *mountains, valleys, hilly, flat*).

This surface is displayed using AVS [2] (Application Visualization System), which allows rotation of the figure in several ways, as well as zooming when necessary and some other interesting transformations.

The main goals of a DLS are:

- To provide an abstract representation of the performance of the program.
- To provide useful information for the user, allowing detection of unknown bottlenecks using 3D displays.
- To provide scalable views for programs running on thousands of processors.

By analyzing a DLS, the user can see particular performance features like load balance (i.e. *flat* surface, which means that every processor is taking the same amount of time to execute the do-loop), communication delays (e.g. *mountains* in the surface), and general patterns.

Why do-loops? A do-loop represents one of the most important sections of the program, since it is generally where the main computation takes place. Additionally, a programmer may understand more about do-loop structures than communication directives. A DLS is, therefore, appropriate in this sense.

A DLS is also scalable. It is represented by a single picture that can be zoomed if necessary and a general view of the surface will determine which regions require a more detailed analysis. Although we have only produced trace data from up to 64 processors, we expect to get data from 128 processors. However, more realistic measures must be taken on more than 512 processors in order to test scalability.

3 Case study: Matrix Multiply

The purpose of this case study is to show how useful a DLS could be analyzing the performance of a parallel algorithm. A parallel Matrix Multiply algorithm was selected as a case study, mainly for its simplicity, and future work will incorporate real industrial applications.

The parallel implementation of this Matrix Multiply algorithm works in the following way: the matrix A is distributed by rows and the matrix B by columns. At the stage i, the processor which has the row i sends this row to all the other processors (broadcast) and then each processor starts computing the corresponding inner products in order to generate the result (each processor generates a set of elements of the resulting matrix). The matrices of this experiment are square matrices and the size ranges from 100x100, 130x130 and so on up to 400x400.

A trace generation library was written in order to collect the required data per iteration. The only thing that the user has to do in order to obtain trace data, is to add a call to the corresponding trace function at the beginning and at the end of the do-loop. The hardware platform consist of a 64 T800 Parsys Supernode and the program was written in C using PARMACS [12] (communication library).

3.1 Results for a 100x100 matrix on 32 processors

The DLS of figure 1 represents a matrix multiplication algorithm, for two matrices of dimension 100x100, on 32 processors. The values correspond to the main do-loop of the algorithm.

Some clear facts from the picture (that we *already know*) are:

- There are some initialization costs at the beginning of the algorithm (initialization and terminating values have been removed in order to get a clearer picture).
- Since the hardware topology for this experiment is a grid of 4x8, the cost to send messages from one node to another is not the same. Therefore, there is a regular delay that follows like a linear pattern on the surface (like a small hill), and this is repeated three times. This point represents when each processor is working with a row which is in its local memory. At that time, that particular processor has to broadcast that row before starting the multiplication process (i.e. the delay is longer for this processor). For a matrix of size 100x100 and 32 processors, this occurs exactly three times ($100/32 = 3$).

Now, one good question is whether we can improve the performance of the program in some way using the information of the DLS. One possible answer is to try to reduce those hilly parts of the surface (i.e. reducing the delays per processor). Since the communications are synchronous for the broadcasting of rows at this stage of the algorithm, one possibility is trying using asynchronous communication.

The effect on the DLS using asynchronous communication is remarkable, see figure 2. The display is darker (which means lower values for the elapsed time per iteration) and the hills are lower (a colour display will make differences clear). Although the initialization costs are the same, the improvement in performance is extremely good (from 6.48 seconds to 2.15 seconds).

4 Conclusions and Future Work

Performance visualization is an important and useful technique that helps the user to understand and improve complex parallel performance phenomena. This technique has been widely used and interesting research efforts can be found in the literature.

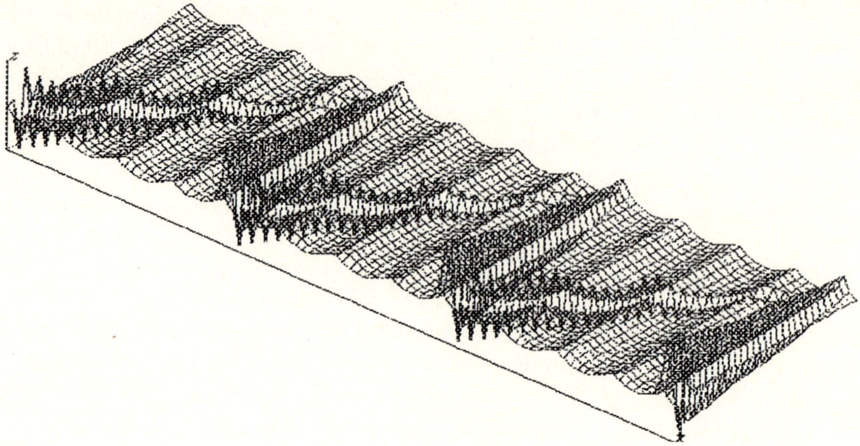

Fig. 1. Matrix Multiply: Do-Loop-Surface (Synchronous communication).

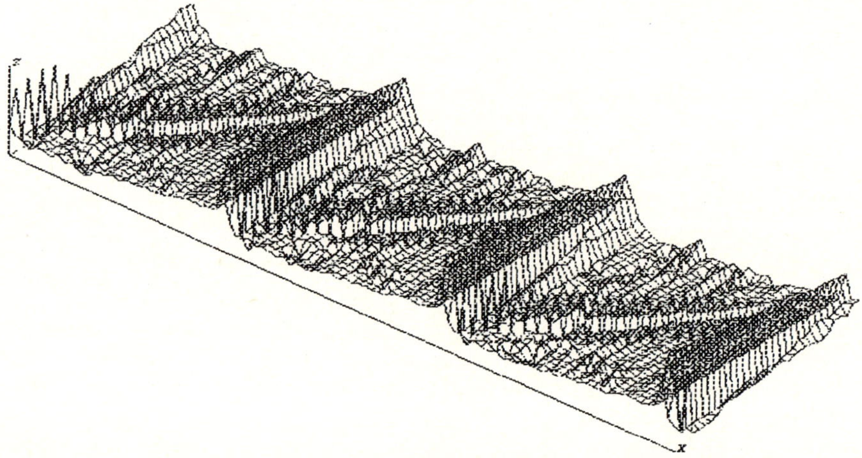

Fig. 2. Matrix Multiply: Do-Loop-Surface (Asynchronous communication).

Popular views like space-time/Feynman diagram (ParaGraph [10]) or event timelines (Express Etool [21]) often provide some insight about program behaviour. Unfortunately, for these tools to be truly useful in the domain of large scale parallel machines they must include abstract high level views [24].

In this paper, the Do-Loop-Surface (DLS) representation of the performance of a particular do-loop in a program has been presented as an alternative to provide an abstract and scalable representation of performance (at least of the performance of a particular do-loop or kernel in a program), using an existing Data Visualization Tool (AVS [2]) for this purpose. One advantage of this approach is that no tool development is required and that every feature of the data visualization tool can be used to find unknown bottlenecks (e.g. rotating a figure may lead the user to discover something that he has not seen before, using a specific module that computes statistics about the data points displayed, etc). One disadvantage is that it is difficult to relate the data to the program, or to do detailed analysis (i.e. zooming) on a particular region of the display (e.g. what information corresponds to a particular processor).

The DLS has been successfully used in order to improve the performance of a Parallel Matrix Multiply Algorithm. By representing the main loop of the computation of this Matrix Multiply Algorithm, it was possible to discover a communication bottleneck. This problem was solved using asynchronous communication and the result was remarkable since the performance was improved by a factor of 3. Although the Matrix Multiply Algorithm is very simple, future work will include real industrial applications on larger parallel systems.

The Do-Loop-Surface is a contribution towards a better abstraction of the performance of a parallel program, but it is not the best and more research is required in this field (including issues like scalability and the capability of tracing back view features to raw data).

Finally, it is important to say that experiences like this allow us to learn more about how to use visualization techniques to represent performance data and to design, modify, and produce tools which incorporate this new knowledge.

References

1. Cliff Addison, James Allwright, Norman Binsted, Nigel Bishop, Bryan Carpenter, Peter Dalloz, David Gee, Vladimir Getov, Tony Hey, Roger Hockney, Max Lemke, John Merlin, Mark Pinches, Chris Scott, and Ivan Wolton. The Genesis Distributed Memory Benchmarks-I. Methodology and General Relativity benchmark with results for the SUPRENUM Computer. For submission to Concurrency: Practice and Experience, March 1992.
2. Advanced Visual Systems Inc. *AVS User's Guide, Release 4*, May 1992.
3. G. Almasi, B. Alpern, C. Berman, Larry Carter, and D. Hale. A Case-study in performance programming: Seismic Migration. In *2nd Symposium on High Performance Computing*, pages 195–206. North Holland, October 1991.
4. Arndt Bode and Peter Braun. Monitoring and visualisation in topsys. In *Workshop on Performance Measurement and Visualization of Parallel Systems*, Moravany, Czecho-Slovakia, October 1992.
5. Larry Carter. Private Electronic Mail Communication. January 1993.
6. Alva Couch. Categories and Context in Scalable Execution Visualization. *Journal of Parallel and Distributed Computing*, 18:195–204, 1993.
7. Joan Francioni, L. Albright, and J. Jackson. Debugging parallel programs using sound. In *SIGPLAN Notices*, volume 26, pages 68–75, 1991.
8. Joan Francioni, L. Albright, and J. Jackson. The sounds of parallel programs. In *Proceedings of the Sixth Distributed Memory Computing Conference.* IEEE Computer Society, 1991.

9. Joan Francioni and Diane Rover. Visual-Aural representations of performance for a scalable application program. In *Scalable High Performance Computing Conference, SHPCC-92*, pages 433–440. IEEE Computer Society, April 1992.
10. M. Heath and J. Etheridge. Visualizing the performance of parallel programs. *IEEE Software*, pages 29–39, September 1991.
11. Michael Heath. Recent Developments and Case Studies in Performance Visualization using ParaGraph. In *Workshop on Performance Measurement and Visualization of Parallel Systems*, Moravany, Czecho-Slovakia, October 1992.
12. R. Hempel. *The ANL/GMD Macros (PARMACS) in FORTRAN for Portable Parallel Programming using the Message Passing Programming Model. User's Guide and Reference Manual.* Pallas GmbH, 1991.
13. Institut für Informatik, Technische Universität München. *TOPSYS User's Overview, Version 1.0*, December 1990.
14. T. LeBlanc, J. Mellor-Crummey, and R. Fowler. Analyzing parallel program executions using multiple views. *Journal of Parallel and Distributed Computing*, 9(2):203–217, 1990.
15. Allen Malony and Gregory Wilson. Future directions in parallel performance environments. In *Workshop on Performance Measurement and Visualization of Parallel Systems*, Moravany, Czecho-Slovakia, October 1992.
16. John Merlin. HPF Visualization Tools - Proposal. Technical report, Southampton University, April 1993.
17. Barton Miller. What to draw? when to draw? An essay on parallel program visualization. *Journal of Parallel and Distributed Computing*, 18(2):265–269, 1993.
18. Bernd Mohr. SIMPLE: A Performance Evaluation Tool Environment for Parallel and Distributed Systems. In *EDMCC2*, Munich, April 1991.
19. Oscar Naím and Alejandro Teruel. Consideraciones sobre el Paralelismo en SIMPAR (FASE I). Technical Report IT-1991-001, Department of Computer Science& Information Technology, Universidad Simón Bolívar, Caracas-Venezuela, 1991.
20. Pallas, GmbH. *PA-Tools, Performance Analysis Tools*, 1991.
21. Parasoft Corporation. *ParaSoft Express. User's Guide*, 1990.
22. Daniel Reed, Ruth Aydt, Tara Madhyastha, Roger Noe, Keith Shields, and Bradley Schwartz. The PABLO performance analysis environment. Department of Computer Science, University of Illinois at Urbana-Champaign, 1992.
23. Diane Rover and Charles Wright. Visualizing the Performance of SPMD and Data-Parallel Programs. *Journal of Parallel and Distributed Computing*, 18:129–146, 1993.
24. Sekhar Sarukkai, Doug Kimelman, and Larry Rudolph. A methodology for visualizing performance of loosely synchronous programs. In *Scalable High Performance Computing Conference, SHPCC-92*, pages 424–432. IEEE Computer Society, April 1992.
25. Margaret Simmons and Rebecca Koskela. *Performance Instrumentation and Visualization.* ACM Press, Frontier Series, 1990.
26. Brian Wylie, Michael Norman, and Lyndon Clarke. High Performance Fortran: A Perspective. The University of Edinburgh, EPCC-TN92-05.04, May 1992.

A GRAPHIC DISTRIBUTED MONITORING SYSTEM FOR UNIX-BASED ARCHITECTURES

G. De Pietro[2], A. Esposito[1], G. Reitano[2]

[1] Italian Air Force Academy, Via Domitiana, Pozzuoli, Italy
[2] IRSIP, National Research Council of Italy, Via P. Castellino 111, Naples, Italy

Abstract. The monitoring of the activities of a computing system is fundamental for performance evaluation, system tuning and resource utilization. In this paper a distributed on-line monitoring system, DOMINE, is presented; its portability on Unix platforms and the powerful graphic interface make DOMINE well suited for distributed and heterogeneous systems.

1 Introduction

There are several reasons for establishing performance control and evaluation of computing systems. For instance, the response time evaluation is fundamental for many applications in manufacturing process control and for all systems controlling critical applications. Moreover, the program response time knowledge is very useful to schedule the activities for large computer systems with heavy workloads: it can be used in order to establish a deadline or a future-knowledge scheduling policy. Controlling a large system is a complex task and many operating systems are provided with resource management facilities, able to handle different work types and modify relative priorities of the active jobs, according to specific policies. In this case, the workload is subdivided into classes with assigned service specifications and the dispatching control is performed by measuring resource consumption by the active jobs.

With the advent of parallel computers the monitoring problem has become topical again; the complex interaction of many architectural, hardware and software features of parallel and distributed systems make difficult to well understand the performance characteristics of machines and user programs [2,8]. Typically, three levels of monitoring tools users can be identified:

- technicians needing data to determine exactly how the system functions;
- users requiring selected data pertaining to their applications;
- managers requiring accounting results and trends.

In this case, not only one single instrumentation tool, but rather a system of distributed instrumentation tools is required [3,4,5,7]. Moreover, formal models need to determine the most effective way for exploiting the high performance capabilities of parallel systems and/or investigating program behavior. In fact, a model can support the choice of the actions on workload, scheduling and resources that allow optimal values of performance indexes according to specific requirements (Fig. 1) [4,6].

In this paper a Distributed On-line MonItoriNg Environment (DOMINE) is presented; it is a modular, flexible, monitoring tool for Unix-based architectures, provided with a powerful graphic interface.

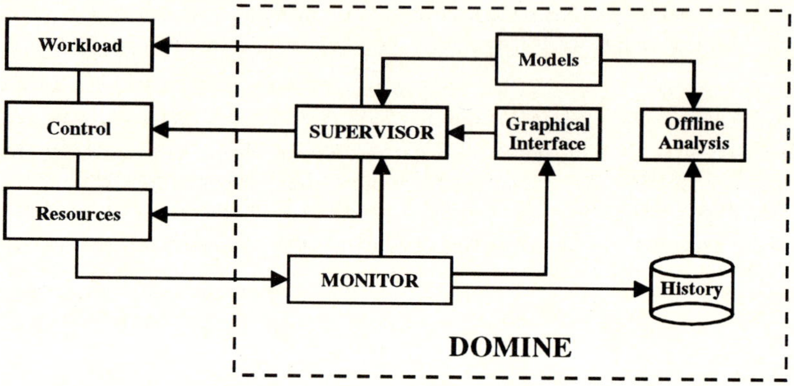

Fig. 1. Reactive System Schema.

2 Monitor Design Issues

The first problem in the design of a monitor is the selection of the events of interest: the designer has to define a "low-level" event set, which can be also used to specify further events of higher hierarchical level. Clearly, the structure of the monitor could totally change if the low-level event set is defined at hardware level (e.g. the monitor has to be able to observe a memory read/write operation) or at software level (e.g. operating system or user code). The following step in the design phase is the choice of a technique for the events recognition; a first approach is to periodically analyze the status of the system under monitoring, in order to derive statistical information on the events of interest (event sampling monitors). Another possible technique is to provide mechanisms for intercepting the events as they occur (event driven monitors). It should be noted that, because of non-determinism of parallel programs, all the choice made in the design phase have to take into account that the overhead introduced by the monitoring system could change the behavior of parallel programs [2,4].

The proposed monitoring system is an on-line, software, event sampling monitor which has been designed according to these fundamental criteria:

1. Portability: the monitor has to run on parallel and distributed systems which support the Unix operating system;

2. Easy comprehension: the monitor is provided with a very flexible and user-friendly distributed graphic monitoring interface (GMI);
3. Flexibility: the monitor can adapt iteself to specific user or environment requirements;
4. Low interference.

DOMINE can be mainly regarded as a performance evaluation tool: our goal is to provide a system manager of a distributed system (or some tool of a reactive distributed system) with information and statistics (e.g. CPU time, I/O time, memory usage, etc) related to the activities of the nodes composing the system (a node can be a single processor of a parallel machine or a single workstation or supercomputer). At the same time, the monitor gives user information about his programs, also when they run in parallel on several nodes; moreover, the user can profitably access to a (restricted) number of global status information of the distributed system (e.g. in order to run his program on lightly loaded nodes). However, whenever the user needs profiling of his programs, DOMINE provides graphic interface for postmortem analysis of programs traced by using the standard Unix tools (e.g. gprof).

3 DOMINE

DOMINE is composed by a master module (MMM) running on a particular node (chosen at the start-up of the monitoring environment) and several slave modules (SMMs) running on the other system nodes (Fig. 2). The difference between MMM and SMM is that only MMM is demanded the calculation of parameters and statistics concerning the distributed system in the whole, besides local statistics. At fixed time intervals, each SMM collects local information and computes local statistics; MMM collects this information making available in this way also global data. The sampling interval is chosen at the start-up of the monitoring system; note that data can be updated at lower rates according to specific requirements.

To start the monitoring of a program, the user has to perform no modification on the original source codes. All the monitoring actions are executed by the SMM (MMM), which accesses (in a transparent way for users) the Unix kernel process table and the u.area of the single process. This strategy, which makes the monitor independent of a particular programming environment, has the advantage that many measured values for a process are not affected by the monitor overhead. In fact, the SMM (MMM) is a daemon-like process which periodically performs its actions; clearly, the presence of SMM (MMM) in the process queue of each node increases the elapsed time of user processes, but the resources usage of the SMM (MMM) is not added to any user process.

The graphical monitoring interface (GMI) is the front-end of the experimenter with respect to the monitoring system. Each user can activate an instance of GMI from a node which he is logged on. GMI is composed by a control unit (GMCU) connected to the local monitor module (Fig. 3); on command, GMCU generates a set of child windows (GMCWs), each one supporting the visualization of numerical values and diagrams representing performance indexes and statistics. The diagrams show dynamic system state via different views. Detailed performance measurements and hierarchical analysis of data are also provided; clearly, the monitored data can be saved in a log file for future examinations.

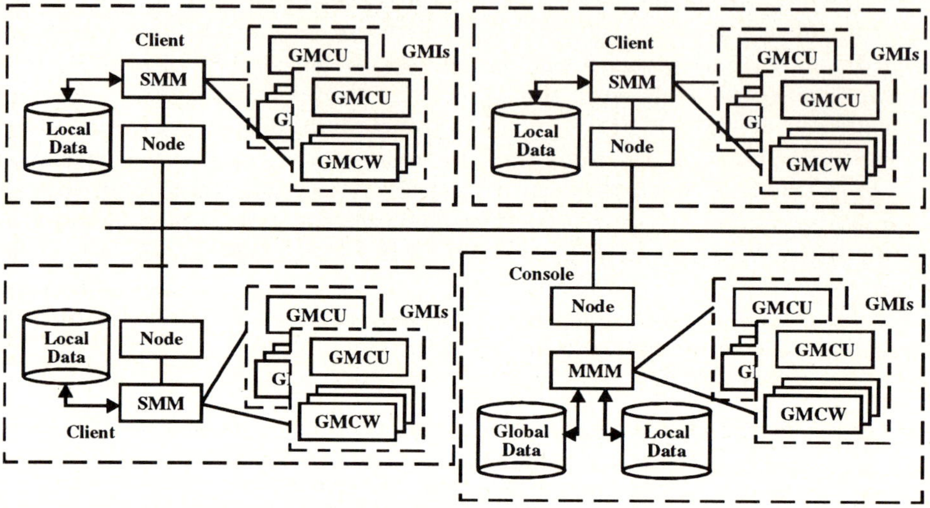

Fig. 2. DOMINE Architecture

In order to meet the goal of portability, the GMI has been built by using OSF/MOTIF libraries; in such a way the interface can virtually run on every UNIX machine. Note that GMI could be placed on nodes not pertaining to the monitored system. GMI supports two modalities:

- Super-user: the behavior of the whole distributed system is analyzed, by giving information regarding all system activities and all user processes, according to the system manager point of view;
- Common user: the user is provided only with information about its processes (and some global statistic). It should be noted that, whenever a user is logged on different machines with different user names, he has to provide the GMCU with a machine-login table.

In the last case the user can specify data filters in order to analyze only some specific process (or group of processes). Even through the graphic interface, the user can perform the following operations:

- set-up of the monitoring environment: the MMM and SMMs are spawned on the distributed system (this operation can be performed only in Super-user mode). The Super-user must provide a configuration file specifying the nodes on which the daemons have to run;

- start-up of a monitoring session: the user is able to monitor all the system activities related to his programs at different abstraction levels;
- data visualization: the user is able to chose for his data different kinds of representation (Fig.4).

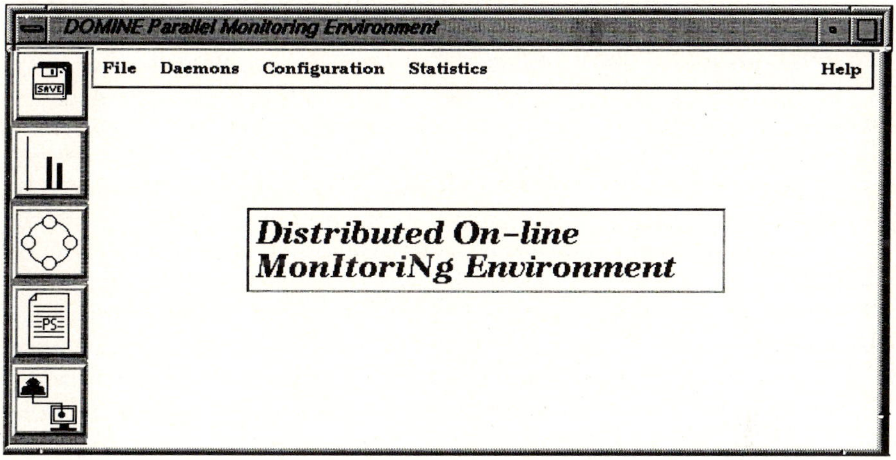

Fig. 3. GMCU View.

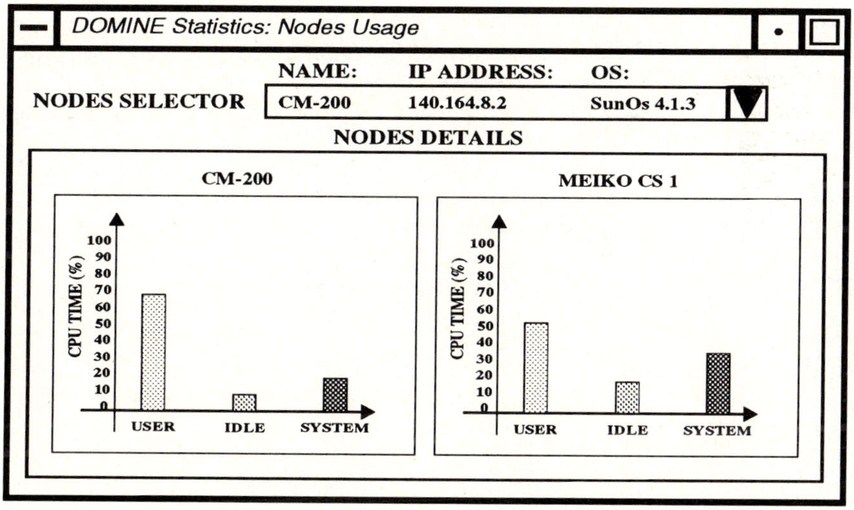

Fig. 4. GMCW Example.

4 Implementation Notes

The software of the monitoring modules has been written in C language, while the data communications among modules are performed by using PVM 3.2 communication primitives; this implies that all the nodes of the distributed system must provide PVM environment [1,7]. This is no effective constraint (PVM is a public domain software); however, next releases of DOMINE could utilize different communication mechanisms (e.g. UNIX sockets). As different UNIX versions can be present in the distributed system to be monitored, DOMINE has to be properly configured for the specific machines constituting the system.

DOMINE has been tested on a heterogeneous distributed system composed by a Connection Machine CM-200, a Meiko Computing Surface CS-1, a Meiko Relational Data Cache, and SUN workstations; all these systems are connected by a LAN Ethernet. Several experiments have been performed, testing DOMINE in many different situations. Particular care has been given in choosing the sampling interval; we found that 0.1 sec seems to be a good compromise to obtain a high accuracy and a low overhead. Note that the monitor overhead affects essentially the elapsed time of the user processes rather than the program behavior, because a distributed system with LAN Ethernet with CSMA-CD access technique is non-deterministic of its own. At present, a more complete version of DOMINE which includes other platforms (e.g. IBM Risc 6000, Meiko CS-2) is under development.

References

1. Beguelin, A., Dongarra, J.J., et alii.: PVM and HeNCE: Tools for Heterogeous Network Computing. in Environments and Tools for Parallel Scientific Computing (J. J. Dongarra and B. Tourancheau eds.) North-Holland (1993) 139–153
2. Cantone, G., Esposito, A., Gragnani, F. S.: Predicting Temporal Behavior of Highly Distributed Processes. EC Newsletter, 4, 1 (1992) 85–95
3. De Falco, I., De Pietro, G., Russo, D., Vaccaro, R.: POMOS: Parallel On-line MOnitoring System. CNR Project Report 3/208 (1993) (in italian)
4. De Pietro, G., Esposito, A.: Estimating Execution Time of Parallel Programs. Proc. Wshop on Comp. Architecture Technology, Napoli (1992)
5. Jacobs, P., Pluvinage, D.: DIMOS: Distributed Monitoring System for the Realization of a Nuclear Power Plant Supervision System. Proc. Int. Wshop on Real-Time Programming, Bruges (B) (1992) 61–66
6. Klar, R., Quick, A., Sotz, F.: Tools for a Model-driven Instrumentation for Monitoring. in Computer Performance Evaluation (G. Balbo and G. Serazzi eds.) Elsevier (1992) 165–179
7. Lange, F., Kroeger, R., Gergeleit, M.: JEWEL: Design and Implementation of a Distributed Measurement System. IEEE Trans. on Parallel and Distriibuted Systems,3,6, (1992) 657–671
8. Lawson, H. W., Svensson, B.: An Architecture for Time-Critical Distributed/Parallel Processing. EUROMICRO Wshop. Parallel & Distributed Processing, Gran Canaria (SP) (1993) 65–70

References

1. M. van Steen, T. Vogel, A. ten Dam, Specification of the DES, HAMLET internal document, AEG Electrocom (ed.), Konstanz, Germany, 1993.
2. M. van Steen, T. Vogel and A. ten Dam, "ADL: A Graphical Design Language for Parallel Real Time Applications." In Proceedings World Transputer Congress 1993, J.H.R. Grebe, S. Hilton, M. Jane, P. Welch (ed.). IOS Press, 1993, pp 365-379.
3. T. Bemmerl, O. Hansen and T. Ludwig, "PATOP for Performance Tuning of Parallel Programs", In Proceedings of the CONPAR 90 - VAPP IV Conference, Springer-Verlag, 1990, pp 840-851
4. O. Hansen, T. Bemmerl, W. Obelor and H. Willeke, "Adapting the Portable Performance Measurement Tool PATOP to the Multi-Transputer Monitoring System DELTA-T", In Working Conference on Programming Environments for Parallel Computing, IFIP, 1992.
5. C.A.R. Hoare, "Communicating Sequential Processes." In Communications of the ACM, 21(8) pp 666-677, 1978.
6. Hamlet Consortium, "Application Requirements, Deliverable 1.1" AEG Electrocom (ed.), Konstanz, Germany, 1992.
7. INMOS Ltd., ANSI C Toolset, IMS D0314-DOCA, Bristol, 1992.
8. B. Stroustrup. The C++ Programming Language, Addison-Wesley, 1986.
9. W. Huiskamp, R Kiel and M.H. Smit, "HPC takes the Bus!" In Proceedings World Transputer Congress 1993, IOS Press, 1993.
10. POSIX 1003.4 and 1003.4a, IEEE, New York, 1992.
11. J.P. Kitajima and B. Plateau, "Building synthetic parallel programs: the project ALPES", In Programming Environments for Parallel Computing, North-Holland, 1992, pp 161-170.
12. J.P. Kitajima, C. Tron and B. Plateau, "ALPES: a tool for the performance evaluation of parallel programs", In Environments and Tools for Parallel Scientific Computing, North-Holland, 1993, pp 213-228.
13. B. Boehm "Software Engineering Economics", Prentice Hall, 1981.

8 Acknowledgments

This work has been carried out within the context of the HAMLET project and is based on a fruitful cooperation between CAP, TNO-TPD, TUM and INESC. All partners contributed step-by-step by constructive discussion to the elaboration of the principles for the environment and to its implementation. All these participants are acknowledged for the work we made together. We would also thank the HAMLET application builders, AEG, TNO-FEL, DLR, CASA, HITEC and Gabriel who contributed by explaining their needs and assessing the delivered tools in a constructive manner.

On-line Distributed Debugging on Scaleable Multicomputer Architectures*

Thomas Bemmerl[1] and Roland Wismüller[2]

[1] Intel Corp., European Supercomputer Dev. Center, D-85622 Feldkirchen, FRG
RWTH Aachen, Lehrstuhl für Betriebssysteme (LfBS), D-52056 Aachen, FRG
[2] Technische Universität München, Institut für Informatik, D-80290 München, FRG

Abstract. Debugging parallel programs is one of the most tedious jobs in programming scalable multiprocessor architectures. Due to the distributed resources of these machines, programming is often architecture dependent. Most development tools still reflect this dependency even during the analysis phase of parallel programs. This paper presents the distributed debugger DETOP, which offers a global name space and hides architectural features like the mapping of processes. DETOP is part of the integrated tool environment TOPSYS implemented on iPSC hypercubes, networks of SPARCstations and partly on Transputer systems.

1 Introduction

Some compute intensive applications, e.g. fluid dynamics and simulations, require computing performance far beyond the performance of today's supercomputers. Many computer scientists claim that the performance necessary for these "grand challenges" can only be reached with parallel distributed memory computers.

Although some of these computers already offer hardware concepts to hide the specific architectural features (e.g. topology is hidden by cut-through routing and virtual channels), programming these machines is still more time consuming than writing programs for workstations [5]. A lack in adequate programming tools for parallel architectures boosts this effect. In particular the design and implementation of on-line debuggers is a challenging task due to the following problems:

- The distribution of resources, time relationship between resources and consistency of states.
- The complexity of the target system (large number of processes, processors, channels).
- Highly dynamic process models and applications.
- The natural non-determinism of parallel programs.
- The interference between debugger and user program, that may change its dynamic behaviour (probe effect).

* Partly funded by the German Science Foundation, Contract: SFB 0342

2 State of the Art and Related Work

The techniques to solve these problems can be divided into four main categories explained below.

Off-line Debugging. An off-line debugging session consists of two phases. In the execution phase information on the program's behaviour is recorded in trace files for each node or process. In the second phase, these traces can be analyzed with tools that offer either a graphical data representation or database like information retrieval. Since all information is acquired within a single program run, nondeterminism is not a problem. However, storing detailed traces needs an enormous amount of memory (and time).

On-line Debugging. On-line (interactive) debuggers allow to stop the target program at any point of the user's interest (breakpoint). Once the program is halted, its state can be examined or modified. Finally the program is continued until another breakpoint occurs. To get information on previous states, the program is usually restarted ("cyclic debugging"), so techniques for deterministic re-execution are useful.

Several methods to specify distributed event predicates triggering a breakpoint have been proposed, e.g. behavioural abstraction [1] or event based approaches [8, 6]. Once the breakpoint is triggered, all processes must be stopped in a consistent state, i.e. a state that may occur during normal execution. Stopping should be as fast as possible, since if a large number of statements is executed after the event occurrence, the program's state may no longer be useful.

Deterministic Re-execution. Since the order of messages arriving at a process may depend on occasional delays, parallel programs are usually nondeterministic, i.e. may behave differently when re-executed. "Instant replay" [7] achieves deterministic re-execution by logging the order of messages in the first program run. During re-execution, the original message order is enforced by delaying the receipt of early messages.

Static Analysis. In contrast to above techniques, static analysis allows to detect some classes of program errors (e.g. deadlocks or access anomalies) without ever executing the program. Since static analysis examines all possible executions, even errors are detected that don't occur in a particular program run.

In the following chapter, we will focus on the event based approach and introduce a transformation-based method for efficient event recognition.

3 Event Based Debugging with the DETOP Debugger

3.1 Programming and Debugging Model

We assume a programming model based on light weight processes and message passing as provided by the programming library MMK [4]. MMK offers three kinds of programming objects, that can be created and deleted dynamically:

Tasks, i.e. light weight processes for computing, *mailboxes* for communication and *semaphores* for synchronization. Objects can be accessed independently of their current location in the distributed system by means of globally unique identifiers.

This location transparency simplifies both program coding and debugging, since the user need not have in mind the location of the programming objects. However, the debugger must provide a global view of the distributed program and some kind of (virtual) global time. The ability to dynamically create and delete objects also influences the debugger. The problems to solve are how to name these objects and how to keep the debugger informed of all existing objects and their locations without a large communication overhead.

To support parallel debugging, DETOP adopts the event action model. The user can specify events, e.g. receipt of a message or execution of a statement, and relationships between events. DETOP uses two different methods to define these relationships: On the user level, a simple event description language is used, while event recognition is based on deterministic finite automata. Once events, relationships and actions have been defined, the debugger permanently monitors the specified events. When they satisfy the relationship, the actions are performed, e.g the program is halted. This scheme helps users to move from sequential to parallel programming environments, since it is a natural extension of sequential debugging methods. It may also be used for other purposes, e.g. performance monitoring or visualization.

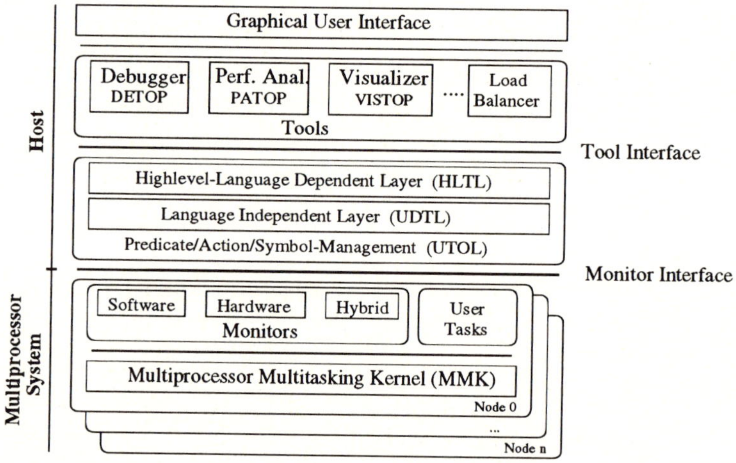

Fig. 1. Hierarchical model of TOPSYS

3.2 Architecture of the DETOP Debugging System

DETOP is part of the TOPSYS programming environment [2], that is built in a hierarchical manner, as shown in fig. 1. We have defined two important interfaces:

The **monitor interface** allows to observe a target program at the machine level. TOPSYS uses a distributed monitoring system with a monitor attached to each node of the multicomputer. Each monitor recognizes local events (occurring on the monitor's node), tests relationships between these events and performs local actions. To implement global predicates and actions, the monitors can exchange messages via a virtually fully connected communication network. Beside a pure software implementation, there is also a hybrid version that uses special hardware and a dedicated communication bus to detect and combine events [3].

The **tool interface** offers the same functionality at the level of source language and programming model and provides a global view of the distributed system. So while the tool interface allows to specify global events related to the source code, e.g. 'execution of line 23 in file foo.c' or 'sending a message to mailbox A', the monitoring system is based on machine code and hooks in the operating system, e.g. 'execution of address $1e34' or 'insertion into send queue'.

A central layer named UTOL is responsible for the transformations between these abstraction levels and the management of predicates, actions and symbol tables. To increase portability there are two sublayers: the high-level language dependent part (HLTL) contains parsers for commands and expressions and also handles complex data types. The language independent layer (UDTL) translates symbolic names into addresses and vice-versa. It also implements the predicate transformation described in the next chapter.

Execution Events	Data Events	Communication Events
execute(task,procedure)	write(task,variable)	send(task,mailbox,msg_ptr)
execute(task,line)	read(task,variable)	receive(task,mailbox)
	assign(task,variable,value)	request(task,semaphore,units)
		release(task,semaphore,units)

Table 1. User level events (wildcards for objects are allowed)

3.3 Monitoring of Global Predicates

As stated before, we use a simple event description language to define global predicates at the user level. A predicate consists of an arbitrary number of events (see table 1) that may be combined with any of the following operators:

$\vee$: $A \vee B$ becomes TRUE when A has become TRUE or B has become TRUE
$\wedge$: $A \wedge B$ becomes TRUE when both A and B have become TRUE
$\rightarrow$: $A \rightarrow B$ becomes TRUE when B becomes TRUE after A has become TRUE

In contrast to other approaches our monitoring system does not directly interpret the global user predicate. Instead, each monitor processes only those parts of the predicate that can be supervised locally. These parts are determined by inspecting the objects that participate in an event.

The mapping between object identifiers and node numbers is established by a localizer module within the UTOL. Since objects may be created and deleted dynamically, an object's node cannot be determined without communication with the target system. In order to keep this communication infrequent, we use a cache-based approach. The localizer holds an internal table containing object identifiers and corresponding node numbers. If an identifier is found in this table, no communication is needed. In the other case, the localizer requests each monitor to send the identifiers of all existing objects on its node and updates the table. If an object has been deleted, but is still in the localizer table, a monitor may receive an event description referring a non-existent object. In this case the event description can be ignored, since the event can never occur.

To achieve distributed global event detection we use a concept called "crosstriggers". Crosstriggers are flags that are initially FALSE and can only be set to TRUE. They are used to implement both communication between monitors and the '∨' operator. For example, assume that $P = (a_0 \longrightarrow b_1) \vee (c_2 \longrightarrow d_2)$, where the indices indicate the nodes that can detect the subpredicates. Distributing this predicate using crosstriggers results in $P = CT0;\ CT1 \ \models a_0;\ CT0 \ \models CT1_1 \rightarrow b_1;\ CT0 \ \models c_2 \rightarrow d_2$. The '|=' operator denotes that the crosstrigger on the left hand side is set when the right hand side evaluates to TRUE.

The software monitor implements crosstriggers as messages, where $CTx \models P$ means "associate action 'send message of type x' with predicate P", while CTx_i on a right hand side denotes 'message of type x arrives at node i'. In the hardware monitor a crosstrigger is a single wired-or signal in a special bus.

Although the set of local predicates could be monitored directly, we decided to compile it into a deterministic Mealy type automaton. This automaton, that generates sequences of local actions as its output, is built by simulating the parallel evaluation of all predicates on a node. This step requires additional computing effort when a predicate is defined. However, it reduces the monitoring overhead, since the event detection algorithm is now a simple automaton interpreter, that can also be efficiently implemented in hardware. In addition, predicate transformation may include some optimization, e.g. to reduce communication, so the scalability of the monitoring scheme is further increased.

4 The Distributed Debugger DETOP

Based on the monitoring scheme introduced above, we have built the distributed debugger DETOP. The debugger uses a graphical interface offering commands that fall into five major groups:

1. **Execution control:** This group contains commands to start, stop and single step tasks.
2. **Inspection of program state:** These commands allow to retrieve information about the program's state, e.g. a list of all currently existing objects, their mapping to processing nodes, scheduling state of tasks, message and task queues of mailboxes, value and type of variables.
3. **Modification of program state:** Currently only modification of variables is supported.
4. **Breakpoints and traces:** As stated in chapter 3.3 distributed breakpoints can be defined based on the events in table 1. The user can also specify events that will be logged to a trace. Starting and stopping the trace can be controlled by a predicate with an associated trace trigger action.

5. **Miscellaneous:** Beside configuration menus and on-line help, multiple listing windows can be used to view source code, to define execution events and to display the current line of execution of a task.

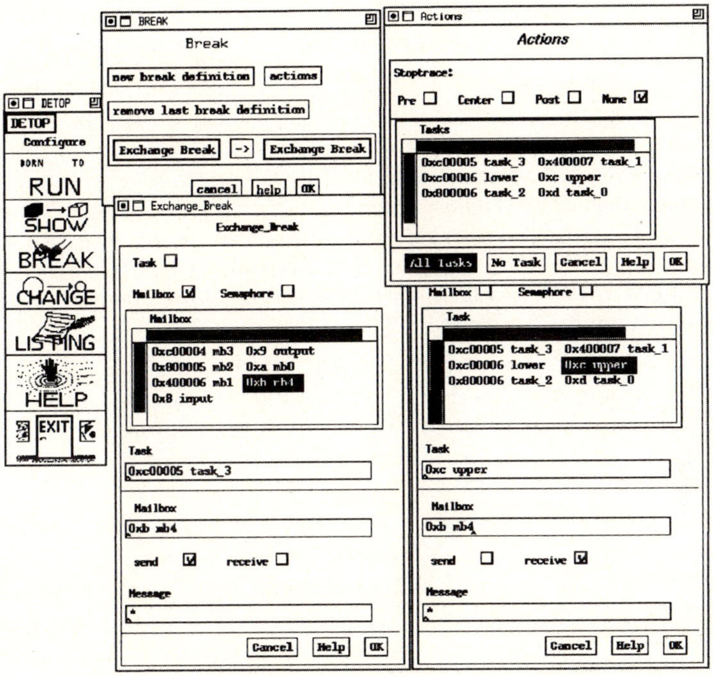

Fig. 2. Definition of a breakpoint with DETOP

Figure. 2 shows how breakpoint definitions are supported by the user interface. In the small window in the upper left, the user defines the overall structure of the predicate, i.e. chooses between different event types and operators. The detailed definition of each event and the associated actions is done in separate windows in order to keep the display clear. All objects are accessed with symbolic names whenever possible. In the example, all tasks are stopped, when task *upper* receives a message from mailbox *mb4* that has been sent by *task_3*.

References

1. P. Bates and J. C. Wileden, "An Approach to High-Level Debugging of Distributed Systems", In *Proc. ACM SIGSOFT/SIGPLAN Software Engineering Symposium on High-Level Debugging*, vol. 18(8) of *ACM SIGPLAN Notices*, pp. 107–111, Aug. 1983.
2. T. Bemmerl, A. Bode, P. Braun, O. Hansen, T. Treml, and R. Wismüller, "The Design and Implementation of TOPSYS", Report 342/16/91 A, Technische Universität München, July 1991.

3. T. Bemmerl, R. Lindhof, and T. Treml, "The Distributed Monitoring System of TOPSYS", In *Proc. CONPAR 90 - VAPP IV Conference*, Zürich, Schweiz, Sept. 1990.
4. T. Bemmerl and T. Ludwig, "MMK - A Distributed Operating System Kernel with Integrated Dynamic Loadbalancing", In *Proc. CONPAR 90 - Vapp IV Conference*, Zürich, Schweiz, Sept. 1990.
5. G. C. Fox, M. Johnson, G. Lyzenga, O. S. W., J. Salmon, and D. Walker, *Solving problems on concurrent processors*, Prentice Hall, Englewood Cliffs, 1988.
6. D. Haban and W. Weigel, "Global Events and Global Breakpoints in Distributed Systems", In *Proc. Twenty-First Annual Hawaii International Conference on System Sciences*, vol. II, Sortware Track, pp. 166–175, 1988.
7. T. J. LeBlanc and J. M. Mellor-Crummey, "Debugging Parallel Programs with Instant Replay", *IEEE Trans. Comput.*, vol. C-35, no. 4, pp. 471–481, Apr. 1987.
8. B. P. Miller and J. D. Choi, "Breakpoints and Halting in Distributed Programs", In *Proc. Eighth International Conference on Distributed Computing Systems*, pp. 316–323, Los Alamitos, California, 1988.

The FTMPS–Project: Design and Implementation of Fault–Tolerance Techniques for Massively Parallel Systems[1]

Johan Vounckx[3], G. Deconinck[3], R. Lauwereins[3 2], G. Viehöver[4], R. Wagner[4], H. Madeira[5], J.G. Silva[5], F. Balbach[6], J. Altmann[6], B. Bieker[7], H. Willeke[7]

[3] Katholieke Universiteit Leuven, ESAT, K. Mercierlaan 94, 3001 Heverlee, Belgium, tel: +32–16–22 09 31 – fax: +32-16-22 18 55 – johan.vounckx*esat.kuleuven.ac.be

[4] Parsytec GmbH (D)

[5] Universidade de Coimbra (P)

[6] F.A. Universität Erlangen-Nürnberg (D)

[7] Universität-GH Paderborn (D)

Abstract. The FTMPS-project provides a solution to the need for fault–tolerance in large systems. A complete fault-tolerance approach is developed and being implemented. The built-in hardware error-detection features combined with software error-detection techniques provide a high coverage of transient as well as permanent failures. Combined with the diagnosis software, the necessary information for the OSS (statistics and visualisation) and the possibly reconfiguration is collected. Backward error recovery based on checkpointing and rollback, is implemented.

1 Introduction

Fault-tolerance is now more than ever indispensable in computer systems: even if the *massively parallel systems* (MPS) may grant the growing demand for computational power, execution times of weeks and months are still required for heavy number-crunching applications. Though the probability of the failure of a single chip decreases due to better technologies, the statistical chance that one element in these large systems breaks down during run time is not at all negligible. However, the failure of one component should not result in the failure of the complete system. Hence, the failures which will occur, must be tolerated, without influencing the results of the computations.

Most users of MPS which are used for scientific and industrial applications do not require that these systems are continuously running with their *full* capabilities. As long as the system is usable, producing *correct results* and getting back to full speed within an *acceptable period*, they allow reduced system performance, due to failures of some components or down-times due to preventive maintenance.

[1] Supported by the EC as ESPRIT-project 6731

[2] Senior Research Associate of the Belgian National Science Foundation

This need for correctness, continuity and availability motivates the fault-tolerance techniques for long-running number-crunching applications developed within ESPRIT-project 6731. The acronym FTMPS - A Practical Approach to fault-tolerance in Massively Parallel Systems - explains its primary objective: developing fault-tolerance concepts to manage failures in massively parallel computers which are immediately applicable to the market. Project-partners are the KU Leuven (Belgium), the University of Coimbra (Portugal), the Universities of Paderborn and Erlangen-Nürnberg (both Germany), British Aerospace (UK) and Parsytec Computer GmbH (Germany).

In the next section the target machine is described for which the FTMPS software is developed. In the third section we give the fault-tolerance concept followed within the project. The next section gives two additional developments of the project which support the software for the operator and enhance its applicability for other MPS. Finally, we end this paper with a conclusion and an outlook to the future of this project.

2 Target Machine

In this section we describe the target architecture for our fault-tolerance techniques. To make the system software as hardware independent as possible a Unifying System Model (USM) is introduced. The applicability of the FTMPS approach is proven on Parsytec's GC series. In the second subsection we will describe these computers.

2.1 Unifying System Model

In the USM, the massively parallel system consists of two logically divided parts. The *D-net* (data network) is used to execute user applications. It is divided into partitions (space-sharing), which correspond to the set of nodes assigned to a single application. The *C-net* (control network) is used to execute the system (control) software. The global C-net is shared by all partitions. A local C-net is used by a single application. These divisions are necessary to provide fault-isolation and prevention of influences from one application to an other.

By assuring that the system software corresponds to this USM, it is possible to obtain a high degree of architecture independence, applicable to a wide range of MPS.

The USM does not impose any network topology. However, each topology requires another routing approach. In the FTMPS-project we focus on mesh-based architectures. Indeed, this topology covers a wide range of massively parallel systems [8], [7], [3] thanks to its expandability and routing simplicity [11].

2.2 Parsytec GC Series

The Parsytec GC series covers a wide range of (massively) parallel computers. The GCel [8] consists of a network of T805 transputers connected in a 2D-grid. Statical routing switches and a control network allow space sharing by assigning a partition to each user. The built-in spare is already a first fault-tolerance means.

The GC/T9 [7] is based on the T9000 transputer and dedicated hardware routers minimising communication delay. These routers must be programmed to set up the partitions. Again spares are available. The hierarchical structure is 3D-grid based.

The nodes of the GC/PPC are connected into a 2D-mesh like the GCel. Each node consists of two powerful PowerPC's for computational purposes and four T805's for communication. Statical switches are provided to set up the user-partitions. Spares are equally integrated in the system.

3 Fault-Tolerance Techniques

In this section we focus on the fault-tolerance concept of the FTMPS-project. The concurrent error-detection's goal informs the diagnosis software upon a fault. This fault is then analysed and classified. The system must possibly be reconfigured and the application restarted from a saved checkpoint. A statistics tool (Section 4.1) is provided to help diagnosis and reconfiguration. The following subsections describe each of the subtasks in more detail.

3.1 Error-detection

The error-detection is based on two complementary techniques. *Structural error detection* techniques are based on codes for memory and communication. Classically used techniques such as parity bits, error detecting and correcting codes, possibly checksums must be included in the system. *Behaviour based techniques* detect errors in the subsystem formed by the processor, bus and memory. In this approach, information describing a particular aspect of the behaviour (e.g. the program control flow) is previously collected (e.g. at compile/assembly time). At run time this information is compared with the actual behaviour. An excellent survey of this family of error detection techniques can be found in [5].

3.2 Diagnosis

The next step is the evaluation of the data delivered by the fault detection mechanisms in order to localise the faulty components and to classify the fault. The fault diagnosis software handles an error when an error message is received by the control processors (from an error-detection mechanism) or when a faulty component omits to send *I'm alive* messages. The algorithm consists of two parts running on the control processors. The first part supervises the application processors and the data net; the second part checks the control processors and control net. If a fault cannot be diagnosed by the control processors, the host diagnoses the fault. In addition to this, the host is the interface to the statistics database, which stores the diagnosis results and delivers necessary information. The result of the diagnosis is passed to the recovery algorithms which - if necessary - reconfigure the system and restart the application (Sections 3.3 and 3.4).

3.3 Reconfiguration

A partition which seems *undamaged* for the application is needed. Hence, permanent errors require a reconfiguration of the system before the application may continue. This reconfiguration is user-transparent and consists of two parts.

Rerouting: when a component has failed permanently, the routing tables must be reprogrammed such that those failed entities are detoured. The GC uses *interval routing* [9] which is very well suited for an MPS because of the compactness of its routing information. Adaptation of the routing tables to overcome failures while keeping the information compact is quite complicated. Solutions are shown in [10].

Remapping: when processors fail they must be remapped on spare processors to allow the application to continue. The repartitioning algorithm must find a partition with sufficient working processors for the application.

3.4 Application Recovery

The recovery-software must also initialise the restart of the involved applications. To avoid that long-running applications must be restarted from scratch, *backward error recovery* is integrated. It is based on *checkpointing and rollback.* This means that during normal execution, the status of the application program is saved to stable storage. This set of information about the status is called a checkpoint. In case of a failure the application can be rolled back to a checkpoint and restarted from there.

Recovery of parallel applications has to cope with the *consistency problem.* After rollback the application must obviously restart from a consistent state. This means not only a consistent status of each processor on his own, but also the consistency among several checkpoints corresponding to different processors must be guaranteed. Since the different nodes communicate and no global time is available, problems arise. An overview of existing solution may be found in [2].

In the FTMPS-project an application-wide checkpointing technique is used which has the advantage that during normal fault-free operation overhead is produced only when saving the checkpoints. *Fail time bounded behaviour* is incorporated which does not assume fail-stop, but allows an error detection latency. The user-driven implementation is a non-blocking approach which saves the minimal amount of information at the cost of a limited user-involvement.

The user-transparent approach freezes the application and relieves the user of this task.

4 Applicability

The next section describes two important aspects to enhance the applicability of the project results. Focus is put on two aspects: a system operator interface which facilitates the use of the system and serves as backbone for the FTMPS-software and the portability of the software.

4.1 OSS (Operator Site Software)

For the maintenance staff, it is important to know which boards are damaged and have to be replaced. Manufacturers try to localise weak points in their hardware. For these reasons an *automatic error log* is integrated. Additionally, a *software monitor* [1], [4], [6] provides data about the system's workload in order to reveal failure/load relationships. New problems are faced due to the amount of data which has to be routed to and evaluated on the control host of an MPS. This OSS supports both the other fault-tolerance software (providing history facts and system status) and the system operator (visualising statistics and status, and interfacing for interventions, e.g. in exceptional cases, system crashes, repairs, changes in the partitioning, upgrades, etc.).

The OSS can be thought of as the front-end of the fault-tolerance software. The built-in *visualisation* features simplify the handling of massively parallel systems for the operator.

4.2 HIL (Hardware Independence Layer)

The Hardware Independence Layer (HIL) provides hardware component independence for the operating system and the FTMPS software. This enables *portability* of this software across different platforms containing different types of processors and communications. The cost of incorporating this software on other or updated hardware will then be reduced as only the HIL must be adapted. In defining the HIL a trade-off is made between minimising the necessary recoding and maximising the efficiency of a single implementation by taking the advantage of specific hardware facilities. For a programmer, the HIL should be transparent and not affecting the functionality of the services offered by the operating system and fault-tolerance extensions. Hence, the HIL provides a *virtual processor* interface to the system software, which may be unmodified. The HIL therefore consists of a library of functions which execute only under control of the operating system.

5 Conclusion

In this paper, we presented a specification of a global fault-tolerance approach for a wide range of massively parallel systems. The real need of fault-tolerance in large systems was described. We explained the target hardware on which this project is being implemented together with the fault-tolerance software-modules. The built-in hardware error-detection features combined with software error-detection techniques provide a high coverage of transient as well as permanent failures. Combined with the diagnosis software, the necessary information for the OSS (statistics and visualisation) and the possible reconfiguration is collected. From the applications' points of view, backward error recovery based on checkpointing and rollback, is implemented. Especially for long-running number-crunching applications this seems an advantageous approach. By now the project has finished a first prototype demonstrating the applicability and flexibility of the developed fault-tolerance techniques.

References

1 Castillo F., Siewiorek D.P.: Workload, Performance, and Reliability of Digital Computer Systems. IEEE Proc. of FTCS-11, pp. 84-89, June 1981.

2 Deconinck G., Vounckx J., Lauwereins R., Peperstraete J.A.: Survey of Backward Error Recovery Rechniques for Multicomputers Based on Checkpointing and Rollback. IASTED Intl. Conf. on Modelling and Simulation, Pittsburgh, PA, USA, May 1993, pp. 262-265.

3 Esser R., Knecht R.: Intel Paragon XP/S - Architecture and Software Environment. Proceedings of Supercomputer 93, Mannheim, June 1993.

4 Iyer R.K., Rossetti D.J.: A Measurement-Based Model for Workload Dependence of CPU Errors. IEEE Trans. on Computers, C35(6):511-519, June 1986.

5 Mahmood A.: Concurrent Error Detection Using Watchdog Processors - A Survey. IEEE Trans. on Computers, 37(2), 1990.

6 Maehle E., Obelör W.: DELTA-T, a User-Transparent Software-Monitoring Tool for Multi-Transputer Systems. Proc. EUROMICRO 92, Microprocessing and Microprogramming, 32(9):245-252, Sep. 1992.

7 Parsytec GmbH: Technical Summary Parsytec GC, Version 1.0. Parsytec GmbH, 1991.

8 Tiedt F.: Parsytec GCel Supercomputer, Technical Report, Parsytec GmbH, 1991.

9 van Leeuwen J., Tan R. B.: Routing with Compact Routing Tables. Technical Report RUU-CS-83-16 Rijksuniversiteit Utrecht, Nov. 1983.

10 Vounckx J., Deconinck G., Cuyvers R., Lauwereins R., Peperstraete J.A.: Network fault-tolerance with Interval Routing Devices. Proc. of the 11th IASTED Int. Symp. Applied Informatics, pp. 293-296, Annecy, France, May 1993.

11 Vounckx J., Deconinck G., Cuyvers R., Lauwereins R., Peperstraete J.A.: Multiprocessor Routing techniques. Deliverable O3.1.1/L of ESPRIT Project 6731, July 1993.

High Performance Fortran Languages: Advanced Applications and Their Implementation *

Barbara Chapman[a] *Piyush Mehrotra*[b] *Hans Zima*[a]

[a]Institute for Software Technology and Parallel Systems,
University of Vienna, Brünner Strasse 72, A-1210 Vienna, Austria
E-Mail: {barbara,zima}@par.univie.ac.at

[b]ICASE, MS 132C, NASA Langley Research Center,
Hampton VA. 23681 USA
E-Mail: pm@icase.edu

Abstract

High Performance Fortran Languages such as Vienna Fortran and High Performance Fortran (HPF) allow the programming of massively parallel machines at a relatively high level of abstraction, based on a user-specified distribution of data across the processors of the machine. In this paper we examine the parallelization of two advanced applications – which require irregular data and work distributions – in Vienna Fortran and identify the reasons why the current version of HPF does not provide adequate functionality for formulating efficient parallel versions of these codes.

1 Introduction

Programs for massively parallel machines, such as the Intel Paragon or Meiko's CS-2, have been traditionally developed by manually restructuring sequential codes into parallel programs with explicit message passing. This process is difficult, time-consuming, and error-prone. High Performance Fortran Languages allow the programming of these machines at a higher level of abstraction, based on the data-parallel Single-Program-Multiple-Data (SPMD) model.

Vienna Fortran [15, 2] was the first fully defined Fortran language extension for massively parallel machines. It provides the following features:

*The work described in this paper was partially supported by the Austrian Research Foundation (FWF Grant P8989-PHY) and by the Austrian Ministry for Science and Research (BMWF Grant GZ 308.9281- IV/3/93). This research was also supported by the National Aeronautics and Space Administration under NASA Contract No. NAS1-18605, while the authors were in residence at ICASE, NASA Langley Research Center, Hampton, VA 23681.

- **Abstract processor arrays**, identifying the processors which execute the program, may be explicitly declared. One or more structures (*processor views*) may be imposed on such arrays.
- Array declarations may be annotated with a specification of the array **distribution**, which determines a mapping from array indices to abstract processors. In addition to replication and basic intrinsic functions *BLOCK* and *CYCLIC* for regular distributions, Vienna Fortran provides *general block*, *indirect* and *user-defined* distributions.
- The distribution of arrays may be static, or change **dynamically** during the execution of the program.
- In **procedures**, formal array parameters may be explicitly distributed or inherit the distribution of the actual argument.
- The **FORALL** construct permits explicitly parallel loops to be written. Intrinsic reduction operations are provided, and others may be defined by the user. Loop iterations may be executed on a specified processor, where a particular data object is stored, or as determined by the compiler.

In 1993, **High Performance Fortran (HPF)** [6] was defined as a language extension of Fortran 90. The main concepts in HPF have been derived from a number of predecessor languages, including CM Fortran [12], Kali [9], Fortran D [3], and Vienna Fortran. HPF follows Vienna Fortran closely in a number of features. This includes in particular abstract processor arrays, the distinction between static and dynamic distributions, the definition of the procedure interface, and FORALL loops (called *independent* loops in HPF).

On the other hand, a number of advanced concepts of Vienna Fortran have **not** been included in HPF. In particular, only the basic distribution functions *BLOCK* and *CYCLIC* are provided. This omission makes HPF unfit to express advanced algorithms using, for example, irregular or adaptive grids. The discussion of this issue is the main topic of this paper.

In Section 2, we give a short characterization of irregular and dynamic problems and identify the related requirements with respect to language, run-time support, and compilation mechanisms. The subsequent two sections discuss these issues in the context of two examples, a particle-in-cell (PIC) code and a sweep over an unstructured mesh. We finish with concluding remarks in Section 5.

2 Irregular and Dynamic Problems

There are a number of scientific codes where an efficient distribution of some of the major data structures is not possible at compile time. In applications such as particle-in-cell (PIC) codes or PDE solvers using unstructured and/or adaptive meshes, the work distribution changes as the computation progresses.

In such codes, the data needs to be redistributed dynamically in order to rebalance the workload. While HPF offers features for dynamically redistributing arrays, it cannot express the irregular distributions occurring in such codes. In contrast, the advanced distribution mechanisms of Vienna Fortran provide the functionality to handle these codes efficiently.

When dealing with irregular problems, arrays are usually accessed indirectly via subscripted (pointer) subscripts. The compiler can then no longer determine the dependence and communication structure of the problem. As a consequence, *explicitly parallel loops* must be provided by the language, and certain analysis functions must be performed at run time. We now discuss such loops and the associated compilation techniques. Our treatment of this topic is based on work by Saltz, Mehrotra, and Koelbel, in particular on Koelbel's Ph.D. Thesis [7], which provides a detailed discussion.

Forall loops are explicitly parallel loops.[1] By definition, they do not contain loop-carried dependences: this means that a variable defined in one iteration of the loop is not defined or used in any other iteration; as a consequence, all iterations can be executed in parallel. Consider the example below:

```
FORALL  I = 1,N ON OWNER(C(K(I)) )
  Y(K(I))=X(I)+C(K(I))*Y(K(I))
ENDDO
```

The *on-clause* specifies that the i-th iteration ($1 \leq i \leq N$) of the loop is executed on processor *OWNER(C(K(i)))*. The processor may also be specified explicitly, such as in **ON** $R1(I)$, where $R1$ is a processor array. The array K serves as a pointer array, whose values are determined at run time. As a consequence, the access pattern associated with the use of C and Y cannot be statically analyzed. The compiler can not generate communication statements nor can it determine which processor must execute a specific iteration of the loop. Moreover, since it cannot be decided whether or not separate loop iterations assign values to the same element of array Y, this loop would be executed sequentially if written as a standard DO loop. Thus an explicit language construct or directive is essential to enable parallel execution of code containing one or more levels of indirection.

A well-known strategy for handling a forall loop is the **inspector-executor paradigm**. This strategy generates two code phases for forall loops, known as the **inspector** and the **executor**.

The inspector analyzes the loop and computes the communication and iteration sets. It begins by performing a dynamic loop analysis: a simplified version of the loop is executed, in which only those components are analyzed that are relevant for the generation of communication. For each iteration to be executed in a processor p, the accesses to non-local elements are determined along with

[1] Note that the parallel loop introduced here, called a *forall loop*, is not the forall loop proposed during the development of Fortran 90.

```
      PARAMETER (NCELL = ..., NPART = ...)

      INTEGER BOUNDS($NP)
      REAL FIELD(NCELL,NPART,...) DYNAMIC, DIST( BLOCK,:,:)

C       Compute initial position of particles
      CALL initpos(FIELD, NCELL, NPART, ...)

C       Compute initial partition of cells
      CALL balance(BOUNDS, FIELD, NCELL, NPART, ...)
      DISTRIBUTE FIELD :: GENERAL_BLOCK(BOUNDS)

      DO k = 1, MAX_TIME
C         Compute new field
        CALL update_field(FIELD, NCELL, NPART, ...)
C         Compute new particle positions and reassign them
        CALL update_part(FIELD, NCELL, NPART, ...)

C         Rebalance every 10th iteration if necessary
        IF ( MOD(k,10) .EQ. 0 .AND. rebalance() ) THEN
          CALL balance(BOUNDS, FIELD, NCELL, NPART, ...)
          DISTRIBUTE FIELD :: GENERAL_BLOCK(BOUNDS)
        ENDIF

      ENDDO
```

Figure 1: High level PIC code in Vienna Fortran

the associated processors: this yields the sets of elements to be *received* in p. Based on this information, the inspector then computes, as a result of a global communication phase, for every processor the sets of values which must be *sent* to other processors prior to execution of the loop.

Although it is superior to individual communications of values, the inspector phase nevertheless represents a significant run time overhead. It is therefore important to recognize situations in which one execution of the inspector suffices to organize the communication for multiple executions of the executor [10, 5].

The **executor** is the second phase in the execution of the forall statement; it performs the actual computation. When the executor commences, all communication and iteration sets have been computed in the inspector. For each processor p, the executor first sends all local data of p that are required by other processors. Then all iterations accessing only local elements of p are executed; in parallel, non-local data required in p are received from the other processors and stored in a temporary buffer. Finally, the executor performs the remaining iterations, accessing the corresponding buffer elements.

We have not shown the final stage of a forall loop: if values have been assigned to non-local data, then there must be a concluding communication phase which transmits these to all processors which own them.

The **Parti** routines ([13, 11]) represent a library of primitives that have been constructed to support the handling of irregularly distributed arrays, whose distributions are specified indirectly via **mapping arrays**, where the value of a mapping array element is the number of the processor storing the array element with the same index. The mapping array is very costly in terms of storage space, since it is as large as the original array, however it permits the specification of an arbitrary distribution. Parti routines receive and transmit irregularly distributed non-local data, and perform reduction operations on them. The strategy adopted generalizes the *inspector-executor paradigm* discussed above.

On top of the Parti routines, the CHAOS system [10] handles the dynamic redistribution of arrays depending on the communication pattern in a loop, and a corresponding redistribution of the FORALL iterations by integrating a dynamic **partitioner**. Both the Parti and CHAOS routines have been designed so that they can be inserted into code by a compiler or used directly by programmers. They have been successfully integrated in the Vienna Fortran compiler and other compilation systems.

3 Particle-in-Cell Code

Consider a simulation code, which can be used to study the motion of particles in a given domain, such as plasmas for controlled nuclear fusion, or stars and galaxies. The computation at each time step can be divided into two phases. In the first phase, a global force field is computed using the current position of particles. In the second phase, given the new global force field, new positions of the particles are determined. The program can be structured by dividing the underlying domain into cells with each cell owning a set of particles. The particles move from one cell to another as they change positions across the domain. Since the computation in each cell is dependent on the number of particles in the cell, the workload across the domain changes as the computation progresses.

Figure 1 shows the outermost level of a simplified version of a PIC code as expressed in Vienna Fortran. The code omits details irrelevant to the discussion here. The cells are represented by the first dimension of the array *FIELD*. There are a maximum of *NCELL* cells and each cell is restricted to have a maximum of *NPART* particles.

The main goal here is to distribute the cells across the processors such that the work per processor is approximately equal. This means that the distribution of the array *FIELD* across the processors must reflect the distribution of particles across cells, and thus is a function of values computed at execution time. Clearly, *BLOCK* and *CYCLIC* distributions alone are inadequate to handle such a situation.

We solve this problem here by using *general block distributions*. These are similar to regular block distributions in that the index domain of an array dimension is partitioned into contiguous blocks, except that they do not require that blocks must be of the same size: arbitrary partitions are allowed. Thus, this class of distributions provides irregularity while retaining the contiguity property, which plays an important role in achieving target code efficiency. In the PIC code described here, the block sizes are selected so that each processor has roughly the same number of particles on its local part of the domain.

The array *FIELD* is declared to be **DYNAMIC** with the first dimension initially distributed into regular blocks. The procedure *initpos* determines the initial position of the particles and places them in the appropriate cells. Using the number of particles in each cell, the procedure *balance* computes the block sizes to be assigned to each processor and stores these in the array *BOUNDS*, such that *BOUNDS*(p) specifies the block size for processor p. This array is then used to redistribute *FIELD* via the the distribution function *GENERAL_BLOCK*.

In each time step (represented by one iteration of the outer loop), the procedure *update_field* computes the new force field based on the current particle positions. Then, the procedure *update_part* is called to update the positions of the particles. Based on the new positions, the new owner cell for each particle is determined. If a particle has moved from one cell to another, it is explicitly reassigned. This obviously requires communication if the new cell is on a different processor. Since this communication is based on the locations of the current and the new cell, it is highly irregular in nature. Thus, the compiler will have to generate runtime code using the inspector/executor paradigm [8, 11] to support this particle motion.

If the number of particles on each processor remains roughly equal for the duration of the simulation, then load balance will be maintained. Some problems of this kind display sufficient uniformity such that a simple block distribution will suffice to provide a reasonable load balance. For other problems, the motion of particles during the simulation may lead to a severe load imbalance. The code, as shown here, checks on every 10th iteration (by calling function *rebalance*) whether rebalancing is required. If so, a new *BOUNDS* array is computed and the cells redistributed to balance the workload.

General block distributions can be represented in a very compact way and implemented efficiently. They were first implemented in the SUPERB parallelization system [14, 4]. For a detailed description of the associated compilation techniques see [16]. However, they offer only limited flexibility. More general methods for data distributions, as described in the following section, may be needed.

4 Sweep Over Unstructured Meshes

Here, we look at an abstraction of a two-dimensional unstructured mesh Euler solver. The mesh is represented by triangles and the flow variables are stored at the vertices of the mesh. We reproduce only one part of the computation, which

```
PARAMETER(NNODE = ...)
PARAMETER(NEDGE = ...)

REAL X(NNODE)  DYNAMIC DIST( BLOCK)
REAL Y(NNODE)  DYNAMIC CONNECT (=X)
INTEGER MAP(NNODE)  DIST( BLOCK)
REAL EDGE(NEDGE,2)  DYNAMIC DIST( BLOCK)

...
CALL PARTITION( MAP, EDGE )

DISTRIBUTE X  :: ( INDIRECT(MAP))
DISTRIBUTE EDGE :: (FDIST(MAP, EDGE, NEDGE, NNODE))

...
FORALL I =  1, NEDGE   ON OWNER( EDGE(I,1) )
  INTEGER N1, N2
  REAL  DELTAX

  N1 = EDGE(I,1)
  N2 = EDGE(I,2)

  DELTAX = F(X(N1), X(N2))

  Y(N1)  SUM= - DELTAX
  Y(N2)  SUM=   DELTAX
END FORALL
...
END

DFUNCTION FDIST(MAP, EDGE, N, M)

TARGET  A(N,*)
   REAL MAP(M)  DIST(*)
   INTEGER EDGE(N,2)  DIST(*)

    DO 10 I = 1, N
       A(I,:)  DIST TO $P(MAP(EDGE(I,1)) )
10        CONTINUE
END
```

Figure 2: Code for Unstructured Mesh

consists of accumulating at each node the contribution from each of the edges incident upon it. The computation is implemented as a loop over the edges: the contribution of each edge is subtracted from the value at one node and added to the value at the other node.

Figure 2 shows one way in which this computation may be specified in Vienna Fortran. The mesh is represented by the array $EDGE$, where $EDGE(I,1)$ and $EDGE(I,2)$ are the node numbers at the two ends of the Ith edge. The arrays X and Y represent the values at each of the $NNODE$ nodes.

Consider the distribution of the data across the (implicit) one-dimensional array of processors. Each of the arrays has to be dynamically distributed, since the mesh is to be distributed at runtime, in order to balance the computational load across the processors.

The array X, representing a data value at each node, is declared to be dynamically distributed with an initial block distribution. Further below, this array is explicitly distributed via the indirect distribution mechanism provided by Vienna Fortran. The indirection is based on the mapping array MAP, defined in the user specified routine $PARTITION$ depending on the structure of the mesh. (The code for $PARTITION$ has been omitted from the example.) The value of the Ith element of the array MAP, which must be declared with the same size as X, is the number of the processor in the implicit one-dimensional processor array, **$P**, to which the Ith element of the array X is distributed.

Y is also declared with the keyword **DYNAMIC** and is assigned the same distribution as X; its distribution is, moreover, connected with that of X by the **CONNECT** attribute. This means that when X is redistributed, Y is automatically redistributed with exactly the same distribution function.

The array $EDGE$ is also declared with a dynamic distribution and an initial distribution by block. Given the structure of the computation, it would be useful to distribute $EDGE$ in such a way that the values at one or both of its nodes are on the same processor. We have chosen to distribute the elements of $EDGE$ to the processor which owns the values for the first of its nodes. Such a distribution cannot be described by the intrinsic functions, so it is specified by the user-defined distribution function (**DFUNCTION**) $FDIST$ in Figure 2.

DFUNCTIONs are similar to regular Fortran functions, but have a special argument declared with the keyword **TARGET**. It represents the array that is being distributed. Here, the distribution function $FDIST$ takes as arguments the arrays MAP and $EDGE$ and the special argument A. The function body then specifies that the Ith row of the array A is to be distributed to the processor whose number is given by $MAP(EDGE(I,1))$. Thus, when the distribution function $FDIST$ is accessed in the distribute statement, the special argument A is associated with the array being distributed, i.e., $EDGE$, so that $EDGE$ is distributed as required.

The computation is specified using a **FORALL** loop. The variables $N1$, $N2$ and $DELTAX$ declared within the **FORALL** loop are called private variables and conceptually each iteration is allocated a private copy of each of them. Thus assignments to these variables do not cause flow dependencies between iterations of the loop. For each edge, the X values at the two incident nodes are read and used to compute the contribution $DELTAX$ for the edge. This contribution is then accumulated into the values of Y for the two nodes, using the reduction operator **SUM**.

The most important feature of this code as far as its compilation is concerned is that the values of X and Y are accessed via the edges, hence a level of indirection is involved. We distributed the arrays in such a way that the values at the first node of an edge are always local to a loop iteration, but the values at the second node may not be. The data distribution of each of the arrays is determined at run time; thus the compiler cannot detect which references are local and which are not. In such situations, runtime techniques such as those discussed in Section 2 are needed to generate and exploit the communication pattern.

5 Conclusion

This paper gave an overview of Vienna Fortran and HPF and examined the applicability of these languages for solving irregular and dynamic problems. While HPF provides dynamic data distributions and has a language construct to express explicitly parallel loops, its data distribution primitives are inadequate for such problems. In contrast, the generality of the Vienna Fortran data distribution concept allows a concise and efficient formulation of irregular problems. We expect that Phase 2 of the HPF effort, which is scheduled to start in 1994, will address this problem as one of the major issues to be resolved.

References

[1] S. Benkner, B. Chapman, and H. Zima. Vienna Fortran 90. In *Proceedings of the SHPCC Conference 1992*, 51–59, April 1992.

[2] B. Chapman, P. Mehrotra, and H. Zima. Programming in Vienna Fortran *Scientific Programming* 1(1):31-50, Fall 1992.

[3] G. Fox, S. Hiranandani, K. Kennedy, C. Koelbel, U. Kremer, C. Tseng, and M. Wu. Fortran D language specification. Department of Computer Science Rice COMP TR90079, Rice University, March 1991.

[4] H. M. Gerndt. *Automatic Parallelization for Distributed-Memory Multiprocessing Systems.* PhD thesis, University of Bonn, December 1989.

[5] R.v.Hanxleden. Handling Irregular Problems with Fortran D – A Preliminary Report. Proc. Fourth Workshop on Compilers for Parallel Computers, Delft, The Netherlands, December 1993.

[6] High Performance Fortran Forum. High Performance Fortran Language Specification Version 1.0. Scientific Programming 2(1-2):1-170,Spring and Summer 1993.

[7] C. Koelbel. *Compiling programs for nonshared memory machines.* Ph.D. Thesis, Purdue University, August 1990.

[8] C. Koelbel and P. Mehrotra. Compiling global name-space parallel loops for distributed execution. *IEEE Transactions on Parallel and Distributed Systems*, 2(4):440–451, October 1991.

[9] P. Mehrotra and J. Van Rosendale. Programming distributed memory architectures using Kali. In A. Nicolau, D. Gelernter, T. Gross, and D. Padua, editors, *Advances in Languages and Compilers for Parallel Processing*, pp. 364–384. Pitman/MIT-Press, 1991.

[10] R.Ponnusamy, J.Saltz, A.Choudhary. Runtime Compilation Techniques for Data Partitioning and Communication Schedule Reuse. Technical Report, UMIACS-TR-93-32, University of Maryland, April 1993.

[11] J. Saltz, K. Crowley, R. Mirchandaney, and H. Berryman. Run-time scheduling and execution of loops on message passing machines. *Journal of Parallel and Distributed Computing*, 8(2):303–312, 1990.

[12] *CM Fortran Reference Manual, Version 5.2.* Thinking Machines Corporation, Cambridge, MA, 1989.

[13] J. Wu, J. Saltz, H. Berryman and S. Hiranandani. Distributed memory compiler design for sparse problems. ICASE Report 91-13, January 1991.

[14] H. Zima, H. Bast, and M. Gerndt. Superb: A tool for semi-automatic MIMD/SIMD parallelization. *Parallel Computing*, 6:1–18, 1988.

[15] H. Zima, P. Brezany, B. Chapman, P. Mehrotra, and A. Schwald. Vienna Fortran – a language specification. ICASE Internal Report 21, ICASE, Hampton, VA, 1992.

[16] H. Zima and B. Chapman. Compiling for Distributed Memory Systems. *Proceedings of the IEEE, Special Section on Languages and Compilers for Parallel Machines*, February 1993.

Evaluation of High Performance Fortran on Some Real Applications *

Thomas Brandes
German National Research Center for Computer Science (GMD),
P.O. Box 1316, 53731 Sankt Augustin, FRG
e-mail: brandes@gmd.de

Abstract

Due to the existence of a global name space, the data parallel programming model is very comfortable to use. All communication requirements are implicit and therefore left to the compiler. To support this model even to general classes of parallel architectures, i.e. MIMD machines with distributed memory, High Performance Fortran was developed. Beside a data parallel point of view the programmer has the ability to specify data distributions explicitly via directives.

Some real application programs have been investigated to show the usefulness of High Performance Fortran. Therefore these programs have been transformed into the data parallel style and a prototype compilation system has been used to translate them to message-passing programs running on different platforms.

The results verify that the generated message-passing programs scale and can achieve nearly the same performance as their hand-written counterparts. The experiences have also shown where the data parallel programming model has difficulties and where additional optimizations are required.

1 Introduction

Within the ESPRIT-6643 project PPPE (Portable Parallel Programming Environment) some real application programs have been evaluated. The goal of this evaluation was to investigate how partitioning tools and future High Performance Fortran (HPF) compilers can actually help for the parallelization of more complex application codes and how far HPF programs can be competitive with hand-written message-passing programs.

For this purpose some programs of the RAPS (Real Applications on Parallel Systems) benchmark suite have been chosen. As there are also hand-written message passing programs of these codes available, a comparison of data parallel programs and message passing programs was possible.

The sequential versions of the codes written in Fortran 77 needed some changes to become HPF programs. Some situations have been identified where the current HPF definition is not sufficient enough as the current compiler technology still requires more information about the code to generate efficient programs.

Performance results are available by using a prototype HPF-like system. Though hand written message-passing programs will be faster in any case, current compilation systems can achieve nearly the same performance.

*This work was funded by the Esprit-6643 project PPPE (Portable Parallel Programming Environment)

2 The Application Codes

2.1 AVL FIRE Code

FIRE [1] is a fully interactive fluid dynamics package, including powerful, menu-driven pre- and post-processing, developed specially for computing compressible and incompressible turbulent fluid flow as encountered in engeneering environments. 3D and 2D unsteady or steady simulations of flow and heat transfer within arbitrary complex geometries with moving or fixed boundaries can be performed.

Some solvers of this code are part of the RAPS benchmark suite (every solver has about 350 lines of code). These solvers are iterative ones working on unstructured grids. Structured grids are represented by two- or three-dimensional arrays, whereas unstructured grids are represented by one-dimensional arrays to reduce memory requirements. But then neighborhood information must be represented in integer arrays that will be used for indirect addressing within all programs.

Though for the evaluation all three benchmark solvers have been considered, only the results for one solver (GCCG, orthomin with diagonal scaling) will be presented.

2.2 IFS Code

In cooperation between GMD and ECMWF (European Center for Medium-Range Weather Forecasts) the ECMWF's production code for medium-range weather forecasts, the IFS (Integrated Forecasting System), has been parallelized. The solution method employed in the IFS is the spectral transform technique, in which three different function spaces are involved in the computations, namely grid point space, Fourier space and spectral space.

For the evaluation a sequential program of the 2D model of the IFS has been investigated (about 22.000 lines of code). This version contains already all relevant data structures and algorithmic components of the corresponding 3D model. It should be mentioned that the same code has already been parallelized successfully by hand [GJS93].

3 Rewriting Applications in HPF

HPF is a language that supports the data parallel programming model [Hig93]. This model avoids explicit communication and stands for a single thread of control, global name space, and loosely synchronous parallel computation. It is easy to use and data-parallel programs usually scale very well.

For transforming sequential Fortran 77 programs into HPF it is necessary to choose a suitable data layout and to identify the data parallelism by using array operations or parallel loops.

A tool which can greatly simplify the task of porting serial Fortran 77 programs to the data parallel model is the CMAX Converter [TMC92]. The CMAX tool has been derived from the FORGE tool of APR (Applied Parallel Research) [APR93]. It converts sequential programs into data parallel CM Fortran programs [TMC91] by considering the serial loops with its dependences and transforming them either to array operations or forall loops if

[1] FIRE is a registered trade-mark of AVL LIST Gmbh

possible. Furthermore, the layout or distribution of all array variables is determined by using interprocedural analysis.

CM Fortran programs can be rewritten straightforwardly to HPF. This requires in most cases only little syntactical changes.

3.1 Rewriting the AVL FIRE Code

The sequential benchmark solver has been translated to Connection Machine Fortran by using the CMAX Converter. Some small modifications of the original code were necessary to get the solver code successfully translated. Some cleaning up and hand optimizations of the original code have been done to get much more better performance results on a CM-2 and on a CM-5.

The main loop within one iteration computes a new value for every cell by using the old values of this cell and of the six neighbored cells. This loop has no dependences and is directly translated by CMAX to a forall loop that is equivalent to the following vector statement.

```
      DOUBLE PRECISION DIREC1(NNCELL), DIREC2(NNINTC)
      INTEGER LCC (6,NNINTC)
      ...
      DIREC2(1:NNINTC) = BP(1:NNINTC)*DIREC1(1:NNINTC)
     x        - BS(1:NNINTC)*DIREC1(LCC(1,1:NNINTC))
     x        - BW(1:NNINTC)*DIREC1(LCC(4,1:NNINTC))
     x        - BL(1:NNINTC)*DIREC1(LCC(5,1:NNINTC))
     x        - BN(1:NNINTC)*DIREC1(LCC(3,1:NNINTC))
     x        - BE(1:NNINTC)*DIREC1(LCC(2,1:NNINTC))
     x        - BH(1:NNINTC)*DIREC1(LCC(6,1:NNINTC))
```

This statement is very inefficient as it requires six indirect accesses to the array DIREC1. Transformations by hand were necessary to reduce them to one indirect access.

3.2 IFS Code

For the 2D model of the IFS, a 1D partitioning of the data in each of the different data spaces is adequate [GJS93]. During the computations in grid point space and in Fourier space, the partitioning is over latitudes, i.e. different processes are responsible for the calculations of different latitudes. The spectral coefficients are partitioned with respect to wave numbers m such that for a given m all corresponding values are mapped onto the same process. Because of the different distributions there is a redistribution of the data in the Fourier space required. One distribution is with respect to latitudes and the second one is with respect to wave numbers m.

Using HPF layout directives for this distribution of the different spaces was impossible as the corresponding data structures in the code are not two- or three-dimensional arrays but one-dimensional arrays that are used as working spaces with additional integer arrays for indexing. The advantage of these data structures is of course the optimal memory requirements. But it is not possible to use HPF layout directives in such a way that the partitioning is conform to the distribution of the spaces in the logical view.

Therefore a restructuring process was necessary to transform the work spaces into two or three-dimensional arrays (see figure 1). This work has to be carried out by hand. Afterwards HPF layout directives can be set that specify exactly the wanted distribution.

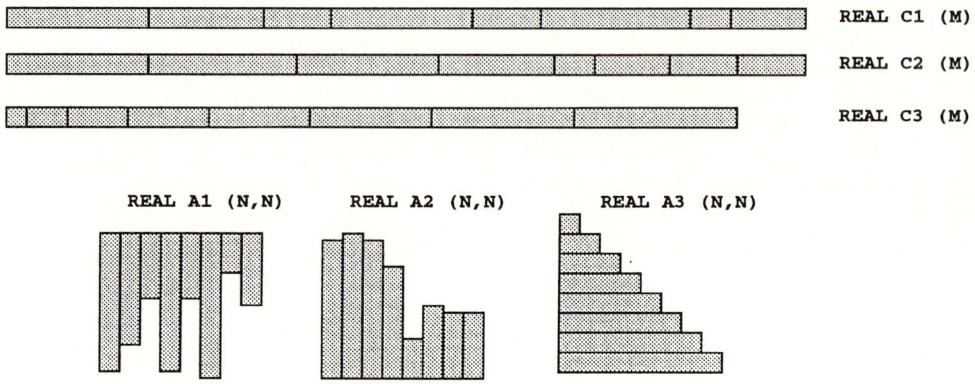

Figure 1: Restructuring of Work Spaces to Structured Arrays

In HPF, an assignment between two arrays with different layout directives results in a redistribution of data. By this way the redistribution of the Fourier space can be realized. HPF contains also a redistribution directive, but this directive is not part of the subset. Some other smaller changes were necessary to identify the parallel loops and the reductions for calculating the spectral norm.

Using the CMAX tool was not possible for this code as this tool would only detect the fine-grained parallelism, but the given parallelism is coarse-grained. In the most relevant parts, the code is composed of loops calling complex subroutines that can be executed independently. This parallelism cannot be detected automatically and must be specified by hand using the HPF INDEPENDENT directive.

The current HPF definition has no directives for specifying private arrays and independent loops that require absolutely no communication. As compiler technology is far away from detecting this automatically, this information must also be given by additional directives to achieve better performance. Such directives are not part of HPF.

4 Compiling the Data Parallel Programs

The data parallel versions of the application programs have been translated to message passing programs by using the Adaptor tool. Adaptor (Automatic Data Parallelism Translator) is a system developed at the GMD for compiling data parallel Fortran programs to equivalent Fortran 77 message passing programs [Bra93]. Only some small modifications were necessary to get the codes successfully translated by Adaptor with its current restrictions.

Some special directives of Adaptor have been used to identify private arrays and parallel loops without communication in the IFS code.

The runtime system of the Adaptor tool is available for many parallel architectures and the programs did actually run on all of these parallel machines. In the following only results for

tjunc (13845 cells)	NP = 1	NP = 2	NP = 4	NP = 8	NP = 16	NP = 32
Adaptor	–	–	71 s	37 s	25 s	16 s
Adaptor (optimized)	74 s	41 s	22 s	13 s	9 s	7 s
Hand-Coded	74 s	39 s	19 s	11 s	7 s	5 s

Table 1: Results for AVL benchmark solver on CM-5 (no vector units)

the Connection Machine CM-5 are presented. The vector units have not been used as the node programs of the message passing programs could not take advantage of them.

5 Results

The performance of the automatically generated program for the AVL benchmark solver was very low due to the high overhead for indirect addressing (see first row in table 1).

The hand-written message passing programs take advantage of the fact that the data decomposition is also a domain decomposition and that the communication pattern does not change between the iterations. This implies that there are only small boundaries between processors (see figure 2) and the necessary communication is reduced to a minimum.

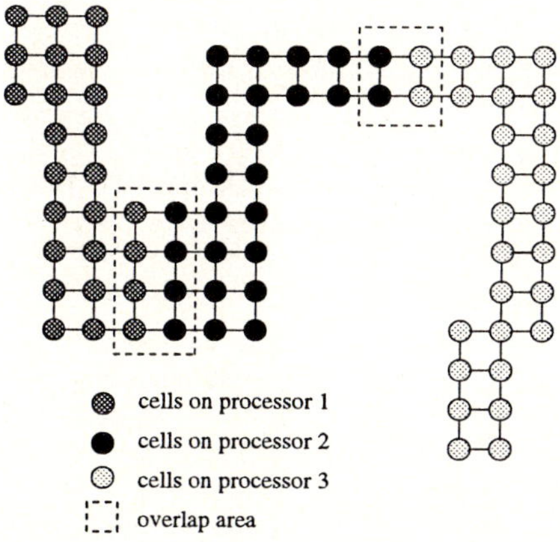

Figure 2: Domain Decomposition of an Unstructured Grid

Adaptor supports also this kind of decompositions, but some small modifications of the generated code were necessary to get similar results as the hand coded version of the solver (see second row of table 1).

Table 2 shows for a typical problem size of the IFS code the runtimes in seconds. The automatically generated message passing program has nearly the same performance as the hand-coded message passing program. Indeed both codes use the same parallelization strategy, but the data parallel version uses nearly the double space of memory. It has also to be mentioned that there is still a high potential for optimizations in the Adaptor compilation system.

CM 5, T63	NP = 1	NP = 2	NP = 4	NP = 8	NP = 16	NP = 32
Adaptor	71.0	35.9	19.9	10.0	5.5	3.2
Hand-Coded	64.5	34.0	17.5	9.0	4.6	2.6

Table 2: Results for T63 on CM 5 (no vector units), Adaptor 2.0

6 Conclusion

High Performance Fortran is on the way to become a useful alternative to writing message passing programs. In contrary to message passing programs, less straightforward work is to be done and data layout can be changed very easily.

If some users still expect to get their old unchanged codes running efficiently on parallel systems, they will be disappointed. Also HPF requires parallel thinking and the employment of a good parallelization strategy at all. Also some knowledge of HPF compiler techniques might be necessary.

While hand-written message passing programs can take advantage of nearly every additional information concerning the data and program structure, compiler for data parallel programs are restricted to the information that they can detect in the program at compile time. Especially better support for irregular data structures is needed before HPF and HPF compilers can be actually competitive.

References

[APR93] FORGE 90: xHPF 1.0 Automatic Parallelizer for High Performance Fortran on Distributed Memory Systems - User's Guide. Technical report, Applied Parallel Research, Inc., April 1993.

[Bra93] T. Brandes. Adaptor: A Compilation System for Data Parallel Fortran Programs. In *International Workshop on Automatic Distributed Memory Parallelization, Automatic Data Distribution and Automatic Parallel Performance Prediction*, Saarbrücken, March 1993. Vieweg.

[TMC92] Thinking Machines Corporation. Using the CMAX Converter. Manual, TMC, September 1992.

[GJS93] U. Gärtel, W. Joppich, and A. Schüller. Parallelizing the ECMWF's Weather Forecast Program: The 2D Case, Technical Documentation and Results for the IFS-2D Model. Arbeitspapiere der GMD 740, Gesellschaft für Mathematik und Datenverarbeitung mbH, March 1993.

[Hig93] High Perforamnce Fortran Forum. High Performance Fortran Language Specification. Final Version 1.0, Department of Computer Science, Rice University, May 1993.

[TMC91] Thinking Machines Corporation. CM Fortran Programming Guide, Version 1.0. Manual, TMC, January 1991.

Experiments with HPF Compilation for a Network of Workstations

Fabien COELHO (coelho@cri.ensmp.fr)

Centre de Recherche en Informatique, École des mines de Paris,
35, rue Saint-Honoré, F-77305 Fontainebleau Cedex, FRANCE.
phone : +33 1 64 69 48 52, fax : +33 1 64 69 47 09

Abstract. HIGH PERFORMANCE FORTRAN (HPF) is a data-parallel Fortran for Distributed Memory Multiprocessors. HPF provides an interesting programming model but compilers are yet to come. An early implementation of a prototype HPF optimizing compiler is described. Experiments of PVM 3-based generated code on a network of workstations are analyzed and discussed. It is shown that if such systems can provide very good speedups at low cost, they cannot allow scalable performance without specific communication hardware. Other early implementations of HPF compilers from academic and commercial groups are presented and compared to our work.

Introduction

The most promising parallel machines seem to be the Distributed-Memory Multiprocessors (DMM), such as the Intel's Paragon or the Thinking Machine's CM5. They are scalable, flexible, and offer good price/performance ratio. However their efficient programming using the message-passing paradigm is a complex and error-prone task, which makes coding hard and expensive. To ease the programmer's burden, new languages have been designed to provide a uniform name space to the user. The compiler must handle the communications, and the machine can be used as a Shared-Memory Multicomputer.

High Performance Fortran (HPF) is a new standard to support data-parallel programming for DMMs. The HPF forum, composed of vendors, academics and users, specified HPF [6] in 1992. It is intended as a *de facto* standard, supported by many companies. The language is based on Fortran 90 with additions to specify the mapping of data onto the processors of a DMM (namely directives `align` and `distribute`), parallel computations with independent and data-parallel loops (`independent` directive and `forall` instruction), reductions, plus some other extensions like new intrinsics to query about the system at run-time. The specification effort has restarted in January 1994 to address problems left aside in 1992 such as parallel I/O and irregular computations.

Section 1 gives a brief overview of the implementation and the optimizations performed by our compiler. Section 2 describes results of runs of Jacobi iterations on a network of workstations, and Section 3 analyzes what can be expected from this kind of applications on such systems. Section 4 describes the current status of other HPF compilers and compares the shortcomings of the different implementations with respect to our experiments.

1 Compiler implementation

A prototype HPF compiler [5] has been developed within PIPS [10] (Scientific Programs Interprocedural Parallelizer) at CRI. It is a 15,000 lines project that generates SPMD (Single Program Multiple Data) distributed code. Fortran 77 and various HPF constructs such as independent loops, static mapping directives and reductions are taken as input. The full semantics of the HPF mapping is supported, e.g. replicated dimensions and arbitrary cyclic distributions are handled. From this input, a 2PMD (2 Programs, Multiple Data, see Figure 3) Fortran 77 message passing code is generated. The first program mainly deals with I/O to be performed by the host processor, and the other is an SPMD code for the nodes. The code uses a library of PVM 3-based [7] run-time support functions. Thus the compiler output is as portable as PVM. Two files are also generated to initialize run-time data structures describing the distributed arrays.

The compilation is divided into 3 phases:

First, the input code is parsed and normalized (e.g. temporaries are inserted to avoid indirections...), the directives are analyzed and new declarations are computed for the distributed arrays. These new declarations reduce when possible the amount of allocated memory on each node.

The second phase generates the run-time resolution code [4] for the host and nodes as a double rewriting scheme on the abstract syntax tree of the program. The *owner computes rule* is used to define the processor that performs the computations. Accesses to remote data are guarded by tests and communications if necessary. This rewriting scheme has been formalized, which enabled us to prove parts of the correctness of the compilation process. For instance, the balance of communications can easily be proved by checking that each rewriting rule generates as many sends as receives with complementary guards and destination.

The third phase performs optimizations when necessary conditions are met. An overlap analysis for multi-block-distributed arrays [8] is implemented. Alignment shifts at the template level are used to evaluate the overlap width in each directions. Guards are generated for non contributing nodes. Messages are vectorized by the process, and moved outside of the loop body. Reductions are compiled through calls to dedicated run-time functions.

2 Experiments

Experiments have been performed on an unloaded Ethernet network, with up to 8 Sparc Stations 1. The application (see Figure 1 with HPF directives) computes 100 Jacobi iterations on a 2D plate. The computation models heat transfers in an homogeneous square plate when the temperature is controlled on the edges. This application is fully parallel and few communications are needed. The kernel comes from [12], with a few I/O and initializations added. The communication pattern induced by the computation kernel, as well as the different initializations of some areas within the plate, are representative of stencil computations such as wave propagation in geophysics. The arrays are aligned and block-block distributed to minimize the amount of data exchange. Figure 2 shows extracts from the generated code for the machine nodes: It is an SPMD code parametrized by the processor's identity. Declarations are reduced to what is necessary on one processor, and extended to store remote data in overlap areas. Run-time support functions are prefixed by `hpfc`. The `north` vector initialization introduces a guard so that only the appropriate processors execute the loop. The local loop bounds are computed by each processor before the loop. The last part of the code shows the first send within the kernel of the computation: Each selected processor first computes to which neighbor it has to send the data, then packs and sends them. The last line is the comment that introduces the corresponding receive. All codes were compiled with all compilers' optimizations set on.

The measures are given for 1, 4 and 8 processors, and for plate width of 20 to 1,000 points (up to 2,000 points for 8 processors). They are based on the best of at least 5 runs. Figure 4 shows the Mflop/s achieved by the sequential runs when the plate width is scaled up. From these measures, 1.45 Mflop/s is taken as the Sparc 1 performance on this application. It matches most experimental points, and cache effects explain the other results. This reference is scaled to the number of processors to provide a realistic peak performance for the network of workstations used. Other measures are displayed as the percentage of this peak performance reached by the best run. This metric (e) is called *relative realistic efficiency*. Real speedups were rejected because of the artefacts linked to cache effects: A good speedup may only mean a bad sequential performance for a given plate width. Moreover sequential experiments were stopped because of memory limitations on the tested configuration. An absolute measure (e.g. Mflop/s) would not have clearly shown the relative efficiency achieved. Note that $p.e$ (p processors, efficiency e) is a speedup, but not a measured one.

Figures 5 and 6 show the experimental data using this metric and theoretical curves derived from realistic assumptions in the next section. Large computations lead to up to 80–90% efficiency. The complementary part evaluates the loss due to latencies and communications. These results are used to test the formulas derived in the next section. These formulas are then used to precisely analyze the performance which can be expected from such applications run on networks of workstations when the parameters change.

3 Analyses

The theoretical curves (doted lines on Figures 5 and 6) are based on assumptions about the network bandwidth ($\gamma = 700$ KB/s through PVM), the realistic peak performance of one Sparc 1 ($\pi = 1.45$ Mflop/s) and an offset ($\alpha p + \delta$) to model the initialization times. It is assumed (a) that floats are 4 bytes long, (b) that the application is block-block distributed, (c) that communications and computations do not overlap, and (d) that the communications are sequentialized on the medium. If p is the number of processors, n the plate width and t the number of iterations, then the total time complexity $\Theta_t(n,p)$ to run the program is:

$$\Theta_t(n,p) \simeq \frac{4n^2t}{\pi p} + \frac{16n(\sqrt{p}-1)t}{\gamma} + \alpha p + \delta \qquad (1)$$

The first term is the computation time and the second the communication time. If $\mu = \frac{\pi}{\gamma}$, the continuous regime relative realistic efficiency is:

```
      program jacobi
      parameter (n=500)
      real tc(n,n), ts(n,n), north(n)
chpf$ template t(n,n)
chpf$ align tc(i,j), ts(i,j) with t(i,j)
chpf$ align north(i) with t(1,i)
chpf$ processors p(2,4)
chpf$ distribute t(block,block) onto p
chpf$ independent(i)
      do i=1,n
         north(i) = 100.0
      enddo
      ...
      do k=1,time
c     kernel of the computation
chpf$ independent(j,i)
      do j=2,n-1
        do i=2,n-1
          ts(i,j) = 0.25 *
     $      (tc(i-1,j) + tc(i+1,j)
     $     + tc(i,j-1) + tc(i,j+1))
         enddo
      enddo
      ...
```

Fig. 1. Jacobi iterations kernel

```
      program node
      include 'fpvm3.h'
      include 'parameters.h'
      ...
      real*4 north(1:125),
     $     ts(1:250,1:125), tc(0:251,0:126)
      call hpfc_init_node
      ...
      if (mypos(1,1).eq.1) then
        call hpfc_loop_bounds(i_5,i_6,1,500..
        do i_4 = i_5, i_6
          north(i_4) = 100.0
        enddo
      endif
      ...
      do k = 1, time
c p(1:2,2:4) send tc(1:250,1) to (-1)
      if (mypos(2,1).ge.2) then
        call hpfc_cmpneighbour(-1)
        call hpfc_pack_real4_2(tc, ...)
        call hpfc_sndto_n
      endif
      ...
c p(1:2,1:3) receive tc(1:250,126) from (+1)
```

Fig. 2. Node code extract

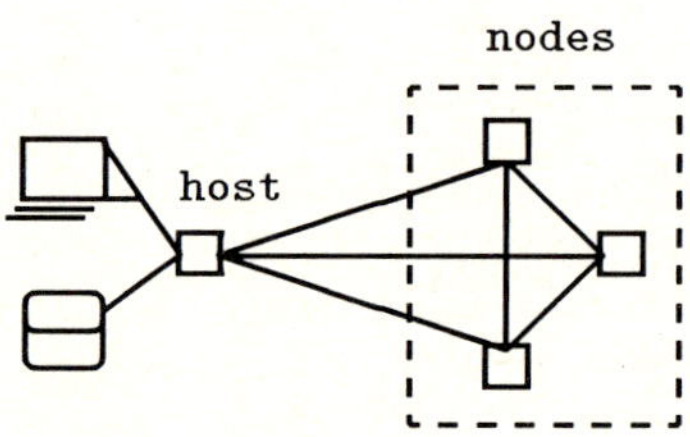

Fig. 3. Machine model

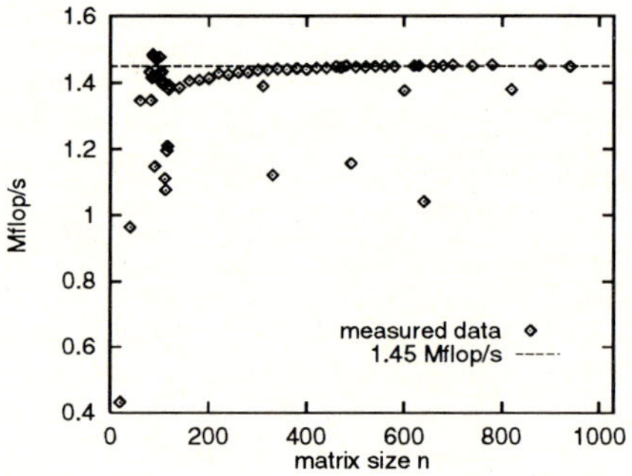

Fig. 4. Sequential Mflop/s

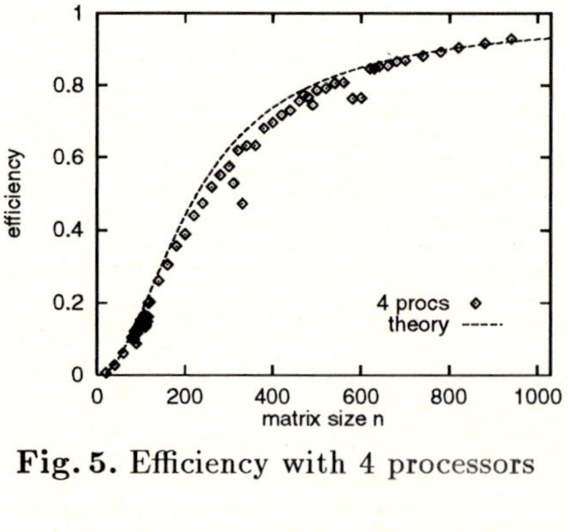

Fig. 5. Efficiency with 4 processors

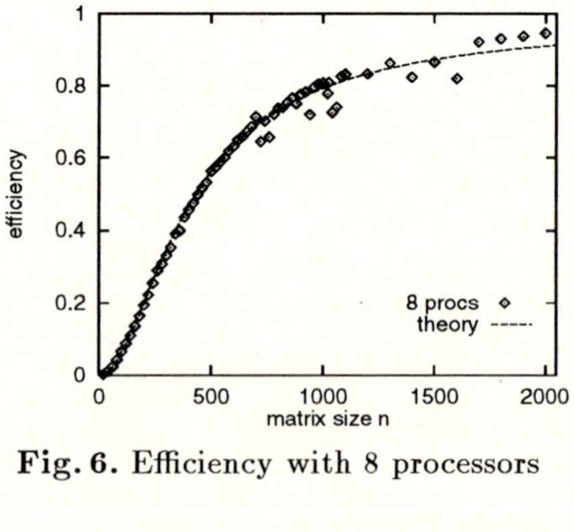

Fig. 6. Efficiency with 8 processors

$$e_\infty(n,p) = \lim_{t\to\infty} \left(\frac{4n^2t}{\pi p}\right) \Theta_t(n,p)^{-1} = \left(1+\mu\frac{4p(\sqrt{p}-1)}{n}\right)^{-1} \quad (2)$$

These functions match very well the experimental points as can be seen on the Figures. They can be used to see what can be expected from such applications on networks of workstations. The interesting point is not to scale up the problem size for better efficiency, but to analyze what happens when the number of processors is scaled with a constant problem size: The efficiency quickly decreases. The minimal size to get efficiency e with p processors can be computed (3). An optimal number of processors is also easily derived (4), for which 2/3 of the network bandwidth is used.

$$n \geq \left(\frac{4e}{1-e}\right)\mu p(\sqrt{p}-1) \quad (3) \qquad\qquad p \simeq \left(\frac{n}{2\mu}\right)^{\frac{2}{3}} \quad (4)$$

The μ parameter is expected to belong to a large range of values as processor and network performances change. For a network of RISC 6000 on Ethernet, $\mu \simeq 100$[1], while for SS1 $\mu \simeq 2$. For a realistic application with $n = 1000$, $\mu \simeq 100$ gives the optimal number of processors $p = 3$, a 1.5 speedup and an overloaded network! This clearly shows that a set of fast workstations linked by Ethernet is definitely not an underused massively parallel machine, even for an embarrassingly parallel program like Jacobi iterations. Scaling the problem size to show better results is a fake, because the convergence speed and other requirements of the algorithms [11] would dramatically slow down the resolution.

The first problem is the low bandwidth of the network, especially when compared to processor speed. The local networks should be upgraded as much as the workstations to get good performance. The second problem is the complexity in p of the functions since the communications are sequentialized on the medium. The network is the bottleneck of the system.

4 Related work

A lot of work about compilation and prototype compilers for DMMs was published during the last few years. The Vienna Fortran Compiling System [13] and Fortran D [12] are early developments of data-parallel languages on which HPF is based. The Fortran D prototype allows only one dimension to be distributed, and no I/O. Adaptor [2] is a pragmatic and efficient public domain software which implements some features of HPF and which was initially based on CM-Fortran. Many vendors have announced commercial compilers: Applied Parallel Research, Digital Equipment, Pacific-Sierra Research, the Portland group...These products are not yet available, or do not yet implement all HPF features. Moreover the performances of these systems will depend on the implemented optimizations, and many points are still an open research area. Performance figures for some of these prototypes are available [9, 3], but comparisons are difficult because the applications and the machines are different.

[1] This figure is based on the peak performance of a RS 6000 running at 62.5 MHz

Conclusion

Our optimizing compiler supports the full HPF mapping semantics and produces portable code. Experiments with Jacobi iterations on a network of workstations were performed with the compiler output. Very good efficiencies were measured for large problem sizes. These results have been analyzed and discussed, and it has been shown that networks of fast workstations cannot provide good performance without specific communication hardware.

Some HPF features, such as procedure interfaces and the `forall` instruction, are missing. Moreover I/O are not yet efficiently compiled. Future work will include a better handling of I/O, experiments using more realistic programs and real parallel machines (Paragon, CM5, Alpha farm...), as well as implementation of new optimization techniques [1].

References

1. C. Ancourt, F. Coelho, F. Irigoin, and R. Keryell. A linear algebra framework for static HPF code distribution. In *Workshop on Compilers for Parallel Computers, Delft*, Dec. 1993. Also available as TR EMP A/250/CRI.
2. T. Brandes. Adaptor: A compilation system for data parallel fortran programs. Technical report, High Performance Computing Center, German National Research Institute for Computer Science, Aug. 1993.
3. T. Brandes. Results of Adaptor with the Purdue Set. Internal Report AHR-93 3, High Performance Computing Center, German National Research Institute for Computer Science, Aug. 1993.
4. D. Callahan and K. Kennedy. Compiling programs for distributed-memory multiprocessors. *The Journal of Supercomputing*, 2:151–169, 1988.
5. F. Coelho. Étude de la compilation du *high performance fortran*. Master's thesis, Université Paris VI, Sept. 1993. Rapport de DEA Systèmes Informatiques. TR EMP E/178/CRI.
6. H. P. F. Forum. *High Performance Fortran Language Specification*. Rice University, Houston, Texas, May 1993. *Version 1.0*.
7. A. Geist, A. Beguelin, J. Dongarra, J. Weicheng, R. Manchek, and V. Sunderam. *PVM 3 User's Guide and Reference Manual*. Oak Ridge National Laboratory, Oak Ridge, Tennessee, May 1993.
8. H. M. Gerndt. *Automatic Parallelization for Distributed-Memory Multiprocessing Systems*. PhD thesis, University of Vienna, 1989.
9. S. Hiranandani, K. Kennedy, and C.-W. Tseng. Evaluation of compiler optimizations for Fortran D on MIMD Distributed-Memory machines. In *ACM International Conference on Supercomputing*, 1992.
10. F. Irigoin, P. Jouvelot, and R. Triolet. Semantical interprocedural parallelization: An overview of the PIPS project. In *ACM International Conference on Supercomputing*, June 1991.
11. J. Pal Singh, J. L. Hennessy, and A. Gupta. Scaling parallel programs for multiprocessors: Methodology and examples. *Computer*, pages 42–50, July 1993.
12. C.-W. Tseng. *An Optimising Fortran D Compiler for MIMD Distributed Memory Machines*. PhD thesis, Rice University, Houston, Texas, Jan. 1993.
13. H. Zima and B. M. Chapman. Compiling for distributed-memory systems. *Proceedings of the IEEE*, Feb. 1993.

HIGH PERFORMANCE FORTRAN

Dr. G. M. van Waveren
member of ISO/WG5 and HPFF
e-mail: <waveren@xs4all.hacktic.nl>

1. Introduction

High Performance Fortran consists of a set of extensions to Fortran 90, which make it possible to develop efficient data-parallel applications for massively parallel computer systems. Typical data-parallel applications are seismic applications, the Fast Fourier Transform, computational fluid dynamics and weather simulation.

The advantages of using parallel processing technology in industrial applications lie in the field of cost reduction and turnaround time improvement. For example in seismic production, the improvement in turnaround time can lead to lower costs and quicker results for clients. Also in product development where computer simulations play a significant role, for instance drug design, aircraft design and flow meter design, the use of parallel processing technology leads to a decrease in the time-to-market.

In the development of parallel applications, the use of the emerging software development standards has the advantage that the applications are portable between platforms, making the user less dependent upon the vendors. The user can then switch relatively easily between vendors.

In this lecture, firstly an overview of High Performance Fortran 1.0 will be given. Secondly the incorporation of High Performance Fortran 1.0 into the ISO standards will be discussed. Thirdly the experience of vendors and users gained in 1993 will be discussed. This lecture will end with a discussion of the plans of the High Performance Fortran Forum for 1994.

2. Overview of High Performance Fortran, version 1.0

High Performance Fortran (HPF) [1] is a set of extensions to Fortran, which make it possible to write efficient data parallel programs for massively parallel systems. It was developed between March 1992 and March 1993 by the High Performance Fortran

Forum (HPFF). HPF seems likely to become the language standard for massively parallel systems. In this paragraph, the main features of HPF will be discussed.

A data distribution model has been introduced in the language to allow the user to advise the compiler on the allocation of data objects to processor memories, with the assumption that operations on two data objects will complete faster if the objects are on the same processor. This is specified by specially formatted comments called directives. The distribution directive can divide an array into equal-sized pieces (BLOCK distribution) or assign elements to processors in round-robin fashion (CYCLIC distribution). Additional directives allow more complex patterns, dynamic data remapping, and passing special information about procedure arguments. In the model the data objects are mapped to abstract templates and distributed on abstract processors. The compiler subsequently maps the abstract processor distribution to physical processors. In figure 2.1 this is graphically illustrated.

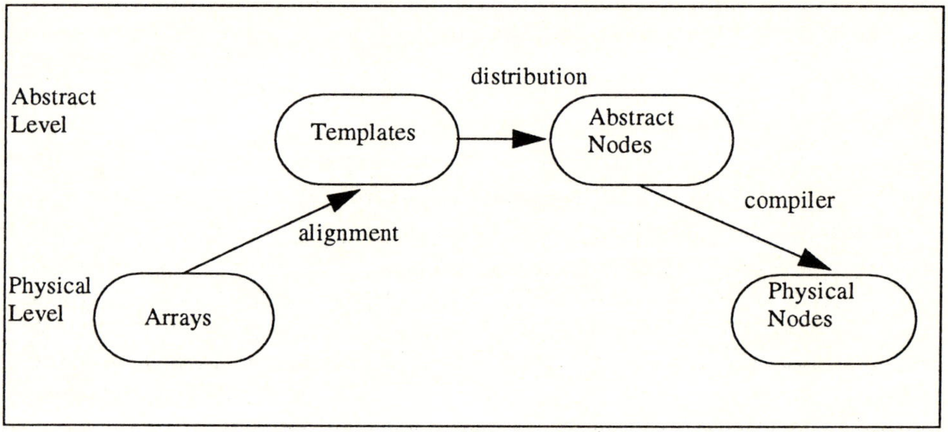

Fig. 2.1: Graphical illustration of data distribution model. Firstly a set of abstract nodes is defined in the software. Secondly templates of arrays are defined and distributed in block or cyclically along the abstract set of nodes. Thirdly the arrays in the software are aligned along the corresponding template. The translation of the abstract set of nodes to the physical nodes is left up to the compiler.

Simultaneous operations on large groups of array elements can be assigned using the Fortran 90 array notation and the FORALL statement and construct. In the Fortran 90 array notation, array sections are treated as objects and simultaneous assignments can be made for these objects. The FORALL statement and construct also allow such parallel assignments, but also provide a wider range of array section shapes and the ability to apply user-defined functions elementally.

Other HPF features include the HPF library, PURE functions, and EXTRINSIC procedures. Space does not allow discussion of these features and the reader is referred to the HPF Language Specification [1].

3. ISO standardization

The ISO working group on Fortran met in 1993 and agreed upon the principle that the ISO Fortran standard should be extended in such a manner, that most HPF programs will conform to it. For ISO standardization purposes, the HPF extensions were subdivided into language constructs and non-language constructs.

The language constructs will be included in the next Fortran revision, i.e. Fortran 95. These consist of the FORALL statement and construct and some minor extensions to intrinsic functions. Fortran 95 addresses itself only to pure language constructs. Thus, the non-language constructs, i.e. the directives and the HPF_LIBRARY module, will be included into another standard document than Fortran 95.

4. Vendor- and User experience with HPF 1.0

During a meeting in january 1994 in Houston, Texas, USA, vendors and users gave presentations on their experiences with HPF 1.0. This paragraph is meant to give to the reader an account of these discussions.

4.1. Vendor experience

The vendors Thinking Machines Corporation, DEC, IBM, the Portland Group, Applied Parallel Research and Convex gave presentations at this meeting. Some of their experiences are listed below:

- The development of a compiler for HPF is an incentive for the development of a compiler for Fortran 90.
- HPF is efficiently implementable.
- The language is expressive.
- The language must be used carefully. Small syntactic changes can cause enormous dfifferences in performance.

4.2. User experience

Fox classified user applications with respect to their parallelization properties. The following four classes emerged:

- *Synchronous applications:* Applications where the data structure is simple to parallelize. Examples are crystalline molecular dynamics or Monte Carlo and Fast Fourier Transform. These applications are typically data-parallel and can be efficiently implemented using HPF.
- *Embarrassingly parallel applications:* Essentially independent execution of disconnected components. The independent components can be quite complicated. Examples are the calculation of matrix elements of an Hamiltonian and quantum Monte Carlo calculations. These applications are also efficiently implemented in HPF.
- *Loosely synchronous applications:* Applications where the data structure is hard to parallelize. Examples are direct methods for sparse matrix solvers and multipole methods for particle dynamics. The expression of these applications in HPF 1.0 is uncertain.
- *Asynchronous applications:* Applications with functional and/or data parallelism that is irregular in space and time. Examples are event driven simulations and transaction analysis. These applications are currently outside the scope of HPF.
- *Metaproblems:* Asynchronous collection of (loosely) synchronous components. The different components are data-parallel and can be expressed in HPF.

5. Plans of the High Performance Fortran Forum for 1994

The High Performance Fortran Forum has set itself the following four tasks for 1994:

- HPFF wants to encourage 'industrial strength' implementations of HPF by vendors. This means that the HPFF will develop more notes to implementors, collect and publish practical programming kernels and support the establishment of a validation suite.
- HPFF will turn out clarifications, corrections and interpretations of HPF 1.0. This includes clarifying the ways that HPF 1.0 already supports coarse-grained parallelism. Any individual or organization needing a clarification or interpretation, can make his or her request known to the HPFF. The electronic mail addresses for sending in requests are <hpff-interpret@cs.rice.edu> for interpretations and <hpff-comments@cs.rice.edu> for comments.
- HPFF will identify and flesh out requirements for HPF 2.0. However these will not be developed in 1994. During 1994 a decision will be taken whether to develop them

in 1995. Candidates for requirements are parallel I/O, irregular grids and additional tasking.

- An HPF 1.x document will be produced during 1994.

A general meeting will take place in early 1995 to discuss the results and experiences reached in 1994 and to make plans for 1995.

Acknowledgements

The author wants to thank Schlumberger Ltd, the Netherlands Fortran Specialists Group and the Nederlands Normalisatie Instituut for help towards the trips to the standardization meetings, necessary for writing this article. He thanks Chuck Koelbel of Rice University for reviewing the article. He also wishes to thank Marisa do Nascimento for her support during the writing of this article.

References

[1] High Performance Fortran Forum: High Performance Fortran Language Specification, May 3, 1993. This document is available via anonymous ftp from the file servers located in the US at Rice University, Oak Ridge National Laboratory and in Europe at GMD-I1.T (Sankt Augustin, Germany).

Value-Based Distributions in Fortran D*

Reinhard v. Hanxleden[1] and Ken Kennedy[1] and Joel Saltz[2]

[1] CRPC, Department of Computer Science
Rice University, Houston, TX 77251.
E-mail: {reinhard|ken}@rice.edu
[2] UMIACS, Department of Computer Science
University of Maryland, College Park, MD 20742.
E-mail: saltz@cs.umd.edu

Abstract. Compiling irregular applications written in a data-parallel language, like High Performance Fortran, presents a challenging problem of growing importance. One difficulty with irregular problems is the lack of access locality when distributing data and computation naïvely, based on simple functions of array and iteration indices. *Value-based distributions* extend index-based distributions to conveniently express for example the locality characteristics of an underlying physical problem. This gives the compiler an opportunity to improve both inter- and intra-processor locality, resulting in better performance and scalability, even when this locality is not reflected by the sequential data structures and access patterns.

1 Introduction

Data-parallel languages promise user-friendly and machine independent programming of parallel computers. Examples include High Performance Fortran (HPF) [9], Vienna Fortran [1], and Fortran D [4]. Here the applications programmer uses a dialect of sequential Fortran and annotates it with high level distribution information. From this annotated program, data-parallel compilers will generate codes in different native Fortran dialects for different parallel architectures. For regular problems, *i.e.*, applications with relatively simple array subscript functions and fixed communication requirements, these compilers have had considerable successes [12]. However, irregular problems, such as unstructured mesh codes, molecular dynamics, galaxy simulations, or computational fluid dynamics, have turned out to be significantly harder to parallelize [11].

One principal problem with irregular problems is the general lack of access locality when distributing data and computation naïvely. For example, assume that the value assigned to some array element $a(i)$ depends on some other array element $b(j)$. In a regular problem, there will typically be some simple relationship between i and j, for example that they are related to each other via a linear function known at compile time. For irregular problems, subscripts i and j may

* This work is supported by an IBM fellowship, and by the National Aeronautics and Space Administration/the National Science Foundation under grant #ASC-9349459.

each depend on some complicated function or an array lookup, the outcome of neither one known at compile time. Furthermore, even if the compiler would know the values of the i's and j's, there would often still be no way to achieve good locality via regular, index-oriented distributions (like **BLOCK** or **CYCLIC**). For example, if i and j are different vertices in a mesh, then $a(i)$ and $b(j)$ might depend on each other if i and j are linked together by an edge. Most meshes number their vertices in a way that makes it hard to predict whether two vertices are linked together by just looking at their index. Therefore, distributing mesh points and the computation associated with them across processors by dividing their index space in some regular fashion typically results in many off-processor accesses and poor load balancing.

To allow more general access patterns, index-based mapping arrays [14] or mapping functions [1] can be used. For these, however, the programmer has to provide arrays or functions that explicitly map indices to processors. These "irregular" distributions are typically harder to debug and manage than regular distributions and present an additional level of complexity beyond general message-passing style programming. High level library routines, such as CHAOS [2], can assist in tasks like global-to-local name space mappings, communication schedule generation, and schedule based communication. Such libraries are essential for keeping code complexity and programming difficulties in reasonable limits. However, since each application still has its own individual communication requirements, the proper usage of such routines and preprocessing for generating their arguments is still a non-trivial task one would rather leave to the compiler.

Fortunately, many scientific applications lacking any index-based locality that a compiler might take advantage of do offer another kind of locality, which we will refer to as *value-based locality*. This kind of locality, which will be introduced in more detail in the next section, naturally lends itself to *value-based distributions*. Value-based distributions were initially proposed as an enhancement of Fortran 77D [6]. A variant of it, based on a *GeoCoL* (**Geo**metrical, **Co**nnectivity and/or **L**oad) data structure, has since then been implemented in a Fortran 90D prototype compiler by Ponnusamy et al. [10].

In this paper we introduce language extensions to express value-based distributions, illustrate its usage within a scientific application, and provide experimental results. An extended version of this paper describes the compiler technology specific to handling such distributions and its relationship to other aspects of the compiler [8]; that paper also provides an example of the output generated by the Fortran D compiler, a formal extension syntax, and additional experimental results. For a discussion of other, equally important aspects of compiling irregular applications, such as communication analysis and preprocessing, we refer the reader to other publications [3, 7].

2 An example application

An example where data are not related by indices, but values, is molecular dynamics, in which programs such as GROMOS [5] simulate biomolecular sys-

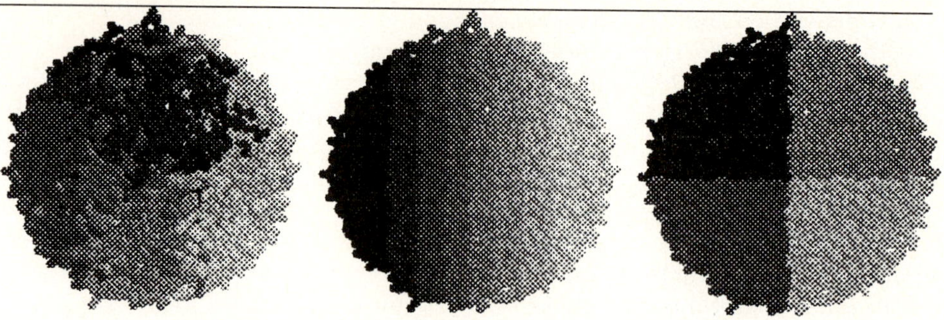

Fig. 1. Atoms of an SOD molecule colored according to the processor they are mapped to, using three different distribution schemes for an eight-processor configuration. Shown are (from left to right) an index-based `BLOCK` distribution and value-based distributions of atoms along one and three dimensions, respectively. Note the varying degrees of locality and surface-to-volume ratios.

tems. One important routine common to molecular dynamics programs is the non-bonded force (NBF) routine, which typically accounts for the bulk of the computational work (around 90%). An important characteristic of the NBFs is that their intensities decay very rapidly with increasing distance between the atoms involved. This locality characteristic is exploited by using a *cutoff radius*, R_{cut}, beyond which the NBF interactions are ignored and not computed. A parallel NBF implementation can take advantage of this locality by distributing the data associated with each atom based on the value of their physical coordinates.

The atom numbering itself is not related to the coordinates[3]; therefore, a traditional, index based distribution would lose this locality. In fact, since a processor needs to know about all atoms within R_{cut} of each atom it owns, a regular distribution typically results in each processor accessing all data, with accordingly high communication and storage requirements.

We extended the Fortran D compiler at Rice University to handle *value-based distributions*, which allow the programmer to express value-based locality as a simple extension of the regular distribution mechanism employed in data-parallel languages. Figure 2 shows a Fortran D implementation of the NBF kernel using value-based distributions. Given such a program, the Fortran D compiler generates a message passing Fortran program annotated with calls to the CHAOS runtime library for supporting irregular distribution and communication patterns. Figure 1 illustrates the effect of index and value-based distributions for a 6968 atom solvated superoxide dismutase (SOD) system.[4]

[3] Atoms are typically numbered according to some data bank standard, like the Brookhaven protein data bank, which considers amino acid types, peptide bonds, solute/solvent classifications, etc. – an ordering which is rather difficult for a compiler to take direct advantage of without user assistance.

[4] SOD is a catalytic enzyme that converts the toxic free-radical, O_2^{-4}, a byproduct of aerobic respiration, to the neutral molecules O_2 and H_2O_2 [13].

```
        PROGRAM nbf

        INTEGER i, j, p, t, n$proc, atomMax, pMax, stepMax
        PARAMETER (n$proc = 8)
5       PARAMETER (atomMax = 8000, pMax = 250, stepMax = 30)
        INTEGER inb(atomMax), partners(atomMax, pMax)
        REAL x(atomMax), f(atomMax), force

    C   Fortran D directives
10      DECOMPOSITION atomD(atomMax)
        ALIGN inb, x, f, partners(i,j) WITH atomD(i)
        DISTRIBUTE atomD(BLOCK)

    C   Initialize data
15      CALL read_data(x, inb, partners)

    C   Redistribute atomD according to coordinate values
        DISTRIBUTE atomD(VALUE(DIM=1,VALS=x,WEIGHT=inb))

20  C   Loop over timesteps
        DO t = 1, stepMax

    C      Reset forces to zero
           DO i = 1, atomMax
25            f(i) = 0
           ENDDO

    C      Computes forces
           EXECUTE (i) ON_HOME f(i)
30         DO i = 1, atomMax
              DO p = 1, inb(i)
                 j = partners(i, p)
                 force = nbforce(x(i), x(j))
                 f(i) = f(i) + force
35               f(j) = f(j) - force
              ENDDO
           ENDDO

    C      Push atoms
40         DO i = 1, atomMax
              x(i) = x(i) + delta(f(i))
           ENDDO
        ENDDO
        END
```

Fig. 2. Fortran D version of Non-Bonded Force kernel (with coordinates and forces shown 1-D for simplicity). During each of the `stepMax` time steps, forces are first reset to zero, then they are computed based on the distances between atoms, and finally the forces are used for updating coordinates. Note the index-based distribution directive in line 12, followed by a value-based redistribution in line 18. Note also that the strict owner computes rule is overridden in the NBF calculation itself via an `on_home` directive.

3 Experimental Results

We compiled the Fortran D kernel shown in Figure 2, but with 3-D instead of just 1-D coordinates and forces. For this kernel, the Fortran D compiler-generated output is practically identical to a hand-coded parallel program using the same CHAOS run-time support. Therefore we are mostly interested in the performance gain obtained by value-based distributions relative to index-based distributions. We compared the following data distribution schemes:

1. Index-based, block-wise: for N atoms and P processors, processor p gets assigned atoms $(p-1)N/P+1 \ldots pN/P$ (assuming P divides N). This corresponds to using the original `BLOCK` distribution (line 12) throughout the run (*i.e.*, no redistribution in line 16).
2. Value-based, 1-dimensional bisection, no load balancing: the physical problem domain gets divided along the x-axis, assigning each processor an equal number of atoms. This corresponds to a "`DISTRIBUTE atomD(VALUE(DIM=1, VALS=x))`" directive (*i.e.*, no "`WEIGHT=inb`" parameter).
3. Value-based, 1-dimensional bisection, with load balancing: each atom's work load is measured by the number of interaction partners, and the partitioner divides the physical problem domain such that each processor has an even workload. The appropriate directive is already shown in Figure 2.
4. Value-based, 3-dimensional bisection, no load balancing: the physical problem domain gets recursively divided along the x, y, and z-axes, assigning each processor an equal number of atoms. The directive here is "`DISTRIBUTE atomD(VALUE(DIM=3, VALS=x,y,z))`."
5. Value-based, 3-dimensional recursive bisection, with load balancing. This is achieved with a "`DISTRIBUTE atomD(VALUE(DIM=3, VALS=x,y,z, WEIGHT=inb))`" statement.

For each distribution strategy, the output of the Fortran-D compiler was compiled with `if77` onto an iPSC/860 with 32 nodes, 8 of which having 16 Megabytes of memory, the others having 8 Megabytes. The subsequent parallel runs simulated 30 time steps using pairlist data and physical coordinates from an SOD simulation using an 8 Å cutoff radius; SOD itself is of size $53 \times 55 \times 52$ Å^3. We were able to run all strategies on all processors sizes, except for 1 and 2 processors, where the value-based strategies where too memory intensive.

Figure 3 shows the timings measured for the 3-dimensional, balanced recursive bisection, and it summarizes the speedups obtained for the various distribution methods. In the processor ranges measured, the overheads associated with preprocessing, redistributing data, and communication are about an order of magnitude lower than the cost of the actual computation. The cost of preprocessing (including the inspector which enables message vectorization) gets well amortized for the given number of time steps. However, it is also apparent that the scalability of the run-time support may become critical for larger numbers of processors. The value-based distributions significantly outperform the index-based distribution, and explicit load balancing provides an additional advantage.

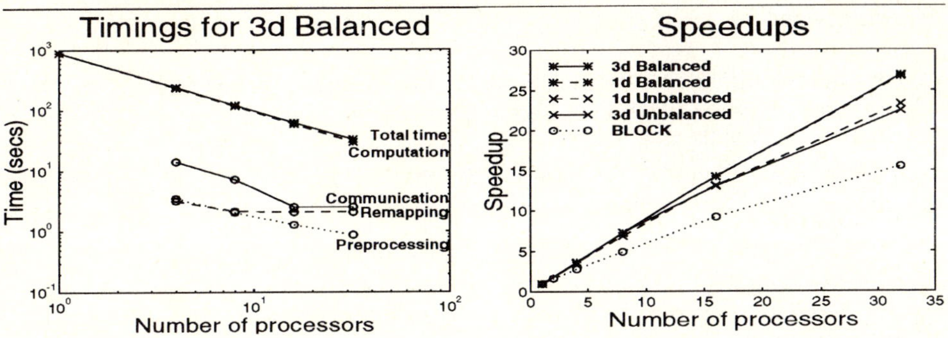

Fig. 3. The timing breakdown (excluding I/O) for varying machine sizes, using a 3-dimensional, value-based balanced bisection with different processor numbers (left), and the speedup obtained with different processor numbers and distribution strategies (right).

4 Summary and Conclusions

Data-parallel languages, such as HPF or Fortran D, promise a user-friendly, efficient programming environment for parallel machines. However, one of their weaknesses so far has been the lack of support for irregular problems. Here access patterns and work load distributions are not very amenable to the data parallel paradigm based on index and iteration space decomposition.

Value-based distributions provide a specific kind of expressiveness that had been missing so far; they can give the compiler locality information that cannot be described in terms of array indices. While this is only one aspect of parallelizing irregular problems, we believe that it widens the range of important applications that can be implemented efficiently in data-parallel languages.

Acknowledgements

We thank Seema Hiranandani and Chau-Wen Tseng, who developed the Fortran D compiler support for regular problems. Paul Havlak provided much of the symbolic analysis used in the Fortran D compiler.

We appreciate the help from Raja Das, Ravi Ponnusamy, and Yuan-Shin Hwang, who developed much of the compiler/run time technology involved in this project. Jim Humphries wrote the dynamic memory allocator.

Special thanks to Terry Clark, Ridgway Scott, and Bernie Brooks, who offered their broad expertise with molecular dynamics and pointed out many practical issues when compiling irregular real-world codes. Terry also provided the molecule test data used for the experiments in Section 3.

The molecule graphics were produced by the RasMol visualization program written by Roger Sayle.

References

1. B. Chapman, P. Mehrotra, and H. Zima. Programming in Vienna Fortran. *Scientific Programming*, 1(1):31–50, Fall 1992.
2. R. Das, Y.-S. Hwang, M. Uysal, J. Saltz, and A. Sussman. Applying the CHAOS/PARTI library to irregular problems in computational chemistry and computational aerodynamics. In *Proceedings of the Scalable Parallel Libraries Conference, Mississippi State University, Starkville, MS*, October 1993.
3. R. Das, J. Saltz, and R. v. Hanxleden. Slicing analysis and indirect accesses to distributed arrays. In *Proceedings of the Sixth Workshop on Languages and Compilers for Parallel Computing*, Portland, OR, August 1993. Available via anonymous ftp from `softlib.rice.edu` as `pub/CRPC-TRs/reports/CRPC-TR93319-S`.
4. G. C. Fox, S. Hiranandani, K. Kennedy, C. Koelbel, U. Kremer, C. Tseng, and M. Wu. Fortran D language specification. Technical Report TR90-141, Dept. of Computer Science, Rice University, December 1990. Revised April, 1991.
5. W. F. van Gunsteren and H. J. C. Berendsen. GROMOS: GROningen MOlecular Simulation software. Technical report, Laboratory of Physical Chemistry, University of Groningen, Nijenborgh, The Netherlands, 1988.
6. R. v. Hanxleden. Compiler support for machine independent parallelization of irregular problems. Technical Report CRPC-TR92301-S, Center for Research on Parallel Computation, November 1992. Available via anonymous ftp from `softlib.rice.edu` as `pub/CRPC-TRs/reports/CRPC-TR92301-S`.
7. R. v. Hanxleden. Handling irregular problems with Fortran D — A preliminary report. In *Proceedings of the Fourth Workshop on Compilers for Parallel Computers*, Delft, The Netherlands, December 1993. D Newsletter #9, available via anonymous ftp from `softlib.rice.edu` as `pub/CRPC-TRs/reports/CRPC-TR93339-S`.
8. R. v. Hanxleden, K. Kennedy, and J. Saltz. Value-based distributions in Fortran D — A preliminary report. Technical Report CRPC-TR93365-S, Center for Research on Parallel Computation, December 1993. Available via anonymous ftp from `softlib.rice.edu` as `pub/CRPC-TRs/reports/CRPC-TR93365-S`.
9. C. Koelbel, D. Loveman, R. Schreiber, G. Steele, Jr., and M. Zosel. *The High Performance Fortran Handbook*. The MIT Press, Cambridge, MA, 1994.
10. R. Ponnusamy, J. Saltz, A. Choudhary, Y.-S. Hwang, and G. Fox. Runtime support and compilation methods for user-specified data distributions. Technical Report CS-TR-3194 and UMIACS-TR-93-135, University of Maryland, November 1993. Available via anonymous ftp from `hyena.cs.umd.edu`.
11. J. P. Singh and J. L. Hennessy. An empirical investigation of the effectiveness and limitations of automatic parallelization. In *Proceedings of the International Symposium on Shared Memory Multiprocessing*, Tokyo, Japan, April 1991.
12. C. Tseng. *An Optimizing Fortran D Compiler for MIMD Distributed-Memory Machines*. PhD thesis, Rice University, January 1993.
13. Y.-T. Wong, T. W. Clark, J. Shen, and J. A. McCammon. Molecular dynamics simulation of substrate-enzyme interactions in the active site channel of superoxide dismutase. *Journal of Molecular Simulation*, 10(2–6):277–289, 1993.
14. J. Wu, J. Saltz, H. Berryman, and S. Hiranandani. Distributed memory compiler design for sparse problems. ICASE Report 91-13, Institute for Computer Application in Science and Engineering, Hampton, VA, January 1991.

Basic Linear Operators in Fortran 90

Richard Hanson and Tim Leite

Visual Numerics, Inc. (IMSL)
9990 Richmond Avenue
Houston, TX 77042, USA

Abstract. Standard F90 lets a programmer define operators, corresponding to mathematical operations, that apply to arrays or more complicated classes of objects: The matrix-vector and matrix-matrix products $y = Ax$ are expressed in F90 as *defined operations*. Use of more complex linear algebra operations is simplified with *generic functions*. Combined, these yield standard decompositions or matrix operations.

1 Defined Operations

The F90 operation, `y = A.x.x` implements the matrix-vector product $y = Ax$, and is defined by functions packaged and hidden in a Fortran 90 *module*. Usage of this operation requires invoking the module with an F90 `USE` statement, followed by declaring the arrays `A` and `x`. The F90 compiler then provides the interface to the appropriate function that performs the computation. A welcome side-effect of this interface is user code that is easier to read and write than a Level 2 BLAS subprogram [4], `CALL _GEMV ('N', M, N, 1.0, A, LDA, X, INCX, 0.0, Y, INCY)`. Also note the related works [3], [5].

1.1 The Operations Themselves

Our goal is to provide our users with a suite of defined operations, combined with F90 intrinsic array operations, that are useful for algebraic manipulation of rectangular matrices. We therefore implemented matrix products, matrix inverses, a Moore-Penrose (M-P) inverse, multiplication on either side by inverses, and multiplication by adjoints of matrices. We wanted our software to be efficient when computing inverses, so an LU factorization is used with non-singular, square matrices. For singular, square matrices, or rectangular matrices, we express the M-P inverse using a QR factorization. The user's code is the same for all cases. Let `A` denote an $m \times n$ array of any of the four F90 intrinsic data types. Thus the code `y = A.ix.b` results in the mathematical operation $y = A^{-1}b$, if $m = n$; the solution of minimum Euclidean length, if $m < n$; and the least-squares solution, if $m > n$. Although we recommend that users perform the operation using `.ix.`, they may elect to use the mathematically equivalent operation `y = .i.A .x.b`, that corresponds to $y = (A^{\dagger})b$, where $A^{\dagger}$ is the M-P inverse.

The defined operations interface with functions, packaged as F90 modules, matching type, kind and rank of arrays. Within the code for an individual function it is often desirable to use efficient replacements that are based on fast algorithms that depend on vendor hardware.

Table 1. VNI Defined Operations for Rectangular Matrices

Defined Operation	Matrix Operation
`A.x.B`	AB
`.i.A`	A^{-1}
`.t.A; .h.A`	A^T; $A^H = A^*$
`A.ix.B; B.xi.A`	$A^{-1}B$; BA^{-1}
`A.tx.B; B.xt.A`	A^TB; BA^T
`A.hx.B; B.xh.A`	A^HB; BA^H

2 Completing the Tool Suite

The algebraic operations presented in the last section are augmented by matrix functions that compute decompositions and other attributes of matrices. One function name is used with an operation for any intrinsic data type. An example is the computation of a vector or matrix norm, $||A||$. This value is required to verify the quality of results. For example given an $n \times n$ nonsingular matrix A, an approximation to the solution $x = A^{-1}b$ must yield a residual vector $r = b - Ax$ such that $||r||/(||A|| \times ||x|| + ||b||)$ is approximately equal to machine precision.

2.1 The Generic Matrix Functions

We have provided optional arguments for several of the functions. These are enclosed in square braces, `[ ]`. For example the `SVD( )` function will provide the complete singular value decomposition $A = USV^H$. Those users who require the decomposition will execute the statement `S = SVD(A, U=U, V=V)`. Another usage, with only the singular values required, is `S = SVD(A)`. If the singular values and the right singular vectors are required, then execute `S = SVD(A, V=V)`.

The `EIG( )` function is complicated by the fact that even for the case of real data, the eigenvalues and eigenvectors may be complex. When users know that both the values and vectors are real, they may use the optional real array `V=V`, for the vectors. When the eigenvectors are truly complex the complex array `W=W` must be present, if eigenvectors are required. The eigenvalues themselves are always returned as a complex rank-1 array. If the user assigns a real array on the left-hand side, a loss of the imaginary parts of the values will occur. This is a side effect of Fortran assignment rules, and not a fault of our software per se. For the ordinary eigenvalue problem one expects the residual matrix `R = A.x.V - (V.x.diag(E))` to have a small norm, relative to `NORM(A)`. In those case where the vectors are complex the residual matrix becomes `R = A.x.W - (W.x.diag(E))`. In the case of the generalized eigenvalue problem the optional argument `B=B` is used. The same rules as noted apply when choosing a real or complex array for the vectors. One expects the residual matrix `R = A.x.V.x.diag(D) - (B.x.V.x.diag(E))` or `R = A.x.W.x.diag(D) - (B.x.W.x.diag(E))` to have a small norm, relative to `NORM(A)+NORM(B)`.

An important side comment concerns rules about using parentheses in the above examples: F90 gives the highest precedence to a user's unary defined operation, and the lowest precedence to a binary operation,[1], page 232.

Table 2. VNI Generic Linear Algebra Functions

Array Function	Matrix Operation
`S = SVD(A[,U=U,V=V])`	$A = USV^H$
`E = EIG(A[[,B=B,D=D],V=V,W=W])`	$AV = VE,\ AWD = BWE$
`R = CHOL(A)`	$A = R^H R$
`Q = ORTH(A,[,R=R])`	$A = QR,\ Q^H Q = I$
`U = UNIT(A)`	$A = [a_1, \ldots],\ U = [u_1, \ldots] = [a_1/\|a_1\|, \ldots]$
`F = DET(A)`	$f = det(A) = determinant\ of\ A$
`K = RANK(A)`	$k = rank(A) = rank\ of\ A$
`Y = NORM(A)`	$y = \|A\| = s_1$
`C = COND(A)`	$c = s_1/s_{rank(A)}$
`Z = EYE(N)`	$Z = I_N$
`A = DIAG(X)`	$A = diag(x_1, \ldots)$
`X = DIAGONALS(A)`	$x = (a_{11}, \ldots)$

3 Some Elementary Linear Algebra

To get the impact of using defined operators, we recall basic properties of inverses, norms, condition numbers and matrix products. Some of this development is found in [2], pages 12-19, and illustrates the principles using random matrices and numerical matrix inversion.

In our development each matrix is a dimensioned array with a fixed precision. These can be declared with the following statements in a program unit:

```
USE linear_operators
integer, parameter :: n=6, m=3
real (kind(1d0)) :: one = 1d0, err
real (kind(one)), dimension(n,n) :: A, P, X
```

3.1 Powers of Matrices

We have not provided a defined operation for powers. The following F90 assignment and loop computes A^m: `P=EYE(n); do i=1,m; P=P.x.A; end do`. See [6], page 442, for algorithms that are more efficient when m is replaced by a larger value.

3.2 Inverses of Square Matrices

The relations are $X = A^{-1}$; $AX = I_n$; $XA = I_n$. The expressions follow. We expect the computed value of **err** to be about the working precision, provided by the F90 intrinsic function **epsilon(one)**.

```
A = rand(A); X = .i.A
err=(norm(EYE(n)-(A.x.X))+norm(EYE(n)-(X.x.A)))/cond(A)
```

4 Acknowledgements

We thank Mr. Naoki Iwata, of NEC Systems Laboratory, The Woodlands, TX, for his contribution to VNI consisting of implementing most of the defined operations and matrix functions.

References

1. Adams, J., Brainerd, W., Martin, J., Smith, B., Wagener, J.: Fortran 90 Handbook. Complete ANSI/ISO Reference, McGraw-Hill, New York, NY, (1992)
2. Gantmacher, F. R.: Matrix Theory, Volume I. Chelsea Publishing Company, New York, NY, (1959)
3. Lawson, C., Hanson, R., Kincaid, D., Krogh, F.: Basic Linear Algebra Subprograms for Fortran Usage. ACM Trans. Math. Soft. **5**, (1979) 308-325
4. Dongarra, J., DuCroz, J., Hammarling, S., Hanson, R.: An Extended Set of Fortran Basic Linear Algebra Subprograms. ACM Trans. Math. Soft. **14**, (1988) 1-32
5. Dongarra, J., DuCroz, J., Duff, I., Hammarling, S.: A Set of Level 3 Basic Linear Algebra Subprograms. ACM Trans. Math. Soft. **16**, (1990) 1-28
6. Knuth, D. E.: The Art of Computer Programming, second Edition. Addison-Wesley Publishing Company, Reading, MA, (1981)

parLisp - Parallel Symbolic Processing with Lisp on the Distributed Memory Machine MANNA

Angela Sodan and Hua Bi

GMD Institute for Computer Architecture and Software Technology, Germany
email: sodan@gmd.de, bi@gmd.de

Abstract. The parLisp system consists of a parallel run-time system and a set of tools for parallel symbolic processing with Lisp on the distributed memory parallel machine MANNA. The parallel run-time system provides and implements efficiently language features and mechanisms for expressing parallelism appropriately and for handling the data access problem by either explicit copying or by Virtual Shared Memory. A set of tools for detection of parallelism, mapping, profiling and visualization supports the process of getting efficient parallel symbolic applications.

1 Introduction

parLisp is a parallel Lisp system developed for MANNA which is a massively parallel computer with distributed memory [1]. Each node consists of 32 M byte memory and two i860 processors - one of them can be used as pure communication processor. The nodes are linked by a fast hierarchical crossbar system which allows to connect up to several thousand nodes. MANNA's operating system PEACE provides a Virtual Shared Memory System (VSM) which maintains a global shared address space and automatically transfers objects or pages accessed but not available in the node's memory. VSM ensures consistency of the data throughout the system by driving special protocols.

Symbolic applications like expert systems, theorem provers, computer algebra etc. differ from numeric ones in that control flow is input-dependent and irregularly shaped (often resulting from recursions with search trees of differing breath and depth) and that data structures are linked ones and created dynamically. Therefore special mechanisms for allocating and passing data and for mapping the dynamic control structures are necessary for a parallel Lisp system. In addition, tools for detection of parallelism, profiling and visualization are important for getting efficient parallel symbolic applications.

2 Parallel Run-Time System

Most parallel Lisp systems have been designed for shared memory architectures like Multilisp [2] but there also exist some Lisps on distributed memory systems like Concurrent Scheme [3]. Other ongoing research exists in respect to architecture-independent systems, e.g. in relation to Eulisp [4]. parLisp is a modified and extended version of the public domain Common Lisp system AKCL (compiles to C so that parLisp is portable). We provide some quite-standard (within the Lisp-world) additional features for expressing and controlling parallelism based upon so-called *futures* (asynchronous value return). In comparison to the general future mechanism, however, our features are expressed in an object-oriented way, and explicit synchronization is required. As a more important extension parallel tasks can be grouped in respect to balancing and synchronization for making the logical relation of processes explicit and allowing a better mapping.

Special attention is paid in parLisp to the argument handling. Arguments can be passed by reference or by copy. Copying passes data immediately in the call with packing and unpacking the linked data structures. When data passed by reference is accessed it is fetched automatically via VSM (and kept consistent by its protocol). Copying arguments is used only when it is legal and more efficient. Besides to consistency reasons VSM may be preferable if only part of the data structure is accessed and that part is unknown in advance. Efficiency considerations, however, depend on the concrete machine parameters and are therefore done by the mapping system. The user only specifies what is semantically legal.

parLisp is configured for VSM such that its address space is at least partly common (data guaranteed to be used locally only can be allocated in local areas). Each node maintains a different part of the common address space for creation of new objects (to avoid unnecessary conflicts on pages). In many symbolic applications garbage collection time is a significant part of the overall runtime. Garbage collection is done locally on each node for the node's own data. Local heaps per process reduce the individual breaks from garbage collection (important for communication and load balancing).

3 Performance Results

parLisp currently runs on MANNA as well as on a SUN workstation net. Performance results for the Triangle benchmark program on MANNA are shown in table 1. Load balancing has not yet been integrated when measuring these results, and performance will increase when added.

no. nodes	sequential	3	6	10	13	∞(simulated)
run-time	97.2s	56.4 s	33.3 s	22.9 s	18.1 s	6.7 s

Table 1: Sequential and parallel run-times for Triangle

4 Programming Environment

In addition to the basic Lisp system, we provide a set of tools to assist users in detecting parallelism from a sequential Lisp program, in dynamically mapping the resulting parallel tasks to machine nodes (by granularity control and load balancing) and in getting information about dynamic behaviors of programs by profiling and visualization.

5 Summary and Future Work

We presented parLisp's general framework for solving the problems raised by the symbolic application's dynamic behavior and gave an overview of the concepts and implementation of the kernel system. We demonstrated with our parLisp system that distributed parallel symbolic processing is possible. parLisp is portable by being based on AKCL and PEACE, and the first performance results indicate an efficient implementation.

The perspective for further research is in automatic parallelization and mapping. We will do that as well as more experiments with real-life applications in the European HCM project VIM (Virtual Multicomputer for Lisp) in which we are a partner.

References

1. W.K. Giloi, M.A. Montenegro, S. Pletner. Eine Billion Operationen. Design & Elektronik, Sept. 1993, special issue "Zukunftstechnologien".
2. Robert H. Halstead. Parallel Computing Using Multilisp. In Janusz S. Kowalik (Ed.). Parallel Computation and Computers for Artificial Intelligence. Kluwer Academic Publishers, 1988.
3 R. Kessler, H. Carr, L. Stoller, and M. Swanson. Implementing Concurrent Scheme for the Mayfly Distributed Parallel Processing System, Lisp and Symbolic Computation, 1992, No. 5.
4. Neil Berrington, Peter Broadbery, David DeRoure, and Julian Padget. Eulisp Threads: A Concurrency Toolbox. Lisp and Symbolic Computation Journal, Vol. 6, Aug. 1993.

Parallelizing compilers: what can be achieved ?

Michèle Dion[1], Jean-Laurent Philippe[2] and Yves Robert[1]

[1] Laboratoire LIP, CNRS (U.R.A. n° 1398)
Ecole Normale Supérieure de Lyon
69364 LYON Cedex 07, France
email: [mdion,yrobert]@lip.ens-lyon.fr
[2] Société Archipel
PAE des Glaisins, 1 rue du Bulloz
74940 Annecy-le-Vieux, France
e-mail: philippe@dosadi.archipel.fr

Abstract. We discuss automatic parallelization techniques that take a sequential program as input and produce executable code for massively parallel distributed memory machines. Target programming style is SPMD data-parallel. Target language is High Performance Fortran. We review the whole design trajectory: data dependence extraction, scheduling and mapping onto virtual processors, code generation for execution on physical processors. With concrete examples we explain all the difficulties we have to face. We show that fully automatic parallelization can be achieved for simple computational kernels arising from scientific applications, namely loop nests programs with uniform or affine dependences.

1 Introduction

This text is intended to give a brief survey of current techniques and tools for state-of-the-art compiler-parallelizers. The goal of automatic parallelization techniques is to transform a sequential program into a program executable on parallel machines. Motivations are obvious, we quote three among the most important: (i) Reduction of conception, design and implementation times, which is particularly useful for non-specialist users; (ii) Portable programming style; and (iii) Simpler and correct programming.

High Performance Fortran (HPF) has been a major step towards providing a portable language that programmers can use for more easily developing application programs onto massively parallel machines. Indeed, with HPF, a program for a parallel multiprocessor computer could be written almost as if it were for a monoprocessor computer.Targeting the HPF language, we aim at automatically extracting the parallelism present in nested loops, in order to automatically generate the HPF directives for the parallelization of such programs.

2 High Performance Fortran

HPF [14] provides support for high performance programming on a wide variety of machines, including massively parallel SIMD and MIMD systems and vector processors [14]. Language extensions and feature selection for Fortran aim at supporting:

- data parallel programming (defined as single threaded, global name space, and loosely synchronous parallel computation),
- top performance on MIMD and SIMD computers with non-uniform memory access costs,
- code tuning for various architectures.

HPF is defined as full Fortran 90 with restrictions on storage and sequence association, augmented by language features in three areas:

- directives in the form of comments to provide information to a compiler to enable optimization and parallelization,
- a FORALL statement construct,
- extended intrinsic functions and support library.

The official subset HPF is defined as a selected set of features from Fortran 77 and Fortran 90, plus a subset of the HPF directives and intrinsics (as defined in Section 8 of the HPF Language Specifications, Version 1.0).

Now HPF's success or failure will depend upon the effectiveness of the first compilers in generating efficient code for various target architectures. If it is a success, HPF could help break down one of the most formidable obstacles to progress in the high performance computing industry, namely the absence of a vehicle for expressing data parallel programs in a machine-independent way.

The current version of HPF is helpful only for regular problems. In the long term, HPF cannot be a complete success unless it can also help with problems on irregular or adaptative meshes. This is part of the second round for defining HPF, called HPFF2, that has convened early this year for the kick-off meeting.

Prototypes for compiling HPF already exist at the current time. In the following sections, some prototypes and ongoing efforts for providing HPF compilers are presented.

2.1 Fortran D

A Fortran D compiler for massively parallel MIMD distributed-memory machines has been developed at Rice University. Fortran D is a version of Fortran that provides data decomposition specifications at two levels: data objects are first aligned relative to one another, and then distributed onto abstract processors through a set of data distribution functions. Main Fortran D features have been reused during the definition of HPF and the specifications of the two languages are simular in many points [18].

The compiler is organized around three main functions: program analysis, optimization, and code generation. Its strategy is based on the *owner computes* rule: each processor computes its own data only.

Data mapping Fortran D requires the user to specify the two levels of data parallelism: *problem mapping* (how arrays are aligned with respect to one another), and *machine mapping* (distribution of data onto the parallel machine). The statements used are ALIGN, DECOMPOSITION and DISTRIBUTE.

The DECOMPOSITION statement is used to give a name to each problem mapping. Arrays are then mapped to the decomposition with the ALIGN statement. Arrays mapped to the same decomposition are automatically aligned with each other.

The mapping of the decomposition to the physical parallel machine is specified with the statement DISTRIBUTE. DISTRIBUTE assigns an ATTRIBUTE to each dimension of the decomposition, the three possible attributes are: BLOCK, CYCLIC and BLOCK_CYCLIC. One attribute may be assigned for each dimension of the decomposition, multidimensional decompositions may have different combinations of distribution patterns.

FORALL loops Fortran D defines FORALL to be loops such that each iteration can only *use values defined before the loop or within the current iteration.* When a statement accesses a memory location, it will not get any value written by a different iteration in the loop. It will get the *old* value at that memory location (*i.e.*, the value before the beginning of the loop).

The major benefit of a FORALL loop is that since no values depend on other iteration, the loop may be executed in parallel without communication. However, communication may still be required before the loop begins to acquire non-local values, and after the loop to update or merge non-local values.

2.2 Adaptor

ADAPTOR (Automatic DAta Parallelism TranslatOR) is a tool for transforming data parallel programs written in Fortran with array extensions, parallel loops, and layout directives to parallel programs with explicit message passing. The source language of Adaptor is Fortran 77 with many features of Fortran 90, Connection Machine Fortran (CMF) and High Performance Fortran (HPF). The generated message passing programs will run on different multiprocessor systems with distributed memory, but also on shared or virtual shared memory architectures [3, 4, 5].

Distribution of Arrays A layout directive enables the user to specify the dimension of an array which should be distributed. For the current version, only block distribution along one dimension is supported.

2.3 Commercial HPF compilers

See the extended version of this paper [9] for a description of HPF compilers announced by PGI (*The Portland Group, Incorporated*), DEC, APR (*Applied Parallel Research*), and Lahey.

2.4 EuroTOPS

EuroTOPS (European Toolset for Open Parallel Software) is a European EUREKA project. The consortium currently consists of:

- Archipel (project leader), ESI, Simulog, and LIP in France;

- DEC in UK;
- ACSET in Belgium;
- Iberdrola, and Barcelona Tecnologia (BTSA) in Spain.

Other potential partners are:

- Olivetti, ACS, and R&S Informatica in Italy.
- NA Sofware, and University of Liverpool in UK.

EuroTOPS is aimed at providing a standardized set of software tools for the development of applications on massively parallel computers. These tools will be portable across various hardware platforms and will be compatible with the present software standards and include consideration for emerging software standards, in particular MPI (Message Passing Interface) and HPF.

3 Compiling full potential parallelism of loop nest programs

In this section we deal with very simple programs, namely perfect loop nests with uniform dependences. Our goal is to show that it is possible to automatically extract the full potential parallelism lying inside such nests (in other words, to compile the best FORALL loops) and to map data and computations so that communications are minimized (in other words, to generate the best ALIGN directives).

3.1 Target example

We define perfect loop nests with uniform dependences as in Banerjee [2]. Here is a well-known example taken from Peir and Cytron [17]:

Example

for $i = 0$ to N do
  for $j = 0$ to N do
    begin
    { Program P }
      { Statement S_1 } $a(i,j) = b(i,j-6) + d(i-1,j+3)$
      { Statement S_2 } $b(i+1,j-1) = c(i+2,j+5)$
      { Statement S_3 } $c(i+3,j-1) = a(i,j-2)$
      { Statement S_4 } $d(i,j-1) = a(i,j-1)$
    end

In this example, the computation domain is a square: $Dom = \{p = (i,j) \in Z^2, 0 \leq i \leq N, 0 \leq j \leq N\}$. In fact, N is a size parameter, and we should write $Dom(N) = \{x, Ax \leq Nb\}$, where $A = \begin{pmatrix} 1 & 0 \\ -1 & 0 \\ 0 & 1 \\ 0 & -1 \end{pmatrix}$ and $b = \begin{pmatrix} 1 \\ 0 \\ 1 \\ 0 \end{pmatrix}$.

The variable $a(i,j)$ is produced by statement $S_1(i,j)$ and consumed by statement $S_4(i,j+1)$, hence a dependence from S_1 to S_4 of vector $d_{1,4} = (0,1)$. Similarly, we check that all dependences are uniform, and we obtain the dependence matrix

$$D = (d_{1,3}, d_{3,2}, d_{2,1}, d_{1,4}, d_{4,1}) = \begin{pmatrix} 0 & 1 & 1 & 0 & 1 \\ 2 & -6 & 5 & 1 & -4 \end{pmatrix}$$

Usually the loop nest is represented as an oriented graph with k nodes (the statements) linked by edges corresponding to the dependence vectors. See Figure 1: there are two dependence cycles, namely $C_1 = (S_1, S_3, S_2)$ and $C_2 = (S_1, S_4)$. The dependence graph is here strongly connected.

[htbp]

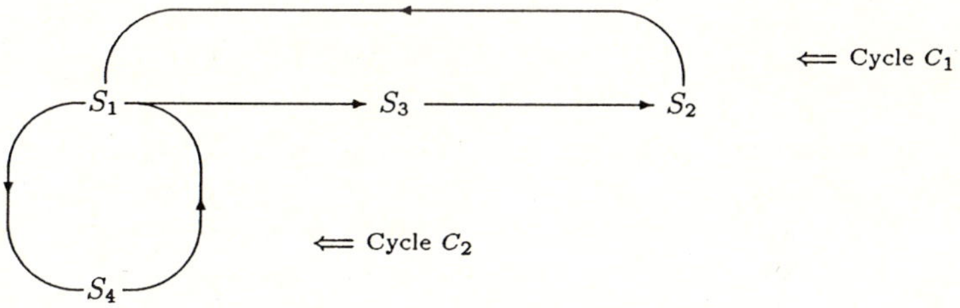

Fig. 1. Reduced dependence graph of Example 1

We illustrate only two steps, scheduling and mapping, of the whole design trajectory summarized in Figure 2 by working out this example. See the extended version of this paper [9] for further information.

We point out that the space-time transformation techniques presented here apply to a much more general class of programs called affine loop nests. In short, affine loop nests [10] are programs composed of scalar and array assignments. Data types are restricted to multi-dimensional arrays of integers or reals, and control constructs are limited to the sequence and the *for* loop. Loops bounds and access functions to arrays are **affine functions** of the iteration counters of the surrounding loops and of the parameters. The main extensions are the following: (i) loops are not perfectly nested; (ii) dependences are no longer uniform; (iii) there can be several size parameters. These extensions induce considerable technical difficulties.

3.2 Why loop nests ?

The importance of loop nests in terms of applications is evident: in many scientific programs, the time spent in the execution of a small number of loops represents a large fraction of the total execution time, while the potential parallelism of these loops is very important. On one hand, restricting our analysis to uniform or affine loop nests is not a severe limitation. Even the very simple class of uniform nests is so important in practice that it has motivated a considerable amount of research since the pioneering work of Lamport [15]. Next, when considering general affine

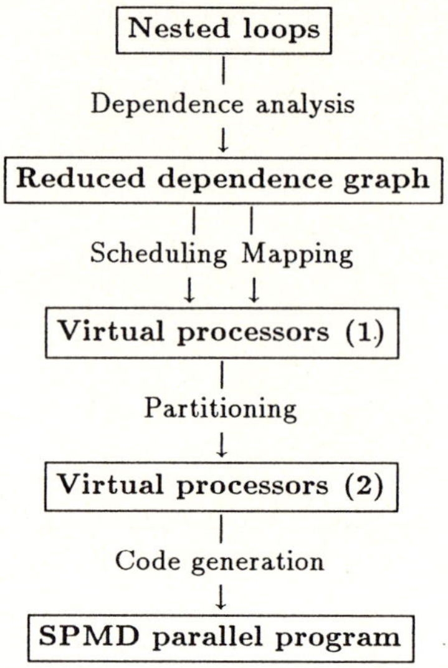

Fig. 2. Compilation steps: the whole design trajectory

loop nests as defined above, we see that most computational kernels from digital signal processing or numerical linear algebra can be expressed in such a framework.

On the other hand, the regular and repetitive structure of affine loop nests is the key to efficient loop transformation techniques that can be applied at compile-time and that are based on sophisticated mathematical tools such as linear programming and integer matrix manipulations. Indeed, the general problem of finding the optimal scheduling for a task system on a parallel machine is known to be difficult. However, in the case of affine loop nests, it is possible to analytically derive transformations that lead to a parallel scheme of execution while preserving the semantics of the sequential version. This is the aim of this paper to derive such transformations. The key-features that distinguish scheduling techniques applied to affine loop nests as opposed to general task systems are the following:

Cyclicity The whole task system does not need to be fully processed. Owing to the regular and repetitive structure of the nest, the search for an optimal schedule is conducted on the *reduced* dependence graph. Therefore compile-time depends only upon the size of the program, not upon the number of computations that are performed.

Genericity It is possible to find out *generic* schedules that are valid for any values of the parameters. No need to re-compile each time the parameters change.

Evaluability We can assess the quality of the schedules and prove optimality theorems, as opposed to the general case where we have to rely on heuristics.

3.3 Scheduling

There are various approaches for scheduling uniform loop nests. The most widely used technique consists in searching for a scheduling vector π so as to transform the nest into the following scheme:

for $time = 0$ to $time_{max}$ do
    execute in parallel all $p = (i_1, \ldots, i_n)$ such that $\lfloor \pi.p \rfloor = time$
endfor

This is nothing else than Lamport's hyperplane method [15]. Node p in *Dom* is scheduled at time $\lfloor \pi.p \rfloor = time$, where π is a rational vector such that $\pi D \geq 1$ (this constraint comes from the fact that dependences must be preserved). Methods for determining an optimal scheduling vector π, i.e. a scheduling vector for which the total execution time is minimum, are proposed in [6, 11]. In our example, the best scheduling vector is $\pi = (7, 1)^t$, and the total execution time is $T_{opt} = 8N$.

Rather than considering the k statements of program P as a whole block, we can try to schedule them separately. A first technique consists in introducing a different constant for each statement: instance p of statement S_i is executed at time $\lfloor \pi.p + c_i \rfloor$. A second technique consists in using an affine scheduling for each statement: with a different timing vector for each statement, node p of statement S_i is executed at time $\lfloor \pi_i.p + c_i \rfloor$. In both cases, these techniques can be refined to compute *generic* schedules that smoothly depend upon the size parameter N. We summarize all these solutions:

(1): linear A single scheduling vector, no scheduling constant. The scheduling is given by the function $p \longrightarrow \lfloor Xp \rfloor$.

(2): affine with same linear part A single scheduling vector, a constant per statement. The scheduling for statement i is given by the function $p \longrightarrow \lfloor Xp + c_i \rfloor$.

(2)bis: parametrized affine with same linear part Each constant is a linear function of the parameters. In the case of a single parameter N, the scheduling for statement i is given by the function $p \longrightarrow \lfloor Xp + Nc'_i + c^*_i \rfloor$.

(3): affine-by-statement A scheduling vector and a constant per statement. The scheduling for statement i is given by the function $p \longrightarrow \lfloor X_i p + c_i \rfloor$.

(3)bis: parametrized affine-by-statement Each constant is a linear function of the parameters. In the case of a single parameter N, the scheduling for statement i is given by the function $p \longrightarrow \lfloor X_i p + Nc'_i + c^*_i \rfloor$.

See [6] for optimality results. In our example, we find that solution (2)bis and (3)bis are equivalent, because the reduced dependence graph is strongly connected. The best solution is $X = (\frac{11}{7}, -\frac{1}{7})$, $c'_1 = 0$, $c'_2 = -\frac{1}{7}$, $c'_3 = \frac{9}{7}$ and $c'_4 = \frac{8}{7}$, leading to a total execution time of the order of $\frac{12}{7}N$, which is less than one quarter of the previous solution.

To summarize in a sentence, note that determining the best "regular" schedule is not easy, as naive loop manipulations are far from sufficient. But the good news are that constructive and efficient methods are available.

3.4 Mapping

The general problem of optimally mapping affine loop nests onto virtual processors is NP-complete [16, 1]. More surprisingly, this negative result still holds for uniform loop nests [7]. However, in the simple case of uniform loop nests, one can still determine optimal mappings or apply efficient heuristics, as detailed in [7].

To summarize the procedure, starting from an uniform loop nest of depth n and with k statements over a parametrized domain $Dom(N) = \{Ax \leq Nb\}$, our target machine is a virtual $(n-1)$-dimensional mesh operating in SPMD mode. More precisely, we will have k superimposed grids, one for each statement, i.e. as many virtual cells as there are distinct projections of computation points $S_i(p), 1 \leq i \leq k, p \in Dom(N)$.

We have many allocation functions, one for each variable and one for each statement, thereby extending the "owner computes" rule [12]. In our example, we have a 2D problem ($n = 2$) and four arrays a, b, c and d. For each array we define an affine allocation function. Consider for instance array a: we want to assign element $a(i,j)$ to a virtual processor on a 1D-array. We use an affine allocation function which is the composition of a projection defined by a 1×2 matrix M_a and of a translation by a constant α_a:

$$\text{alloc}(a)(i,j) = M_a(i,j) + \alpha_a$$

Similarly we map element $b(i,j)$ onto virtual processor $M_b(i,j) + \alpha_b$, element $c(i,j)$ onto virtual processor $M_c(i,j)+\alpha_c$ and element $d(i,j)$ onto virtual processor $M_d(i,j)+\alpha_d$.

Where will we execute each instance of each statement? Instance (i,j) of statement S_1, i.e. computation $S_1(i,j) : a(i,j) = b(i,j-6)+d(i-1,j+3)$ will be assigned to virtual processor

$$\text{alloc}(S_1)(i,j) = M_{S_1}(i,j) + \alpha_{S_1}$$

Similarly, computations $S_2(i,j)$, $S_3(i,j)$ and $S_4(i,j)$ will be assigned to processors $M_{S_2}(i,j) + \alpha_{S_2}$, $M_{S_3}(i,j) + \alpha_{S_3}$ and $M_{S_4}(i,j) + \alpha_{S_4}$ respectively.

To execute computation $S_1(i,j)$, processor $\text{alloc}(S_1)(i,j)$ needs to receive $b(i,j-6)$ from processor $\text{alloc}(b)(i,j-6)$ and $d(i-1,j+3)$ from processor $\text{alloc}(d)(i-1,j+3)$. After the computation, processor $\text{alloc}(S_1)(i,j)$ has to send $a(i,j)$ to processor $\text{alloc}(a)(i,j)$.

If we analyze all the required communications for processing Example 1, we can draw the communication graph of Figure 3. The communication graph captures the communications that are required given a mapping of data and computations onto the virtual processor mesh.

There are nine edges in the communication graph, hence as many possible communications. Our goal is to minimize their number. We have many parameters to play with: the eight alignment constants α, and the eight allocation matrices M. But we do not have full freedom because of the cycles in the communication graph. See [8] for technical results. In a word, for uniform loop nests it is always possible to have the same allocation matrix M for all data arrays and computations (it remains to determine best alignment constants), while for affine loop nests this is not the case (much research is ongoing in this area, e.g. [1, 7, 13, 16]). In the example we end up with a single communication, although there were up to nine edges in the communication graph.

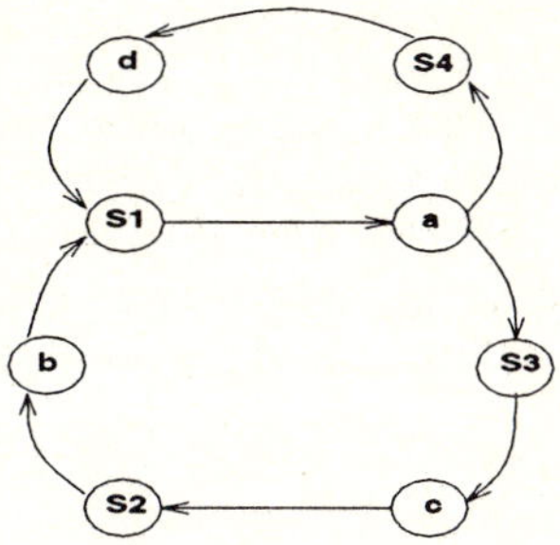

Fig. 3. Communication Graph

4 Conclusion

We have briefly described HPF main features and current prototypes. We have shown that source to source transformation is possible for single loop nest programs, thereby automatically generating HPF directives. This is a small step towards the sequential programming of parallel machines. We hope to achieve new developments in the framework of the *EuroTOPS* project.

References

1. Jennifer M. Anderson and Monica S. Lam. Global optimizations for parallelism and locality on scalable parallel machines. *ACM Sigplan Notices*, 28(6):112–125, June 1993.
2. Utpal Banerjee. An introduction to a formal theory of dependence analysis. *The Journal of Supercomputing*, 2:133–149, 1988.
3. Thomas Brandes. Adaptor language reference manuel - version 1.0. Technical report, German National Institute for Computer Science, 1993.
4. Thomas Brandes. Adaptor the distributed array library - version 1.0. Technical report, German National Research Institute for Computer Science, 1993.
5. Thomas Brandes. Adaptor users guide. Technical report, German National Research Institute for Computer Science, 1993.
6. Alain Darte, Tanguy Risset, and Yves Robert. Loop nest scheduling and transformations. In J.J. Dongarra and B. Tourancheau, editors, *Environments and Tools for Parallel Scientific Computing*, volume 6 of *Advances in Parallel Computing*, pages 309–332. North Holland, 1993.
7. Alain Darte and Yves Robert. A graph-theoretic approach to the alignment problem. Technical Report 93-20, Laboratoire de l'Informatique du Parallélisme, Ecole Normale Supérieure de Lyon, July 1993. To appear in Parallel Processing Letters.
8. Alain Darte and Yves Robert. Mapping uniform loop nests onto distributed memory architectures. Technical Report 93-03, Laboratoire de l'Informatique du Parallélisme, Ecole Normale Supérieure de Lyon, January 1993. To appear in Parallel Computing.
9. Michèle Dion, Jean-Laurent Philippe, and Yves Robert. Parallelizing compilers: what can be achieved ? Technical report, Laboratoire de l'Informatique du Parallélisme, Ecole Normale Supérieure de Lyon, February 1994.
10. Paul Feautrier. Dataflow analysis of array and scalar references. *Int. J. Parallel Programming*, 20(1):23–51, 1991.

11. Paul Feautrier. Some efficient solutions to the affine scheduling problem, part i, one-dimensional time. Technical Report 92-28, Laboratoire MASI, Université Pierre et Marie Curie, Paris, May 1992. to appear in Int. J. Parallel Programming.
12. Seema Hiranandani, Ken Kennedy, and Chau-Wen Tseng. Compiler optimizations for FORTRAN D on MIMD distributed-memory machines. In *Supercomputing 91*, pages 86–100. IEEE Computer Society Press, nov 1991.
13. C.H. Huang and P. Sadayappan. Communication-free hyperplane partitioning of nested loops. In Banerjee, Gelernter, Nicolau, and Padua, editors, *Languages and Compilers for Parallel Computing*, volume 589 of *Lecture Notes in Computer Science*, pages 186–200. Springer Verlag, 1991.
14. Charles H. Koelbel, David B. Loveman, Robert S. Schreiber, Guy L. Steele Jr., and Mary E. Zosel. *The High Performance Fortran Handbook*. The MIT Press, 1994.
15. Leslie Lamport. The parallel execution of do loops. *Communications of the ACM*, 17(2):83–93, feb 1974.
16. Jingke Li and Marina Chen. The data alignment phase in compiling programs for distributed memory machines. *Journal Parallel Distributed Computing*, 13:213–221, 1991.
17. J.K. Peir and R. Cytron. Minimum distance: a method for partitioning recurrences for multiprocessors. *IEEE Transactions on Computers*, 38(8):1203–1211, aug 1989.
18. Chau-Wen Tseng. An optimizing fortran D compiler for MIMD distributed-memory machines. Technical report, Rice University, 1993.

A Family of Data-Parallel Derivations *

M Clint[1], Stephen Fitzpatrick[1], T J Harmer[1], P L Kilpatrick[1] and J M Boyle[2]

[1] The Queen's University of Belfast, Department of Computer Science, Belfast BT7 1NN, Northern Ireland
[2] Mathematics and Computer Science Division, Argonne National Laboratory, Argonne IL 60439, USA.

1 Introduction

A good programmer attempts to minimize architecture-specific detail when writing a sequential implementation of an algorithm. Such good programming practice makes it possible to transport the implementation to other hardware architectures and thus minimize programmer effort. Indeed, high-level programming languages attempt to hide the detail required by particular machine architectures and thus make it easier to construct programs and transport them.

When using traditional methods to implement an algorithm for an advanced parallel architecture, the programmer faces the dilemma of

- writing the algorithm implementation in an architecture-independent way and thereby, inevitably, achieving disappointing execution performance (when compared to the architecture's theoretical execution performance); or
- writing the algorithm implementation in an architecture-dependent way and thereby achieving good execution performance, but in the process producing an implementation dedicated to a particular parallel architecture.

With the scientific community's insatiable desire for increased performance, a programmer will generally choose the latter course. However, the increasing variety of parallel computer architectures and the speed of technological change make this course an expensive one, since it requires a new implementation to be prepared when a new parallel architecture is considered.

The problem that we address in this paper is how to enable a programmer to obtain high performance from an implementation without having to write a low-level, machine-specific implementation. The approach that we use is to write high-level, machine independent specifications of algorithms in a pure, functional programming language (a subset of the SML programming language[8]).

Such *functional specifications* can be executed, and indeed often are executed in the initial stages of development to give confidence that an algorithm has been correctly described. However, we intend our functional specifications to be a clear statement of the algorithm that captures its essence without consideration

* This work is supported by SERC Grant GR/G 57970, by a research studentship from the Department of Education for Northern Ireland and by the Office of Scientific Computing, U.S. Department of Energy, under Contract W-31-109-Eng-38

for execution efficiency. Such a specification executes prohibitively slowly using available functional language compilers (if such a compiler is available for the architecture at all), much more slowly than could be expected of a hand-crafted, imperative implementation of the algorithm.

So, rather than compile a functional specification, we *derive* imperative implementations, normally expressed in some dialect of Fortran, from the specification. Many imperative implementations can be derived from a single specification; each implementation is tailored for the hardware to be used and the data to be manipulated.

The derivation of an implementation from a specification is performed by automatically applying *program transformations*. A transformation is a simple rewrite rule that produces a change in a program; normally, a single application of a transformation produces a minor, local change. A derivation effects the implementation of a functional specification by applying many transformations, each transformation being applied many times. We have demonstrated that it is possible to derive highly efficient implementations from our functional specifications; indeed, these implementations are comparable in performance to implementations written by a programmer using a conventional approach [6].

2 A Family of Transformational Derivations

The implementation of a functional specification is a complex task; its complexity may be reduced by identifying *intermediate forms* between the specification language and the final implementation language. For example, rather than make the transition directly from SML to Fortran, a specification is first converted into the λ-calculus, then into Fortran:

$$\text{SML} \longrightarrow \lambda\text{-calculus} \longrightarrow \text{Fortran.}$$

Each of these transitions may also be sub-divided into further intermediate forms, to whatever degree is convenient. A derivation to implement a specification is correspondingly divided into *sub-derivations*; one sub-derivation being used to create each intermediate form.

There are advantages to such division beyond simplifying the task of implementation: the sub-derivation that creates the λ-calculus form is independent of the final implementation language, and so may be combined with another sub-derivation to create, say, an array processor implementation (for example, for the AMT DAP). Similarly, the λ-calculus to Fortran sub-derivation is independent of how the λ-calculus form was created, and may be combined with another sub-derivation that converts another specification language into the λ-calculus.

$$\left.\begin{array}{c}\text{SML}\\ \text{Lisp}\\ \text{Miranda}\end{array}\right\} \longrightarrow \lambda\text{-calculus} \longrightarrow \left\{\begin{array}{c}\text{Fortran}\\ \text{Cray Fortran}\\ \text{DAP Fortran}\\ \text{C}\end{array}\right.$$

4. Determining the "best" preference combination

Once preferences have been determined this information must be used to construct all the preference combinations suggested by each statement. Each statement generates at least one preference combination, in which each array has a particular preference. We reduce the number of preference combinations for a phase to a feasible number by only considering those preference combinations generated by statements in that phase; all other possible combinations of preferences are ignored.

4.1 The preference combination construction strategy

Having generated all the preference combinations for the phase we consider each "partial" preference combination, ie. each preference combination containing an ANY semi-preference. In order to estimate performance using a particular preference combination it is preferable that the preference combination concerned is complete (ie. not partial). However, we seek to replace ANY's with more relevant semi-preferences than simple, arbitrary defaults, which represent only a last resort. Consequently we endeavour to combine partial preference combinations where possible. This is illustrated below:

preference combination_1: ANY{}, BLOCK ; BLOCK, ANY{} ; BLOCK, ANY{}
preference combination_2: BLOCK, BLOCK ; ANY{}, ANY{} ; ANY{},BLOCK
preference combination_3: ANY{}, ANY{} ; BLOCK, ANY{} ; BLOCK,BLOCK

These three preference combinations may be "composed" into a single (partial) preference combination: BLOCK, BLOCK ; BLOCK, ANY{} ; BLOCK,BLOCK which satisfies all statements generating preference combinations 1, 2, and 3. Any outstanding ANY{} semi-preferences are set to a default preference, CYCLIC(1). If a dimension of an array is sufficiently small then replication of that dimension is considered, rather than distributing it and incurring communication costs which exceed the computational time saving.

Each preference combination is sent to the Performance Estimator in order to estimate the execution time of the current phase using the combination of array distributions represented by this preference combination, after which a "best" preference combination is selected by comparison of execution time estimates.

4.2 Determination of a distribution scheme for the entire program

Due to the high cost of array redistribution between phases, a phase's computational content must be such that the redistribution cost penalty would be outweighed by the saving due to the use of an appropriate preference combination rather than an inefficient one. It seems probable that redistribution will only be worthwhile for phases of extensive computation. Hence the essential nature of a phase is that it identifies iterations. A phase is therefore defined as an array-syntax DO-loop which does not contain other array-syntax DO-loops (an array-syntax DO-loop is a DO-loop containing array-syntax assignment statements or WHERE masks in its body). A phase may be nested within other DO-loops.

The scanner detects the phases in the program, building up a representation of the program in terms of the phases it contains. Then, for each phase, the best preference combination is determined as described above. The formulation of the overall distribution scheme for the program is carried out using this information and a "distribution tree" abstraction in which each path from root to leaf represents a particular combination of redistributions between the best preference combinations. The overall scheme is derived heuristically and inserted into the source code as a series of distribution and redistribution actions to be performed at particular points.

5. Conclusion

In the general case, the fully automatic determination of data distributions for distributed memory MIMD machines appears intractable. The vast majority of researchers in the field of parallelizing compilers for such machines have interpreted this result as a cue to adopt a semi-automatic approach, involving the programmer annotating the input program [4]. The FCS project addresses the fact that there is a subset of problems which consists of simple, regular, data-parallel computations which should be amenable to fully-automatic treatment. The FCS is currently being implemented in C++ using the NeXTStep environment.

Acknowledgement

Philip Crooks is supported by a Research Studentship (Distinction Award) from the Department of Education for Northern Ireland.

References

[1] B. Chapman, P. Mehrotra, H. Zima: "Programming in Vienna Fortran" Scientific Programming. Vol. 1, No. 1, Autumn 1992, pp 31-50.

[2] High Performance Fortran. Scientific Programming. Vol. 2, No. 2, Spring 1993, pp 1 168.

[3] F. Bodin, P. Beckmann, D. Gannon, et al : "Sage++: A Class Library for Building Fortran90 and C++ Restructuring Tools: DRAFT 0.1"

[4] P. Crooks, R.H. Perrott : "Language Constructs for Data Partitioning and Distribution", Internal Report, Dept. of Computer Science, Queen's University, Belfast, June 1993

Some Synthesis Aspects for Data Parallel Programming

Guy-René Perrin

University of Franche-Comté, F-25030 Besançon
e-mail: perrin@comte.univ-fcomte.fr

Introduction

Among the different parallel programming models, scientific users praise data parallelism for this approach does not impose major changes in their way of programming. This interest is clearly illustrated in the HPF Language [5]. In this model one can hope efficient data distributions and memory cache transfers on massively parallel architectures, as soon as the source code expresses data alignments on virtual processor grids, and run-time communication shapes, such as broadcasts or neighbouring shifts.

So, a major current issue is to define a safe and efficient source-to-source translator, in order to transform existing codes in a convenient dialect for a data parallel form. Such a translator can be founded on well mastered parallelization techniques, which were developped in the last decade for loops restructuring ([1], [2]), or systolic arrays design ([7], [11], [8]). Indeed, in practice these parallelization techniques are mainly powerful in program fragments as nested loops.

In order to achieve proper statements for data parallelism from such given pieces of programs, some particular problems have to be solved. The aim of this presentation is to address the way parallelization techniques can answer to these probems. According to the data dependence modelling they involve and the space-time allocations that can be synthesized, we emphasize the problems of spreads, local communications and virtual processor count minimization.

1 Recurrence equations and parallelization techniques

1.1 Affine recurrence equations

We consider statements expressed as systems of recurrence equations. They are abstract forms of nested loops, in which the only dependencies are flow-dependencies, since such statements apply the single assignment rule. In practice, we assume that dependencies are affine functions of the iteration indices and the iteration space is a convex polytope of Z^n, where n is the depth of the nest. An affine recurrence equation is of the form

$$X(\mathbf{z}) = f(\ldots, Y(g(\mathbf{z})), \ldots) \qquad \mathbf{z} \in D \subset Z^n, \tag{E}$$

where g is an affine function. The initialization of the recurrence defined by equation (E) is specified by some input equations.

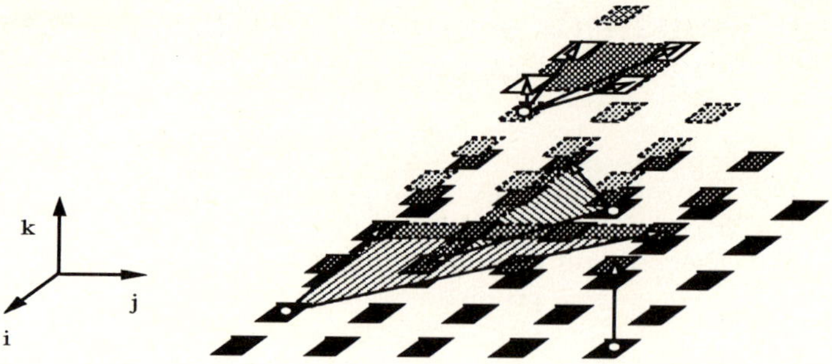

Fig. 1. Dependencies for the Gaussian elimination

Example 1. The Gaussian elimination problem.

$$\begin{array}{ll} \text{A(i,j,k)= A(i,j,k-1) - A(i,k,k-1)} \times \text{A(k,j,k-1) / A(k,k,k-1)} & \\ & i \in k+1..N, \;\; j \in k+1..N, \;\; k \in 1..N-1 \\ \text{A(i,j,0)=}\ a_{i,j} & i \in 1..N, \;\; j \in 1..N \end{array}$$

1.2 Dependence analysis

The detection of depending operations in a program is called the dependence analysis. Similarly dependence analysis defines the data dependencies occurring in recurrence equations. Assuming the variables are fully indexed, the vertices of the extended dependence graph associated with equations are the integral points inside the iteration space and the dependencies can be defined by dependence vectors $\mathbf{d} = \mathbf{z} - g(\mathbf{z})$ in Z^n. So, for the previous example, dependence vectors link points $(i_0, j_0, k_0 - 1)$ with some points (i, j, k_0). They are :

$$\begin{array}{ll} \mathbf{d}_1 = (0, 0, 1) & \mathbf{d}_2 = (0, j - k_0 - 1, 1) \\ \mathbf{d}_3 = (i - k_0 - 1, 0, 1) & \mathbf{d}_4 = (i - k_0 - 1, j - k_0 - 1, 1) \end{array}$$

In the context of data parallelism, it becomes important to model these dependencies in such a way that underlying communication shapes can be synthesized in order to benefit by communication primitives such as broadcasts. This supposes a global approach, while many parallelization techniques suffer from a piecewise criterion which only specifies needed data for each elementary calculation. It is the reason why, considering an equation, the *utilization set* $\{\mathbf{z} \in D \mid g(\mathbf{z}) = \mathbf{z}_0\}$ of points using an occurrence $\mathbf{z}_0$ is introduced [10]. It is a convex polytope in an affine subspace of Z^n, whose underlying vectorial space is $Ker(g)$. It is generated by *utilization vectors* which are meaningful in the translation towards a data parallel program.

Example 2. The Gaussian elimination problem (continued).
Figure 1 shows four examples of utilisation sets of an item. They are either

a singleton, or a line segment, or a square depending on the dependence vector. The following table presents utilization vectors that can be associated with dependence ones.

dependence vectors	*utilization vectors*
$\mathbf{d}_1 = (0,0,1)$	$\mathbf{u}_1 = (0,0,0)$
$\mathbf{d}_2 = (0, j - k_0 - 1, 1)$	$\mathbf{u}_2 = (0,1,0)$
$\mathbf{d}_3 = (i - k_0 - 1, 0, 1)$	$\mathbf{u}_3 = (1,0,0)$
$\mathbf{d}_4 = (i - k_0 - 1, j - k_0 - 1, 1)$	$\mathbf{u}_{4,1} = (1,0,0)$ $\mathbf{u}_{4,2} = (0,1,0)$

1.3 Space-time allocation

From such a modelling, space-time allocations can be determined. They describe restructurations of the initial nested loops. These techniques are known as the Lamport wavefront method [6] and are founded on projections in Z^n. A schedule specifies the instant of execution of any elementary calculation. It is defined from a vector $\boldsymbol{\lambda}$: *"fronts"* are hyperplanes perpendicular to $\boldsymbol{\lambda}$ and supported by a $(n-1)$-dimensional vectorial space denoted as $Ker(\boldsymbol{\lambda})$. A space mapping specifies virtual processors on which calculations take place. It is a linear mapping σ from Z^n to Z^{n-1} : it maps any occurrence $\mathbf{z}$ onto the virtual processor $\sigma\,\mathbf{z}$, by projection along a direction $\boldsymbol{\xi}$. The loop restructuration is then a change of basis in Z^n defined by

$$P = \begin{pmatrix} \boldsymbol{\lambda} \\ \sigma \end{pmatrix}$$

Some properties are attached to such a change of basis. Some of them specify simple cases : for example the unimodularity of matrix P simplifies the scanning of the resulting polytope in terms of loops. Other ones are conditions for the schedule and the space mapping to be valid.

Proposition 1. *An affine schedule is valid if and only if its linear part* $\boldsymbol{\lambda}$ *satisfies* $\boldsymbol{\lambda} \cdot \mathbf{d} > 0$ *for any dependence vector* $\mathbf{d}$. *Moreover, a vector* $\boldsymbol{\xi}$ *defines a valid space mapping if and only if* $\boldsymbol{\lambda} \cdot \boldsymbol{\xi} \neq 0$.

Last, a condition can be given to characterize data parallel solutions which can involve broadcasts. In this case virtual processors arrays can be synthesized according to the following property :

Proposition 2. *An affine schedule yields a broadcast on some utilisation set (i.e. along dimensions of the virtual processor set) iff* $Ker(\boldsymbol{\lambda}) \cap Ker(g) \neq \mathbf{0}$, *i.e.* $\boldsymbol{\lambda} \cdot \mathbf{u} = 0$ *for some utilization vector* $\mathbf{u} \neq \mathbf{0}$.

These conditions yield the resolution of integer linear problems, e.g. the synthesis of an optimal affine schedule [4]. But, as *Proposition 1* says, the global determination of a space-time allocation is not a linear problem with some global constraint. Hence, for a given schedule, many space mappings can suit. Their convenience can be relative to various criteria, which can be opposite : activity ratio of the processors, geometry of the array or of the communication links, virtual processor count, etc.

2 The Data parallelism case

2.1 Synthesis of spreads

Fortunately, the modelling of data dependencies we recalled hereabove is a good framework to synthesize space-time allocations since a criterion is chosen. For instance, as *Proposition 2* says, a schedule such that fronts contain some utilization vector leads to a data parallel solution with data spreads. In this case, the linear problem to solve is :

$$\begin{cases} \boldsymbol{\lambda} \cdot \mathbf{d} > 0 & \text{for any dependence vector } \mathbf{d} \\ \boldsymbol{\lambda} \cdot \mathbf{u} = 0 & \text{for some utilization vectors } \mathbf{u} \end{cases}$$

with an objective function which yields an optimal affine schedule generating spreads. If a solution exists, regarding spreads, all the space mappings satisfying *Proposition 1* define equivalent geometries of the virtual processor sets. So, for a spread associated with some utilization vector $\mathbf{u}$, any space mapping defined by $\boldsymbol{\xi}$ such that $\boldsymbol{\xi} \cdot \mathbf{u} = 0$ can be considered as a canonical mapping. It is generally partially determined by these equations. The full determination of $\boldsymbol{\xi}$ can depend on a minimization criterion, as suggested in [9]. This leads to nice data parallel programs with data spreads and minimal communications.

Example 3. The Gaussian elimination problem (continued).
Regarding the utilization set associated with the pivot elements, the dependence and utilization vectors yieds the following linear problem :

$$\begin{cases} \lambda_3 > 0 & \lambda_1 = 0 \\ \lambda_2 + \lambda_3 > 0 & \lambda_2 = 0 \\ \lambda_1 + \lambda_3 > 0 & \end{cases}$$

whose optimal integer solution is the vector $\boldsymbol{\lambda}^T = (0, 0, 1)$. In this case, the canonical mapping is fully determined as $\boldsymbol{\xi}^T = (0, 0, 1)$.

This example emphasizes a data parallel solution with a global broadcast of the pivots in the virtual grid. Since each element of any pivot row and each element of any pivot column have a one-dimensional utilization set, generated by a subset of the utilization vectors of the pivot itself, these items are also spread, but only along one dimension of the grid. The canonical mapping is fully determined : it is such that any point (i, j, k) is allocated to the virtual processor (i, j) in the grid. Array A is then aligned on a template $(1 : N, 1 : N)$.

Other schedules are valid too, and determine one-dimensional spreads in the virtual grid. They are defined by vectors $\boldsymbol{\lambda}^T = (1, 0, 1)$ or $(0, 1, 1)$ or else $(1, 1, 1)$. The broadcast implied by this last schedule can be removed by a rewriting of the initial equation, introducing a preliminary division of the pivot row (or the pivot column) by the pivot element. This yields a data parallel program whose communications are regular neighbouring shifts, in a well-known systolic fashion.

Example 4. The Gaussian elimination problem (continued).
Vector $\boldsymbol{\lambda}^T = (0,1,1)$ generates one-dimensional spreads in the grid. It is such that $\boldsymbol{\lambda} \cdot \mathbf{u}_3 = \boldsymbol{\lambda} \cdot \mathbf{u}_{4,1} = 0$. The canonical space mapping is then partially determined by $\xi_1 = 0$. In order to minimize the communications, one can choose a direction which generates a utilization set. Here the direction $\mathbf{u}_2 = \mathbf{u}_{4,2}$ is a good candidate. It determines $\boldsymbol{\xi}^T = (0,1,0)$ which yields a solution where communications are only one-dimensional spreads or neighbouring shifts. Any point (i,j,k) is allocated to the virtual processor (i,k). Array A is then aligned on one dimension of the grid, one row per virtual processor (see Fig. 2(a)).

2.2 Minimizing the size of the virtual grids

Virtual grids derived by a linear space-time allocation present many qualities such as regular and local communications or data spreads. In the previous examples the grid and the matrix have the same size, equal to the *"potential parallelism"*. Unfortunately, in real life virtual processors can have a non-optimal parallelism ratio. This phenomenon arises in two situations : either processors are rythmically active, or some processors have disjoint activity periods. That is the reason why re-allocation techniques are defined. They only deal with space mapping and yield minimized size grids.

In the first situation *clustering* techniques can apply. The clusters defining a paving of the initial grid should have regular shapes such as rows, or more general parallelipiped or regular polygons whose edges are either parallel to the array borders or parallel to the projection of some dependence vectors. An example is presented in [3] for the Gaussian elimination, considering the systolic solution characterized by $\boldsymbol{\lambda}^T = \boldsymbol{\xi}^T = (1,1,1)$.

In the second situation *folding* techniques can apply. They consist in mapping some initial virtual processors with disjoint activity periods into a single (virtual or physical) one. So, this technique is either a way for minimizing the size of the virtual processor grid, or a compiling technique to distribute templates and instructions on a physical architecture. The new architecture can be determined by observing that, at run-time, active processors can be drawn inside a shifting cone. So, processors can be paired one with each other, since they appear on different borders of the cone. When applied regularly, this technique leads to regular toroidal meshes and defines new data and code distributions.

Example 5. The Gaussian elimination problem (continued).
The solution defined by $\boldsymbol{\lambda}^T = (0,1,1)$ and $\boldsymbol{\xi}^T = (0,0,1)$ has a one-dimensional spread of every element of the pivot row along its column. Although it does not minimize communications, this mapping emphasizes a nice solution by folding. Since any point (i,j,k) is allocated to virtual processor (i,j) and regarding the activity period of each processor, template $(1:N, 1:N)$ can be reduced by half. Communication links follow a one-dimensional toroidal mesh (see Fig. 2(b)) and data distribution can be defined by a `CYCLIC` directive.

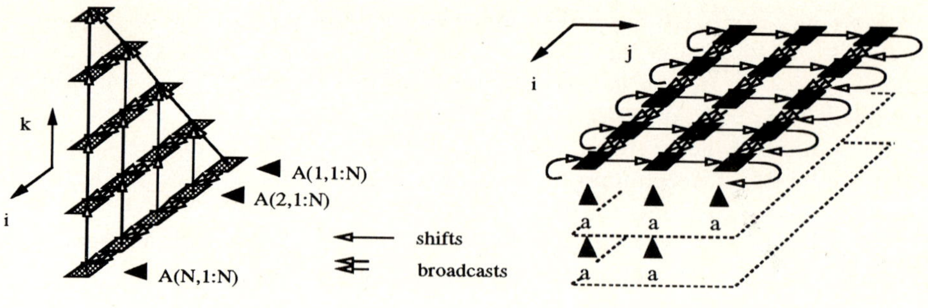

(a)

(b)

Fig. 2. Two solutions : (a) a data alignment (b) a toroidal mesh

References

1. Allen J.R., Kennedy K. (1984). Automatic Loop Interchange. *ACM SIGPLAN'84 Symp. on Compiler Construction.*, SIGPLAN Notices, **19-6**, 233–246.
2. Banerjee U. et al. (1993). Automatic Program Parallelization. *Proc. of the IEEE*, **81-2**, 211–243.
3. Clauss P., Mongenet C., Perrin G.R. (1992). Calculus of Space-Optimal Mappings of Systolic Algorithms on Processors Arrays. *J. of VLSI Signal Proc.*, **4**, 27–36.
4. Darte A., Robert Y. (1992). Scheduling Uniform Loop Nests. *Research report 92-10, Laboratoire de l'Informatique du Parallelisme, ENS Lyon.*
5. Draft, High Performance Fortran Language Specification. *High Performance Fortran Forum, January 1993.*
6. Lamport L. (1974). The parallel execution of DO loops. *Com. ACM*, **17-2**, 83–93.
7. Moldovan D.I. (1983). On the Design of Algorithms for VLSI Systolic Arrays. *Procedings of IEEE*, **71-1**, 113–120.
8. Mongenet C. (1985). Une Méthode de Conception d'Algorithmes Systoliques, Résultats Théoriques et réalisation. *PhD. Thesis, INPL, Nancy.*
9. Mongenet C. (1993). Data compiling for systems of recurrence equations. *Dagsthul Seminar 9325 on Parallelization Techniques for Uniform Algorithms.*
10. Mongenet C., Clauss Ph., Perrin G.R. (1991). Geometrical Coding to Compile Affine Recurrence Equations on Regular Arrays. *Int. Parallel Processing Symposium, IEEE, Anaheim, CA, USA.*
11. Quinton P. (1984). Automatic Synthesis of Systolic Arrays from Uniform Recurrence Equations. *11th Int. Symp. on Computer Architecture, Ann Arbor, MI, USA, IEEE Computer Society*, 208–214.

Influence of Fortran 90 Features on Performance on Cray Vector Computer Systems

Uwe Küster, Manuela Zürn

RUS,

Allmandring 30, D-70550 Stuttgart,

kuester@rus.uni-stuttgart.de, zuern@rus.uni-stuttgart.de

Abstract. To formulate data structures suited to numerical problems like selfadapting multilevel algorithms several data constructs, conditions and attributes are necessary. These constructs are offered by languages like C++ or Fortran 90.
A selection of features which seem to be useful in programming certain algorithms are pointer, derived types, dynamic memory management, some array constructs etc. In the first point we were interested in the newly developed programming language Fortran 90. Cray was the first company in developing a real Fortran 90 compiler which has been released in December 1993. This paper gives an impression of how using some single Fortran 90 features does influence the speed of the scalar part of a program.

1 Introduction

1.1 Numerical Motivation

Modern techniques in the solution of partial differential equations are guided by unstructured grids, multi level techniques and self adaption.

Data structures for unstructured grids consist of long vectors of derived types or some kind of trees or linked lists of derived types. The derived types contain data for the status and geometric variables and pointers to or index numbers of the neighbouring cells, sides, edges and node points.

In the case of topologically identical cells (triangles, tetraedra) the number of these pointers resp. index number is fixed. In the case of complex cells with arbitrary number of sides and nodes the cell data structure must be dynamical in some sense for example by pointer arrays of dynamical length.

Handling data structures for unstructured grids can be done by accessing long vectors involving strides > 1 in the case of access to the cell data itself. The neighbourhood is accessed by index vectors in the case of cell vectors or by (vectors of) pointers. In any case indirect access is needed. In the case of cells with arbitrary number of sides and nodes it is harder to vectorize.

Direct and indirect access to vectors of derived types with and without pointers is important. Difficulties with strides can occur.

The multi level case needs additional pointers/index arrays between the cell levels.

Selfadapting techniques, that is generation and deletion of cells within the grid at run time in dependence on the solution, need dynamic memory management and data structures which enable the handling of changes in the neigbourhood. In many cases this is done by trees of derived types with pointers to the cell neighbours which can be changed simply. The data are accessed in the trees by recursively called subroutines. Data access still can be vectorized by an alternative data access via "arrays of pointers". Fast access to pointers is essential as well as a fast memory management.

The generation of new cells in multi level under certain conditions, for example of new triangles without hanging points (red, green and blue refinement) generates recursive procedures which are hardly vectorizable and difficult to parallelize. The scalar power of a machine is stressed here. Small times for accesses to pointers and for subroutine calls are important.

Modern numerical techniques of this kind on a vector computer therefore force fast (vectorizable) access to data (pointer or not) in derived types, small pointer handling times in scalar and vectorizing context, fast allocation and deallocation of fixed data objects, fast subroutine calls, and flexible inlining. We have investigated all these points besides the last one in this paper because inlining was not yet available in the first release of CF90.

1.2 Fortran 90 Features

All of the new features in Fortran 90 are useful but might be dangerous in extensive usages. The new Fortran 90 features are generally not performance improving.

Most of the inquiries depend on the Cray Y-MP system in combination with the special release CF90 compiler. It is doubtful that trends will be others on other vector computer systems. We looked at data structures and new Fortran 90 features but less at optimization and vectorization aspects. The statements we can give are based on a not released alpha- and beta- compiler version from October/November/December 1993 and the released version of December 1993. Changes of times in any ways are possible.

Measuring times in small contexts on Cray vector computer systems
We used the timing function *irtc* and the Cray interactive simulator *sim*. The function *irtc* returns wall clock values. To overcome the inaccuracy of measured times by clock calls especially for very short times we used the Cray interactive simulator *sim* where possible.

Any results are given in number of clock periods (CPs) to get a better idea of the costs of the operations in relation to the floating point performance which is 2 op/CP on a Cray Y-MP.

2 Pointer

On Cray vector computer systems a single pointer has a length of 6 words. Therefore "arrays of pointers" (via an additional derived type) need much memory. For each triangle element 3 to 10 pointers are necessary. An array pointer (pointer on an array) has 3 extra words per dimension.
The pointer assignment statement in scalar context takes about 45 CPs on a Cray Y-MP in contrast to scalar assignment which takes only 17 CPs.

It is quiet cheap (20 CPs) to nullify a pointer. In contrast to this the intrinsic function associated takes more than 170 CPs. It is not clear what else happens within the function apart from checking the one pointer word containing the pointer's association state.

For allocation of small sized objects e.g. new elements in selfadapting meshes it is still better to write own memory allocation modules (see later section for allocation times). If more pointers to a fixed data type are needed e.g. in creating a tree recursive list there is a possibility to avoid the allocation of each single pointer in allocating a large array of this data type (having the target attribute) at once and assign just the pointers in the tree generation. This allocation technique is much less expensive than the allocation of each single pointer.

Vectorization of pointers

Fortran 90 pointers are less restrictive with respect to vectorization than C pointers. The following table shows loops handling arrays and "arrays of pointers" with pointer or target attribute or without any attribute in a subprogram.

Loop construct	array pointers	"arrays of pointers"
others1(i) = others2(i) + others3(i)	vectorized	not vectorized
others(i) = pointer1(i) + pointer2(i)	vectorized	not vectorized
pointer(i) = others1(i) + others2(i)	vectorized	not vectorized
pointer1(i) = pointer2(i) + others(i)	not vectorized	not vectorized
pointer1(i) = pointer2(i) + pointer3(i)	not vectorized	not vectorized
others(i) = target1(i) + target2(i)	vectorized	not vectorized
target(i) = others1(i) + others2(i)	vectorized	not vectorized
target1(i) = target2(i) + others(i)	vectorized	not vectorized
pointer(i) = target(i) + others(i)	not vectorized	not vectorized
target(i) = pointer(i) + others(i)	not vectorized	not vectorized
others(i) = pointer(i) + target(i)	vectorized	not vectorized
pointer(i) = target1(i) + target2(i)	not vectorized	not vectorized
target(i) = pointer1(i) + pointer2(i)	not vectorized	not vectorized
target1(i) = target2(i) + pointer(i)	not vectorized	not vectorized
target1(i) = target2(i) + target3(i)	vectorized	vectorized

Array syntax is an alternative to do-loops with array pointers. Dependencies between left and right hand side of the assignment are eliminated by syntactical definition because in array syntax a temporary is introduced which contains the result of the operation on the right hand side of the assignment. This temporary is copied on the result array on the left hand side of the assignment afterwards. The copy generates additional overhead which is significant for loops with small operation to load relation.

Using array syntax instead of do-loops with "arrays of pointers" is not possible in any way because the pointer is at the right hand side of an array section with nonzero rank which is not allowed per definition.

3 Derived Type Access

There is no difference in times between the access to a real variable and a real derived type component which has no pointer component. Derived type hierarchies without pointer components are handled as one simple derived type. The access to components of derived types of any level are realized through only one additional simple address offset which causes no additional costs. That means structuring of code by derived type hierarchies is not performance decreasing if no pointer components are involved and is therefore strongly recommended (see section 4 for strides). Arrays of fixed length used as components of derived types are handled as a set of variables or as a vector dependent on the context. They cover a contiguous space in the memory within the other derived type components and vectorize in loops.

Pointers as components of derived types must be handled carefully to assure fast data access. Too many levels of derived types should be avoided if they are related through pointers. Each pointer stands for an additional indirect access to the derived type component.
The pointee can be dynamic. The length of the derived type is not influenced by the length of the pointee. If a pointer component exists which points to another derived type, the pointee cannot be copied in the higher level derived type by the compiler as it would be without the `pointer`-attribute. For this reason access to pointer components in a derived type array in a vector loop is much slower than access to non pointer components. In a loop construct the access through all of the pointer relations is not repeated in any loop execution. If possible pointers in frequently referenced nested derived types should be avoided.

Pointer as alias

In derived type hierarchies pointers can be used as aliases pointing to a lower level in the hierarchy to simplify the code.
Using pointers as aliases should be handled carefully to improve performance. The more statements use the alias the more worthwhile is it. In a derived type hierarchy with an array pointer as lowest level it almost makes no change in times to access array pointer aliases or the whole hierarchy in a loop because an internal alias is set before the loop is executed.
In a derived type hierarchy with an array of the highest level derived type an ordinary do-loop to access the derived type hierarchy vectorizes. The derived types may contain pointers to the lower level derived types. A loop containing pointers used as aliases for the hierarchy above still vectorizes.

Linked lists

Linked and tree recursive lists via recursive data type definitions are useful e.g. in sparse matrix structures if the matrix can be split up into several blocks or if a fill in during elimination occurs and in multilevel algorithms to relate parents with their children. They should be used rarely because data access by recursion is not vectorizable.
The intrinsic function *associated* is often used in loops to catch the end of a recursive list. This function is expensive compared to the number of needed calls. If possible the intrinsic function `associated` in this context should be avoided (substituted by loop with known length).

The following table shows the access times in a very simple linked list in Fortran 90 on a Cray Y-MP and in C on a Cray Y-MP and on an IBM RS/6000-580 workstation (66.6 MHz, 128 KBytes data cache, 256 KBytes instruction cache). The times are given in number of cycles per element.

Number of elements	Fortran 90 Cray Y-MP without *associated*	Fortran 90 Cray Y-MP with *associated*	C Cray Y-MP	C IBM RS/6000
10	≈ 108 CPs	≈ 264 CPs	≈ 359 CPs	≈ 125 CPs
1000	≈ 98 CPs	≈ 270 CPs	≈ 34 CPs	≈ 31 CPs

The table shows that the equvalent code in C is 8 (!) times faster than the Fortran 90 loop.

Tree recursive list

In selfadaptive multilevel algorithms for the solution of partial differential equations it is convenient to organize the data of elements, their children and parents in tree recursive lists because it is simple to add new elements and to delete unnecessary ones.

One list element in the binary tree recursive list built up in this example contains a real value and two pointers to children. The tree recursive list contains $2^{n+1} - 1$ elements for n levels starting with level 0. The following table shows two different access variations, one via the tree recursive list (TRL), the other via an "array of pointers" (AOP) on Cray Y-MP and IBM RS/6000-580 in Fortran 90 and C. The times are given in clock periods (CPs) per element.

Number of Levels	Number of Elements	F90 (TRL) Cray Y-MP	F90 (AOP) Cray Y-MP	C (TRL) RS/6000	C (AOP) RS/6000
0	1	576.90	327.85		
2	7	541.47	48.49	135	
6	127	530.498	5.533	28	
13	16383	529.85	3.2199	23	11

Data access by "array of pointers" is naturally faster then going through the links. The loop to access the tree recursion by an array of pointers can be vectorized with the help of a compiler directive. The more elements the list contains the less cycles per elements are needed. The calling overhead of the recursive calls is dominant. For frequent access to the derived type data the alternative way is recommended. The table shows that the calling overhead for cache based superscalar architecture of the RS/6000 is much smaller.

4 Length of Derived Types and Strides

This section is based on the CF90 compiler on Cray computer systems. It is related to the Cray hardware which is word addressable with a length of 8 bytes per word. All recommendations can differ on other machines. However the principles won't change.

The stride is the constant linear memory distance in a regular vector access and is very important in context with array access. Cray Y-MP and C90 hardware architecture is almost

insensible to odd strides and strides of 2 and 4. This stride should not have $2^n, (n \geq 1)$ as divisor. A critical stride can be made harmless by inserting an additional dummy variable.
If derived types turn up in loop constructs the stride is the sum of the lengths of all data objects which are components of the derived type. Data objects can be of intrinsic or derived type with or without pointer attribute. If a derived type component is a real array with size m the length of the array is m words (m is product of extents in each dimension). The size of a character string as a derived type component is ((length of the string) / 8) + 1 words.

The influence of the kind-parameter on the length of data objects

While compiling a program or subprogram, the length of any intrinsic type with any kind parameter is fixed. The usage of the `kind`-parameter instead of instrinsic data types has no special influence on performance. It influences the strides and arithmetic.
The length of data objects are determined without any kind-parameter.

5 Fortran 90 Arrays

Array syntax vectorizes respectively parallelizes by definition. This is also true if the involved arrays are pointer arrays or targets because the compiler introduces a temporary between the right and the left hand side of the assignment resulting in additional loads and stores. If an array expression can be replaced by a do-loop this loop is generally faster (after a possible insertion of an `IVDEP` compiler directive) because of the omitted loads and stores.

This seems to be also true if it should syntactically be possible to avoid this copy back in the assignment. This results in a performance loss especially for complex do-loops involving a lot of temporary scalars which can be held in vector registers. These loops are restructured in a lot of different array expressions increasing the memory traffic. Array syntax is not applicable if pointers are to the right of the vector subscript.

Solving partial differential equations array syntax is useful only in handling structured techniques. It does not simplify coding of unstructured methods.

Array syntax is necessary in programming SIMD computers like Maspar and CM-2 but seems not to be helpful on vector computers.

Array sections

An array section is a group of elements within an array that can be used as an operand in an array expression. Array sections can be used as actual arguments to external or intrinsic functions. It is possible in Fortran 90 to use an array pointer as a pointer to array sections of another array. Do-loops handling different array sections assigned in the same program unit do not vectorize.
In Fortran 90 it is possible to pass array sections to subroutines. This can cause a slowdown of the program for non contiguous array sections, due to the copy-in and copy-out operations. Passing an array section as an array pointer does not call the copy-in and copy-out functions. A loop handling this array section in the subroutine does not vectorize.
Loops do vectorize if the array subsection is passed as an assumed shape array. In this case the copy-in and copy-out functions are called with the subroutine call.

Array inquiry functions

The usage of array inquiry functions seems to be unintelligible expensive. There are 4 functions for inquiries about the bounds, shape and size of an array of any type. The result depends only on the array properties, the array needs not be defined.
In the following example an array of the form below has been passed to a subroutine and was analyzed in its shape, size, bounds and status there:

```
real,dimension(-2:max , 5:max+2) :: array  ! in main program
                  :
real,dimension(:,:)               :: array  ! in subprogram
```

array inquiry function		time in CPs	array inquiry function		time in CPs
allocated	≈	259 CPs	lbound(aa)	≈	28 - 76 CPs
shape(aa)	≈	3520 CPs	lbound(aa,2)	≈	288 CPs
size(aa)	≈	804 CPs	ubound(aa)	≈	2870 CPs
size(aa,1)	≈	274 CPs	ubound(aa,2)	≈	288 CPs

Array inquiry functions could be very helpful e.g. in determining loop sizes and sizes of automatic arrays but they need much more time than transfering the values as parameters.

6 Allocation and Deallocation of Dynamic Data Objects

Allocation and deallocation of small sized data objects are expensive features of Fortran 90. It is better to avoid the *allocate* statement whenever possible and generate own memory allocation modules, or allocate at least more data objects in one allocate statement. Allocate and deallocate statements for frequently used small data objects should be avoided.

The allocation of an "array of pointer" could theoretically be vectorized but is not.

The allocation of a single real pointer takes more than 1700 CPs! Allocating a real array takes about 2400 cycles if the size of the array is not too large (≈ up to 100 000). The allocate statement for a derived type (list element of tree recursive list) takes about 1942 cycles. The respective statement with *malloc* from a C program takes about 1250 cycles.
The Fortran 90 *deallocate* for the same derived type takes 1403 CPs . A call to *free* from a program written in C takes 560 cycles. It takes 2406 CPs to deallocate a real array of size (100 000).

(De-)allocation of multiple data objects in one statement can reduce the overall time.

Allocation and deallocation of Fortran arrays in subroutines

Fortran 90 offers different kinds of dynamic arrays which are automatic arrays, allocatable arrays and array pointers. The following table shows the allocation (deallocation) times of these arrays entering (leaving) a subroutine.

FORTRAN 77 array argument :	≈ 74 CPs		
automatic array alloc. :	≈ 158 CPs	automatic array dealloc. :	≈ 93 CPs
allocatable array alloc.:	≈ 2719 CPs	allocatable array with dealloc. :	≈ 2916 CPs
		allocatable array without dealloc.:	≈ 1672 CPs
array pointer alloc.:	≈ 2663 CPs	array pointer with dealloc.	≈ 2489 CPs
		array pointer without dealloc.	≈ 73 CPs

This table shows that that automatic array allocation (on stack!) should be used whenever possible.

7 Explicit and Implicit Interfaces

Explicit interfaces offer the possibility of simple inlining which is not implemented in CF90 yet but will be in a further release. Therefore the times for subroutines via explicit interfaces will change.

Call to internal and external subroutines

Passing array pointers to internal subroutines is about 50-70 CPs cheaper than passing real assumed shape arrays. The more arguments are passed the more expensive the subroutine call is.

Calling an internal subroutine without any arguments takes at least 75 CPs.

External subroutines can either have an implicit interface (as known from Fortran 77) or an explicit interface by an interface block in the calling program unit.

It takes up to 12 cycles less to pass array pointers and assumed shape arrays to external subroutines than passing them to internal subroutines via explicit interfaces in both cases. It doesn't make a change in the times if the subroutine has an explicit or implicit interface.

8 Conclusions

The new features in Fortran 90 are useful and offer everything expected and required from a modern programming language. But some features are dangerous in extensive usages because they decrease performance.

Fortran 90 pointers are not as restrictive in being vectorized as C pointers but Fortran 90 pointers are slower than C pointers. Array syntax improves the vectorization of array pointers but it is not faster than ordinary loops. Array inquiry functions are expensive in general. Derived types have no influence on performance besides the stride. Apart from automatic arrays dynamic data objects are expensive.

To sum up we can say that luxury is expensive.

References

1. J.C. Adams, W.S. Brainerd, J.T. Martin, B.T. Smith, J.L. Wagener, *Fortran 90 Handbook*, McGraw-Hill Book Company, New York 1992

The BBN Butterfly Family : An Overview

Jasir S. Alherbish
Department of Computer Science and Engineering, University of Connecticut
Storrs, CT 06269

Abstract: **Parallel architecture has become an important way of providing high performance computation to users. For the last few years many high performance computers have been built. The BBN Butterfly family of multiprocessor systems is one example of such systems. This family supports both shared memory and message-passing models of computation. This paper reviews two BBN Butterfly systems; the BPP and the GP1000. The review highlights the architecture, the operating system, and the programming environment supported by each machine. Some applications that has been conducted on these two machines are also mentioned.**

1 Introduction

Two BBN Butterfly machines will be investigated in this paper with examples of real application on these machines. The first machine is the BBN Butterfly Parallel Processor (BPP) system, and the other is the BBN GP1000 system. The BPP is the first version of the BBN family which uses an interconnection network to connect N processors with N memory modules. Despite some disadvantages faced in the real life applications such as the poor operating system and the lack of a floating point co-processor (see [BRN88]), the BPP has been a successful machine in the market and it is claimed that over 100 BPP systems have been delivered [RAN90]. The GP1000 was introduced to the market as an enhancement of the BPP. While the general architecture of the BPP was maintained in the GP1000, the major improvement was the use of a UNIX-based portable flexible operating system called Mach 1000.

2 The BBN Butterfly Family

2.1 The BBN Parallel Processor System (The BPP)

The BPP system consists of up to 256 processing nodes connected by a switching network. In early machines, each processing node is an 8 MHz MC68000 with 24-bit virtual addresses and up to 1 Mbyte of local memory (4 MBytes with additional memory boards). A 2901- based bit-slice co-processor called the processor node controller (PNC) interprets every memory reference issued by the 68000 and is used to communicate with other nodes across the switching network. All of the memory in the system resides on individual nodes, but any processor can address any memory through the switch, and perform block transfer and atomic operations.

The BPP operating system is Chrysalis operating system. This operating system provides operations for process management, interprocess communication, and memory management. Many of the most common operations are implemented in microcode in the processor node controller (PNC). The user-level view of the memory architecture is defined by several Chrysalis system calls. The tightly coupled shared memory architecture of the Butterfly creates a program execution environment where tasks can be distributed to processors without regard to the physical location of the data associated with the tasks [ELI88]. This programming methodology, called *the Uniform System,* has evolved into an application library of functions for storage allocation and processor management. The Uniform System greatly simplifies programming the Butterfly and permits effective use of the multiple processors and memories.

2.2 The Butterfly GP1000

The GP1000 is an enhanced version of the prescribed BPP system. In general, the architecture of the GP1000 is similar to the BPP architecture. Both of them are MIMD system that incorporates up to 256 processing nodes connected via a multistage interconnection switching network that uses Butterfly switch. Also, the GP1000 is a NUMA multiprocessor system. The memory of the machine is shared among all processors in this way; each processor node includes 4 MBytes of memory (compare to 1 MByte in the BPP) that can be accessed from any processor in the system via the network. The time ratio between a local access and remote access with no other processors active is up to 1:15, depending on the types of the access [ZHA91]. The enhancement that has been achieved in the GP1000 includes the use of the MC68020 processor in the processing node instead of the MC68000. Also, each node has a 68851 paged memory management unit for virtual memory processing. However, the major improvement that has been achieved in this machine is the use of the operating system Mach 1000.

The GP1000 operating system, Mach 1000, is a system based upon the Mach operating system developed at Carnegie Mellon University. Mach has been designed to provide a standard for extending the UNIX environment into the multiprocessor arena. It provides the complete Barkeley 4.3BSD compatibility while significantly extending the UNIX notions of virtual memory management, processor management, and interprocess communication.

3 Examples of Applications

The first version of the BBN Butterfly machines was introduced to the market in 1985. Since that year, over 100 Butterfly systems have been delivered, see [RAN90]. Examples of applications performed using the Butterfly BBP system include:
- Medical applications such as the one described in [ALB88],
- Performance analysis tools like the University of Indiana Sigma System, see [DEN88],
- Image processing packages such as the one developed at the University of Rochester, see [BRN88],
- Mathematical algorithms like the Blocked Gaussian Elimination algorithm performed using the BPP, see [ELI88].
- Performance prediction and evaluation of parallel processing systems , see [ZHA91].

4 Conclusion

A commercial multiprocessor family has been reviewed in this paper. The BBN Butterfly family represents a Non-Uniform Memory Access architecture. The review included the BBN BPP system, as the first release of the BBN Butterfly systems, and the GP1000 which is considered an enhanced version of the BPP. The paper also listed some real applications that have been conducted on the BBN Butterfly machines. As a summary of findings we say:
- Since the BBN machines are NUMA multiprocessors they have the potential to scale to very large numbers of nodes.
- The BBN family can support a distributed memory multicomputer environment in which data sharing and communication are conducted by message-passing through the network. However, it is found that the message-passing on the GP1000 is not very efficient because the overhead cost is relatively high.
- The parallel tasks may be distributed and processed without regard to the physical location of the data associated with the tasks using the Uniform System as a parallel programming environment.
- Both data partitioning and functional partitioning are supported in the BBN family.
- The GP1000 operating system is Mach 1000. It is a flexible and portable UNIX-based operating system that achieve its flexibility by taking an object-oriented approach to operating system services . The use of Mach 1000 avoids retraining and migration costs for the users while providing an extensible environment for the development of new, truly parallel applications.

The ongoing research at the BBN Systems and Technologies Corporation promises many improvements over the prescribed BBN machines. As an example, Rettberg and others presented a prototype of the newest member of the BBN Butterfly machines called The Monarch (see [RAN90]).

References

[ALB88] Albert B., "The modification of a rule-based Diagnostic System for Routinized Parallelism on the Butterfly Parallel Processor", *in Proc. 3rd Int. Conf. Supercomput.*, 1988, vol2, pp. 149-155.

[BRN88] Christopher B., "Parallel Vision with the Butterfly Computer", *in Proc. 3rd Int. Conf. Supercomput.*, 1988, vol1, pp.54-68.

[DEN88] Dennis G., "The Sigma System: A Tool for Parallel Program Design", *in Proc. 3rd Int. Conf. Supercomput.*. 1988, vol2, pp. 157-163.

[ELI88] Elizabeth J., "Blocked Gaussian Elimination on the BBN Butterfly Multiprocessor", *in Proc. 3rd Int. Conf.*

Architectural Principles of the RPM

Yury A. Mamatov and Vladimir P. Yemelin
Institute for Computer Science, Russian Academy of Sciences
18 Sovetskaya St., Yaroslavl, Russia 150000

Extended Abstract

The Recursive Parallel Machine (RPM) is designed to solve scientific and technological tasks of high complexity. From the point of view of architecture, the RPM occupies an intermediate position between the parallel systems with shared memory and the distributed "message passing" systems. Developing the RPM architecture we tried to eliminate the shortcomings while preserving the advantages of the given systems. The architectural concept of the RPM allows to find a comp-romise among the modular organization, the shared memory, the complexity of the communication network with many nodes, and the dynamic parallelizing. The implementation of a computing module based on the given concept allows to create modular expanding parallel systems of various configurations - up to a supercomputer.

The main shortcomings of the "message passing" parallel systems are their insufficient effectiveness of the processor loading because of following: (1) the lack of dynamic parallelizing support which allows to reveal the parallelism and generate parallel processes during computations depending on the values of processed data; (2) the static parallelizing excludes a possibility of the parallel processes migration with the purpose of the dynamic balancing of the processor loading; (3) under static parallelizing the programmer himself must remember about a concrete system configuration and develop the programs considering this configuration making programs with poor portability.

The parallel shared memory systems are free from the shortcomings of the static parallelizing. However, this systems with many (about 1000) processors have a very expensive organization of the commutation system and the shared memory. Also, there are problems of the so called "hot spots" and "bottle neck" affecting the incorporation of many processors.

The typical reasons of the "hot spots" are a bad organization of the parallel reduction computations (when the accumulation of the reduction result occurs in a single memory bank) or an access to the centralized shared resources (for example, the sequential access to the queue of ready for execution parallel processes).

The RPM architecture is desinged to overcome above problems while preserving the advantages of the given system classes.

The following principles is a base of the RPM architecture:

1. the composition of hierachical model of parallel computations for shared memory and message passing model;

2. the recursive principle of dynamic parallelizing supported by system software and hardware;

3. the hierachical organization of the RPM memory to solve the following tasks: *decrease the load on the commutation network* in order to facilitate the hardware implementation of the network; *provide the regular load on the commutation network* in order to prevent the effect of "hot spots" that leads to the degrading of the network throughput; *organize the background parallel access* to the distributed shared memory and the dis-tributed external memory; *extend the volume of the main RPM (local and shared) memory* at the cost of organizing a two-level virtual memory.

Recursion describes dynamically generated parallel processes as procedure activations, that make it possible to: execute dynamic balancing of the PM loading by the parallel processes migration; develop parallel programs that are invariant to the hardware configuration; represent the parallelism depending on the values of processed data, i.e. the parallelism that can only be discovered in the process of computation.

In oder to perform dynamic balancing of the PM loading in RPM, the number of generated parallel processes must be more than the number of PM. Otherwise dynamic redistribution of work among PMs shall be impossible. When developing an RP program the user task is to provide sufficient number of activations for dynamic balancing, on the one hand, and, on the other hand, activations must be capacious enough to keep insignificant the expenses for their generation.

The non-started up processes but already called ones will migrate. In this case only small descriptor of the process and its parameters will actually migrate between PMs. The dynamic balancing itself is concealed from the user and is executed by the RPM system means considering PMs current busyness. A distinguished feature of the used balance algorithm is that it is distributed, i.e. there is no centralized queue of the parallel process and the algorithm supports the recursive parallelizing technique. Recursion and the means of dynamic balancing provide a high speed of the expansion of parallel processes over the system PMs. The expansion mechanism is similar to the chain reaction.

The RPM is a modular expanding computing system incorporating up to 128 clusters with up to 128 Processor Modules (PM) in each. The RPM has a shared memory that is physically distributed over the processor modules of the system. The RPM performance and the shared memory capacity encrease proportionally to the number of PMs. In the maximum configuration The RPM can perform up to 128 parallel I/O channels, through which a parallel access is performed to different external devices and also a parallel access to files.

Applications Performance on Intel Paragon XP/S-15

Subhash Saini* and Horst D. Simon*
Numerical Aerodynamic Simulation Facility
NASA Ames Research Center, Mail Stop 258-6
Moffett Field, CA 94035-1000, USA

Abstract

The impact of two different operating systems OSF, and SUNMOS available on the NAS Paragon, on the performance of applications has been studied and investigated. In OSF, paging of the unused part of the server and management of the virtual memory by the operating system degrades the performance of the applications by as much as by 40% in some of the cases studied. The influence of the data cache on the performance of the applications under both OSF and SUNMOS using one-dimensional (1-D) Fast Fourier transform (FFT) and three-dimensional (3-D) FFT has also been investigated. The performance of NAS Parallel Benchmarks is reported, and the scalability issues of the machine and the algorithms under both OSF and SUNMOS are considered.

1: Introduction

The Numerical Aerodynamic Simulation (NAS) Systems Division received an Intel Touchstone Sigma prototype model Paragon XP/S-15 in February 17, 1993. It was found that performance of many applications, including the assembly-coded single node BLAS 3 routine DGEMM, was lower than the performance on the Intel iPSC/860. This finding was quite puzzling since the clock of the microprocessor i860 XP used in the Paragon is 25% faster than the microprocessor i860 XR used in the Intel iPSC/860. It was also found that the performance of the NAS Parallel Benchmarks (NPB) is enhanced by about 30% if they are run for a second time in a DO loop. Furthermore, the performance of DGEMM was identical for the first run and the second run on a service node, but on a compute node the performance of the second run was about 40% better than the first run. These anomalies in the performance on the Paragon led us to investigate the problem in more detail. This in turn led us to propose a method of dynamic allocation of memory that increases the performance of the applications by about 30% to 40% [1-4]. In Section 2, we give a brief overview of the Paragon system including the two operating systems (OSF and SUNMOS). Section 3 gives the description of the BLAS kernels, FFTs and NPB used in the investigations. Section 4 discusses the results. Section 5 presents some conclusions.

2: Paragon Overview

2.1: NAS Intel Paragon XP/S-15

A single node of the Paragon XP/S-15 consists of two i860 XP microprocessors with 50 MHz clock: one for computation and the other for communication. The compute processor is for computation and the communication processor handles all message—protocol processing, thus freeing the computation processor to do computations. Currently, the communication processor is not used in the NAS Paragon. Each compute processor has 32 MB of local memory, but at NAS under OSF only about 24 MB is available for applications, the rest being used for the micro kernel, OSF server and system buffers. Under SUNMOS 31.5 MB per node is available for the applications but currently only up to 24 MB per node can be used. The NAS Paragon has 208 compute nodes, eight support nodes (one boot node, four service nodes, three ethernet nodes), and eight I/O nodes attached to the RAID disk drives. Theoretical peak performance for the NAS Paragon is 15.6 GFLOPS.

2.2: Paragon Operating System

On NAS Paragon the following two operating systems are available:

2.3.1: Open Software Foundation (OSF/1 AD)

The Unix operating system was originally designed for sequential computers and is not very well suited to the performance of massively parallel applications. The standard operating system on the NAS Paragon is based on the Open Software Foundation Advanced Development system (OSF/1 AD). The OSF/1 AD is based on the Mach microkernel from Carnegie Mellon University and the OSF/1 Unix implementation. The OSF/1 AD provides all the Unix features including virtual memory; shell, commands and utilities; I/O services; and networking support for ftp, rpc, and NFS. Each Paragon node has a small microkernel irrespective of the role of the node in the system. The Paragon operating system provides programming flexibility through virtual memory. In theory, virtual memory simplifies application development and porting by enabling code requiring large memory to run on a single compute node before being distributed across multiple nodes. The application runs in virtual memory which means that each process can access more memory than is physically available on each node. At NAS, OSF/1 AD runs on 144 compute nodes and on all service nodes.

2.3.2: SUNMOS

The chief drawbacks of OSF/1 AD are (a) OSF takes about 6 MB of memory on each node of the Paragon, (b) messages can be sent at a bandwidth of 30 MB per second compared to 200 MB per second peak advertised rate, (c) latencies are of the order of 100 microseconds using Intel NX calls under OSF. All these drawbacks can be minimized by using a new operating system called Sandia University of New Mexico Operating System (SUNMOS). SUNMOS was originally developed and ported to nCUBE-2 in 1991. SUNMOS was ported to Intel Paragon in 1993. SUNMOS takes only 250 KB of memory on each node of the Paragon and can send messages at bandwidth of 170 MB per second with latencies of 70 microseconds. However, SUNMOS provides a very limited compatibility with Intel NX calls under OSF/1 AD. It only supports hostless programs and does not support host-node programs. In addition to this limitation, SUNMOS has very limited support for I/O and absolutely no support for parallel I/O. NAS Paragon runs SUNMOS on 64 compute nodes and these nodes do not appear under the compute partition. Furthermore, jobs running under SUNMOS get a fixed amount of heap, stack, and communication space at load time. SUNMOS does not support virtual memory.

3: Applications Used

3.1: Basic Linear Algebra Subprograms

BLAS 1, 2, and 3 are the basic building blocks for many scientific and engineering applications. For example, the dot product (BLAS 1) is a basic kernel in Intel's ProSolver Skyline Equation Solver (ProSolver-SES), a direct solver using skyline storage, useful for performing Finite Element Structural analysis in designing aerospace structures. BLAS 3 (matrix-matrix) kernels are basic kernels in Intel's ProSolver Dense Equation Solver (ProSolver-DES), a direct solver that may be applied in solving computational electromagnetics (CEM) problems using Method of Moments (MOM). BLAS 2 and BLAS 3 are basic kernels in LAPACK. In the present paper, we have used a BLAS 3 routine called DGEMM to compute C = A*B, where A and B are real general matrices. The DGEMM is a single node assembly coded routine and, as such, involves no interprocessor communication.

3.2: Fast Fourier Transforms

The FFT has become a basic tool in various scientific and engineering applications ranging from artificial intelligence to oil exploration. At NAS, distributed three-dimensional FFT is used to solve Poisson partial differential equation. We have measured the performance of radix-2, -3 and -5 complex to complex FFT on Paragon. We have used 1-D single node, and 3-D distributed FFTs to study the imapct of data cache and scalability issues under OSF and SUNMOS on Paragon. Intel supplies only radix-2 1-D FFTs on Paragon.

3.3: NAS Parallel Benchmarks

The NPB were developed to evaluate the performance of highly parallel supercomputers. One of the main features of these benchmarks is their pencil and paper specification, which means that all details are specified algorithmically, thereby avoiding many of the difficulties associated with traditional approaches to evaluating highly parallel supercomputers. The

NPB consist of a set of eight problems each focusing on some important aspect of highly parallel supercomputing for computational aerosciences. The eight problems include five kernels and three simulated computational fluid dynamics (CFD) applications. The implementation of the kernels is relatively simple and straightforward and gives some insight into the general level of performance that can be expected for a given highly parallel machine. The other three simulated CFD applications need more effort to implement on highly parallel computers and are representative of the types of actual data movement and computation needed for computational aerosciences.

4: Results and Discussion

Figure 1(a) shows the results for the assembly coded BLAS 3 routine DGEMM for a matrix size of 1024x1024 on one compute node for the first and second run. The performance is 27 MFLOPS for the first run and 46 MFLOPS for the second run.

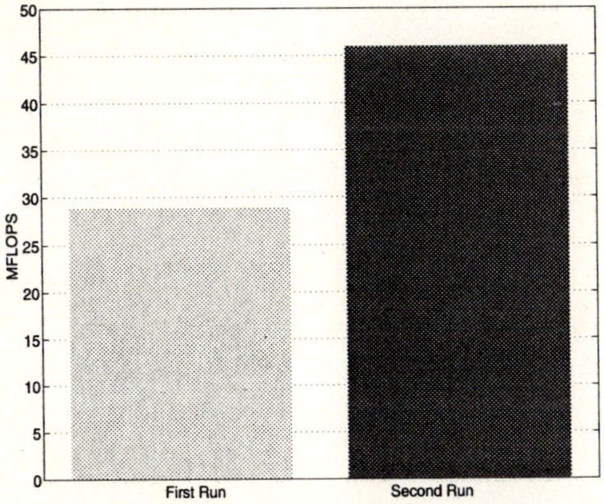

Figure 1(a): DGEMM on a Compute node under OSF.

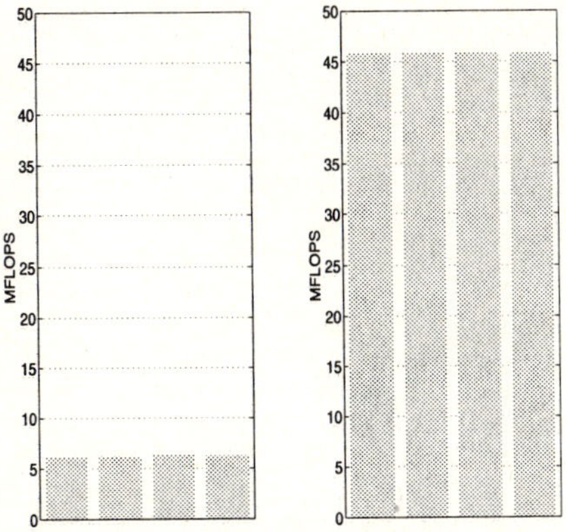

Figure 1(b): DGEMM on four compute nodes.

The performance obtained by the second run is about 40% better than the performance obtained by the first run. This degradation in performance is not acceptable since users will always run their code once. The left of the Figure 1(b) shows the performance of DGEMM on four compute nodes. The MFLOPS rate has decreased from 27 MFLOPS to about 6 MFLOPS. This problem can be eliminated by using dynamic allocation of memory. The performance of DGEMM using dynamic allocation of memory is shown on the right side of Figure 1(b). For details see reference [4].

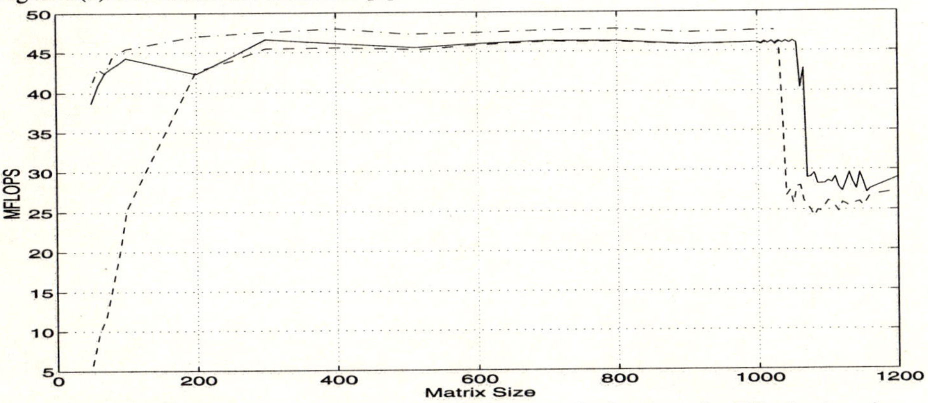

Figure 2: MFLOPS Vs. Size of the matrix. - . - .- . - SUNMOS; - - - - first iteration under OSF using dynamic allocation of memory, —— second iteration under OSF using dynamic allocation of memory.

The performance of DGEMM as function of size of matrix is shown in Figure 2. SUNMOS results are about 5% better than corresponding OSF results probably due to a better memory access mechanism. However, under SUNMOS, for a matrix size larger than 1024 either the system hangs or crashes and therefore results could not be obtained. Under OSF we could run our matrix beyond 32 MB per node but with 40% decrease in performance. Figure 3 (a) shows the performance of assembly coded 1-D FFT. Performance is much better when twiddle factors are in cache. The performance is maximum at x=512, corresponding to a size of 4 KB data cache. The other peaks reflect higher harmonics at multiple of 512. Figures 4(a) and 4(b) are similar to Figure 3 but are for Fortran coded 1-D FFT. Notice that the performance does not decrease after x=512 but remains constant due to better cache management. Also Fortran coded 1-D FFT is for radix-2, -3 and -5 whereas assembly coded 1-D FFT supplied by the Intel and used in Figure 3 is radix-2.

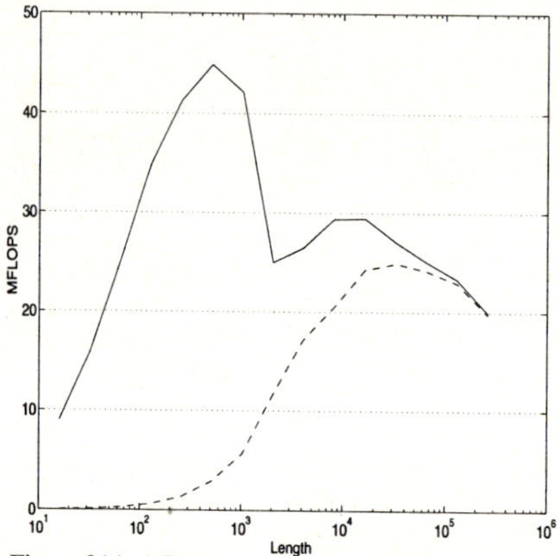

Figure 3(a): 1-D FFT, - - - first iteration; — second iteration. Both are assembly coded under OSF.

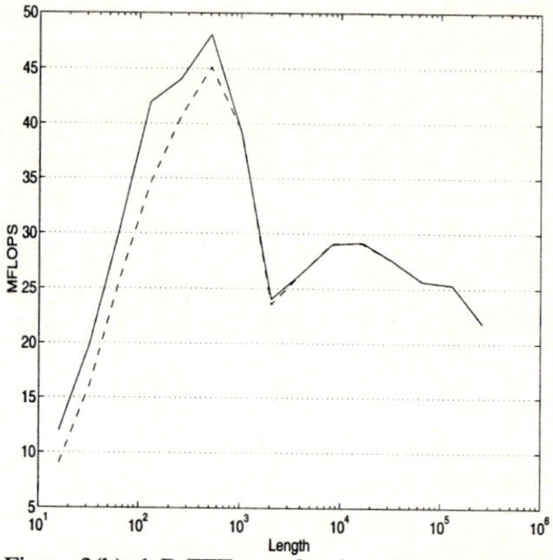

Figure 3(b): 1-D FFT, - - - first iteration; — second iteration. Both are assembly coded under SUNMOS.

Figure 5(a) shows the performance of NPB under OSF for 128 nodes. Performance is under 1 GFLOPS except for benchmarks EP, FT and BT. The benchmark EP involves almost no communication. The kernel FT uses assembly coded 1-D FFT and BT uses an assembly coded block tridiagonal solver for most of the computations. Figure 5(b) shows the performance in MFLOPS per node for NPB. The average performance is about 5 MFLOPS except for EP, FT and BT for the same reasons as discussed before.

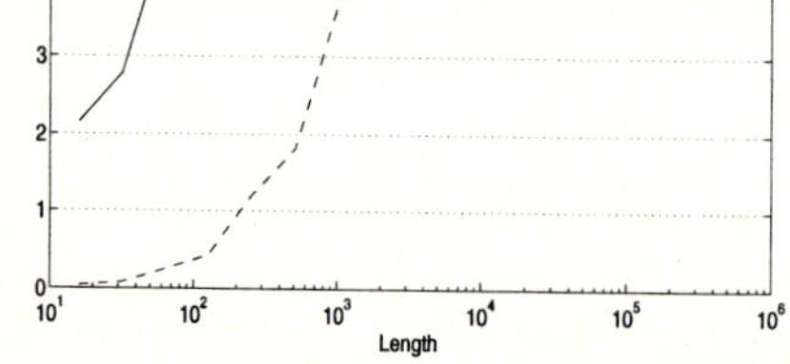

Figure 4(a): 1-D FFT, - - - first iteration, - second iteration. Both are Fortran under OSF.

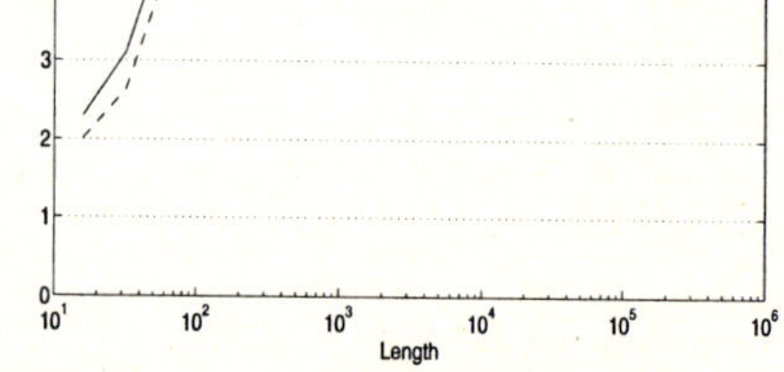

Figure 4(b): 1-D FFT, - - - first iteration, - second iteration. Both are Fortran under SUNMOS.

Figure (6a) shows the performance in MFLOPS of 3—D FFT as a function of the number of compute nodes for a fixed problem size with n_1=256, n_2=256, n_3=128. Under OSF, performance does not scale, whereas under SUNMOS it seems to scale because of higher communication bandwidth. Figure 6(b) shows the performance of 3-D FFT as a function of the size of the FFT for a fixed system size (128 nodes) for OSF and SUMOS. Here also the scalability under SUNMOS is better than OSF.

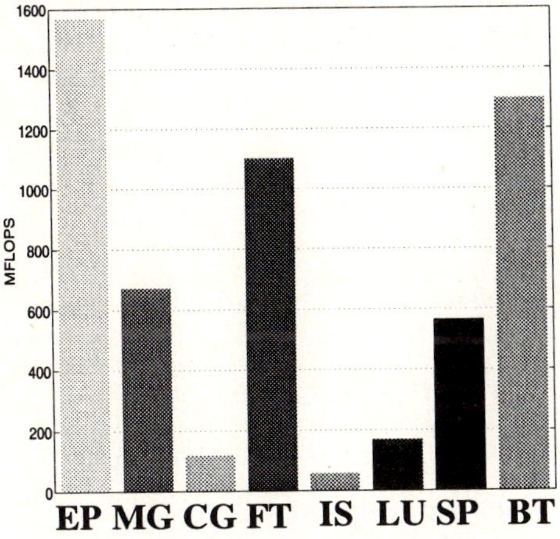

Figure 5(a): NPB on 128 nodes under OSF

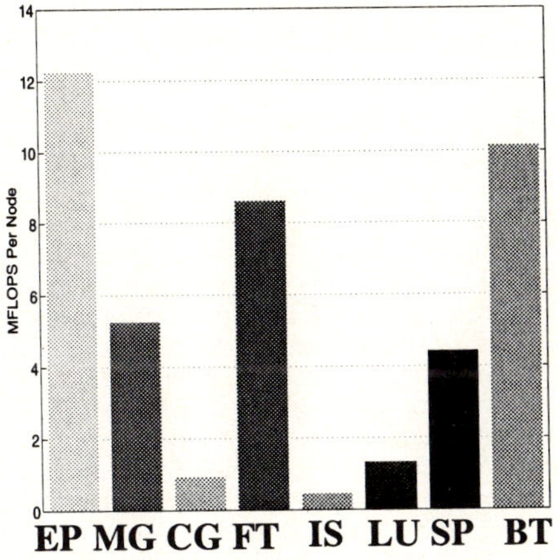

Figure 5(b): MFLOPS per node for NPB under OSF

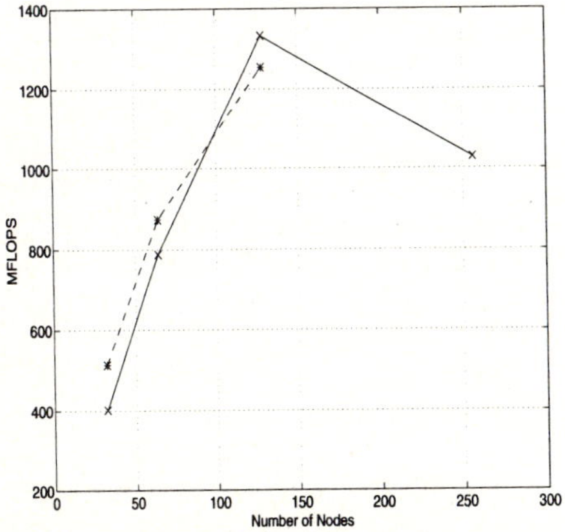

Figure 6(a): MFLOPS Vs. number of nodes.
—— denotes results under OSF and
- - - - denotes results under SUNMOS.

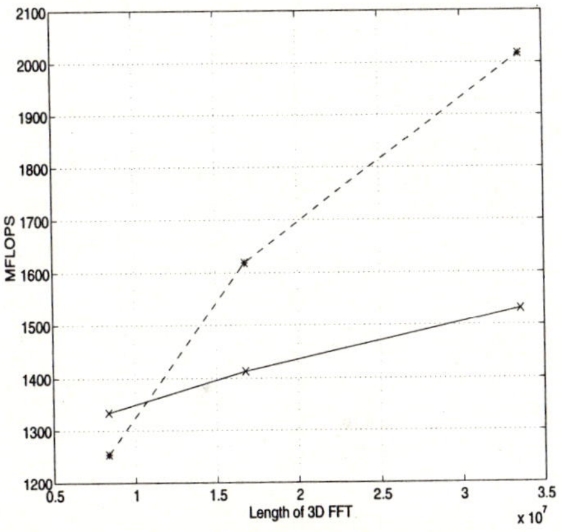

Figure 6(b): MFLOPS Vs. length of 3-D FFT.
—— denotes results under OSF and
- - - - denotes results under SUNMOS.

The utility YOD is used to allocate a partition of the SUNMOS to a portion of the mesh and load the executable. This utility runs in the service partition and handles all requests from the SUNMOS compute nodes that it controls. Aborting a job under control of YOD by KILL -9 leaves the nodes allocated and prevents the use of these nodes in subsequent runs until the system is rebooted. Among others, there are three arguments to YOD which need careful attention. These are COMM, HEAP and STACK. The argument STACK reserves the space for stack. In many examples studied, inadequate allocation of stack gave run time errors and benchmark could not be run. The switch COMM is used for buffering messages for which no receive has been posted. The default size for COMM is 256 KB. If the communication buffer overflows during execution of the application, it causes unrecoverable error and sometimes the system hangs and needs to be rebooted. The argument HEAP reserves the space for heap. The default is to allocate the remaining memory left on each node after the COMM, STACK, program (text and data) and OS space have been allocated. Currently, size of heap cannot be more than 16 MB. When the application needs more than 16 MB per node, specifying the heap to be 16 MB will not run the application and gives the message that not enough space is available for running the application. The application can be still run up to 25 MB per node if the argument heap is not used. Occasionally, the application hangs or the system crashes. The application always hangs the system or crash it if the application needs more than 25 MB per node. To run the application successfully, one has to be extra careful in allocating adequate space for COMM, HEAP and STACK.

5: Conclusions:

1. In SUNMOS, loading of data from memory to the processor is much faster than of under OSF. This is clearly shown by the better performance of first iteration of 1—D FFT kernel.
2. In SUNMOS, one can not use more than 24 MB of memory per node although SUNMOS needs only 250 KB of memory per node. This means that on a 32 MB per node Paragon about 7.5 MB memory is wasted due probably to the hardware problem.
3. In SUNMOS, there is no paging effect, i.e., performance of the first iteration and the second iteration are always the same. Under OSF the dynamic allocation of memory enhances the performance of the applications.
4. In SUNMOS, there is no virtual memory. Even in the absence of the Paragon's hardware problem, the maximum memory per node that can be utilized by the application will never exceed 31.5 MB. Currently, use of 24 MB per node hangs or crashes the system.
5. In SUNMOS, to run the application successfully either for a fixed problem size and varying number of nodes or for a fixed number of nodes and varying size problem, one has to adjust either any or all of the following (a) The size of the communication buffer, (b) The size of the heap, (c) the size of the stack. Choosing any one of them incorrectly either hangs or crashes the system or causes the system to be unusable until it is rebooted.
6. In SUNMOS, the performance of the applications is generally (but not always) better than that under OSF.
7. In SUNMOS, some enhancement of the applications' performance is attributed to the ability of SUNMOS to allocate the mesh as close to the "square" as possible.
8. On 128 nodes of the Paragon only two NPB codes (FT and BT) exhibit performance of more than 1 GFLOPS. This high performance is due to use of optimized assembly routines 1-D FFT in FT benchmark and block tridiagonal solver in BT benchmark.
9. For most of the NPB codes the performance is less than 5 MFLOPS per node except that of EP, FT and BT. The high performance of 12 MFLOPS for EP is due to almost no communication. Message passing is used to collect the results from different nodes. The high performance of FT (9 MFLOPS) and BT (10 MFLOPS) is due to the use of optimized assembly routines (1-D FFT in benchmark FT and block tridiagonal solver in BT)
10. In OSF, the 3—D FFT kernel does not scale as the number of nodes are increased from 32 to 256.

* The authors are employees of Computer Sciences Corporation. The work is supported through NASA contract NAS2-12961.

References:

[1] S. Saini and H.D. Simon, "Performance of BLAS and NAS Parallel Benchmarks on NAS Intel Paragon XP/S-15" in *Proceedings of Intel Supercomputing User's Group Meeting*, Oct. 3-6, 1993, St. Louis, Missouri, USA.

[2] S. Saini and H.D. Simon, "Performance of BLAS 1, 2 on NAS Intel Paragon XP/S-15" in *Proceedings of Scalable Parallel Libraries Conference* organized by IEEE, Oct. 6-9, 1993, Mississippi State University, Starkville, Mississippi, USA.

[3] S. Saini and H.D. Simon, "Performance of BLAS and NAS Parallel Benchmarks on NAS Intel Paragon XP/S-15", Abstract on page 77 of *Final Program for SC '93*, Supercomputing '93, November 15-19, 1993, Portland, Oregon, USA.

[4] S. Saini and H.D. Simon, "Enhancing Applications Performance on Intel Paragon through Dynamic Memory Allocation", Report RNR-93-017, November 1993, *NAS Systems Division, NASA Ames Research Center*, Moffett Field, California 94035, USA.

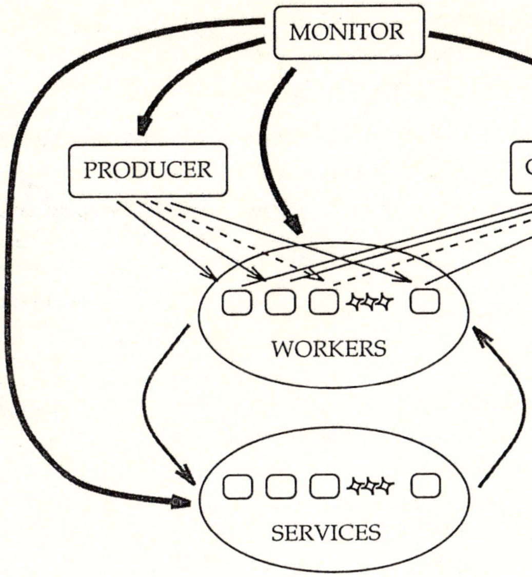

Fig. 1. The parallelization topology

implemented to take care of global operations, like histogramming, updating of statistical tables and alike. The system is fault-tolerant in the sense that, thanks to dedicated controls on the data structures at producer and consumer level, occasional worker failures can be recognized and lost packets (if any) can be recovered.

4 Data Structures

In order to be able to perform the tracking of all primary particles of an event, each processor running a *scalar* version of GEANT must contain all the static and dynamic informations mentioned in a previous section. Most of the ZEBRA structures containing this data (e.g. geometry) can be initialized independently by each process. The informations to be exchanged are only:

- producer: initial kinematics
- worker: initial kinematics for the initialization of the intermediate structures; output data (hits, and, possibly, digits)
- consumer: output data (hits, and, possibly, digits)

Unless some shared-memory resources are available, data reproducibility is not achieved when running the parallel version of GEANT. In fact, in this case,

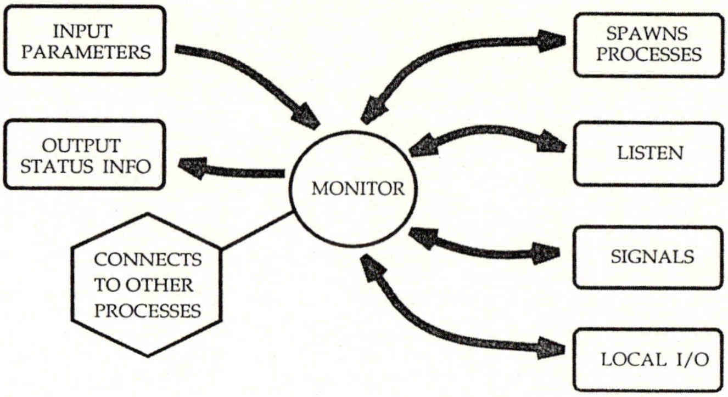

Fig. 2. The monitor structure.

all worker variables are local to the single process, and dynamic changes via common blocks from external processes, as a sequential random numbers generation requires, are not allowed. Anyway, an independent sequential generation, starting from the initial seeds, of a new random number for each packet to be sent to the worker, seems to be safe enough. As in the sequential case, the last generated seeds can be saved in memory and used, if necessary, for the next event.

For sake of simplicity, we decided to keep our software as close as possible to the original one, enclosing almost all the standard tracking routines in the worker task, while writing from scratch the producer, consumer and, of course, the communication codes.

The simplest configuration is essentially composed of one producer, a number of workers, one consumer (plus additional servers, but they can be ignored in this discussion). In addition to the fact that the workers operate *on demand*, in order to ensure load balancing, we proceeded as follows: since the time spent to process one event is proportional to the total event energy E (which is a constant for events produced at colliders), and the number of workers N is set before processing starts, nearly the same amount of energy (and hence of load) can be distributed among the workers by building packets of primary tracks, whose energy sum is of the order E/N. Figure 3 shows the splitting of the LIFO stack JSTAK into a linear chain of banks, each one containing the event header, vertically connected to the tracking informations banks (including the random seeds), organized in packets with linear connections among them. This ZEBRA structure has the advantage that the link to the single packet of data depends only on the address of the top bank JSTAK.

At the end of the simulation process, fragments of events (hits, digits) are obtained. The consumer recognizes the packets and rebuilds the events. Each packet is identified by run, event and packet progressive number. Each event structure is headed by event features (number of tracks and packets).

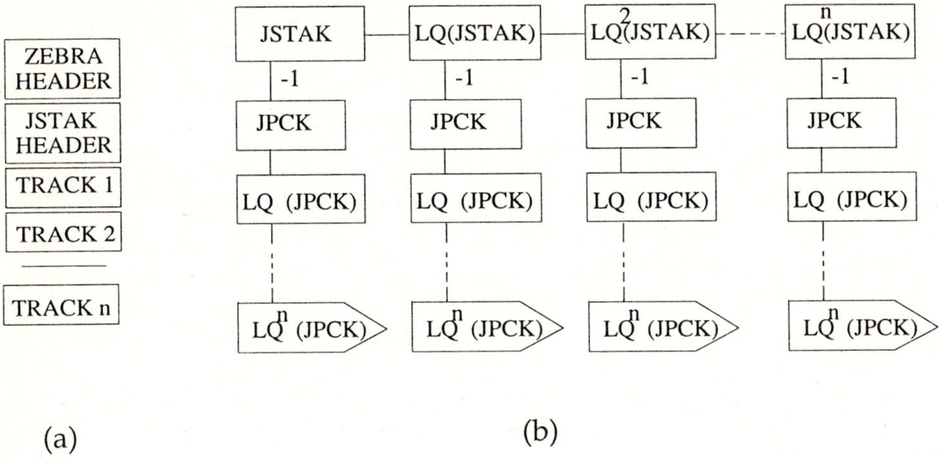

Fig. 3. The data structure JSTAK: (a) original; (b) after splitting

5 Arnia

In the parallelization of codes, especially of large ones, the development of high level programming tools is usually recommended to provide direct support to the programmers. ARNIA is a product engineered by ACS which consists of a set of libraries, each one implementing a different parallelization technique. Among the ARNIA libraries, MSlib provides direct support for the parallelization of applications that can be decomposed following the Master/Slave computational model, while CSlib provides direct support for the parallelization of applications following the Client/Server model. The high level communication routines are implemented on a message passing layer called Stratos, presently interfaced to CSTools, Express and PVM.

5.1 Parallel Computational Frame

The approach explained in the previous paragraph is well suited for simple applications, which can be parallelized following a unique decomposition model; when the problem to solve is inehrently complex, the ARNIA libraries can be combined at the cost of a stronger programming effort. This is the evidence for a higher level tool, which permits to easily combine the ARNIA libraries.

The proposed approach is based on a precise programming methodology: the programmer has to decompose the problem according to the different patterns in which parallelism can arise. Each one of these patterns represents a subproblem of the original one. This methodology should be iterated until each one of the obtained frames obeys to one of the basic models.

We name *Parallel Computational Frame* (PCF) [3] the different parallelization techniques and PCF *instances* the patterns obtained through the problem decomposition just described.

A PCF instance is composed of all processes belonging to a given context covered by one of the ARNIA libraries (so we speak of PCF Master Slave instance, PCF Client Server instance etc.). Each process is identified by the role played inside the PCF instance, in such a way that to each process is associated a process type (for example master or slave in the PCF Master Slave) describing its behaviour inside the instance.

A PCF application consists of a set of PCF instances possibly intersecating: each intersection is due to the fact that at least a process belongs to more than one PCF instance (and calls functions from more than one ARNIA library). From the programmer's point of view, the only overhead is the need to declare for each process of the application the list of the PCF instances to which it belongs.

The Parallel Computational Frame library (PCFlib) implements the concept of Parallel Computational Frame and provides the user with the possibility to easily combine the ARNIA libraries.

5.2 The Configuration Language

PCFlib is based on the declaration of the structure of the parallel application in terms of PCF instances. The way in which the user can specify it is twofold. Firstly, the user can declare explicitly the fact that a process belongs to a certain PCF instance using PCFlib functions, which take care of instances creation and management by creating data structures which implement PCF concepts. Secondly, the user can declare the structure of its application using PCL (Parallel Configuration Language): a simple ad hoc configuration language to specify the PCF instances building a PCF application.

6 Conclusions

We have achieved the decomposition of the GEANT program into a set of functional units. The implementation of the resulting model on a MIMD machine, as well as on a heterogeneous cluster of workstations is a clear evidence of portability. We also developed a set of tools to assist the implementation of complex topologies. Further tests are needed to test the scalability and to measure the efficiency of our approach.

Acknowledgments

This work has been carried out with the financial contribution of the Sardinian Regional Authorities and of the Commission of the European Communities.
We would also like to thank Federico Carminati (CERN, Geneva) for many fruitful discussions and hints.

References

1. F. Carminati (editor), GEANT Users Guide, Program Library **W5013**, CERN, Geneva.
2. B. Adeva *et al.*, The L3 Database System, Nuclear Instruments and Methods in Physics Research **A 309** (1990) 318.
3. P. Stofella *et al.*, Parallel Computational Frames: an Approach to Parallel Application Development Based on Message Passing Systems, Proceedings of the I2U Convention **92**, 597.

A Practical Experience in Parallelizing a Large CFD Code: The ENSOLV Flow Solver *

Marcello Amato, Alfonso Matrone and Pasquale Schiano

C.I.R.A., *Centro Italiano Ricerche Aerospaziali, Via Maiorise 81043 Capua, Italy*

Abstract. The aim of this paper is to show a practical experience in parallelizing a large CFD code starting from a sequential version. Major steps developing this activity for a 30000-Fortran-statements code are showed. This is done focusing on difficulties, techniques, "open" problems and solutions that a multidisciplinary group faces during the work. As a case study, the parallel implementation of a 3D Thin Layer Navier-Stokes code, originally developed in collaboration with Alenia and NLR , for the simulation of the subsonic/transonic flow around a complex aerodynamic configuration is considered. The message passing, for the data transmission among processors, is handled by PVM. The target parallel architectures are several MIMD machines (including cluster of workstations); a comparison of the results, in terms of performance, with the current most powerful supercomputers is presented.

1 The ENSOLV code

The ENSOLV code is part of a flow simulation system originally developed in collaboration by C.I.R.A., NLR (The National Aerospace Laboratory, The Netherlands) and Alenia /DTT. This system is composed of three codes: **ENDOMO** (**E**uler **N**avier-Stokes **DO**main **MO**deller), **ENGRID** (**E**uler **N**avier-Stokes **GRID** generator), and **ENSOLV** (**E**uler **N**avier-Stokes Flow **SOLV**er). **ENDOMO** is an interactive code running on current generation of workstations. It has the functionality of splitting the flow domain into simple subdomains (i.e. blocks)[2]. In practice, starting from the reference geometry, the topological and geometric al data, that define the decomposition into blocks are produced. The geometrical data include the new representation of the aerodynamical configuration. In fact , the starting geometry is defined by pathches with a topology that does not match, in general, the final blocking.

These data constitute the input of **ENGRID**[3]. The grid generator runs interactively on workstations platforms and in batch mode on different supercomputers (NEC SX3, CRAY-YMP, CONVEX C3860). The interactive mode is used for the grid dimensioning and tuning. The tuning is performed on a base

* This paper is a part of a common contribution to the HPCN Europe '94 conference by the European Aerospace Research Centers (CIRA, DLR, DRA, FFA, INTA, NLR, ONERA) participating to the GARTEUR Working Group on Informatics

(coarse) grid. If the grid to be generated is quite fine, the data produced interactively are used to run the grid generator in batch mode on supercomputer. The aerodynamical, numerical and boundary conditions data are input to the flow solver. shortly described in the next section.

The ENSOLV code employes the Multizone (MZ) approach as flow model [1]. The Thin-Layer Navier-Stokes (TLNS) equations, completed by the Baldwin-Lomax turbulence model, and the Euler equations are used. A cell-centred finite-volume method is used to discretize, in space, the flow equations. The solution procedure is based on an explicit time-marching multigrid method. Different boundary conditions are implemented: slip solid wall, no-slip solid wall, far field conditions, and three options for the propulsion systems simulations.

CIRA and Alenia/DTT (Pomigliano) are cooperating to extend and upgrade the flow simulation system [5].

2 A guideline of the Parallel Implementation

The current available tools on parallel machines (compilers, debuggers etc.) are not easy to use for end-users.

The development of an efficient parallel version of large codes is still a work for specialists. This is a strong limiting factor for a wide-spreading of parallel machines in the industrial environment.

Here the guidelines that were followed to perform the parallelization of a large CFD code are given.

The ENSOLV code is composed of 130 subroutines and more than 30000 Fortran lines, with a large number of functionalities (convergence accelerators, several boundary conditions, multizonal approach) that can be set up by the user.

Our initial efforts were addressed in designing a proper parallel structure of the code. This structure had to cope with the complexity arising from the multiblock technique that is adopted in the code.

Previous experiences [6, 8] on simpler codes suggested us to applies a Domain Decomposition Technique (DDT). The entire computational domain was divided in subdomains, each to be assigned to a processor. Initially each subdomain was constituted by integer numbers of blocks. However, our final goal is a more efficient, but more complicated, decomposition named Masked Multiblock (MMT) [7] that is superimposed on the original multiblock structure of the code. With MMT it will be also possible to obtain subdomains composed by non-integer numbers of blocks allowing a real computational load balancing among processors [4].

This problem has to be carefully considered for the ENSOLV code. In fact, the blocking is unstructured, different kind of topological degeneration are allowed, the computational weight largely varies among blocks (due to different number of grid points and also to the multizonal approach) and this is a serious limit to perform an hand-made computational balancing. To overcome this problem, for the first version of the code using the DDT it was built up a pre-processor code based on genetic algorithm to obtain an acceptable computational load among processors [9]. Apart from a general overview on the followed approach to obtain the parallel version of the ENSOLV code, it is felt to be useful to outline the simple strategies adopted, and moreover the problems solved, during our work.

A Master-Slave model was adopted. The master process had to perform the I/O functionalities of ENSOLV (reading of the grid cells, boundary conditions, aerodynamic parameters, etc. and writing of the whole flow field) and the distribution to the slaves of the needed data to perform the computational work over the assigned subdomains.

In the predesign phase, the static tree of the sequential version routines was analyzed and subdivided in two groups: one belonging to the master and the second to the slaves processes (or to both). These were placed in two separate directories with proper Makefile for an easy handling of several versions of the code.

Subsequently, the data type and the data flow from the master to the slaves (and viceversa) were studied. PVM2.4 was choosen as message passing tool. Several routines were developed to send initial data to the slaves and to collect data from each slave back to the master.

As far as the use of PVM is concerned we had to face two main problems. One related with the handling of 64-bit precision and a second concerning the debugging of new routines. When using 32-bit precision we did not meet problems with PVM Fortran routines. On the contrary the usage of a compiler option to translate all variables from single (32-bit) to double precision(64-bit) generated deadlock in the code. To overcome this problem, due to the lack of a compiler option permitting the conversion only for real variables, it was necessary to declare real*8 every floating point variables used along the 130 routines of ENSOLV. Luckly, this work was simplified by the good documentation released with the code, and moreover by the decision of the original developpers of the code not to use implicit declarations for the variables.

During the work the lack of efficient debugger tools on parallel architectures was manifest. The debugging phase had to be realized by means "check" print was necessary and a long time was spent in this activity.

The part requiring the higher efforts was the routines to update the boundary conditions of the subdomains. After estabilishing the data type and the data flow, PVM-based swapping routines were built according with the existing blocking coupling algorithm. In order to update the internal boundary conditions a "face-marching" procedure was adopted. For each elementary face the adjacent blocks were determined, then running on the face the halo-cells of the two blocks were updated.

3 Results

Here some results in terms of time, speed-up and efficiency are presented. The parallel machine used is the Convex Metaseries: a cluster of 8 HP-PA 735 workstations connected by a FDDI ring. The parallel version of the code is developed by using PVM 2.4 as message passing tool.

Tab. 1 shows results (time, speed-up and efficiency) for an inviscid solution around a NACA 0012 4-block airfoil geometry (computation balanced).

The second table shows results for a more-CPU demanding solutions: Eulerian flow calculations around a two component airfoil, 29 blocks (not perfectly balanced).

In both cases a comparison of results with traditional single processor supercomputers (Convex C3400 and C3800, CRAY Y/MP) is also given.

Machine	Metaseries			CRAY	C34	C38
Number of processors	1	2	4	1	1	1
Time (sec.)	2326	1273	698	423	2835	1135
Speed-up	-	1.83	3.33	-	-	-
Efficiency	-	.91	.83	-	-	-

Table 1. NACA0012 airfoil, 4 blocks, 4 grid levels, 1500 iterations per level

Machine	Metaseries				CRAY	C34	C38
Number of processors	1	2	4	8	1	1	1
Time (sec.)	14058	7655	4261	2780	2375	16038	6390
Speed-up	-	1.83	3.3	5.50	-	-	-
Efficiency	-	.91	.82	.63	-	-	-

Table 2. Two components airfoil, 29 blocks, 3 grid levels, 2000 iterations per level

References

1. J.C.Kok,M.Amato,"Mathematical-Physical modelling for multiblock NaS/Euler flow simulation, NLR-CR- 91235 L.
2. J.W.Boerstoel, S.P.Spekreijse, P.L.Vitagliano,The design of a syst em of codes for the industrial calculations of flows around aircraft and other complex aerodynamic c onfigurations",AIAA-92-2619-CP.

3. S.P.Spekreijse, J.W.Boestoel, P.L.Vitagliano,"New Concepts for M ulti-Block Grid Generation for Flow Domains around Complex Configurations",NLR-TP-91046 L, 3rd Int. Conf. Num. Grid Gen. in Comp.Fluid Mech. and Rel. Fields, Bacrcelona, J une 1991.
4. M. Amato, "Memorandum on Definition of the Project M4ENAS", CIRA-DILC-EST-TM-343
5. M. Amato, "Memorandum on Definition of the Project M4ENAS", CIRA-DILC-EST-TM-343
6. S. Borrelli, A. Matrone, P. Schiano, "A Multiblock Hypersonic Flow Solver for Massively Parallel Computer", Proc. of Parallel CFD '92, May 1992, North-Holland, 1993.
7. C. de Nicola, L. Paparone, V. Puoti, R. Tognaccini, "A Strategy for load balancing problems in advanced CFD Multiblock solvers on distributed memory machines", Proc. of Parallel CFD '93, to be published
8. P. Schiano, A. Matrone, "Parallel CFD applications: experiences on scalable distributed multicomputers",Proc. of Parallel CFD '93, to be published
9. D. Quagliarella, "Optimal Domain Decomposition for Parallel Multiblock Flowfield Solvers using Genetic Algorithms", to appear

Fig. 1. Grid around a Two component airfoil

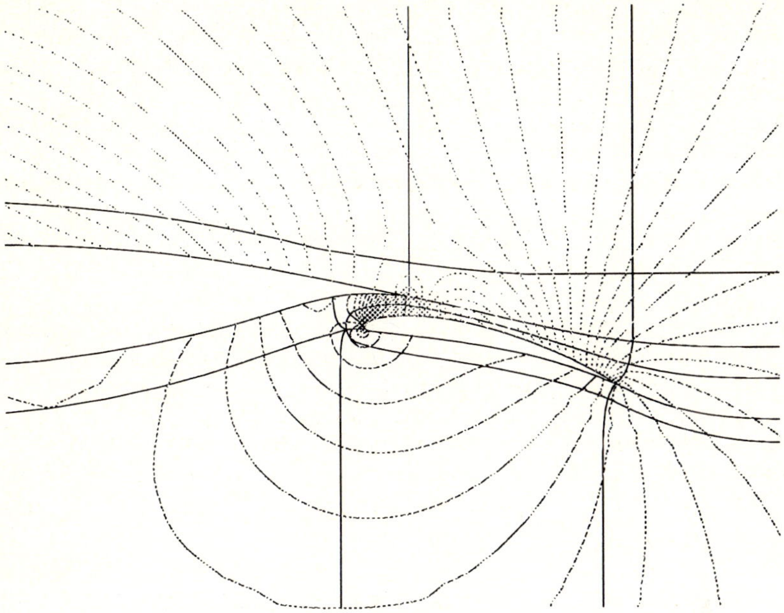

Fig. 2. sequential solution (pressure)

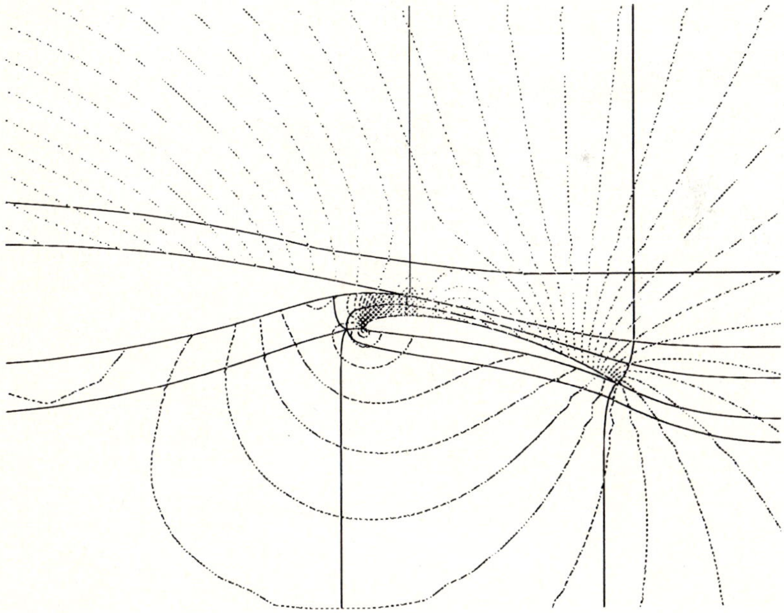

Fig. 3. parallel solution (pressure)

Author Index

Lecture Notes in Computer Science

For information about Vols. 1–719
please contact your bookseller or Springer-Verlag

Vol. 720: V.Mařík, J. Lažanský, R.R. Wagner (Eds.), Database and Expert Systems Applications. Proceedings, 1993. XV, 768 pages. 1993.

Vol. 721: J. Fitch (Ed.), Design and Implementation of Symbolic Computation Systems. Proceedings, 1992. VIII, 215 pages. 1993.

Vol. 722: A. Miola (Ed.), Design and Implementation of Symbolic Computation Systems. Proceedings, 1993. XII, 384 pages. 1993.

Vol. 723: N. Aussenac, G. Boy, B. Gaines, M. Linster, J.-G. Ganascia, Y. Kodratoff (Eds.), Knowledge Acquisition for Knowledge-Based Systems. Proceedings, 1993. XIII, 446 pages. 1993. (Subseries LNAI).

Vol. 724: P. Cousot, M. Falaschi, G. Filè, A. Rauzy (Eds.), Static Analysis. Proceedings, 1993. IX, 283 pages. 1993.

Vol. 725: A. Schiper (Ed.), Distributed Algorithms. Proceedings, 1993. VIII, 325 pages. 1993.

Vol. 726: T. Lengauer (Ed.), Algorithms – ESA '93. Proceedings, 1993. IX, 419 pages. 1993

Vol. 727: M. Filgueiras, L. Damas (Eds.), Progress in Artificial Intelligence. Proceedings, 1993. X, 362 pages. 1993. (Subseries LNAI).

Vol. 728: P. Torasso (Ed.), Advances in Artificial Intelligence. Proceedings, 1993. XI, 336 pages. 1993. (Subseries LNAI).

Vol. 729: L. Donatiello, R. Nelson (Eds.), Performance Evaluation of Computer and Communication Systems. Proceedings, 1993. VIII, 675 pages. 1993.

Vol. 730: D. B. Lomet (Ed.), Foundations of Data Organization and Algorithms. Proceedings, 1993. XII, 412 pages. 1993.

Vol. 731: A. Schill (Ed.), DCE – The OSF Distributed Computing Environment. Proceedings, 1993. VIII, 285 pages. 1993.

Vol. 732: A. Bode, M. Dal Cin (Eds.), Parallel Computer Architectures. IX, 311 pages. 1993.

Vol. 733: Th. Grechenig, M. Tscheligi (Eds.), Human Computer Interaction. Proceedings, 1993. XIV, 450 pages. 1993.

Vol. 734: J. Volkert (Ed.), Parallel Computation. Proceedings, 1993. VIII, 248 pages. 1993.

Vol. 735: D. Bjørner, M. Broy, I. V. Pottosin (Eds.), Formal Methods in Programming and Their Applications. Proceedings, 1993. IX, 434 pages. 1993.

Vol. 736: R. L. Grossman, A. Nerode, A. P. Ravn, H. Rischel (Eds.), Hybrid Systems. VIII, 474 pages. 1993.

Vol. 737: J. Calmet, J. A. Campbell (Eds.), Artificial Intelligence and Symbolic Mathematical Computing. Proceedings, 1992. VIII, 305 pages. 1993.

Vol. 738: M. Weber, M. Simons, Ch. Lafontaine, The Generic Development Language Deva. XI, 246 pages. 1993.

Vol. 739: H. Imai, R. L. Rivest, T. Matsumoto (Eds.), Advances in Cryptology – ASIACRYPT '91. X, 499 pages. 1993.

Vol. 740: E. F. Brickell (Ed.), Advances in Cryptology – CRYPTO '92. Proceedings, 1992. X, 593 pages. 1993.

Vol. 741: B. Preneel, R. Govaerts, J. Vandewalle (Eds.), Computer Security and Industrial Cryptography. Proceedings, 1991. VIII, 275 pages. 1993.

Vol. 742: S. Nishio, A. Yonezawa (Eds.), Object Technologies for Advanced Software. Proceedings, 1993. X, 543 pages. 1993.

Vol. 743: S. Doshita, K. Furukawa, K. P. Jantke, T. Nishida (Eds.), Algorithmic Learning Theory. Proceedings, 1992. X, 260 pages. 1993. (Subseries LNAI)

Vol. 744: K. P. Jantke, T. Yokomori, S. Kobayashi, E. Tomita (Eds.), Algorithmic Learning Theory. Proceedings, 1993. XI, 423 pages. 1993. (Subseries LNAI)

Vol. 745: V. Roberto (Ed.), Intelligent Perceptual Systems. VIII, 378 pages. 1993. (Subseries LNAI)

Vol. 746: A. S. Tanguiane, Artificial Perception and Music Recognition. XV, 210 pages. 1993. (Subseries LNAI).

Vol. 747: M. Clarke, R. Kruse, S. Moral (Eds.), Symbolic and Quantitative Approaches to Reasoning and Uncertainty. Proceedings, 1993. X, 390 pages. 1993.

Vol. 748: R. H. Halstead Jr., T. Ito (Eds.), Parallel Symbolic Computing: Languages, Systems, and Applications. Proceedings, 1992. X, 419 pages. 1993.

Vol. 749: P. A. Fritzson (Ed.), Automated and Algorithmic Debugging. Proceedings, 1993. VIII, 369 pages. 1993.

Vol. 750: J. L. Díaz-Herrera (Ed.), Software Engineering Education. Proceedings, 1994. XII, 601 pages. 1994.

Vol. 751: B. Jähne, Spatio-Temporal Image Processing. XII, 208 pages. 1993.

Vol. 752: T. W. Finin, C. K. Nicholas, Y. Yesha (Eds.), Information and Knowledge Management. Proceedings, 1992. VII, 142 pages. 1993.

Vol. 753: L. J. Bass, J. Gornostaev, C. Unger (Eds.), Human-Computer Interaction. Proceedings, 1993. X, 388 pages. 1993.

Vol. 754: H. D. Pfeiffer, T. E. Nagle (Eds.), Conceptual Structures: Theory and Implementation. Proceedings, 1992. IX, 327 pages. 1993. (Subseries LNAI).

Vol. 755: B. Möller, H. Partsch, S. Schuman (Eds.), Formal Program Development. Proceedings. VII, 371 pages. 1993.

Vol. 756: J. Pieprzyk, B. Sadeghiyan, Design of Hashing Algorithms. XV, 194 pages. 1993.

Vol. 757: U. Banerjee, D. Gelernter, A. Nicolau, D. Padua (Eds.), Languages and Compilers for Parallel Computing. Proceedings, 1992. X, 576 pages. 1993.

Vol. 758: M. Teillaud, Towards Dynamic Randomized Algorithms in Computational Geometry. IX, 157 pages. 1993.

Vol. 759: N. R. Adam, B. K. Bhargava (Eds.), Advanced Database Systems. XV, 451 pages. 1993.

Vol. 760: S. Ceri, K. Tanaka, S. Tsur (Eds.), Deductive and Object-Oriented Databases. Proceedings, 1993. XII, 488 pages. 1993.

Vol. 761: R. K. Shyamasundar (Ed.), Foundations of Software Technology and Theoretical Computer Science. Proceedings, 1993. XIV, 456 pages. 1993.

Vol. 762: K. W. Ng, P. Raghavan, N. V. Balasubramanian, F. Y. L. Chin (Eds.), Algorithms and Computation. Proceedings, 1993. XIII, 542 pages. 1993.

Vol. 763: F. Pichler, R. Moreno Díaz (Eds.), Computer Aided Systems Theory - EUROCAST '93. Proceedings, 1993. IX, 451 pages. 1994.

Vol. 764: G. Wagner, Vivid Logic. XII, 148 pages. 1994. (Subseries LNAI).

Vol. 765: T. Helleseth (Ed.), Advances in Cryptology - EUROCRYPT '93. Proceedings, 1993. X, 467 pages. 1994.

Vol. 766: P. R. Van Loocke, The Dynamics of Concepts. XI, 340 pages. 1994. (Subseries LNAI).

Vol. 767: M. Gogolla, An Extended Entity-Relationship Model. X, 136 pages. 1994.

Vol. 768: U. Banerjee, D. Gelernter, A. Nicolau, D. Padua (Eds.), Languages and Compilers for Parallel Computing. Proceedings, 1993. XI, 655 pages. 1994.

Vol. 769: J. L. Nazareth, The Newton-Cauchy Framework. XII, 101 pages. 1994.

Vol. 770: P. Haddawy (Representing Plans Under Uncertainty. X, 129 pages. 1994. (Subseries LNAI).

Vol. 771: G. Tomas, C. W. Ueberhuber, Visualization of Scientific Parallel Programs. XI, 310 pages. 1994.

Vol. 772: B. C. Warboys (Ed.),Software Process Technology. Proceedings, 1994. IX, 275 pages. 1994.

Vol. 773: D. R. Stinson (Ed.), Advances in Cryptology - CRYPTO '93. Proceedings, 1993. X, 492 pages. 1994.

Vol. 774: M. Banâtre, P. A. Lee (Eds.), Hardware and Software Architectures for Fault Tolerance. XIII, 311 pages. 1994.

Vol. 775: P. Enjalbert, E. W. Mayr, K. W. Wagner (Eds.), STACS 94. Proceedings, 1994. XIV, 782 pages. 1994.

Vol. 776: H. J. Schneider, H. Ehrig (Eds.), Graph Transformations in Computer Science. Proceedings, 1993. VIII, 395 pages. 1994.

Vol. 777: K. von Luck, H. Marburger (Eds.), Management and Processing of Complex Data Structures. Proceedings, 1994. VII, 220 pages. 1994.

Vol. 778: M. Bonuccelli, P. Crescenzi, R. Petreschi (Eds.), Algorithms and Complexity. Proceedings, 1994. VIII, 222 pages. 1994.

Vol. 779: M. Jarke, J. Bubenko, K. Jeffery (Eds.), Advances in Database Technology — EDBT '94. Proceedings, 1994. XII, 406 pages. 1994.

Vol. 780: J. J. Joyce, C.-J. H. Seger (Eds.), Higher Order Logic Theorem Proving and Its Applications. Proceedings, 1993. X, 518 pages. 1994.

Vol. 781: G. Cohen, S. Litsyn, A. Lobstein, G. Zémor (Eds.), Algebraic Coding. Proceedings, 1993. XII, 326 pages. 1994.

Vol. 782: J. Gutknecht (Ed.), Programming Languages and System Architectures. Proceedings, 1994. X, 344 pages. 1994.

Vol. 783: C. G. Günther (Ed.), Mobile Communications. Proceedings, 1994. XVI, 564 pages. 1994.

Vol. 784: F. Bergadano, L. De Raedt (Eds.), Machine Learning: ECML-94. Proceedings, 1994. XI, 439 pages. 1994. (Subseries LNAI).

Vol. 785: H. Ehrig, F. Orejas (Eds.), Recent Trends in Data Type Specification. Proceedings, 1992. VIII, 350 pages. 1994.

Vol. 786: P. A. Fritzson (Ed.), Compiler Construction. Proceedings, 1994. XI, 451 pages. 1994.

Vol. 787: S. Tison (Ed.), Trees in Algebra and Programming – CAAP '94. Proceedings, 1994. X, 351 pages. 1994.

Vol. 788: D. Sannella (Ed.), Programming Languages and Systems – ESOP '94. Proceedings, 1994. VIII, 516 pages. 1994.

Vol. 789: M. Hagiya, J. C. Mitchell (Eds.), Theoretical Aspects of Computer Software. Proceedings, 1994. XI, 887 pages. 1994.

Vol. 790: J. van Leeuwen (Ed.), Graph-Theoretic Concepts in Computer Science. Proceedings, 1993. IX, 431 pages. 1994.

Vol. 791: R. Guerraoui, O. Nierstrasz, M. Riveill (Eds.), Object-Based Distributed Programming. Proceedings, 1993. VII, 262 pages. 1994.

Vol. 792: N. D. Jones, M. Hagiya, M. Sato (Eds.), Logic, Language and Computation. XII, 269 pages. 1994.

Vol. 793: T. A. Gulliver, N. P. Secord (Eds.), Information Theory and Applications. Proceedings, 1993. XI, 394 pages. 1994.

Vol. 796: W. Gentzsch, U. Harms (Eds.), High-Performance Computing and Networking. Proceedings, 1994, Vol. I. XXI, 453 pages. 1994.

Vol. 797: W. Gentzsch, U. Harms (Eds.), High-Performance Computing and Networking. Proceedings, 1994, Vol. II. XXII, 519 pages. 1994.

Vol. 800: J.-O. Eklundh (Ed.), Computer Vision – ECCV '94. Proceedings 1994, Vol. I. XVIII, 603 pages. 1994.

Vol. 801: J.-O. Eklundh (Ed.), Computer Vision – ECCV '94. Proceedings 1994, Vol. II. XV, 485 pages. 1994.